W9-AEY-064

The American Critical Archives is a series of reference books that provide representative selections of contemporary reviews of the main works of major American authors. Specifically, each volume contains both full reviews and excerpts from reviews that appeared in newspapers and weekly and monthly periodicals, generally within a few months of the publication of the work concerned. There is an introductory historical overview by the volume editor, as well as checklists of additional reviews located but not quoted. *Henry James: The Contemporary Reviews* presents the most comprehensive gathering of newspaper and magazine reviews of James's work ever assembled. Other volumes in the American Critical Archives series concentrate on reviews from American publications, but because of the importance of James's British connection, this book also generously samples reviews from British newspapers and other periodicals. The focus here is on the novels, but reviews of James's most important travel narratives are included as well. The volume ends with reviews of *The American Scene,* James's impressionistic depiction of his relationship with his birthplace. This collection also reprints many rarely seen notices written by the most important female reviewers of the late nineteenth and early twentieth centuries. Each chapter ends with a checklist of additional reviews not presented here. The Introduction surveys the major themes of the reviews and shows how they influenced James personally and in his work.

AMERICAN CRITICAL ARCHIVES 7
Henry James: The Contemporary Reviews

The American Critical Archives

GENERAL EDITOR: M. Thomas Inge, Randolph-Macon College

Henry James

The Contemporary Reviews

Edited by
Kevin J. Hayes
University of Central Oklahoma

CAMBRIDGE
UNIVERSITY PRESS

Published by the Press Syndicate of the University of Cambridge
The Pitt Building, Trumpington Street, Cambridge CB2 1RP
40 West 20th Street, New York, NY 10011-4211, USA
10 Stamford Road, Oakleigh, Melbourne 3166, Australia

First published 1996

Printed in the United States of America

Library of Congress Cataloging-in-Publication Data
Henry James: the contemporary reviews / edited by Kevin J. Hayes.
p.   cm.—(American critical archives; 7)
Includes index.
ISBN 0-521-45386-0
1. James, Henry, 1843–1916—Criticism and interpretation.
I. Hayes, Kevin J.   II. Series.
PS2124.H463   1995
813′.4—dc20   95-8077
CIP

A catalog record for this book is available from the British Library.

ISBN 0-521-45386-0 hardback

For Hershel Parker

Contents

Series Editor's Preface

The American Critical Archives series documents a part of a writer's career that is usually difficult to examine, that is, the immediate response to each work as it was made public by reviewers in contemporary newspapers and journals. Although it would not be feasible to reprint every review, each volume in the series reprints a selection of reviews designed to provide the reader with a proportionate sense of the critical response, whether it was positive, negative, or mixed. Checklists of other known reviews are also included to complete the documentary record and allow access for those who wish to do further reading and research.

The editor of each volume has provided an introduction that surveys the career of the author in the context of the contemporary critical response. Ideally, the introduction will inform the reader in brief of what is to be learned by a reading of the full volume. The reader then can go as deeply as necessary in terms of the kind of information desired—be it about a single work, a period in the author's life, or the author's entire career. The intent is to provide quick and easy access to the material for students, scholars, librarians, and general readers.

When completed, the American Critical Archives should constitute a comprehensive history of critical practice in America, and in some cases Great Britain, as the writers' careers were in progress. The volumes open a window on the patterns and forces that have shaped the history of American writing and the reputations of the writers. These are primary documents in the literary and cultural life of the nation.

M. THOMAS INGE

Introduction

After *Roderick Hudson* was published in the United States, Henry James eagerly anticipated reviews of the work, his first separately published, book-length work of fiction. He wrote his brother, father, and mother, asking them to send any notices from local newspapers and magazines, and he also wrote William Dean Howells, asking about another *Roderick Hudson* review.[1] Seldom again would James express such interest in the opinions of his reviewers. Over the course of his career, his attitude toward contemporary critics shifted from enthusiasm to disgust. James's surviving letters to family, friends, and publishers reveal an emerging disdain toward the critics that ultimately approached intolerance. By the 1890s, James, according to the letters, had begun taking pains to avoid reading reviews. With a few exceptions, he came to see his reviewers as thick-witted bumblers with little sensitivity to the English language and little understanding about what made a good book.

Responding to his brother's curiosity about the American reception of *Roderick Hudson*, William James wrote: "Roderick Hudson seems to be a very common theme of conversation, to be in fact a great success, though I can give you no saying about which is memorable for its matter or its source. Every one praises the end, including myself."[2] William James exaggerated, but *Roderick Hudson* reviews were mainly positive. Several readers, however, did not mask their uneasiness. Sometimes, the book's characters were unsympathetic, and other times they seemed unrealistic. The author's tone appeared somewhat heartless. Excessive details sometimes weighed the story down. Despite these occasional negative comments, nearly all the reviewers recognized James as a writer of power. Overall, *Roderick Hudson* indicated his tremendous potential and seemed to foreshadow a brilliant career. Because the critics recognized James's superior writing ability, however, they would subsequently hold him to higher standards than those applied to other novelists of his time. The contemporary response to Henry James illustrates the clash between a writer's artistic ideals and critics' unrealistic expectations.

The minor criticisms leveled at *Roderick Hudson* became more pronounced in reviews of *The American* and *The Europeans*. James's manner was becoming increasingly cold-blooded; his characters, even more unsympathetic. Both books were censured for their endings. The St. Louis *Post-Dispatch* reviewer, for example, commented that while reading *The Europeans*, "there was a vague suspicion all the way through that it wasn't going to end in anything in particular, as it proves at last."[3] In *The American*, the New York *Tribune* complained, the "action simply stops, leaving matters very much as they were before." Christopher Newman had been likeable enough through much of the book, but he lost the reader's sympathy by the end. His final lack of forcefulness and perseverance seemed incongruous with his early activities as a go-getting, self-made American. Through much of the book, the *Scribner's* reviewer found Christopher Newman believable, engaging, and manly, but by the end, "the successive steps of the story grow more and more disheartening, and we finally close the volume, conscious victims of misplaced confidence." The New York *Times* went as far as to suggest an alternate ending: "It would have been better for Mr. James's literary fame to have blown the convent up with nitroglycerine, and had Newman carry off Mme. de Cintré . . . than to have allowed him to end his love affair in what is vulgarly termed a fizzle."

The book's title was part of the problem. Setting up Newman as *the* American did not sit well with the nationalistic American critics. Contemporary English readers, free from the jingoism of their American counterparts, responded somewhat differently. George Saintsbury's review indicates how the work was received in England. Saintsbury saw Newman as a "typical Yankee" and found "something exceedingly jarring" in the idea that Newman would revenge himself for personal slight by making use of a family secret. Saintsbury asked, "How could he think of doing such a thing?" whereas American critics asked, "How come he didn't go through with it?"

Though more open-minded, the English reviewers were not always kind. After reading reviews of *The American, The Europeans,* and the English edition of *Roderick Hudson* (the publication of which had been delayed until 1879), James expressed skepticism about his contemporary readers in letters to his family. Sending a copy of the *Saturday Review* notice to his brother William, he wrote, "The shabbiness of its tone is such as really—n'est ce pas?—to make one think more meanly of human nature."[4] A review in the *Spectator,* James wrote his mother, "depressed me by its essential *unintelligence* and the extreme narrowness which lurks under its liberal pretensions."[5]

Still, he was not without enthusiasts. W. E. Henley was his favorite English reviewer of the early novels. Reviewing *The Europeans* for the *Academy,* Henley found James an "exponent of the refined, eclectic realism of Turgénieff" and found the book the "purest piece of realism ever done." James made sure Henley promptly received copies of his next works. When *Daisy Miller* appeared, James wrote his publisher, "I enclose you a rather long list, as usual, of people to whom I should like 'Daisy Miller' sent. Will you kindly see that the copy for *Henley* (the 1*st*) goes *immediately?* He is an admirable reviewer to whom I promised an early one."[6]

After its publication in 1878, *Daisy Miller* quickly became James's best-liked book up to that time. Although the character of Daisy Miller was not totally sympathetic, she was recognizable, reminding readers of many young American women traveling abroad. Some saw the work as a cautionary tale. Richard Grant White, for example, hoped the book would have "some corrective effect" but accurately prophesied, "the probability is that, on the contrary, Daisy Miller will become the accepted type and her name the *sobriquet* in European journalism of the American young woman of the period." American reviewers of *Daisy Miller* analyzed how James's title character measured up as a national type just as they had for Christopher Newman. English critics, on the other hand, saw the book as more than merely an illustration of national character and recognized other aspects of James's writing such as his narrative technique. The *Pall Mall Gazette* reviewer, for example, approved James's use of an internally focalized, third-person narrative: "We know no more about them [the characters] than the *dramatis personae* see, and in this way our curiosity is kept alive."

James was delighted with the English reception. He wrote his brother William from England, "I am very glad indeed that you were pleased with 'Daisy Miller,' who appears (*literally*) to have made a great hit here. 'Every one is talking about it' &c, & it has been much noticed in the papers. Its success has encouraged me as regards the faculty of appreciation of the English public; for the thing is sufficiently subtle, yet people appear to have comprehended it. It has given me a capital start here." [7] James's words both convey his enthusiasm and suggest what he believed to be a writer's ultimate goal: to create a literary work that satisfies both creator and audience. Never again would James's artistic quest and his desire for public acceptance so happily coincide.

Reviews of James's fiction from *Confidence*, first published in late 1879, through *The Aspern Papers* in 1888 reflect the differences between his approach to fiction writing and his contemporary reader's understanding of the novel. The author, most readers believed, should reflect some sympathy in his characters, but James seemed devoid of sympathy. With his "mental microscope," to borrow a term the Chicago *Tribune* applied to describe the technique he used in *The Bostonians,* James scrutinized the thoughts and actions of his characters just as a biologist treated specimens. Scientific diction pervades the critical language applied to the works of James's middle period. *Washington Square,* the New York *Times* quipped, portrayed "a few marked specimens of the *genus Americanum*." [8] Reviewing *Confidence,* the New York *Herald* stated that when James's narrators found "a young lady worthy of their interest they impale her as a naturalist might a butterfly and make a careful and scientific investigation of her nature." In his fine overview of James's readers, Henry Nash Smith noticed the many times reviewers used the graphic surgical term "vivisection" to describe James's penetrating analysis. [9] The field of physics also provided appropriate metaphors. The *Critic* said that *The Princess Casamassima* would be "endlessly delightful . . . to the lover of interpretations, of emotions analytically examined, of hairs radiantly split, of spectroscopic gratings capable of dividing a ray of light into 32,000 lines to the square inch, or of intellectual engines describing 150,000 sensations to the twenty pages."

James sometimes claimed the right to enter the heads and hearts of his characters at will, and many readers found this authorial prerogative disturbing. Reviewing *The Bostonians,* Horace E. Scudder commented on James's "habit of reporting the mind as well as the conversation of his baser characters in a sort of third personal evasion of elegance." Julia Wedgwood, too, criticized the narrative point of view in *The Bostonians:* "To be told not only what his *dramatis personae* express but what they thought and kept to themselves, what they felt inclined to express and why they refrained . . . seems to us a violation of every conceivable rule of literary good breeding, and affects us in fiction with not less sense of fatigue and unfitness than such an experience would in life." The most perceptive readers, however, accepted James's minute delineation of thought and feeling and tried to understand his narrative strategies.

Some found that James made excessive demands on his readers. Rather than straightforwardly explain the action taking place, James more often seemed to force his readers to fill in important details. One reviewer had become accustomed to James's endings by the early 1880s and saw *The Portrait of a Lady* as a kind of mathematical proof. He wrote, "when at last the demonstrator breaks off in the abrupt way which has startled all his readers, it is with the air of saying, 'I have furnished all the points and shown you how to proceed. Find the answer for yourselves.'"[10] While many resented the demands James made on his readers, others were pleased. Describing *Confidence,* the *Scribner's* reviewer noticed: "We see, too, the influence that their emotion exerts on their conduct, but not the real emotion itself. For all that, the reader who can supply the missing links and rewrite the love passages for himself, can only admire the whole outgrowth of the conditions." Sometimes this complicity between author and reader became uncomfortable for the reader. Robert Bridges remarked that in *The Aspern Papers,*

> the reader is entrapped into a keen interest in the hunt for the love-letters of the poet *Aspern.* When the indelicacy and even cruelty of the whole plot are suddenly flashed upon you, you feel something of the shame and humility which at last overtook the literary ghoul. You are to a degree *particeps criminis,* and understand the weak point, in human nature which has led to so many unpardonable literary sins.[11]

By the late 1880s, James had created a large enough body of work that reviewers had a fair idea of the "Jamesian" novel.[12] Concerning *The Aspern Papers,* the *Saturday Review* commented, "Though readers who have followed his [James's] past career will know what awaits them at the end of the story, there is still an interest in watching the passes of the swords." In other words, the reviewer is saying, simply accept the fact that although James's endings would remain disappointing and unresolved, his telling of the tale would nevertheless be worth reading. When George Bernard Shaw was reviewing books for the *Pall Mall Gazette* during the late nineteenth century, he apparently did not have the opportunity to review any of James's works, but on one occasion he did manage to mention James and characterize his way of ending a book. Complaining of an author who mixed both old and new writing styles and incongruously placed the new before the old, Shaw made an analogy with James's writing: "It is as if a publisher not quite abreast of his time had commissioned Mr. James to write a novel, and, finding the last chapter inconclusive and unsatisfactory, had called in Miss Braddon to marry the lovers, kill the villain, and wind up the business on the strictest principles of poetic justice." [13] Shaw recognized that the Jamesian dénouement marked an advance over the typical romantic ending. Ambiguity and lack of resolution, Shaw's remark suggests, were infinitely preferable to cliché.

During the decade from *Confidence* to *The Aspern Papers,* James's attitude toward his reviewers changed drastically. Early in the period, he remained eager to know how his work was being received. After *Washington Square* appeared, for example, James, then in San Remo, wrote Frederick Macmillan, "Have there been any (noticeable) notices of my book? Perhaps you have sent two or three to Bolton St. I should be glad to see the few that appear in the important papers: for the others I don't care." [14] Macmillan wrote back promising to send "anything of interest." [15] On a trip home to America after the publication of *The Portrait of a Lady,* James was pleased to find the critics responding positively. He again wrote Macmillan, "Also my book is selling—largely, for one of mine. I hope it is doing something of the kind *chez vous*. I have seen a good many English notices, & appear to myself to have got off on the whole very well. Look, if you can put your hand on it, at a Review in the *Tribune* for Dec. 25th—very glowing, & well-written." Although James did not admit it to his publisher, the *Tribune* review had been written by his good friend John Hay.[16] With the appearance of *The Bostonians,* James's attitude soured. "I even confess," he later recalled, "that since the *Bostonians* I find myself holding the 'critical world' at large in a singular contempt. I go so far as to think that the literary sense is a distinctly waning quality." [17]

After the critics got hold of *The Princess Casamassima,* James abandoned hope about his reviewers. Those who disliked the book heartlessly said so. Still, he was not without sympathizers. William Dean Howells had written a "rousing eulogy" on the work,[18] and Edmund Gosse wrote to console James for the scathing *Athenaeum* review. James responded to Gosse, "Yes, the notice in the Athenaeum of my 'Princess' is singularly discreditable. But this sort of thing is a very old story to me—I have nothing more to learn about it . . . though it disillusionizes one for art & letters." [19] Another sympathizer wrote mentioning the negative review in *Punch*. James responded, "You exaggerate the importance of that contemptible little notice in *Punch,* of the *Princess:* these things are not of my ken or my care. This sounds sublime—but really the idiocy and ill nature of the journals of my time have made me so. Don't speak of them." [20] In 1890, James wrote his publisher, reversing his instructions of nearly ten years before, "Kindly instruct that no 'notice' of any kind be sent me." [21]

James's attitude about the reviewers is poignantly reflected in a letter to his brother written after finishing *The Tragic Muse* but before it was published:

> I hope you will have received promptly a copy of *The Tragic Muse,* though I am afraid I sent my list to the publishers a little late. I don't in the least know, however, when the book is supposed to come out. I have no opinion or feeling about it now—though I took long & patient & careful trouble (which no creature will recognise) with it at the time: too much, no doubt; for my mind is now a muddled, wearied blank on the subject. I have shed and ejected it; it's over & dead—& my feeling as to what may become of it is reduced to the sordid hope it will make a little money—which it won't. [22]

James was wrong about how critics would respond to *The Tragic Muse.* It actually received the most praiseful reviews of any James work since *Daisy Miller.* The *Christian Union* reviewer found a "gain in freshness of feeling and vigor of treatment. . . . The impression that one receives is that the story is a *tour de force* of a very accomplished and brilliant man." The New York *Times* also enthusiastically approved the work. Unlike the typical James story, the story was full of movement and the ending was good: "Mr. James's former work appears to have been a schooling for this latest book, which takes its place, for the present at least, as a masterpiece." And the Manchester *Guardian* found *The Tragic Muse* a "brilliant rendering of the kaleidoscopic effects which play on the surface of society life."

For much of the last decade of the nineteenth century, James devoted his creative energies to play writing. He did publish collections of short fiction during the early 1890s, but these received little critical notice. During the autumn of 1896, James published *The Other House,* a work originally written as a play and his first novel since *The Tragic Muse* more than six years before. Prior to its publication, James wrote to his publisher Frederick Macmillan to reiterate his earlier instructions: "Kindly, when *The Other House* is published, neglect, as far as I am concerned, the reviews. I mean, please *don't* forward them." [23] It is important to understand that although James tried to avoid reading the reviews, often he could not help but read them. A letter he wrote to his brother a month and a half later suggests that, despite the instructions to Macmillan, Henry James had learned of the critical response to *The Other House.* Most reviewers liked the book, but James was hardly pleased. He knew that *The Other House* was a slight work compared to some of his earlier efforts that the reviewers had disliked. He wrote his brother, "*The Other House* . . . by the way, shows symptoms of being the most successful thing I have put forth for a long time. If *that's* what the idiots want, I can give them their bellyfull." [24] In light of this letter to his brother, Henry James's letter to Macmillan seems to convey a deliberate pose. For his publisher, James fashioned himself as a literary artist who cared little for what the public thought about his work. For his brother, however, James freely admitted that he was both aware of the reviews and disturbed by their superficiality.

During the six-year hiatus in which James published no novels, an important new scientific discovery had been made—Wilhelm Röntgen had discovered X rays. Literary critics suddenly had the ideal scientific metaphor with which to describe James's technique. Commenting on *The Spoils of Poynton,* the novel that appeared next after *The Other House,* the Chicago *Tribune* reviewer stated, "Like the up-to-date doctor who makes his patients swallow an electric light bulb and turns the X rays on them to boot, Mr. James illumines the whole interior of his characters and calmly dissects their thoughts while you wait." Similarly, the narrator of *The Sacred Fount* was characterized by one reviewer as a "Röntgen-ray-eyed guest," and another called him "an X-ray-eyed narrator." [25]

Although critics had a new metaphor to describe James's fiction after the mid-1890s, the X ray comments were, after all, merely an extension of the "mental microscope" and "vivisection" metaphors applied to the fiction of James's middle period. What made these later reviews different from the earlier ones was the amount of respect critics began to give James. The New York *Times* closed its review of *The Spoils of Poynton* with the following:

> It is sad to think that not one novel reader in ten thousand, probably, will be able to comprehend his [James's] and Mrs. Gereth's and Fleda Vetch's views of life, art, and conduct, leaving sympathy out of the question. But the appreciation of the one in ten thousand is worth working for, and the knowledge Mr. James must have that his delight in the book's subtlety and refinement, the grave, thoughtful piquancy which is its substitute for humor, will be keen while it lasts, is, perhaps, a sufficient reward. And counting all the tens of thousands of novel readers in the English speaking world, one from each of the tens of thousands will make up a company that is worth while. So that we need not grieve for Henry James.

James's next novel, *What Maisie Knew,* elicited similar comments from the *Pall Mall Gazette* reviewer, who adapted Milton's words to describe James's readers as an "audience fit, though few."

The Two Magics, published a year after *What Maisie Knew,* contained "The Turn of the Screw" and "The Covering End." Most reviews concentrated on the first tale. Nothing James had written before had prepared the critics for "The Turn of the Screw." To be sure, they found his characteristic subtlety, but unlike in earlier works, they found that the subtlety in "The Turn of the Screw" enhanced rather than obscured the story. The *Athenaeum* reviewer called the use of subtlety in "The Turn of the Screw" "triumphant" and remarked that James "only adds to the horror of his conception by occasionally withholding the actual facts and just indicating them without unnecessarily ample details." The *Illustrated London News* was similarly impressed: "He has rarely written anything so subtle, so delicate in workmanship, so intense in feeling, so entirely artistic." The Manchester *Guardian* reviewer also liked James's use of subtlety. He "presents his details with a fine economy, and their accumulation and elaboration prepare us for the intenser moments."[26] The London *Daily News* stated that "The Turn of the Screw" showed James's

> subtlest characteristics, his supreme delicacy of touch, his surpassing mastery of the art of suggestion. . . . The story is a masterpiece of artistic execution. Mr. James has lavished upon it all the resources and subtleties of his art. . . . The workmanship throughout is exquisite in the precision of the touch, in the rendering of shades of spectral representation.[27]

Reviewers of *The Two Magics* were thrilled by James's departure from his usual subject matter, which one deprecatingly called "things of sublime inconsequence." They were pleased that James had abandoned the petty insignificance of the sitting room and the parlor to grapple with the elemental forces of good and evil. After reading "The Turn of the Screw," the *Athenaeum* reviewer had hopes that James would give his readers "more of the natural man, and less of the intricate criticism and of the excessive sense of the importance of his subject" that, the critic implied, had marred several of James's previous works. The reviews of James's other works often expressed anger that he seemingly wasted so many words and so much creative energy on trivial things. No one made that complaint about "The Turn of the Screw."

According to many of his critics, James could hardly have followed up "The Turn of the Screw" with two less important books than *The Awkward Age* and *The Sacred Fount*. The New York *Tribune* review of *The Sacred Fount* begins:

> When Mr. James published "The Turn of the Screw," in the fall of 1898, he must have inspired in many a breast the wish that he would trust himself again in the train of speculation so powerfully exploited in that eerie narrative. It carried him, for the moment, away from the trivialities which have too often engrossed him, and enabled him to breathe the spiritual airs of creative imagination. In the following summer came "The Awkward Age," an anti-climax, if ever there was one.

Reviewing *The Awkward Age,* the *Spectator* concluded, "On the whole, we never remember to have read a novel in which the disproportion between the ability employed and the worth or attractiveness of the characters was more glaring."[28] Another English review of *The Awkward Age* was titled "Mr. Henry James Exasperates" and stated that "James has refined refinement, subtilized subtlety, and suggested suggestion to bewilderment."

Reviews of *The Sacred Fount* were much the same as those of *The Awkward Age*. The Chicago *Tribune* stated, "It justifies to the full every adverse criticism ever passed upon his work by those who do not like his methods." More than one reviewer explicitly called the work a parody of James himself, and several others suggested much the same thing. *Current Literature* said that "James has out-Jamesed himself," and the London *Daily Chronicle* contrasted James's "later manner" with his "more charming earlier style." With every book, the reviewer suggested, "his manner, so to say, gets later and yet more late." James tried to stay above the reviewers, but he could not avoid reading the notices altogether. He wrote a correspondent who had sent him a clipping, "Many thanks about the 'Notice.' I have seen but one—the one in the *Times,* but I shan't trouble you for any—as it is my eccentric practice to see as few as possible. No 'press-cuttings' agency ever had access to me. This is the fruit of a long life." [29]

The Wings of the Dove, The Ambassadors, and *The Golden Bowl* brought admirers or, perhaps more accurately, confirmed the admiration of many long-time James enthusiasts—despite the fact that, as Montgomery Schulyer claimed, James had become a "harder taskmaster than ever." [30] To be sure, the intricate syntax of these late works made them less approachable than the early works, but critics found something else they had not found within the earlier fictions. James, it seems, had finally learned how to express sympathy with his characters. The *Times Literary Supplement* suggested that James had written nothing to compare with *The Wings of the Dove,* except possibly *The Tragic Muse* and *Roderick Hudson,* but "in neither of these works do we find the same element of grave and penetrating tenderness." [31] None of the reviewers had found tenderness in James's early works. The *Pall Mall Gazette,* which had greatly disliked *The Awkward Age,* called *The Ambassadors* James's "finest novel." Similarly, Edward Garnett called the work the "finest and subtlest piece in the long gallery of his many achievements." [32] The *Athenaeum* review of *The Golden Bowl* expressed a unique sentiment: The reviewer wished the book were longer!

The Golden Bowl was James's last published novel, but he had one master-work left in him. *The American Scene,* a work Ezra Pound would later call the "triumph of the author's long practice," [33] described James's impressions of America upon his return after an absence of nearly a quarter century. In the book, James had characterized himself as the "restless analyst," and his reviewers found the phrase a fitting epithet. Several American readers disliked the book, but most English critics were awed by it. Much like the novels, *The American Scene* illustrated James's late manner. Edmund Gosse remarked,

This strange and eloquent book, divided by such a chasm from all ordinary impressions of travel made by the competent and intelligent stranger, is highly typical of Mr. James's later manner of writing. It is produced in that curious mode of his, by which an infinity of minute touches, each in itself apparently unemphatic, are so massed and arranged that out of them arises, when the reader least expects it, perhaps—a picture which absolutely controls the imagination.

Gosse called the book the "most durable surface-portraiture of an unparalleled condition of society which our generation is likely to see."

After reading the *Daily Mail* review, James wrote his friend Gosse, "I have just come up to town, & I gave myself this morning very promptly to the beatific perusal of your beautiful notice of *The American Scene* in the D.M. It has given me extraordinary pleasure—more, I can emphatically say, than any Appreciation of any book of mine has *ever* given me. Therefore my eyes really fill with tears as I very devoutly thank you."[34] James's heartfelt response to Gosse reflects a considerably different stance than had earlier letters such as those to Macmillan. James may have told others that he had no desire to read his reviews, but, these thankful remarks make clear, he never stopped wanting to be read, appreciated, and understood.

The present study represents the most thorough gathering of James's reviews ever assembled, but it would not have been possible without the pioneering research into James's contemporary reception begun fifty years earlier. The study of the critical response to Henry James started with Richard Nicholas Foley's Catholic University dissertation, *Criticism in American Periodicals of the Works of Henry James from 1866 to 1916* (1944), and Donald McLeish Murray's New York University dissertation, "The Critical Reception of Henry James in English Periodicals, 1875–1916" (1950), part of which appeared as "Henry James and the English Reviewers, 1882–1890" in *American Literature* (1952). Subsequent studies have treated the reception of individual works, such as Richard Dankleff's University of Chicago dissertation, "The Composition, Revisions, Reception, and Critical Reputation of Henry James' *The Spoils of Poynton*" (1959), and Rosalie Hewitt's "Henry James's *The American Scene*: Its Genesis and Its Reception, 1905–1977," *Henry James Review* (1980). Perhaps the best short treatment of James's contemporary readers is Henry Nash Smith's "Henry James II: The Problem of an Audience," in *Democracy and the Novel: Popular Resistance to Classic American Writers* (1978). Linda J. Taylor's *Henry James, 1866–1916: A Reference Guide* (1982) provides an excellent list of James's reviews in American newspapers and magazines but, curiously, lists almost no English reviews. Still, I am immensely grateful for Taylor's work. It helped me locate many American reviews of James's books that would otherwise have escaped my attention, and it was especially helpful for compiling the checklists of additional reviews that close each section of this book. For items concerning James in American newspapers and other periodicals that appeared during his lifetime other than book reviews, readers should consult Taylor.

Contemporary notices of James's works have been reprinted in many different places. Casebooks and critical editions of several important works—*The American,* "Daisy Miller," *The Portrait of a Lady,* "The Turn of the Screw," and *The Wings of the Dove*—reprint reviews. Other collections of critical essays, such as James Gargano's two-volume *Critical Essays on Henry James* (1987) and Roger Gard's *Henry James: The Critical Heritage* (1968), reprint others. The checklists of additional reviews that end each section of the present book are cross-referenced to other reprints of James's contemporary notices to allow readers to access easily those reviews that space constraints prevented me from including here.

Late nineteenth- and early twentieth-century critics had the habit of quoting lengthily from works they reviewed. In this edition, I have abbreviated overlong quotations to the first and last sentences from the quoted passage and replaced with ellipses the intervening text. After each abbreviated quotation, I have bracketed references to the page numbers on which the quotation appears. For works from *Roderick Hudson* (1875) to *The Tragic Muse* (1890), I conveniently cite page numbers from the Library of America editions: *Henry James: Novels 1871–1880,* ed. William T. Stafford (1983); *Henry James: Novels 1881–1886,* ed. William T. Stafford (1985); and *Henry James: Novels 1886–1890,* ed. Daniel Mark Fogel (1989). For those works published after 1890, I cite page numbers from the original editions.

Many people deserve credit for making this work possible. My fascination with Henry James began in graduate school during J. A. Leo Lemay's seminar "Complicity in American Literature." An essay I wrote for Professor Lemay's course eventually became the basis for " 'The Turn of the Screw' and the Aesthetics of Response," a paper that helped to shape the present work and which I presented separately at the 1993 American Literary Realism conference in Cabo San Lucas. I also thank M. Thomas Inge for establishing this series and for his work on this book as series editor. Further, I thank the newspaper and microfilm librarians at the University of Central Oklahoma, the University of Delaware, the University of Illinois, Indiana University, the Library of Congress, the University of Michigan, the University of Oklahoma, and the University of Virginia. I am especially grateful to Doylene Manning and the Interlibrary Loan Department at the Max Chambers Library, University of Central Oklahoma. Of course, I thank Richard and Carole Hayes for their encouragement and support from the beginning. Finally, I am grateful to Hershel Parker, who first taught me the techniques for, and the value of, finding reviews. To him this book is dedicated.

Notes

1   Henry James to William James, 3 December 1875; *The Correspondence of William James,* ed. Ignas K. Skrupskelis and Elizabeth M. Berkeley (Charlottesville: University Press of Virginia,

1992–   ), 1:244–45. Henry James to Henry James, Sr., 20 December 1875; Henry James to Mrs. Henry James, Sr., 24 January 1876; Henry James to William Dean Howells, 3 February 1876; *Henry James Letters,* ed. Leon Edel (Cambridge, Mass. The Belknap Press of Harvard University Press, 1974–84), 2:12–23.

2   William James to Henry James, 12 December 1875, *The Correspondence of William James,* 1:247.

3   St. Louis *Post-Dispatch,* 7 December 1878, p. 2. Quotations from reviews reprinted in this volume will not be separately documented.

4   Henry James to William James, 1 May 1878, *The Correspondence of William James,* 1:302.

5   Henry James to Mrs. Henry James, Sr., 6 July 1879, *Henry James Letters,* 2:250.

6   Henry James to Frederick Macmillan, 17? February 1879, *The Correspondence of Henry James and the House of Macmillan, 1877–1914,* ed. Rayburn S. Moore (Baton Rouge: Louisiana State University Press, 1993), p. 30. Four months later, James wrote Macmillan again, asking him to send copies of the English edition of *Roderick Hudson* to Henley and to Matthew Arnold; *Correspondence of Henry James and . . . Macmillan,* p. 33.

7   Henry James to William James, 23 July 1878, *Correspondence of William James,* 1:305–6.

8   New York *Times,* 28 November 1880, p. 10.

9   *Democracy and the Novel: Popular Resistance to Classic American Writers* (New York: Oxford University Press, 1978), p. 146.

10   *Lippincott's Magazine* 29 (February 1882), 213–15; reprinted in this volume.

11   For my notions of complicity in American literature, I am indebted to my teacher J. A. Leo Lemay.

12   My use of the word "Jamesian" here is not an anachronism. The earliest use of the adjective "Jamesian" that I have located occurs in the Detroit *Free Press* review of *The Princess Casamassima* in 1886.

13   "A Novel by Mr. Julian Hawthorne," review of Julian Hawthorne, *Love—or a Name, Pall Mall Gazette,* 30 December 1885; reprinted in Brian Tyson, *Bernard Shaw's Book Reviews Originally Published in the Pall Mall Gazette from 1885 to 1888* (University Park: Pennsylvania State University Press, 1991), p. 76.

14   James to Macmillan, 27 February 1881, *Correspondence of Henry James and . . . Macmillan,* p. 61.

15   Macmillan to James, 4 March 1881, *Correspondence of Henry James and . . . Macmillan,* p. 62.

16   James to Macmillan, 27 December 1881, *Correspondence of Henry James and . . . Macmillan,* p. 67. See also George Monteiro, *Henry James and John Hay: The Record of a Friendship* (Providence: Brown University Press, 1965).

17   James to William Dean Howells, 2 January 1888, *Henry James Letters,* 3:210.

18   On 10 March 1887, William James wrote Henry James, "Howells told me the other night that he had written a rousing eulogy of your *Princess* for the next Harper, and he hadn't a fault to find with it. Rev. John Brooks, a good man, interested in Socialism was here this morning and called it 'a superb book.'" *Correspondence of William James,* 2:59. James W. Gargano, *Critical Essays on Henry James: The Early Novels* (Boston: G. K. Hall, 1987), pp. 64–65, reprints the *Harper's* review of *The Princess Casamassima* without attributing it to Howells.

19   James to Edmund Gosse, 8 November 1886, *Selected Letters of Henry James to Edmund Gosse 1882–1915: A Literary Friendship,* ed. Rayburn S. Moore (Baton Rouge: Louisiana State University Press, 1988), p. 44.

20   James to Francis Boott, 26 November 1886, *Henry James Letters,* 3:139.

21   James to Frederick Macmillan, 29 May 1890, *Correspondence of Henry James and . . . Macmillan,* p. 162.

22   Henry James to William James, 16 May 1890, *Correspondence of William James,* 2:135.

23 James to Messrs Macmillan & Co. [New York], 17 September 1896, *Correspondence of Henry James and . . . Macmillan,* p. 184.
24 Henry James to William James, 30 October 1896, *Correspondence of William James,* 2:416.
25 *Academy* 1503 (23 February 1901), 165–66; "Mr. Henry James' New Novel," *Current Literature* 30 (April 1901), 493; both are reprinted in this volume.
26 Manchester *Guardian,* 11 October 1898, p. 4.
27 Quoted in "Book Reviews Reviewed," *Academy* no. 1391 (31 December 1898), 561.
28 *Spectator* 3697 (6 May 1899), 647; reprinted in Roger Gard, ed., *Henry James: The Critical Heritage* (London: Routledge & Kegan Paul, 1968), p. 282.
29 James to James B. Pinker, 18 September 1902, *Henry James Letters,* 4:242.
30 *New York Times Saturday Review of Books and Art* 7 (4 October 1902), 658.
31 *Times Literary Supplement* 34 (5 September 1902), 263. Reprinted in Gard, *Henry James: The Critical Heritage,* pp. 319–21; J. Donald Crowley and Richard A. Hicks, eds., *The Wings of the Dove: Norton Critical Edition* (New York: W. W. Norton, 1978), pp. 481–83.
32 Arthur Sherbo, in "Still More on James," *Henry James Review* 12 (1991), 110–12, first located Garnett's review but carelessly said it appeared in the *Spectator.* Garnett's review, reprinted in the present volume, appeared in *Speaker: The Liberal Review* new series 9 (14 November 1903), 146–47.
33 *Literary Essays of Ezra Pound,* ed. T. S. Eliot (New York: New Directions, 1935), p. 327.
34 James to Edmund Gosse, 2 February 1907, *Selected Letters of Henry James to Edmund Gosse,* pp. 225–26.

RODERICK HUDSON

The author of this novel, the "Jr." appended to whose name connects him with a father whose writings are well known for their rare union of subtlety of thought with vigor of style, has heretofore published essays and sketches which have appealed to the taste of the more cultivated and thoughtful part of the reading public. His last published article, that on Balzac in the November *Galaxy,* is a fine piece of thorough and delicately appreciative criticism, and is also a very characteristic exhibition of Mr. James' habit of thought, of his taste, and his style of writing.[1] As he has thus far exhibited himself to us, Mr. James—considering him as a writer—is the result of culture, and the observation of cultivated society operating upon a mind naturally perceptive, receptive, and yet fastidious. He has shown no indications of qualities of a robust natural growth; but it cannot hence be justly inferred that he is without them. Circumstances may have given his mind the cast it has worn hitherto, and we may see him, as he attains conscious strength and wins confidence in his powers by their exercise, developing original traits which have hitherto been repressed by the combined influences of doubt and discipline. We heartily hope that such may prove to be the case, for he has already shown that he is what so many of our "popular" writers are not—a literary artist.

Roderick Hudson is Mr. James' first published attempt at sustained creative work. As a first novel it must be regarded as remarkably successful. Its theme and its personages are quite removed from common-place; some of the latter have a very considerable degree of vitality; the story is on the whole cleverly although not vigorously constructed, and after we are once, with a little determination, well launched on it, we are not content until we are safely in port at the end of the voyage. *Roderick Hudson* is a rarely-gifted man, a sculptor, in whom egoism is absolute and supreme, and to egoism he adds selfishness, a quality which often, but by no means always, accompanies the other. Some of the greatest and best men the world had seen have been egoists; but goodness and selfishness cannot go together. Roderick's genius is first recognized by Mr. Rowland Mallett, a New-England gentleman of fortune and of the highest character and culture, who finds in the house of his cousin a little statuette in bronze which the unknown sculptor, then a student of law in the village in which the lady lived, had modeled and given to her. And here, upon the threshold of Mr. James' story, we find an example of a fault in literary art which yet commands a certain admiration. Cecilia, Rowland Mallett's widow cousin, is the mere occasion of his meeting with Roderick. She has no other function whatever in the story. She has no more connection with it than the stakes driven to mark out the space for the foundation of a building have to do with the building. And yet Mr. James wastes some very careful work, and many pages, and some of his readers' time upon her. She is minutely portrayed, both as to her surroundings and her individuality. We are even taken so far into the details of her character as to be told that she had "a turn for sarcasm, and her smile, which was her pretty feature, was never so pretty as when her sprightly phrase had a lurking scratch in it"—a description which leads us first to say that this Cecilia was a very good sort of woman to flee away from. We believe that it is Alexandre Dumas *fils* who wisely says, "*N'epouse jamais une fille railleuse. Dans une fille le raillerie est un symptome d'enfer.*" This Cecilia, who is so carefully drawn and finished, immediately disappears, and is no more seen, heard of, or referred to. She is the mere wicket gate at the beginning of our pilgrimage, and we resent having been thus interested in her for nothing. We are inclined to think that this fault is not one into which Mr. James has unwittingly fallen; but that it is a conscious or half-conscious imitation of Balzac, the greatest error of whose art, and at the same time the greatest exhibition of whose skill, was in the impertinent elaboration of mere accessories.

Mr. Rowland Mallett, who is about going to Europe, offers to take Roderick with him and to give him opportunities of study. The offer is accepted; but before they depart a perplexing little triangular arrangement of personages takes place. There is staying with Roderick's mother a certain Mary Garland who, as Cecilia says, is "a sort of far-away cousin; a good, plain girl, but not a person to delight a sculptor's eye." Nevertheless, this Mary Garland has a very captivating smile, and is represented as a person of strong character and deep but quiet feeling. With her at very short notice Mr. Rowland Mallett falls in love, only to discover, however, just on the eve of departure, that Roderick, finding that she loved him, fancied that he loved her and engaged himself to marry her as soon as he was prosperous.

After brief study of the art of the Old World, which he understands by intuition, Roderick goes to work, and (having, it will be remembered, modeled successfully and mastered all the mechanism of his art at home,) achieves success at a bound, and at once becomes talked of—almost famous. But before he makes his first great statue an incident occurs of no little importance to all the personages of the story. As the two young men were sitting together in the grounds of the Villa Ludovisi, a middle-aged and rather overdressed and pompous lady attended by a little elderly man passed them; and then there sauntered in their wake a young lady about twenty years old, very elegantly dressed, leading a fantastic poodle. The poodle was so absurd that Roderick smiled rather aggressively, whereupon:

> "The young girl perceived it and turned her face full upon him, with a gaze intended apparently to enforce greater deference . . . I wonder if she would sit to me." [*Novels 1871–1880*, p. 229]

That is very strongly imagined. The picture is clearly outlined, full of color and full of life. And, indeed, we are inclined to regard this group of people, albeit the characters of all of them are very extravagant, as the most natural, congruous, and vital in the whole story. They are, Mrs. Light, an American woman, once a great beauty, now something of an adventuress upon a large scale; the Cavaliere Nameless, who is also *cavaliere servieute* to Mrs. Light, and Christina Light, the daughter of the latter, for whom her mother is scheming to make a great marriage. After Roderick achieves his success, they, who have till then—and a year has passed—utterly disappeared from view, visit his studio, and there Christina Light plays with her poodle, talks nonsense, and a kind of careless sarcasm with a tone of studied indifference. Roderick asks permission to model her bust. She calls across the studio, "Mamma this gentleman wishes to model my bust. Please speak to him." Then soon she says, "Is it very tiresome? I have spent half my life sitting for my photograph in every conceivable attitude, and with every conceivable coiffure. I think I have posed enough." Her mother hesitates, when Christina bluntly or, rather, coldly says that it is because her mother does not know whether Roderick means the bust shall be paid for, adding, "I assure you she will not pay you a sou;"

4

and again she says to her that if Roderick gives the bust to her, instead of carrying it about, she "can always sell it." But Roderick carries his point. He makes the bust, and he falls hopelessly in love with the original.

Christina Light is no mere dawdling rich-husband-catching beauty. She has character, intelligence, and even a heart. She loathes the position in which she is placed by circumstances, and by her adventuress mother's schemes, and she plays a part. She is not exactly true and sound all through; and yet she is capable of sacrificing the most brilliant success in marriage, such a success as her mother could not have hoped for, to her womanly feeling and for a marriage that would satisfy the cravings of her heart. The Prince Casamassima becomes a victim of her charms. He is of the ancient nobility; his fortune is colossal; he is not vicious; he is merely a very weak brother in every way. Yet when he is introduced to her at a ball and asks her to dance, she brushes him aside for Roderick Hudson, and that not for mere coquetry or caprice, as amply appears afterwards. Her mother is in despair. And well she may be, for Christina roasts her Prince-Croesus of a lover thus. They are all, Roderick included, on a pretty terrace, which leads Mrs. Light to speak inquiringly of the terrace at the Prince's castle. He replies:

> "It is four hundred feet long, and paved with marble. . . . What did you inform me was the value of the hereditary diamonds of the Princess Casamassima?" [*Novels 1871–1880*, p. 319]

Thus does the poor girl scoff at the weak-brained, weak-bodied, weak-willed princeling who offers to buy her with his golden carriages and his quarts of diamonds. And she delights to show her scorn of herself and of the position in which she is placed in the presence of the mother whom she despises. She becomes deeply interested in Roderick, and yet does not quite love him with her whole heart; a heart that is ready we see to love with total abandonment upon good occasion. That occasion Roderick does not give. With all her admiration of his genius and of himself she feels that he is not quite manly. The virile force to which her feminine nature longs to render due submission, she does not find in his brilliant but unstable, untrustworthy nature. And so under pressure she engages to marry the hero of the terrace, the golden carriage, and the diamonds. He has at least those, and the title of Prince to boot, all of which Roderick is without, and, as she fears, true manliness besides. Roderick becomes moody, listless, nervous, helpless. He has not broken off his engagement with Mary Garland; and at Mr. Rowland Mallett's suggestion he sends for his mother and his promised wife. The result is not exactly what Mr. Mallett hopes. For not only does Roderick soon confess to him that his mother and Mary "bore" him, but the presence of Miss Garland piques Christina Light. She sees her rival, observes her, treating her not with petty jealousy but in the grand style, and soon to the surprise of all and the consternation of her mother and the Cavaliere, the Prince is sent about his business in a very decided and unmistakable fashion. In her despair Mrs. Light appeals to Mr. Mallett to help her to bring Christina to her senses; and this is done in a scene which we should only mar by quoting from it, but which is very cleverly managed somewhat in the manner of Dickens, for Mrs. Light, although she is a scheming adventuress, is a fool. This scene shows us the author's nearest approach to humor, which does not seem to be a strong element in his composition. Mr. Mallett has an interview with Christina which is interesting, but utterly in vain as far as the Prince is concerned, she remaining firm in her determination against him, whatever may be the fate of Roderick's suit. But to his surprise he hears next day that she not only recalled the Prince, but was married to him that very night. The cause of this catastrophe is intimated to us very plainly. Mrs. Light, and the Cavaliere, told Mr. Mallett that they had yet one pressure in reserve; and this proves to be that Christina is the daughter, not of Mr. Light, but of the Cavaliere, and that besides, her mother is involved in such disgraceful money affairs that only great wealth can save them all from ruin.

Roderick and his party, Mallett included, go off to live a while in Switzerland. There, in a lonely walk among the mountains, Roderick is overtaken by an awful storm, in the darkness and turmoil of which he falls from a precipice and is killed. He is found by Mallett and a fellow-artist, not mutilated, not bloody, for the rain has washed away all traces of such injury, and, as Mr. James beautifully says, "it was as if violence having done her work had stolen away in shame." The body is borne home, the mother and Mary come out to meet it. "Mrs. Hudson tottered forward with outstretched hands and the expression of a blind person; but before she reached her son Mary Garland had rushed past her, and in the face of the staring, pitying, awe-stricken crowd had flung herself with the magnificent movement of one whose rights are supreme, and with a loud, tremendous cry, upon the senseless vestige of her love."

This is the story of Roderick Hudson, and it must be admitted that it does not lack a great and a peculiar interest. It shows unmistakably that its author has the constructive and the narrative faculty, and that he possesses also no small share of dramatic power; and yet its defects are chiefly those of characterization. In detail, in the portrayal of minute traits, Mr.

James is very skillful. It is in the expression of a strong unity that he is least successful. With one or two exceptions, his personages are aggregations rather than single conceptions; and when he seeks to impress a character upon us by implication he fails. Mary Garland is an example in point. She is evidently intended to leave upon us the impression of a strong, rich, passionful, and truly womanly nature, one whose passions, and even whose passing emotions, are kept under restraint, a nature whose power is in reserve. But the result is that she is tame and colorless. We see what the author means her for; and yet we think of her as a plain, rather prim and awkward, somewhat shy, New-England woman in an ill-fitting stuff gown—a woman who, in the eye of a much better man than Roderick Hudson, could not stand up a moment before the much less estimable Christina Light. Nor is it only the beauty of the latter which gives her her advantage. For, as we have seen, she is no mere beauty. And, by the way, we must remark, in passing, that the author shows great skill in bringing her beauty before our mind's eye. The task is not an easy one. It is not to be accomplished by mere description of form, of feature, and of color. Mr. James makes us feel the effect of her marvelous loveliness of person.

Another personage upon whom Mr. James has spent much labor, Mr. Rowland Mallett, fails to produce an impression of vital individuality. He is an impossible and not a very attractive character, to begin with. He is altogether too perfect to live, and too consciously perfect to be endured. And although we see what he was meant to be, he remains almost a lay figure, a stiff model of oppressive excellence and wisdom, always saying and doing exactly the right thing at the right time. Roderick himself is better, not because he is morally inferior; but because, good or bad, he is not made up, but imagined. And yet he is somewhat repulsive from his extravagance. Indeed, all through the book we long for some simple, truthful portrayal of our common human nature.

With all this there is a sameness that is monotonous in the talk of these people. Excepting the Light group, they all talk pretty much in the same way, the way of Mr. Henry James. Jr. Mallett might be a male Mary Garland, and Mary Garland a female Rowland Mallett, Esquire.

But delicate and charming touches of character are not lacking, and of these not a few are spent upon Mrs. Hudson, who is altogether the most natural and living of the New-England group. When she first sees Christina Light and is told that Roderick has made her bust:

"'Her bust! Dear, dear!' murmured Mrs. Hudson, vaguely shocked. 'What a strange bonnet!'"

The same old-fashioned New-England, shrinking from delight in the beautiful, appears with delicately bright characterization, as the mother, son, and Mary Garland are sitting together under a rarely beautiful Italian night.

"'It is a night to remember on one's deathbed,' Miss Garland exclaimed. 'Oh, Mary, how can you!' murmured Mrs. Hudson, to whom this savored of profanity, and to whose shrinking sense indeed the accumulated loveliness of the night seemed to have 'something shameless and defiant.'"

In a certain time of great trouble with Roderick, whom his poor mother cannot but regard as having been ruined by Europe, and, therefore, by Mr. Mallett, who is present, she "divided her time between looking askance at her son, with her hands clasped about her pocket-handkerchief, *as if she were wringing it dry of the last hour's tears,* and turning her eyes much more directly upon Rowland in the mutest, the feeblest, and the most intolerable reproachfulness. She never phrased her accusations, but he felt that in the unillumined void of the poor old lady's mind they loomed up like vaguely-outlined monsters." Again, on the same occasion, "somehow, neat, noiseless, and dismally lady-like, as she sat there, *keeping her grievance green with her soft-dropping tears,* her displeasure conveyed an overwhelming imputation of brutality." This is very fine and highly-finished work.

Mr. James' style is remarkably neat, clear, and, we might say, picturesque, if it were not for a conscious primness which is too often apparent. It is generally very correct, and so very rarely at all pretentious that we are shocked at reading of "anfractuosities of rain." *Anfractuosities* is a good enough word to be put into a dictionary—and to be left there. But it is not a word for living men and women to be called upon to read in cold blood. We observe with some surprise slips in the use of *would* and *should*. For example—"I used to think that if any trouble came to me I *would* bear it like a stoic" (p. 416.) "'Suppose you had fallen,' said Miss Garland, 'I believed I *would* not fall'" (p. 428.) This from a writer of Mr. James' quality and a man of his New-England breeding is astonishing.

On the whole, Roderick Hudson is a book of marked merit and of unusual interest, one of the best novels produced in America of late years. It gives us much now and promises more hereafter.

Note

1   "Honoré de Balzac," *Galaxy* 20 (December 1875), 814–36.

Chicago *Tribune*, 11 December 1875, p. 1.

Judging from the specimen before us, Mr. James' talent as a novelist lies in a broad, rich style, in brilliant colloquy, and in a rare faculty for making impossibly-sumptuous characters, electric in their intense vitality. But, judging again from the same example, he wants the firm, sure, even power of a finished artist, who, while composing splendid effects, brings into harmony with them the smallest accessories, and suffers none of the minor passages to degenerate into weakness and vacuity.

Roderick Hudson is a magnificent scapegrace, a sculptor gifted with genius, with physical beauty, with captivating traits of disposition, and, if we may add it in the same connection, with a total lack of the moral sense. His rival-figure in the book, poor Christina Light, is, like him, superbly endowed by nature, and a victim destined for immolation by inexorable circumstance. The tragedy of her fate moves us to pity: for her noble instincts, inextinguished by a pernicious education, should have gained her a happier fortune. Rowland Mallet and Mary Garland, the reputable pair brought into the foreground for purposes of contrast, are tame and uninteresting in their undeviating goodness. It is here that the novelist has shown his weakness. In the attempt to depict a couple of straightforward, single-hearted personages, he has failed to produce strong and distinct individualities. When they occupy the scene, as they do too much of the time, we are invariably wearied with their dull respectability.

Here is a grave fault, to our mind, too, in the plot. Rowland should have recognized the exacted worth of Christina's native character, and by marrying and lifting her out of an evil atmosphere give her the opportunity that she helplessly strove for, of salvation. By regarding the law of counterparts, Mr. James would have given a far more artistic creation. However, despite of the blemishes we have mentioned, the novel is to be distinguished from the innumerable hosts of its tribe by its power to furnish very agreeable recreation.

Appleton's Journal 14 (18 December 1875), 793.

As specimen of ingenious and sustained psychological analysis, Mr. Henry James, Jr.'s, "Roderick Hudson" (Boston: J. R. Osgood & Co.) is a wonderful production; but as a novel it fails to stand the crucial test. It is surprising, indeed, that a book which is so good in many ways—so subtle in its insight, so full of the finest fruits of culture, and so eloquent withal—should fail so utterly in the essential point of impressing us with the objective reality of the people to whom it introduces us. The difficulty seems to be that, with all his knowledge of human nature and insight into character, Mr. James cannot conceive a *person*. The motives of any given course of action, the influence of antecedents and circumstances upon character, and the complex effects which in human life flow from an apparently simple cause, he can trace with marvelous skill; but he does not seem able to construct in thought the process by which a person reveals his personality, and becomes individual in the apprehension of others. The characters in "Roderick Hudson" are far from being mere puppets, and yet the action of the story is curiously suggestive of a puppet-show. The author discourses elaborately in explanation of the qualities and characteristics of his several *dramatis personæ,* and then they come on the stage and say or do something to demonstrate the acuteness of his insight. They do not reveal themselves—they have no chance to reveal themselves—they are dissected beforehand with a precision and minuteness which leaves no opportunity for the spontaneous or the unexpected. The very conversation is for the most part a reflection of Mr. James's own mental processes, and even Christina Light, the spoiled child of fashion, talks like a trained metaphysician.

But for this deficiency of dramatic faculty on the part of the author, "Roderick Hudson" might be accepted without hesitation as the long-expected "great American novel." The story is finely conceived, and the book has an indescribable charm. The history of a genius must always be fascinating and impressive, especially if it have *vraisemblance,* and the story of Roderick Hudson's rise and fall is almost terrible in its fidelity to psychological truth. But the great charm of the book lies in the atmosphere of Rome which pervades it— the very flavor of Italy. In no other work, except Hawthorne's "Marble Faun," is the Eternal City made so familiar to our imaginations. It infects one irresistibly with the "Roman fever," and we feel as we read that, if all roads do not in fact lead to Rome, at least none is worth traveling which does not promise to lead there.

[Thomas Powell].
New York *Herald,* 26
December 1875, p. 3.

If we could go into a gallery of statuary and breathe life into the marble figures posing gracefully around us we would experience the same strange sensations we have after reading one of Henry James, Jr.'s, romances. None of his characters are real men and women. They have too much dignity to be called puppets and too much warmth to be called statues. Yet they are more like marble figures than real flesh and blood. We have no human sympathy with his heroes and heroines, still we are drawn to them by an irresistible fascination. Mrs. Hudson is the only real person in this last book of Mr. James', and consequently she is the least interesting. Roderick is a type of genius exaggerated, let us hope, but not impossible in a milder form. It is not so much for the story that Mr. James' books are charming as for their beautiful language and wonderful descriptive powers. Mr. James is not a story teller any more than Hawthorne was a story teller. He is a romancist, and one of the best living. He is cosmopolitan in literature as well as in life, and his models are the best of foreign masters. None of his books end in a conventional way, probably because he is not a conventional writer, and those who look for "and they lived together happily ever after" at the end of the last chapter of any of his novelettes will be disappointed.

In Roderick Hudson we find a young man of genius who was growing up untaught and unappreciated in a retired New England village. A fairy godmother turns up in the person of Rowland Mallet, a rich young fellow, with a taste for the fine arts. Rowland has just arrived at the village to say goodby to his cousin Cecilia before he sails for Europe. There he meets Roderick and is shown a bronze figure of his designing, which strikes the connoisseur as being of great promise. He immediately proposes taking Roderick along with him to Europe, and the proposition is accepted. Before the two young men set sail Rowland meets a cousin of Roderick's, Mary Garland, in whom he becomes very much interested, but tries to forget when he finds that she is engaged to Roderick. The reader cannot sympathize with this singular fancy on the part of a man of the world like Rowland. She was plain in face, dress and manner. The expressions of her face "followed each other slowly, distinctly gravely, sincerely, and you might almost have fancied as they came and went that they gave her a sort of pain." There was no reason in the world that Roderick should have loved her either, and we don't believe that he ever did, at any rate not very deeply. When the two arrive in Rome they meet Christina Light, the beautiful daughter of a semi-adventuress, and Roderick becomes enamored and evidently forgets all about Mary. Christina had a pair of extraordinary dark blue eyes, a mass of dusky hair over a low forehead, a blooming oval face of perfect purity, a flexible lip, just touched with disdain, and the step and carriage of a princess—just such a vision as would turn any young man's head, particularly an artist's. Roderick worked well when he first came to Rome, and quite distinguished himself, and his statues were bought by Rowland. But after he became in love with Christina he behaved like a lunatic. In fact, he was little better than insane at the best of times. Christina only liked him as a plaything; he was too weak a character for her. She was so uncertain of herself that she could not have loved as a husband a man of inferior will. Rowland was the unwilling confidant of both parties, for he did not at all approve of Roderick's conduct. Roderick is the most exasperating character; he has all the eccentricities of genius. He would not work unless he felt a certain inspiration. A Michael Angelo could not have been more whimsical. He hung around Christina everywhere she went, and really thought that she loved him. But what woman could love such a weakling? He was handsome and talented, but he was conceited and bad tempered also. When Christina

really dropped him and married another man he acted in the most outrageous manner. He simply gave himself up to despair. He refused to turn his hand to anything, and he said that his brain was dead. He begged Roderick to shoot him and put him out of his misery. Altogether his conduct was unmanly and unbearable. He did not pretend to love Christina after her marriage, but abused her right and left. "She's as cold and false and heartless as she's beautiful," he said in his rage, "and she has sold her heartless beauty to the highest bidder. I hope he knows what he gets!" She would have done worse had she married Roderick, for his heartlessness would have shown itself after the honeymoon. He was not meant for a finished man. Only a butterfly existence could suit such a character. With the proper ingredients in his make-up he would have been a great man; as it was, he was a great failure.

"James's *Roderick Hudson*." *Scribner's Monthly* 11 (February 1876), 588–99.

Less than a year ago, Mr. James, long known as a writer of brilliant magazine stories, published his first volume, a collection of the same. We now have his first novel before us. The interval is too short to warrant us in looking for any new growth in this book, by which to measure more accurately the merits and place of "The Passionate Pilgrim;"[1] and, indeed, we find it to be very much the same in substance and quality with the shorter tales. They were rich samples: this is a sort of extended Bayeux tapestry. We must accord to it the same excellences which we noted in the former volume, and we find ourselves also assigning to it the same limitations which we pronounced upon that. Let us, for a moment, put ourselves in the situation of a semi-disappointed admirer of Mr. James. Such a person, we think, might make some curious comments on the work. He would ask, for instance, "Is it a novel at all, in the common acceptance of that word? Instead of being a dramatic and diverting tale to take the reader captive by the strange charm of improvisation, and instruct or elevate him while under the influence of that spell,—is it not rather a biography, a curious psychological study based on types, more convenient when thus arbitrarily adopted than if fettered by the facts which limit any description or study of an actual life? To be sure, this is the primary condition of all novel-writing, that the novelist arranges types and conditions to suit himself; but there is something about Mr. James's book which gives this motive an undue prominence. One cannot say it is because the story seems unreal, for, in fact, it has a vigorous reality. Perhaps it is the excessive elaboration of details, which oppresses one with a sense of its determination to be very life-like, in order to counteract the rather abstract nature of the interests involved. Whatever the cause, it seems written too much for the sake of writing a novel of some sort; too little generated by some strong, untamable artistic impulse. The main interest is certainly remote from the ordinary scope of most readers' cares and hopes and susceptibilities. A tremendous young genius in sculpture is thrown on our hands, and we are tacitly required to feel a sufficient suspense respecting the success or failure of his artistic development, to carry us through some four hundred and eighty ample pages. One or two guys, of course, are thrown out—to assist us in walking this extended tight-rope—in the shape of Roderick's engagement to the simple and sweet Miss Garland, of Northampton, and his friend and patron Rowland's suppressed affection for her; also of Roderick's infatuation for Christina Light, in Rome. This latter proves to be inwoven pretty closely with the central fiber of the story (which, however, remains always the sculptor's æsthetic progress), and at length gives way, letting us down into the gulf of tragedy at the end. But, in the main, the subject is too cold and hard, and the treatment, brilliant as it is, is saturated with a sophistication that at times becomes almost repellent."

Such objections as these of the semi-disappointed admirer we do not sympathize with entirely, yet we can see that they have some ground to rest on. They do not do justice to the splendid workmanship of the author, or the sinewy and elastic movement of his characters, who are made of real flesh and blood. Every one of them is distinct, and the intensity of passion in some of them is huge. We have our doubts whether they are quite worth learning to know so thoroughly. Mrs. Light is too pitiable; the Cavaliere and the Prince are sad, faded, wearisome figures; Rowland is exceedingly monotonous; none of these are remunerative, they result in no clear gain to author or reader, so far as we discern. Mary Garland is a reverent study which comes nearer to beauty than Mr. James's studies commonly do.

The other figures of Americans are treated with a barren sneer, though they are sketched in a way that would otherwise be amusing. Some of the author's little habits also, such as putting the obsolete "nay" into the mouths of characters in common talk, the excessive use of "prodigious" and "inordinate," and a recurrence of scratching the head or wiping the forehead, on the part of Roderick and Rowland when embarrassed, seriously blemish his rich style. Still, with all that we have hinted in derogation, it must be said that

11

few novels of the season can, on the whole, take higher rank than "Roderick Hudson." Mr. James is an artist, and has it in his power to give us admirable compositions.

Note

1 *A Passionate Pilgrim, and Other Tales* (Boston: James R. Osgood, 1875).

F. M. Owen. *Academy* [England] new series 197 (12 February 1876), 142–43.

It is strange that American novels should not be better than they are. The literature for children is excellent. The stories written with "a high moral purpose" are often clever and seldom miss their mark. Why is it that Hawthorne still occupies the highest place among American novelists, and that we are acquainted with no one of them who comes near him? It is not that originality is lacking, for the short stories which reach us in American magazines or in cheap reprints have enough original matter in them to make more than one of the three-volumed novels which flood our own country, and are of a far higher order of merit: there is a very large amount of nervous force in the style; there is a superabundant command of language; there is "a desire to understand and record what is true;" and yet they fall short of being great. In *Roderick Hudson* we find an amusing passage in which the hero speaks of American art:—

> "He didn't see why we (Americans) shouldn't produce the greatest works in the world; we were the biggest people, and we ought to have the biggest conceptions. The biggest conceptions of course would bring forth in time the biggest performances. We had only to be true to ourselves, to pitch in and not be afraid, to fling imitation overboard and fix our eyes upon our national individuality."

And this seems to us what their novelists fail to do. The story of Roderick Hudson was a "big conception," but it is not a "big performance."

Roderick is an obscure sculptor in a New England village. Rowland Mallet, a lover of art who "has never done anything handsome for his fellow men," discovers genius in a small bronze statuette which Roderick, the attorney's clerk, has made, and forthwith takes him to Rome, thereby removing him from the home influence of his mother and his betrothed, Mary Garland, which seems to have been his best inspiration. For a while the genius flares up in Rome, and produces after six months (!) an Adam and an Eve which make a sensation; then it begins to fail, it wastes itself in a passionate love, flickers awhile and goes out miserably. The story is as sad as any story need be, but it would have been pathetic if Roderick had been more skilfully handled. It is entirely inartistic to make him so unpleasant that we are unable to sympathise with him. Towards the end of the book he is simply unbearable; how the people round him could have tolerated him is a problem; but they spoil him, pet him, give way to him in everything, and mildly remark to each other that he is "fatally picturesque," whatever that may mean. If they had said he was "fatally ill-mannered" or "fatally idiotic," it would have been more comprehensible. And yet no one can help being sorry for him when in the closing interview with his patron Rowland he discovers the nobility of his friend, and in the fierce light of that

12

purity knows himself so vile that his own artistic instinct is offended, and his last words are "I am hideous." Much of the plot of the story is laid among artists in Rome, but nothing is elaborated except a group of four or five characters:—Rowland, the dilettante patron whose kindness killed where it meant to save, and whose patient self-abnegation and bitter disappointment in the object of it are finely drawn; Christina Light, the young lady who plays the part of Will o' the wisp to Roderick, and wearies us by her affectation, her acting, and her selfishness; Mary Garland, who is little more than a lay figure, and about whom we are unable to rouse ourselves to Rowland's admiration; Mrs. Hudson, the mother, who appeals to us more than any of the other women in the book from her blind worship of the genius of the son with whom she has no real sympathy; and the sculptor himself, with his erratic moods, and fancies, his profound selfishness and egotism, his promise and his failure. In spite of all faults there is talent in the book and interest enough to repay the reader, who will feel that the idea of the author has been considerably greater than the power of execution, and that the story would have been more effective if it had been told in simpler language.

[Grace Norton].
"*Roderick Hudson.*"
Nation 22 (9 March 1876), 164–65.

The readers of Mr. James's other writings, who rightly appreciate them, are justified in looking for a great deal of pleasure in the reading of this new novel, and after finding this pleasure, they will recur with all the keener enjoyment to his earlier stories; for while the qualities connected with thoughtful and elaborate observation have here more complete expression than Mr. James has given them before, their very excellence makes them serve as an admirable foil for the greater simplicity of his earlier work. In saying this we are thinking especially of those stories of Mr. James's of which the scene is laid, as for the most part is the case with this, in Europe—that charming series which began with the 'Passionate Pilgrim' and ended with 'Madame de Mauves,' including among others, the plaintive tale of the young French girl, pretty, graceful Gabrielle, and the more passionate sorrows of the Italian woman at Isella.

Though the scene of 'Roderick Hudson,' as we have said, is laid in Europe, with Rome for the background of its sombre incidents, which succeed each other in an unbroken file, and with the precipices and storms of Switzerland causing the closing catastrophe, the *dramatis personæ* are all Americans, and each one—it would almost appear, as if unconsciously to the author—is in his or her individual way a constant reminder that Americans lose much of their rightful charm and interest when transplanted from their own habitat and exhibited among the more cultivated growths of foreign life. The bare plot of the story is this: Rowland Mallet, the hero *de facto*, meets at Northampton, in the State of Massachusetts, Roderick, the hero *ex officio*, and, discovering in him an unrecognized genius for sculpture, transports him on the wings of his own large fortune and Rowland's enthusiasm to Rome. On the eve of leaving home Roderick engages himself to a certain Mary Garland, in whose serene solidity Mr. Mallet, in a very few interviews, has on his side felt that charm which is but love, while Roderick's love is but the flower of that other charm which lies in familiar companionship. In mid-ocean, Roderick's careless communication of his relations with Miss Garland reveals to Rowland a future of self-sacrifice—of self-sacrifice, as he despairingly hopes, for her sake. But the self-sacrifice becomes mingled with poignant self-questionings for poor Rowland when the young artist plunges through dissipation into passion—a very headlong and headstrong fall—and becomes the slave of a certain very uncertain Miss Light. Miss Garland and Mrs. Hudson, the sculptor's mother, are summoned to the scene, but they are, of necessity, powerless to aid, and after a time Roderick's death brings an end to one period of unhappiness for his friends and at the same time imposes on them the misery of endless regrets. So it is still compassion and not congratulation that is felt for Miss Garland and Mr. Mallet, though the wonderfully complete mental training which the ever-improving Mary has received, first from love and then from sight-seeing, must somewhat break the force of the blow to her and the force of the sympathy felt for her sufferings.

Poor Rowland we leave comfortably wretched, but how could one be otherwise who had already given ample evidence of the vein of insanity which runs through every man's brain in the madness which leads him to carry a Northampton boy to Italy as a lump of fine potter's clay, to be shaped according to his unforeseeing will on the wheel of fate? The anomalous relation of these two young men, who are sometimes comrades on the footing of good fellowship, and sometimes separated into a modest and most conscientious and responsible patron, and a ward now wholly self-surrendering and endearing, and again obstinately resisting and repelling, is so strange a flaw in the story as to damage it throughout. Even Americans, with all their pliability, do not twist themselves into such odd arrangements as these.

The odd arrangements and circumstances which surround Miss Light's career are (all but an insufficiently accounted for Cavaliere) more in keeping with what has been observed before of human nature. Miss Light—Christina Light—is the *beautiful* heroine; and one looks to Miss Garland to take the role of *ingénue,* and to Miss Light to be *première amoureuse*; but, when all is said and done, Miss Light stands revealed in the passionless feebleness of successful, self-scorning worldliness, while the highly-educated Miss Garland poses as a very stalwart Truth.

We may jest a little, for our jests play on a very solid ground of admiration. The serious intention to do the author's best is everywhere felt in this story, and it produces most excellent results. The simplicity and directness and quietness of the plot make the interest of its gradual development a matter of very considerable artistic skill, since it relies wholly on the phases and transformations of the characters involved. No small amount of delicate strength of purpose and power of vigorous execution is to be perceived in the life given to the subordinate characters—Sam Singleton, Mrs. Hudson, Madame Grandoni, Mr. Leavenworth, and especially Miss Blanchard—each of which is to a very unusual degree self-existent, independent of its author; not at all pulled by puppet-strings as part of a show, but walking about actively on legs of its own; and, at the same time, the subordination of these characters to the two principal personages, Christina and Roderick, is always cleverly, and more than cleverly, managed.

It is one of the noteworthy points in considering the artistic construction of the story that Roderick's character is seen wholly through the eyes of others. The author never gives us his own interpretation of Roderick's actions, but only that of the bystanders. We have only an outside view of him from the first page to the last, and the success of his portraiture is less likely to be recognized than if the workings of his mind were more boldly revealed. We know him chiefly through Rowland, and Rowland does not always understand him.

The figure of Rowland himself is perhaps, on the contrary, over-elaborated, or at least it seems unnecessary to acquaint us with his prehistoric loves, or to trace the line of his qualities through the biographies of his parents and grandparents in a work not intended to set forth the doctrines of heredity, and not written by Balzac. And we must remonstrate against his name. Why should Mallet be anybody's name in a story of which the hero is a sculptor; and if anybody's, why not the sculptor's own, after Thackeray's fashion?

Athenaeum [England] 2697 (5 July 1879), 12–13.

Every one is familiar with the novel in which the hero is the centre of the whole story, and either tells it himself or else it comes immediately from the author's hand—the normal novel, as it may be called. There is also another kind, which a few years back was very popular, in which the author is concealed behind a fictitious personage, who plays no great part in the events, but is in a position to see them all, and who recounts them for the reader's benefit. This is a good method, especially when the hero is of an unamiable character, and has, if we mistake not, been em-

ployed with effect by Mr. Wilkie Collins. Mr. James has struck out a somewhat different line. He retains the narrative in his own hands, but yet does not lead the reader to identify him with the hero, as is often the case where no personage interposes between the author and his creations. He does this rather ingeniously by introducing the reader to another person first. The book is, as it were, an episode in the history of Rowland Mallet, embracing the period of his acquaintance with Roderick Hudson. This arrangement gives a great air of life-likeness to the story. The chief personage comes in, as it were, incidentally, and we are rather concerned with his doings as they affect his acquaintances than with theirs as they affect him. The story is the old tale of "the soul possessed of many gifts, that did love beauty only"; the moral, that the motto "Everything for art and by art" will not serve as a working canon of ethics. It is a well-worn theme, but as good as another to hang a study of characters and manners upon. Mr. James has done this so well that he has quite established his right to choose even a more hackneyed *motif* if he will. It is impossible to quote much, but one or two specimens will show the neatness of his phrasing. In the opening scene Rowland Mallet touches himself off in conversation with a clever widowed cousin, with whom he is just not in love, and to whose "sense of the irony of things" he "suspected awkwardly that he ministered not a little":—

" 'Do you know, I sometimes think that I am a man of genius, half-finished? The genius has been left out, the faculty of expression is wanting, but the need for expression remains, and I spend my days groping for the latch of a closed door.' 'What an immense number of words,' said Cecilia, 'to say you want to fall in love!' "

However, if he cannot be the rose, Rowland will at least live near it and cultivate it, so he carries off the genius of Northampton, Mass., a youth named Roderick Hudson, of great promise as a sculptor, to Rome; and the story is mainly occupied with what befell them there. It is very sad, and the impression is strengthened by the way in which the author is at no pains to gather up his ends, but leaves them as they are apt to be left in real life, loose and ready for tying on, if the chance comes, elsewhere.

The women are all well conceived. There is, for instance, Christina Light, the typical daughter of a typical mother, an adventuress who trades equally on her own shame, for Christina is not her husband's child, and on her daughter's beauty; using the one to beat down by fear of its disclosure her daughter's scruples at selling the other to the highest bidder. The reader learns almost to pity the poor girl, utterly untrustworthy as she is, even towards her own self. She

"had a fictitious history in which she believed much more fondly than in her real one; and an infinite capacity for extemporized reminiscence adapted to the mood of the hour."

Her counterpoise is Mary Garland, the New England girl, Roderick's cousin and betrothed.

"She did you the honours of her mind with a grace far less regal. . . . If in poor Christina's strangely commingled nature there was circle within circle, and depth within depth, it was to be believed that the object of Rowland's preference [for his genius for falling in love has found its scope here], though she did not amuse herself with dropping stones into her soul and waiting to hear them fall, laid quite as many

sources of spiritual life under contribution."

'Roderick Hudson' is so much the best novel by Mr. James that we have seen, that we regret to find it is not his latest, having been, as a prefatory note informs the readers, originally published in Boston some four years ago. We regret it, because its date precludes the critic from regarding it as a counter-assurance to certain fears respecting Mr. James's future as a novelist which this journal expressed when noticing his last volume of stories. Perhaps it may be that the form of the more sustained work after all suits him better. He puts some excellent remarks on the question of "keeping it up" into a conversation among some of his Roman artists. It is to be hoped his readers may accept the omen for himself!

W. E. Henley. *Academy* [England] new series 379 (9 August 1879), 99.

Mr. Henry James, it is pleasant to reflect, is rapidly and steadily making himself a name and a place among English novelists. Not long ago he gave us that brief and charming book, *The Europeans;* then we had of him *Daisy Miller* and *Four Meetings,* a couple of psychological studies of a merit almost as rare in English as the method they example; and now, in orthodox three-volume form, he sends us *Roderick Hudson.* It is practically a new book, though it was first published in Boston some three or four years since. To say that it is strongly suggestive of an admiring acquaintance with Ivan Tourguenieff is as much as to say that it is tolerably unhappy throughout, and that its ending is miserable indeed. Tourguenieff loves to treat of wasted lives; he finds his materials among the bankrupts of humanity; he is the sardonic, unsympathetic Shakspere of a world of petty and trivial Hamlets. Mr. James is not averse from practising the study of the same section of social pathology. Fortunately for his readers, however, he has the gifts of intellectual charm and good temper, and is saved thereby from the reproach of grimness and cruelty that else might possibly attach to him. *Roderick Hudson,* like most of its kindred, is only pleasantly discomfortable. Told by a man of the fashionably inexorable temper, it would be intolerable; but Mr. James's tact and serenity keep him always on the right side of the hedge, and *Roderick Hudson* is a singularly readable as well as a singularly vigorous and clever book. Perhaps in the end you are inclined to owe Mr. James a grudge for killing off his hero instead of letting that poor creature go away to Lucerne after Christina Light, and enjoy himself in his own natural and immoral way; but you forgive him at once when you recall how amiably and intelligently he has been discoursing to you from the first, what a deal of brilliant and striking work his three volumes contain, how many picturesque and original persons they have introduced to you, and how much that is new and true they have told you about men and things. After all, too, if Mr. James does murder his hero, there is something from his own point of view to be said in excuse of that feat, and it does not come home to you with such bitterness as is yours over the shameful violence done to Lucy Feverel and Neville Beauchamp. Roderick Hudson, as a man in love, and very creditably in love, is interesting, and not unworthy of regard; but despite the certitude of insight with which

he is apprehended, and the athletic ease and cleverness with which he is done, I find him the weakest fact about the book. Perhaps he suffers a little in the neighbourhood of such figures as Christina Light and Rowland Mallet, as Augusta Blanchard and Mr. Leavenworth, as Mrs. Hudson and the Cavaliere Giacosa, which seem to me as good work of their kind as later literature can show.

Checklist of Additional Reviews

Boston *Evening Transcript,* 23 November 1875, p. 6.

Boston *Daily Advertiser,* 27 November 1875, p. 2.

Chicago *Inter-ocean,* 27 November 1875, p. 5.

New York *World,* 29 November 1875, p. 2. Reprinted in James W. Gargano, ed., *Critical Essays on Henry James: The Early Novels* (Boston: G. K. Hall, 1987), pp. 32–35.

St Louis *Globe Democrat,* 5 December 1875, p. 6.

New York *Daily Graphic,* 9 December 1875, p. 299.

Independent 27 (23 December 1875), 8.

Philadelphia *North American,* 27 December 1875, p. 1.

Saturday Review [England] 41 (29 January 1876), 154.

Atlantic Monthly 37 (February 1876), 237–38.

Graphic [England] 13 (25 March 1876), 306.

[Sarah Butler Wister]. "James's Roderick Hudson." *North American Review* 122 (April 1876), 420–25.

Pall Mall Gazette [England], 26 June 1879, p. 12.

[R. H. Hutton]. *Spectator* [England] 2662 (5 July 1879), 854–55. Reprinted in Roger Gard, ed., *Henry James: The Critical Heritage* (London: Routledge & Kegan Paul, 1968), pp. 75–77.

British Quarterly Review 70 (October 1879), 529–30. Reprinted in Gard, p. 78; Gargano, pp. 35–56.

[J. R. Wise]. *Westminster Review* [England] 15 (October 1879), 619.

THE AMERICAN

New York *Tribune,* 8 May 1877, p. 6.

Mr. Henry James, jr., inherits from his father a diction so rich and pure, so fluent and copious, so finely shaded yet capable of such varied service, that it is, in itself, a form of genius. Few men have ever been so brilliantly equipped for literary performance. Carefully-trained taste, large acquirement of knowledge, experience of lands and races, and association with the best minds, have combined to supply him with all the purely intellectual requisites which an author could desire. His use of these rare advantages, and consequently the question of his highest success depends therefore upon that subtle element of temperament which can neither be inherited nor acquired—that passion, springing equally from the intellect and the moral nature, which makes creation a necessity. It is this that tinges the colorless ichor of the brain with the strong, ruddy hues of the heart, and forces the very pulses of an author's life, whether he will or not, to beat upon his pages.

We cannot yet distinctly feel the presence of such an informing power in Mr. James's stories and novels. He sits beside his characters, observing and delineating their qualities and actions with marvelous skill, yet apparently untouched by any sympathy with them. His objectiveness is that of the *savant* rather than that of the novelist or dramatic poet. His conceptions are not forged in the heat of his mind, but hammered from cold steel, the temper of which has been tested in advance. This gives a stamp of security to his work, which, up to a certain point, is both an advantage and a charm. He approaches fine psychological problems with a confidence which the reader involuntarily shares, and rarely falls short of the limits within which he has decided to solve them. Yet most of his figures have something of the character of bas-reliefs: they can only be seen from one side, and are best seen in one light. In some of his former stories, their selected peculiarities are presented with such care and vividness, that we nearly lose all other aspects of their individualities, even their sex.

In "The American," Mr. James has to some extent overcome this tendency. Every character is cut like an intaglio; the outlines are so sharp and clear; and they are never allowed to blur. The picture of the Bellegarde family, with its meanness, selfishness, and the impregnable pride of the *vieille noblesse,* is equal to anything of the kind in Balzac. In fact, heartily as we detest its members, and much as we admire the pluck and good-nature of Mr. Newman, the American manufacturer, who is determined to buy the finest piece of Sèvres porcelain for a wife, we find some of our respect given back to the former, at the close of the story—if it can be called a close where the action simply stops, leaving matters very much as they were before. As in "Roderick Hudson," Mr. James gives us the various stages of a problem, and omits the solution. Or, if the fact that Newman has utterly failed, in spite of the pluck and shrewd natural diplomacy he has exhibited throughout the story, must be accepted as a solution, it is one which takes him down from his heroic pedestal and casts a suspicion of stupidity over his goodness of heart. Our interest in "The American" would be greater, if we could have the least faith in Newman's professed love, or Madame de Cintré's amiable inclination. But we contemplate them as coldly as we feel the author must have done, and, after a few chapters, only value them as subjects for his rapid, keen, sure dissecting hand. Valentin de Bellegarde and Mdlle. Noémie are the two for whom we most care, because they have a slight clothing of flesh-and-blood. The parts they play are of little consequence, seeing that so little comes of them, but they are as well-drawn as need be.

The great charm of the story lies in the dialogue and by-play of the principal persons. We overlook the occasional lapses of dramatic consistency, while listening to conversation so brilliant, so subtle, and so abundant in finely-contrasted touches of character. Herein Mr. James is easily a master. In the descriptive passages, also, he is never at fault: he knows so well what to paint, that he rarely misses a stroke. Hence we regret all the more keenly the absence of that profound and universal human sympathy which is needed to temper the severity of his scientific apprehension of the natures of men and women. We cannot escape the impression of an indifference, never expressed, perhaps because it is congenital and thus not distinctly conscious to the author's mind; and it is an indifference which does not predict a later cynicism, since the very quality of the latter implies at least a hostile interest. In a word, Mr. James writes like a man who has never known an enthusiasm,—like one who, finding that in certain rare and refined intellectual qualities he is the superior of most of those whom he meets, is easily led to overlook the intrinsic value of other forces in human nature. With his remarkable ability, it is not likely that he should have deliberately assumed the restrictions we have indicated: they are probably natural and inevitable.

"Henry James's Latest Novel." New York *World*, 14 May 1877, p. 2.

It would be saying a good deal to say that Mr. James's new novel is better than its immediate predecessor, and we shall hardly take the risk of saying so, with the impression left by "Roderick Hudson" still fresh in our minds; but it certainly is not inferior to it. And it is so entirely different from "Roderick Hudson" that any attempt to compare them is useless. The later work is, perhaps, more equable than the former; it is not so intense; but is a trifle more mature; it is broader and more comprehensive in scope; more finished and polished in detail even, but it is not so single and simple in its aim and its effectiveness. When "Roderick Hudson" appeared we remember remarking upon the difference between the attention that Mr. James bestowed upon the stars of his company and that given to their support. The difference then seemed due to two circumstances; first, Mr. James's lack of personal interest in what is superficially uninteresting, and in the second place the excellence of Mr. James's power of expression—the one made his minor characters lifeless and the other made them monotonous. It is quite impossible to note either of these circumstances with any emphasis in "The American;" and all that has prevented our pleasant disappointment at this impossibility is the conviction that we have had since reading "Roderick Hudson" that its author's next book would display, in a marked way at least, neither of these defects—that they were defects which an increasing maturity and an increasing experience in the writing of fiction would easily remedy. And they are certainly remedied if not entirely cured here. It would have been a little singular perhaps if this improvement had not been wrought at the expense of some sacrifice, and so we are prepared to find no character in "The American" so admirably portrayed and endowed with so much life as well as life-likeness as any of the three principal figures in "Roderick Hudson," while at the same time the minor characters of the book are not only more life-like but more living than their predecessors.

This is the story: Christopher Newman, the American, having begun to earn his fortune at the age of ten, or thereabouts, finishes that occupation after the various ups and downs of Western life, at the age of thirty-six, and the story opens by introducing him to the reader as he sits in the Louvre looking wearily at the pictures, and making a business of enjoying the freedom from affairs that his fortune has earned him. There he meets a countryman, resident in Paris at whose home he becomes a frequent guest, and listens good-humoredly to Mrs. Tristram's banter, and the rather placid bickerings of husband and wife. He is unmarried, but disposed not to remain so if he can find "the right person," and Mrs. Tristram undertakes with alacrity to find him a wife who shall fill the rather exacting requirements of her new-made friend. So he gets introduced to Mme. Claire de Cintré and, the prologue over, the first act begins: Mme. de Cintré *ætat.* twenty-five, is the only daughter of the late and sister of the present Marquis Henri-Urbain de Bellegarde; she had been sold to the late M. de Cintré and so earned freedom from all family dictation that she did not choose to respect. Her mother and the present Marquis are of the old Legitimist aristocracy of France, the Bellegardes' traceable ancestry going back to Charlemagne at the latest, in spirit as well as in blood and position. Mme. de Cintré probably feels as much regard for the rank that is but the guinea's stamp as her experience of the institutions therewith connected has left her; and her younger brother, Valentin, none at all perhaps that is not inherent and only half-conscious. With Valentin, Newman makes friends at once. The youth has a heartiness that earns for him the appellation "Anglomane" among his French acquaintance, and he warms towards Newman from the first. The latter proposes to marry Mme. de Cintré forthwith, and the very coolness of the proposal gets him a hearing at the hands of Marquise de Bellegarde. He is asked how much his income is, and he is accepted as a suitor for the hand of Mme. de Cintré. For six months he swims in a sea of delight, his regard growing into affection and finally into love. Mme. de Cintré at the end of that time accepts him, and also at the end of that time the Bellegardes have become convinced that it will be impossible for them to allow such a misalliance between nobility and plebeian blood. A "commercial" person has become a stench in their thin nostrils—beyond all their previous imaginings. Valentin, meanwhile, who has been conducting a small flirtation with a small grisette, gets into a small fuss over her with an Alsatian; a duel ensues, and the catastrophe of the novel comes with unexpected suddenness. Newman gets his *congée* from the Marquise de Bellegarde and her son, and a despatch saying Valentin is dying, almost at the same time. He remonstrates, storms, gets furious, at the treachery of the Bellegardes. Mme. de Cintré has been *commanded* to give him up, and she does so with shame and sorrow, and so he hastens, torn by a whirl of emotions, to the bedside of Valentin. The dying youth divines the cause of his perturbation, and apologizes to him with failing breath for the wrong done him, and confides to him a secret with which he may avenge himself at the least. But Mme. de Cintré goes into the convent of the Carmelites, is lost to him irretrievably, and after due reflection Newman burns his slip of paper, throws away his chance of bringing the Bellegardes low, and the book closes.

We have given an outline only of the narrative, which is as good in detail as it is in mass, so to speak, and is in mass of too delicate a texture to adequately photograph within our limits; but from the summary here given it can readily be seen that a very large social question is presented by "The American." Evidently the complete artistic presentation of that question was Mr. James's chief design—not the solution of it by any means, not even the discussion of it, but the objective statement of it, interesting and full of meaning, to be discussed or solved by the reader if he choose, and doubtless by different readers differently, just as any phase or problem of life is viewed differently by different observers. A better scheme for the presentation of this question can scarcely be imagined—certainly there can be nothing more extremely patrician than the Legitimist French nobility, and nothing more extremely plebeian than a mining-stock speculator from San Francisco. And in no other way could the two be brought so forcibly into contrast as they are in "The American"—an extreme, rather than a typical, representative of the New World civilization, and extreme, rather than typical, representatives of the Old World's. And herein, we think, lies the defect of Mr. James's book—he has, curiously for him, rather overstated differences; we do not remember to have ever noticed too great obviousness in him hitherto. In order to make his problem appear as difficult of solution as it really is he has made it unnecessarily hard. He has made the Bellegardes a trifle too haughty and Newman a good deal too plebeian. The latter is certainly true; and if Mr. James had refrained from supplying his hero with a "cerulean cravat" and a broad expanse of shirt-front, had not insisted on his stretching his legs so often and so far, and had curbed his disposition to refer to his wash-tub manufactory, the statement of this social question would have been more satisfactory and more complete. The wonder now is not that Newman and the Bellegardes did not travel in company, but that the Bellegardes should have ever imagined that they could. And besides the more satisfactory and complete presentation of his social problem which Mr. James would have secured by refraining from overstating differences, there is the more important point still to be considered, that in that event his portrayal of character would have been more satisfactory and complete. For if it be the whole of a novelist's function to portray life, the chief of the elements which make up that whole is certainly the portrayal of character. And it should be sacrificed to no consideration whatever, not even to the obvious statement of a social question.

No one appreciates this more thoroughly than Mr. James does, we imagine. "The American" is cumulative evidence of his appreciation of it. And the sacrifice of character-portraiture here is so unconscious, so unwitting, and moreover so slight, that we are tempted to call our notice of it suggestion rather than statement, and to add that we should possibly not have noticed it at all if there had been any more tangible defects in the book. And jealous as we are of Mr. James's least deviation from the requirements of the novelist's art, we are by no means blind to the admirable portrayal of character which "The American" displays. Possibly Mr. James himself would not agree with us that the chief quality of his book is not what it should be, but is the statement of a social problem. At all events, this last and the portrayal of character are so delicately intertwisted and so nicely inter-dependent that we do not greatly insist on the point, and, as we say, we do not fail to recognize the improvement which the figure-painting in "The American" shows over that of "Roderick Hudson," taking the figures as a group. None of the characters in "The American" is as strongly individual as Roderick Hudson, his friend Mallet or Christina Light; none of them stands out so living and so real. But, on the other hand, the minor characters of the book are better and have a more distinct identity—the equipoise of the whole is more perfect. Moreover, Mr. James had set himself a harder task—the task not only of presenting artistically a social problem, but of depicting much less tangible and much more elusive traits. And his success here is surprising, considering his conditions. It was not, of course, an easy matter to portray such a nature as that of Roderick Hudson; still less easy perhaps to vitalize so inconsistent a character as that of Miss Light; but, nevertheless, there was something aggressive about both of them, something that could be handled, moulded, compressed, beaten out, or whatever suited the fashioner of them. Mme. de Cintré, on the other hand, is rather a wraith than flesh and blood—she seems to float rather than walk, to pervade a room rather than to distinctly appear in it; and yet with a marvellous, subtle skill she is made to be felt not the less powerfully and certainly for that the impression she makes is indefinite and undefinable and her influence is not less potent for that the source of it is so elusive. How much it may depend upon the artistic sympathy of the reader we are not prepared to say, but there is certainly unusual charm in the portrait for those who care to examine it, though we can readily understand that many readers of "The American" will deem it a "most unsatisfactory" delineation. At all events, the Marquise and her

eldest son are finely drawn—are made to show themselves with the subtlest kind of art. Their whole behavior, from the moment of their introduction to the end, is a wonderfully delicate study. As we have said, they are made now and then, perhaps, a trifle unnecessarily haughty to meet the unnecessarily rigid requirements of Mr. James's scheme, but for most part they are perfectly painted. Valentin, too—we suspect that the delicacy with which Valentin is described will escape many readers until they notice the nice shade of difference between him and his French seconds after the duel. The different ways in which that institution is abstractly regarded by the American, the Anglo-Frenchman and the Frenchmen themselves, are noted with a nice discrimination that one rarely meets with. And it is quite the same with the other characters, even those which have scarce anything to do with the burden of the story: M. Nioche—especially M. Nioche—his unforgiven daughter, the Tristrams—notably Mrs. Tristram—Mrs. Bread, even the uneasy Unitarian Babcock—they are complete in themselves and distinct from each other. We do not need to say anything of the American himself. In his way he is a masterpiece.

As to the story itself, it seems to us more vitally a part of the whole novel than one usually finds. It is not merely a setting for the characters, possibly not enough subordinated, as we have intimated. But it is organic in a marked degree—it plainly has a beginning, a middle and an end; the catastrophe and the gradual dawn of the inevitable end are finely managed. The end of the story is like that of "Roderick Hudson." Probably it will annoy many people who will call it also "most unsatisfactory." For ourselves we do not know in recent fiction anything so artistic—so almost scientific in its art—as the conclusions of these two novels; so hard it is for an author to know when his tale is told in the first place, so hard for him in the second to relentlessly resist ending it otherwise that it *must* be ended to be true. For the rest we venture the wish that our best American novelist may write for us some day an American novel.

New York *Times*, 21 May 1877, p. 3.

A novel which has occupied the position of chief serial in the *Atlantic Monthly* is apt to attract the notice of a great many persons who are above average as readers of literature something better than light, and, moreover, persons who discriminate and think over the books they read. For this reason the publication in book form of *The American* may be considered a matter of more than usual importance to those who may be called distinctively readers. Mr. James is one of the few men in America who are engaged in a literary life pure and simple, having no relations to any other means of livelihood not literary. He is, moreover, and has been from the start, a writer of an extraordinarily painstaking variety, whose style is evidently the result of much thought and a wide canvassing of various literary models in at least two languages, French and English. Hence, *The American* is sure to be a subject for debate among people who take an interest in such matters, and the question, Do you like it? is sure to be asked in many quarters, and arouse a variety of opinions. Undoubtedly there are people to whom almost all that Mr. James writes is either entirely distasteful, or simply unsympathetic, who rather avoid reading his books and shun any examination of his merits or demerits. But he has also enthu-

siastic admirers, respectful readers, and incisive critics, who find his writings worthy of some sort of regard, ranging from one pole of appreciation to the other.

As the name indicates, the present novel is still moving in the general field which has so long been Mr. James' specialty, viz: Europe. "The American" is a man who has worked hard all his life, at various occupations, in divers parts of the United States, until in his 36th year, when he is already a millionaire, he suddenly feels a longing to see the world, and hastily decamps for Europe. In Paris he comes across an old friend, is taken in hand by the friend's wife, and, on acknowledging that he wishes to make a fine marriage, is introduced by her to a Madame de Cintré, a young widow, who belongs to one of the oldest and most Legitimistic of the ancient families of the Faubourg Saint Germain. He admires her, and pushes the acquaintance with a mixture of naïveté and courage which forms the chief element of his character, is accepted formally by the heads of the house, gains an ally in the youngest son, Valentin de Bellegarde, and is publicly acknowledged as an accepted son-in-law at a ball given in the ancient Bellegarde Hotel to the gathered aristocracy of Bourbonistic Paris. After this ball, the match is broken off suddenly by Mme. de Cintré, at the command of her mother and elder brother, who cannot support the want of breeding and rank of Newman. Valentin is mortally wounded in a duel, but, before he dies, tells his friend, the American, that they wish to marry her to an English cousin, a Lord Deepmore, and that there is some frightful secret about the death of the old Marquis de Bellegarde. The Bellegardes having gone to their country-place, Newman, the American, follows them there, and by tampering with an old English housekeeper whom Valentin had designated, gets possession not only of the secret, but of proof that the death of the old Marquis had been hastened by poison administered by his wife. While he is "working up the case" Mme. de Cintré yields to the further demands of her mother and elder brother and enters a convent in Paris. Newman shows the Bellegardes that he has them in his power, but they defy him. He does not use his knowledge to ruin them, but flies off to America, only to return to Paris again with the intention of seeing at least the convent in which his Claire is immured. This is the real finale of the novel:

> "Newman found himself in a part of Paris which he little knew—a region of convents and prisons, of streets bordered by long dead-walls and traversed by few wayfarers. . . . Everything was over, and he too could rest." [*Novels 1871–1880*, pp. 867–68]

The woman whom he had played for, and lost just as he expected to win her, is certainly indicated in a charming way. Mme. de Cintré reminds one of the woman into whom Gabrielle de Bargerac, the heroine of one of Mr. James' most charming short stories, might have grown.[1] She is of a peculiarly French type, not beautiful in face, but beautiful in general—full of grace and harmony. The younger brother, Valentin, is also a typical young Frenchman. As to old Mme. de Bellegarde and her dear son, they are English after a fashion, she being the daughter of an English Earl, and her son taking after his mother. Noémie Nioche, a Parisian Becky Sharp, who caused the death of Valentin, as well as her obedient father, are also well drawn from a more accessible class than the Bellegardes, with equal excellence. In regard to the Americans, there are two besides Newman. The friend, resident in Paris, is in outlines not a bad characterization of the floating American abroad, who has neither business nor hobby nor other absorbing pursuit save his club. But he is not very distinct or of much importance; nor can much more be said of his wife, though she is better. When it comes to Newman himself, his character appears to be a kind of patch-work. He does not act consistently from the standpoint of a man who has lived the life we are told he has. He is blunt in consequence of having fought for money for 20 years or so, without thought of people or things, but he says surprisingly sharp and Parisian things. His conduct is not that of so unsophisticated a man; we learn that he impresses others with his barbarism, but he does not act or talk like a barbarian. The sensations, likes, and dislikes which Mr. James attributes to him are those that he, Mr. James, might have, but not a Californian handler of stocks, who has to learn French at the age of 36. Again, there is an adage to the effect that he who loves late loves violently, but Newman's love, from beginning to end, strikes one as more the feeling of an amateur for a fine statue or a lovely picture than a woman. Newman acknowledges that he never was in love before; he gets to the gently glowing stage over Mme. de Cintré, and when formally invested with the title of her fiancé he beams; but it seems a lack-lustre affair when the positive and uncorrupted nature of the man is taken into consideration. This amounts, in the end, to a lack of vitality, of the living quality in Newman. It is one of Mr. James' faults that we are always being reminded of how clever it all is, instead of taking the characters into our sympathy. Early in the book we are sure that no matter what happens to Newman it will be merely a question of curious speculation—not for laughter or for tears. We come nearest to tears at the death scene with Valentin, but even there, where the dying man is a joyous, reckless, engaging young Frenchman, some cool consideration shuts off our sympathy and makes us think, how clever! As to the finale of the novel, we look to hear a chorus from those who read Mr. James in deprecation of such an end. A modern French novelist has introduced a cool young American millionaire in Paris as the hero of a quartet of novels. His name is *Le Colonel Chamberlain*. But the Frenchman's hero is not left with empty hands when his American experience has earned him the right to carry his point against whatever odds may arise. It would have been better for Mr. James' literary fame to have blown the convent up with nitroglycerine, and had Newman carry off Mme. de Cintré on an engine captured and managed for that purpose by the hero himself, than to have allowed him to end his love affair in what is vulgarly termed a fizzle.

Note

1 "Gabrielle de Bergerac," *Atlantic Monthly* 24 (July–September 1869), 55–71, 231–41, 352–61.

[T. S. Perry].
"James's *American*."
Nation 24 (31 May 1877),
325–26.

The American whose adventures are here recorded is named Christopher Newman. At the time the story opens he is thirty-five years old, having served in the war, from which he came out a brigadier-general by brevet, and accumulated since a large fortune by dealing in leather, wash-tubs, and stocks. His instruction from books had been slight, for he tells us he celebrated his tenth birthday by leaving school; he had, however, seen many men and cities before the whim seized him of going to Europe to enjoy his fortune, not after the fashion of the majority of his fellow-countrymen; but quietly, rationally, with a vague notion of supplying the missing foundation-stones in his education. He meets an old friend named Tristram in Paris, who introduces him to his wife, and she, finding herself entrusted with a good-looking, rich bachelor, who, moreover, is not averse to matrimony, naturally turns to match-making, and looks about for a wife for him. The woman she has in view is a French lady of excellent family, who had early married a man a great many years older than herself and is now a widow. She and Mrs. Tristram had been schoolmates. Without much difficulty she manages to introduce Newman to her friend, Madame de Cintré, and the romance fairly begins. The action does not hurry on from this point, however, for Newman is first dismissed for the summer that he may take French lessons, visit picture-galleries, examine the architecture of churches, and in general rid himself of the dust of the prairie which might have made him too conspicuous for the houses of the French nobility. With the winter he returns to Paris, having carried with him throughout the summer a very distinct memory of Madame de Cintré's dark eyes. What follows next is very entertaining, as Mr. James gives the reader a most interesting study of the way the intricacies of a complex society pass unnoticed by our fellow-countryman, who suddenly finds himself in better company than he was ever in at any time of his life. The difficulties that would beset even the most successful stock-speculator from San Francisco in his attempts to enter the houses of the Legitimist nobility are ingeniously put out of the way by the proper exercise of the novelist's art, so that nothing seems more natural than that Newman should be stretching out his long legs in one of the most exclusive houses in Paris. His own position is made very clear. He had no diffidence, and his education had not encouraged in him the habit of cringing before the aristocracy, so that with his frankness and manliness he makes an attractive contrast to the artificial creatures he meets in this new world. For Valentin de Bellegarde he has that warm affection which a man has only for the favorite brother of the woman he is in love with; and Valentin, a capitally-drawn young *gentilhomme,* consistent throughout, certainly deserved this affection. Newman does not disgrace himself in his new surroundings, except so far as sprawling one's legs in company is a disgrace; at times, to be sure, cold shivers must have run down the backs of his new acquaintances at his allusions to the past when he was struggling in business, but his self-possession keeps him from being uncomfortable, and he never finds it necessary to bolster up his courage by bragging about himself or his native land. He is conscious of his wealth and of its value, because he amassed it himself, but he is above all vulgar ostentation. Then, too, he is supremely good-natured, and he endures the scorn of the mother and other brother of Madame de Cintré, of Urbain de Bellegarde namely, with great composure; indeed, generally these cold-hearted aristocrats when they descend to trying to snub their visitor get, as the phrase is, as good as they give.

In spite of their noble prejudices they consent to receive Newman as a suitor for Mme. de Cintré's hand because he is wealthy and there is no very violent objection to be urged against him; but in their hearts that half of the family hate him. Even Valentin is startled when he first hears from Newman's lips of his audacious hopes and plans, but he consents not merely to refrain from throwing obstacles in his way, but even to do what he can in furtherance of his suit. As for Madame de Cintré, she finds herself for the first time in her life thrown with a man who is genuine, sincere, and as simple as a child, whose virtues stand out in sharp relief against the affectations and hollowness of the society in which she lives. Newman's quaint ways are to her the evidence of originality, and naturally she is not blind to the force of his affection for her. By a capital touch she is represented as very shy—she is overridden by her despotic mother and brother; but when the time comes she is bold enough in accepting Newman with all his imperfections on his head. Their love-making is for the most part discretely [*sic*] cool: even Urbain, the marquis, might have sat by without casting too heavy a gloom upon Newman while he was wooing, and without receiving any great shock to his patrician susceptibilities. There is but one sure test, however, of the excellence of any method of courtship, and if it is applied here, it must be confessed that Newman's way was a wise one, for the woman he loved promised to marry him. So far everything had gone on as he wanted, but soon he comes on crags and sunken rocks in the shape of the perfidy of the mother and her favorite son. Newman is introduced to a number of the most aristocratic friends of the family at a ball given in honor of the engagement, when suddenly the firm ground gives way under his feet, and he is told by Madame de Cintré at his next visit that she has decided not to marry him. The reason of this suddenly altered determination is that her mother has asserted her authority, and expressly forbidden her taking that step. Her obedience to this command seems in no way impossible; we have already had plenty of proof of her great shyness, and it can be seen that with that quality and her detestation of a family quarrel, she felt her incompetence to keep a bold front against combatants as well trained as her own mother and brother, and that for the sake of peace she would consent to sacrifice even her own and her lover's happiness. She was a timid creature, and she was bullied into this renunciation of her hopes. So much is intelligible and consistent. But here comes the great disappointment of the story, which is Newman's conduct in this altered state of affairs.

It is very natural that novelists should grow tired of ending their stories with a fine wedding and the imaginative statement that the newly-married couple always lived happy afterwards. But it is also to be remembered that if readers ask that a love-story should end with a marriage or a definite statement of some satisfactory reason why the marriage did not occur, it is because they know that a real passion leads to marriage unless there is some insuperable obstacle in the way, and that this is a law which does not admit of exceptions. It may very well happen that a slight matter may turn off a half-hearted man who has deluded himself with an unfounded notion that he is in love, when he is only interested; but if he is ever in earnest he is earnest then unless he has deceived himself in some way. Now, it is impossible to suppose that Newman had not his whole heart in this matter. It was the one love of his life, and all the mothers and brothers in Christendom would have been no more guard for Madame de Cintré than half a dozen cobwebs. A man who has made his way so successfully in the world since he was ten years old is not one who can be rebuffed by his mistress's sense of duty to her family. He would know, and he would make it plain to her, that her duty lay elsewhere. She might not have been strong enough to take the responsibility of action upon herself; but he could have assumed it and have brought their troubles to a satisfactory end. This is what the reader feels. It is to be remembered, too, that Newman was no theorizer who formed his decisions first and then acted upon them; he was emphatically a man of action, who felt that he wanted something and at once put out his hand for it. He cares nothing for these enemies of his, but he lets the wave break over his head and thinks how badly he has been treated on account of his commercial pursuits. Even before he has lost all chance he gets into his hand a bit of paper, by means of which he might turn the tables on the Bellegardes, and possibly get their consent to the marriage, or, at any rate, inflict a lasting revenge upon them, and he goes to see an old lady, one of their intimate friends, who would take extreme pleasure in spreading scandal about them; but instead of taking his vengeance he lets the chance go by, and the plot of the Bellegardes is perfectly successful. There is no *mésalliance* in the family, Newman is shuffled out of the way, secret and all, as if the Bellegardes in their interview with him saw in him something the reader does not see, which told them that he would be a week-kneed adversary whom they could despise.

Now, either the reader has been all along mistaken about Newman's real feeling for Madame de Cintré, or this hero is totally unworthy of the sympathy that is surely given him. A man of his sort cannot sacrifice his life's happiness, and, what is more, that of the woman he loves, who had never known what happiness was, for a mere whim. It was very well for him to let the sixty thousand dollars go which he mentions early in the book, but there is no analogy between that renunciation and the final one, for he had plenty of money besides, whatever became of those thousands, while there was no woman who could replace Madame de Cintré. It is here that the element of passion is wanting, and it is not satisfactorily replaced by the drawing of Newman's extreme goodnature. Its absence is the more noticeable because in the account of Newman's wooing there is a beautiful passage where Madame de Cintré accepts him, which promises real ardor in the energetic American.

But, apart from this, how much there is to admire in the novel! The different threads are managed with rare skill. The episodical story of Valentin, and his doings is told most admirably, and it serves the purpose of bringing out more clearly the excellence of Newman's character. There is great completeness and symmetry in these chapters. But the best thing of all, in our opinion, is the delicacy with which Madame de Cintré is drawn, with her shyness and gracious delicacy. The success here, attained as it is by that apparent simplicity which is the height of art, gives the novel a place among the best modern studies of society, and makes it an honorable example of Mr. James's serious endeavor to attain excellence only by careful choice of methods.

Atlantic Monthly 40 (July 1877), 108–9.

It is perfectly manifest that The American takes a place in advance of Roderick Hudson: it has the same sort of merits and the same sort of faults, yet on the whole it must be rated as more successful than Mr. James's former effort. Precisely why it deserves this distinction may not be a thing fully explainable; but there are at least three points that support the claim: the characters are better chosen, the hero and heroine and Madame de Bellegarde having far more intrinsic interest than any corresponding persons in Roderick Hudson; the movement, the grouping, and final disposition of all the persons contain more of that symbolic quality essential to the best artistic successes; and lastly, the author's treatment has gained perceptibly in approaching nearer to an air of simple human fellowship. It would be hard, among recent novels, at least, to find a more acute or vigorous full-length portrait than that of Christopher Newman, in the first pages of this book. We will transfer only this description of Newman's countenance: "It had that typical vagueness which is not vacuity, that blankness which is not simplicity, that look of being committed to nothing in particular, of standing in an attitude of general hospitality to the chances of life, of being very much at one's own disposal, so characteristic of many American faces." This is one out of a hundred similar bits of vivid picturing woven into Mr. James's pages with a lavish hand. It is a little too long for the point involved; and in general Mr. James begins to show as a distinct trait of style a fluency which tends at times to the verbose; but we cite it as recalling the perfect clearness, combined with ease, which the author commands at will. This "touch" of his stands him in good stead for familiarizing the reader with a situation and a scenery rather unusual. The scheme of bringing a keen, hardy, broad-hearted but intensely commercial American into contact with a French family of the old *régime* is, so far as we know, entirely new; and Mr. James has carried it out with a brilliancy and a nice application of details that make his novel delightful to a refined taste. He is untiring in accumulating the details requisite for illustrating the diversities of these alien elements, and the contrast between the healthy, sagacious Newman and the thoroughly Parisian Valentin de Bellegarde, in their respective dealings with Mademoiselle Nioche, is very effectually enforced. There is something very neat, too, in the distribution of destinies as the story comes to a close. Yet we are bound to take some serious exceptions. The episode of young Babcock, the feebly æsthetic Unitarian, is expanded beyond all proportion. We cannot at all countenance Mr. James's optimistic estimate of young Valentin, whom he expressly calls "the best fellow in the world," and otherwise gilds beyond his deserving; and the fate which overtakes the person whose side the reader is compelled to favor is to our thinking not a fair reward for one's sympathy. A more mature consideration might very possibly have shown Mr. James that Madame de Cintré, Newman, and their pathetic auxiliary, Mrs. Bread, were by no means forced by their circumstances to the wretched condition he assigns them. Merely as a question of artistic obligation, it seems to us that having introduced the element of intrigue, in Newman's discovery of the paper criminating old Madame de Bellegarde, Mr. James should have treated this element more consistently. One may disdain incident of that sort, but the appetite which it excites for some striking and dramatic result is a perfectly lawful one. The plot having been turned into the channel of intrigue, therefore, our æsthetic sense is not satisfied by the event here led up to. Mr. James pleads indirectly for a judgment that this issue was made inevitable by the character of Newman. It was his "fundamental good-nature," we are told, which caused him to refrain from publishing the Bellegarde secret to the *beau monde;* and on this good-nature the Bellegardes relied. Perhaps we ought to accept this reasoning, but it seems to us that good-nature is a meagre excuse for a man so profoundly in love as Newman with Madame de Cintré. So insufficient is it that the course which he takes in destroying his paper makes his passion appear suddenly and totally to evaporate, notwithstanding Mr. James's careful portrayal of his despondent and blighted after-years. We may admit that Newman could not have disgraced the family and then married Madame de Cintré as a daughter of that family; the attitude of triumph would

have been too petty, even if practicable. But is it any more dignified for him to exult in having at least given Madame de Bellegarde a terrible scare? Another defect is that this French noble family are far from likely to have had the faintest conception of that American good-nature on which Mr. James hints that they relied. The logic of fiction is not that of philosophy, and this story might have had a different ending without defeating consistency. Nevertheless it is good as it stands. It is an impressive composition, and will repay a second reading. That it so naturally raises the question just discussed is a fact in proof of its force; and even if one should be seriously dissatisfied with the termination, it is worth considering whether the catastrophe was not essential in order to show how venomous and fatal is the power belonging to aristocracy when it has been warped by age, avarice, and falsehood.

Galaxy 24 (July 1877), 135–38.

Mr. Henry James, who needs no other passport than his name to the favor of the readers of "The Galaxy," has just published another novel which is so good that we regret very much that it is not better. For, as it seems, it so easily might have been made better, that we feel as if defrauded of a perfect enjoyment which, in the nature of things, we ought to have. Mr. James's purely literary work is always good, neat, finished, with an air of elegance about it which is too rare in the writing of American authors. In this respect "The American" is better than its predecessor, "Roderick Hudson." The writer's hand is steadier, and the work is of more even excellence. But we are not sure that in the former book there are not isolated passages of greater vivacity and stronger imaginative power than can be found in this one.

The plot of "The American" has the great merit of originality, and it is well constructed. Mr. Christopher Newman—well chosen name—is an American who, having left school at ten years of age, is knocked about the world, tries various modes of getting a living, even to making washtubs, fails, or at least does not succeed, and finally goes to California, where he strikes a lead, in business if not in mining, and ends by accumulating a very large fortune before he is forty-five years old. He is an exceedingly good-natured person, and gives up a prospective gain of sixty thousand dollars and the pleasure of victimizing in that amount a rival who has behaved shabbily to him, doing so simply because he don't care much for the money, and don't care much to take his revenge. He goes to Europe determined to see everything, and have everything of the best. Europe to him means chiefly Paris, of course; and there we find him desiring, among other things of the best, to have a very fine wife. He falls into the hands of an American lady, a Mrs. Tristram, who has long been a resident of Paris, and who, learning from him his inclinations toward marriage, if he can find a first rate woman, one who is up to his mark, informs him that she has such a woman among her French acquaintances, and promises him an introduction to her, which she brings about. It must be confessed that Mr. Newman's notions as to the woman with whom he is willing to share his fortune are sufficiently exacting. She must be beautiful, well born, well bred, intelligent, accomplished, of kindly nature, and unexceptionable character. The only point upon which he is not exacting is just that upon which European men are very particular—money. Of that he asks none; he has no need of it, and he is generous as well as good-natured.

He is first shown to us in the Museum of the Louvre, somewhat jaded and worn with sight seeing. With "head thrown back and legs outstretched," he is lounging upon a divan, looking at one of Murillo's Madonnas; a man "long, lean, and muscular, he suggested that sort of vigor that is commonly known as 'toughness.'" In the gallery he scrapes an acquaintance with a very pretty young woman who is copying a picture, a Mlle. Noémie Nioche. He buys her copy for two thousand francs, which is just two thousand francs more than it is worth—doing so partly from good nature, partly in his utter ignorance of art. She turns out to be a thorough little adventuress, whose real object in life is to get some man to "take care of her." She fails entirely to succeed with Newman, but her fortunes become somewhat involved with his, and her conduct has a very considerable influence upon his fortunes and upon the story. The introduction of this exemplary young person is very adroitly managed, and her connection with the course of events in which Newman becomes involved is very skilfully wrought out; her character being, moreover, one of the finest delineations in the book.

The lady to whom Mrs. Tristram introduces Newman with match-making intent is Mme. de Cintré, who is of the Bellegarde family, one of the ancient *haute noblesse* of France. She is a widow, having been married in early youth against her will, and as it proves against her father's will, to M. de Cintré, a repulsive man, old enough to be her grandfather. He soon dies; and she is understood to be disinclined to a second marriage. Her father is not living; her mother, the dowager Marquise de Bellegarde, is, although of Irish birth, a thorough French *grande dame* of the old school, haughty, hard, polished, unscrupulous, and scheming. She has two brothers, the Marquis, a worthy son of such a mother, and the Vicomte Valentin de Bellegarde, a good-hearted, somewhat cynical representative of the *jeunesse dorée* of the Faubourgh St. Germain; not very heavily gilded, however, for the Bellegardes are in need of money.

Into this family Christopher Newman, some time maker of washing-tubs, and present California millionaire, is dropped, somewhat to the amazement of all its members. To the still greater surprise of all, he soon announces himself as the suitor of Mme. de Cintré. For that lady meets all his expectations, fulfils all his desires in a wife. She has an elegant, slender figure, a fine fair face, with large, beautiful blue eyes, all the womanly charms and graces, and her manner is perfection. When he proposes to her she does not send him off or forbid him to speak again, but only imposes a period of probation, and *château qui parle et femme qui ecoute va se rendre. A conseil de famille* is held, the consequence of which is that the American ex-washing-tub maker, and present millionaire, is accepted as a candidate for the hand of the daughter of the house of Bellegarde. Ere long the lady yields; the engagement is formally announced, and a grand evening party is given by the old Marquise de Bellegarde, to which all the swells of the ancient *régime* are invited, that Christopher Newman may be introduced to them as the future husband of Mme. de Cintré.

Meantime the younger brother, Valentin de Bellegarde, who has nobility as well as generosity of nature, and who forms a strong friendship for Newman, becomes enamored of the pretty little adventuress Mlle. Nioche. At the same time he has penetration enough to see through that young woman thoroughly, and character enough to feel that any connection with her would be a mistake. Nevertheless he hovers around her, and finding her one evening at the opera, flirting with the son of a German brewer, who makes himself disagreeable, and finally becomes insulting, he challenges the young son of malt, and goes off, in spite of Newman's entreaties and protests, to fight the duel, in which he is mortally wounded. While Valentin is on this bloody expedition his prospective brother-in-law learns, to his surprise, that Mme. de Cintré is about leaving Paris for the Bellegarde country seat, without a word to him. He seeks an interview at once, which he obtains in the presence of the family, and is informed by all of them that the marriage is broken off because the dowager Marquise and the Marquis cannot finally bring themselves to consent to receive "a commercial person" into their family. In the midst of this complication he is summoned by telegraph to the deathbed of his dear friend Valentin. He goes at once, and Valentin manages to extort from him the truth as to the breaking of the engagement. The young man is shocked and ashamed at the bad faith of the proceeding, and apologizes to Newman in the name of the ancient family of the Bellegardes. In addition he gives him some information which he may use to further his cause, which is that the old Marquis de Bellegarde was poisoned by his wife, with the connivance of her eldest son, the present Marquis, to get rid of his opposition to the marriage with De Cintré. Newman worms the whole secret out of an old Englishwoman, an attendant upon the Marquise, to whom Valentin refers him. He faces the old Marquise and the Marquis with his evidence of the truth, and threatens them with exposure. Although startled and frightened, they show a bold, polished front, and defy him. He is baffled in his real purpose, which is to get his wife; and as to exposing the high-born poisoners, his good nature leads him to abandon that entirely. Mme. de Cintré takes the veil as a Carmelite nun; and there the story ends as regards the principal personages. But Mlle. Nioche is not neglected. Whatever the cause, the occasion of the breaking off of the match was the appearance in Paris of Lord Deepmere, a fiftieth cousin of the Bellegardes, to whom, instead of Newman, the old Marquise conceives the project of marrying her daughter. Lord Deepmere, finding how matters are between Mme. de Cintré and Newman, is too good a fellow, although a rather weak one, to step between them and their prospective happiness, and Mme. de Bellegarde is baffled. But Newman leaves Paris for London; and there in Hyde Park he finds Mlle. Nioche, and with her Lord Deepmere, who, as he could not have Mme. de Cintré in marriage, takes Mlle. Noémie upon her own terms.

It must be confessed that, with such possibilities in the story, this is rather a lame and impotent conclusion. A story ought to have a manifest and impressive end, just as much as a house ought to have a manifest and characteristic entrance. The interest of Mr. James's story culminates when Mme. de Cintré finally enters the Carmelites; and this incident, together with that of the discovery of the murder of the old Marquis, which is very well conceived, and the effect of which is visible in the earlier parts of the story, might have been worked up into a very dramatic finale. Instead of this, the close of the American's career, the retirement of Mme. de Cintré from the world, the bringing to light of a deed of darkness that would have ruined the ancient house of Bellegarde, all are frittered away, and the end of the story "peters out" just as some tropical rivers which are deep and strong soak away in the sand and really flow no whither. When we merely learn in an incidental way that Mme. de Cintré takes the veil, that the Bellegardes, after being a lit-

tle frightened, but not too much to keep them from bluffing it out, retire to their ancient seat of Bellegarde, and that Christopher Newman, Esq., resumes his travels, we wonder what all this fuss was for. As to the glimpse that we get of that pure and impulsive creature Mlle. Noémie in company with the husband whom the Bellegardes wished to impose on Mme. de Cintré instead of Newman, gratifying although it is, we are most distinctly of the opinion that it does not meet our natural and reasonable expectations of a catastrophe. Mr. James's story is like some pieces of orchestral music which really end, although in no very marked way, some time before they stop, but which go on afterward, and on, about nothing very important, and at last give out rather than come to a decent end.

We have another fault to find with Mr. James, which is with the title of his book, and the inferences which it measurably warrants abroad. Mr. Christopher Newman is certainly a fair representative of a certain sort, and a very respectable sort, of American; but he is not such a man that Mr. James, himself an American living in Europe, is warranted in setting him up before the world as "*The* American." Men like Newman are already too commonly regarded as the best product, if not the only product, of two hundred and fifty years of American life, and a hundred of republican institutions. But let us argue a little *ad hominem,* and ask Mr. James if Christopher Newman fairly represents the larger number of his associates when he is at home. We fancy not. Why then put him forth thus set up on the pedestal of the definite article? If Mr. James had chosen to write his novel with Newman for hero, and to call it by his name, or Mme. de Cintré's, or any other, and to let Newman go as a representative of a certain kind of American who gets rich in California, very well; but to have an American hold this man up to the world as *the* American is not highly satisfactory.

And this objection has to do with another of more importance, which is that Mr. James's hero is entirely insufficient for the part which he is called upon to play. The motive of the book is the bringing of a representative, supposed to be admirable, of a democratic and trading community into contact with persons of the oldest and highest aristocratic family connections and traditions of Europe, and the presentation of the former in such a light that he carries with him the sympathies of the reader. Other than this the book can have no conceivable motive at all. Now to produce such an effect, Mr. James's hero should have been a man of some mark, clever, if not brilliant, a man of the best breeding that his country could produce, of engaging manners, of dignified bearing, in short a man who by the force of his own personality might be likely to break down the social prejudices at least of the woman who consents that he may make love to her. Whereas, Newman, although an honorable and respectable man, intelligent in his way, and well-behaved enough, is so entirely lacking in attractive personal qualities, and, although not exactly uncouth, so raw in his manner, that no one wonders why the Bellegardes, being at heart dishonorable people, seize the first opportunity of getting rid of him. He is after all only just what Mr. James makes them call him, "a commercial person," which he might be, and yet be all the rest that he is not. Our only wonder is how a woman like Mme. de Cintré can be brought to look upon him with eyes of personal favor. We are speaking of a woman such as the figure of Mme. de Cintré stands for. For as to the heroine herself, her personality is of the vaguest. She leaves no impression of individuality upon us; we are told certain things about her, indeed, but she is almost a lay figure.

Again, as to Newman, there are certain gross inconsistencies which prevent us from accepting him as a real living personage. We see that he is in mind and body rather strong; he is also in mind and body rather *gauche*. Nevertheless Mr. James from time to time puts words into his mouth and thoughts into his mind which only belong to a person of social and intellectual culture and of delicate apprehension. The old Marquise de Bellegarde, who does not conceal her haughtiness or her family pride from him, says to him one day frankly, "I would rather favor you on the whole than suffer you. It will be easier." To which Newman at once replies, "I am thankful for any term. But for the present *you have suffered me long enough.* Good night." And he takes his leave. Again, in reply to a cynical remark by Valentin as to the virtue of old M. Nioche, Newman says, "It seems to me that you [he and Mlle. Noémie] are very well matched. You are both hard cases, and M. Nioche and I, I believe, *are the only virtuous men to be found in Paris.*" Now the delicate retort of the first of these speeches, and the irony of the second, are not in keeping with the rest that we see of Newman, nor are they consistent with the natural character of a man who left school at ten, and who drifted round the far West in his youth, and in early manhood grew rich in California.

It is only with his hero and his heroine, however, that Mr. James has been unsuccessful. His French people and his French-Americans are admirable. They have the air, all of them, of careful studies from the life, and more. For that they might be and yet lack life themselves; but on the contrary, they live. The old Marquise de Bellegarde is clearly strongly imagined. How truthful the delineation may be as the type of a *grande dame* of the legitimist society of France can only be told by those who have had the opportunity of entering that society, but it has the air of truth about it, as certain portraits have of which we have not seen the originals. So it is with the brothers Bellegarde, the elder of whom, although he is a weak creature, kept erect only by family pride, still impresses us with his individuality, even when he "walks up and down the drawing-room in silence like a sentinel at the door of some smooth-fronted citadel of the proprieties;" while poor Valentin lives and breathes and wins us to love him and to mourn his death, his behavior as to the cause of which is thoroughly and exquisitely French. But perhaps the most vivid portraiture in the book is that of Mlle. Noémie. She is at least the Marquise's rival in this respect; and how the crime-blackened old *grande dame* would have drawn herself up at the thought of even the mention of Noémie's name and hers together! Mr. James has very deftly made this thoroughly Parisian young person reveal herself to us, instead of describing her himself. He has had the skill to show us what she is by the impression that she makes on others, and by acts and words of her own that rather suggest than tell plainly what is passing in her mind. And her father, poor old broken down reprobate, trying to cover up his consent to her life from his own eyes—he too is admirable and pitiable. Mr. James's book, for the sake of those personages, although somewhat disappointing at the end, will richly repay reading.

Literary World [Boston] 9 (July 1877), 29–30.

The American is a very modern novel; with no flavor of the past and no prophecy of the future, but on the exact level of the present. Mr. James's forte consists in placing Americans in a European setting—always a difficult task, as the writer is apt to fail either in the environment or the character. Mr. James fails in neither; he knows his own countrymen, and he knows Europe. His delineation of French character here is as thorough and accurate as that of the American. The story is exceedingly simple and devoid of incident. The "American"—a highly successful man and a thoroughly "good fellow"—is suddenly seized with a disgust for business, the hidden and better qualities of his nature having asserted themselves. He goes to Europe to see and enjoy the world, not in a low, nor yet in a high, but in an extremely natural way. He has no vulgar tastes nor bad habits; does not even smoke; still is no purist, and is not shocked by the rather too vivid glimpses of Parisian wickedness disclosed in the course of the story, as some of its readers will be. He is thoroughly a man of the world, with an excellent opinion of himself and corresponding good sense; sound-hearted, intelligent but not cultivated; and as to manners, hovering about the point that separates the vulgar from the well-bred; in reality belonging to the latter, but by association carrying the marks of the former. The story turns upon this blending of manners—a clever hit on the part of the author; and consists of the history of a courtship in an impoverished family of the Bourbon aristocracy, the American's money being the ground of favor with the family, and his manners and antecedents the offsets; the attachment between the parties themselves being strong and genuine. Its varying fortunes, with a duel in which our hero did not share, an ugly family secret, sundry glimpses of characters and conduct that might better have been kept in the background, a semi-tragic ending on the part of the heroine, and a general clearing up in the mind and heart of the hero, constitute the main features of the story. The story in itself is too slight to interest, the *denouément* being evident at the outset; half the characters are utterly detestable, and the other half without attraction. No gentle reader will shed a tear or heave a sigh over the most tragic of its pages. The characters are not presented for sympathy but for inspection, and in truth they stand out very clearly, but we do not care to prolong the acquaintance. What then is the charm of the book? One less dull was never written, and it has enough weight to hold the attention of the most exacting reader. Its power consists in the brilliancy of its literary execution, and in the accurate delineation of character. It is a clear-cut book. The characters are more than photographed; they walk through the pages. There is none of the mistiness that enveloped our recent friend, Mr. Deronda.[1] Every person and scene are thoroughly eliminated from their surroundings, and brought before us clear and precise. We can say nothing better of its literary quality than that it affects us like good painting. That one art should carry the effect of another is skill indeed. We trust Mr. James will not take it amiss if we suggest that his book has too much of these fine qualities to accompany its tone; they are not in the "concatenation accordingly," as Tony Lumpkin says in the play.[2] It is not agreeable to witness Pegasus ploughing. Nearly the finest thing in the book is the keen sarcasm of the morbid moral sensitiveness of the young Unitarian clergyman, but we incline to think that as between the author and the preacher, the latter has the best of it, and that the former could not do a better thing than to place himself under the ministrations of the Rev. Mr. Babcock before beginning his next book. Or, if that be impossible, let him ponder the maxim "art for art" till he thoroughly feels its hollowness. Seriously, we think Mr. James's admirable talent de-

mands a better field and atmosphere than he here allows himself, and a nobler set of characters to be used for the illustration of some higher purpose. The author evidently has a dread of the serious; it is his weakness. We must object also to the company into which he introduces us. This bright American book comes perilously near being a French novel, from which may the good Lord long deliver us!

Notes

1 George Eliot, *Daniel Deronda* (1876).
2 A character from Oliver Goldsmith, *She Stoops to Conquer* (1773).

"*The American.*" Scribner's Monthly 14 (July 1877), 406–7.

Those who have faith in the growth of literature according to seed and soil, have long cherished the hope—deferred from season to season—that the "great"-ness which characterizes so many American things would soon develop itself in fiction. A great American novel has seemed to many a confident and hopeful patriot to be heralded with the incoming of each new writer. Mr. James early showed qualities which justified the turning of expectant gaze in his direction. The "Passionate Pilgrim," "A Modern Madonna," and "The Last of the Valerii," showed some qualities which might well grow to greatness.[1] It is true that in "Madame De Mauves" and in "Roderick Hudson," expectation received a warning; but Mr. James had given such unmistakable evidence of originality and delicacy, and of skillful *technique,* that when the first chapters of "The American" made their appearance we were justified in looking for a novel thoroughly American in character and sufficiently good to satisfy our national literary longing. It was evident that the movement of the story was to be on foreign soil—where its author is so much at home,—and that but one of its important characters was to be of our own people, but this one character was so thoroughly of the best typical American sort as to afford a safe basis for the highest hopes that might be built upon it. Big, rich, frank, simple-hearted, straightforward, and triumphantly successful, he satisfied us entirely by his genuine and hearty manliness, and he seemed to carry in his very blood a genius for success in any direction toward which his modest strength might be turned.

Though deficient in cultivation, and though possessed of no artificial advantages that might not be readily traced to a manly character, and to the sort of career to which such a character naturally turns in our most active haunts of business, he had a breezy and wholesome confidence in himself, and a kindliness toward all his fellows which made him a thoroughly engaging hero. Up to the time of Valentin's death, we had gained such faith in his stability and in his straightforward determination to attempt only what was right, and to follow up his attempt to crowning success, that it would have seemed the most natural thing in the world for him not only to marry Madame de Cintré, but to become the guiding head of the whole house of Bellegarde, gaining a controlling respect within the circle of the *haute noblesse* of which that house was a center.

The process by which Mr. James created in the minds of his readers an ideal so different from that which he himself had conceived, is not easy to explain, unless by the suggestion that he set forth external evidences which had fallen uncomprehended under his notice, and which meant far more to us than they did to him. Traits in which he found only material for artistic delineation, indicate to those who really know the type of American to whom they belong, a nobility and heroism which it seems never to have been his good fortune to detect. Certain it is that while in drawing this character he furnishes food for admiring contemplation, he was himself quite ignorant of its significance.

For many chapters after the fatal duel there is nothing in the movement of the story to disturb our faith in its hero. He followed the clue that Valentin had given him, and came into full possession of the tragic secret of the Bellegardes. Madame de Cintré quailing before her fiendish mother, and her stone-hearted older brother, cowered away into her Carmelite novitiate. A strong, clean-souled, upright, and resolute American, whose inmost life she had stirred with an admiring and satisfying love, held the power to overcome their stern will, and to bring her back to such happiness as, under their hard heel, she never could have known. Up to this point Mr. James had the full sympathy of his readers. Thenceforth, save for a waning hope that at the last moment he might still not betray our trust, the successive steps of the story grow more and more disheartening, and we finally close the volume, conscious victims of misplaced confidence.

Briefly stated, Newman, by a carefully studied and minutely defined chain of events, which had begun with the sacrifice of a happy and engaging young life, and the later links of which had been forged, one by one, with the best skill of Mr. James's hammer, had been armed with the means for vigorous battle. In the Parc Monceau the very moment of his victory was at hand. Then, with one dull, slow, cold look, the Marquis de Bellegarde measured his enemy's strength and found that it was only weakness. He brushed Newman almost unheeded from his path, and Madame de Cintré, in default of the manly help that Newman alone could give her, sank into the sad, lonely, life-doomed "Sœur Véronique."

The only purpose of Valentin's life or death, so far as the conduct of the story goes, was to develop the character of that extremely objectionable and repulsive young person, Mademoiselle Nioche. And later, while our hearts are sad over the sufferings of the real heroine, and before hope is quite dead, that the hero may yet feel one throb of masculine vigor, we have thrust upon us an unmeaning and offensive delineation of this girl. Save in the postscript of Mrs. Tristram's letter, we have no word of Madame de Cintré, but there is page after page of Nioche. Newman, on the very morrow of his defeat, goes mooning off to England, where he passes three months in purposeless and listless wandering. There and in America, and again in Paris, he proves himself to be, as Mr. James expresses it, "a hopeless, helpless loafer, useful to no one, and detestable to himself."

In palliation of the conspicuous failure of this attempt at novel-writing, reviewers have been profuse in praise of Mr. James's excellent "style,"—a style where delicate and skillful diction are seconded by that trick of suggestive "under-statement" toward which modern fashion so greatly tends. With occasional awkward lapses, Mr. James's style is very good indeed, and a good style is essential to a good novel; so is good dress essential to the completeness of a well mannered and charming person. But the most easy and graceful writing, unsustained by a living subject, hangs tame and unsatisfying, like fine raiment on a clothes horse. It may be suggested that Mr. James aimed at some other ending of his story than the conventional marriage. To this we answer that a marriage with Madame de Cintré need not

have ended the story; it might have been used only as a means for placing Newman in a position to show the value of his rare good qualities. Also, a marriage was by no means necessary to the success of the story. Madame de Cintré might have taken the black veil and Newman's career might have ended in sadness and desolation. But it was an imperative condition that he should have *tried* to marry the woman he loved, and if he must fail, that his failure should be in no wise weak and spiritless. Any man with the force of character needed to make the manufacture of washtubs a stepping stone to a great fortune, whether he were an American or not, would have had that in him which would have driven him even to a desperate effort to reclaim a promised wife, whose selfish relations were stealing her away from him, and whom they were dooming to a life of hard seclusion.

It is the best compliment we can pay to Mr. James's writing, to say that he gave us such a living interest in his hero, that we are made angry by his own failure to comprehend the character he had created. Can it be that we owe such a fiasco in some degree to the fact that the author has been unconsciously twisted out of his own individuality by the strong influence of Tourguéneff's example? Tourguéneff, however, would justify so miserable an ending; he is remorseless, but he does not shock nor disappoint.

Note

1 "A Passionate Pilgrim," *Atlantic Monthly* 27 (March–April 1871), 352–71, 478–99; "The Madonna of the Future," *Atlantic Monthly* 31 (March 1873), 276–97; "The Last of the Valerii," *Atlantic Monthly* 33 (January 1874), 69–85; "Mme. de Mauves," *Galaxy* 17 (February–March 1874), 216–33, 354–74; all reprinted in *A Passionate Pilgrim* (1875).

Athenaeum [England]
2593 (7 July 1877),
14–15.

Mr. James's 'American' will interest English readers greatly, as a clever presentment of a characteristic type of his countrymen, in search of adventures in the paradise to which good Americans go. His face "had the typical vagueness which is not vacuity, that blankness which is not simplicity, that look of being committed to nothing in particular, of standing in an attitude of genial hospitality to the chances of life, of being very much at one's own disposal, so characteristic of many American faces." His nature does not belie this description of his appearance. Newman maintains the freshness of view he brings with him, in spite of a tragic experience of the conventionalities of a world which is quite new to him. The contrast between the honest self-satisfaction of the hero, as he treads upon all sorts of prejudices and threads his way over slippery places in the paths of society, and the coldness with which his advances are received in the high circles which he penetrates, is extremely amusing. The sombre termination of the book is, perhaps, a necessity, where there is so hopeless an antagonism between inclination and supposed duty as in Madame de Cintré's case; but the general impression left is humorous. Whether lightly discussing the situation with Valentin, his gay young friend, a fine type of a French aristocrat of a modern kind, or fencing with the authorities of the house of De Bellegarde, the Marquise and her son, who are as impenetrable in their pride and as satisfied of the excellence of their motives as if the ordinary rules of morality were set aside in their favour, there is an incisiveness mingled with *naïveté* about the American which makes the dialogue unusually spirited. Withal he is a thoroughly good fellow, and the reader's sympathies follow him throughout his hopeless struggle with the polished wickedness of his opponents. Madame de Cintré's character is also very happily drawn. The want of backbone which causes her to fail in her engagement to Newman, under the pressure of what she has been taught to regard as her primary duty to her family, is only what might be expected from a virtuous young Frenchwoman brought up in the aristocratic *faubourg*. Her faithfulness to her attachment, which drives her to the convent for escape, is only another side of the same loving and submissive nature. Mdlle Noemie and her miserable father, who does *not* play the part of Virginius, are amusing in their wretched way. On the whole, Mr. James's story breaks fresh ground, and will be read with interest.

George Saintsbury.
Academy [England]
new series 271 (14 July
1877), 33.

We have but one thing against Mr. James and we wish we could say as much for most of the novelists whose work comes before us. He has read Balzac, if it be possible, just a little too much; has read him until he has fallen into the one sin of his great master, the tendency to bestow refined dissection and analysis on characters which are not of sufficient intrinsic interest to deserve such treatment. No doubt this is a fault which savours of virtue; but still it is a fault, and a fault which renders it extremely difficult to fix one's attention

41

on *The American* until the excellence of Mr. James's manipulation fairly forces one for very shame to interest oneself in his story. The hero and heroine are the chief stumbling-blocks. He is a typical Yankee who, after serving with distinction in the civil war, has set to work at making a fortune, and has made it by the help of things in general—washtubs, soap, and oil being more particularly specified. He comes naturally to Paris to spend the fortune, and to look out for something exceedingly superior in wives. Unfortunately for himself, he has proposed to him a certain Countess de Cintré, an angel in herself, but appertaining to a by no means angelic family, who represent in race and character the stiffest types both of English and French nobility. They, of course, cannot away with the washtubs, even though transmuted into dollars, and by working on Mdme. de Cintré's filial ideas they at last succeed in getting the match broken off. There are several minor characters who are decidedly better than the principals. Such are the old Marquise, who bears, however, a rather perilous likeness to Lady Kew; her younger son, a capital fellow and a partisan of the ill-treated Yankee; a match-making and platonically flirtatious American matron, and others. Also we have a ghastly family secret, a fatal duel, and a retirement to a convent; so that Mr. James has been by no means stingy of what some people will regard as the solids of his feast. But we wish we could like his chief figures. The portrait of his countryman must of course be taken as accurate, and is evidently sympathetic. But if not only the *naïf* consciousness and avowal of being as good as anybody else, but also the inability to understand how the anybody else may possibly differ from him on this point, be taken from life, the defect of repulsion strikes us as a serious one. There is, moreover, something exceedingly jarring to our possibly effete nerves in the idea of a man who seriously entertains the idea of revenging himself for a personal slight by making use of a family secret which he has surreptitiously got hold of. It is true he does not do it, but he threatens to do so, and tries to make profit of the threat. After this we cannot help feeling on the side of his enemies, scoundrels as they are. And the lady, though her temperament and French ideas of duty explain her conduct not insufficiently, is far too shadowy and colourless. The book is an odd one, for, though we cannot call it a good book, there is no doubt whatever that it is worth a score of the books which we are wont truly enough in a sense to call good.

Appleton's Journal new series 3 (August 1877), 189–90.

The position of an American, fresh from the comparative crudity of the New World and confronted with the maturer social forms, the stereotyped ideas, and the artistic riches of the Old, seems to have an inexhaustible interest for Mr. Henry James, Jr. It furnishes the motive for most of his short stories, it was the dominant feature of "Roderick Hudson," and it is almost the sole theme of his latest work, "The American." For this reason there is a certain sameness in his work which, but for his fertility of invention, would detract seriously from its interest; and yet, in spite of identity of situation and similarity of externals, there is an almost complete contrast between "Roderick Hudson" and "The American." In the former the interest is almost exclusively personal and individual—the characters are more important than, and substantially independent of, their surroundings; in the latter, the individual is subordinated to the social type, and beneath and around the persons whose little drama nominally occupies the stage we are made to see and feel the warring forces of two opposing civilizations. The situation certainly is one of deep and many-sided interest. Christopher Newman is a typical American, who "began to work for his living when he was a baby," as he says, and who, after encountering many vicissitudes and having various experience of life in the army and in the Far West, finds himself at thirty-four the possessor of an enormous fortune, in which he takes undisguised satisfaction, not for its own sake, but because it stamps the unmistakable seal of success upon his efforts. Though uneducated and totally destitute of social polish, he is a fine, manly fellow, physically and mentally, with unimpaired sensibilities and plenty of aspiration of a practical and democratic kind. Having got enough, he determined to leave off money-making and go to Europe, "to get the biggest kind of entertainment a man can get—to see the tallest mountains, and the bluest lakes, and the finest pictures, and the handsomest churches, and the most celebrated men, and the most beautiful women." Among his other wants is a wife, who must be not only beautiful, but as good as she is beautiful, and as clever as she is good—in fact, as he says, "the best article in the market;" and in Paris a female friend undertakes to introduce him to such a one, a Madame de Cintré, sole daughter of the noble house of Bellegarde, whose lineage dates back to the ninth century, and whose existing representatives live in proud seclusion because they refuse to recognize the *régime* of the "*parvenu* emperor.*" Strange to say, Newman not only wins the love of this lady and the cordial friendship of her brother, but gains the reluctant consent of her haughty mother and of the loftily-aristocratic Marquis de Bellegarde. On the eve of his

marriage, however, a combination of motives and circumstances, so complex that Newman himself fails to comprehend them, frustrates his hopes, consigns Madame de Cintré to a convent, and drives him forth a wanderer over the world. The situation is the same as that in "The Spanish Gypsy," which Fedalma describes when she says, pathetically, to Don Silva:

"Our dear young love—its breath was
    happiness!
But it had grown upon a larger life,
Which tore its roots asunder. We
    rebelled—
The larger life subdued us." [1]

Without going more deeply into the plot, and thus impairing the pleasure of those readers who have not yet perused the book, we could not do justice to the many admirable and delightful qualities of the story. It teems in every part with the overflowings of a rich and full mind; and an indefinable atmosphere of culture, and refinement, and high thought, imparts a charm over and above the more special attractions. The descriptive portions are as delightful as in all Mr. James's work, the social perspective is admirably harmonious and sustained, and the characters pique curiosity where they do not inspire a more genuine interest. Newman himself is hardly so impressive a personage as Roderick Hudson, but Mr. James has never hitherto produced anything equal to the portrait of Madame de Cintré, whose presence pervades the book like a delicate and exquisite perfume. The minor characters, too, are exceptionally well defined and vividly delineated, and throughout there is a sense both of power and of power well applied. If one pronounced opinion upon it after reading two-thirds, we could understand how it should be considered not only a good novel but a great one; but it must be confessed, as a serious qualification of our praise, that the story breaks down sadly toward its close. It is not merely that the end is painful and disappointing—the most unobservant reader must know that in real life love does not always result in wedding-bells; but in the great crisis of their lives even Madame de Cintré fails to fulfill our ideal of her, and Newman conducts himself so that we almost resent the affectionate interest that we have allowed ourselves to feel for him. Our minds are diverted from the great pity we would otherwise feel for his unhappy fortune by the doubt whether, after all, he really knew what love was, and by the suspicion that we have from the beginning overrated both his moral fibre and his intellectual capacity. This is a sad flaw, indeed, but it is the only drawback upon such work as we seldom have the opportunity of enjoying, and is by no means sufficient to deter the intelligent reader from participating in the feast. "The American" is a book to be read slowly and reflectively, and read thus it will leave a flavor upon the palate as of rich Falernian.

Note

1   George Eliot, *The Spanish Gypsy* (1868).

Eclectic Magazine new series 26 (August 1877), 249–50.

The first thought that occurs to one after reading "The American" is that the opulence of power displayed in it ought to have made it a novel of the first rank, and precisely why it fails of being such it is somewhat difficult to say. The plot is consistent and well-constructed if somewhat commonplace, the characters are without exception piquant and interesting, the descriptive portions are remarkably brilliant and picturesque, and the entire book is pervaded by that atmosphere of elegant culture which is so grateful to refined and educated minds. The "situation," too, is very effective—that of an American, a self-made man, fresh from the crudities of his wild Western home, confronted with the aristocratic prejudices and the inflexible social standards of the most exclusive society of the Old World. But we fear that it was the very effectiveness of this situation—its wide-reaching suggestiveness and interest—that spoiled Mr. James's book as a novel. In his anxiety to point the contrast and essential antagonism between two such alien civilizations as those of Republican America and Bourbon France, he has subordinated his characters to the machinery of his story, so to speak, and thus deprived them of that personal individuality and self-determining force without which neither real nor fictitious persons can establish any strong claim upon our sympathies or interest. No doubt in actual life men and women are constantly entangled in the web of fate and circumstance, their purposes thwarted and their aspirations turned away; but in such cases there must be co-operating conditions in their own nature, and it reduces them to the level of puppets in our eyes if we see too plainly the external predetermining agencies by which they were crushed. Hence, the reader is dissatisfied with the manner in which "The American" ends, not because it is painful, but because it mars the conception which he has been led to form of the two principal characters in the story; because it seems incongruous with what has gone before; and because it is manifestly the result, not of spontaneously-acting natural causes, but of a preexistent social theory in the author's mind.

In order to reach cause for fault-finding, however, it is necessary to go very deep into the structure of the novel; for its salient qualities, taken separately, we have nothing but heartiest praise. The portrait of Madame de Cintré would be sufficient by itself to lift the book altogether above the level of current fiction; yet there are half a dozen other characters whose natures are laid bare to us with scarcely less delicacy and precision of touch. The incidents are plausible and sufficiently varied, the accessories partake of the multifarious splendors of Paris, and the affluence of resource exhibited in every direction renders the story at once a stimulus and an enjoyment.

Checklist of Additional Reviews

Nation 24 (11 January 1877), 29. Notice of serial publication. Reprinted in William T. Stafford, ed., *The Merrill Studies in The American* (Columbus, OH: Charles E. Merrill, 1971), pp. 27–28; James W. Tuttleton, ed., *The American: A Norton Critical Edition* (New York: W. W. Norton, 1978), pp. 389–90.

Boston *Evening Journal,* 12 May 1877, Supp., p. 2.

St. Louis *Missouri Republican,* 12 May 1877, p. 4.

Louisville *Courier-Journal,* 13 May 1877, p. 3.

Hartford *Daily Courant,* 17 May 1877, p. 1.

Independent 29 (17 May 1877), p. 9. Reprinted in Tuttleton, p. 391.

Chicago *Times,* 20 May 1877, p. 11.

Chicago *Tribune,* 26 May 1877, p. 12.

New York *Daily Graphic,* 26 May 1877, p. 610.

Springfield [Mass.] *Republican,* 31 May 1877, p. 3.

Indianapolis *Journal,* 1 June 1877, p. 5.

New Orleans *Daily Picayune,* 3 June 1877, p. 12.

Boston *Evening Transcript,* 6 June 1877, p. 6.

Spectator [England] 50 (21 July 1877), 925. Reprinted in Tuttleton, p. 411.

Saturday Review [England] 44 (18 August 1877), 214–15. Reprinted in Tuttleton, pp. 411–12.

Library Table 3 (30 August 1877), 154–55. Reprinted in Tuttleton, pp. 402–3.

Edward L. Burlingame, *North American Review* 125 (September 1877), 309–15. Reprinted in James W. Gargano, ed., *Critical Essays on Henry James: The Early Novels* (Boston: G. K. Hall, 1987), pp. 37–40; Tuttleton, pp. 403–6.

Graphic [England] 16 (8 September 1877), 230. Reprinted in Tuttleton, p. 412.

Academy [England] 15 (10 May 1879), 408. Reprinted in Tuttleton, pp. 412–13.

British Quarterly Review 70 (July 1879), 268–69. Reprinted in Gargano, pp. 40–41; Tuttleton, pp. 413–14.

[J. R. Wise]. *Westminster Review* [England] 57 (January 1880), 285–86. Reprinted, but unattributed, in Tuttleton, p. 414.

THE EUROPEANS

W. E. Henley.
Academy [England] new series 336 (12 October 1878), 354.

If Mr. Henry James's new novel could only be regarded as the harbinger of a whole noise of such fowl, the pleased critic would look forward to the coming season very cheerfully. As it is, and with every reason to believe that *The Europeans* is alone in the world, he is glad to welcome it for its own sake. It is an extremely clever book, and a book withal that is readable from first line to last. It is scarcely so touching as *Daisy Miller,* which is out and away the best thing of its kind in recent English; but it is a piece of work so capable and original, so vigorous, and to a certain point so telling, as to be worthy of equal praise and study. Mr. James, who would seem to be an exponent of the refined, eclectic realism of Turgénieff, has produced in it a novel remarkable for complete absence of intrigue, of didactics, of descriptiveness. There is not any plot in *The Europeans;* there are scarcely any landscapes or interiors; and such good things in the way of phrase or generalisation as occur in it are quite inseparable from their context, and would seem commonplace outside of it. And yet it is not possible to read *The Europeans* without the admiration of absorption. It has all the qualities of a rare etching: of an etching, that is to say, the beauty of which is a beauty of line, and depends in no measure on a property of tone or an arrangement of masses. The effect of the whole thing is that of something colourless and cold, but so subtle and right, so skilful and strong, as to force the attention first and afterwards the respect of those who consider it. Mr. James has a sufficient contempt for prettiness and obviousness. His form is ascetic even to uncomeliness; he has nothing whatever to say that is not absolutely essential; and he suppresses all signs of his own personality with such austerity as could scarcely have been believed to be within the compass of a modern novelist. His purpose has been, not at all to write a book, and still less to write a story, but to show off the spiritual machinery of some six or eight men and women, all of whom are interesting from a certain human point of view, but none of whom are in any degree heroic or even extraordinary; and to do this with as much art and as little apparent excuse for it as could possibly be imagined. In this aim he has been altogether successful. His people are so completely apprehended and so intelligently conveyed that, as he himself has written of the greatest of living novelists, "you believe as you read." All are handled with equal acuteness and with equal sympathy, so that the reader's intelligence of one and all is for the nonce as perfect as the writer's. The book is, in fact, a remarkable book: in its merits as in its shortcomings. As it stands, it is perhaps the purest piece of realism ever done. And there seems every reason to believe that, if Mr. James could, or would, endow such work as in it he approves himself capable of with the interest of a high tragic passion, he might be not only one of the ablest but also one of the most renowned novelists of his epoch.

"The Europeans."
Pall Mall Gazette
[England] 22 October
1878, p. 10.

Mr. Henry James, although an American by birth, belongs by literary sympathies and antecedents essentially to Europe, and in Europe to France. In that country his first important attempt at fiction is laid, and to the modern school of French literature he has devoted an admirable collection of essays.[1] The tendency of recent fiction in France is all in the direction of psychological study of character as against plot or story proper. Frequently the latter plays a very subordinate part, or at least the sensational element is relegated to the final chapters. The bulk of the book is generally given up to incidents of every-day life and conversation, during which the characters are allowed gradually to develop and to grow upon the reader. We are not, of course, speaking of the ordinary run of novelists, who in France as elsewhere work on the imagination of their readers by whatever means is most handy; but of the great masters of the art of Malot and Feuillet. Take, for instance, Feuillet's "Julia de Trécœur," in its narrow limits perhaps the most finished work of fiction produced by this school during the Second Empire. The greater part of the story treats of the ordinary complications of French family life—a mother marrying a second husband much against the wish of her growing-up daughter. Ostensibly nothing happens, and even the original family quarrel seems on the point of being settled to the satisfaction of everybody. Only very gradually does the idea dawn upon us that under this calm surface terrible passions are at work which bring about the final catastrophe with the necessity of a natural event. Mr. James has followed exactly the same course—but for the final catastrophe. The ordinary reader goes on wading through pages after pages of commonplace though refined talk, thinking that something must turn up at last to reward his patience. But the author is inexorable; the end of his story is as eventless as were the beginning and the middle. A brief account of what Mr. James very improperly calls a sketch—for the book nearly extends to ordinary novel-size, and the working out is, if anything, over-finished—will illustrate our meaning.

The Baroness Münster, a lady of American origin but European birth and antecedents, and her brother, an artist, arrive at Boston in search of their Transatlantic cousins, whom for reasons of their own they intend to honour with a visit. As to the nature of these reasons we are not left in the dark. The Baroness has been married morganatically to a German prince, who, having become tired of her, is eager to buy her consent to a dissolution of the marriage. In the meantime supplies are stopped; a circumstance by no means pleasant to a lady of Mdme. Münster's habits. The lady's brother is willing enough to work for their common wants, but a few hundred francs from the illustrated papers are of little avail under such circumstances. In this emergency the thought of their American relations has struck them as a last resource. "I count upon their being rich and powerful, and clever and interesting, and generally delightful. Tu vas voir," says Felix, the brother. In due course the relations are discovered. They live in an old-fashioned country house a few miles from Boston, and are as simple-minded and kindly people as any scheming cousins can desire: Mr. Wentworth, a ceremonious gentleman of the old school, his two charming daughters, Gertrude and Charlotte, and

50

his very youthful and somewhat dissipated son. Of the latter the Baroness very soon takes possession, varnishing his rudeness with the gloss of European refinement, and in a general way fascinating him: But the daughters, and to some extent the old gentleman himself, are equally under her spell. Her title, her aristocratic habits, even the domestic arrangements of a charming summer-house, placed at her disposal by Mr. Wentworth, exercise a strange exotic charm on the unsophisticated Americans. In addition to these the lady succeeds in enticing a Mr. Acton, who has been to China, and on that account is admired as a great traveller and experienced man of the world by the little family circle. Between him and the younger Wentworth as the more desirable prize the clever Baroness may choose.

In the meantime Felix has not been idle. He is one of those irrepressible natures whom no misfortune can daunt, no coldness in personal intercourse deter. He is young, handsome, and his lips are shaded by "a light moustache that flourished upwards as if blown that way by the breath of a constant smile." Such a stereotyped smile may be the expression of a debonair nature; it may also be the impenetrable mask of a villain. Gertrude is decidedly of the former opinion. She has been submitting half-unwillingly to the addresses of an excellent clergyman, but that homely suitor has no chance against the fascinating stranger. Naturally of a romantic turn of mind, she begins to chafe at the narrowness of her existence, and her only desire is to follow Felix into the world, with whose splendour he has filled her innocent mind. This is the situation at which we arrive comparatively early, and which continues through chapter after chapter without much change or progress. At every moment we think that something surely must happen. For what object, we begin to conjecture, do these two brilliant strangers bear the monotony of New England country life? Is it the heart or the purse of their simple-minded cousins they are aiming at? Will the Baroness obtain a divorce from her prince and marry one of her admirers? or will brother and sister disappear one fine morning, leaving broken hearts and ruined fortunes behind them? Nothing of all this happens. The Baroness, it is true, returns to Europe, but the best wishes of her relatives accompany her on board the steamer; and as to Felix, he settles down into an exemplary husband and citizen. His beaming countenance was, after all, the mirror of a genial mind which sheds its brightness on all around. Not satisfied with being happy himself, he also contrives to bring together the disappointed suitor of his wife and her sister Charlotte, who had been nurturing a silent and hopeless passion for the worthy pastor. Other minor characters also find suitable partners, and the tale concludes amidst the polyphonous peals of marriage bells.

All this is satisfactory enough; and so indeed are the descriptions Mr. James gives of his various characters—of the life they lead and of the scenery which surrounds them. The author is evidently a careful student of human nature. His *dramatis personæ* are painted with life-like touches, which would do credit to Balzac himself. And, unlike that great painter of human nature, Mr. James has preserved intact his sympathy with the phases of life which he has subjected to such keen observation. There is, indeed, a peculiar poetic charm about these quiet scenes of New English home life. These are qualities of the utmost value to a novelist, but they are not alone sufficient to fix the reader's attention through two volumes. Mr. James is mistaken if he thinks that by calling his book a sketch instead of a story he can avoid the necessity of providing some kind of dramatic background for his clever delineations of character. In a master's hand a novel may occasionally do without a hero; but no hero can entirely dispense with the narrative and dramatic ingredients which the ordinary mind connects with the idea of the novel.

Note

1 *French Poets and Novelists* (London: Macmillan, 1878).

"*The Europeans.*" Chicago *Tribune*, 2 November 1878, p. 9.

"The Europeans" will go far to establish Henry James' rank among the first of American writers of fiction. He is in some respects superior to any of those who might successfully dispute the claim to pre-eminence with him. He has much of Hawthorne's power of analysis, and even a more complete synthetic faculty. He has Howells' charm of style, with more than his energy. He has not yet exhibited the dramatic skill of Mrs. Stowe, in her solitary great work, but has surpassed her in every other quality of a good novel.

Mr. James has properly offered this book to the public as "a sketch." It lacks the element of a great and sufficient motive, and the robust tone which we are accustomed to associate with full-grown books. But it has things which are more necessary than these. It has admirable studies of character, a loving appreciation of local coloring in and about Boston, and a cosmopolitan sympathy with strange ideas and tastes—that is to say, with human nature modified by surroundings. The character with whom the author has evidently taken the most pains is Mr.

Wentworth, the Puritan father—we had almost said forefather—of the story. He is, in the words of one of the Europeans, "a tremendously high-toned old fellow; he looks as if he were undergoing martyrdom, not by fire, but by freezing." Mr. Wentworth, with his rigid countenance and freezing ways, reminds one of another distinguished New Englander whose reputation in political circles is something of the same kind. The Puritan of the story has more than the average New England horror of the Roman Catholics and foreigners, whom he groups together by some mental process which he has never fairly worked out. There is hardly anything better in the book than the dialogue between this old man and his nephew, one of the Europeans, peculiarly effervescent in his manner and habit of thought. Felix is a good amateur artist, and talks of taking his uncle's portrait.

> "I should like to do your head, sir," said Felix to his uncle one evening before them all. . . . "You are a beau vieillard, dear uncle," said Mme. Munster, smiling with her benign eyes. [*Novels 1871–1880*, pp. 931–32]

Mr. Wentworth, it must be said, at first distrusted the morality of the two Europeans merely because they were foreigners. But Felix had a joyous, sunny disposition and an essential honesty which nearly disarmed all suspicions before the end. The Baroness on the other hand was disingenuous. Besides, she had been married morganatically to a German Prince, and the word "morganatic" overawed all of Mr. Wentworth's tender susceptibilities; "it reminded him of a certain Mrs. Morgan whom he had once known, and who had been a bold, unpleasant woman." Even without this unfortunate reminiscence, there was reason enough for a clashing between the Europeans and the Puritan household from which they were separated by a generation in time and two centuries in education. Gertrude was the only member of the Wentworth family who seems ever to have imagined that the chief end of man was not to glorify God by being miserable. "There must be a thousand different ways of being dreary," she once said, "and sometimes I think we make use of them all." The Europeans, on the other hand, had never done much else than to seek after their own enjoyment. The whole purpose of this little sketch is found in the contrast between the two modes of living and thinking presented by the different branches of the family. For the rest, there is much good conversation, love-making, scheming, and idling; and the sauce piquante is, if anything, too abundant.

Detroit *Free Press,* 15 November 1878, p. 8.

Following so closely upon a work so meritorious as "The American," and reaching its first audience in that most trying of all forms, the serial, it would not be remarkable if "The Europeans" failed to command the highest encomiums of the critics. That it does command them under such circumstances may be reasonably accepted as the best possible evidence of desert. It is in many respects superior to "The American," though it nowhere suggests an effort on the author's part to improve upon the latter. Indeed it scarcely suggests the latter at all, save in a certain finished elegance of style, which is one of the author's chief characteristics. And yet it is the other side of the picture presented in "The American," its object being to present European life as it appears to American eyes, as the object of the former

work was to present American life as it appeared to European eyes.

The story is subordinate to the object, but it has abundant attraction, considered merely as a story. The characters are sketched with the pencil of a true artist, and the suggestive hints and touches by which the action of the story is gently moved forward without dragging or being dragged, is as artistic as the character sketching. In writing it Mr. James has established himself, if he never did before, in the front rank of modern novelists.

Graphic [England] 18 (16 November 1878), 511.

"The Europeans: a Sketch," by Henry James (2 vols.: Macmillan).—Mr. Henry James, who has already won considerable reputation by some critical essays on modern French literature, seems likely to achieve no less distinction as a novelist, his "Americans" having already won him considerable popularity. It is true that there is hardly an attempt at plot in this present story—or rather, as he calls it, "sketch"— of his; but, thin as is the thread of narrative, it is yet strong enough to hold together a group of characters most of them wonderfully life-like and original. Foremost among these stands Felix Young, an American by descent, but born and brought up in Europe, a young fellow who has roamed about the Continent as actor, singer, and artist, settling to nothing, but always enjoying himself, and making the most of life, and as incapable of serious wrong-doing as he is of fixed and definite aims. Together with his sister, the Baroness Munster—she is the morganatic wife of a German Princeling, whose family are seeking to set aside the marriage—this airy young gentleman finds himself paying a visit to America, bent, at the instigation of the Baroness, on making the acquaintance of certain extremely well-to-do cousins who are living in the near neighbourhood of Boston. Of this Baroness we need not say much, for though she is drawn sufficiently well to make us understand that she is a clever, scheming, and not over-scrupulous woman, she does not fill that space in the reader's mind that the author, we fancy, intended her to occupy. But the contrast between Felix, with his brilliancy, his versatility, and his genial sunny nature, to which everything is full of interest for the opportunities of enjoyment it may afford, and his grave and sedate Puritan relatives, whose habitual mood is somewhat joyless and depressed from an overstrained conscientiousness and sense of the solemnity of life, is brought out in the happiest manner; many of the conversations by which this result is effected being as dramatic as they are exquisitely humorous. In particular, how this gay Bohemian, who for all his levity is yet so entirely amiable and worthy of confidence, gradually comes to exercise influence over the serious uncle, fatigued and overwhelmed by the ever-present feeling of his "responsibilities," to whom at first Felix, "as a young man extremely clever and active, and apparently respectable, and yet not engaged in any recognized business," is "an unfortunate anomaly," so that in the end Mr. Wentworth comes to consent to his nephew's marriage to his cousin Gertrude, is sketched with admirable vivacity and skill. We are, in short, in the book taken on new ground, and introduced to characters almost, if not altogether, novel and striking, who, unfamiliar as they are, yet impress the reader at once as real and living men and women. Mr. James ought to have a really brilliant future before him.

Independent 30 (21 November 1878), 9.

Turning now to Mr. James's "sketch," we shall find a proof of the immense interval between the American and the "European" mind to accept for a moment such broad generalizations, and a proof too of the difficulty with which one mind comprehends the other. For Mr. James scarcely describes "Europeans" as seen from an impartial point of view. He gives, rather, the critical impression of Europeans as contemplated by a distinctly American mind. His story describes the experiences and the impressions of Felix, happily so named, the light-hearted amateur of painting, and of his morganatically married sister, an equally irresponsible person. These persons are by descent American. We see them in New England, on a visit to their Puritan cousins, to whom their "European" lightness is fascinating and shocking at the same moment. There is some not very spontaneous love-making in the due course of the situation, ending in the marriage of Felix to Gertrude Wentworth, the heiress and the least prime of the cousins. Plot and incident are of slight texture; but so they are in many an admirable story, as in Daudet's "Petit Chose," for instance, which we lately had the pleasure of commending.[1] Why is this story less interesting? Because of its deficiency in sympathy, and its consequent failure in truth. The sympathy and truth which make the charm of Daudet's work or Cherbuliez's are not what one will look for in Mr. James's.[2] The interest of his writing is analytic, not epic. *The Europeans* is essentially a criticism, not a novel. And in this instance his critical view is the popular American view—that all

Frenchmen are frivolous and all New Englanders melancholy. Mr. James works out this commonplace very cleverly; but his view remains only sublimated commonplace, after all.

Mr. James's style has been praised both duly and unduly. It abounds in implications, in subtleties; there are delicate touches of recording observation; there is frequent cleverness of phrase, though these ingenuities are sometimes pressed to the impairment of the meaning. A more serious defect of it is a certain labored quality, a certain lack of spontaneity. It is the reverse in this respect of Thackeray's, for instance. It reminds us, too often for full enjoyment, of a well attired person who is somewhat uneasily conscious of his dress. The last secret of literary style, the *ars celare artem,* is still a secret for Mr. James to master.

Notes

1 Alphonse Daudet, *Le petit chose; histoire d'un enfant* (Paris, 1868).
2 Victor Cherbuliez (1829–99).

Appleton's Journal new series 6 (January 1879), 94–95.

Readers of Mr. James's "The Americans" [*sic*] will naturally expect to find in "The Europeans" a companion or complement to that subtile and elaborate study; but in the latter Mr. James has experimented in another field and aimed at quite different literary effects. "The Europeans" is truly described as "a sketch"—events and persons being outlined rather than analyzed, and large dependence being placed by the author on the cooperation of the reader's imagination with his own. Yet, in spite of its slightness, "The Europeans" will be generally admitted, we think, to contain Mr. James's best and most artistic work. The picture of the Wentworths, as a typical American family, is an unmistakable achievement of genius, and is sufficient of itself to lift the story into the domain of genuine creative art. The art with which it is painted is very delicate and unobtrusive, but its effectiveness and power and imaginative truth are proved by the persistency and clearness with which it arises in the mind after the book is laid aside and mere details have sunk into hazy indistinctness. The family as a whole, indeed, is a greater conception than any individual member of it. Charlotte is the only one whose portrait is painted at full length, and this is chiefly owing to the essential commonplaceness and simplicity of her character, which, however, is not without a certain reposeful charm of its own. Gertrude, who is in a sense the heroine, baffles the reader to the end quite as much as she puzzles her relatives and friends; and the austere personality of Mr. Wentworth is hinted at rather than portrayed. The family, as we have said, dominates and subordinates its constituent factors; and it would be difficult to conceive a finer and truthfuler picture of that high-minded simplicity, that serene fidelity to a somewhat ascetic conception of duty, that physical and moral cleanliness, and that virginal purity which characterize American life at its best, and which dwarf into insignificance its comparative deficiencies on the side of grace, and amenity, and social complaisance.

Very great skill is expended upon the figure and character of the Baroness—greater, we think, than is justified by the part which she plays in the story—but she never quite succeeds in pleasing, and after one or two experiments, as it were, is

55

gradually relegated to the background. It is as if the author shrunk from following her character along its natural and logical pathway; and though at the beginning she promises to take the part of leading lady in the drama, she proves on trial incongruous with her surroundings, and is speedily assigned to a subordinate and not very interesting *rôle*. Equally skillful in execution and much happier as a conception is the character of her brother, Felix Young— American by parentage, European by birth and nurture, and Bohemian by profession and practice. He is the apostle, exponent, type, and examplar of happiness as a creed and as a standard of conduct; and his influence upon the story is similar to that of a joyous smile upon a beautiful human face. The contrast between European and American life on their moral side, as exemplified in the Baroness, is only hinted at by the author; and we have reason to be grateful for the protest which Felix Young embodies against the ascetic ideals, the hyper-puritanic standards, the strained conscientiousness, and the distrust of everything that takes the semblance of pleasure for pleasure's sake, which make American life, in spite of a certain austere nobleness and purity, the most colorless, joyless, physically wearing and mentally exhausting, in the world.

We have already referred to the delicacy and refinement of Mr. James's art, and we return to the point only to remark that it is almost too subtilely delicate for its purpose. The reader has to be constantly on the alert, must meditate over passages in order to secure their full flavor, and even when the story is finished must go over it again to catch those delicate *nuances* which constitute its atmosphere and tone. The model of the workmanship is to be sought, not in English or American, but in French fiction; and not less conclusively than his essays on French novelists, "The Europeans" demonstrates that Mr.

James's studies in this field have been profound and fruitful.

Eclectic Magazine new series 29 (January 1879), 123.

In our notice of Mr. James's "The American" at the time of its appearance we praised it for the minute elaboration of its character-studies, for the vivid realism of its portraiture, for the versatility of resource which it exhibited on the part of the author, and for the opulence and amplitude of its style. "The Europeans" deserves even higher praise, but on quite different grounds. It is described by the author as "a sketch," and such it is in comparison with either "The American" or "Roderick Hudson." Details are well-nigh ignored, accessories are glanced at instead of being emphasized and obtruded upon the attention, painstaking elaboration of minor points is carefully avoided, and the characters, their surroundings, their individual traits, and the social background against which they are projected, are all painted in bold, distinct, rapid, and luminous outlines. At the same time, there is no lack of definiteness in the design or of finish in the execution. On the contrary, the story is remarkably artistic in construction, and the refinement of method and polish of style are almost too obvious. The essential difference between this and Mr. James's previous novels is that he has substituted the dramatic for the analytical method, and portrays persons and character by showing them in action rather than by a subtle analysis of motives. The gain is great both in vividness and in brilliance; and "The Europeans" will be generally accepted, we think, as Mr. James's most artistic, most satisfactory, and most characteristic work. It would claim a permanent place in our literature, if for nothing else, for the exquisite picture of a typical American family and home which it contains—a picture so true, so real, so vivid, and yet so gracious and pleasing that it causes the reader to feel a sort of conscious pride in being an American. Yet the portraits of the two Europeans are quite as skilful and effective, and only a degree less pleasing.

If we go on, however, we shall reveal more of the story than we ought; so we will content ourselves with recommending it to all who can appreciate thoroughly artistic, refined, and finished work.

Richard Grant White. *North American Review* 128 (January 1879), 101–6.

Mr. James's latest work in fiction of any importance is "The Europeans," which is intended, of course, as a companion piece to "The American." The author of "The Europeans" styles it upon his title-page a sketch, probably recognizing himself, by that word, its absence of plot, and confessing that in writing it he did not propose to himself to interest his readers strongly in the fate of his personages. And indeed the sayings and doings of these shadowy people are not such as to trouble us much as to what becomes of them. Their sayings are many and their doings few. The Europeans are two European-born Americans of very Bohemian type and tendency: a youngish woman, Eugenia Young, who as the morganatic wife of a German prince has received the title of Baroness Munster, and her brother, a clever draughtsman,

half amateur, half professional, who is engaged in furnishing sketches to an illustrated journal in Europe. To put the matter plainly, the Baroness Munster is an adventuress, nothing more nor less. As an adventuress she became a morganatic wife of the brother of a petty German grand duke (it was thirty years ago), and now as an adventuress she comes to America to try her fortune in finding some rich American to take her in some fashion—as a wife preferable of course—off her German prince's hands. In the first place it is difficult to see why these people are called "the Europeans." They are in a certain sense indeed the product of the conditions of society upon the continent of Europe, as the Marquis of Brotherton and Dean Lovelace are the product of the conditions of society in England. But they are not, like the Marquis and the Dean, indigenous products of that society, integral parts of it; they are waifs and strays—Europeanized Americans of a not very admirable sort. It was a little fretting to see Mr. Newman set forth as "the American" by Mr. James; that personage being hardly, we think, what Mr. James himself would like to have accepted as a fair representative of the social product of his country. But Mr. James's Europeans have really no claim whatever to the style and title which he bestows upon them; being simply cosmopolite Bohemians of European origin; folk which the real people of no country would acknowledge as being of themselves, not to say take pride in owning.

These adventurers find their New England kinsfolk living in one of the suburbs of Boston, and are kindly received by them and placed in a pretty cottage near their own house. There the Baroness and her brother remain week after week, month after month, visiting the big house, doing nothing, suffering nothing, getting into no trouble and therefore getting out of none, making no material for a story even of the slightest kind, but revealing their own characters and drawing out those of their cousins, young and old. These cousins are a father, Mr. Wentworth, and two daughters, Charlotte and Gertrude, who seem to be presented as types of New England people of their condition. And what character they have, it may be acknowledged, is New-England-ish. Their common trait seems to be a pale, intellectual asceticism; but besides this they have very little character at all. Their coldly moral view of life is admirably described by Mr. James. As he makes Felix say to Gertrude, who is falling in love with him, she and her family "take a painful view of life." This is also indicated reflexively by Gertrude, who, going from the bare neatness and respectability of New England to the Baroness's drawing-room in the little cottage, which the latter has decked and softened with curtains and colored drapery (some of it rather dingy), looks at it, and then " 'What is life, indeed, without curtains?' she secretly asked herself; and she appeared to herself to have been leading hitherto an existence singularly garish, and totally devoid of festoons." These Yankee girls have none of the conventional reserves to which Felix has been accustomed; and the effect upon him is thus delicately suggested: "He had known fortunately many virtuous gentlewomen, but it now appeared to him that in his relations with them (especially when they were unmarried) he had been looking at pictures under a glass. He perceived at present what a nuisance the glass had been—how it perverted and interfered, how it caught the reflection of other objects and kept you walking from side to side." These traits of character and others like them, on both sides, are touched by Mr. James with a dainty and skillful hand.

Although Mr. James's Wentworths may be recognized as possible New England people, they can not be accepted as fair representatives, mentally or physically, of their class. His description of the young ladies personally is puzzling. Gertrude, whose slumbering love for the vanities of the world is aroused by the Baroness's festoons, and who finally captivates Felix, is described as being "tall and pale, thin and a little awkward; her hair was fair and perfectly straight; her eyes were dark and they had the singularity of seeming at once dull and restless—differing herein, as you see, fatally from the ideal fine eyes, which we always imagine to be both brilliant and tranquil." Her sister Charlotte "was also thin and pale; but she was older than the other; she was shorter, and she had dark smooth hair." And yet these most unattractive young ladies are afterward referred to more than once as beautiful. The truth seems to be that Mr. James, clever literary artist as he is, is not strong in imagination. His personages do not exist, even for himself, as living, independent, "self-contained" human beings. They act and speak only as he wishes them to act and speak from time to time. He has no personal respect for them. How could it be otherwise? How could he treat them with any deference when they plainly have no existence for him out of the range of his own consciousness? He calls "The Europeans" a sketch; and indeed its effect is very sketch-like as well as very French. It brings to mind some of those very clever things of which so many are done by French painters: a mere outline, with a dot or a line suggestive of light and shade set here and there, and then filled with color very faintly washed in; the whole thing indicative of the great skill that comes from careful training, but nevertheless a very shadowy hint of humanity, demonstrative rather of great half-exercised powers on the part of the artist than of the solid and vital personality of the subject. The author seems to be making his sketches, just as Felix did his, to send them to his illustrated paper. Hence it is, probably, that while they are touched off so cleverly they are so unsatisfactory. And yet this lack of individuality and vital force in their personages is the great defect of all Mr. James's novels. His men and women, although they talk exceedingly well, are bloodless, and remind one of the "vox et præterea nihil" of his youth. This shadowy, bloodless effect is not at all the consequence of the particular type of New England personage depicted in "The Europeans"; for, besides that it is manifest in the peopling of all of Mr. James's novels, let the Wentworths, any or all of them, be compared with Madame Launay in Trollope's recent "Lady of Launay," which is a mere sketch no longer than Mr. James's own "Daisy Miller." It consists chiefly of a pair of every-day lovers, and of an old lady who is ready to sacrifice everything and everybody, herself included, upon what she regards as the altar of duty. The lovers have the virtue of constancy; the old lady, Madame Launay, that of inexorable firmness. She is ill, she is almost bed-ridden, she becomes a shadow; but there is more strength, more individuality in this attenuated old woman than in a regiment of Mr. Wentworths. There is one scene in this little sketch in which Philip Launay faces his mother and wins a victory over her, partly by his boldness in assaulting her fortress of will, and partly by the treachery of love within the walls, in which that young man outweighs a ton of such men as are in "The Europeans," although one of them, Mr. Brand, is an enormous specimen of muscular Christianity, and the other is the sinfully positive and joyous Felix Young. This is the question in regard to Mr. James's ultimate success as a novel-writer—whether he will be able to bring before us living personages in whose fate we take an interest. As to his literary skill there is no question. The impression which Felix, always gay, always a little aggressive in his fullness of animal spirits,

makes upon the shy and shrinking Charlotte, is illustrated—we might say illuminated—with a little flash of wit of which the most brilliant French writer might be proud: "Poor Charlotte could have given no account of the matter that would not have seemed unjust both to herself and to her foreign kinsman; she could only have said—or rather she never would have said it—that she did not like so much gentlemen's society at once."

The moral pedantry and the chilly unemotional life characteristic of a not inconsiderable part of New England society in past generations are delicately exposed all through the book. These might have depressed a much less sybaritic person than the Bohemian Baroness. As the story, if story it must be called, draws to a close, these motives find happy expression in the view taken by Mr. Wentworth of the love affairs of Gertrude, who was with his approval to have been given to Mr. Brand, the big young minister, but who with that gentleman's consent transfers herself to Felix. When the change was made known to him, "Where are our moral grounds?" demanded Mr. Wentworth, who had always thought that Mr. Brand would be "just the thing for a younger daughter with a peculiar temperament." And soon after, when he is urged to consent to the marriage, he again reverts to his cherished view of her case: "'I have always thought,' he began slowly, 'that Gertrude's character required a special line of development.'" This brings to mind Mr. Howells's humorous presentation of the same trait of character in his charming "Lady of the Aroostook," yet incomplete. When the Rev. Mr. Goodlow's advice is asked in regard to the unfortunate circumstance of Lydia Blood's being the only woman on board that vessel, and her making the voyage to "Try-East" in company with five men, exclusive of the crew, he replies, "I think Lydia's influence upon those around her will be beneficial, whatever her situation in life may be."

"James's *The Europeans.*" *Scribner's Monthly* 17 (January 1879), 447.

After "The American," Mr. James gives us "The Europeans," a story that was received with marked favor when the first chapters made their appearance in "The Atlantic."[1] The situation was well calculated to show the best powers of a writer who is noted for the neatness and finish of his work, for the delicateness of his satire and the care with which he studies his characters. Eugenia, a woman half American by descent, and morganatically the wife of a German princeling, finds herself on a gloomy day in a Boston hotel, accompanied only by her brother, a joyous and talented youth. Both are still in doubt as to their reception by relatives named Wentworth. They have never seen them. The view of a church-yard from their window puts Eugenia into a despondent frame of mind—Felix, however, is a very Mark Tapley of a youth; gloom and slush only make him more sure that the Wentworths are charming, and that the venture to America will be a success. And in the end it is a success for him; but the result, so far as Eugenia is concerned, tallies with her own presentiments. It all comes to nothing in her case, although she is the main character, the only heroine in a story without heroes. Mr. James seems to have aimed at consistency in finishing the story after such a method, just as the musician closes his piece by striking once more the note with which he began.

As the Wentworth family are slowly revealed in all the modern dilution of the ancient Puritan conscientiousness, the contrasts between the lively Bohemianism of the Europeans, and the solemn self-doubt of the New Englanders become still more piquant. We feel that here are the elements for something worth reading without intermission to the end. The unfolding is slow, but irritation at the slowness is rather pleasant than otherwise. Yet, after all is over, we become aware that something more was expected than the tame return to Europe of Eugenia, and the equally tame marriage of Felix with Gertrude Wentworth. It may be urged that Mr. James is highly consistent. The Baroness really could not be expected to stand the dullness of life in the suburbs of Boston. Robert Acton, whom she attracts, could not be expected to love her enough to keep her away from the fascinations of Europe, nor to excuse sufficiently the numerous small untruths of which, first and last, she is guilty. Nevertheless, the story lacks a strong satisfactory close. It has weakness at the end, as so many of this charming writer's stories have. It will neither please the main bulk of novel-readers, nor the fastidious few who demand to be stirred by an author. But its audience will be found in a highly respectable and well-read class, which may be termed the "upper middle cultured;" for they will be delighted throughout with its air of gentlemanliness, excellent diction, and fastidious turns of thought, while they will not miss the want of life and incident. On every page there is something to show how earnest and observant a literary artist Mr. James is. It is not his fault, if he does not strike a ringing note. Meanwhile, it is saying a great deal that he steadily improves in his style and methods. In certain points, he takes the lead among American writers; with such a foundation, there is no reason why he should not achieve far higher laurels.

Note

1 "The Europeans," *Atlantic Monthly* 42
(July–October 1878), 52–72, 155–77, 262–
83, 404–28.

Atlantic Monthly 43 (February 1879), 167–69.

To read Mr. Henry James, Jr., is to experience a light but continuous gratification of mind. It is to be intellectually *tickled*, provided one is capable of such an exercise. It is to take a pleasure so simple and facile that it seems only one step removed from physical content in the lavish cleverness of an almost incessantly witty writer,—a pleasure enhanced, no doubt, by a lurking sense that one must be a little clever one's self in order to keep pace with such dazzling mental agility. To people who have read a good deal of French, and read it because they liked it,—and why else should an Englishman or an American ever advance in that literature beyond the absurd Racine of his school-days?—the writing of Mr. James has the additional interest of offering the best of proof that the English language approaches the French much more nearly than is usually supposed, in its capacity for what may be called *current* epigram. Occasionally, also, Mr. James comes strikingly near to showing that our "sober speech" might, under proper cultivation, blossom as richly as that of the lively Gaul, into what Mr. Mallock calls "that perfect flower of modern civilization, the innuendo." But to do our countryman justice, he is too truly refined to indulge more than sparingly in this exotic species of literary ornament. The clean turns and crisp graces of his style are such as peculiarly befit an essayist, and some of his critical sketches are extremely admirable; but he is too freaky and irresponsible to be always a safe guide, even in matters of bookish opinion, and it is as a novelist only that we propose to consider him.

Within the last three years, Mr. James has written two noteworthy stories, both of which appeared first in these pages. One and the same purpose animates them, and that is to illustrate the different types of character and manners produced by European and American civilization; or, more strictly speaking, by European civilization and American semi-barbarism. On this one point our author keeps all his bright faculties intently focused, and studies the human specimens, which he has first carefully selected, with the methodical minuteness and ecstatic patience of a microscopist.

In The American, as the readers of The Atlantic undoubtedly remember, the hero, Christopher Newman, a self-made Yankee who has gathered a great fortune before the age of thirty-five, and gone to Paris to spend it, naïvely resolves to take him a wife out of the Faubourg St. Germain, gets the *entrée* in a sufficiently unlikely manner of that difficult stronghold and very nearly succeeds in carrying out his project. His wife is in fact promised him by her high-bred and fastidious family. But when these potentates see an unexpected chance of marrying her to an imbecile Irish lord they break their pledge. The passive bride, whose heart had really been won, has just spirit enough to baffle them by going into a Carmelite convent, and the American, after one rueful promenade round the walls of his lady's sepulchre, takes the self which he had made away to parts unknown.

In The Europeans, which came as a kind of *per contra* to The American, we have a brother and sister of mixed Swiss and American parentage, who have passed all their lives (they are both in the neighborhood of thirty) on the continent of Europe. The sister, Eugenia, has made a morganatic marriage with a German prince, which, for state reasons, the reigning family desire to annul; and the brother, Felix, though a pleasant fellow and a clever artist, is virtually a penniless adventurer; so the two come to seek their fortune among their American cousins. These prove to be people of wealth and the highest respectability, living puritanically and yet with dignified abundance at a fine old country-seat, seven miles and a half from Boston,—say in Watertown; and the equable currents of suburban life are of course terribly disturbed by this unlooked-for foreign irruption. In the end, Felix wins and carries away to the Parisian heaven the younger and more enterprising of his pretty cousins; while Eugenia, after a course of the most finished coquetry with a gentleman retired from the India trade, returns as she came. But whether it was because she could not, at the last, quite bring her own mind to the flavorless conditions of a virtuous New England life, or because Mr. Acton could not reconcile himself to her constitutional duplicity, we are left, after three steadfast perusals of this part of the narrative, absolutely in doubt.

It will be perceived at a glance that all these plans—they cannot be called plots—afford abundant opportunities for humor of situation, every one of which, it need hardly be said, Mr. James brilliantly improves. Newman, before the old Marquise de Bellegarde, replying to her slow and pompous explanations of the uncompromising pride of the race he dared seek to come among by the cheerful assurance that *he* wasn't proud, and didn't mind them; Felix expatiating to his blameless uncle, sitting reluctantly for his portrait, on the ravishing novelty of "calling on twenty young ladies and going out to walk with them," sitting in the evening on the piazza and listening to the crickets, and going to bed at ten o'clock; Mr. Brand making a pale, intrepid confession of Unitarianism to the heathen strangers who had never heard of that form of faith; and the Rev. Benjamin Babcock taking a small bag of hominy with him to all the principal Continental hotels, and passing sleepless nights because he cannot make Newman feel, as he does, the overwhelming "seriousness of art and life,"—all these are spectacles that minister a malign delight. It is in single scenes, detached portraits, and episodes like those of Valentin's duel and Newman's summer tour with Mr. Babcock, that Mr. James is at his very best. The habit of his mind is so irresistibly analytic that he must needs concentrate himself in succession upon each separate detail of his subject. His romance is a series of situations imperfectly vivified by action. There is a scene in The American,—a stormy night in the Rue de l'Université, when Madame de Cintré goes to the piano and plays,—and there are a dozen idle scenes in the more languid Europeans, which have absolutely no connection with the thread of the story. In like manner his portraits are a succession of uncolored features, and his philosophy is a succession of admirably quotable aphorisms. Here probably we have the reason suggested why we can hear Mr. James's characters so much better than we can see them. In the nature of things only one word can be spoken at a time, and Mr. James is an acute listener and an alert reporter; so that his conversations, except when he endeavors to put into the mouths of his creatures some of his own oversubtle considerations, are exquisitely real and just. But over and above all the items of aspect, whether in places or people, there is a physiognomy, a *look*, and this is what Mr. James never imparts. He tells us clearly, and with an almost anxious emphasis, that Claire de Cintré had a "long, fair face;" that Gertrude Wentworth had "sweet, dull eyes;" that his delightful and deplorable Valentin de Bellegarde had "a round head high above the ears," and "a crop of short silky hair;" and that the Wentworth mansion in Watertown had white wooden pilasters in front, supporting a pediment with one large central window and two small ones. And we listen as if we were blindfolded, and credit our informant certainly, but do not see at all.

It is a question whether Mr. James himself sees. He is so *spirituel,* and his conceptions are so subtle, that he has not *sense* enough (the term is used metaphysically and with entire respect) to give them form, still less flesh. And so, although a most entertaining chronicler, he escapes being an artist, for an artist must *portray.*

The American is perhaps the finest fragment in modern fiction, but it is only a fragment. The Europeans is much less fine, but equally unfinished. His narratives are so fine-spun and so deficient in incident, so unpicturesque as a whole and weak in the way of sensuous imagery, that they are specially ill fitted for serial publication. His flavor is too delicate to be suspended and superseded for a month. But he never wrote anything which was not well worth a connected reperusal, and nothing strikes one with more surprise in re-reading him than the unremembered, one might almost say unintentional, *goodness*—pure and simple—of some of his characters. Christopher Newman is as noble a fellow, in essentials, as ever breathed. He is the soul of honor as distinguished from its code, which is gracefully personified in Valentin de Bellegarde. He is generous, gentle, and gloriously frank; he is delicate-minded and true. He has wrath and scorn only for what is vile, and in his forgiveness of the base injury done him by the elder Bellegardes, and the relinquishment of his vengeance, there is the essence of a Christianity usually considered as much too fine for every-day use as unalloyed gold would be. Yet all this sterling worth seems to be held not merely lightly, but cheaply, by Newman's biographer. Our final impression of this simple hero is of a man disconcerted and disheartened, and who more than half deserved his bitter discomfiture for the undeniable social enormities of having telegraphed his engagement to America, and shaken hands on his introduction to a duke with the affable remark that he was happy to make his acquaintance.

Again, in The Europeans Felix beguiles Gertrude away from a home, austere indeed, but singularly safe, dignified, and refined, into the dark ways of European Bohemianism; and Eugenia seems to have missed the affluent settlement which she had exiled herself to secure, because she disgusted a high-minded suitor by lavish and inappropriate lying; yet we cannot help feeling—and who but Mr. James makes us feel?—that Felix won a victory and Eugenia made an escape.

In general, one cannot help wishing that our native authors would have done with this incessant drawing of comparisons between ourselves and the folk in Europe, and our respective ways of living, thinking, and talking. Publicly to compare one's self with another is always ungraceful and undignified. It always proclaims self-consciousness, usually self-uneasiness. It was very well for Count de Gasparin, once upon a time, to write of America before Europe, but for America herself to be passing between two mirrors looks rather silly.[1] We have our own life to live, our own resources to unfold, our own crude and complex conditions finally to compel into some sort of symmetry, our own youth to train. If we do not evolve some new forms adapted to our new environment, it will show pretty conclusively that there is small health in us. At all events, let us concentrate our wits on our affairs for a time, and not worry about our looks.

Notes

1   Agenor Comte de Gasparin, *America before Europe* (1862).

Checklist of Additional Reviews

London *Examiner,* 12 October 1878, pp. 1303–4.

New York *Commercial Advertiser,* 15 October 1878, p. 1.

New York *Daily Graphic,* 17 October 1878, p. 744.

Chicago *Inter-Ocean,* 19 October 1878, p. 10.

Hartford *Daily Courant,* 21 October 1878, p. 1.

Spectator [England], no. 2626 (26 October 1878), 1334–6.

Christian Union 18 (30 October 1878), 361.

Philadelphia *North American,* 31 October 1878, p. 4.

Chicago *Inter-Ocean,* 2 November 1878, p. 10.

G[eorge] W. S[malley]. New York *Tribune,* 2 November 1878, p. 8.

New York *Times,* 4 November 1878, p. 3.

New York *World,* 4 November 1878, p. 2.

Boston *Daily Advertiser,* 7 November 1878, p. 2.

Boston *Evening Transcript,* 4 December 1878, p. 6. Reprinted in James W. Gargano, ed., *Critical Essays on Henry James: The Early Novels* (Boston: G. K. Hall, 1987), p. 43.

St. Louis *Post-Dispatch,* 7 December 1878, p. 2.

Atlantic Monthly 43 (January 1879), 106–8. Reprinted in Roger Gard, ed., *Henry James: The Critical Heritage* (London: Routledge & Kegan Paul, 1968), pp. 66–69.

Harper's New Monthly Magazine 58 (January 1879), 309. Reprinted in Gard, p. 70.

International Review 6 (January 1879), 95–96.

Literary World [Boston] 10 (January 1879), 28.

DAISY MILLER

New York *Times*, 10 November 1878, p. 10.

In *Daisy Miller* Mr. James has surpassed all his previous writings for the clearness of his conception and the accuracy of his observation. The tragical sketch of a young girl from Schenectady may not be recognized as a portrait of any maiden of that old Dutch town, who traveled in Europe only to find her grave in the Eternal City. Schenectadians—if that be the right term to use—may not be pleased to find their town identified with a young person of bad manners. Nor is it likely that Schenectady, or any other town of the Middle States, would produce just such a compound as the pretty, independent, but very ill-advised damsel whose name is Daisy Miller. But take her as a type that embraces the characteristics of various young women from America now journeying about Europe with more money at their disposal than discretion, and the truth and cleverness of this sketch will appear—even to a patriot of Schenectady. It is a hackneyed remark that Americans continually shock the prejudices of Europeans. When the prejudices relate to unimportant things, it may be well to pay no more attention to them than to avoid, as much as possible, hurting their feelings. But when the question relates to the reputation of a young girl, it is worse than folly to persist in defying public opinion. This must be the view Mr. James takes; for his sketch, although satirical, deals gently, toward the end, with the unwise, untrained young woman whose pranks in Europe he has chronicled. In this case the author is, therefore, something more than heretofore. His previous books have been elaborate and well finished. The new story, which appeared, inappropriately enough, in an English magazine, shows that he is possessed of a sincere patriotism, since he consecrates his talents to the enlightening of his countrywomen in the view which cynical Europe takes of the performances of American girls abroad. And he enlightens them in the happiest style and with fully as much gentleness as the circumstances warrant. Excellent is the method of adding stroke to stroke until the character of Daisy is complete. She comes on the scene directly after her little brother, a monstrous child, who is decidedly overdrawn and unnatural. Her mother follows her, and in her way is as well drawn as the daughter. Then comes the courier, Eugenio, who is on the most intimate terms with the family. The young American who discovers this interesting and in many ways typical family at Vevay [*sic*] is of a type often seen in Mr. James' works. He is supposed to be in love with the heroine, but is really nothing but a detective following her about. Winterbourne is too much scandalized by the escapades of Daisy to continue the friendship when he follows her to Rome, and the pathos of the story lies in a hint that the poor girl, though flirting with Giovanelli, the Roman fortune-hunter, was really in love with the serious, pedantic youth who frowned on her mode of conduct. In thinking over the writers of fiction in England and America, we fail to remember any one who can write so well balanced and clever a short story as this last by Mr. James.

[Richard Grant White]. *North American Review* 128 (January 1879), 101–6.

Daisy Miller is a beauty, and, without being exactly a fool, is ignorant and devoid of all mental tone or character. She dresses elegantly, has "the tournure of a princess," and is yet irredeemably vulgar in her talk and her conduct. She shocks all Europeans and all well-bred Americans by the terms on which she is with the courier of her party, and by making chance acquaintances with men and flirting with them. She has a grand affair of this kind in Rome, which, after excluding her from the society of more reserved American women, ends in her going to see the Coliseum by moonlight with her Roman cavalier, who is not a gentleman, and taking there the fever of the country and dying. In Daisy Miller Mr. James has undertaken to give a characteristic portrait of a certain sort of American young woman, who is unfortunately too common. She has no breeding, little character, a headstrong will, in effect no mother, and with all this has personal attractions and a command of money which are very rare in Europe, even among people of rank. As she flares through Paris, and flits from place to place over the continent, attended but not controlled by her parents, she is the wonder and horror of all decorous people, American and European. Mr. James's portrait is very faithful. He has succeeded to admiration in the difficult task of representing the manner in which such people as Mrs. and Miss Miller talk; the difficulty being caused by the extremely characterless nature of their conversation, which is never coarse, or very vulgar, or even very fool-ish. It is simply inane and low-bred, and is marked by certain slight perversions of language; for example, "going around," instead of "going about," of which one phrase, by the way, Mr. James makes rather too much. It is perhaps well that he has made this study, which may have some corrective effect, and which should show European critics of American manners and customs the light in which the Daisy Millers are regarded by Americans themselves. But the probability is that, on the contrary, Daisy Miller will become the accepted type and her name the *sobriquet* in European journalism of the American young woman of the period.

[John Hay]. *Atlantic Monthly* 43 (March 1879), 399–400.

To read the silly criticisms which have been printed, and the far sillier ones which are every day uttered in regard to Mr. James's Daisy Miller would almost convince us that we are as provincial as ever in our sensitiveness to foreign opinion. It is actually regarded as a species of unpardonable incivism for Mr. James, because he lives in London, to describe an under-bred American family traveling in Europe. The fact that he has done so with a touch of marvelous delicacy and truth, that he has produced not so much a picture as a photograph, is held by many to be an aggravating circumstance. Only the most shiveringly sensitive of our shoddy population are bold enough to deny the truth of this wonderful little sketch. To those best acquainted with Mr. James's manner (and I believe I have read every word he has printed) Daisy Miller was positively startling in its straightforward simplicity and what I can only call *authenticity*. It could not have been written—I am almost ready to say it cannot be appreciated—except by one who has lived so long abroad as to be able to look at his own people with the eyes of a foreigner. All poor Daisy's crimes are purely conventional. She is innocent and good at heart, susceptible of praise and blame; she does not wish even to surprise, much less outrage, the stiffest of her censors. In short, the things she does with such dire effect at Vevay and at Rome would never for an instant be remarked or criticised in Schenectady. They would provoke no comment in Buffalo or Cleveland; they would be a matter of course in Richmond and Louisville. One of the most successful touches in the story is that where Daisy, astonished at being cut by American ladies, honestly avows her disbelief in their disapproval. "I should not think you would let them be so unkind!" she cries to Winterbourne, conscious of her innocence, and bewildered at the cruelty of a sophisticated world. Yet with such exquisite art is this study managed that the innocence and loveliness of Miss Miller are hardly admitted as extenuating circumstances in her reprehensible course of conduct. She is represented, by a chronicler who loves and admires her, as bringing ruin upon herself and a certain degree of discredit upon her countrywomen, through eccentricities of behavior for which she cannot justly be held responsible. Her conduct is without blemish, according to the rural American standard, and she knows no other. It is the merest ignorance or affectation, on the part of the anglicized Americans of Boston or New York, to deny this. A few dozens, perhaps a few hundreds, of families in America have accepted the European theory of the necessity of surveillance for young ladies, but it is idle to say it has ever been accepted by the country at large. In every city of the nation young girls of good fam-

ily, good breeding, and perfect innocence of heart and mind, receive their male acquaintances *en tête-à-tête*, and go to parties and concerts with them, unchaperoned. Of course, I do not mean that Daisy Miller belongs to that category; her astonishing mother at once designates her as pertaining to one distinctly inferior. Who has not met them abroad? From the first word uttered by Miss Daisy to her rampant young brother in the garden at Vevay, "Well, I guess you'd better be quiet," you recognize her, and recall her under a dozen different names and forms. She went to dine with you one day at Sceaux, and climbed, with the fearless innocence of a bird, into the great chestnut-tree. She challenged you to take her to Schönbrunn, and amazed your Austrian acquaintances whom you met there, and who knew you were not married. At Naples, one evening—*Eheu, fugaces labuntur anni;* it is not worth while to continue the enumeration. It makes you feel melancholy to think she is doing the same acts of innocent recklessness with men as young and as happy, and what the French call as unenterprising, as you were once.

As to the usefulness of this little book, it seems to me as indubitable as its literary excellence. It is too long a question to discuss in this place, whether the freedom of American girls at home is beneficial or sinister in its results. But there is no question whatever as to the effect of their ignorance or defiance of conventionalities abroad. An innocent flirtation with a Frenchman or Italian tarnishes a reputation forever. All the waters of the Mediterranean cannot wash clean the name of a young lady who makes a rendezvous and takes a walk with a fascinating chance acquaintance. We need only refer to the darker miseries which often result from these reckless intimacies. A charming young girl, traveling with a simple-minded mother, a few years ago, in a European capital, married a branded convict who had introduced himself to them, calling himself, of course, a count. In short, an American girl, like Daisy Miller, accompanied by a woman like Daisy's mother, brought up in the simplicity of provincial life in the United States, has no more chance of going through Europe unscathed in her feelings and her character than an idiot millionaire has of amusing himself economically in Wall Street. This lesson is taught in Mr. James's story,—and never was necessary medicine administered in a form more delightful and unobtrusive.

Athenaeum [England] 2679 (1 March 1879), 276.

Mr. James's three stories[1] are pleasant reading, and it may, therefore, be assumed, taking the converse of a well-known rule, that, slight as they appear, they were not written without plenty of trouble. At the same time, and perhaps for this very reason, they do not enable a critic to feel quite sure of Mr. James's potential excellence as a writer of fiction. He is little more than a beginner, and he already writes with the *aplomb* of a veteran; he has almost acquired a manner. But, after all, his stories lack substance. All three have that melancholy touch, as of one conscious rather of the irony of fortune than of more cheerful possibilities, which we have learnt to consider a necessary element in this kind of short sketch. In 'Daisy Miller' a young American makes the acquaintance of a pretty girl, his compatriot, at Vevey. He is more or less disposed to be in love with her, and, as we gather, she with him; but she disgusts him by outrageous flirtation, and dies of Roman fever

before an explanation is possible. The story is called "a study"; but a study is generally taken from nature, with a view to its being introduced into a larger composition. Both these requirements seem to fail here. There is that shade of exaggeration by which a study is turned into a caricature; and moreover, as far as we see, the subject is worked out to its possible limits. Character and incident are alike too slight to be capable of further development. 'An International Episode' is fresh in the memory of readers of the *Cornhill*. It is an excellent magazine story, and the sketch of American life in New York and Newport would seem to be admirable. 'Four Meetings' is purely sad, with the saddest of all sadness, a gentle and generous nature compelled to associate with sordid vulgarity. The writers by whose influence Mr. James is most affected are, we suspect, strange as the juxtaposition may at first seem, Balzac and Mr. Trollope. The latter offers by far the easier example to follow, both in his merits and in his faults; and unless Mr. James takes care he will, even while believing that the great French story-teller is his model, become little more than a reflection of a writer in whose later work, at all events, the faults decidedly predominate.

Note

1 The two-volume English edition of *Daisy Miller* (London: Macmillan, 1879) also included "An International Episode" and "Four Meetings."

"Mr. Henry James's Sketches."
Spectator [England] 2644 (1 March 1879), 277–78.

Mr. Henry James is certainly a very re-markable illustration of the tendency of our age to subdivide in the finest way the already rather extreme division of labour, till a very high perfection is attained in producing articles of the most curiously specialised kind, though apparently without the power of producing anything outside that kind. For a long time we have had novelists who are wonderfully skilful in a particular form of novels, but who seem almost unable to master more than one form for themselves. But Mr. Henry James, though he has attained a very great perfection in his own line, seems not to aim at anything quite so considerable as a story of human life of any sort. He eschews a story. What he loves is "an episode," *i.e.,* something which by the nature of the case is rather a fragment cut out of a life, and *not* a fair or average specimen of it, nor even such a part of it as would give you the best essence of the whole,—but rather an eddy in it, which takes you for an interval out of its main current, and only ends as you get back into the main current again, or at least at the point at which you might get back into the main current again, if some event (accidental, in relation to the art of the story) did not occur to cut off abruptly the thread of the narrative. The *Europeans* was essentially an "episode." *Daisy Miller,* called here "a study," is also and truly an episode. The second story is called by Mr. Henry James himself "An international episode," and certainly the whole flavour of it depends on its episodical character. And the third,

called *Four Meetings,* though the most like a whole, the nearest thing to a study which is not episodal, but rather genu-inely characteristic of the nature and des-tiny it is intended to delineate, is yet so ef-fective as it is, because it paints a nature intensely and even morbidly concentrated on one of the episodical interests of life as if it were the main interest, and which is yet able to sacrifice this dream of youth at the bidding of a motive of the same illusive and romantic kind, though the act of yielding to it involves a final blight to all the brightness and joy of existence. It seems as if life interested Mr. Henry James only in its episodes; as if, in order to catch his attention, it were almost necessary that men and women should not be pursuing the main threads of their lives, but should be engaged in a little by-play, which presented them in a less real and less organic relation to the rest of the world, than that which they usually care to fill. What he seems to desire to do most is to paint human nature in its semi-capricious moods, when it is rather out for a holiday excursion, in some beat of life for which it is not particularly well fitted, than when it is weaving for itself its permanent character and destiny. It is perfectly true that in the little sketch called *Four Meetings,* Mr. James has, as we have already admitted, really produced a very touching and deli-cate, though mild and rather pallid, trag-edy, with a real integrity and a natural end. But then the beauty of the picture seems almost to have depended in his mind on the fact that its heroine, Miss Caroline Spencer, has fostered for herself a vivid, though delicate passion out of the mere fancy for European travel,—long cherished, and its gratification long de-layed,—and that when at last she is on the point of gratifying that passion, the same gentle romance which sowed it in her heart turns her home again, in order to provide the means for helping a worthless cousin and his equally worthless wife, who have managed to appeal to the unselfish spirit which is part and parcel of her romance. But even this story would not have been so striking as it is, had it not been the sketch of a nature which provides us with an episode in the story of human nature generally. Romance is not usually unselfish, as it is in Miss Caroline Spencer. There is nothing more selfish than the so-called romantic side of many human hearts. The desire for those great excitements which have managed to kindle the imagination, is one of the most selfish of desires. But now and then, as in the case of the heroine of *Four Meetings,* you find a mind "delicately agitated," as Mr. Henry James happily expresses it, by some train of fancies and associations containing no selfish element in them, and the gratification of which can be resigned, if need be, at the impulse of the very same kind of purely imaginative motive which brought them into being.

No doubt there is a wonderful skill in the writer who, avowedly refusing to tell you what can properly be called a story—loving above all things to depict excursions of the heart and mind which fade away and end in nothing,—can yet interest you so deeply as he does in his delineation of these unfulfilled intentions of men, these *manqué* and tentative deviations into regions not adapted for embodiment into the substance of life. One might perhaps say that Mr. Henry James has discerned in relation to literature what has long been known in relation to art—that with artists of any genius, "sketches" are apt to be more satisfying than finished pictures. But then the sketches we like so much in artists' studios are, though unfinished pictures, still pictures of what the painter has been most struck with, pictures in which he has given all that struck him most, and left only what did not strike him to be filled in by the fancy of the pub-

lic. Now Mr. Henry James does not give us sketches of the striking features in what he sees of human life and passion, so much as finished pictures of the little nooks and bays into which human caprice occasionally drifts, when the main current of life's deeper interests has left us for a moment on one side, and rushed past us. He does not half-paint what is striking; he prefers rather to paint with wonderful care and precision what is not striking, or only striking by its contrast with what is usually thought so. As in his "study" of Daisy Miller, he loves to paint that aspect of life which is commonly mistaken for its main aspect, when it is not its main aspect; or if it is so, is so only because, in the particular case of the character he thus studies, the preparatory antecedents of action or passion as they show themselves in other beings, have taken up an accidental preponderance, and superseded the interest of the action or passion to which they are usually only preparatory. Mr. Henry James is not so much a novelist as an episodist, if such a term be allowable. But he is a wonderful episodist.

"*Daisy Miller.*" *Pall Mall Gazette* [England], 20 March 1879, p. 12.

All English novel-readers are to be congratulated upon the appearance of these stories of Mr. James's in the peculiar form which publishers in this country reserve for new works of fiction. The author has hitherto been known as an American, and his most popular books have made their way across the Atlantic to this country, bearing their transportation with no loss of success, but still on their arrival here wearing the garb of strangers. In the present instance, however, Mr. James meets with the full honours due to an English novelist.

Daisy Miller is an American young lady, brilliantly dressed and dazzlingly pretty, who makes her appearance on a hot summer evening in the garden of a hotel overlooking the Lake of Geneva, and at once begins to prattle confidentially to the hero of the story, himself a well-educated, well-travelled American. Miss Miller is not well educated, nor has she gained much experience from her wanderings with her family over Europe, although the party is superintended by the most unexceptionable and patronizing of couriers. The young man is immediately fascinated by her prettiness and the perfect frankness of her conversation, while his fancy is stimulated by a doubt whether she is perfectly unsophisticated and simply intent on getting as much amusement as she can out of things, or whether she is a hardened flirt. In vain his aunt assures him most positively that she must be a horrid girl; he is completely charmed, devotes himself to her most assiduously, answers all her questions about himself, and is much flattered, though slightly embarrassed by the liking she shows for him without any reserve. After a few days of this sort of intercourse, he goes off, not exactly in love, but very much interested and well satisfied with himself. In the winter they meet at Rome, in fulfilment of a summer agreement. Miss Miller is unfeignedly glad to see her friend, greets him most warmly, and at once drags him for a walk to the Pincian, where she has agreed to meet a certain Giovanelli, a handsome, good-for-nothing Italian. Winterbourne, our American hero, is disgusted to find that the young lady is carrying on, only in an intensified form, the same sort of flirtation which he had found so charming himself in the summer. Rome,

however, is not a good place in which to pursue tactics so open as Miss Miller's. Every one is scandalized by her proceedings; Winterbourne himself is fairly puzzled; Daisy is perfectly friendly, perfectly open with him, laughs at his expostulations, explains nothing, does not seem aware that there is anything in her conduct to explain; and, although once or twice she shows that she is really hurt by rebuffs which she meets in society and which show only too clearly what people think of her, she does not give in to popular prejudice, but goes on, fluttering about like a butterfly, always in the company of her Italian. Winterbourne feels she is honest but the evidence is getting too strong for him. At last, late one night, coming home from a party, he finds the pair enjoying the sentimental moonlight in the Colosseum. It is too much for him; hitherto he has only remonstrated; this time he, also, throws his stone, and sees that his insult has hit her hard. She goes home, catches a fever, and dies, leaving a message which shows the young man that he has been wrong, and that a real opportunity is lost to him for ever.

"An International Episode" is less sad; and the situation, though to a certain extent the same, is less complicated. Two young Englishmen, one, Lord Lambeth, the eldest son of the Duke of Bayswater, the type of an honest, stupid, cheerful, sensible man, go to America, and are most hospitably entertained by Mrs. Westgate, a fashionable New York lady whose husband is always too busy to get away from his work, and her unmarried sister, Miss Bessie Aden. The young lord shows strong signs of having fallen in love with this young lady; but is hurried back to England away from danger by his companion, who feels that the heir of an English title must not marry an unknown American, however charming she may be. Lord Lambeth's friends, however, find the difficulty recur, when Mrs. Westgate and her sister come over to England on their way to the Continent, and the young man shows himself quite devoted, escorting them to the Tower of London and other incongruous places. For some time we are in doubt whether Miss Aden is really in love; Lord Lambeth's family, however, assume, naturally enough, that she must be bent on capturing a lord, and at last make a demonstration in force to show the Americans that their position is untenable. The grand ladies swoop down on the hotel where Mrs. Westgate and her sister are staying, and pay a solemn visit of petrifying affability. Mrs. Westgate has something of the spirit of a general; and, thinking that her sister is not seriously affected, is anxious to hold her ground and fight the matter out. At this juncture the knot is abruptly cut by Miss Bessie, who refuses the young man, and so the story ends.

It will be seen from the sketch we have given that the motive of these stories is very slight. In both it is the same, a girl who by her simplicity of manner and unaffected enjoyment of life gets to be looked on with suspicion by the people with whom she is brought into contact, while in reality she is entirely honest and sincere. The great art of Mr. James consists in the perfect proportion which he maintains between the importance of the subject and the method in which he treats it. Light plots of this nature are easily overladen; they have to be elaborated in detail, and detail is apt to destroy their compactness. It is to the preservation of this balance throughout that the stories owe much of their piquancy. Another clever device of Mr. James's is the objective form in which he presents the characters of his heroines to the reader. We know no more about them than the *dramatis personæ* see, and in this way our curiosity is kept alive to a degree which cannot be attained by any of the so-called analytical studies of character which are nowadays so fashionable. Writers of fiction are usually supposed to be omniscient within the limits of their stories. Mr. James shows how effective the opposite method of developing a plot may be: he avoids the two dangers which beset all dramatic narrative; the heroines are not driven to unfold their inner selves in long egotistical speeches, and they are not so like life as to be uninteresting and to make the reader disinclined to solve the motives which actuate them. Mr. James tells sufficiently little to keep our curiosity alive, and enough to prevent our being puzzled.

The outline which we have given does not pretend to have done full justice to these stories. Their interest is by no means confined to the principal characters; the accessories are all as fresh and amusing as can be. Daisy Miller herself, in a modified form, is a familiar figure to all frequenters of hotels abroad. Travelling Americans are a tempting subject, and many people have attempted to describe them, but Mr. James deserves the credit of having discovered how to do so in a really successful manner. Indeed, he has revealed to many of us a new distinct variety of womankind in these sketches of American girls. Nor can we omit all mention of Daisy's brother Randolph, who deserves a permanent place in the gallery of horrid little boys whose literary portraits have won immortality. Again, in the "International Episode" there is an admirable picture of life at Westport, the watering-place where the fashionable world of New York fly for coolness during the summer months. The description is admirably vivid, and the scene is unlike anything we can remember to have met in books. Apart, however, from the novelty of the subjects, which no doubt renders these stories exceptionally striking, the thoroughness of Mr. James's workmanship would win success, whatever he touched: as is proved by "The Four

Meetings," the last story in the book, the conception of which is comparatively commonplace and hackneyed, while the writing is as delicate and the management of details as ingenious as anything can be. In the first two stories, on the other hand, it seems to us that Mr. James has shown a touch of that spirit of invention which is the essence of all fiction, and without which other qualities are comparatively worthless; whether he has this gift in sufficient quantity and of quality sufficiently robust to furnish out a really good novel we cannot tell. The Americans and the Europeans rank high in the second class, but they are not perfect in the way in which these shorter stories are. It is impossible to prophesy in such cases, but, whatever Mr. James may do in the future, whether he risks his reputation in a more ambitious effort or whether he remains content on the humbler field in which he is sure of success, we shall always welcome his name.

Graphic [England], 5 April 1879, p. 342.

"Daisy Miller, a Study; and Other Stories," by Henry James, Jun. (2 vols.: Macmillan).—What is most characteristic about these stories—there are three of them altogether, "Daisy Miller," "An International Episode," and "Four Meetings"—is that, if the Hibernicism may be pardoned, they are not properly "stories" at all. Stories, even the slightest of them, have an end; whereas to Mr. Henry James it seems as if incompleteness were in itself fascinating. What he gives us here are sketches—sketches executed with wonderful finish and delicacy—of mere episodes in certain lives, which are brought

more or less accidentally to a termination and seem to leave no results behind them. The author, it may be, recognises this peculiarity in the character of his work by styling the second of the pieces here "An International Episode." Here, for instance, we have no hint that the relations between Lord Lambeth and the American girl, Bessie Alden—relations which only just fall short of becoming tender—had any effect upon the life of either of them a twelvemonth afterwards. Daisy Miller, again, and her strange freaks and caprices, are altogether an episode in the life of Winterbourne, the man through whose eyes we are made to view her. Whether readers in general, who are accustomed to tales in which everybody, or, at least, everybody of interest, either dies or lives very happy ever after, may not feel impatient that so much pains should have been, as they may say, wasted upon what comes after all to nothing, is more than we can say, but for our own part we feel that Mr. Henry James is too perfect an artist in his own line, somewhat odd as it is, for us to experience any wish that he would lay it aside for another.

Saturday Review [England] 47 (3 May 1879), 561.

Mr. Oliver Wendell Holmes says somewhere that America offers the largest market in the world for intellectual green fruit. This is true, and shows itself in more ways than one. Not only are young writers unwilling to wait till they have something to say, or till they have found out that they have nothing to say, but men of real power and merit are freed from the wholesome restraint of knowing that they are addressing a public which can distinguish their best from their second best. It is probable that Mr. Holmes's remark has less force now than when it was made a few years ago. And certainly, if anybody were disposed to find fault with Mr. James's work, it would not be on the score of immaturity or want of finish. It would rather be for a sort of instinctive unwillingness—the result very often of the critical faculties being highly cultivated—to have much to do with the elementary feelings of human nature. Mr. James is a remarkable observer of all that can be seen with the eyes or heard with the ears. The appearance, the costume, the tones and inflections of voice, the movements, the gestures, the little tricks of speech and manner of his characters are reproduced with a microscopic accuracy. The details all the while are never overdone. Only what is characteristic is selected; and, so far as the outward man and woman are concerned, or those parts of their characters which may be called the external parts, one knows them as well as one knows a personal friend. But further than this Mr. James declines to go. What sort of people they all are at bottom he refuses to tell us. He devises a situation with great skill. He interests us in all his actors. A number of incidents, selected in the most judicious manner in the world, lead up to a final crisis admirably adapted for a complete revelation of character. But at the last moment, when our curiosity is on tiptoe, when we are fidgeting to see what the next page will tell us, when all is arranged for a *dénouement,* as necessary for the completion of the plot as for the development of the characters, they either stand still and do nothing at all, or else they do something purely capricious and unaccountable. In a novelist of less ability we should take what we can get, and be thankful for it. But one is forced to regret this inequality in the work of a writer in many respects so admirable and accomplished as Mr. James.

Daisy Miller is just the sort of tale which shows Mr. James's writing at its best. The scene is laid first on the Lake of Geneva, and afterwards in Rome among the nondescript society which peoples the hotels of the former and the Anglo-Italian or Americo-Italian drawing-rooms of the latter. Daisy Miller is a girl from the State of New York, who imagines that all which is permissible for a young lady on that side of the Atlantic is equally in accordance with the manners and customs of Continental Europe, or, if not, that there is no reason why she should not act as if it were. She is a good and pure girl from beginning to end of the story; but by her cheerful, free-and-easy disregard of all social conventions makes people first stare at her, then shake their heads significantly, and finally cut her dead. It is only towards the end of the story that she seems herself to have any clear notion of the damage she is doing to her reputation. She first appears in the garden of one of the hotels at Vevay, where Winterbourne, a young American, said by his friends to be "studying" at Geneva, and by those who were not his friends to be attending on a foreign lady who resided there, is resting for a season from his labours. An intimacy springs up between Winterbourne and Daisy Miller with a rapidity which scandalizes the aunt of the former, who is a lady of position both in her own country and in Europe. Daisy, it must be said, is not an everyday type of the American girl; but most people who have known a fair number of Americans will be able to recall one or two to whom she bears a strong likeness. Good girl as she is, and with many of the qualities of a lady, there is certainly something underbred in her ready familiarity, and something blunt in the perceptions which do not tell her how her conduct will be looked on by the world. She is, in plain words, common, but still interesting and almost charming. The ease and self-possession with which she violates the social code of Europe, whenever it suits her whim to do so, is thrown into stronger relief by contrast with a characterless and wholly imbecile mother, "a small, spare, light person, with a wandering eye, a very exiguous nose, and a large forehead decorated with a certain amount of thin, much-frizzled hair." The presence of a chaperon like this, whose parental guardianship never goes beyond a feeble, half-apologetic remonstrance, just enough to irritate, but utterly useless to check, naturally makes Daisy all the more wilful and headstrong. When Winterbourne meets her in the following winter at Rome, he finds her provided with anything but an enviable renown. She is on terms of great friendship with several Italian gentlemen, not of the choicest sort, particularly with one Giovanelli, with whom she walks, drives, sings, goes to parties, makes calls, and presents herself in the afternoon on the Pincio before the assembled society of Rome. The mixed and dubious world which is all that most English and American travellers see in Rome, if they see anything of society at all, is sketched briefly, but with admirable truth. Daisy finds it as easy to get male assistance in setting the *convenances* at defiance as a handsome young lady might be expected to do. It is she, unfortunately, who has to pay all the penalty. Throughout her follies, which she advertises to all the world with a curious naïveté and audacity, and to the last without fully understanding what they are taken to mean, she does not lose her hold of the reader's sympathy, interest, and pity. Considering the interest which Mr. Winterbourne feels in her, and the terms of intimacy on which they stand, he might fairly be expected to do a little more to open the girl's eyes. Something he does do—but feebly, and in vain. This is indeed just an instance of Mr. James's practice in those of his tales which we have read— shall it be added, that it is his method?— to leave the reader in doubt as to the real nature and purpose of his characters. What Winterbourne's genuine feeling for Daisy is, or Daisy's for either Winterbourne or Giovanelli, and why they all keep standing on the brink of doing something decisive and never do it, it is impossible to say. The situation is too good a one to be left without a solution, nor is the crisis grave enough to require that Daisy should be put to death and the solution thus evaded. Yet this is what happens. She goes one evening all alone with Giovanelli (whom Winterbourne, by the way, treats all through with exemplary forbearance, not to say politeness) to see the Colosseum by moonlight, and there catches a fever, of which she dies. Winterbourne returns to Geneva—to "study," as his friends say— to resume attendance on the foreign lady, as is averred by others.

The other stories in this book—"An International Episode," and "Four Meetings"—show the same accurate and minute observation, the same power of telling a tale pleasantly and readably, and the same adroitness in keeping the reader's curiosity alive to the last moment. But, like the first story, they balk one at the critical instant. Everything goes on charmingly till the moment arrives for decision and action—the moment when the veil is lifted, and people are forced to show what they are and what they are good for. And just then the characters which have been admirably lifelike hitherto suddenly become shadowy and unreal. Even when the step they take is intelligible, the feelings which prompt them to it remain in the dark. No doubt great difficulties are avoided by this ignoring of all deeper psychological analysis, but great opportunities are also lost by it. Still, notwithstanding this defect, Mr. James's stories have great and unusual merit. They have, above all, the great and unusual merit of being readable a second and third time.

Checklist of Additional Reviews

Philadelphia *North American,* 8 November 1878, p. 4.

Hartford *Daily Courant,* 11 November 1878, p. 2.

New Orleans *Daily Picayune,* 24 November 1878, p. 5.

[Mary Eliot Parkman]. *Nation* 27 (19 December 1878), 386–89. Reprinted, but unattributed, in William T. Stafford, *James's Daisy Miller: The Story, the Play, the Critics* (New York: Charles Scribner's Sons, 1963), p. 106.

Springfield [Mass.] *Republican,* 31 December 1878, p. 2.

Harper's New Monthly Magazine 58 (January 1879), 310. Reprinted in Stafford, p. 105.

International Review 6 (January 1879), 95–96.

Mrs. F. H. Hill. London *Daily News,* 21 March 1879, p. 6. Reprinted in J. Don Vann, *Critics on Henry James* (Coral Gables: University of Miami Press, 1972), pp. 17–18.

British Quarterly Review 69 (April 1879), 267.

Blackwood's Edinburgh Magazine 126 (July 1879), 107. Reprinted in Stafford, p. 109.

CONFIDENCE

Athenaeum [England] 2723 (3 January 1880), 16.

Mr. James is in his more cheerful mood this time. In his conception of the man who first takes an unfavourable view of the girl whom his friend wants, or thinks he wants, to marry, and then, when the friend has married someone else, falls in love with her himself and becomes engaged to her, there are all the elements of a fine domestic tragedy. Happily this is avoided, mainly through the perspicacity of the young lady herself, who has the wit to see that her former admirer and his actual wife care more for each other than casual observers or even they themselves suppose. This is really the entire nucleus of the story, but from this Mr. James develops two volumes of narrative, as imponderable but yet as delightful to the observer as the tail of Donati's comet. Siena, Baden, the Norman coast, are all brought before the reader with that seemingly light but really careful touch of which Mr. James more than any living English writer possesses the secret. Nor are the characters less admirably indicated. Take the hero, Bernard Longueville:—

> "He was almost always spoken of as 'accomplished'; people asked why he did not do something. This question was never satisfactorily answered, the feeling being that Longueville did more than many people in causing it to be asked."

In one point the story will perhaps jar a little upon the feelings of British readers, who are hardly accustomed to the ease with which the marriage tie is loosed in America, and will therefore be a little startled at the notion of a man proposing to put away his wife at a moment's notice on the ground of mere "incompatibility," and letting her go off with another man, while he renews his offer to a woman who has twice refused him, and who is, moreover, the affianced bride of his best friend. However, the possibility of this is only stated to be dismissed with contumely by the lady chiefly concerned; and, as has been said, her good sense brings the whole affair to the right issue. We have no other criticism to make; and, in truth, Mr. James's novels are better fitted to be read and enjoyed than to be criticized.

"Confidence." Saturday Review [England] 49 (3 January 1880), 25–26.

Mr. Henry James's fictions seem to us at this moment to follow each other in course of publication a little too rapidly for the full enjoyment of their attractions. His stories are apt to dwell in the memory, and it seems to us but the other day that we had the pleasant task of writing about his collection of tales called the *Madonna of the Future;*[1] and with the taste of that, so to speak, yet in our mouths, we have *Confidence* put before us. To carry further a gastronomic metaphor, we might not appreciate the flavour of caviare if it were a thing of constant recurrence so well as by consuming it only now and then. Although it certainly cannot be said of Mr. James's works that they are caviare to the general, in the sense that they are not popular, if "the general" stands for the reading public who get their supplies from the circulating libraries, yet it may be doubted if more than half the people who read his books appreciate, or try to appreciate, their finer qualities. A long course of Mérimée or of Tourgenieff might be trying to a conscientious reader, and, as has before been pointed out in these columns, Mr. James has more affinity with these two writers than with any English-writing novelist of whom we can think.[2] In other words, Mr. James's fiction has the quality of rarity both in thought and expression, and in his branch of art frequent production is a disadvantage, not perhaps to him or to his public, but to his reviewer. We remember once to have heard a young man infected with the aesthetic cant of the day profess that he objected strongly to the exhibition of fine works in picture galleries because it "vulgarized" them. This of course was rank nonsense; but it may not be altogether paradoxical to say that such delicate work in writing as Mr. James's suffers from being put too continuously before his readers. One cannot take in a good novel so readily as a good picture, and, like the writers to whom he has been compared, Mr. James has a way of always leaving something not unimportant to the imagination of his readers. He works out his problem to a certain point and then leaves them to deal with it as they will, and in *Confidence* he has sprung a new puzzle upon us almost before we had forgotten to be "intrigued" over those which he last set before us. It must be said that in his present book the puzzle takes a comparatively mild form. One marriage which we have been looking forward to has taken place; another, apparently made with some rashness, has, we may presume, been turned from discontent to happiness; and we are only left to wonder what is the exact nature and tenor of the unusually long letter which the older writes to the younger bridegroom who has been for years his closest friend, and whom he has lately regarded, not altogether unjustly,

with feelings which could not be completely friendly. It may well be that only a minority of Mr. James's public will trouble their heads over this matter; but we are inclined to think that in this minority will be found his most faithful and appreciative readers, to whose feelings he might with advantage make some concession. However, in certain things, and perhaps in such things as this, the artist must be allowed to be his own best critic; and that Mr. James is an artist will not be denied.

It is one of the author's characteristics to open his books by presenting one of his chief characters in circumstances and scenery which serve to give a general idea of his nature. "The American," if we remember rightly, was discovered in the galleries of the Louvre, oppressed by an "aesthetic headache." The hero of the present work is also an American, but of a very different type. "The American" was an admirably studied specimen of a self-made man, possessed of an innate strength and dignity, set off by innumerable great and little traits of character, which were difficult to analyse, but which all combined to produce a harmonious and pleasing result. The American, Bernard Longueville, who takes the principal part in *Confidence* belongs to the naturally well-off and educated class of his countrymen. Dignity, if not strength, has come to him with his bringing-up; and his is a more complex, if a less striking, character than that of the hero of the novel by which, as far as English readers were concerned, Mr. James first made his mark. Longueville, when we meet him in the first page of the book, has been spending the winter in Rome:—

He had travelled northward with the consciousness of several social duties that appealed to him from the further side of the Alps, but he was under the charm of the Italian spring, and he made a pretext for lingering. . . . He re-

82

marked to himself that this was always his luck, and the remark was characteristic of the man; it was charged with the feeling of the moment, but it was not absolutely just; it was the result of an acute impression made by the particular occasion; but it failed in appreciation of a providence which had sprinkled Longueville's career with happy accidents—accidents, especially, in which his characteristic gallantry was not allowed to rust for want of exercise. [*Novels 1871–1880*, p. 1041]

We learn, further, of this personage—who becomes more interesting in proportion to the unexpected influences brought to bear upon him—that "he was clever indeed, and an excellent companion; but the real measure of his brilliancy was in the success with which he entertained himself. He was much addicted to conversing with his own wit, and he greatly enjoyed his own society. Clever as he often was in talking with his friends, I am not sure that his best things, as the phrase is, were not for his own ears. And this was not on account of any cynical contempt for the understanding of his fellow-creatures; it was simply because what I have called his own society was more of a stimulus than that of most other people." In spite of this he was "a very sociable animal"; and after this it will be readily "admitted at the outset that he had a nature which seemed at several points to contradict itself." The description reads like a study from life, and the impression that this is so is deepened as the story, or rather the finely-touched narration of events which hang together, goes on. It must not be inferred from this that there is anything bald, or, to use a paradoxical phrase, too life-like, in the following out of Longueville's character. Mr. James is a singularly keen observer, but he has plenty of the artistic instinct and skill which prevent a novelist from producing an impression of tiresome adherence to the naked result of observation. There is probably more than one Longueville in the world, and yet Mr. James's Longueville never fails to be interesting.

More remarkable, perhaps, is Mr. James's skill in the treatment of Gordon Wright, who is more or less to Longueville what "Charles, his friend," is to the hero of a certain kind of comedy, and who also affords an admirable foil to Longueville's more finely-strung nature, to which, with an odd contradiction which the author's fine faculty of observation has happily seized, the more robust one of Wright is ever prone to turn for counsel. These characters are both American. Mr. James is less happy in his representation of Captain Lovelock, who, in spite of a fortunate touch here and there, is little more than the typical army Englishman of a hundred English novelists. That he should be represented as heavily bearded may perhaps be regarded as a sin of mere detail—or perhaps the author may advance the theory that the length of his beard was in proportion to that of his leave. But in one scene we find what we cannot but regard as a blunder, which is a thing very uncommon in Mr. James's work. Longueville and Lovelock are on those terms of close acquaintance which spring from constantly meeting in the company of the same people at the same place; the place in this instance being Baden-Baden in the gambling days. Lovelock is supposed to be, if not very wise, well born and well bred. The two meet after the party of ladies in whom both are interested have suddenly and without warning moved their camp. " 'Damn it, they're going—yes, they're going,' said the Captain, after the two young men had exchanged a few allusions to current events." The Captain says "damn" so often that one could almost think the author had been studying old-world French caricatures just before he wrote his book, and that stray recollections of them had stuck to him. After this he falls into a confidential mood, in which he recounts among other things his bad luck "at those filthy tables." He has lost heavily, and Longueville has just won a quantity of money at the same tables the winning of which has given him no pleasure; Lovelock accepts from him a loan which both know will not be repaid, and which both know will be employed at "those filthy tables." What is more odd is what will be found in the following quotation:—

> I'll take fifty pounds with pleasure, thank you, and you shall have them again—at the earliest opportunity. My earliest convenience—will that do? Damn it, it *is* a convenience, isn't it? You make your conditions? My dear fellow, I accept them in advance. That I'm not to follow up Miss Evers; is that what you mean? Have you been commissioned by the family to buy me off? It's devilish cruel to take advantage of my poverty! Though I'm poor, I'm honest. But I *am* honest, my dear Longueville; that's the point. I'll give you my word, and I'll keep it. I won't go near that girl again—I won't think of her till I've got rid of your fifty pounds. It's a dreadful encouragement to extravagance, but that's your look-out. I'll stop for their beastly races, and the young lady shall be sacred.

This from a writer of Mr. James's power is little short of astounding when the conditions of Lovelock's existence are remembered. But the drawing of this character is throughout, it seems to us, unworthy of Mr. James's talent and reputation.

With one of the women of the story, Miss Evers, the author is as successful as he has ever been; the character is well conceived and admirably executed in every detail. But with the heroine, Miss Vivian, he seems less successful. He tells us at once too much and too little of her. He has aimed, it would appear, at painting such a strange character as Musset loved to illuminate with the brilliant flashes of his undated comedies.[3] To try this in a novel of modern life is a bold experiment. Mr. James seems to us to have lost himself to some extent in the intricacies devised by himself. Brilliant flashes are thrown from time to time upon Miss Vivian's nature; but they scarcely suffice to give any definite and abiding impression. The key to the character is no doubt possessed by the author; but he does not hand it on to the reader. Mrs. Vivian's character, on the other hand, strikes us as being an ordinary one, which its depicter has vainly attempted to invest with mystery. These are the faults which we find with a novel which can, in spite of them, be recommended to all who care for Mr. James's fine style and method. We do not propose to give any clue to its story, for, as is usual with Mr. James, that part of his work hangs entirely upon his treatment of character, and to tell it merely as a succession of facts would be obviously unjust. If we might venture to give a word of counsel to the author, it would be to avoid all temptation to deliberate obscurity.

Notes

1 *Madonna of the Future and Other Tales* (London: Macmillan, 1879).

2 Prior to 1880, James had reviewed Prosper Mérimée three times. See "Dernières Nouvelles," *Nation* 18 (12 February 1874), p. 111; "The Letters of Propser Mérimée," review of *Lettres à une Inconnue, Independent* (9 April 1874), pp. 9–10; and "Lettres à une autre Inconnue," *Nation* 22 (27 January 1876), pp. 67–68. James had reviewed Turgenev twice and translated a Turgenev poem. See "*Frühlingsfluthen. Ein König Lear des Dorfes. Zwei Novellen. Von Iwan Turgéniew*," *North American Review* 118 (April 1874), pp. 326–56; *Nation* 23 (5 Oc-

tober 1876), p. 213; *"Terres Vierges," Nation* 24 (26 April 1877), pp. 252–53.
3 Alfred de Musset (1810–1857).

"*Confidence.*"
Pall Mall Gazette [England], 23 January 1880, p. 12.

If Mr. James were anxious to appear to take a systematic view of life in his novels, the nine volumes of fiction he has produced within the year might have been published as parts of a comprehensive whole to be called "Amours de Voyage," after the title of Clough's poem.[1] Love must obviously be a very different affair to an American travelling for pleasure and to an Englishman tied and bound in the chains of domesticity. Mr. James's ideal tourist is, above all, unattached and irresponsible; he has cut the knot of duty and left behind the cares of life. His mind, too, is in a condition peculiarly susceptible to fresh impressions, and a *table d'hôte* supplies in its most attractive form that element of juxtaposition which Clough declared and the Widow Wadman proved to be more than half the battle of love. At home society is so arranged that people as a rule know all about one another before they meet. But at a popular place of holiday resort every prepossessing toilet is an enigma soliciting solution; while men, athirst for new experiences of whatever kind, can pursue their experiments with an audacity which could not exist under the critical glances of friends and relations. Moreover—and this is the supreme advantage of a roving flirtation—the man who feels that circumstances are growing too strong for him can seek safety in flight.

After indulging in sentimental promenades at midnight, when wisdom comes with morning he has only to take the early train and seek distraction from a trouble never very serious. It is notorious how Clive Newcome's passion for his cousin Ethel was much harder to bear in London than it was at Baden, whence he escaped to Rome, where he took his pastime in the company of the Misses Freeman and the third Miss Balliol. But England is a land of short holidays. Only painters and Americans have leisure to appreciate all the varied delights of travel.

It is not, however, to be supposed that Mr. James's heroes defy the proverb, and by a run across the Atlantic change not only climate but also their inner selves. Rather they are so constituted that life at home is unbearable to them. Their minds are devoid of the ballast of the weightier emotions and are absorbed by the single quality of intellectual curiosity. All they desire is to know the most charming objects the world has produced, and those they pursue at their leisure through every country of Europe. Mr. James's range is necessarily cramped by the exclusion of the business and family side of life from his novels. His books, however full of acute observation and just discrimination they may be, resemble the exploded pastorals of last century inasmuch as they attempt to represent the graces and adornments of life, without allowing them to be disfigured by any trace of the toil and suffering of ordinary existence. They are worldly idylls, as lifelike and as unreal as porcelain figures. Thus Mr. James's cosmopolitanism has the same defect of narrowness as the provinciality of American society, against which he railed so bitterly in his recent volume upon Hawthorne, but with a difference.[2] The provincial is often narrow only because he is not yet developed; if the proper stimulant be applied, he will expand in a number of unexpected ways. Excess of sensibility, on the other hand, frequently ends in a collapse of the sympathetic powers. The cosmopolitan, with his single intelligent view of life, is really at the last gasp. Bent on refined enjoyment, he is in danger of being left with nothing to fall back upon but a sense of gratitude that at any rate his refinement survives. However, Mr. James's practice sufficiently refutes his theory of the unsuitability of American life to the purposes of a novelist. The pictures he has himself given of America in various books, and especially in the opening of "Roderick Hudson" are in themselves far more interesting than his most brilliant Continental sketches. Yet while he continues to write descriptions as good as those in this volume, it is perhaps unreasonable to wish him to change his field. The reader is taken to Siena, Baden, and the coast of Normandy in turn. Dissimilar as these places are, Mr. James reproduces very skilfully not only the physical features, but the local flavour and atmosphere of each. He never proceeds, sandwich fashion, by alternating slices of narrative with layers of description, but manages to infuse a sense of external circumstance into his account of the sayings and doings of his personages.

It may readily be guessed that by "confidence" is meant a violation of trust. However, the situation in which the hero is placed by the too implicit confidence of a friend is so delicate that his conduct may perhaps pass muster under the code of ethics applicable to the ideal tourist we have attempted to describe. At Siena Angela Vivian falls in love with Bernard de Longueville. At Baden Gordon Wright falls in love with Angela, but, before he proposes, sends for Bernard, his confidential friend, to pronounce upon the young lady, and goes off to London, leaving Bernard to study Angela's character. She discovers Bernard's design, and very naturally behaves rather inconsistently to him. He is puzzled and piqued, and warns Gordon to have nothing to do with her, whereon Gordon goes off and marries a most unsuitable person in disgust, with whom he is not at all happy. Three years afterwards, on the coast of Normandy, Bernard meets Angela, and discovers that he is in love with a delight as naïve as Arthur Pendennis's, when he woke on the morning after the eventful night on which he saw the Fotheringay.[3] Bernard proposes and is accepted. Gordon, on hearing the news, is furious, and makes a scene; but thanks to Angela's tact the story is made to end happily and hurriedly, somewhat after the fashion of the winding up of modern comedies. Mr. James has worked out this plot with his usual ability, which is saying not a little. He writes semi-dramatically from the point of view of his hero, the reader knowing no more about the other characters than Bernard does. For instance, it is not till he is engaged that we are given the clue to Angela's conduct by being allowed to find out that she fell in love with Bernard at first sight; and similarly when all the personages are more or less at cross-purposes, the reader is not in a position to hold the balance evenly among their various claims on his sympathy. Mr. James succeeds in making this perplexity very attractive, as all readers of his book will discover for themselves.

Notes

1 Arthur Hugh Clough, "Amours de Voyage," first appeared in the *Atlantic Monthly* (1858).

2 *Hawthorne* (London: Macmillan, 1879).

3 William Makepeace Thackeray, *The History of Pendennis* (1848–50).

"*Confidence*."
New York *Herald,* 23
February 1880, p. 8.

In Henry James, Jr.'s new novel, "Confidence" (Houghton, Osgood & Co.), we find a great deal of the same material used in his former stories. The episodes are all international and the characters, if not brothers and sisters, are at least cousins. Blanche Evers is only Daisy Miller done over, and Angela Vivian is not unlike the heroine of "Roderick Hudson." The men are always the same. There is a dull Englishman, an amiable American, and an American who dissects the people he meets in a fine Bostonian way; but we do not find fault with a sameness that is so pleasing. As for plot, there is very little in "Confidence." One can see from the very first that Bernard Longueville is to marry Angela Vivian. And there really is no love in a flesh and blood sort of way. The courtships of Mr. James' heroes are not like Romeo's. They make studies of character, and if they are pleased with the result marriage follows. If they think a young lady worthy of their interest they impale her as a naturalist might a butterfly and make a careful and scientific investigation of her nature. The poor body cannot quiver under this treatment without that expression of emotion being subject to analysis. "Confidence" is as clever a bit of workmanship as Mr. James has given us for some time, and those persons who have cried out at what they call his unpatriotic treatment of his country or his countrymen will be satisfied with the way both are treated in this story. Mr. James has a very happy faculty of drawing mothers; he has given us many types in his various stories and each one calls up a vivid picture.

Mrs. Vivian is one of his most striking mothers; a quiet little creature, but a power in her way. With Gordon Wright we have little sympathy. A man who depends upon another man's analysis of the woman he loves rather than his own feelings deserves to lose her. If Gordon loved his silly little wife he had a very poor way of showing it, and it only proves how clever Angela Vivian was that she made the discovery. While it is not hard to pick a flaw here and there in Mr. James' story, it is much easier to praise it. A book like "Confidence" contrasted with the novels of the day stands alone.

New York *Tribune,* 5
March 1880, p. 6.

In this novel Mr. James has succeeded in framing an interesting dramatic narrative from a remarkable paucity of materials. The plot is diversified with little incident; the actors in the scene are few in number, and are made to stand for exhibition in a variety of situations; while the movement of the story is carried on by brief, brisk flashes of dialogue which throw a vivid light on the workings of passion and character. The prominent figures are two young friends, who with the best intentions toward each other, have both fallen in love with a countrywoman of their own, a handsome American maiden, who like themselves is roaming through the capitals of Europe, seeking enjoyment and satisfaction and finding none. In the development of the slight plot, they all become entangled in a network of cross-purposes, reciprocal misunderstandings and recriminations, hard words and harder thoughts, evil surmises and bitter jealousies, from which it tasks the curious ingenuity of the author to extricate them without placing the young girl in a false position, or bringing a cloud over the romantic and ardent friendship of her lovers.

Bernard Longueville, the favored hero of the story, is an amateur artist, who, while travelling in Italy, is idling away a few days in the old city of Siena in order to gratify his fancy for sketching. He was a young fellow of moderate fortune, given to strange whims and conceits, fond of musing and airy speculations, not without a taste for serious studies, but without the smallest tincture of pedantry or literary affection. He had gained many friends, and was an excellent companion, but preferred his own society to any other, and was greatly addicted to conversing with his own fancies. One morning he was out sketching on a favorite spot in the suburbs of the city, when he saw a young woman whom he had previously noticed at an inn opposite his own, duly accompanied by her mother. She turned her eyes upon the graceful artist who for some reason or other suspected that she had been looking at him for some moments before he perceived her. She turned away almost as soon as she met his eyes, leaving the impression that she was a handsome creature, but rather bold, and most decidedly an American. She stood before him long enough to let him see that she was a person of easy attitudes, and then walked away slowly presenting her back to Longueville, and gazing upon rural Italy, as she rested her arms upon a high stone ledge in the vicinity. The young artist went on with his sketch perhaps less attentively than before, and soon became aware that she had placed herself in the very centre of his foreground. His first feeling was that she would spoil the picture; his second that she would improve it. She stood motionless, almost as if she were there for the purpose of being drawn. Her delicate and thin profile defined itself against the sky in the clear shadow of a coquettish hat; her figure was light and waving; she wore a gray dress, fastened up as was then the fashion, displaying the broad edge of a crimson petticoat. There was no doubt that she would improve the picture. Longueville could not quite make up his mind whether she was posing for his benefit; but at all events, he resolved to put her into his sketch. "It will give it a human interest," he said to himself, "and there is nothing like having a human interest." Thus thinking, he introduced the figure of the girl into his foreground, and at the end of ten minutes had almost made something that had the form of a likeness. She now turned away, looking Longueville in the face, as she passed near him, with an expression which a few minutes before he had mentally characterized as bold. Her hair was dark and dense. She was a strikingly handsome girl. The acquaintance thus whimsically commenced is continued in a remarkable dialogue, of which there are not a few similar specimens, presenting a foretaste and illustration of the quality of the book:—

> "I am so sorry you moved," he said, confidently, in English. "You were so— so beautiful." ... "You pose admirably," said Longueville. [*Novels 1871–1880*, pp. 1045–47]

Meantime affairs advanced at a moderate pace, and at length Bernard, while on a visit in Venice, receives an extraordinary letter from his bosom friend, Gordon Wright, who was then lingering among the shades of the Black Forest in the lovely retreat of Baden-Baden. Gordon Wright confesses that he had been making love all Summer long, and finds that it takes such an immense amount of time that everything gets terribly behindhand. He bids his friend to come at once to Baden, and give his opinion of the lady of his heart, whom he describes as an extremely interesting girl and uncommonly handsome. Bernard obeys the summons and starts at once for Germany. On the journey from Venice to Munich he amuses himself with a mental sketch of the character of his friend. Gordon Wright, he finds, had not a particle of imagination. He compares his want of it to a bottomless pit, out of which once in one could never come up alive. Every phrase of Gordon's letter seemed to march in thicksoled boots. It was wonderful that he should invite him to come and make a chemical analysis of the idol of his love. Gordon, he thought, has no idea of the difficulty in forming or expressing an opinion, or in accepting it when expressed. "His mind," he went on to himself, "has no atmosphere, his intellectual process goes on in the void. There are no currents and eddies to affect it, no high winds or hot suns, no changes of season and temperature. His premises are neatly arranged, and his conclusions are perfectly calculable." Still Longueville had a strong affection for the man on whose character he so freely exercised his critical shrewdness. They had been great cronies in their college days. The strongest link in their friendship was a sort of mutual respect. Their pursuits and tastes were different, but each of them had a high opinion of the other's character. It may be said that they were easily pleased, for neither of them certainly had ever performed any very conspicuous action. They were both highly civilized young Americans, born to an easy fortune and tranquil destiny, and with no desire to embrace a career. Wright was deeply interested in physical science. He was fond of experiment, and spent much time in that line of research. Bernard had a relish for fine quality, and greatly appreciated the simple, manly, affectionate nature of his friend. Gordon Wright had a tender heart, a strong will, a rare combination which is often the motive of admirable actions. The general impression which he produced was that of intelligent good-nature. Longueville was certainly equipped with a greater variety of gifts. He was tall, dark, agile, perfectly finished, good-looking to a fault, so good-looking that he might be forgiven even if he had been a fool. But he was very far from being a fool. He had many talents, of which he had made something by study and discipline. He was almost always spoken of as accomplished, but people wondered why he had accomplished so little. He had no career, but at all events he enjoyed himself, and without dispute was a very charming fellow, urbane, free-handed, with ready wit, and with that fortunate quality in appearance known as distinction. With this rehearsal of the prominent characters in the drama, the sequel can easily be imagined, but not the subtle artifice and fine invention with which Mr. James has conducted his unpretending plot to a natural and credible dénouement. The study of this in his own pages will prove an exercise of aesthetic discipline, as well as a provocation to curiosity, and a piquant source of mental enjoyment.

The interest of the story is by no means confined to the figures which occupy the foreground of the canvas, but many of the side scenes are of a singularly attractive character, and drawn with the consummate skill of a master in his kind. Mr. James possesses an equal gift for the illustration of social qualities and the description of natural beauty. His pictures of European scenery are as exquisite as they are faithful, derived from artistic observation and a suggestive fancy. Nor does anything peculiar and significant in the many-colored phases of human life escape his piercing notice. Little Blanche Evers, the conjugal humming-bird that hovers around the domestic tree of Gordon Wright, Captain Lovelock, the bumptious, good-natured, reckless English swashbuckler, and good Mistress Vivian, the matronly mamma of the heroine, are all admirable, amusing sketches. The last-named personage is brought out as a type of character peculiar to Boston, but softened and secularized by a residence in the more sunny atmosphere of New York. She was a little elderly lady with an expression of amorous vigilance, and a band of hair as softly white as a dove's wing. She was of old New-England stock, shy and scrupulous of habit, of the original Boston temperament, but the Boston temperament sophisticated, perverted a little, not to say corrupted, the local east wind, in fact, with an infusion from climates less tonic. Mrs. Vivian might indeed be called a Puritan grown worldly, a Bostonian relaxed. The prominent feature in her character that concerns the reader of this history is her preference of Gordon Wright, with an income of thirty thousand dollars, as the husband of her daughter, to Bernard Longueville, whose revenue amounted to a considerably smaller sum.

The lovers of sensational fiction and prismatic narratives, glittering with all the colors of the soap-bubble and abounding in high-wrought scenes of human misery and human rapture, will find little to admire in this creation of a genius more remarkable for acute observation, deep insight, and refined analysis than for gorgeous word-painting and strange and grotesque inventions. It has few incidents, and those are mostly drawn from the dusty routine of common life. Mr. James is not epic, nor tragic, in his artistic tendencies, but psychical, if so hard a word may be allowed. He delights in the study and the representation of personal traits, which, though not eccentric, are original, and illustrate natural but suggestive qualities of human character. He experiments with the passions, as the old alchemists did with the metals, not so much with the view of transmuting dross into gold, as of

exhibiting accustomed forms in novel and striking combinations. Mr. James's style has been so justly commended as a model of terse, and vigorous, and elegant expression as to call for no sign of admiration in this place; but we must demur at his extravagant use of certain favorite terms, the adjective *clever,* for instance, often occurring two or three times in a single page, and as superfluous as the white daisies in a field of grass. To make the matter worse, the word is used in the English sense of *clever,* which has not yet become so familiar to American ears, as to be without a certain savor of affection. "It's only *me,*" "I feel *like* doing so and so" are not legal-tenders, and "I *ain't*" was surely never uttered by an educated Englishman, like the incomparable Captain Lovelock.

[W. C. Brownell]. *Nation* 30 (25 March 1880), 239–40.

Like his last book, Mr. James's 'Confidence' is a study rather than a story, and what demerits it has arise from the necessity—urgent, we suppose—of presenting it as a story instead of as a study. The probability of his situation being taken for granted, almost everything else follows naturally, and is captivating reading. But if the reader has no difficulty in esteeming perfectly natural the conduct of a fastidiously honorable man in instituting a kind of spiritual clinic in the case of a young woman, at the instance and for the benefit of a sensitively honorable man who is in love with her, and in concealing from this "curious impertinent"—by the way, the scheme is not unlike that of the 'Don Quixote' story modernized—the fact that he has already met the subject of his diagnosis; no difficulty in reconciling the said young woman's conscious share in the transaction with her character as it is portrayed; and none in accepting the sundry apparent incongruities that arise out of all this, he will, we suspect, be more fortunate than Mr. James himself has been. There is on various accounts so little inherent likelihood in even a modified and modernized story of Lothario, peopled with everyday characters whose respect for conventions amounts to a code of morals, such as all Mr. James's best people have been of recent years, that a good deal of the author's cleverness, which we could wish to see otherwise employed, is expended in bolstering his scheme, and with, at the best, but doubtful success. In the case of a purely romantic writer this would make little difference. A purely romantic writer has a dispensation from being anything but entertaining. But verisimilitude is the *sine qua non* of realism, and however imaginative his method may be, Mr. James has been wholly given over to realism ever since he wrote his 'Roderick Hudson.' Apart from its structure, 'Confidence' is remarkably good, however. The characters are very much alive, very individual, and, if we except the somewhat stolid and ridiculous Wright, very interesting. The best of the lot, to our mind, is the chattering and absurd Blanche, whom it is a very nice touch to bring out so well at the end. The details, it need not be said, are very well done. Indeed, with Mr. James the details are apt to count fully as largely as the main thing. Blanche's monologues are exquisite, and from them and certain subtle chess-playing with intricate motives, so to speak, one gets not only the entertainment which a good thing of the kind always affords, but an intimate pleasure in recognizing their life-likeness and relations to the talk and actions of "people we have met." One's only regret is that 'Confidence' should be more closely related to the 'Daisy Miller' series than to 'The American,' or even 'The Europeans.'

British Quarterly Review 71 (April 1880), 269.

Mr. Henry James could not write without showing insight into characters of a certain type, or without some gleam of a humour peculiar to him. But in all sincerity we cannot help thinking that he is writing too much and allowing himself to fall into the habit of facile expansion instead of concentrating his matter. 'Confidence' is very clever—after a certain conventional society ideal—but it will not do anything to raise his reputation. All Mr. Henry James's peculiar sentiments about certain social arrangements are here implicitly, for, in spite of his air of disinterestedness, he is a preacher; and though cosmopolitan in tone and air, to the extent of carrying us through one-half the fashionable resorts of the Continent, he never once succeeds in really making us realize the places. The American of culture is with us again. We confess to being interested at the outset in Mr. Bernard Longueville, with his mixture of *amour propre,* languor, and superficial good-natured affection for Gordon, which is about as far as he could go; in this same Gordon Wright; in Mrs. Vivian; and in the young ladies; but the constant strain on them is to us like the wearing of a violin string, and we do get wearied. At length, when the conclusion comes, it is a pure *fiasco.* We have been led all this way and been beguiled to listen to lisping society talk of a polished but astonishingly thin kind all along these shifting-scene ways, and all for nothing. Mr. Henry James has approved himself capable of better work than this, and it is a pity that he should try the good nature and indulgence of his readers with such experiments. Or is 'Confidence' not an earlier effort, refurbished up to sell now that the market for the marked wares is open?

Susan Coolidge.
"Mr. James's *Confidence*." *Literary World* [Boston] 11 (10 April 1880), 119–20.

Mr. Henry James's new story opens in the lovely and quaint town of Sienna. There is a sketch, given with his unerringly happy touch, of a certain little grass-grown terrace which lies before an old church; a terrace with "an old, polished parapet about as high as a man's head, above which was a view of sad-colored hills;" and on this terrace, Mr. Bernard Longueville, a young American, sits one day, taking, or trying to take, a sketch, when a young lady, also American, emerges from the church and occupies the foreground of the picture. This young lady is handsome; her name is Angela Vivien. Bernard puts her into his drawing. Presently her mother, "a delicate little gentlewoman, with a light step," joins her, and there is a brief talk. Here we have three of the characters in the coming drama, lightly and skillfully introduced upon the scene. There is a good deal of art in doing this with so little visible effort. It is one of Mr. James's happy knacks that he succeeds so well in this. Mrs. and Miss Vivien and Mr. Longueville dawn on us in

this opening chapter as real people do in real life, accidentally as it were, without premeditation and without awkwardness. We are aware of, but not surprised by, their advent, and the gray silences, shot with color of the rich old Umbrian city, make effective background for them.

Presently the scene changes to Baden; Baden in the joyous days before reform, when the click of the roulette, and the call of the croupier, and the excited rustle and stir of those who waited to learn their fate, were matters of every day. Here we come again upon our Siennese trio, and upon other characters as well. There is Gordon Wright, a rich American, with a taste for science, who takes chemistry under his protection as it were, and is the intimate friend of Bernard Longueville; there is Blanche Evers, one of those limpidly foolish, beautifully dressed American girls whom Mr. James delights to hit off, though not always successfully; there is also a certain English Capt. Lovelock. The game of cross-purposes goes on. Gordon Wright fancies himself in love with Angela; but his passion—if passion it is—takes the form of uneasy analysis; a reflection, possibly, from his chemical bent. He is distrustful of himself, still more so of her; he worries himself (and Bernard) almost to death in the attempt to gauge and comprehend his own sensations; he theorizes, and deduces, and hesitates, and winds up with twice offering himself to Miss Vivien, and twice being rejected. The relation between Bernard and Angela is still more complicated. It is flirtation expressed in innuendo. There is much of that amatory fencing in which Mr. James excels, but the hands of both combatants seem perfectly steady, and the by-stander can detect no blood on the foils. In the end the party breaks up suddenly, and separates to the four quarters of the globe, after the wont of Americans who meet in

Europe. Bernard goes to the East, and, returning to New York at the end of two years, finds his friend married to the pretty, chattering Blanche Evers. Under the promptings of a restlessness which he can neither repress nor define, he returns to Europe, and, stumbling casually on the Viviens at the little Norman watering-place of *Blanquet les Galets*, becomes suddenly aware that he is, and for two years has been, desperately in love with Angela! We confess to having paused at this point of the story with bated breath. Mr. James's heroes are but too apt to terminate their sentimental adventures by doing something exceedingly queer. A flight to the antipodes is the manner by which they frequently testify the integrity of their passion, and it was with sinking heart that we became aware that Mr. Bernard Longueville was packing his portmanteau. But, no! It was but to test himself by a month's absence that he went; and with unspeakable relief we find him, a little later, pulling the bell of Mrs. Vivien's apartment in Paris. Once there, we are bound to confess that he comports himself as foolishly, is as much in love, as unreasonable and impetuous, as any other writer's hero! All is speedily settled, and the marriage day draws near, when Mr. and Mrs. Gordon Wright, accompanied by the inevitable Capt. Lovelock, arrive in Paris.

And now opens what Mr. James would perhaps claim to be the most subtle and interesting part of the story, but what, to our mind, is its irredeemable failure. It is not to be conceived that a loyal, simple-hearted gentleman like Gordon Wright could be capable of a sudden hallucination under which he resents as an unpardonable wrong the fact that his friend should have won a woman who had rejected his own suit two years before, during which years Gordon Wright himself had married another woman. More impossible still, that in cold blood he should ask Angela to "Wait—give me another chance;" and when she says, "You speak as if you were going to put an end to your wife," reply:

> She is rapidly putting an end to herself. . . . As soon as they have left Paris I will let you know; and then you will of course admit that, virtually, I am free! [*Novels 1871–1880,* p. 1235]

More extraordinary still, that, supposing the possibility of this conversation, the other actors in it, instead of clapping Mr. Gordon Wright into a *maison de santé* on the spot, listen quietly, and, for the sake of pacifying him, feign to acquiesce in his arrangements. Angela, with a perspicacity which can only be termed superhuman, discovers that the true difficulty is that Gordon is madly in love with his wife—the wife whom he so coolly proposes to dismiss to dishonor! Under her advice, Bernard retires to London, leaving her to bring Gordon Wright to his senses and reconcile him to Blanche. A crazier and more unclean situation it would be difficult to find in romance. That Mr. James should make it end happily, with wedding gifts and hand-shaking all round, only shows that he knows how to avail himself of the novelist's power over the beings of his own creation, to make them *faire l'impossible*. In real life, such an imbroglio would have terminated in murder or the mad-house; and it is real cause for regret, that an author whose pen is capable of such refined and delicate work should have indulged in a plot so objectionable and preposterous, for the pleasure of showing with what cleverness he can disentangle his own ingeniously tangled snarl of circumstance.

Christian Union 21 (28 April 1880), 398.

M. Gautier's attitude toward his characters [in *Captain Fracasse*] is that of a disinterested spectator, so that one comes to feel toward them rather a speculative interest than a warm sympathy.—It is this feeling in a still greater degree that the reader entertains toward the personages in Mr. Henry James's *Confidence*. (Houghton, Osgood & Co.) They are not unfamiliar persons. We have met them under various other names in Mr. James's other books, where they have gone through nearly the same motions and said substantially the same things. From old acquaintance and from the insight we are permitted from time to time to have into their mental processes we ought to have come to a pretty clear understanding of their several characters, and yet when we attempt to define any one of them to ourselves the picture disappears. Mr. James has analyzed it to the vanishing point. It is true we are let into their minds, but we are never quite sure whether there is not some mental reservation which we are not allowed to see. We can never get over a lingering distrust of their actions and their motives, and even when the author gives us his own word for it that these are frank and open we hesitate to accept the testimony. Ordinarily, however, Mr. James declines to express any opinion of the sort, and the reader is left to his own unaided sense, embarrassed by a lot of contradictory analysis, to form a judgment. In "Confidence" the author is, perhaps, less inflexibly neutral toward his characters than usual, but it cannot be said that one gets a much clearer idea of their personality, or that his keen unemotional men, and his cool calculating women, who form one set of his automata, or his insipid volatile women and dull, stolid men who make up the other set, are in any sense representatives of average American society; or that the fragmentary and mysterious dialogues in which they indulge throw much light upon American conversational talent.

Eclectic Magazine new series 31 (May 1880), 634–35.

The style and manner of Mr. James are so delightful that the reader is apt to be beguiled into indifference as to his subject and method of treatment; and except for this it must be confessed that "Confidence" would be a far from encouraging work to those who have erected large expectations upon the basis of the author's previous stories. It shows an increasing command over his materials, and an exquisite gracefulness and delicacy of art which in itself almost implies genius; but, on the other hand, to our sense, it reveals no growth of imaginative vigor, and no widening of that "vision and faculty divine" which is quite as indispensable to the creative novelist as to the poet. Influenced, perhaps, by the remarkable success and popularity of the "Daisy Miller" sketches, Mr. James has allowed himself to be led into the attempt to give an elaborate and exhaustive study of the genus with one of whose species the "Daisy Miller" sketches were concerned—the American sojourner abroad; and though the result is amusing, its lack of definite interest, and the slight hold which it gets upon the reader's sympathies seem to show that, however well adapted they may be for light touch-and-go portraiture, both the people and the situations are too flimsy and artificial to justify the serious delineation of them by a really great and skilful artist.

Like everything else that Mr. James has written of late, "Confidence" makes very charming reading—the supreme excellence of its art would suffice to render it charming to such as can appreciate its rare quality; but those who have looked to see Mr. James manifest a higher order of power than that of merely pleasing will not only be disappointed with the story itself, but will regret the tendency which it seems to reveal on the part of the author to avoid the broad currents of human life while exploring more curiously than they deserve the little side eddies.

"James's *Confidence*."
Scribner's Monthly 20
(June 1880), 311.

It must always remain a matter of wonder to those who admire Mr. James most sincerely, that, being so great as he is, he is no greater; that with all the artistic perfection of his style, the keenness of his observation and the strength and brilliancy of his thought, he has yet so little real depth of insight. Would any one, for instance, venture to assert that Mr. James's writings display an adequate conception of what love is? In "Confidence," the cardinal passion manifests itself chiefly as a vague unrest which has the power of propelling its victim an indefinite number of times and in either direction across the Atlantic Ocean. It causes young ladies to behave in an enigmatical fashion (which of course is perfectly proper), and up to the moment of the happy consummation makes everybody mildly and discreetly miserable. However, this is undeniably the form in

which love most frequently asserts itself in the over-civilized "international" society with which Mr. James's books are concerned; it is a gentle and easily manageable emotion, not a passion with a spark of Plutonian fire in it.

Within these limitations, "Confidence" is an entertaining and skillfully constructed novel. Close up to the line of real emotion, we see the whole inner life and character of Mr. James's men and women. We see, too, the influence that their emotion exerts on their conduct, but not the real emotion itself. For all that, the reader who can supply the missing links and re-write the love passages for himself, can only admire the whole outgrowth of the conditions. Judged by itself, each character is a skillful study, and is accepted into the circle of our literary acquaintance to a degree not usual even with those which have stirred us more. The absurdly conscientious Gordon Wright, with his interminable letter-writing; the chattering little coquette Blanche Evers and her redoubtable English adorer Captain Lovelock, are all so originally and so piquantly portrayed as almost to impress us as new creations. And yet Captain Lovelock is quite a common type in the English novel of the day, and Blanche Evers, in her deliciously inane chatter, reminds us constantly of Daisy Miller, of whom she is an improved and further elaborated edition. Mrs. Vivian, the "perverted Puritan," is also very vividly conceived, and the mixture of timid worldliness and minute conscientiousness in her character has a quaint, serio-comic effect. Angela is so needlessly enigmatical that we doubt if Mr. James himself understands her; but this does not deprive her of attractiveness and fascination. Bernard Longueville, the nominal hero, is a slightly modified repetition of the author's favorite type. Apart from his very clever talk and his cosmopolitan tendency to roam the world over at a moment's notice, he is in no wise remarkable, and we are inclined to think that he was blessed beyond his deserts in gaining Angela. The plot, as usual with Mr. James, is conspicuous chiefly for its simplicity, but contains, nevertheless, a series of delightful surprises dexterously managed. Especially masterly is Angela's successful stratagem for restoring the disaffected Gordon to his innocent flirt of a wife.

[T. S. Perry].
Atlantic Monthly 46 (July 1880), 125–26.

Mr. James's Confidence is really not a novel, but a study of an ingeniously devised situation, that is analyzed and described with the utmost skill. To take the work too seriously, as a profound treatise on life, would be a lamentable mistake; it is a sketch of the mutual relations of half a dozen people, whom we get to understand better than we do most of our acquaintances. They are a set of life-like figures, whose positions in regard to one another are distinctly drawn, and watching their movements is like looking at a well-played game of chess. And as in this but little attention could be given to the observer who should complain that, while the castle moved in straight lines and the bishop on the diagonals, the knight was to be condemned for his irregular gait, so in speaking of the book one feels that it is one's duty to take it for what it pretends to be, and not to demand, as some have done, that this light and graceful structure should be overburdened with moral teaching or social ethics. One might as well lament that it throws no light on Mr. James's views concerning the third term.

As a bit of what may be called social imagination, the story is deserving of high praise. From very slender materials Mr. James has woven a complicated plot about the distinctly defined heroes and heroines, and the ins and outs of the game form as entertaining a book as one can care to read. The main hero, Bernard Longueville, is the thoughtful, clever fellow, the observer, who is not uncommonly found in Mr. James's stories; and we have, too, a new specimen of the large class of chattering American girls, one Blanche Evers, whose artless prattle is capitally given. The other heroine is of sterner stuff, a really serious character, and her mother is the well-known American matron, who when well on in years does her hair in as complicated involutions as if she were a girl in her teens. The relations in which these people stand to one another are sufficiently intricate, and their social skirmishing does them credit. The chief heroine, Angela, plays her part with especial skill; her swift comprehension of the position in which she is placed in regard to the two men—which should serve as a warning against those unhealthy alliances—and her handling of the tangled threads at the end of the book are certainly entertaining reading. More than this, the change in Bernard from the position of willful observation to that of a partaker in the game is distinctly well drawn.

In execution, the story is of course most admirable; it runs on brightly, and he will be a hardened reader of fiction who does not feel something like breathless interest in the story. The *donnée* of the book is a light one, to be sure, and we are no less grateful for the amusement to be got from it when, under the inspiration of the miasmatic conscience of New England, we ask that Mr. James should not confine himself to those simply entertaining, though exceedingly entertaining, novels, but that, with his generous equipment for the task, he give us novels of a higher flight.

Checklist of Additional Reviews

Spectator [England] 53 (10 January 1880), 48–49. Reprinted in Roger Gard, ed., *Henry James: The Critical Heritage* (London: Routledge & Kegan Paul, 1968), pp. 83–86; James W. Gargano, ed., *Critical Essays on Henry James: The Early Novels* (Boston: G. K. Hall, 1987), pp. 43–46; Herbert Ruhm, ed., *Confidence (1880)* (New York: Grosset and Dunlap, 1962), pp. 220–22.

London *Times*, 5 February 1880, p. 3.

[James Davies]. *Academy* [England] 17 (7 February 1880), 101. Reprinted in Ruhm, p. 223.

Chicago *Times*, 21 February 1880, p. 8.

Hartford *Daily Courant*, 21 February 1880, p. 1.

Boston *Evening Journal*, 9 March 1880, p. 1.

Independent 32 (18 March 1880), 11.

Detroit *Free Press*, 20 March 1880, p. 3.

St. Paul *Daily Pioneer Press*, 29 March 1880, p. 4.

"Mr. Henry James's Latest Novel." New York *Evening Post*, 29 March 1880, p. 1.

Harper's New Monthly Magazine 60 (May 1880), 945–46.

M[ayo] W[illiamson] H[azeltine]. New York *Sun*, 23 May 1880, p. 57.

Boston Book Bulletin 3 (June 1880), 40–41.

Californian 2 (July 1880), 92.

National Quarterly Review (July 1880). Reprinted in Ruhm, pp. 228–29.

WASHINGTON SQUARE

[Thomas Powell]. "*Washington Square*," New York *Herald*, 6 December 1880, p. 5.

If you imagine a cynical dandy lying back in his easy chair and telling a story leisurely to a friend or two, you have a fair idea of Mr. Henry James, Jr.'s, manner as a novelist. Sometimes he seems to shake out a perfumed handkerchief; presently he is knocking the ashes from a cigar; anon he absolutely puts his hands in his pockets, as who would let the world wag without giving the old pendulum a push. A little priggish with his perfume sometimes; the least bit dreamy with his tobacco smoke, and playing the *rôle* of "stony-eyed god" with his hands in his pockets. If the gods who used to look with unconcerned eyes on human joy or sorrow lived on Fifth avenue or Belgrave square they would express neutrality by putting their hands in their pockets. There is nothing particularly offensive in this way of telling one's stories, provided they are worth listening to. We don't want Hugo with his brandished flambeau all the time. On the contrary, there is a certain piquancy in the little dainty turns given by this easy chair narrator. Disraeli wore three feet of gold chains and used hair oil, and Benjamin had brains. He did not, however, tell his stories lying back in his easy chair, but sat up and gesticulated. Bulwer was called "the man who wears the stays," but in his novels he does not seem stiff or trussed up, though there is much musk and lavender in them. It is Mr. James' way to lie back and sketch a little, sneer a little, make a little love and point his story with a little epigram. As to "rounding it out"—positively these people have been helped along far enough—he puts his hands in his pockets and lets them shift for themselves. In "Washington Square"—republished in book form by the Harpers—he does all these things. You understand old Dr. Sloper, his plain faced daughter and the mildly flighty old maiden aunt. You learn as much of their existence as he can tell you just now. Mr. Morris Townsend's steadiness of character is fairly clouded in. Certain houses in Washington square that were palaces in their way forty years ago still look comfortable, and Miss Sloper after loving that adventurer fellow, manages to live without him, even to refuse him when he comes back ten years later. All this may be rather thin, but so are certain cool, acidulous drinks we swallow with avidity in the hot weather or at crowded receptions. Perhaps we have indicated why and how a great many people will read and relish this book. Du Maurier's illustrations are disappointing.

Chicago *Tribune*, 18 December 1880, p. 10.

What one critic is pleased to call "Mr. Henry James' latest completed exercises in his art of definition," referring by that expression to his latest novel, "Washington Square," has been published in book form after running through the pages of *Harper's Magazine* for some months.[1] Mr. James is not one of our favorite authors. He is too supercilious, too dilettante, talks too much and says too little. He never puts himself to the exertion of finishing out a character or roundly developing a plot. He called "Daisy Miller" a "study," and he might with equal propriety call "Washington Square" a sketch. The scenes are laid in New York City some thirty or forty years ago, and the characters are no strangers to metropolitan residents to-day. Mr. James has found a strong and popular chord apparently in treating of American character. And it must be admitted that he has depicted certain types with remarkable accuracy and fidelity. *Doctor Sloper* is a not exaggerated type of the fashionable physician, as his daughter is also of a not uncommon style of female found occasionally in what is called the best society. But that does not make her any the less dull and uninteresting. As a heroine she is a lamentable failure, and the worthy Doctor is a much more pleasing character. He is a successful man without deriving success from his talents. "It was an element in *Doctor Sloper's* reputation that his learning and his skill were very evenly balanced; he was what you might call a scholarly doctor, and yet there was nothing abstract in his remedies,—he always ordered you to take something. Though he was felt to be extremely thorough, he was not uncomfortably theoretic; and if he sometimes explained matters rather more minutely than might seem of use to the patient, he never went so far (like some practitioners one had heard of) as to trust to the explanation alone, but always left behind him an inscrutable prescription. There were some doctors that left the prescription without offering any explanation at all; and he did not belong to that class either, which was, after all, the most vulgar. It will be seen that I am describing a clever man, and this is really the reason why *Doctor Sloper* had become a local celebrity." "Washington Square" does not strike us as a work of absorbing interest. The substructure is weak and the superstructure uninviting. The strong points of the book are in the character-drawing, which is well done, the *Doctor* and *Aunt Penniman* being the best examples. Of Du Maurier's illustrations the less said the better. Not only do they fail to illustrate, but they are not at all in harmony with the book, being as thoroughly English in construction and design as the latter is un-English and American in locale and in detail.

Note

1 "Washington Square," *Harper's New Monthly Magazine* 61 (July–November 1880); 287–301, 413–26, 593–607, 753–66, 907–18; 62 (December 1880); 129–44.

Dial 1 (January 1881), 195–96.

It is perhaps scarcely necessary to proffer the information that Mr. James's "Washington Square" is distinguished by that author's characteristic modesty and moderation. These qualities are very becoming to him; and his consciousness of the fact may be inferred from the continued exercise of his self-restraint and his apparent reluctance to undertake anything more complicated in plot than these simple "studies" in which he has been so fortunate. No one is afraid of being wearied, or of having the feelings unduly harrowed, by Mr. James. His stories, never dull and never dangerous to the nerves, have the sort of agreeableness found in those rare people who never do or say anything in excess. Thus his readers, if not profoundly moved by him, are always in a good humor toward him, and, though unconsciously, cannot fail to be grateful not less for what he refrains from attempting than for what he so admirably accomplishes. It is much for a novelist to avoid exciting his readers' animosity by making them uncomfortable; and this art Mr. James understands to perfection. He attempts no statement or solution of great social or moral problems, no dissemination of pessimistic theories: he simply draws in outline the characters of men and women supposed to represent the types he has observed and studied in society, and artistically arranges these sketches into groups with more or less relationship to each other. The most striking of these characters in "Washington Square" are Dr. Sloper, the wealthy and highly respectable physician, whose intense individuality is thoroughly manifest; his daughter Catherine, a simple-minded and right-minded girl, who, when the one romance of her life is ended by the faithlessness of her lover, quietly accepts the result and lives out her lonely life with a fortitude and self-reliance which prove more than a match for her father's determined obstinacy; Morris Townsend, a "beautiful" young man of society—a "dangler" in the eyes of Dr. Sloper, and a transparent fraud to everybody but Catherine and her romantic aunt;—and, best of all, this aunt, Mrs. Penniman, a fatuous and absurd old jenny whose meddlesome solicitude for others is pretty certain to prove in the end the greatest calamity that can well befall them. This character is a most amusing and delightful one, and might be sufficient to make the reputation of a literary artist less a master of this kind of portraiture than is Mr. James. One should perhaps not look too closely for consistency of action in a work like this; but it is difficult to understand the motive of Catherine's lover in deserting her—an episode on which the slight plot chiefly hinges. Adventurers of his type are not apt to turn away from ten thousand dollars a year because they cannot get forty thousand. The book has a number of cuts of a style which is more common in English than in American novels; and the publishers, Harper & Brothers, are to be complimented on the very tasteful cover which they have given it.

New York *Tribune*, 6 February 1881, p. 8.

. . . "Washington Square" is neither a very good story, nor a very lively sketch of character and society; the scene is laid in New-York about forty years ago, and all the personages except one are rather ordinary ladies and gentlemen of the place and period. No travelling foreigner is brought into this quiet company to point a contrast, in Mr. James's favorite manner, between the old civilization and the new: and those sensitive Americans who are forever accusing Mr. James of turning up his nose at his countrymen will find nothing here to inflame their patriotic anger or even to stir their suspicions. Such glimpses as we catch of the social aspect of Washington Square about the year 1840 are too vague and evanescent to provoke attention. The actors in this little domestic play trot their little round at an easy pace, never disturbed by the occurrence of exciting events or the intrusion of people with habits and ideas unlike their own. Their troubles arise from the conflict of sentiments in common-place minds, which are described with a leisurely minuteness queerly in harmony with the lazy movement of the tale. The suggestion is a little grotesque; but it really seems as if Mr. James must have written "Washington Square" after an over indulgence in the prolix perplexities of some of Mr. Anthony Trollope's heroines.

It is no new discovery that Mr. James

lacks the constructive art of the novelist. He is a charming sketch writer, and in many of his short and earlier pieces there were pages of vivid description, fragments of dramatic dialogue, and ingenious situations which gave [of] promise success in more elaborate works fiction. This promise has not been fulfilled. "The American" was one of his most ambitious efforts, and it showed very plainly at once the elegant finish of his art and its narrow scope. The plan of the book was ingenious and original, and many of the incidents were boldly devised and told with remarkable power. But after laying out the scheme of a forcible story, adroitly marshalling his personages into position, and describing with consummate skill the complicated springs of action which lay in their various and effectively opposed characters, the author seemed unable to go any further. The threads of the plot dropped from his hands. "The American" came to an end not by any process of development, but simply by exhaustion. "The Europeans" approached somewhat nearer the orthodox form of the novel so far as this, that it wound up with a few marriages, but in point of construction it was really almost as weak as the other story. As Christopher Newman, in "The American," was thrust into the society of an old legitimist French family, and after serving to expose the pettiness, the cruelty and the folly of their pride, was quietly withdrawn from the scene, so Eugenia, the central figure in "The Europeans," having emerged from a little German principality in order to set off a picture of domestic life in a suburb of Boston, vanished serenely across the ocean when she had played her part. The characters in "Washington Square" are presented and withdrawn in the same artless and easy manner. Nothing happens in the book except that a brilliant fortune-hunter jilts a dull and confiding girl when he finds that he cannot get money with her, and then she lives on quietly as an old maid. There is not the faintest attempt at the invention of a plot, or even at the arrangement of events whose natural course is to bring about the intended conclusion. "Washington Square" is no more than the narrative of a rather sluggish life, enlivened by admirable bits of dialogue and humorous characterization, but ending without a catastrophe—we might almost say without incident. We refer to this deficiency not in the spirit of fault-finding, but because it must be taken into account if we wish to understand in what the power of Mr. James really lies. He has been harshly criticized for not doing what he has perhaps decided not to attempt. He is not bound to write novels; and while he gives us essays in fiction and satire so fascinating in their way as the best of his books certainly are, we need not vex ourselves that he sees fit to display his beautiful workmanship upon fabrics of a light substance.

By far the best character in "Washington Square" is Aunt Lavinia Penniman. This romantic dame, with her passion for wholly superfluous mysteries and her good-natured but mischievous intermeddling in the love affairs of her niece, is drawn with a masterly skill: "Mrs. Penniman took too much satisfaction in the sentimental shadows of this little drama to have for the moment any great interest dissipating them. She wished the plot to thicken, and the advice that she gave her niece tended in her own imagination to produce this result. 'You must act, my dear; in your situation the great thing is to act,' said Mrs. Penniman, who found herself altogether beneath her opportunities. Mrs. Penniman's real hope was that the girl would make a secret marriage, at which she should assist as brideswoman or duenna. She had a vision of this ceremony being performed in some subterranean chapel; subterranean chapels in

New-York were not frequent, but Mrs. Penniman's imagination was not chilled by trifles; and of the guilty couple—she liked to think of poor Catherine and her suitor as the guilty couple—being shuffled away in a fast whirling vehicle to some obscure lodging in the suburbs, where she would pay them (in a thick veil) clandestine visits; where they would endure a period of romantic privation; and when ultimately after she should have been their earthly providence, their intercessor, their advocate, and their medium of communication with the world, they would be reconciled to her brother in an artistic tableau, in which she herself should be somehow the central figure." She wrote innumerable unnecessary letters to Mr. Morris Townsend—much to that astute young gentleman's annoyance; and she appointed meetings with him, which she called "interviews," and always approached with great parade of secrecy. For the first of these trysts she fixed upon an oyster saloon in Seventh Avenue, kept by a negro—an establishment of which she knew nothing save that she had noticed it in passing. She sat with Morris for half an hour in the duskiest corner of the shop "and it is hardly too much to say that this was the happiest half hour that Mrs. Penniman had known for years. The situation was really thrilling, and it scarcely seemed to her a false note when her companion asked for an oyster stew and proceeded to consume it before her eyes." It is quite in keeping with the sentimental and effusive temperament of this fantastic lady that twenty years after Morris's desertion of his affianced, when Catherine is a placid and contented old maid, she brings about a meeting between the two old lovers, and flutters about the entry while Morris is vainly trying to renew his suit in the parlor. Catherine is a personage with whom it is impossible for the reader to feel much sympathy; she is too dull, too foolish, too

profoundly, hopelessly commonplace; while her cold-blooded father, Dr. Sloper, who watches her mental sufferings with the same curious interest with which he might study a strange case of disease, is almost repulsive. He tells his sister, Mrs. Almond, that Catherine has surprised him; "she must have been so deucedly divided and bothered," between adoration of her father and infatuation with her lover. He is trying to fix the point where filial adoration stops; if one sentiment ceased where the other began the case would be simple enough: "but the two things are extremely mixed up, and the mixture is extremely odd. It will produce some third element, and that's what I'm waiting to see. I wait with suspense—with positive excitement; and that is a sort of emotion that I didn't suppose Catherine would ever provide for me. I am really very much obliged to her."

That a book contains no character whom the reader can like and none with whom the writer himself seems to be on terms of respect or cordiality is a serious blemish. We suspect that the dubious quality of Mr. James's popularity is to be accounted for in a large measure by the frequency of this fault, which gives a cynical and mocking tone to so many of his best sketches. He takes the keen delight of an artist in presenting effective contrasts of character, speech, manner and habits of thought, by bringing together the types of different nationalities—the American in Europe or the European in America—and in doing this he is not at the pains of cultivating anybody's sympathies. His analyses are as cold-blooded as Dr. Sloper's psychological study of the mixture of sentiments in the distresses of his daughter Catherine. The hero of "The American" is one of Mr. James's most careful creations, but it is impossible for us to care much about him, principally because his inventor does not care much. Newman is amiable and generous, but there is a broad streak of vulgarity in his composition of which we are never allowed to lose sight. Even his love making is vulgar; he undertakes the acquisition of the very finest attainable wife as a rich American with somewhat different tastes might set about the purchase of the biggest house or the most costly picture. The author never tells us that Newman is vulgar but we feel that with all his intrinsically noble qualities he is a person for whom we are not to entertain a very high respect, a product of thrift and enterprise to whom a fastidiously cultivated society might properly feel itself superior. So, on the other hand, when Mr. James, in the companion novel of "The Europeans," sets off the sophisticated polish of Felix and Eugenia against the stiff simplicity of the Wentworth family, we are conscious that he is smiling in a lofty and tolerant and not altogether becoming way at these pure and excellent New-Englanders; and the unpleasant effect is not materially lessened by the fact that the contrast between them and their foreign visitors is altogether to the Wentworth's advantage. That Mr. James holds himself above his countrymen, that he loves to point out the crudities of American society as compared with that of more aristocratic lands, we confess that we find nothing in his stories to show. He appears to regard all countries and all classes from the point of view of a dispassionate outsider; and if he has ridiculed the ideas and customs that prevail upon one side of the Atlantic more than those that distinguish the other, the discrimination has certainly not been against us. "Daisy Miller," which we suppose must have been the cause of more heartburning and feminine wrath than any of his other stories, will perhaps be cited in contradiction of this estimate. But "Daisy Miller" is pure satire of the most trenchant and legitimate kind. Nobody can have observed those curious products

of our civilization, the American hotel young lady and the American hotel mother, without recognizing the rare fidelity of this sketch of a grave social abuse, and appreciating the substantially just and kindly spirit with which the censor has tempered his severity. We should be glad indeed if Mr. James would forsake for a while the painting of amusing but upon the whole rather unprofitable and unsympathetic character pictures, such as are displayed in "Washington Square," and devote himself to the wholesome satire of which "Daisy Miller" was such an excellent example. America has great need of an earnest satirist, and Mr. James, we think, might undertake the office not only with profit to his countrymen but with great advantage to himself in the strengthening and development of powers which as yet seem to be uncertain of their proper field.

Athenaeum [England] 2781 (12 February 1881), 228.

Mr. James's countrymen complain that he is too fond of Europe; that he has deserted America for the society of the Old World; and that if he condescends to notice Americans at all it is only to satirize their weaknesses. This notion may be merely a symptom of the over-sensitiveness with which educated Americans are apt to observe English opinion; but in any case 'Washington Square' ought to do something towards dissipating it. The theme of a girl, in herself not attractive, being sought for her money's sake by a plausible and fascinating adventurer, to whom she in all good faith becomes deeply attached, is not exactly novel; but Mr. James has contrived, as he usually does, to throw a new charm over the old story, and to give his readers at the same time a view of the American young lady in a totally new character. Caroline Sloper, the quiet, steadfast, unattractive girl, is the sort of person whom we expect to meet with in an English country parsonage, rather than as an heiress in a fashionable part of New York; and her blind faithfulness to her unworthy suitor and her deference to her critical father are qualities which we have not been taught to look for in a Yankee girl. In depicting this character Mr. James must certainly be considered to atone for the less favourable idea of his younger countrywomen which many of his previous portraitures have given. Of course the reader lays down the book with that feeling of tranquil melancholy which most of the author's stories inspire; but it is tempered by the reflection that Caroline was probably much happier as an old maid in easy circumstances than she would have been as the wife of an adventurer; and the pain of disillusion is, after all, less sad to contemplate than the misery which arises when a well-grounded anticipation of happiness is unfulfilled. Mr. James's style is as pleasant as ever, though once or twice the desire to put things smartly has made him obscure. We have utterly failed, for example, to discover the meaning of the following sentence:—

"As regards this [an early tendency to greediness in the heroine], however, a critical attitude would be inconsistent with a candid reference to the early annals of any biographer."

Of the stories which accompany 'Washington Square,' 'The Pension Beaurepas' is rather pointless.[1] 'A Bundle of Letters' introduces some amusing characters, especially the innocent young woman from the state of Maine, who travels alone in Europe for greater advantages in the way of culture, and goes to the Palais Royal Theatre because it is marked in her guidebook with two stars: also the aesthetic youth from Boston, who writes of an English girl, "It is a very gracious, tender type," and calls her brother "purely objective." But is not the German professor wrong in saying that this youth "is an illustration of the period of culture in which the faculty of appreciation has obtained a preponderance over that of production"? If what Mr. James's countrymen call "slinging ink" be a form of production, the congeners of this young man possess a pretty considerable faculty of it.

Note

1 The English edition of *Washington Square* (London: Macmillan, 1881) also included "The Pension Beaurepas" and "A Bundle of Letters."

Appleton's Journal new series 10 (March 1881), 274–75.

The critic who is in the habit of analyzing his impressions must sometimes have been puzzled by the discovery that the so-called "light literature" is generally the heaviest reading that he undertakes to do. To lounge on the rainbow and read eternal romances of Crébillon was Campbell's ideal of happiness, and dawdling over the "last new novel" is now perhaps the favorite form of intellectual lotos-eating; but we are divulging no secret, we hope, when we acknowledge that for the professional critic there is in general no more appalling task than that which presents itself in the shape of an accumulated pile of "recent novels," all of which must be read to the bitter end. Sheridan used to declare that the way in which some critics prepare themselves for giving an opinion upon a book is to cut the leaves and smell the paper-knife; but, however applicable this compendious process might be to some classes of books which come under the reviewer's notice, in the case of novels nothing short of actual and thorough perusal will suffice. To the errors of judgment to which one is liable in estimating a work of the imagination, one dare not add the further risk of falling into errors of fact; and whether Lucy is a satisfactory heroine, and whether Edward is a "snob," a "cad," or a "gentleman," can be pronounced upon with confidence only after acquiring a knowledge of their several histories.

The task would be less arduous if all novels possessed the merits of Mr. Henry James's "Washington Square"; for it is short and it is lively—it can be read quickly, and the interest is seldom allowed to flag. At the same time, it must be confessed, the story is a rather disappointing one. The title leads the reader to expect more than he actually finds; for, while such local color as there is is probably faithful enough, the book does not reproduce with any degree of adequacy either the period or the society of which Washington Square might be regarded as typical. On the contrary, it depicts neither a place nor a period, but belongs to the order of novels which might be classified as character-studies. It is a study of a woman, not beautiful, not brilliant, not clever, not piquant, not even eccentric, but who, on the physical and intellectual side at least, is thoroughly and remorselessly commonplace. Such charm as Mr. James has bestowed upon his heroine is exclusively a moral charm, so to call it—the charm of a thoroughly sincere, straightforward, simple, and upright nature. In "Jane Eyre," Charlotte Brontë avowedly set herself the task of rendering fascinating a woman who was without physical beauty, but who possessed in an eminent degree what would now be described as a "magnetic" temperament. Mr. James appears to have set himself the far more difficult task of arousing our sympathy and even regard for a woman who is as commonplace in sentiment as in appearance; who is dull, if not quite stupid; narrow-minded, if large-hearted; whose very virtues take on the aspect of faults, and to whom is denied even the slender endowment of good taste in dress. That he quite succeeds in his undertaking can hardly be said; for, though we come to feel a great pity for Catherine in her trouble, she is not one of those imaginary sufferers whose story takes a profound and lasting hold upon our memories.

Such enjoyment as may be derived from consummate literary skill is obtainable from all Mr. James's stories, and from "Washington Square" in equal measure with the rest. Mr. James is beyond doubt the cleverest writer who now entertains the public with fiction; and even in portraying a dull woman his cleverness loses none of its point—in fact, it has the piquancy of a suggested contrast. Quite independent of the substance of what he says, there is a constant satisfaction in noting the manner in which he says it; and there is a flattering accession of self-esteem on the part of the reader in the perception that the author has bestowed painstaking care upon even the minor details of his work. The attention is constantly pricked with compendious little epigrams, the interest of which lies rather in what they suggest than in what they express, as where he periphrastically refers to woman as "the complicated sex." There is characteristic humor in the remark about Doctor Sloper that, on a certain occasion, when Catherine had been unexpectedly meek in her submissiveness, "he said to himself, as he had said before, that, though it might have its momentary alarms, paternity was not, after all, an exciting vocation." There is a caustic humorousness about the entire portrait of Doctor Sloper, and more of the causticity and less of the humor about the companion portrait of Mrs. Penniman, Catherine's mischief-making aunt. Morris Townsend, the fortune-hunting sneak, is one of the neatest and most finished society-portraits that Mr. James has painted; and there are none of those impersonal lay-figures that usually crowd the canvas in stories of this kind, where so much has to be compressed into brief space.

How distinctly Mr. James is a student of men and women and of manners is very strikingly indicated by little touches here and there, as well as by the texture and theme of his stories themselves. The descriptions of natural scenery, of which most modern novelists are so fond, are resorted to by him only when he desires to vary his background; and one feels that he sympathizes cordially with Dr. Johnson's preference for "the full tide of human life at Charing Cross." The reader can, perhaps, recall the cruel reference to Northampton, Massachusetts, in "Roderick Hudson"; and at the opening of "Washington Square" he represents the offer of a home in New York City as being "accepted with the alacrity of a woman who had spent ten years of her life in Poughkeepsie." These touches, be it observed, are not merely amusing—they are eminently characteristic of the author and his work. No living writer of fiction makes less use of those externals and surroundings that furnish such aid in fixing the "atmosphere" of a story, and to which Mr. Black, for example, gives his chief attention. The evolution of character under the bent of its own inherent impulses, and as influenced by the other personalities with which it is brought into contact, isolated as far as possible from the "environment"—this is the only portion of his work that seems really to attract Mr. James, or to call for the full exhibition of his powers.

"James's *Washington Square.*" *Scribner's Monthly* 21 (March 1881), 795–96.

Unless it be Mr. Thomas Hardy, there is no one now writing novels in English who brings to the task so complete a training and so fine a hand as Mr. Henry James, Jr. The English writer has elements of superiority which it may be never in the life of Mr. James to equal; he has an imaginative side that the American lacks. But merely as an artist in the management of a novel, Mr. James can readily afford to give him odds. The comparison between the two comes to be instituted all the more easily and naturally, since they have been publishing novels side by side in the same great popular magazine, "Harper's." Mr. James is especially remarkable for the patient care which he bestows upon his style, and the elaboration of his notes on modern society. More cool-headed than Hawthorne, and quite as industrious, he stores away the most minute observations on the daily conduct of people of all kinds. It is not the exceptional person who interests him particularly; he is rather occupied with cataloguing his impressions of commonplace characters such as one meets every day. In that respect he is eminently an observer such as the present quarter of the century has to show in other paths of research; men who are not rebuffed by the dryness of a task, or the amount of time involved in an examination of facts, so long as the result is some small gain to science. "Washington Square" is a tale that seven novel-readers out of ten vote dull; but to us it seems one of the best and cleverest Mr. James has produced. In the first place, he has shifted his old ground completely, and writes of people upon American soil, for the trip the heroine takes to Europe is too slightly sketched to make any appreciable mark on the book. Some weakness, it is true, results from the removal of his scenes to a country which either is not as suggestive to Mr. James, or else is not so thoroughly examined. The view of New York City, between 1820 and 1840, is more like that of a foreigner, who has lived a good portion of his life in America, than that of a person American-born. And every now and then, one comes upon a touch which is distinctly French, not American, nor even English in its origin. An exact analogy to this curious fact in Mr. James's novels may be seen in the kindred touch on the canvases of our young painters who have studios in France. With a writer it shows in modes of expression foreign to Americans, in turns of thought, and, less often, views of the relative positions of people toward each other in society, which are not usual here. Particularly liable to misconstruction are the delicate adjustments of the relations between young girls and young men. In the United States it requires a great deal of patient study to reach the truth on this matter, for no one rule, indeed, no ten rules, govern it. In Europe the matter is, or is conventionally supposed to be, simple, and practically invariable. It cannot fairly be said that "Washington Square," with all its realism, shows a thorough understanding of this relationship of the unmarried sexes. Yet, with such modification, the picture offered is exceedingly good. The society physician, who is disappointed that his daughter, the child of a brilliant

man and his brilliant wife, should be a dull, plain, timid creature, is an admirable study; his unusual hardness being easily explainable as gradually growing upon him, and leading him in the end to a relentless cruelty to the unhappy girl, which he could not have entertained at first. He watches her "case" intellectually and morally, as he had learned to watch the symptoms of his patients. In all of Mr. James's novels there is some such cool observer, who is "watching the case." It is Mr. James himself, who stands in his own novels with note-book and pencil in hand, conning the foregone facts, jotting down the new, and trying to make up his mind as to the probable course of the coming situation.

The character of Catherine Sloper is a true triumph for Mr. James; it is one of the best outcomes of his generalizing realism. Some women may readily be exasperated at such a picture as she presents intellectually; but she is true to the life; are there not Catherine Slopers all around us—good, amiable girls, who have hosts of friends who admire them from a distance, but at close quarters find them unutterably dull? This is the kind of women Mr. James, who is a biting cynic under the calm flow of his novels, chooses for his heroines. It is no wonder that people ask, why does Mr. James select the dullest of a dull class for a Catherine Sloper, the worst educated of a badly brought-up class, for a Daisy Miller. From a nation celebrated for brilliant and beautiful women, why does he select the most faulty, those that represent the bad minority, instead of painting types of the better majority? To such impatient questionings the answer is: Mr. James prefers to—and one must not quarrel with an artist's choice. It is sufficient if he carries out what he attempts.

Notwithstanding his realism, Mr. James does not dare to make these commonplace types truly real. They talk and act after a superior fashion, and in fact, if they are to be located in any one town of the United States, belong to Boston rather than to New York. The atmosphere in which they move is not exactly that of New York, even in 1820; they are a trifle too precise, and a trifle too provincial. There is a grimace of intellectual superiority in Dr. Sloper which is hard to fit into the surroundings. His sister is a character who must be found everywhere—from remote New England villages to the bayous of Louisiana. Without any sort of doubt, the aunt who enjoys twice as much as Catherine the love affair of the latter, and in trying to be a clever match-maker only contributes to her niece's confusion, is the best character in the novel. She forms a pendant to the little old lady in "Middlemarch," who is guilty of "little beaver-like noises." To consider the novel from the close, we must again admire the workmanship, and notice again a recurring trait in the books of this able writer. This is the want of force in the *dénouement*. Like most, and perhaps all of his novels, "Washington Square" seems to have been worked up with extraordinary care and skill—and come to nothing. We do not care two straws for the fate of the actors; we are merely concerned with the evident cleverness of the author.

"*Washington Square.*" *Pall Mall* Gazette [England], 4 March 1881, p. 11.

Washington-Square is situated in the centre of what may be called the Bloomsbury of New York, and within the limits of the square the action of the novel is rigorously confined. The heroine is a young lady whose body and mind are in harmony with such a setting, incapable of conceiving existence under any other circumstances than those in which it has pleased Providence to place her, and content to accept the ills of life as they come without criticising them or even consciously wishing that they might be otherwise. A story of this scope is, indeed, a new departure for Mr. James, who has hitherto been nothing if not cosmopolitan, and in whose books one great element of charm has been the perpetual play of contrast between his personages and the incongruous influences to which they are exposed. But on the present occasion by his choice of subject he has burned the ship which has carried him on so many and so successful literary ventures. "Washington Square" is the introduction, we hope, to a series of American "Scènes de la Vie de Province"—a heading under which none of the author's previous stories can be ranged, not even "The Europeans," the point of which depended in great measure on the contrast between the loose-laced strangers and their prim Transatlantic cousins. Indeed, a critic can only wonder why Mr. James has avoided till to-day a topic so rich. America is at once near and remote, familiar and strange enough to awaken sympathy and curiosity in England—a combination of feeling most auspicious for a novelist. And what more could the heart of a writer desire than to have a new world at his feet waiting only to be written about and an audience waiting only to read? Now that Mr. James has proved how capable he is of turning to account the opportunities of his subject, it is his bounden duty to give us from time to time pictures of the Americans who stop at home as well as of those who go abroad.

It is not in scenery alone that "Washington Square" is unlike Mr. James's previous novels. His heroine is in complete contrast to the clever, impressionable, critical, self-absorbed persons whom he has hitherto delighted to describe. As we have said, she is neither pretty nor clever, and for these reasons she is rather a disappointment to her father, a rich, clear-sighted, cold-blooded widower, who, though he is fond of her in a way, yet feels little compunction about acknowledging to himself that she is a fool. Catherine Sloper, for so the realistic author has christened his heroine, meets an agreeable young man at a party who pays her the greatest attention—a sort of homage to which she is not at all accustomed; and when he proposes to her, as he does in due course, she finds she is in love, not desperately, for that would be impossible to her temperament, but irrevocably. And then, having pledged herself, she begins to realize that the stream of her life, which has hitherto flowed in one sluggish current of home duties, must henceforth be split into two. Her father, she knows, dislikes the dashing Townshend, and it is with some terror that she announces her engagement. Dr. Sloper, however, is quite prepared for the news, and has made his arrangements accordingly. He informs Catherine that her lover is an adventurer, and bids her tell him that, if he marries her, it must be without a dowry. The Doctor, as usual, is right. The young man is an adventurer, but he thinks not unreasonably that, Catherine holding firm, her father is sure to give in sooner or later. The rest of the book describes the campaign fought between the two men, with Catherine's heart as the seat of war. She is too loyal to the traditions in which she has been brought up to entertain any hope of being able to reconcile the conflicting claims of father and lover. She sees with the clear-sightedness of stupidity that she must fail in her duty to one or the other. And she receives no assistance from either. Townshend naturally does not wish to precipitate matters; it is obviously his interest to wait. Dr.

Sloper, on the other hand, having delivered his ultimatum, is so pleased with his own perspicuity, so certain that Townshend will do nothing without a satisfactory settlement, that he lets things take their course without making any real effort to help his daughter in her scrape. On the contrary, he lets her understand that she is her own mistress, free to marry Townshend, if only she can dispense with her father's benediction and he with his father-in-law's fortune. At last Catherine screws her courage to the sticking point, and proposes to her lover that they should marry without further delay. And then, poor woman, the bubble bursts, and she is left alone, abandoned by her lover and alienated from her father. As for the Doctor, he does not enjoy his triumph as much as he expected. It is true he is proved to be in the right, but the victory is won at a cost which might perhaps have made defeat preferable. It is with fine irony that Mr. James shows the father's mistake.

"Washington Square," it will be seen from this sketch, is a version of the plot of "Eugénie Grandet," with this fundamental alteration, that the story is transferred from the grimmest regions of tragedy to those of comedy.[1] Indeed, so far as the two novels can be compared, it is for the sake of the contrast, not the similarity between them. What would Eugénie have been if her father had been considerate, though unsympathetic, and her lover had flung himself upon her generosity? Catherine Sloper is not nearly so romantic a heroine as Eugénie Grandet, and it would have been easy for the author to make her troubles appeal more loudly to the reader's sympathy if she had been represented as the victim of extraordinary and not of ordinary circumstances. But Mr. James has too much common sense—a quality with which the greatest writers alone can afford to dispense—to force more into a subject than nature intended it to hold. In

112

one respect the representation of Catherine is an advance on the author's previous work. Mr. James is an acknowledged master in the art of analyzing complex natures open to every variety of conflicting impulse; but it requires solider, if less brilliant, qualities to do justice to the earnestness of a simple character like Catherine's. Such a description as the following carries with it a conviction that it must be true:—

> The girl was very happy. She knew not as yet what would come of it; but the present had suddenly grown rich and solemn. If she had been told she was in love, she would have been a good deal surprised; for she had an idea that love was an eager and exacting passion, and her own heart was filled in those days with the impulse of self effacement and sacrifice. Whenever Morris Townshend had left the house her imagination projected itself with all its strength into the idea of his soon coming back; but if she had been told at such a moment that he would not return for a year, or even that he would never return, she would not have rebelled nor complained, but would humbly have accepted the decree, and sought for consolation in thinking over the times she had already seen him, the words he had spoken, the sound of his voice, of his tread, the expression of his face. Love demands certain things as a right; but Catherine had no sense of her rights; she had only a consciousness of immense and unexpected favours. Her very gratitude for these things had hushed itself; for it seemed to her there would be something of impudence in making a festival of her secret.

The minor personages of the Washington-square drama are excellent. Best of all is a sentimental aunt who derives much vicarious satisfaction from her niece's romance, and who drives Townshend mad by her interference, as the following scrap of dialogue will show:—"'I have been thinking a great deal, Mr. Townshend,' said Mrs. Penniman. 'You think too much.' 'I suppose I do; but I can't help it, my mind is so terribly active. When I give myself, I give myself. I pay the penalty in my headaches, my famous headaches—a perfect circlet of pain. But I carry it as a queen carries her crown. Would you believe that I have one now?'" Of the short stories which eke out Mr. James's volumes, space only permits it to be said that they contain three delightful new types of Americans—two ladies who shop, two more who pride themselves on their "point of view," and an aesthetic Bostonian, who is satirized with such relish, such vigour, and such justice that we wish Mr. James would take certain Cockneys in hand.

Note

1 Honoré de Balzac, *Eugénie Grandet* (1833).

Leonora B. Lang. *Academy* [England] new series 462 (12 March 1881), 185–86.

In *Washington Square* Mr. James has struck a new chord and achieved a new success. He has not only had the audacity to choose for his heroine a girl plain, awkward, and wholly devoid of charm, and the skill to enlist all our sympathies on her side, but he has allotted the other parts in his drama to three people whom we either disapprove or dislike, while we yet regard their strategic movements with absorbing interest. Finally, he has dared to fill a volume and a-half with the discussion of a possible marriage between the rich heiress and her penniless suitor, though contriving to the very last to keep us in suspense as to the result. Nothing, it may be said, can exceed the simplicity of the problem to be solved. Catherine Sloper—who we feel sure was destined by nature to be called Charlotte—was the daughter of a New York physician in good practice, who had married a rich lady now dead. At the age of twenty she had not outgrown her childish unattractiveness, and it was consequently a matter of surprise and gratitude to her to become the object of the attentions of handsome young Morris Townsend. Her father, considering the matter from the point of view of the most unprejudiced observer, decided at once that the young man was mercenary, and that a stop must be put to the whole affair. In this, however, he found that he had reckoned without his daughter. Catherine opposed a dutiful but steady front, and was supported in her resistance by the counsels of her aunt, Mrs. Penniman, ever anxious to be romantic by proxy. Mrs. Penniman is one of the most delightful people it has been our lot to meet with in fiction. Her elaborate affectations, her untiring efforts to produce a sense of mystery about her surroundings, and the extraordinary inappropriateness of her expressions when speaking of the result, all make up a whole which is one of the very best sketches of the sort that has ever been done. Only once have we seen anything at all like her, and that was in the representation of Dame Pluche by Mdme. Jouassain. Mrs. Penniman is absolutely without moral sense as we understand it. It was nothing to her that she was encouraging Catherine to disobey her father, that she was urging her to risk her happiness in a clandestine marriage, and that she was receiving in her brother's house a guest of whom she knew he disapproved, for Mrs. Penniman had long since sacrificed truth,

sense, and taste on the altar of Romance. So she was quite at ease when she made an appointment with the unwilling Mr. Townsend in a low restaurant in the purlieus of New York, going with a reticule on her arm in order to look "like a woman of the people," the object of the interview being to entreat him to marry Catherine at once and trust to the doctor relenting afterwards. She had no scruples when, in giving her sister an account of an interview she had had with Catherine, in which the latter had not only declined to pour out any confidences, but had very nearly turned her aunt from the room, she observed that Catherine had told her "she had a genius for consolation," because to have stated the facts as they really were would have spoilt the attitude of love-lorn maiden which it was proper her niece should assume. No better foil could have been provided for Catherine. In her we see a maiden about as different from the introspective heroines of latter-day novels as can well be imagined. Her nature, commonplace in most respects, was lifted into something almost like heroism by its steadfastness. She was true, not only to her idea of her lover and to her duty to her father, but also to her duty to herself. In spite of continued want of sympathy and occasional brutality on the part of her father, she was willing to wait till she could gain his consent, without ever showing, in voice or manner, that she considered herself harshly treated—a neglect of her opportunities deeply resented by Mrs. Penniman. It was only when she had been stung by a long course of irony and insult that she made up her mind to take the matter into her own hands; but even then her revolt, though open, was reticent. One fine touch we cannot help noticing. When near the close of his life, Dr. Sloper asked Catherine to give him a promise that she would never marry the man whose mercenary schemes had been years before placed beyond a doubt. She declined to give the promise, though a large portion of her fortune was at stake. She knew she could never marry Morris Townsend as he had revealed himself to be, but she instinctively felt that the refusal must be the result of her own nature, and not the result of external pressure. Mr. James has frequently been charged with not being able to tell a story; but is there one among his novels where we can guess with certainty how the characters will act, or what the end is to be? Even in *Washington Square* we tremble at the last; for when the Ethiopian had changed his skin to that extent that Mrs. Penniman had held her tongue for seventeen years on the subject of Catherine's matrimonial intentions, we cannot predict that a similar change may not have taken place in Catherine herself. Fortunately, she found she could not piece together the broken Dagon, and replace him on his pedestal. Those who have been oppressed by the dreariness of the foreign tour taken by Dr. and Miss Sloper will turn with delight to the boarding-house experiences of Miss Miranda Hope in Paris. *A Bundle of Letters* contains the sketches of the inmates of this Parisian establishment by each other's pens, beginning with a young lady of enquiring mind from Bangor, U.S., to whom everything was real interesting, who could see no impropriety in anything out of the Decalogue, but whose innocence and simplicity had instinctively shielded her. We have the sweet, elegant, somewhat prolix letter of the high-born English girl, whose long, clinging, embroidered dress, decorated with a row of "spinal buttons," called forth the admiration of the gentlemen and the reprobation of the ladies. A young American aesthetic gentleman pours forth his experiences to his kindred spirit in Boston, and classes days according to the schools of painting to which they belong, and speaks of a past episode in his life as

"gray and cottony—he might almost say woolly," in tone. These and many more equally characteristic make up some of the most amusing pages Mr. James has ever written.

Californian 3 (April 1881), 376–77.

Mr. James's new book belongs eminently to the small class of works of art whose execution is well nigh perfect, and whose design is a blunder. The blunder of design in *Washington Square* is that of handling tragedy by the dispassionate, realistic method. A more completely tragic history (if we may be allowed to use the adjective with regard to a calamity wrought out by purely psychologic methods, and devoid of external incidents) could hardly be conceived than this of Catherine Sloper. The author has started, like a spiritualized Zola, with the assumption that the legitimate subject-matter of tragedy is the infliction of suffering on a human being. He has, therefore, created with a marvelous skill and delicacy, with an all but infallible accuracy both of analytic and constructive power, a character endowed with the utmost receptivity to pain and the least resources or defenses against it; has subjected her to precisely those experiences holding the utmost possibilities of pain to the temperament in question, and has filled in even minor details with an almost complete avoidance of any alleviation. All this is most excellently done. Mr. James is not usually at his best in portraiture. He analyzes too much—overloads with detail, and obscures the broad lines that impress our memories. But in "Catherine Sloper" he has given us a fine portrait, all the finer because it is in the very extreme of the "low-toned" method. The artists are few indeed who can paint character in neutral colors, and Mr. James has not merely painted "Catherine" in neutral colors. He has, with a fine artistic feeling for quietude, put her against as neutral a background as possible. He has hardly allowed to her whole history a single outwardly dramatic moment. The drama consists solely of her own mental experience, and affects no one else especially, not even her supposed lover, while this drama remains to the end unexpressed by speech, action, or even look, except in the merest fragments. So far as the skillful description of the way in which such a girl was made the victim of life goes, Mr. James has left little to be asked. Nothing could round out the quiet desolation of her fate more perfectly than the summary of her life ten, fifteen, twenty years after her brief romance:

> "From her own point of view, the great facts of her career were that Morris Townsend had trifled with her affections, and that her father had broken its spring. Nothing could ever alter these facts. They were always there, like her name, her age, her plain face. Nothing could ever undo the wrong or cure the pain that Morris had inflicted on her, and nothing could ever make her feel toward her father as she felt in her younger years. There was something dead in her life, and her duty was to try and fill the void."

No delicate touch is omitted that could heighten the tragedy (always assuming that tragedy means intensity and completeness of misfortune). "Catherine's" perfect blamelessness, not only in action, but in the most subtle refinements of spirit and motive, and the fact that the hardest part of her misfortune, if not the whole, was the logical result of her very blamelessness, is an element in her fate that, while true enough to nature, verges on the intolerable.

Now, we repeat, with all these elements of tragedy at hand, and all most finely managed, Mr. James has not written anything in the least resembling a tragedy. He would, no doubt, repudiate with horror the idea of ever doing such a thing. A dignified quietude, a masterly dispassionateness, and a matter-of-fact realism, are qualities without which he would find it as impossible to appear in print as he would find it to appear in the street without his coat and shoes. And these qualities we, for our part, should be utterly unwilling to lose from his writings. But he ought not to try, under their bonds, to treat of such things as love at its utmost depth, crushed hearts, spoiled lives. Not that he makes himself ridiculous, as if he were playing Hamlet in an immaculate shirt-bosom and studs. His taste is too perfect for that. On the contrary, he makes the very mention of love and heart-break in a passionate way seem ridiculous. It is more as if some accomplished psychologist, who knew the details about Hamlet, sat down and told us in smooth tones and with a genuine scientific interest all that the royal Dane had suffered; told it so well and appreciatively that we realized perfectly all that was distressing in the story, and yet were not lifted above the painfulness of it by any passion of sympathy or any tragic fervor.

The result is that *Washington Square* is painful reading, and leaves an unpleasant taste in the mouth. One is inclined to look for a volume of Mark Twain after laying *Washington Square* down, to take the taste out. It is quite as if Mr. James, with the most admirable skill, had performed a difficult vivisection for us to witness. If we are psychologists enough to appreciate the skill, and not sensitive to pain (in others), our admiration is unmixed; otherwise, we feel that the piercing of live flesh in cold blood is bad art, and only justifiable when some beneficent end is to be gained. If young men were to be made less unscrupulous, old ladies less silly, clever fathers more sympathetic, and loving girls more shrewd by this book, it would be worth while to make the reader uncomfortable; but we need hardly say that it is not calculated to have any such effect. The breaking of hearts, again, in Turgeneff, Shakspere, and George Eliot, is more analogous to the cutting of flesh and shedding of blood in warfare than in vivisection. No matter how true to life the psychology, how close the realism, there is always the passion and fervor, the sound of trumpets, and the great onward movement of something irresistible. The author is always in a subjective attitude (without necessarily quitting the objective); there is always a certain fitness and necessity in the result that warrant a "piling up" of suffering to any hight in such tragedies as "Prometheus" or "Œdipus" or "Lear." In Mr. James's other books that "turn out badly"—*The American* and *Daisy Miller*—there is such a necessity in the very nature of things for the result, and the result itself, though sad enough, falls so far short of intolerableness, and is so lightly sketched, that we accept it as the right thing. Nevertheless, in general Mr. James's exceeding cleverness is of too unemotional a character to be employed on pain and misfortune. Mr. Howells, whose cleverness is as great, and of a warmer and richer quality, sets a wise example in the avoidance of tragedy.

Mr. James is strongest, in all his books, in "clever talk." He sometimes slips into the habit of making all his characters talk with equal cleverness and similar diction. In *Washington Square* the cleverness is distributed to the right people, though it must be remarked that the three clever ones—the Doctor, Mrs. Almond, and Morris Townsend—say bright things of a precisely similar cast, and turn their epigrams in just the same way, and it may be further added that it is remarkably similar to the way in which the distinctively clever people in all Mr. James's other books turn their epigrams. Nevertheless, the individualities in *Washington Square* are all clear. The book is brief and sketchy enough to have all its characters drawn more or less in outline, and Mr. James can always make a consistent and clear sketch of character. It is elaborate portraits that he obscures. The book is in charming English, crammed with keen and discriminating observation of society and of human nature, thoroughly original, and is pervaded by the author's own refined good taste and educated intelligence, and, for these reasons, is good reading, and earns the comment so often made on Mr. James's books, "Whether it is, on the whole, a success or not, I like to read it, it's so cleverly written."

Checklist of Additional Reviews

New York *Times*, 28 November 1880, p. 10.

Boston *Evening Transcript*, 2 December 1880, p. 6.

Philadelphia *Public Ledger and Daily Transcript*, 4 December 1880, Supp., p. 2.

Boston *Evening Traveller*, 8 December 1880, p. 1.

New York *Daily Graphic*, 10 December 1880, p. 297.

Cleveland *Daily Plain Dealer*, 15 December 1880, p. 2.

Hartford *Daily Courant*, 16 December 1880, p. 1.

"Henry James' *Washington Square*."

Louisville *Courier-Journal,* 17
December 1880, p. 4.

Philadelphia *North American,* 17
December 1880, p. 4.

Chicago *Inter-Ocean,* 18 December
1880, p. 14.

Portland *Morning Oregonian,* 29
December 1880, p. 1.

Literary World 12 (1 January 1881), 10.

Lippincott's Magazine 27 (February
1881), 214–15. Reprinted in James W.
Gargano, ed., *Critical Essays on Henry*

James: The Early Novels (Boston:
G. K. Hall, 1987), pp. 46–47.

R. H. Hutton. *Spectator* [England] 54 (5
February 1881), 185–86. Reprinted in
Roger Gard, ed., *Henry James: The
Critical Heritage* (London:
Routledge & Kegan Paul, 1968), pp.
88–90.

London *Times,* 19 April 1881, p. 9.

Horace E. Scudder. *Atlantic Monthly* 47
(May 1881), 709–10. Reprinted in
Gard, p. 92.

THE PORTRAIT OF A LADY

Athenaeum 2822 (26 November 1881), 699.

It is impossible not to feel that Mr. James has at last contrived to write a dull book. 'The Portrait of a Lady' is of enormous length, being printed much more closely than is usual with three-volume novels; and a large part of it is made up of page after page of narrative and description, in which the author goes on refining and distinguishing, as if unable to hit on the exact terms necessary to produce the desired effect. There is, of course, plenty of dialogue as well, but not very much of a kind to make the reader wish, as he may have done in the case of some of Mr. James's stories, that he had himself been a sharer in it. Here and there a tiresome artifice is employed, that of indicating a conversation by giving one person's remarks only, much as a cross-examination is reported in the newspapers. The theme is one which seems to possess an inexhaustible attraction for the author. An American girl, brought up more or less unconventionally though among ordinary people, conceives high but somewhat undefined notions of her duty, refuses some excellent men on the ground that she does not want to marry anybody, and in a few months is caught by the first aesthetic impostor whom she comes across. After this the history becomes fragmentary; but we find on our next meeting with the heroine that her husband, on perceiving that he has married a woman with views of her own and disinclined to take her place among his *bibelots,* has begun to hate her. Finally, a revelation is made to her about some passages in his former life, and the reader fancies that Mr. James intends to bring about a crisis; yet the only result is to decide her to take a journey against her husband's wishes, and the story leaves her just started back to rejoin him. Nor is the least hint given to show in what way their subsequent relations are to be modified either by her knowledge of his past offences or by her disobedience to his orders. That is to say, this so-called "portrait of a lady" is left unfinished just at the point where some really decisive and enlightening strokes begin to be possible. It may, of course, be wrong to assume that the portrait to which the title refers is that of the heroine. There are other ladies in the story of whom we form a far clearer conception than of Isabel Osmond. For example, there is her friend Miss Stackpole, the lady-correspondent of the *New York Interviewer,* who is really an admirable representative of the literary lady—hard-headed and tender-hearted, shrewd and naïve, unconventional to the verge of scandal, yet as ignorant of evil as a child. There is Isabel's aunt, Mrs. Touchett, who "agrees to differ" from her husband, and lives, *more Americano,* in Italy when she is not at New York or on the way between the two, the husband being domiciled wholly in England. There are, indeed, portraits of ladies enough and clear enough; the only one who is not portrayed so as to make the reader understand her is the heroine. This may be a bit of mystification on Mr. James's part; if so, it can only be said that it is not a novelist's business to mystify his readers, certainly not at this length. That he has aimed at brevity may sometimes excuse an author for being obscure; but obscurity through three long volumes is unpardonable. Mr. James sins in a small matter of style. He has taken to coining and using some very awkward words. "Modicity" as the noun of *moderate,* "superurban" of a house on a hill above a town, "fine" in the sense of *clever* (French *fin*), are not desirable additions to the language. Nor does the epithet "weary" as applied to the brickwork of an old house add much to the picture. When we read of "doors perched upon little 'stoops' of red stone, which descended *sidewise* to the street," we are disposed to smile alike at the ingenuity with which the writer repudiates one term belonging to the English of the United States and the simplicity with which he adopts another. To revert once more to general criticism: there is no doubt that reticence is a virtue in a novelist, but it may be carried too far, and this Mr. James, from a feeling, probably, of repugnance for the gushing and sensational, seems to have done. He should remember that much of human life cannot be painted in "tertiary" tints, and that if he wishes to be a master in the art of portraying it he must furnish his box with some stronger colours, and lay them on boldly.

M[ayo] W[illiamson] H[azeltine]. "Mr. James's New Novel." New York *Sun,* 27 November 1881, p. 2.

It is doubtless true that Mr. Henry James, Jr., has not exhibited the mastery of the emotions displayed by the greatest novelists, and for which, among living writers of fiction, Mr. Bret Harte is conspicuous. But although he may never draw a tear, he can evoke a sustained and earnest sympathy on behalf of many of his characters; and while he does not provoke a laugh, the reader is often moved to smile, and the prevailing mood is one of unclouded satisfaction and calm delight. The author's observation is so keen and fine, his judgment is so shrewd and trustworthy, his tact so delicate, and his taste so refined, that you gain from his books the same kind of entertainment and instruction that the conversation of an accomplished man, long conversant with the best society of both hemispheres, is able to impart. The phases of life which Mr. James has made the object of study are, of course, much more circumscribed and more subdued in tone than those which we see portrayed in the works of Fielding, Dickens, George Eliot, and Bret Harte, or, in other words, the mirror which he holds up to nature is not a pier glass but a hand glass. It is, indeed, a curious fact that in his whole range of novels the author has not depicted, or even outlined, a figure which had not at least some outward pretensions to social respectability. He has not even ventured on a reproduction of that high life below stairs with which Thackeray, conscious of his own limitations, sought to widen and diversify his theme. But for the very reason that Mr. James confines himself exclusively to the study of good society, of men and women who, to a careless eye, all seem to dress alike, to think alike, and to act alike, and who are distinguished from one another, not by sharp divergences of contour and color, but by slight linear variations and faint diversities of shade, he is compelled to use only pencils of the finest point and pigments of a soft and exquisite graduation: that is to say, he must demonstrate an unusual command over the resources of our language. It is, in fact, his style which constitutes Mr. James's capital merit. The adroitness, the flexibility, the neatness of his diction—his felicitous projections of an illusive thought, his arch suggestiveness, his pregnant reticence, his irony, his innuendoes—the smoothness and the gleam which yet betray no mark of graving tool or burnisher on phrase or sentence; all these, and kindred proofs of technical excellence, are incessantly encountered in Mr. James's narratives. It is this power of expression which is more and more noticeable in the work of this patient and conscientious artist, and in none of his books has it been more vigorously and admirably displayed than in *The Portrait of a Lady* (Houghton, Mifflin & Co.).

In this, as in so many other stories by the same hand, Americans supposed to represent the best social traditions of their own country are brought in contact with English people of the higher class. A young lady, Miss Isabel Archer, is taken by her aunt from an old-fashioned house in Albany to an English country house belonging to the American partner in a London banking firm. We are given to understand that the banker's title to our close and respectful attention depends upon the fact that he has obstinately refused to be Anglicized; but inasmuch as he has long retired from active business, the reader cannot help inquiring why he does not return and finish his days in the country to which he professes such unwavering fidelity. Indeed, the one substantial proof with which Mr. Touchett—such is the banker's name—supports his patriotic pretensions is the frequent interjection of the phrases "I guess" and "I aint" in language which otherwise conforms to the English idiom. We should be much more impressed, however, by these verbal shortcomings if the author did not make an English viscount say "I wont" for "I will not." His son, Ralph Touchett, is a much more distinctly conceived and interesting person. He has been at Oxford, where all traces of his American origin were effaced; but inasmuch as residence in England, even when followed by a complete assimilation of English speech and manner, does not make a man an Englishman in the absence of traditions, relationships, and a clearly marked social status, he is virtually a man without a country, and is fain to call himself cosmopolitan. These unattached citizens of the world are apt to be critics and philosophers in a small, inoffensive way, and Mr. Ralph Touchett is the more inclined to assume this attitude because he is supposed to be disabled for active work by some incurable disease. All the young men who encounter Miss Isabel Archer in Europe fall in love with her, and her cousin Ralph does not escape; it is, indeed, through his intercession that the elder Touchett is induced to leave his wife's niece, who has scarcely a penny of her own, some sixty thousand pounds. Before this fortune fell to her, the young lady had refused one Caspar Goodwood of Boston and an English Viscount. It does not appear that Mr. Goodwood had anything to recommend him, except that he was tall and athletic, and had probably rowed in the Harvard boat, was an honest, straightforward fellow, incapable of wounding or betraying a creature weaker than himself, and had a good deal of money invested in New England factories. But although this robust young person, when compared with Ralph Touchett or Lord Warburton, fails to excite much admiration, he seems to have been the only man who could touch the heart of the heroine. Of Lord Warburton she makes quick work, but the reader is surprised at nothing of this kind when he observes that in her colloquies with the Viscount and the Viscount's sisters, this American young woman, although suddenly transported from Albany to the British islands, is not guilty of a single offence against English idiom. Far from imitating the elder Touchett in his adherence to "I guess," she shows herself, within twenty-four hours after reaching London, as minutely perfect in the colloquial rules of English society as Ralph Touchett himself, whose labors at Oxford we suspect had been mainly concentrated upon that object. Singularly enough, the author in his catalogue of Miss Archer's merits does not allude to this extraordinary, not to say incredible, performance.

The ground on which Miss Archer rejects her first two lovers will seem curious enough to most readers, and yet it is in some sort characteristic of all Mr. James's heroines. She refuses the Viscount—not because she does not love him, for it is nowhere intimated that she deems love a condition *sine qua non* of marriage—while for the young man from Boston, who is also twice or thrice repulsed, she manifestly entertains, as we have said, the warmest feeling of which she seems to be capable. But she does not like either of them or anybody so well as she likes herself. She wants to be free, to see the world, to follow her own inclinations, to obey no one's will but her own, or as she, we imagine, would express it, to stretch her wings, expand her faculties, develop her individuality. She is entirely without the strong propulsion toward marriage which is believed to be instinctive with her sex. She is strong-minded, not in the narrow sense of desiring to compete with man in their specific vocations, but in the sense that her head is much more active than her heart, and that she is conscious of no desire to lean on any one. The great blunder of her life, her marriage in Florence to a specious, shallow American castaway named Gilbert Osborne [*sic*], comes from her essentially masculine trait of self-reliance, with its natural incidents—a resentment of interference, and a relish for protecting one she intuitively recognizes to be weaker than herself. Through the intermediation of an artful adventuress, one Madame Merle, who straightway detects the weak point in Miss Archer's armor, the latter's sympathies are strongly excited for Osmond and his young daughter, whose straitened means and isolated lives are ascribed by her to undeserved misfortune and a noble pride. She pities the man, yet it does not appear that her pity is ever kindled into passionate love; and when she marries him the uppermost feeling in her

mind is one of exultation that her rôle in life is active and not passive; that instead of being a pensioner and a protégée, like most women, she has reversed the normal distribution of parts, and is herself the guardian and benefactor. She had refused to be a viscountess from an apprehension that her own personality would be cramped and overshadowed by her husband's. The outcome of her self-centered aspirations is that she falls an easy prey to an adventuress and a rascal, who need her money partly to make themselves more comfortable, and partly to provide for their own illegitimate child.

In the drawing of these figures, Mme. Merle and Gilbert Osmond, the author's artistic skill is strikingly exemplified. We know of few novelists now writing in English who would not have been apt to mar the life-like effect of these characters by too much emphasis, forgetting that if their speech and normal aspect had not been the perfect cloak we see them to be, they never could have played their parts so long and so successfully in society, and have hoodwinked so completely a very clever girl. It is a notable tribute to the author's conception of the man Osmond, and to the consummate execution of his idea, that we are unable to lay our finger on a single word or overt act which adequately justifies the loathing which, in common with his wife, we gradually conceive for him. Our flesh creeps and our gorge rises as if our eye detected across the path we were to tread the tortuous and slimy track of a noisome snake. It follows that while the whole account of the heroine's relations with her husband may be regarded as a powerful plea in favor of divorce, yet it does not appear that Osmond's post-marital conduct, however detestable, offered any grounds on which a court (unless it were in some of our Western States) could base a decree of absolute separation. The reader, accordingly, cannot fail to share the feeling of hopelessness and shipwreck with which, after a visit to her cousin's deathbed, Mrs. Osmond returns to Italy and recognizes herself as condemned to life-long companionship with her miserable husband.

"Mr. James's Latest Novel."
New York *Times*, 27 November 1881, p. 5.

Mr. James's last story is unsatisfactory in its beginning and in its end. It is spun out too much, and suffers the reader at times to exclaim at its dullness. Nor can it be said that the characters often elicit sympathy from their charm or nobility. For all that, "The Portrait of a Lady" is a deeply interesting study of men and women, of motives and moods. In spite of a certain amount of irritation which it will be likely to excite; in spite of not a little thinness and unnaturalness which belong to the characters; notwithstanding the care with which they have been finished and the skill with which they are presented, one is never quite content to lay aside the volume without knowing what has become of them so far as Mr. James is willing to let his reader know. It is in the accessories rather than the central spirit of his characters that Mr. James is a modern follower of naturalism. The minuteness with which he describes their looks and acts, the apparently unnecessary precautions he takes to follow their every thought and shade of thought, would become unbearably tedious were he less subtle. One thinks, every now and then, of Trollope and his everlasting commonplaces. But Mr. James has the depth or the adroitness, to turn what seems to promise to be merely a commonplace into something that has a point after all. To many readers the point may seem small—so small that it might have been omitted. But it lies with the painter whether he wants to paint a cabinet picture or dash off an impression on a big scale. In "A Portrait of a Lady" he indulges himself more than ever in the pleasure of putting little strokes everywhere, so that at times it is felt that he enjoys the describing and making move Rosier, the vapid Paris-bred youth, who hardly has an idea above chinamania, as much as the characterization of his heroine. The latter will come in for more searching criticism than any other figure, because Mr. James has already drawn the portraits of several young American ladies who were for the time famous enough. Daisy Miller was the most famous. In Isabel Archer we have another variety of girl, one who has been to Europe before, and, though poor, still fairly well educated as the educations of girls go. The problem is much subtler than that of Daisy Miller. The characters are chiefly American. From Mme. Merle, who might be a European did she not acknowledge America as her birth-place, and from Gilbert Osmond, who has lived so long in Italy that he has nothing of the American left in him, the various gradations of American character are marked through Isabel to what is meant for pure and unadulterated American types in Caspar Goodwood and the lady correspondent, Henrietta Stackpole. In this list, near the top, stand Mr. and Mrs. Touchett and Ralph, their invalid son, the cousin of the heroine. The latter has no end of lovers and offers. There is Lord Warburton, the type of the better side of young English titled men of education and radical convictions. There is Ralph, who hides his love. There is Osmond, who loves, but selfishly, and in order to make the second marriage successful—the villain of the play. There is uncompromising Caspar, for whom is re-served, so the reader understands at the last, the perilous and unlikely task of con-soling the heroine for her first mistake in matrimony. It may be doubted whether the reader cares to contemplate this. For Caspar, in spite of his rocklike constancy and his self-abnegation to please Isabel, is a little too arid a rock to rest the eyes upon with pleasure, and if the hint that after the villain husband shall be disposed of—by death or divorce, as the reader may elect—this dry figure should possess all those charms of mind and body which the hero-ine has to dispose of, will not be taken in good part.

The finest passages out of many that merit the word fine are those devoted to Ralph's talks with his lovely cousin. The figure of Ralph is appealing to start with. Wealth, position, education go for noth-ing when ill-health has crippled a man and made him ugly. His death scene is moving to a degree which Mr. James has never be-fore attained; it may well be called his highest-water mark in fiction. There are many passages and many more sentences that would do to quote were there space to introduce much that goes before and comes after. Mr. James's style is rather in-terlaced; it takes hold below before it lets go above; when one comes to look for quotations they are not easily lifted out of the context to place before the critical public. Perhaps the remarks of Miss Stack-pole, the lady correspondent, may serve, such as when speaking to Lord War-burton:

> "I don't approve of Lords as an institu-tion. . . . However, I do think of giving up—the little there is left of it—some of these days." [*Novels 1881–1886,* p. 323]

She has been invited to Gardencourt, the house of an American banker living in London, who is the uncle of Isabel, the heroine. The latter expostulates:

> "There are plenty of other subjects—there are subjects all around you." . . .
>
> "He would have died of it!" Isabel exclaimed—"not of the severity, but of the publicity." [*Novels 1881–1886,* p. 278]

Notwithstanding the excellence of much of the thought which has gone to the making of this novel, there will be few readers who will not resent its length. Some may accuse Mr. James of padding. But this is hardly fair, for certainly no more conscientious workman is now writ-ing for the fiction of the monthly press than Mr. James. Those who are impatient should remember that everything cannot be demanded of a writer. He must have his pet weaknesses like other men. One of the gravest in Mr. James just now is his ten-dency to write two words in place of one. And it should be noted that, although the tone of his novels is not bracing, it is ele-vated. Ralph has beautiful and noble traits. Isabel is a charming, if somewhat unsympathetic, spirit, whose aspirations are high and pure.

"*The Portrait of a Lady.*" *Critic* 1 (3 December 1881), 333–34.

All lovers of the analytical method in novel-writing will find in 'The Portrait of a Lady' the perfection of this form. There is not a single character in the book to whom we grow enthusiastically attached, not one whom we approve of steadily. They are the best when they are left half drawn. Lord Warburton stands out as an honest, big-hearted Englishman, because he is left alone. Caspar Goodwood, who in only meagrely developed, clings to our minds chiefly because he clings to the heart of the heroine. Ralph Touchett, from whom we shrink at first, grows pleasantly companionable after a while. He is the most fully drawn of the male characters. But our attachment to all three seems to come mainly from the fact of their dogged faithfulness to the heroine. They all have substantial qualities, mostly of a negative character. They are all gentlemanly fellows, except when they get intrusive, as they all do sooner or later. The women are none of them quite satisfactory. They are all dominated by some stubborn quality, which gets the better of them. There is one general trait which all the characters have in common. They are all excessively witty and caustic. They bite, and snap, and criticise each other—that is, they bite and snap politely. Mr. James's idea of dialogue seems to be that it is only meant to afford the personages an opportunity to develop each other's character. When he is tired of minute analysis himself, or thinks his reader may be weary of it, he varies the form only, and sets the personages to doing it for him. Each gentleman takes his turn in criticizing the young lady. Each lady seems bent on some inquisitorial proceeding—all in a polished, refined way, of course, but persistently. The author has no skill in making action tell the story. It must be done by the analytical method, or not at all. And the characters develop themselves, not to the reader alone, but to each other. The action is nowhere abundant, but the analysis is protracted—not tiresome, or dull, or unilluminated—but still protracted through scores on scores of pages. It is only in description that the author lets a word do the work of a page, and here he shows great skill. His touches, while without the illumination which a spiritual imagination might supply, are happy, neat, and very effective. He presents what scenery he needs, but seems to be easily overcome with ennui, as if some editorial function had brought him acquainted with many young ladies' journals, or as if reading many books of travel had made him mad. Yet who ever gets tired of Hawthorne's descriptions? Our author seldom gives us the *tout ensemble* of a drawing-room; but threading the assembly carefully, he brings us at once to the corner where his persons are. We are almost tempted to say that his victims are isolated at once, that the process through which they are to be put may be unhampered. Here again we lose an atmosphere, or the possibility of one. Perhaps this is the vice of his methods. We hardly dare say that it is the only one. He seems able to deal with but one thing at a time. When we have finished Lord Warburton, as we think, pretty effectually, then we may take up Madame Merle. When she is labeled and ticketed we may have Mr. Osmond. When Mr. Osmond is well under way and has lost our sympathy, we may start afresh with his daughter; and as Lord Warburton by this time shows signs of life, we may stop long enough to knock him on the head—ah, that was a harsh word, and we take it back; we will only stretch him on the table. We say little of the nationality of the characters, because they seem to us to represent national peculiarities only in a gross way. Most of the persons are American, but so alienated that the type is confused. In Henrietta Stackpole we recognize very clearly the American girl turned journalist, and a certain freedom of motion and social forwardness in all is pretty distinctively American. But all the persons are on their travels. We recognize the girls in American social life, but they are second-rate. In good society in any of our large cities they would be considered peculiar. Still with all his limitations, we are disposed to place Mr. James among our keenest and most vigorous character painters.

"The Portrait of a Lady." Pall Mall Gazette [England], 3 December 1881, p. 20.

The doctrine of renunciation is older than Goethe, and has been practised by celebrated persons both before and since his time, independently of Christian influences. Mahommed applied it to Damascus, the late President Garfield to the latter chapters of "Pickwick." We have often thought that an English novel reader, especially of the more critical kind, would do well to apply it to the novels of Mr. Henry James, except that the application would be rather hard upon Mr. James. For Mr. James is a most terrible flatterer of us and of our country, and his flattery is all the more insinuating and dangerous to the moral tone because it is indirect, and even, so to say, unconscious. It is not that he does not speak well and think well of England and Englishmen on the whole; but we are proof against that. No Englishman of the old block really cares a straw for foreign praise or blame: it might be better if he did. But what no Englishman—even Englishmen being human beings—can resist is the subtle juxtaposition of unpleasant persons by which Mr. James contrives to throw up English pleasantness; and this juxtaposition becomes all the more terribly seductive when the unpleasant persons are, as they are almost wholly in his books, Americans. The Englishman who can behold any one of Mr. James's clever portraits of his own countrymen and countrywomen without a violent temptation to echo the Pharisee in the parable must be either of a very fine moral fibre or of an intellectual fibre very far from fine. Here, for instance, is this book. We should call it the very best piece of work Mr. James has done if we did not feel that he had bribed us so shamefully. There are many very carefully drawn characters. There is the heroine, who, with the best intentions, wrecks her life in a way which would have been simply impossible to a more unsophisticated person, by mistaking a selfish and superfine snob for a great genius and a man of extreme distinction. She is American. There is her friend Miss Henrietta Stackpole, whose really excellent nature—the nature of clever and amiable women all over the world—is overlaid heavily with the special follies and vulgarities of a certain class of American girl of the period. There is the miserable creature before mentioned who is enabled to hoodwink a few silly women as to his real character merely by means of the special dilettante varnish of the expatriated Yankee. The worst woman of the book, one of the vilest characters in fiction, who acts as a kind of legal and decent procuress to the lover who has cast her off, and who deliberately sacrifices the guileless and trusting heroine, is American. A kind of serious wild animal who pays uncouth courtship to Isabel, the heroine, and who is left "waiting" for her, in wild animal fashion at the end of the book, is a "perpendicular Bostonian" of the purest type, who has taken out a patent for manufacturing something or other. The most tolerable persons of Mr. James's own nationality in the novel are the heroine's uncle, who appears but little, and has lived thirty-five years in England; his son Ralph, born, bred, and educated among us, and, barring a few slips of taste, an excellent fellow; and the Countess Gemini, sister of the dilettante scoundrel, whose manners are queer and her morals non-existent, but who has at least good-nature if not a good heart. What is a modest and blushing British reader to do when an American author determines in this way that the American dogs shall not have the best of it?

To speak more seriously, though we cannot help thinking Mr. James unfair towards his countrymen, this book is a very clever book, and a book of very great interest. If it has a fault it is a curious and certainly a rare one—the fault of demanding and deserving almost too much attention. There is hardly a sentence which has not been written with evident and almost superfluous care, hardly an incident or a remark which has not been inserted with evident purpose. Mr. James demands that his readers shall wrestle with him all through, and not let go their hold for a moment. This intense fashion of writing sometimes produces a slight feeling of weariness in the reader, and often leads to an indulgence on the part of the writer in what for want of a better word we can only call *marivaudage*. It is a very different kind of *marivaudage* from that of Marivaux certainly.[1] But one cannot help thinking, as Mr. James and his characters metaphysically flirt or argue in a strange Bostonian tongue, of Crébillon's capital satire: "Rendez-moi compte exactement de ce que vous avez fait, et non seulement de ce que vous avez pensé, mais même de ce que vous avez voulu penser;" or, again, "Quoi? ne trouver que les mêmes termes, ne pas oser séparer les uns des autres ceux qu'on a accoutumé de faire marcher ensemble? Pourquoi serait-il défendu de faire faire connoissance à des mots qui ne se sont jamais vus et qui croient qu'ils ne se conviendront pas?"[2] We open "The Portrait of a Lady" literally and honestly at hazard, after copying these words of the improper author of "Tanzaï et Néadarné," and we find these words: "I am not bent on being miserable," said Isabel; "I have always been intensely determined to be happy, and I have often believed I should be. I have told people that: you can ask them. But it comes over me every now and then that I can never be happy in any extraordinary way, not by turning away, by separating myself." Oddly enough, this last suppression of the conjunction is Marivaux to the life. Here is another instance: "I don't know; I have no plans." "Happy man! that's a little nude, but it's very free." This sort of "preciousness" is no doubt very attractive to some people, and the ingenuity of some, and the unexpectedness of all of it, is not unengaging at first sight; but by the end of the third volume it sometimes gets a little wearisome.

The situation of the book is a good one and the characters are well grouped round it. Isabel Archer is one of the American girls who, if their biographers are to be trusted, "look at life too much as a doctor's prescription" (as she herself says) and are always wondering whether this and that will do them good; who have (it is again a quotation) "always been expected to have emotions and impressions," and who, as a result of this, present to the possibly prejudiced European a somewhat morbid appearance. She is a good girl, however, and an amiable one; she refuses the perpendicular Bostonian apparently because he is of a type too familiar to her, and she refuses Lord Warburton, an English millionaire, because she cannot make out the type of a reforming English peer at all. Her cousin, who is a hopeless invalid, persuades his father to leave her a considerable fortune to assist her in her experiments upon life. There is no need to tell the history of her complete failure—it has been hinted at sufficiently already. The plot gives scope for a certain amount of pathos and for a good deal of gentle social satire, and Mr. James has availed himself of these opportunities to the utmost. Indeed, the book is, in a simile of his own, "as ripe as an October pear," and the afore-mentioned *marivaudage* is, after all, nothing much worse than the slight approach to "sleepiness" which such a pear often exhibits. One very remarkable thing about it is the extraordinary pains which have been spent even on the minor characters, such as the little American dandy and bric-à-brac hunter, Edward Rosier, and his beloved Pansy, the ingénue. Nor, whatever objection on the score of repulsiveness may be taken to some of them, can any of the characters be said to be unnatural, with one exception, that of Mdme. Merle, the *intrigante*. Mr. James has attempted a very difficult task in endeavouring, like a conscientious novelist, not merely to attribute to her but to exhibit in her an almost supernatural cleverness and social ability. The reader is not in the least deceived by her, nor by Gilbert Osmond, her rascally ex-lover; and Mr. James has not quite succeeded in showing that there were excuses for Isabel in her deception. However, these are points which may be differently judged. There can hardly be much difference of opinion as to the great, if not unmixed, merit of this "Portrait of a Lady." We do not know a living English novelist who could have written it.

Notes

1 Pierre Carlet de Chamblain Marivaux (1688–1763).
2 Claude Crébillon, *Tanzai et Néadarné* (1734).

New York *Herald,* 12 December 1881, p. 5.

Here are two novels which may be considered typical of the modern school of English fiction. "The Portrait of a Lady" is by Mr. Henry James, Jr., an American, and "A Laodicean" is by Mr. Thomas Hardy, an Englishman. Oddly enough, the titles of these novels might be interchanged. It would seem as though Mr. Hardy once said to Mr. James:—"Let each of us write a novel with a young woman who is neither hot nor cold as the central character." To which Mr. James might have replied:—"Very well, mine shall be an American and yours and English girl." So Mr. James made his Isabel Archer, a young lady from Albany with keen wits and piquant independence of character. A young man from Boston, Mr. Caspar Goodwood, whom she apparently loves, is at the start left with his proposal of marriage unuttered because her wealthy aunt, Mrs. Touchett, has come to carry her over to Europe. There Mrs. Touchett's consumptive son, Ralph, and her son's friend, Lord Warburton, fall in love with her, but she refuses each in turn. Ralph induces his father to settle a fortune on her, and Isabel, now in every sense her own mistress, marries a man named Osmond, who proves to be merely a specious adventurer. The novel ends with Isabel refusing to run away with Caspar Goodwood and returning to her worthless husband in a manner suggestive of a sequel. Mr. Hardy's heroine is Paula Power, the daughter of an English railroad contractor, lately deceased. She is immensely wealthy and resides in an old castle formerly belonging to an ancient county family. Thither George Somerset, a young architect, led by a telegraph wire, finds his way at night. He returns in the morning to sketch and remains to make love. He is hired to design an addition to the old castle, and makes a declaration which Paula meets by a curious permission to love her, but a positive refusal to say whether or no she returns it. Then comes Captain de Stancey, a scion of the old but impoverished county family, who, by the excessively odd machinations of his illegitimate son, Willy Dare, is induced to fall in love with Miss Power. The captain urges his suit all over Europe. Somerset being discredited in Paula's eyes by some shallow trickery of Dare's, the lady consents to marry De Stancey. At the last moment, however, all is cleared up and Somerset is the lucky man. In both of the heroines there is the same outward display of insensibility, the same inability to choose definitely on reasonable grounds. Neither is light minded enough to be called capricious; but they are nevertheless girls of strong reasoning powers liable to a sudden whim. Further likeness in the stories may be found in the fact that the scenes of each novel are laid first in old English residences, and that in both the characters go chasing each other over the continent of Europe. But significant as these likenesses are the treatment is widely different. Mr. James reminds one of nothing so much as an artist in fine mosaics. Bit by bit in infinitesimal portions he completes his figures. So deftly is this done that the process has as much fascination as the picture. It is not like painting, for there is no retouching. Every little colored particle is added with a distinctness of purpose that is striking, and thousands of them go to make a complete figure. Such minute analysis and elaborate synthesis are elsewhere unknown to fiction. There are portraits drawn in broader and subtler lines, but nowhere is the process of character building as uninterruptedly kept up to the end. Mr. Hardy has a more picturesque, more tricky method, though his art is quite as great. He leaves his characters often to be half inferred and frequently seems to take more pains about their surroundings than themselves, but he ends by making you believe you have understood them from the beginning. He is Robertsonian, to make a dramatic comparison. He loves to contrive odd rather than heroic episodes. One of his peculiarities is his love to air an intimate knowledge of architecture. Mr. James is so concerned about his figures that he seems never in a hurry to move them about in his picture. Mr. Hardy seems to take a mildly sardonic pleasure in putting his figures in queer positions, where they are constantly on the verge of appearing utterly ridiculous. These writers, reflecting modern society, give one an idea that its most notable feature is self-repression. Mr. James is always at a level of brilliancy in writing which defies a loss of interest, though it seems at times that he should have produced his effects with half the expenditure of force. Mr. Hardy sustains the interest admirably too, the more so that you are never certain when something specially brilliant will shoot out of the ordinary level of his work. Both make you feel somehow that while earnestness may yet exist on earth real seriousness is a thing out of ordinary life; that the best thing life can do nowadays is to furnish us with genteel comedy.

London *Times*, 14 December 1881, p. 3.

Mr. James pays himself a graceful compliment in assuming the forbearance of his readers and reviewers when writing a novel of extraordinary length on a singularly unsensational subject. His portrait of a lady covers a canvas of vast proportions, while it is finished off with the minute detail of the most painstaking miniature painter. Nor is there anything very original about her; on the contrary, she is the old and familiar acquaintance whom we have met in many of his former stories. Isabella Archer is his typical American girl, who joins to her good looks a certain indecision of character which seems to exercise a strange fascination on the Englishmen who try in vain to fathom her. We are persuaded that personally we should have been sorry to marry her; but the only certainty we have beyond that is that she never, under any circumstances, knows her own mind. Naturally, on landing in England, she takes all hearts by storm. She might have counted in the first week or two on at least a couple of brilliant offers, to say nothing of a lover of fortune and talent she has left sighing on the other side of the Atlantic. But Miss Archer will have nothing to say to any of them. When Lord Warburton proposes, whom she really likes, who deserves to be loved, and who is enormously rich, she can only stammer out a hesitating "No," as it seems out of sheer perversity. And as she is morbidly on her guard against attractions, she appears to accept the husband of her choice on an impulse, if not on the principle of repulsions. Of course she is miserable, but, although we know she must be suffering, she still remains an enigma. So much so that we doubt whether the author is right in crediting her with any excessive sensibility; and we rather take her for one of those beautiful, but cold-blooded animals who may be operated upon without appreciable discomfort. There are other characters in the story who are either more engaging or entertaining. There is her cousin Touchett, son of a wealthy Anglicized American banker, who, though wasting away with a mortal disease, nevertheless falls placidly in love with the beauty, and persuades his father to dower her with an ample fortune, which subsequently lands her in her unhappy marriage. There is Henrietta Stackpole, the accomplished and energetic female correspondent of the New York *Interviewer,* who has a weakness for abusing private hospitality by photographing scenes of domestic privacy; but, nevertheless, brings an Englishman of good position to her feet, dragging him along at the wheels of her matrimonial chariot. And there is Mr. Touchett, senior, who, in his semi-dotage and good-humoured imbecility, reminds us of Mr. Wemmick's "Ancient Parent," in Dickens's "Great Expectations." But disagreeable personages decidedly predominate, and the sombre pictures of our imperfect human nature form no unfitting surrounding to the central portrait of the lady.

"Mr. James's *Portrait of a Lady.*" *Literary World* [Boston] 12 (17 December 1881), 473–74.

This is a book that piques both mental analysis and conscience in a very curious fashion. The root fact about it is that it is a representative society novel of the nineteenth century, and as such exposes very grave social drifts and problems. It is a book of conventional life with some highly unconventional people in it, and yet fastidiously clean in its morals and situations. In parts it runs to metaphysics, like George Eliot's novels, to the delay of the plot; yet its style is as clear as crystal and as sharp cut. Put by the side of a novel of Sir Walter Scott's, the style is epigram itself; not stately, picturesque, or poetical, but strong, incisive, and prompt, as the business temper of the age. Full of love scenes and motives, more or less complex, we hardly remember a book of so little sentiment, at least of the effusive and old fashioned kind. It might almost be called a cruel book in its dissection of character and exposure of the nerves and sinews of human actions. It is not a book to inspire, but to instruct and warn. It is curiously free from any disposition to preach morals or religion, and yet in the antitheses of the social life unfolded it is a well-bred but tremendous homily in behalf of something better. Except for a certain twilight of virtue, due possibly to a Christendom yet extant, this book might have been written among or for cultured heathen. This strikes us as a curious sign in literature; perhaps a prophecy. Mr. James is a realistic painter of landscapes with a minuteness in portraiture which reminds us of DeFoe. His analyses are often exquisitely keen and neat; but any sort of enthusiasm is markedly absent from his book.

As everybody is supposed to have read this book, an account of the mental and moral assets of its characters would hardly be in order. They are in general people whose leisure runs into ennui, and whose theories of life tend to cynicism and the repose of fate. Life is not worth living for some of them, and a few are hardly fit to live. Isabel Archer, the heroine, is a high mettled American girl, who goes out to England under the patronage of her aunt, Mrs. Touchett, to see life and culture herself, and sees more of life than is either pleasing or profitable. She is able early in her career to refuse an English lord; escapes the catastrophe of an offer from her own cousin; drives her most persistent American lover, Casper Goodwood, to despair in two hemispheres; has a fortune left her by her uncle; and most unaccountably marries in Florence another expatri-

ated American, a widower and a dilettante, half Italian and wholly selfish, Gilbert Osmond, who, with utter decorum, leads her a most wretched life in a marriage of mistake and misery. Her old lovers flock about her in the free foreign circle to which she belongs, not much to their profit or her own. Finally, in revolt against a marital life which is only a lingering death to soul and body, she goes back to England, against her husband's will, to watch at the bedside of her dying cousin, and afterwards, in the close of the story, Casper Goodwood tempts her in such guise and temper as lessen the offense in both to turn her back upon her marriage and go with him. This, in the book, at least, she does not do, yet the story closes with a neatly arranged puzzle as to whether she will or will not do it some other time. The question of her unrevealed future has, in Mr. James's handling, two very distinct sides to it, and the true answer must depend on what a woman with Isabel Osmond's curious makeup will be prone to do. For our own part we judge she will. This puzzle, we presume, is already at work in the minds of many lady readers. What she ought to do depends, of course, on the standard by which her judges will measure duty.

Of course there is much episode and byplay from other characters. Madam Merle is an eminently European product, who possesses almost every charm but virtue itself, with which she apparently quarreled at a very early age. In her and the Countess Gemmini one beholds what womanhood with elegance but without integrity is worth. Madam Merle, who makes Isabel Archer's match with Osmond, has her own flesh and blood in Osmond's house in the shape of a most charming Italian maiden, Pansy, who passes for Osmond's child, as she is, and as his dead wife's also, as she is not. The situation, of course, admits of contretemps and ill omens, which abound. Two of the most wholesome characters in the book are Henrietta Stackpole, an American newspaper correspondent, piquant, patriotic, inquisitive, and loyal to everybody; who runs about Europe in the most unaccountable way to pick up knowledge for her paper at home; and Mr. Bantling, whom she condescends at last to marry. Mrs. Touchett and her invalid son are possible persons who have their parts in this singular story.

As a representative book this *Portrait of a Lady* is worth study. It is of a new epoch and has its own virtues. The minor notes of the age, we might almost call them notes of despair, run through its pages. If it be not an unhealthy book, it is at least nonhealthy. There is no sea air in it, and its sunshine shows through mists. One bright baby in a happy mother's arms would have more. We hear in this book a semi-wail, as it were, of the latter Roman empire. If life be a fine art, society, as here shown, works in marble. We are so old-fashioned as to say "Let us work in soul." The boulevards have their charm, but so have the wild hills and the sea.

Our old English writers loved to tell of gentle milkmaids and girls that tended flocks. Mr. James and men like him prefer the product of the salon and the casino. *Chacun à son goût.* This book in some respects is not so much "the portrait of a lady" as of the age.

[John Hay].
"James's *The Portrait of a Lady.*"
New York *Tribune,* 25 December 1881, p. 8.

If there is anything in the motto of "art for art's sake," if the way of doing a thing is, as many claim, of more importance in literature than the thing done, then this last novel of Mr. James needs no justification or apology. No work printed in recent years, on either side the Atlantic or on either side the English Channel, surpasses this in seriousness of intention, in easy scope and mastery of material, in sustained and spontaneous dignity and grace of style, in wit and epigram, and, on the whole, in clear conception and accurate delineation of character. The title was a stumbling-block to many, as the story pursued its leisurely course in *The Atlantic Monthly,* and now that it is finished it is the title which affords to criticism its easiest attack.[1] It is claimed that the heroine is of all the characters the one least clearly painted, least perfectly understood. But it would not be difficult to say that we know as much of her and of her motives as the author chooses for us to know, and the interest of the novel comes in great part from the vagueness of our acquaintance with Miss Archer; and after all, when we lay down the book, we cannot deny, if we are candid, that we know as much of the motives which induced her to refuse two gallant gentlemen and to marry a selfish and soulless scoundrel as we do of the impulses which lead our sisters and cousins to similar results. No one can complain of the clearness with which the other characters are drawn. There is hardly a sharper portrait in our literature, and certainly none more delightful, than Ralph Touchett. None who read the opening chapters of the story a year ago can forget the slight shiver of apprehension they felt when Mr. James distinctly announced that Ralph Touchett was clever, and when Lord Warburton declared that "he was never bored when he came to Gardencourt; one gets such uncommonly good talk." It shows a fine arrogance in the most hardened jouster to throw down such a challenge as that. It is said that Shakespeare killed Mercutio early in the play where he appears, for fear of being killed by him; but Mr. James evidently has no such fear of his own creations. From the first chapter to the last, Ralph is "clever, witty and charming," as Mr. James tells us in the beginning, with a charm which overcomes the tedium of hopeless illness and the repulsiveness of death. The book is full of living and breathing characters. Mr. Trollope has never drawn a better English nobleman than Lord Warburton, the splendor of whose environment is delicately suggested, never described, and whose manners are painted in a dozen subtle phrases like these: "He had a certain fortunate, brilliant, exceptional look—the air of a happy temperament fertilized by a high civilization—which would have made almost any observer envy him at a venture"; "his English address, in which a vague shyness seemed to offer itself as an element of good breeding; in which the only defect was a difficulty of achieving transitions." The portrait of Osmond is one of those wonderful pictures in which Mr. James excels, drawn entirely from the outside, but as perfect as if his acts and conversations had been supplemented by voluminous pages of soliloquy. His sister the Countess is equally good; so is the dry, practical, caustic Mrs. Touchett; so is the travelling newspaper woman, Miss Stack-

pole. It is almost worth while, after reading Mr. James's just but unflattering portrait of Henrietta, to look at a novel of Hamilton Aïdé in which the same sort of person is introduced—that you may see the difference between the work of a master and that of a bungler. In Aïdé's story, "Poet and Peer," the American "lady-correspondent" is characterized merely by the copious use of the word "vurry" for "very," "Amarrican" for "American," a taste for filthy scandal, and a propensity to say "right away" in places where no Yankee would ever expect it.[2] Mr. James's method is altogether different, as will be seen from this brief extract. Miss Stackpole is visiting at the house of an American banker domiciled in England, and is discovered to be writing a letter for her newspaper describing the place and the people. Miss Archer protests:

> "I don't think you ought to do that." . . . "Just let me make a note of it, and I will put it in a letter." [*Novels 1881–1886*, pp. 278–79]

Further on, Henrietta, who is a ferocious patriot—though she ends by a dreadful act of recreancy—is attacking Ralph for not sufficiently loving his country, and for having no regular occupation:

> Ralph bespoke her attention for a small Wattean hanging near, which represented a gentleman in a pink doublet and hose and a ruff, leaning against the pedestal of the statue of a nymph in a garden, and playing the guitar to two ladies seated on the grass. . . . "Ah, set it down a little to my natural charm!" Ralph urged. [*Novels 1881–1886*, pp. 281–82]

In every detail of execution this book shows a greater facility, a richer command of resources than any of its predecessors. The delicate verbal felicities which distinguished the author's earlier works are here found in such abundance that quotation becomes an embarrassing task. The description of Touchett's house in the first chapter is altogether admirable for its completeness and its reserve:

It stood upon a low hill, above the river—the river being the Thames, at some forty miles from London. . . . But it was none the less a charming walk down to the water. [*Novels 1881–1886*, pp. 194–95]

Near the close of the book, when the heroine begins to feel that her life has been thrown away, there is another bit of landscape equally remarkable in its way:

The carriage, passing out of the walls of Rome, rolled through narrow lanes, where the wild honeysuckle had begun to tangle itself in the hedges, or waited for her in quiet places where the fields lay near, while she strolled further and further over the flower-freckled turf, or sat on a stone that had once had a use, and gazed through the veil of her personal sadness at the splendid sadness of the scene—at the dense, warm light, the far gradations and soft confusions of color, the motionless shepherds in lonely attitudes, the hills where the cloud-shadows had the lightness of a blush.

There is hardly a page but has its epigram or its picture well worth quoting and remembering. Some of the most remarkable passages of the book are those in which the author allows the character to draw his own picture, like this—it is Mr. Rosier who speaks, a young American who lives in Paris:

"I like the dear old asphalte. . . . I should like to be a diplomatist; but American diplomacy—that is not for gentlemen either. I am sure if you had

seen the last min—" [*Novels 1881–1886*, pp. 411–12]

Of the importance of this volume there can be no question. It will certainly remain one of the notable books of the time. It is properly to be compared, not with the light and ephemeral literature of amusement, but with the gravest and most serious works of imagination which have been devoted to the study of the social conditions of the age and the moral aspects of our civilization. The story is of the simplest possible. A young girl richly endowed in mind, person and character, but with slight knowledge of the world, unexpectedly receives a great fortune. She has previously rejected two men of entirely suitable position and qualities, not because she doubts their worth but because she has certain vague ideals. She falls into the company of a fascinating woman of forty who marries her to an old paramour of her own. There is positively no incident in the book—there is not one word of writing for writing's sake; there is not a line of meretricious ornament. It is a sober, consistent study of a single human character, with all its conditions and environments, in situations not in the least strained or exceptional. There is nothing exceptional about the book but the genius of the author, which is now, more than ever before, beyond question. This simple story is told with every imaginable accessory of wit, observation, description of nature and of life. But the reader must take his pleasure as he goes along. He can get none from the issue of the story, for no one in it really prospers. The heroine and her ideals come to a sorry market. Even the wicked are not happy. The little people who furnish the comedy of the play go out with the half comic despair of children sent to bed without the toys they had been promised. The nearest approach to content is the case of Mrs. Touchett, who, after the deaths of her husband and her only child, reflects "that after all, such things happened to other people and not to herself. Death was disagreeable, but in this case it was her son's death, not her own; she had never flattered herself that her own would be disagreeable to anyone but Mrs. Touchett. She was better off than poor Ralph, who had left all the commodities of life behind him, and indeed all the security; for the worst of dying was, to Mrs. Touchett's mind, that it exposed one to be taken advantage of. For herself, she was on the spot; there was nothing so good as that."

Notes

1 *"The Portrait of a Lady," Atlantic Monthly* 46 (November–December 1880), 585–611, 740–66; 47 (January–June 1881), 1–27, 176–205, 335–59, 449–77, 623–47, 800–26; 48 (July–December 1881), 59–85, 213–40, 338–65, 479–99, 620–40, 751–70.
2 Hamilton Aïdé, *Poet and Peer* (1880).

British Quarterly Review 75 (January 1882), 115.

Mr. Henry James shows here all his characteristic power of reflecting some of the minor distresses of polite life, wrapped up with a sort of refined enjoyment and half-saddened longing after the unattainable. A kind of vague fatality seems to dominate all his brilliant pictures; life to him at the best seems a disappointment, and individual blindness to the irony of the lot alone makes it tolerable. The languid pessimism which is now so fashionable is here, therefore, reflected. Love, at all events, is a game of cross-purposes, in which destiny seems to guide the hands of the players to make many throws, and thus there is a sense of unconscious irony blended with paradox, which gives a kind of piquancy for other than young people, who will enjoy his bright touch, his clever dialogue, and general air of worldly knowledge and *esprit*. We cannot help regretting that in so many features of his novel Mr. James seems to repeat himself. Here, again, we have American types in contact with English society and its influences. In this case, however, the studies have points of originality. The American banker, Touchett, who lives separated from his wife by such amicable agreement that she can enjoy the continent alone and spend a month each year agreeably in her husband's society, is distinctly original; no less than Mrs. Touchett, who brings with her from abroad a niece of hers, Isabel Archer, who soon becomes the centre of a 'game of cross-purposes' in love. She fascinates at first sight a young aristocrat, Lord Warburton, who at once casts a coronet at her feet, and whose sisters—surely in this very unlike English aristocrats in their reserve in these matters to strangers—freely discuss their brother in Miss Archer's hearing, on her first visit to their mansion. She unconsciously ensnares her cousin, Ralph Touchett, who is the mingled result of American birth and education and English training; she leaves behind her in America a lover, who, however, follows her to England, a Mr. Caspar Goodwood, a manufacturer; and there is what one of his rivals calls a 'sterile' dilettante, Mr. Osmond, a widower, who has a daughter Pansy, who is of some use in the story. This is the quartette of lovers—the first quartette. Ralph Touchett has urged his father to bequeath to Isabel Archer, in his will, one-half of the wealth that would otherwise have fallen to him, 'that she may be free.' Old Touchett soon after dies, and Isabel *is* free with a fortune of £70,000. To the surprise of everybody and the chagrin of Ralph and Lord Warburton, she finally bestows her hand on the widower, Osmond. Never did a woman have more reason to rue her choice or to reproach herself for blindness. When her love episodes are ended, then Pansy takes her place. Ralph Touchett would, no doubt, like Lord Warburton, have transferred his affections from the mother to the daughter if he had not been nigh to death, the story of his last moments in Rome being described with not a little art and pathos. The reader must find out for himself how Pansy's love affairs end. It is a delicious little idyl tacked on to a series of more stirring situations, notable amongst which is the one where Ralph gives his opinion of Isabel's engagement to Mr. Osmond, a piece of work in which we feel that there is all the reserve of true art. On the whole, the novel is delightful; it abounds in quick insights, effective situations, and it faithfully reflects the tone of good society. Fine phrases and suggestive sentences abound also, and occasionally come with the sense of surprise. Here is one: 'A woman's natural mission is to be where she is most appreciated.'

Californian 5 (January 1882), 86–87.

"You wanted to look at life for yourself, but you were not allowed; you were punished for your wish. You were ground in the very mill of the conventional." These words, in which the experience of the heroine of Mr. James's novel is summed up for her by her dying cousin, express what the wearied reader of this most skillful book is ever and anon inclined in his wrath to say to the author. There would be justice and injustice in the application. There is certainly real life in these characters; and in the heroine herself there is a great deal of life. But convention is throughout the book wearisomely prominent. "What went we forth into the wilderness for to see?" readers might ask themselves. Reeds shaken by the wind? or half-breed Americans, wearing away an utterly "sterile" and impotent existence in a foreign land? And of the conventions of the most of these sad people, or of their lack of "the conventional," of their sickly, cowardly, deservedly wretched, wholly pitiable existences, wherefore should we learn so much? Still, the hand of the artist can do wonders. We have become accustomed to the thought that great fiction may take for its subject very humble lives. Perhaps the lives of these banished Americans, in the insufferable dullness of their dark ancient houses, of their moral isolation, of their purposeless and meaningless leisure, may be not too humble for the talents of a successful writer of fiction. Surely, more unpropitious subjects could not well be chosen. If a national or tribal life is at the basis of a fiction, the humblest lives and the weakest characters may much more easily be exalted by the medium in which we find them moving. Even the coarseness and the degeneracy of frontier life can be made interesting by the significance always attending the struggle of civilization with brute force. But the contact of the American with the old civilization of Europe—how much less promising is such a subject! For to make good art of what has in itself a very matter-of-fact and mainly didactic interest, is very hard. Europe is to the American of to-day not a mysterious nor a romantic land. It is simply the great original source of his light and knowledge on all non-political questions of very great importance. To Europe we look for instruction. It is our great school-house. We import its fashions, steal its books, follow its thought, imitate its art; and we need all that we get from it.

The American visiting Europe is therefore normally in the position of learner. He wants information that he cannot get at home. He finds his way abroad. Perhaps he is very raw. Then, if young enough, he perhaps improves; if too old, he is disappointed; if incurably Philistine, he is fiercely critical, and is made even rawer than ever. In all such cases, however, he is a somewhat grotesque person, when viewed in European surroundings. Or perhaps years of training make him indistinguishable from the European except by the fact that he has the spirit and feelings of an exile. In such a case, the man is commonly either the dull learner that must remain forever at school, or the worse than dull man that has no aim in being clever, or the unfortunate creature—the wounded bird that flutters away to hide in a foreign thicket. All such characters, save only the last (and he is apt to be a sickly parody of a character), are for fiction unpromising. The novels that deal with learners or with dullards that cannot learn: we know how apt they all are to be poor statements of an obvious moral, unless, indeed, the learner is to be taught by experiences more romantic than are seasons in foreign boarding-houses, or visits to foreign picture galleries. On the other hand, the novels that deal with voluntary exiles have it against them, that the position of the voluntary exile is apt to be essentially a false position—one suggesting, at least, if not actually resulting from, wasted fortune, responsibilities shirked, unhealthy solitude courted, or general incapacity to meet life in the front. Such characters have not the interest of strength.

All these considerations are against the success of Mr. James in his favorite field. If it was his intention in some of his earlier novels, as many seem to hold, to point out to Americans the poverty and provincialism of their national life, then his inten-tion was well founded in our needs, and was very benevolent, but of course could by itself have written no good novels. But if his intention was to write good novels, then the field chosen was a very hard one. M. Turgeneff has indeed succeeded in a field that much resembles this one; but who shall dare compete with a great genius like M. Turgeneff? The old-fashioned novel of foreign adventure was once very successful; but who does not know that its success depended on the romantic character of its incidents? The romantic is just what Mr. James carefully avoids.

Nevertheless, with all these difficulties before him, Mr. James has been in his previous books very successful. And as to the present novel, it is, as a whole, a highly remarkable and moving tale, while in many of its parts it is marvelously dull, and while it is everywhere injured by the essential barrenness of the life depicted.

It is not our intention to spoil the story by any condensed report of it in this place. After saying that every reader of contemporary fiction ought to find time for this book, in spite of its faults, we shall content ourselves with adding a few comments on the characters for the sake of any one who, having taken our advice, and having lived through the book, shall have patience enough to read anything of ours.

Isabel, the "Lady," is remarkable for the strength and worth that in her case seem built upon such a slight foundation. At first she is merely a bright American girl, such as one may often meet; willing to read a great deal, curious to learn about odd things and new people, with an honest interest in the world;—on the whole, innocent and good, but without any definite moral *credo*. She is not definitely selfish, as George Eliot's Gwendolen was. Yet she is confident that she is not destined to be miserable. She is no coquette; yet she has many lovers. With time, a purpose comes into her mind. Here, she holds, is a very noble and lonely man; he is too good for the world; else why should he sit apart from it? He is noble enough for her; and she will be devoted to him. Happiness and duty are in perfect accord. She wishes to make no one miserable. She has done no willing harm to those sad lovers. But now she can please herself, and a lover too. It is a simple theory. But the conflict of duty and happiness comes at last, long after she has been thoroughly disillusioned. In this conflict there is little question of a struggle with a reflective conscience. There is no such religious resolve as George Eliot's heroines make. There is needed no Savonarola to send Isabel back to her husband. Her acceptance of duty and misery, when the two are inseparably bound together, is a choice resulting from a single moment of a vision. Here are good and evil. She sees and passionately desires the evil, and then flies like an arrow towards the hated and dreaded duty. One knows not whether to call it childish worship of convention, or womanly fear of rebellion against what had been fixed principles, or true moral insight. In the result, these come, in such a case, to much the same thing.

The contrast between this perfect submission to the guidance of the right in the case of the heroine, and the perfect if only momentary overthrow of the principles of a resolute and reflective man such as Caspar Goodwood, gives occasion for one of the finest scenes of the book—a scene much better in itself than the oft-cited catastrophe of the "Mill on the Floss." This young Goodwood, with his square jaw, is a very tiresome figure all through the early part of the book, and the outcome shows him to be merely one example of Mr. James's facility for making, in the beginning, a nuisance of what in time is seen to be a very respectable minor character, or even a character of the first importance.

Warburton and Ralph Touchett are introduced as disagreeably as possible; but we grow to think very highly of them. The venerable banker shall receive our honor. But as for the other characters (excepting poor Pansey), it is with difficulty that one can speak politely of them. They are of various degrees of wearisomeness. Since they are rational animals, they in some sort keep our attention whenever we read of them. But they are of a miserable, puny, pigmy race; it really concerns us little to know what newspaper letters they write when they are well-meaning, or what dirt they eat when they are vicious.

Independent 34 (19 January 1882), 11.

In *The Portrait of a Lady* Henry James, Jr., displays his remarkable literary powers, but with the unfortunate result of having produced a story which will irritate, at least, his American readers, who are not likely to be soothed by its tone of brilliant and ingenius superiority. The story begins in "Gardencourt," on an English lawn, with a glimpse of the Thames and a fine old mansion in view. From this respectable beginning the author sets forth with the air of a man who has performed his ablutions and is ready for the business in hand; but he plunges into it slowly. First he introduces the loyal Vermonter, Touchett, English banker and owner of the place, who is soon to die; then his son, an aimless, cynical invalid, who proves better than he seems. Mr. James's Americans have a remarkable way of doing this. "Ralph Touchett" is a striking example. "Lord Warburton" is the high-born English proprietor, drawn as well as Mr. James can draw him. These two fall in love at sight with "Isabel," Mrs. Touchett's niece, from Albany, the lady of the Portrait, who in her conformation resembles Mr. James's qualities as an author, in being a remarkable union of good and bad and whose great ability is impaired by continual misdirection. She leaves behind her a Boston lover, who follows her across the water, and manages to introduce into the general sobriety of his conduct some episodes of extraordinary idiocy. "Isabel" refuses his "Lordship," chiefly on the ground that all the reasons she can think of as applying to the case urge her to marry him, and keeps her poor cousin "Ralph" at a safe distance. The aunt is a singular but, on the whole, interesting fiction, with strong angularities, heartless but sensible, and with a doubt as to the first suggested in her favor. At the critical point in the story "Mr. Touchett" dies. His will, thanks to the generous intercession of "Ralph," of which, however, "Isabel" knows nothing, proves to have enriched her with nearly the one-half of his fortune and transforms her from a penniless beauty to an irresistible heiress. She now goes with her aunt to Italy, where the intrigues of a mysterious Madam Merle end in her marriage to a bad fellow, Osmond. Her lovers hover around in most extraordinary manner. "Ralph" descends rapidly to the grave, and, at last, at the crisis of the story, a dispatch from the aunt summons her to his death-bed at "Gardencourt." Her departure makes an open rupture with "Osmond," but at "Gardencourt" the blundering importunity of "Caspar Goodwood," the old Boston lover, apparently alarms her with a vision of the abyss in her path and brings her to a sudden decision. The morning finds her on her way back to the life of misery with "Osmond." Whether Mr. James proposes a sequel or not we do not know. Certainly nothing remains of the old *dramatis personæ* to construct one of, and there is no call for one, except that the story ends with the knot as tight and hopeless as ever. It is hard to make out the author's purpose in this story. If he had no further end to serve than to unfold a story, we are at loss to understand its allusions or the choice of such unrepresentative people to be portrayed as Americans. But if he had a satiric or didactic purpose in view, his choice of people might naturally enough be explained. Yet it would remain an inscrutable mystery why he should strike so deep with indiscriminate satire and not have a good word left for that plain but manly and always dignified national feeling which is the obvious cure for the frivolous life he describes. We can never say on what terms his characters stand with the author, nor whether he means to sniff at them or to make fun of them. We are haunted with a sort of vexation at the close approximation to impudence in expecting us to be interested in characters for which he entertains so little generous sympathy. If preaching of any kind or in any degree, oblique or inferential, is in the purpose of the book, there is too much of the taint of cosmopolitan indifference in its tone. It reminds us to apply to it the author's own remark (p. 216) that Osmond's talk was like the tinkling of a glass. The title implies a portrait with a distinct and permanent value on the ground of merits of its own; but, with all the deep touches and revelations of the heart of womanhood, there is mixed up much that is purely accidental or ephemeral, and whose presence in the portrait can be justified only on the ground that the author is describing what he wishes to satirize, as if the "Daisy Miller" inspiration hovered over his larger work. "Isabel," as a whole, is an unnatural character. Her career, without being impossible, falls distinctly into the class improbable. We do not object to Mr. James's delineation of that blind impulse toward wider knowledge of the world which drives on his "Lady," nor of the self-willed pursuit of an ideal life which wrecks her

141

in foreign waters; but is there anything peculiarly American in this? Does it show anything more than that the *Welt-Schmerz* has touched the heart of our people also? Besides, Mr. James seems to forget what a break in national traditions is implied in uprooting a girl and in bringing her forward in the foreign world, with the sudden reinforcement of her beauty by indefinite pounds sterling falling to her abroad. Mr. James changes in this book the ground of his previous complaint. "Isabel" is here in good enough training. She keeps decently inside the social *convenances;* but she breaks down through defects which it is implied lay in her nationality. So long as women are women we shall have fine girls enough in every nation on earth to throw themselves away in the same way. Mr. James writes with great literary skill and brilliancy, but he is not above occasional grammatical errors, and we feel, as we trace our way back through his story, that there is a wonderful resemblance in the glitter of his jewels. "Ralph's" wit, "Warburton's," "Osmond's," "Isabel's" are strikingly alike. The difference between his characters do not lie deep and mark them off as strong original individualities. "Henrietta," the foreign correspondent of the "Interviewer," is a burlesque which the author tries hard to redeem by placing a long roll of good-natured virtues to her account, which, as we have already observed, seems to be his way of vindicating his countrymen. The merely literary merits of the book are many and great, so many that we wonder at its unsatisfactory and unhealthy impression. There is no good heart in it; plenty of brightness, acuteness, wit, and good writing; but not enough to redeem it from the defect of literary Pyrrhonism.

Catholic World 34 (February 1882), 716–17.

With the introduction, a few years ago, of the "Ulster" overcoat, oddly enough came in a flood of English ideas and absurd affectations of English manners. In the same way as, when the old republican simplicity of Rome was swamped by the wealth which conquest had brought, the Roman exquisites aped the small arts and the vices of the Greeks, we, too, have our *Græculi,* not in society only but in literature and in the daily press. Our Little Britons of the press studiously boycott whatever is distinctively American, so that if one desires to get at the real sentiment of the great body of the American people he must as a rule turn elsewhere than to what is styled in the English fashion the "metropolitan" journals. Of course this is merely a momentary craze, but in the meantime, like everything else that is insincere, it is doing harm to the moral sense of the people influenced by it. A mild sort of cynicism is one of its perceptible effects.

This cynicism is apparent in all of Mr. James' writings, and shows itself especially in his studied belittling of whatever was formerly supposed to be the particular pride of Americans. Yet, after all, Mr. James is perhaps not so unjust as he is unmerciful. He aims at a minute picturing of manners rather than of character. His lotus-eating Americans abroad, with their small talk, their selfishness, their entire want of moral purpose, are perhaps not so much caricatures as some critics would have us believe. They are, in fact, the types of a generation that has practically thrown off Protestantism, and, remaining without any but the very vaguest notions of religion, is guided by its natural instincts only, instead of by an educated conscience. In this volume of Mr. James', for instance, except two or three Catholic nuns and a young girl brought up by them—and who all, by the way, are given a very stupid look—not one of the personages seems to have any belief in God or any idea whatever of duty. Even their ambitions, when they have any, are petty and unsteady. Apparently they are only saved from becoming real criminals by the lack of courage and of opportunity. Mr. James himself, it is likely, has no ambition to be rated as a satirist, yet all the same he is a satirist, and a tolerably effective one.

Lippincott's Magazine 29 (February 1882), 213–15.

The fortunes of Isabel Archer exact a closer attention and approach perceptibly nearer to the reader's sympathies than any of Mr. James's former themes, while the critical interest which he never fails to excite must be keener than ever in presence of what is in every way—in length, scope, and finish—his most important work. In characterizing it so unreservedly as his *chef-d'œuvre,* we do not mean to imply that "The Portrait of a Lady" exhibits a new development of power, or that it contrasts in any way with its predecessors. Mr. James is not a writer who advances by bounds or strides. His literary career has been throughout a steadily progressive one, but it has been a quiet progression, consisting in refinement and selection. A somewhat finer diction, a little closer analysis, a more careful attention to detail,—these are the slender stakes which mark his course; but if we cast a backward glance over his work, taking up his novels in the order of their succession, we find an unbroken line of such landmarks, indicat-

ing a steady advance in the direction of a definite goal. From the first his work showed distinct individuality, but within a narrow limit; always clever and marked by subtlety of idea, it was crude to begin with, and, moreover, had a certain scrimped and bald air which indicated no large reserves or youthful exuberance of power. It would be difficult to find, however, even among greater writers, an instance of a talent more carefully cultivated, more fully developed, than that of Mr. James. He has used his resources sparingly, but always effectively, keeping all his promises to pay with the utmost fidelity, and ignoring any unfounded hopes which may have been entertained concerning him; and in consequence he has been steadily increasing instead of diminishing his store. Continual practice, far from exhausting, only enlarges his power, giving him a greater command of technical means. His reputation as a sayer of fine and delicate things was made some years ago; but this event did not prove a check to Mr. James, who, like Burke, has gone on refining ever since. His early crudities have long since been dropped, many of them at the foot of the cliff where Roderick Hudson met his death. His limitations all remain, but he has adapted himself to them with an art akin to that of the painter who adapts the lines of his figures to the restrictions of a round frame. In "The American" and "The Europeans," delightful as they were, the early poverty of his pen was still perceptible in a certain unfurnished aspect which belonged to them. The characters were so simple, the accessories so few, that one was haunted afterward by a recollection of large spaces of blank wall. "Washington Square" had the same severity of aspect. In the shorter stories, "Daisy Miller," "An International Episode," and "The Diary of a Man of Fifty," there was no room for bareness, and these stories exhibited some of his most delicate touches. Still, Mr. James's manner has always seemed best fitted to a long work, in which he can have space for analysis and opportunity for a large number of clever *mots.*

"The Portrait of a Lady" is at once finer and closer in workmanship than anything Mr. James had before done. The walls are no longer blank: they are covered with arabesques of ingenious and delicate pattern. Here are more than five hundred closely-printed pages, on which every line is apparently studied, every word happily chosen. One might search in vain throughout the book for any inaccuracy or inadvertency of expression; the style is not only smooth and correct, but it is everywhere at its best; at whatever page we open we find a constant succession of felicities. The accomplishment of such a diction ought alone, we think, to insure a writer not only a literary reputation, but a moral character as well.

The same untiring vigilance which distinguishes the style we find in the thought of the book. The analysis of character and motive, which fills so large a part in Mr. James's writings, is here conducted with all the accuracy and completeness of a mathematical demonstration. The reader is not confronted at once with the intricacies of the problem or fatigued by its length: he is led by logical process from one point to another, his interest being riveted all through by the detail. Each conclusion is clearly marked, all possible aids are given to the memory, and when at last the demonstrator breaks off in the abrupt way which has startled all his readers, it is with the air of saying, "I have furnished all the points and shown you how to proceed. Find the answer for yourselves."

Mr. James's reluctance, or rather his positive refusal, to complete a book in the ordinary sense of the word is a curious trait, and one which piques study. In the matter of detail his books are finished to the last degree, but he cannot bring himself to the vulgarity of a regular *dénouement,* and he lacks the poetic force to substitute for it a suggestive or picturesque climax. Everything in one of Mr. James's books seems to be leading to a simple and satisfactory end, but coming near the goal he sees a crowd there and turns aside in disgust. There is no time to change his destination, but he will not go out at the common turnstile, happen what may.

The same causes which make Mr. James's *dénouements* so unsatisfactory both from a popular and an artistic point of view are traceable in his delineations of character, giving to his figures that delicacy of aspect, that absence of weight and reality, which is characteristic of them. These causes are, first, his instinctive avoidance of commonplace, and, secondly, a peculiarity of organization, which comes perhaps from his having had the misfortune to be born in Boston, a locality in which it is not infrequent. We allude to the habit of looking at an object by reflection and under cross-lights,—of divining and comprehending instead of seeing it. Now, divination, it is well known, can often transcend actual vision, penetrating into finer chinks and crevices: still, as a substitute for straightforward sight it has its inconveniences. The process is certainly seen at its best in the portrait of Miss Archer, which in all other respects than that of reality is a brilliant success. It is original, consistent in every particular, full of distinction, and painted with wonderful delicacy and precision. Mr. James has drawn from an actual though rare type of American girlhood. He has taken it at its highest development and selected all its finer qualities. He has studied every little nerve and fibre, all the intuitions and reasonings which belong to it: as an exercise in mental anatomy the delineation is perfect. The warmth of intellectual interest, the absence of any religious motive, combined with the clearest moral sense, make Isabel a character belonging to the time perhaps rather than the country, but one which is found here at an earlier age than elsewhere. To make Isabel become Caspar Goodwood's mistress at the end would be to destroy the entire texture of her character, and we cannot believe that Mr. James intended to point to that as the solution. A sweeter nature than hers might be one more susceptible of corruption. Isabel was aloof from it rather than above it, and if moral support failed her she was certain to be saved by that other instinct with which the author has endowed her,—the dread of vulgarity.

What the event was before which Mr. James paused and dropped the curtain is a matter which we will not pretend to be wise about. There are various hints in the book, none of which, apparently, lead very far. Did an infinitesimal drop of the poison used by Mr. Osmond for cleaning his *bric-à-brac* accidentally lodge in some flaw of his porcelain person? Or did Isabel and her husband continue to sit in their Roman *salon,* in patient scorn of each other, while Caspar Goodwood waited on indefinitely? Fortunately, it is not a critic's duty to solve conundrums, and we are perfectly willing to let the ends lie where Mr. James has left them.

Of the other characters, who are all intimately associated with Isabel's destiny, Goodwood is too much in the nature of a geometrical line to require any detailed analysis, but every one else is more or less complex, and there are many delicate shades in their delineation. Such is the resemblance between Madame Merle and Pansy, which is touched upon in a number of little ways and suggests their relationship to each other long before circumstances give any hint of it. Pansy is an unfledged Madame Merle, the same nature more carefully trained, as contented and as complete in her innocence as her

mother is at home in intrigue. Madame Merle herself is tolerably vague. She is an ever-present idea, rather than a person. Miss Stackpole, on the other hand, is bright and vivid; and Ralph Touchett is the warmest and truest figure in Mr. James's gallery of portraits, not excepting the more elaborate and finished one of the Lady herself.

[W. C. Brownell]. "James's *Portrait of a Lady.*" *Nation* 34 (February 1882), 102–3.

Mr. James's novel, which caused each number of the *Atlantic Monthly* to be awaited with impatience last year, gains in its complete presentation, and, like most novels of any pretensions, is most readable when read consecutively. Unlike most novels, however, whose fate (and the fortune of whose authors) it is to appear serially, the reason for this does not consist in the condensation which the reader is thus enabled to make in spite of the author, but in the fact that it is a work of art of which the whole is equal to no fewer than all of its parts, and of which there is a certain "tendency," to lose which is to miss one of the main features of the book. In other words, 'The Portrait of a Lady' is an important work, the most important Mr. James has thus far written, and worthy of far more than mere perusal—worthy of study, one is inclined to say. It is in fact a little too important—to express by a paradox the chief criticism to be made upon it—or, at all events, the only impression left by it which is not altogether agreeable. For the first two or three hundred pages one is beguiled by a kind of entertainment always of a high order—the dissection of an interesting character by a clever and scrupulous demonstrator. After that, though it would be misleading to say that the interest flags—the interest being throughout the book remarkable for its evenness—the feeling supervenes that to be still entertained argues a happy aptitude for most serious and "intellectual" delectation. Most persons will recall some experience of the same sensation in first becoming acquainted with undisguisedly philosophical writings—such as the writings of Emerson or Burke. To others it may be indicated by saying that it is just the sensation Carlyle missed in finding the works of George Eliot "dool—just dool." In America, it is well known, we do not find George Eliot dull, and it is upon our appetite for this sort of provender that Mr. James doubtless relies, and undoubtedly does well to rely. Nevertheless, it is possible to feel what Carlyle meant without agreeing with it; and though maintaining firmly the absorbing interest of 'The Portrait of a Lady,' we are ready to admit that once or twice we have laid aside the book for a season, with the exhilaration which Mr. Howells has somewhere observed to be coincident with giving up a difficult task. One of the happiest of the many happy remarks made in 'The Portrait of a Lady' is in Miss Stackpole's characterization of her *fiancé*: "He's as clear as glass; there's no mystery about him. He is not intellectual, but he appreciates intellect. On the other hand, he doesn't exaggerate its claims. *I sometimes think we do in the United States*." The person of whom this is said naturally cuts a smaller figure in the novel than the more complex organizations, in dealing with which Mr. James is most at home; and it is the inference from this circumstance that we have in mind. For not only are the simpler though perennial elements of human nature in general

eschewed by Mr. James, but his true distinction—that is to say, his strength and weakness also—consists in his attempt to dispense with all the ordinary machinery of the novelist except the study of subtle shades of character. In other words, his masterpiece, as 'The Portrait of a Lady' must be called, is not only outside of the category of the old romance of which 'Tom Jones,' for example, may stand as the type, but also dispenses with the dramatic movement and passionate interest upon which the later novelists, from Thackeray to Thomas Hardy, have relied. In a sense, and to a certain extent, Turgeneff may be said to be Mr. James's master, but even a sketch or a study by Turgeneff is turbulence itself beside the elaborate placidity of these 519 pages. This involves the necessity of the utmost care in presenting the material, and accordingly we have that squaring of the elbows and minute painstaking which not only result inevitably in occasional lumbering movement, but which lend the work an air of seeming more important than any book whatever could possibly be; so that it is perhaps fortunate for its popularity (which, by the way, we believe is extraordinary) that we exaggerate the claims of intellect occasionally in the United States.

Even this measure of fault-finding, however, seems a little ungracious, not to say hypercritical, in view of the distinguished success of Mr. James's experiment in applying the development theory to novel-writing, so to speak. We have ourselves followed the succession of his stories since 'Roderick Hudson' appeared with mingled interest and regret, because he has seemed to be getting further and further away from very safe ground, where he was very strong, and into the uncertainties of an unfamiliar region of which it was impossible to tell whether its novelty or its real merit gave it its interest. The elemental characters and dramatic situations of the novel just mentioned were strongly handled, and the work being, comparatively speaking, a youthful one, its promise seemed even greater than its actual qualities. But, almost as if he had been an amateur dipping into another branch of effort after having demonstrated his ability in one, Mr. James immediately abandoned the field of imaginative romance as it is generally understood. He at once made clear his faculty for his new choice, and the field he entered on with 'The American,' and continued with the shorter stories illustrative of American types, became immediately popular. 'Daisy Miller' may almost be said to mark an era in the mental progress of many persons who exaggerate the claims of intellect occasionally; it is wearisome to recall the "discussions" it occasioned in drawing-rooms and in print. There was, to be sure, a Chauvinist view, so to speak, taken of this and its associated sketches, by persons who omitted to perceive that Mr. James had not only made the current mechanical speculations about "the coming American novel" an anachronism, but had also displayed his patriotism and the national genius by inventing a new variety of literature. But naturally Mr. James might be expected to heed rather those of his readers who appreciated and enjoyed his motives and rejoiced in his discovery of romantic sociology. And this seemed his real danger; for though to these readers this reading conveyed a peculiarly refined pleasure, on account both of its novelty and the cleverness of its execution, there was no certainty that this pleasure was not a rather temporary mood, and likely to pass away after the novelty had worn off. Instead, however, of avoiding this danger by a return to the perennially interesting material with which he first dealt, Mr. James has conquered it, *vi et armis,* by a persistence that at one time seemed a little wilful. No one can now pretend, whatever his own literary likes and dislikes may be, that romantic sociology, exploited as Mr. James has shown it capable of being, is not a thoroughly serious field of literature, whose interest is permanent and dignified.

'The Portrait of a Lady' is a modest title, though an apt one. The portrait of the lady in question is indeed the theme of the book, and it is elaborated with a minuteness so great that when finally one begins to find it confusing it becomes evident that the ordinary point of view must be changed, and the last detail awaited—as in a professedly scientific work—before the whole can appear. Miss Isabel Archer is an orphan to whom her aunt gives an opportunity of seeing the world, and to whom her aunt's husband leaves a large fortune, at the instance of his son, who is unselfishly and romantically interested to see what his cousin will make of her life when nothing prevents her from doing as she wishes. The reader at once assumes the position of this young man, and with more or less (less in our own case, we confess) sympathy, watches the progress of the drama which he has set going. At the climax the heroine discovers that she has wrecked her life most miserably. The spiritual transition from the Isabel Archer of Albany to the Mrs. Osmond of Rome is of course accomplished in part by natural disposition and in part by the influence of the numerous characters which surround her. The way in which this influence is exhibited is a marked feature of the book. If George Eliot was the first to make of this important moral phenomenon a distinct study, Mr. James has here in our opinion quite surpassed her. Any one can judge by comparing the reciprocal effect upon the development of each other's characters of the Lydgates in 'Middlemarch' with that of the Osmonds here. The other characters are treated with a microscopy hardly inferior. Osmond himself is one of the most palpable of those figures in fiction which are to be called subtle. Madame Merle, his former mistress, mother of his child, who makes the marriage between him and his poverty and Isabel and her wealth, and who, up to the climax of the book, is Isabel's ideal, is, if anything, even better done. There is something almost uncanny in the perfection with which these secretive natures are turned inside out for the reader's inspection. As for the heroine, the American girl *par excellence*, it seems as if, scientifically speaking, Mr. James had said the last word on this subject; at any rate till the model herself is still further developed. For example (p. 344): "She never looked so charming as when, in the genial heat of discussion, she received a crushing blow full in the face and brushed it away as a feather." There are pages as good.

It has long been evident that Mr. James's powers of observation are not only remarkably keen, but sleepless as well. But 'The Portrait of a Lady' would not be what it is if it did not possess a *fonds* of moral seriousness, in addition to and underlying its extraordinary interest of purely intellectual curiosity. There is a specific lesson for the American girl in the first place; there are others, more general, which accompany every imaginative work of large importance. That these are nowhere distinctly stated is now nothing new in fiction even of a distinctly moral purpose. But Mr. James has carried suggestiveness in this regard further than any rival novelist, and though, unless one has ears to hear, it is entirely possible to miss the undertone of his book, to an appreciative sense there is something exquisite in the refinement with which it is conveyed. Refinement in this respect cannot be carried too far. In strictly literary matters Mr. James's fastidiousness may be objected to, perhaps, if one chooses; he has carried the method of the essayist into the domain of romance: its light touch, its reliance on suggestiveness, its weakness for indirect

statement, its flattering presupposition of the reader's perceptiveness, its low tones, its polish. Upon occasion, where the circumstances really seem to warrant a little fervor, you only get from the author of 'The Portrait of a Lady' irreproachability. Objection to this may easily be carried too far, however; and those who do thus carry it too far, and argue that no people ever spoke and acted with the elegance and precision of the personages here portrayed, must of necessity pay the penalty of ultra-literalness and miss the secret of Mr. James's success. To characterize this secret with adequate fulness would require far more than the space at our disposal; but it may be sufficiently indicated by calling it the imaginative treatment of reality. In this unquestionably lies Mr. James's truly original excellence. 'The Portrait of a Lady' is the most eminent example we have thus far had of realistic art in fiction *à outrance*, because its substance is thoroughly, and at times profoundly, real, and at the same time its presentation is imaginative. On the one hand, wilfulness and fantasticality are avoided, and on the other, prose and flatness. One may even go further, and say that the book succeeds in the difficult problem of combining a scientific value with romantic interest and artistic merit.

Checklist of Additional Reviews

Hartford *Daily Courant,* 19 November 1881, p. 1.
Ida Clare. "Our Boston Letter." St. Louis *Post-Dispatch,* 22 November 1881, p. 2.
Philadelphia *North American,* 25 November 1881, p. 4.

Albany *Evening Journal,* 26 November 1881, p. 1.

John Ashcroft Noble. *Academy* [England] 20 (26 November 1881), 397–98. Reprinted in James W. Gargano, ed., *Critical Essays on Henry James: The Early Novels* (Boston: G. K. Hall, 1987), pp. 48–50.

[R. H. Hutton]. *Spectator* [England] no. 2787 (26 November 1881), 1504–6. Reprinted in Roger Gard, ed., *Henry James: The Critical Heritage* (London: Routledge & Kegan Paul, 1968), pp. 93–96.

New York *Daily Graphic,* 26 November 1881, p. 181.

Boston *Evening Traveller,* 29 November 1881, Supp., p. 1.

Cincinnati *Commercial,* 1 December 1881, p. 7.

Indianapolis *Journal,* 2 December 1881, p. 68.

Chicago *Inter-ocean,* 3 December 1881, p. 10.

"The Portrait of a Lady." Saturday Review [England] 52 (3 December 1881), 703–4. Reprinted in Gard, pp. 98–100.

San Francisco *Chronicle,* 4 December 1881, p. 6.

London *Daily Telegraph,* 6 December 1881, p. 3.

Chicago *Tribune,* 10 December 1881, p. 10.

Minneapolis *Tribune,* 11 December 1881, p. 4.

New York *Tribune,* 11 December 1881, p. 8.

Detroit *Free Press,* 17 December 1881, p. 3.

Portland *Morning Oregonian,* 18 December 1881, p. 4.

American 3 (31 December 1881), 186–87.

Colorado Springs *Weekly Gazette,* 31 December 1881, p. 4.

H. A. Huntington. *Dial* 2 (January 1882), 214–15. Reprinted in Gard, pp. 111–12.

Horace E. Scudder, *Atlantic Monthly* 49 (January 1882), 126–30. Reprinted in Gard, pp. 109–10; Lyall H. Powers, *The Merrill Studies in The Portrait of a Lady* (Columbus, OH: Charles E. Merrill, 1970), pp. 9–12.

Critic 2 (14 January 1882), 1.

Literary World [Boston] 13 (14 January 1882), 10–11.

Churchman 45 (28 January 1882), 97–98.

Charleston *News and Courier,* 28 January 1882, p. 2.

Harper's New Monthly Magazine 64 (February 1882), 474. Reprinted in Gargano, pp. 50–51.

[Margaret Oliphant]. *Blackwood's Magazine* 131 (March 1882), 374–82. Reprinted, but unattributed, in Gard, pp. 101–4.

E. S. P. *Penn Monthly* 13 (March 1882), 233–34.

Atlanta *Constitution,* 16 April 1882, p. 4.

Literary World [England] 26 (21 July 1882), 40–43.

THE BOSTONIANS

London *Daily News*, 25
February 1886, p. 3.

There are critics who think that Mr. James
is most himself, and most successful, in his
short stories, where he is obliged to bring
matters rapidly to a point. In "The Bostonians" the point is long in being reached,
but the novel is full of novelty—a rare
thing in novels—novelty of character, and
even of situation. As to "incidents," in the
novel-readers' sense of the word, there are
none at all. Mr. James's hero and heroine
can go out in a boat together without en-
suring a storm; they can walk on the
sands, and the tide is not promptly possessed with a desire to arise and swallow
them. The interest of the tale, and it is
abundant, is psychological. Mr. James introduces us (one of his ladies is so European that she does *not* introduce her
guests) to a crowd of characters, very original, and most carefully designed by innumerable minute touches. They are not, for
the most part, very agreeable novelties; we
hope never to meet Silas Tarrant, the mesmeric healer; nor Mrs. Tarrant, that fallen
and faded daughter of an "old Abolitionist family"; nor Mr. Pardon, the Press-
man; nor Mrs. Luna, the widow who
flirts, in the flesh. Olive Chancellor, alas!
many of us have met, and dislike as much
as we pity her. But Mrs. Farrinder, the
Juno of the platform, the successful orator
of Women's Rights, a most humorous
study, has her pleasant side; and there is a
melancholy, pessimistic truth and humour
in the pathetic figure of Miss Birdseye, the
selfless old friend of causes that have
ceased to be forlorn. As to Verena, the heroine, it is impossible to over-praise the
originality of this pretty and pure and
enigmatic maiden, whose talk is full of the
slang of the lecture room, and whose heart

is as glad, her soul as fresh, as if she were
a princess in an old fairy tale. But the most
remarkable thing in this novel—which is
too long, full of *longueurs,* full of over
elaborate and alembicated passages—is
the interest with which it holds us, despite
its length and its lack of adventure. This
captivating power is wholly due to the development of character, and perhaps to a
strange unaccustomed foreign air. In the
Boston parlours and the drawing-rooms
of New York, and among the queer earnest natives, we feel in an air more alien
than that of Dostoiefsky's Russia, or Daudet's Provence. Mr. Henry James may not
be American enough for some of his
American critics; he is certainly as far as
possible, in this tale at least, from being
English. However, he is undeniably interesting to an unusual degree, and one
leaves his story with a desire to hear more
about certain of his characters, and with
a hope that the life he describes is only a
passing phase—the measles, as it were, or
hooping-cough of national "culture" in
Boston.

G. Barnett Smith.
Academy [England], series
722 (6 March 1886), 162.

The comedy of human life, in some of its
special phases, has been cleverly set forth
by Mr. Henry James in *The Bostonians.*
The woman question forms the basis of
the novel; and, under cover of the movement for the so-called emancipation of the
fairer half of the community, he admirably
illustrates the interdependence of the
sexes. The true woman knows well
enough that her real sphere is the home;
enshrined in the affection of her husband
and children, she wishes for no other, and

there is certainly no other in which she could wield half her present influence over the destinies of the world. There have been many cases, no doubt, where women have suffered from the selfishness and brutality of man; but the millions of happy homes which have existed from time immemorial prove that these are only the exceptions. Mr. James gives us several types of women who represent the "forward" movement. Olive Chancellor is a young lady who is really filled with a genuine enthusiasm for her sex, believing that it has been maltreated for ages and made the sport of the creature man. Then there is Miss Birdseye, a member of the Short Skirts League, who has all her life been fighting supposed despotisms of all kings. Mrs. Farrinder is one of the orators of the movement. "The ends she laboured for were to give the ballot to every woman in the country, and to take the flowing bowl from every man. *She had a husband, and his name was Amariah*." That is the whole of Amariah's record. Miss Chancellor has visions of the ages of oppression which have rolled over women; she sees "the uncounted millions who have lived only to be tortured, to be crucified"; and she resolves that all this shall end. She attaches to herself Miss Verena Tarrant, the attractive daughter of a couple of vulgar people, who are only bent on "exploiting" her as a means of profit. Verena is a wonderful inspirational speaker, and she is to be a kind of platform Joan of Arc in the redemption of her sex. All goes smoothly until Verena finds her real womanhood by falling in love with a young Southerner from Mississippi; then she recognises the hollowness of all that she has been doing. The book closes with the collapse of Miss Chancellor's hopes; the moral being that all schemes must ultimately fail which seek to uncreate the woman whom God has made, and to reconstitute her as another kind of being. Mr. James's novel is brilliant, full of

points, and eminently readable; but it is rather tantalising not to afford us a few glimpses of the married life of Verena Tarrant and Basil Ransom, and the future of the disillusioned Olive Chancellor.

Athenaeum [England] 3045 (6 March 1886), 323.

Basil Ransom, a young man from the state of Mississippi, comes to practise as a lawyer in New York. He goes to Boston to visit two distant cousins, of whom the elder, Mrs. Luna, is a lively and worldly young widow, while her sister Miss Olive Chancellor is of a highly nervous temperament, morbidly conscientious, and wholly given up to the cause of female "emancipation." Basil is taken by her to a meeting of other supporters of the cause, at which an address is given by a girl named Verena Tarrant, daughter of a vulgar mesmerizing quack, who has an idea of making capital of her "gift," namely, a certain power of continuous utterance in a musical voice. Basil and Olive each in their own way fall in love with the girl. Olive, who is rich, takes her into her own house and trains her as a champion of the cause; Basil gradually resolves to make her his wife. This is the situation into which Mr. James gets his characters by the end of his first volume, and the remainder of the story is occupied with the details of the struggle. It will be easily conceived that even Mr. James's powers of dilution are hard put to it to make so slight a theme furnish forth the regulation number of volumes. In order to do it he has to fill page after page with long analysis of feelings, or minute descriptions, whether of character or scenery, which, subtle and delicate as they often are, produce at last in the reader's mind the same kind of irritation as results from an over-elaborated picture of a subject which might be sufficiently indicated by a few bold strokes. We know Basil Ransom and Olive Chancellor perfectly well by the end of the first chapter; and every fresh touch put upon their portraits after this seems almost an impertinence. It is, perhaps, for this reason that of all the characters in the story the most entirely satisfactory is "Doctor" Mary J. Pranse, a young lady who, having solved the problem of her own "emancipation" in a thoroughly practical and even useful manner, is inclined to treat with a good deal of contempt the methods adopted by Miss Chancellor and her allies. "Well," she says, on being questioned by Ransom as to what they have to say,

> "'what it amounts to is just that women want to have a better time. That's what it comes to in the end. I am aware of that, without her telling me.' 'And don't you sympathize with such an aspiration?' 'Well, I don't know as I cultivate the sentimental side. There's plenty of sympathy without mine. If they want to have a better time, I suppose it's natural; so do men too, I suppose. But I don't know as it appeals to me—to make sacrifices for it; it ain't such a wonderful time—the best you can have?'"

Luckily Dr. Pranse is a subordinate character; she only appears occasionally, so we are left with the feeling which every author should aim at producing, that we should like to have more of her. Another person who serves as a foil to the enthusiasts by profession—by the way, are there *no* male Bostonians?—is Miss Birdseye, a delightful old lady, who was taking Bibles to the negroes "down South," at the imminent risk of being tarred and feathered, before the loaders of the "movement"

were in their cradles. She has boundless faith in all improvement, thereby differing from Dr. Pranse; but both alike are genuine and practical. The final contest for Verena is well told; but the occasion is hardly serious enough to arouse that interest which ought to belong to the culminating point of so long a story. Condensed into one volume 'The Bostonians' would be as good as anything Mr. James has written; expanded into three it is nothing short of tedious.

"Mr. Henry James's New Novel." *Pall Mall Gazette* [England], 15 March 1886, p. 5.

The motive of "The Bostonians" is the familiar theme of love—that Mr. James and his school do not seem able to change, though the novel in their hands has become so far revolutionized that it is no longer a story. But there is a decided novelty about the circumstances. The obstacles to the course of true love arise from the great "Position of Woman" question. Olive Chancellor, a Bostonian *par excellence*, is wrapped up heart and soul in this question. Her interest in the cause and in the people who are promoting it brings her into contact with one Verena Tarrant, a young girl who, thanks to her beauty and singular charm of manner and voice, has entered upon what promises to be a remarkably successful career as an "inspirational speaker." Olive sees in this young creature, who is perfectly simple and genuine, a great champion of the cause. Unfortunately, in obedience to another call of duty—and, indeed, she lives to obey duty—she has invited the acquaintance of a cousin, one Basil Ransom, who has newly come from his home in Mississippi to seek his fortune in New York. Basil is a mere barbarian in Bostonian eyes, not because he is uneducated, for he is not, but because he is a reactionary on all questions of progress. As to the cause for which Olive lives and of which Verena is to be the prophetess, he believes with Tennyson's fat-faced curate, that "God made woman for the man." He loves Verena, and in time Verena comes to love him; and we read in "The Bostonians" of the way in which Olive Chancellor strives to keep her prophetess from him and for the cause. The reader, unless he happens to be very fond of the "novel of analysis," will probably find his interest flag somewhat before he reaches the end. It seemed to us that Mr. James's good things became rarer as we went on. Such epigrams as that Verena had "lived much among long-haired men and short-haired women," that the ends for which Mrs. Farrinder (another famous speaker) had laboured were "to give the ballot to every woman in the country and to take the flowing bowl from every man," such humorous descriptions as that of Olive's dealings with the shop girls, how "she took them much more tragically than they took themselves," how "they could not make out what she wanted them to do," and in "the last analysis cared much more about Charlie than about the ballot"—such things become more sparse in the later chapters. But we need hardly say that there is much excellent work in these three volumes. The happiest effort perhaps in them is Miss Birdseye, the veteran humanitarian. The ludicrous side of her character is the one that we first see, as indeed it would be the first to show itself. We see in her "the confused, entangled, inconsequent, discursive old woman, whose charity began at home and ended nowhere, whose credulity kept pace with it, and

who knew less about her fellow-creatures, if possible, after fifty years of humanitary zeal, than on the day she had gone into the field to testify against the iniquity of most arrangements." But we come to see that she was more than this, that there was something quite heroic in her in her absolute abnegation of self, her thorough altruism, to use the new philosophical slang. Mr. James makes handsome amends for what may be taken as ridicule of causes popular in some quarters in making this old woman, a life-long devotee of causes, the only really loveable character in the book. The scene of her death is not unworthy to be ranked with that of Leatherstocking in the "Pioneers," and of the old Colonel in the "Newcomes."[1] We must not forget to give a word of praise to the admirable figure of Doctor Prince [sic], the severely practical "medical lady," nor to the truly artistic skill with which, just as Horace after his high flight about the martyrdom of Regulus, drops down to the lower note of the "Venafran fields and Spartan Tarentum," Mr. James dismisses his heroine in tears, with the remark, "It is to be feared that with the union, so far from brilliant, into which she was about to enter, these were not the last she was destined to shed." How different from the flourish with which the heroine generally leaves the stage!

Note

1 James Fenimore Cooper, *The Pioneers* (1823); William Makepeace Thackeray, *The Newcomes* (1853–55).

"*The Bostonians.*"
Boston *Evening Traveler,*
19 March 1886, p. 2.

The hearts of the "Bostonians" will doubtless rejoice in the publication in book form of that serial story which for many months decorated the pages of the Century magazine,[1] in which the exponents of culture saw themselves—not, it may well be, as others saw them, but as Mr. Henry James saw them. It was read—when read at all—in the course of its progress in the Century, amid such a tumult of indignation, remonstrance, disgust and exasperation as, perhaps, never before disturbed the serene atmosphere of this city of the gods and muses. Its localities were pointed out even the exact number and ownership of the Charles-street house where Mr. James located his heroine; its characters were identified with the unerring certainty of historical truth; and the name of the author was visited with such contumely that it seemed to be in the nature of a special Providence that no less a barrier than the Atlantic ocean rolled between Mr. James and his readers. Echoes of this, it is rumored, were mysteriously wafted across the sea, and it is certain that the story, a little later on, lost its piquant and tantalizing photographic realism, and seemed to wander in nebulous mazes, quite unlike the usually artistic work of Henry James. The vibrant indignation changed from its indignant interest to a passive weariness, and "The Bostonians" pursued its course with little attention from that position of mankind whose characteristics it was supposed to celebrate in fiction. Letters of protest, recrimination or satire ceased to ornament the columns of the daily press, and the defenders of Miss Birdseye and Mrs. Farrinder sought out fresh fields to subdue. And in truth the author's pictures of the home of his early and pre-historic youth were rather appalling. He conceived of Boston as a city where weird meetings took place,—"like a rendezvous of witches on the Bracken;" where "witches, wizzards, mediums, spirit-rappers and roaring radicals" most do congregate; a city where no one prevaricated, and which was mysteriously given over to "female conventions." There is no discernible plot to the story so far as the average intellect is able to discover. Basil Ransom, a conservative young Southerner, comes to Boston to visit his cousin, by several removes, Miss Olive Chancellor, a wealthy young woman whom Basil Ransom perceived to be at sight "a signal old maid. That was her quality; that was her destiny. There are women," he said, "who are unmarried by accident and others who are unmarried by option; but Olive Chancellor was unmarried by every implication of her being. She was a spinster as Shelley was a lyric poet or as the month of August is sultry." Miss Chancellor is a leader in reforms, and with her, at this time, is her frivolous married sister, Mrs. Luna, from New York. Miss Chancellor's scheme of entertainment for her Southern cousin included taking him on the evening of his arrival to a small gathering of people who were "interested in new ideas," and she interrogates him as to whether he cares for human progress. Mrs. Farrinder, "the great apostle of the emancipated woman," was expected "to speak,"—the verb used with the peculiar Bostonian significance which all to the manner born well understand. Here he would meet Miss Birdseye—"one of the earliest, one of the most passionate, of the old abolitionists." The personal appearance of Miss Birdseye is described with a vividness that Boston will not soon forget. "She looked as if she had spent her life on platforms, in audiences, in conversations, in phalansteries, in séances. . . . No one had any idea how she lived; whenever money was given her she gave it away to a negro or a refugee." Mrs. Farrinder, too, will be well remembered, with the "something public in her eye, which was large, cold and quiet; it had acquired a sort of exposed reticence, from the habit of looking down from a lecture desk over a sea of heads, while its distinguished owner was eulogized by a leading citizen." Mrs. Farrinder "lectured on temperance and the rights of woman; the ends she labored for were to give the ballot to every woman and to take the flowing bowl from every man." Basil Ransom had a general idea that these people interested in new ideas were all "communists, vegetarians or mediums," and on this group enters Dr. and Mrs. Tarrant—he a mesmerist and she of old abolitionist stock—with their daughter Verena, who was a speaker "under inspiration."

It is idle to attempt tracing any threads of this nebulous story, that has apparently no more definiteness of theme or motive than the meadow brook winding idly through the fields. In no sense is it a novel—hardly even a story. It is a series of sketches, with the very slightest possible thread of cohesion. The scenes change from Boston to New York, from South-End philistinism to Fifth-avenue magnificence, with an interlude on the South Shore, and the final tableau in Music Hall. There is neither cohesion, purpose, definite aim, or fusion. It is a series of exaggerations rather than of faithful pictures. It satirizes much that is earnest, noble and true. It is inadequate, even as a satire. All this and more of the same tenor might be said. Yet the truth remains—paradoxical as it may seem—that in "The Bostonians" there is certain material that is not only of present interest but of an enduring value. The types of character in it exist, and they are portrayed to the life. They comprise a series of photographs of very unusual and curiously interesting individualities, and while there is no coherency, or fusion, that would transform this meandering narrative into a novel; while the characters have no especial relation as actors in a drama, they are yet rounded, life-like, perfect portraitures of existing types. This is not saying that they are representative of the various movements with which Mr. James involves them. Miss Olive Chancellor and Miss Verena Tarrant are in no wise exponents of the woman suffrage movement, or representative of its prominent workers. The noble men and women who have stood for sublime ideas of human justice and truth and heroism and all that makes for social progress are not subjects for a caricature or for ridicule. But it is evident that no such purpose as this is in Mr. James's mind. Mr. James is a literary artist. He is not a reformer; and he has looked on all this boiling, bubbling, seething cauldron of miscellaneous activities that have their origin and their centre in Boston, from the standpoint of literary surveillance. It has amused him. He has seen it purely objectively. It struck his artistic fancy, and he essayed to embody it in a story. After it was well under way the echoes of the hue and cry reached him over the sea, and in a little alarm at the photographic realism he was half unconsciously introducing, he drew back, and then the story began to relapse into a nebulous indefiniteness that brought upon it fresh rebuke because it wasn't interesting. No candid observer can look upon this Boston life, with its multitudinous phases of inquiry and pursuit—with its advocates of suffrage and anti-suffrage; its discussions of mind-cure, metaphysical cure, mesmerism, spiritualism, theosophy; its hermetic following, its work for the Indians, the refugees—heaven knows what—without finding all Mr. James's material around us. In "The Bostonians" he has preserved this phase of life somewhat as Mr. Howells did a curious period in "The Undiscovered Country," and in many respects "The Bostonians" will be one of the most permanent value in the series of artistically touched novels that have been written by Henry James.

Note

1 *"The Bostonians," Century Magazine* 29 (February–April 1885), 530–43, 686–700, 893–908; 30 (May–October 1885), 58–66, 256–64, 423–37, 553–68, 692–708, 861–81; 31 (November–December 1885; January–February 1886), 85–98, 205–14, 337–51, 591–600.

Boston *Beacon*, 27 March 1886, p. 3.

Mr. Henry James's *Bostonians,* just published in book form by Messrs. Macmillan & Co. (pp. 449, $2.00), do not justify the tempest in the local teapot which the publication of the earlier chapters excited. It will be remembered that some of the characters were understood to be portraits, and it must be admitted that this mistake was not entirely strange or unnatural. But the sequel showed that Mr. James's purpose was not properly understood, and he himself went so far as to say that the intention attributed to him had caused him much pain. The *Bostonians,* then, must be judged exclusively as a novel. Mr. James's literary mastership it is not necessary to point out. He is easily the greatest of our modern American society novelists, and he shares with Mr. Howells the honor of having founded the analytical school of novel writers—a school hardly as yet represented in England, to which so

many of our people look as the mother country of novel writing. The Bostonians are a typical example of this new school. The people whom Mr. James has elected to draw are not profoundly interesting or attractive. And the analysis of their motives and emotions, however great as a psychological study, does not reveal very much that is particularly pleasing. No doubt, there are just such people as Mr. James describes; but the average reader of novels protests that it is hardly worth while to waste so much literary skill on such distressingly uninteresting persons. In defence of the plain reader it must be confessed, also, that a novel is usually read for pleasure, and that comparatively few can appreciate the delicate refinement, the gentle satire and the happy touches of Mr. James's superfine pen. To be plain about it, people want a story, they like dash and dramatic action, and they do not take naturally to Mr. James's highbred way of viewing things. Bostonians in particular, while unable to deny the truth of Mr. James's art, wish that he had selected a more attractive and agreeable set of characters to go down in literature as the men and women of Boston. But after one has found fault with the author on account of his subject, one feels very much like finding fault with the reader who treats a good novelist and great artist like Mr. James as one treats the newspaper. The latter is taken up, looked-at, skimmed, and then laid aside as not containing anything very important or startling. Now, Mr. James does not intend to startle; he does not intend to instruct; he does not intend to tell a good story that has a complicated plot and the usual number of heroes and heroines. He depicts life as he finds it, and he reveals the sentiments of men and women as they are. If these persons happen to be moderately uninteresting, the fault is not in the novelist, not in the subject, but in society. James's *Bostonians* are not true to nature. They are so true that hundreds of people said he had depicted this or that particular woman. To be sure, most Bostonians in the set that Mr. James draws from, it is to be hoped are infinitely better and less trivial than are the people in his novel. But the novel is true, and because it is true, neither criticism nor devout hope can kill it. It will live. And the literary mastership of the *Bostonians,* will be prized and praised after the fault-finders of today are forgotten.

British Quarterly Review 83 (April 1886), 480–81.

Mr. Henry James is at home in the kind of light comedy which he here undertakes. He is careful never to become too broad in his fun nor to make his earnest purpose too obtrusive. The Bostonians here presented to us let us hope, are not quite representative, though they may be typical enough for his purposes. And he shows art in maintaining our interest in the process of frittering away, or in other words, evaporating the human elements on which interest generally depends. For the Bostonians are mostly 'women with a mission.' Olive Chancellor, the heroine, is filled with a virtuous belief that the 'female woman' has been maltreated, downtrodden for ages—a mere 'thing' for the sport and pleasure of man. Miss Birdseye is a member of the short-skirts league, and Mrs. Farrinder is the great orator of that movement; for whose eloquence, however, the curious have at times to wait with patience. Dr. Prance is indefinite, but useful as a counter-element. Then there is Verena Tarrant, the wonderful inspirational speaker, in whom Olive fancies she has found a pearl in view of her great reform

of woman's rights; but the vulgar couple to whom Verena Tarrant owes her existence are enough to make hopeless that ambition—the more that Verena herself falls over head and ears in love with the brilliant Basil Ransom, from Mississippi, who, though he has come to walk the law courts, at the same time accomplishes the somewhat erratic exploit of walking the courts of love. Verena Tarrant and Basil Ransom are wedded, and Olive Chancellor is disillusioned. Mr. Amariah Farrinder and his kind no doubt found a means of entertainment in that wedding, and did not fail to express the hope that woman's rights 'might never triumph to make and to keep *men* non-entities.' And in that vein the author himself winds up his story—more inclined to leave it clear on the mind than to gratify the curiosity of his readers about the early days of married life. Mr. Henry James has here written an amusing book—full of character and points, whose aim is to justify the life of women in the sphere most natural to it—the sphere of home and family influence, and to show how much is lost alike to her and to the world whenever she makes any attempt to pass beyond it.

"The Bostonians." Chicago *Tribune,* 3 April 1886, p. 13.

It is safe to say that few persons who read Henry James's early novel, "Roderick Hudson," felt any temptation to throw it aside before finishing it. Yet very often in perusing his latest work, "The Bostonians," the consciousness of being trifled with is constantly prompting one to furtively turn the pages without bestowing upon each a due amount of attention.

There are people who grow so intent in speaking about themselves that they become almost indifferent as to whether they are listened to or not—the fact that they are talking being the all-important one. Mr. James, it strikes one, is falling into this deplorable state of ecstatic subjectivity. He has looked into the excess of a certain ethical movement in Boston; and he imagines that the keenness of his perception will make amends for the triviality of the object analyzed. His mental microscope no doubt gives him great delight; but a single peep through it will satisfy those who have a fleeting interest in the larger things of life. The author's realism is becoming sordid. The reader has, of course, some moments of compensation, as when he comes across such a picture as that of Tarrant's home. He is likely to remember it all—the oily old charlatan whose stock in trade consists of "cures" and "manifestations;" the scraping, ambitious wife who goes on hoping and trusting; the inspirational daughter with her red gown and her fluent stream of milky eloquence; finally, the shabby house at Cambridge, with the broken platform in front of it. Those rickety boards strike one as a symbol of the decay within. But, when one comes to Olive Challoner [sic], one has but little patience with the author. She may be a type of those Boston women whose ideas of emancipating and reforming everything came to them from the blood that once felt the flush of indignation in contemplating an enslaved race. She may have been nurtured among Abolitionists who were as sensible, perhaps, as the slaveholders, although Mr. James holds to the contrary. The worst that may be said of her is that her motives are altruistic; and, although Mr. James may not think so, it is difficult to make altruism altogether ridiculous. The moral of the book may be found in the words of Basil Ransom, whose attempt to wrest Verena Tarrant from the woman-suffragist, Miss Challoner, is the subject of the story. He says that he desires to rescue his own sex from feminization:

I am so far from thinking, as you set forth the other night, that there is not enough woman in our general life, that it has long been pressed home upon me that there is a great deal too much. . . . The masculine character—the ability to dare and endure—to know and yet not feel reality—to look the world in the face and take it for what it is, a very queer and partly very base mixture— that is what I want to preserve, or rather to recover; and I must tell you that I don't in the least care what becomes of you ladies while I make the attempt. [*Novels 1881–1886*, p. 1111]

Taking "The Bostonians" all in all, the one criticism to be passed upon it is that, whether Mr. James' ideas of woman-suffrage are right or wrong—and the world will not greatly trouble itself whether they are or not—they do not of themselves constitute what is known as a novel.

Detroit *Free Press*, 3 April 1886, p. 8.

Those who have become accustomed to hear Mr. James ridiculed and his novels decried will probably be mildly surprised to know that "The Bostonians" really is a readable and an interesting story which might almost have been written by a novelist without any peculiar or advanced views as to art in fiction. It is drawn out somewhat, after the English fashion, which requires three volumes to be filled in any event; but a little judicious skipping, which the experienced reader knows how and when to indulge in, reduces it to practicable and entertaining dimensions.

If it must be classified—of which we confess we do not see the necessity—it is a study of the woman's rights question with discursive disquisitions upon a variety of other topics, spiritualism among the number. Olive Challoner [sic], of Boston—and Beacon street—has for relatives in Mississippi the Ransoms, whom the war has impoverished. One member of the family is Basil Ransom, a young lawyer, and him Olive invites to come North. She speedily learns to dislike him because he laughs at her advanced notions—Boston notions; but her widowed sister, Mrs. Luna, who constitutes with her the Challoner family, falls in love with Basil. The latter, however, is captivated by a pretty girl—Verena Tarrant, whose father, Selah Tarrant, is a humbug of the order mountebank. The girl is his tool or accomplice, and it is at a "seance" where the father causes Verena to improvise by putting his hands on her head that Basil is fascinated.

He believes in nothing but the girl's beauty, but Olive takes it into her head that with the right kind of culture Verena can be made an instrument for carrying out her own advanced views. She buys off the father for a yearly stipend; gives the girl masters and takes her to Europe. When she has been duly cultivated and comes back ready to lecture and entrance the world, Basil in some mysterious way prevents her and subsequently marries her. Olive herself is compelled to do the lecturing.

The characters are admirably drawn and nicely balanced, one against the other. There is a good deal of felicity, too, in the choice of names, more in fact than Mr. James has heretofore been credited with. The woman physician, Dr. Prance, and the authors, Mrs. Ada T. P. Foat, are illustrations. The Challoners themselves are judiciously named, respectably and Bostonianly. One of the best drawn characters, though he has comparatively little to do with the action of the story, is Tarrant, who in one place is thus photographed:

> The places that knew him best were the offices of the newspapers and the vestibules of the hotels—the big marble-paved chambers of informal reunion which offer to the streets, through high glass plates, the sight of the American citizen suspended by his heels. . . . Once he thought he had been, and the headings, five or six deep, danced for days before his eyes; but the report never appeared. [*Novels 1881–1886*, pp. 897–989]

M[ayo] W[illiamson] H[azeltine].
New York *Sun*, 4 April 1886, p. 4.

Mr. Henry James has been subjected to some captious criticism on the score of the commonplace characters and trivial aspects of life which—so it is charged—have hitherto been chosen by him for portrayal. The men and women in whom he has usually invited us to feel interested are depicted as persons exceptionally self-observant and laboriously refined, according, at all events, to our normal native standard, which is tacitly assumed to be quite low. Now, although nobody denies that novels may have an educational function, yet most of us expect from them a kind of instruction distinct from the lessons of the dancing master and the injunctions of the manicure. We admit that manners are not idle, but we think their nonfutility should be proved by the unfolding of large aspiration and generous endeavor. Their fruitful exposition seems to call for a deep and comprehensive rather than minute philosophy, and we have been beset with a misgiving lest an author who in volume after volume concentrates his powers of insight and analysis on the pirouettes of small talk and the etiquette of card leaving may have begun at the wrong end. If we may draw deductions from the practice of the masters of prose fiction, there are themes more capacious and inspiring to the novelist than the acquisition of conventional deportment and aesthetic information by introspective and inquisitive Americans in the course of a somewhat prolonged sojourn in Europe. But this has been often said, and in his last story, *The Bostonians* (Macmillan & Co.), Mr. James seems to have determined to repel, once for all, the hackneyed imputations of painstaking emptiness and strenuous superficiality. I, too, he seems to say, have studied something besides the ways of drawing rooms; I, too, have brooded on the primal facts of humanity and nature; *et in Arcadia ego;* and behold the fruit of my excursion in a serious novel.

Indubitably "The Bostonians" is nothing if not earnest. The Bostonians to whom we are presented have nothing in common with the people to whom King's Chapel is a shrine and Harvard University an academe. Theirs is a Boston without Beacon street, a Boston for which the term society has a mystic philosophical rather than conventional significance. No trivial intruders from the spheres of fashion, affluence, and art are suffered to set foot on the austere foreground of this picture, and if forms that seem Philistine cross at times the field of vision, they serve but as foils to the high priests of social regeneration, to the apostles and the martyrs of a transcendental impulse. The world which Mr. James has here elected to delineate is the converse of the world which he has hith-

erto made known to us. It is a world of dreamers and reformers, of cranks, clairvoyants, and hierophants, fanatics, idealists, enthusiasts; a world of cant and rant commingled with sublime endeavor, with ascetic self-effacement, with limitless self-sacrifice, with absolute absorption in emotional or spiritual interests; the world of abolitionist crusaders, of temperance propagandists, of the missionaries of woman's rights. Its denizens are the right heirs of the Anabaptists. Latter-day Saints, and Fifth-monarchy men who scandalized the staider Puritans of Cromwell's commonwealth; only their divagations, fervors, and strivings have in view no longer a religious but a social transfiguration.

For a man so shy of raptures as Mr. James had shown himself—so sedulous to keep the unvexed *via media* of moderation and proportion—to devote himself to the portrayal of such types as these was of itself a positive advance and a veritable honor. It was like the assumption of the *toga virilis;* it was like the resolve of an artist already proficient in *genre* painting to risk his fame in the grand style. That he should be all at once and entirely successful in a field so uncongenial to his predilections and experience was not to be expected. Now and then he seems haunted with a doubt lest his reader may think him insincere; but nowhere is he justly taxable with insincerity. Never is he guilty of the blunder of condescending to his shabby and crotchety, but, as history attests, redoubtable Bostonians. He sees that their heroic age is over, that it culminated in the liberation of the slave, but he feels, and forces us to feel, the unfaded majesty of their lingering traditions and the aureole reflected on the brows of the survivors by a great work done. He does not, indeed, place upon the stage any figure that recalls the mighty protagonists of abolition, but he pays due homage to their power by picturing the uses and the life-long devotion to which a creature so feeble as Miss Birdseye could be wrought by their example. The delineation of Miss Birdseye seems to us one of the most veracious, impressive, and memorable in contemporary fiction. She is alive; we feel that we have seen her and we know that we shall not forget her. And when we reflect upon the art by which the moral beauty and benediction of her life are made to shine through the meanness of her surroundings and the fussy weakness of her intellect, we recognize the presence of a master's handiwork. It is in this portrait of Miss Birdseye that the author of "The Bostonians" touches the highest level of a novelist's achievement. The companion figure of Miss Chancellor is not only less interesting, but less distinct. Verena's patroness and acolyte does not sufficiently explain herself—we would say unbosom herself, if such a word did not appear inapposite, for, as Mr. James allows us to discern, she is not so much unsexed as sexless.

The reader of "The Bostonians" will scarcely pause to notice two or three unimportant slips in matters of fact. One of them, perhaps, is worth correcting. The admiration of a visitor to the American Cambridge is slightly chilled by the remark put in the mouth of a young woman. "You ought to have been at one of those really mediæval universities that we saw on the other side, at Oxford or Göttingen or Padua." Oxford or Padua will do well enough to point a contrast. Not so Göttingen, which happens to be a century younger than Harvard.

" 'The Bostonians,' as Mr. Henry James Sees Them." Critic 8 (17 April 1886), 191–92.

All circumstances seem to combine to make it easy to write an impartial review of Mr. James's last novel. Mr. James himself is in England, as usual; his book is published by a London house having a New York branch; and, since *The Critic* is printed several scores of leagues from the city of Boston, it is certainly both safe and advisable for us to treat all the 'parties' with judicial candor. In the first place, we extend to the afflicted and indignant city whose name is so irreverently handled in Mr. James's title, our frank assurances that we quite agree with it in thinking that Mr. James really meant *some* Bostonians, not Bostonians in entirety. Thus, when Thackeray said '*The* Virginians,' he left out many worthy and praiseworthy gentlemen and ladies entitled to use that name. Mr. James has not paid special attention to the Bostonians of the Somerset, Union, or St. Botolph clubs, of Trinity Church or the Old Corner Bookstore, of the Athenaeum or the Art Museum. King's Chapel is mentioned but once, and the somewhat different 'types' at the Church of the Advent are ignored, though they might have filled a novel all by themselves. Cambridge, to be sure, 'figures prominently,' but it is the Cambridge of 'suburban homes,' 'Monadnoc place,' rotting plankwalks, etc. Can we believe our eyes when we find a gentleman who has enjoyed the privileges of a department of Harvard University speaking of Cambridge, as viewed from Charles Street, in such terms as these: 'The long, low bridge that crawled on its staggering posts across the

Charles;' 'the desolate suburban horizons;' 'the general hard, cold void of the prospect;' 'there was something inexorable in the poverty of the scene, shameful in the meanness of its details,' etc. We will not quote more as to 'puddles,' 'the universal horse-car,' 'sheds and rotting piles,' 'loose fences,' and so on, but will reiterate that this is not all of Cambridge. Indeed, Mr. James himself speaks of 'the irregular group of heterogeneous buildings—chapels, dormitories, libraries, halls—which, scattered among slender trees, over a space reserved by means of a low rustic fence, rather than inclosed, ... constitutes the great university of Massachusetts.' Nay more, he treats Memorial Hall with respect, and seriously states, in the capacity of Mr. James himself, that 'the effect of the place is singularly noble and solemn, and it is impossible to feel it without a lifting of the heart.' We call special attention to this sentence, both as proving that Mr. James intended to satirize objectionable Bostonians alone, and that it is unjust to say that he 'lacks feeling.'

After this, it may be added that his pictures of Dr. Tarrant, the mesmeric healer; his faded and crushed wife, with her aspirations for 'society;' Miss Birdseye, veteran reformer; Mrs. Farrinder, great womans'-rights speaker, who would like to 'reach' Beacon Street by the aid of some initiated member; Olive Chancellor, the intense young woman hunting for a mission in life; and Verena Tarrant, the innocent and self-confident product of suburban Tarrantism—all these are remarkably well drawn. Basil Ransom, the chivalric and impoverished Mississippian; the rich New York Burrages; a pseudo-literary club in this city; and the plump and selfish Mrs. Luna, are more hackneyed characters. To sum up the merits and demerits of the book, one might justly say that Mr. James says nothing, in 449 closely-printed pages, but that he says it with an art that

is constant and charming. Who else, of living writers, has a touch so fine that the reader is content to skip nothing? Each sentence seems as condensed as possible, but the story moves very slowly; indeed, the story—with its comparatively crude devices and inartistic close—is what one cares least for.

Springfield [Mass.] *Republican,* 18 April 1886, p. 4.

"The Bostonians" is also a satire, and the foible of the age it strikes at is the public sphere of woman, in which naturally Mr. James does not believe. The mockery is excessively elaborate, and for several chapters it is a matter of doubt whether there is not to be a novel written. This fond anticipation gradually leaves one in a very curious melange of Mr. James's impressions concerning women's rights, inspirational speaking and persons with "fads" generally—to use a "so-English" word that Mr. James ought to like. The novelist has taken great liberties with Boston people and places; helped himself to the house of a well-known literary couple, almost burlesqued several distinguished idealists and some persons of practical value, and treated the best Boston notions without respect, and in fact with a condescension which is temperamental with Mr. James, and which perhaps he calls cosmopolitan, since he employs it also with regard to New York ways, and in other novels toward those of London and other towns of more or less importance. This condescension is rather more severe toward Boston than to other places, however, since his "Bostonians" are all of them "cranks," from Miss Olive Chancellor, the remnant of an old family which he speaks of as belonging to "the bourgeoisie," a distinction which was surely never drawn in Boston old families before—to pathetic Miss Birdseye,—"a confused, entangled, inconsequent, discursive old woman, whose charity began at home and ended nowhere, whose credulity kept pace with it," and whom he sums up as "a poor little humanitary hack." This is the gentlemanly manner in which Mr. James describes one of the best of women, and the caricature is certainly recognizable. But the persons whose fortunes make all the story there is are Verena Tarrant, a pretty girl who is introduced as an "inspirational" speaker, and is the daughter of a mesmeric healer; and Basil Ransom, a young Mississippian practicing law in New York, who is a cousin of Miss Chancellor and visits Boston at her invitation. Both Miss Chancellor and Ransom fall in love with the fascinating Verena; but while the Bostonian, who is wealthy, carries off her prize to consecrate her to virgin devotion of the cause of woman's elevation—the Southerner comes in after the fashion of man and offers her that mysterious philter called love, which, though with becoming reluctance, she quaffs, and finally disappears in her lover's arms and a hack, leaving a Boston audience exceedingly mad, and poor Olive Chancellor, the very genius of timidity, rushing on the stage to make good the ungrateful desertion.

This is the narrative, and its center of psychological interest in the struggle of Olive Chancellor, whom one forgets to think of as young, since her agonies are desolating in their concentrated morbidity and intensity. It is impossible to accept her as a type, but as an individual study she is most powerfully presented, and the effect of contemplating her is identical with that produced by any examination of insanity,—depressing in the last degree. The part she assumes in the scheme of Mr.

James's satire is much too tragical, it overweights the tale, which becomes a treatise on alienism. This is a mistake in art, for the movement which is the object of satire becomes secondary to this personal interest. As for the rest, the satire is not without its vigor and its partial truth, even though, as a matter of necessity, the real nobility of the movement for equalizing women with men in the rights of a government by the people is utterly scorned. The book is as ably written as anything Mr. James has done, notwithstanding its great tedium, the exceeding absurdity of much of its detail, and the indefensible liberties of his portraitures.

Independent 38 (22 April 1886), 495.

Mr. Henry James's tremendously pretentious-looking *The Bostonians* has duly been laid on our table. Its chapters appeared, group by group, month in and month out, in *The Century*. Even the most appreciative Jamesite fidgeted, admitted that the story was amazingly long drawn out, and that there seemed no way of approximately determining beforehand when it would be finished. In the words of the poet, it would suffice that an end would come—sometime; and then it would be known. In our museums and art-collections there are special departments and galleries devoted to, let us say, Aztec relics, cuneiform inscriptions, the evidences of the stone age, and the like. That these matters are set forth by themselves in clean and very quiet corners, does not mean that nobody in the world takes pleasure in inspecting them, or likes to set eyes on them. Not so. It merely signifies that most of us don't. It is implied that to the general, but by no means uneducated, public the spending an hour or so before those crowded shelves would be an insufferable bore, and make life a burden for the whole afternoon. Very good: Mr. James may nowadays be looked upon as the head of a certain college of savants, a man delighting in writing what to the majority of flesh-and-blood men and women has no excuse for being so praised, and books that grow more and more arid and dull. This long, prosy, carefully written novel was not worth writing, and is unreadable. Only a certain class of readers will be able honestly to say or think that they admire it or find anything in it that takes hold on them. To such we leave *The Bostonians*. Mr. James shall henceforth have his alcove in the literary gallery. Those who want him and what he has discovered in human nature will know where to go and sit down and—shall we say study? The rest of us will know enough to walk quickly by, not blaming the devotees of archaeology and the stone age for their taste, deeply humiliated that we prefer other mental material, but also honest enough to say so. Mr. James has undoubtedly put some of his very best work into this novel; an amount of care that a broadminded critic appreciates with real regret. It is as finished as an ice castle on the Neva. It warms us up just as much.

London *Times,* 30 April 1886, p. 3.

Mr. Henry James is beyond a doubt fully entitled to rank as the leader, or one of the two leaders, of American novelists; and he has, perhaps, by that fact acquired among English readers a reputation for which he might have waited a long time if he had been English himself. Whether "The Bostonians" (3 vols., Macmillan and Co.) is an average sample of his work may be matter of opinion; but certain it is that, in spite of the undeniable cleverness of this novel, it is not calculated to impress critics with the power of the American school. We are not alluding to the subject of the book (which deals largely in women's rights and wrongs) when we say that it is feminine in style, grasp, and matter. But a dilettante treatment and a tendency to minuteness do not prevent "The Bostonians" from being interesting and amusing; to which end it is assisted by (among other things) the author's American gift of coining new turns of expression. We suppose we may take it that "The Bostonians" portrays some actual phase of Bostonian culture; and, if so, we can only congratulate the "hub of the universe" on its activity in the cause of female emancipation. Miss Olive Chancellor, a graceful and cultured young lady, of independent means, and well described by her cousin, Basil Ransom, as a "ticklish spinster," is one of the devotees of the great cause. But she yearns for a great friend, not one of the daughters of leisure and pleasure, but one of the people, to fortify her in her task. The great friend turns up in Verena Tarrant, who is the beautiful daughter of a vulgar "mesmeric healer," and is what is known as an "inspirationist," that is, a person subject to fits of inspired eloquence. Her Miss Chancellor adjures, and with success, to "be her friend, her friend of friends, beyond every one, everything, for ever and for ever." Verena's pedigree prepares us for an imposture; but not so, Verena is consistently *naïve*, honest, and charming. Olive and she work well in double harness for the cause, Verena going into training for her great mission of bursting on the world as a prophetess of emancipation. But as it was in the case of the Princess, so it is in the case of her humbler imitators. Love (in the person of Basil Ransom, almost the only sane person in a book of crotcheteers) comes as the dissolvent of this union, and tears Verena from her shrill and indignant companion. We have ventured to outline the plot because "The Bostonians" has very little plot, and should be considered rather as a study of character. Olive and Verena are good and careful sketches of the virile and the feminine women's-righter respectively. There are several more of the same tribe— Mrs. Farrinder, their chief; Dr. Prance, the lady-physician; and Miss Birdseye, who—

> Belonged to the Short-Skirts League, as a matter of course; for she belonged to any and every league that had been founded for almost any purpose whatever. . . . She looked as if she had spent her life on platforms, in audiences, in phalansteries, in *séances;* in her faded face there was a kind of reflection of ugly lecture-lamps; with its habit of an upward angle, it seemed turned toward a public speaker, with an effort of respiration in the thick air in which social reforms are usually discussed. [*Novels 1881–1886*, p. 825]

After saying that there is little plot in "The Bostonians," we ought to add that there are, in the last chapters of the book, a very humorous and a very dramatic situation. The latter the reader shall discover for himself; for the former we have to thank an irrepressible American reporter.

Horace E. Scudder.
Atlantic Monthly 57 (June 1886), 851–53.

It might be supposed, at first glance, that Mr. James in his latest novel was not going to let us off, but intended to drag us with him into the labyrinth of the woman question. Nothing could be more unjust. Mr. James, with the quick instinct of an artist, saw his opportunity in the strange contrasts presented by a phase of Boston life which is usually taken too seriously for purposes of fiction. We do not remember any more striking illustration of Mr. James's general self-expatriation. He comes back, as it were, to scenes once familiar to him, bringing with him habits of thought and observation which make him seize upon just those features of life which would arrest the attention of an Englishman or Frenchman. The subtle distinctions between the Laphams and Coreys are nothing to him, but he is caught by the queer variety of humanitarianism which with many people outside of Boston is the peculiar attribute of that much suffering city.[1] He remembers, we will suppose, the older form, the abolition sentiment which prevailed in his youth, and now is curious about the later development, which he takes to be a medley of woman's rights, spiritualism, inspirationism, and the mind cure. He notices a disposition on the part of what a clever wit called Boston Proper to break away from its orbit and get entangled in this nebulous mass, and so he takes for his main figure a woman who is young and old by turns, according to the need of the novelist, a Bostonian of the straiter sect, who has yet, by the very force of her inherited rigidity of conscience, martyred herself, and cast in her lot with a set of reformers who are much the worse for wear. Olive Chancellor's high-bred disdain of her seedy associates is mingled with lofty devotion to the cause which they misrepresent, and the composition in character is extremely truthful and skillfully shown. What renders it even more fine as a personal portrait is the admixture of passionate, womanly appropriation of the girl whom she looks upon as the young priestess of the new church of womanhood; and the manner in which the woman is always getting the better of the doctrinaire strikes us as showing more completely than anything else in the book how thoroughly Mr. James has possessed himself of this character.

The second lady of this drama is Verena Tarrant, who was constructed for the purposes of the story, and is, we may say, a purely imaginary being. Mr. James may have had an indefinite image of the Priscilla of Hawthorne's The Blithedale Romance floating in his mind when he built this impossible Verena. Impossible, we say, because, while Hawthorne manages to invest Priscilla with a delicacy of nature in spite of her surroundings, Mr. James, in his analysis of Verena, makes her refined, beautiful, spiritual in her power, and in a hundred ways, when he is not analyzing her, succeeds in betraying a cheap imitation of spiritual beauty. That Olive Chancellor, with a cataract over her inner eye, should fail to perceive the innate vulgarity of the girl is not surprising, but it is too much to ask of us that we should make Basil Ransom stone blind also.

Basil Ransom, however, is in certain ways equally remote from the life which he is supposed to represent. It was a clever notion to bring the antipathetic element from the South, and in a few features this hero of the story has a little likeness to an actual Mississippian; but we cannot resist the conviction that Mr. James has never been in Mississippi, as the phrase goes, and trusts to luck that his readers have not been there, either. We have not much quarrel with him on this ground, however. Perhaps we ought to be thankful, since an intimacy with Ransom's native surroundings might have produced another book of the story, in which the hero should have been built up as patiently and minutely as was the case with the Bostonians themselves. Suffice it to say that the fact of an extreme Southern birth and breeding count for a great deal in orienting this important character.

We have intimated that the book is not in the least a contribution to the study of the woman question, so called. It is rather a study of the particular woman question in this book. Instead of the old, familiar predicament of one heroine and two heroes, one of whom must get and one lose the prize, the two heroes are a man and woman, but the struggle is of the same general character. Who is to have Verena? Shall it be Olive or Basil? That is the question which is asked with great particularity and at great length. The novel is divided into three books: in the first, Basil is barely introduced, but Olive and Verena are built up like a coral reef; in the second, the contesting parties manoeuvre for position; in the third, the conflict takes place, with what may be called a tussle at the end. We hope we may be pardoned for a slight "derangement of epitaphs" and for a possibly flippant manner in stating the argument of the book. The astounding array of particulars invites one to pause and see if he cannot abstract the generals. Indeed, one stands in amazement before the delicacy of workmanship, especially in the first few chapters. The minute touches with which the portraits of Olive Chancellor and Miss Birdseye are elaborated, and the quick, firm strokes that depict Mrs. Farrinder and the Tarrants, have never been excelled by Mr. James. There is a page given to Mrs. Farrinder which is simply a masterpiece in its way; its compactness intensifies its brilliancy, and the wit of its quiet sentences is as keen as it is easy.

The character, however, on which Mr. James has plainly expended the most careful and, we are tempted to say, loving descriptive art is that of Miss Birdseye. At first one fears that the author does not appreciate her, but one ends by seeing that Mr. James knew the pathetic nobility of the figure, and admired it, even while he was apparently amusing himself and his readers. It is not art alone that can do this,—something of personal tenderness must got into the process; and this character is the one redeeming feature of the book, if one is considering the humane aspects. The other persons are either ignoble, like the Tarrants and Mrs. Luna, or they are repellent for other reasons; but Miss Birdseye one falls in love with, quite to the exclusion of the proper heroine.

When we say that most of the characters are repellent, we are simply recording the effect which they produce upon the reader by reason of the attitude which the author of their being takes toward them. He does not love them. Why should he ask more of us? But since he is extremely interested in them, and seems never wearied of setting them in every possible light, we also accede to this interest, and if we have time enough strike up an extraordinary intimacy with all parties. It is when this interest leads Mr. James to push his characters too near the brink of nature that we step back and decline to follow. For instance, the details of the first interview between Olive and Verena in Olive's house carry these young women to dangerous lengths, and we hesitate about accepting the relation between them as either natural or reasonable. So far does this go that in the author's exhaustive reflections upon the subject directly afterward we feel as if another step only were needed to introduce a caricature by Mr. James upon himself. All this is still more apparent in the final scene of the book, which ought to have been the climax; instead of which, by its noise and confusion, and its almost indecent exposure of Miss Chancellor's mind, this scene allows the story just to tumble down at the end.

Mr. James himself is, we fear, somewhat contaminated by the people whom he has been associating with in this study.

His book begins, as we have said, with a remarkable piece of writing, but by and by he falls into a manner which could only have been caught from the Tarrants. His own manner has a trick of being almost too familiar, with its elisions and its easygoing phrases; but his constant resort to the initial *well* in conversation, and his habit of reporting the mind as well as the conversation of his baser characters in a sort of third personal evasion of elegance, add to the general effect of slouchiness which much of the book produces.

We have been drawn by the spirit of the book into a more minute criticism than we had intended, but after chasing with Mr. James so long, it is difficult not to go on chasing him a little. It is when we stop and take the book as a whole that we forget how fine the web is spun, and remember only the strong conception which underlies the book; the freshness of the material used; the amazing cleverness of separate passages; the consummate success shown in so dangerous a scene as the death of Miss Birdseye, where the reticence of art is splendidly displayed; and, in fine, the prodigal wealth scattered through all the pages. There is sorry waste, and one's last thought about the work is a somewhat melancholy one, but we all have a lurking affection for prodigals.

Note

1 William Dean Howells, *The Rise of Silas Lapham* (1885).

Julia Wedgwood.
Contemporary Review [England] 50 (August 1886), 300–1.

We will resist all temptation to criticize Mr. James's last novel from any other point of view than as the production of a clever and brilliant writer whose wit and shrewdness force us to listen with pleasure to an adulteration of familiar truth with vulgar prejudice and a narrative written on a plan that seems to us nothing less than execrable. He is such good company that we sit helpless while he insults our deepest convictions, and listen with irritation to what we would term, with a sense of inadequate virulence, the interruption of a perpetual *aside*. To be told not only what his *dramatis personæ* express but what they thought and kept to themselves, what they felt inclined to express and why they refrained—to be, in short, taken into their inmost confidence on every interview with them—seems to us a violation of every conceivable rule of literary good breeding, and affects us in fiction with not less sense of fatigue and unfitness than such an experience would in life. Intimacy of this close and absolute character should in both cases be an exceptional circumstance, a mark of special interest, not the inevitable result of an introduction. We may not say that it is never in place; there are crises in life when what men and women say or do cease to contain the true narrative of their lives; if you are to understand them you must know what they think and feel. But these crises are wholly exceptional, and to set the tone of a narrative to the key that they demand seems to us as great a mistake as for a sculptor to give all his work the anatomical indication that he needs to express the sudden strain of a Discobolus. The mistake is a result of that obsequious deference which Literature has in these days shown to triumphant Science; an instance of that obliteration of all reserve which the new lawgiver demands and she abhors. "By what he omits show me the master of style," is a maxim our popular writers have forgotten. It is curious that Mr. James should have fallen into this sin. The most earnest, and in spite of some odious associations we will add the most valuable, page in the "Bostonians," is devoted to a protest against what he calls "the damnable feminization of the age." How strikingly a latent touch of conscience accentuates protest! Mr. James is the greatest sinner in this "feminization" that fiction can produce. He gives us on this present canvas at the least three women to one man, and takes not half the trouble over the man that he spends on any of his women. As Mr. James conceives the interests of women, his tiny brush, his perpetual stippling, his touching and retouching every line, are appropriate media of representation, and keeps to the region where this method is legitimate. The novel ends abruptly with the triumph of a man's will over a woman's sense of faithfulness to an engagement; and makes us feel vividly the weakness of woman and the momentum of man. But there is no sense of real strength anywhere.

Checklist of Additional Reviews

Literary World [England] 33 (19 March 1886), 267–68.

St. Louis Missouri Republican, 20 March 1886, p. 7.

Spectator [England] 59 (20 March 1886), 388. Reprinted in Roger Gard, ed., Henry James: The Critical Heritage (London: Routledge & Kegan Paul, 1968), pp. 162–63; James W. Gargano, ed., Critical Essays on Henry James: The Early Novels (Boston: G. K. Hall, 1987), pp. 58–61.

Cleveland Daily Plain Dealer, 21 March 1886, p. 4.

Detroit Evening News, 21 March 1886, p. 2.

Indianapolis Journal, 28 March 1886, p. 9.

New York Daily Tribune, 28 March 1886, p. 6. Reprinted in Gargano, pp. 61–62.

New York Times, 28 March 1886, p. 12.

"Nym Crinkle" [Andrew C. Wheeler]. New York World, 28 March 1886, p. 12.

Indianapolis Journal, 29 March 1886, p. 5.

St. Paul Daily Pioneer Press, 29 March 1886, p. 4.

Catholic World 43 (April 1886), 130.

Graphic [England] 33 (3 April 1886), 378.

Chicago Inter-Ocean, 3 April 1886, p. 10.

Cincinnati Commercial Gazette, 3 April 1886, p. 13.

New York Daily Graphic, 3 April 1886, p. 311.

Chicago Times, 10 April 1886, p. 13.

New Orleans Daily Picayune, 11 April 1886, p. 14.

"Henry James' Latest Work of Fiction." San Francisco Chronicle, 11 April 1886, p. 11.

Louisville Courier-Journal, 16 April 1886, p. 4.

[William Morton Payne]. Dial 7 (May 1886), 14–15.

W. H. Babcock. Lippincott's Magazine 37 (May 1886), 554–56.

Nation 42 (13 May 1886), 407–8. Reprinted in Gard, p. 164.

Albany Evening Journal, 28 May 1886, p. 3.

Saturday Review [England] 61 (5 June 1886), 791–92.

Literary World [Boston] 17 (12 June 1886), 198. Reprinted in Gard, p. 165.

Catholic World 43 (July 1886), 560–61.

THE PRINCESS CASAMASSIMA

Athenaeum [England]
3080 (6 November 1886),
596–97.

If it be not impertinent to hazard a guess at the origins of novels, we should be inclined to surmise that Mr. James had prepared himself for the composition of his present work by a study of some of the Russian novelists, winding up with 'L'Éducation Sentimentale'[1] as a pattern for form and general construction. Not only the secret society business upon which the present story is based, but the frequent insistence upon sordid surroundings and ignoble characters, reminds the reader of Herzen[2] or Dostoievsky; while the fragmentary style of the narrative and the constant abrupt changes of scene recall one of the most irritating characteristics of Flaubert's highly unsatisfactory tale. The result is hardly a success. Socialist conspiracies do not form a congenial theme for Mr. James's Muse; nor has she in the present instance shown herself more capable than heretofore of inspiring a long-continued effort. An enormous quantity of the book (which itself is just about equal in number of words to two average three-volume novels) might be excised without affecting the progress of the story one whit. Unless the author's object was merely to sketch various types of the people who try to improve social unevennesses, it may safely be said that the benevolent Lady Aurora Langrish might go bodily and never be missed. The same applies pretty nearly to her invalid *protégés*. Of course in real life we see a good deal of a great many people whose existence cannot be said to have any perceptible effect on our fortunes, but a literal transcript of real life does not necessarily make a novel any more than a faithful rendering of a view makes a picture. But even if the unessential were eliminated from Mr. James's novel, the remainder would still show that the author and his subject were ill suited. The style in which he has succeeded is adapted well enough for gentle satire on human weaknesses, for tender analysis of such elements of interest as exist in commonplace characters; it fails altogether when it has to deal with the really dark places of human nature. If we understand the present story rightly—that is, if it is anything beyond the mark of a fanciful romance in the Shorthouse manner[3]—the princess is a profligate woman who dabbles in socialism and conspiracy as others in gambling; Paul Muniment is a selfish scoundrel who schemes to take advantage of his friend's genuine enthusiasm, first in order to put him into a post of danger which he dares not take himself, and then by this means to supplant him in the road to a certain social advancement by which his own coarser nature can never profit; while poor Hyacinth himself, with his ambiguous parentage, and the two diverse strains of blood for ever working diversely in him, is the fool and dupe of people morally and intellectually far below him. But if this is what the author means us to see, he gives us trouble enough to get at it. In vulgar phrase he raises the devil, but will not face him. He constantly leads his characters up to a "strong" situation, and then, like Autolycus, "puts them off, slights them, with 'Whoop, do me no harm, good man.'" When the strong situation does come it is strong enough in all conscience, but it is on the last page of the book, and then the reader puzzled and slightly resentful at being brought to this after all by a set of people who, he has learnt to believe, had not among them so much purpose as would be required to drown a kitten. It is an odd feature of the book that nearly all the action, or nearly all of which the date

175

is indicated, takes place on Sundays. Possibly a London week-day suggests a life too strenuous to the lived by the aimless beings whom Mr. James depicts. On one point the author may, we suppose, be congratulated. If people did not now and then "feel badly" or "dreadfully," no one would suppose that the story was not the work of a British hand.

Notes

1 Gustave Flaubert, *L'éducation sentimentale* (1869).
2 Alexander Ivanovich Herzen (1812–70).
3 Joseph Henry Shorthouse (1834–1903). The comment refers to Shorthouse's *John Inglesant* (1880).

Detroit *Free Press*, 13 November 1886, p. 8.

It is a serious test to which to put a 600-page novel, that of publishing it in serial form. A story must be very lively indeed and its interest must be not only admirably sustained but judiciously intensified at the proper periodic points to stand such a test. If the readers lay the story down at any point without some eagerness to get at the coming chapter the story is doomed. It may be read thereafter as a matter of duty, just as some thrifty people eat what is on their plates after appetite is satisfied merely to keep it from being wasted. But no such perfunctory reading counts toward the reputation of a book.

Mr. Henry James' story, "The Princess Casamassima," has been put to this test and has stood it only fairly well. Though very much superior in many respects to the author's previous novels it has tired out a good many readers even of those who

are counted among his admirers. In the book form, where the reader can attack it and leave it at such point as pleases him, it is less likely to prove wearisome; but it cannot fail to impress any candid reader as unnecessarily long. This is not due so much to any superfluity of character or incident or even of detail. It is traceable chiefly to Mr. James' excessive wordiness. Short, sharp, crisp, nobody expects him to be. If he were he would no longer be James. But it certainly does seem that he might be very much less wordy without sacrificing anything essentially Jamesian.

The story is too long—as what has been said clearly indicates—to be even outlined within the limits of a newspaper notice. It is, moreover, a book to which even the fullest outline would do scant justice. We leave it, therefore, to the more or less tender mercies of the reader with the bare statement that it is a story—and in some respects a study of revolutionary socialism in London—in which the long-named Princess and her protege, Hyacinth, play prominent parts.

London *Daily Telegraph*, 18 November 1886, p. 2.

A subject intrinsically sombre is treated by Mr. Henry James in "Princess Casamassima" (Macmillan) with an unwonted tediousness, making it a task of the utmost labour to penetrate the dreary Sahara of this three-volumed Socialistic novel. Neither moral nor wit is to be deducted from the barren record of the folly of Mr. Henry James' hare-brained bookbinder. This misguided youth leans to the yearnings of brother Democrats, and from an ungainly childhood, marked by the utterances of impossibly precocious wisdom, attains manhood without any improvement in his mental condition. Not even the imputation of bastardy nor the suggestion that he has the right to a scoundrel lord's escutcheon, with the addition of a bar-sinister, can galvanise an interest in his tedious descent from birth to self-inflicted obliteration. The affection of Princess Casamassima for this philanthropical monstrosity is incomprehensible except under regard to the tenderness of affinity and the gregariousness of kind. This lady renounces the sumptuousness of her well-stocked palace to wander into the saddest spots of London upon the arm of her youthful democrat, and spy the nakedness of the land through his distorted vision. She disposes of the rank and station which alone could fit her to lead a kindly movement for bettering the condition of the down-cast for the sake of an impossible propaganda and a foolish stripling. Had Hyacinth stuck to his paste pot and mallet it is just possible he might have been a respectable bookbinder, but Mr. Henry James has represented him as a most tedious and vapid hero, whose tragic end is a decided relief. Not Millicent Henning, the delightfully quaint Miss Pynsent, nor any grace of diction or erudition can serve to counterbalance the general tediousness of the book.

"Socialism in Three Volumes."
Punch [England] 91 (20 November 1886), p. 245.

If the Socialists had to sing small on Lord Mayor's Show day, they may perhaps find consolation in other quarters. Flouted by Society, abused by the Press, and checkmated by Sir Charles Warren,[1] they have at least found favour with the Novelist. They seem, indeed, lately to have taken all fiction for their province.

One would hardly, however, have expected the dainty and deliberate Henry James to take anything so violent, so vulgar, so destitute of "sweet reasonableness" as Socialism for his subject. Yet here we find him in his new novel, *The Princess Casamassima,* dealing with Secret Societies, and the Great Restitution. Dealing in his own way, of course, which is, perhaps, hardly the firm and full-blooded way best suited to the theme. Mr. James's specimens of the British proletariat, like his capriciously cosmopolitan Princesses, are very select, and, as the Darwinite would say, "highly specialised" specimens. *Hyacinth Robinson* and *Paul Muniment* are very far indeed from being average British Workmen, and they and their story, it must be feared, would pretty considerably puzzle any handicraft member of the Social Democratic Federation who took up *The Princess Casamassima* with the idea of getting any light upon Culture's view of "the movement."

To the ordinary and not too earnest reader, however, Mr. James's new book is very delightful reading. Poor ill-fated *Hyacinth,* with his tragic antecedents, his mixed nature, his artistic instincts and conflicting sympathies, his small person and his great, if delicate and undemonstrative pluck, and his dismal doom, is a very winning character. *Paul Muniment* is a puzzle and a disappointment. *Pinnie,* the frail and confused but devoted little dressmaker, but touched in very cleverly, with somewhat finical irony in place of somewhat exaggerated humour. She is very real, and seems more vivid and vascular than any other character in the book. As to the miraculously lovely, man-tormenting, convention-defying, emotion-seeking *Princess Casamassima* herself, with her sphinx-like fascinations and her equivocal interest in "uprisings and liberations," one finds her, in the long run, rather irritating, and just a little preposterous.

Mr. James as usual, runs away from his subject, leaves most of his heroes and heroines in the lurch, and his readers pretty much in the dark. It is his way. It is not a satisfying way, at any rate to the ordinary novel-reader, who cares more for a finished story than for a story's "finish," or for fine-spun theories of fictional art.

He has used Socialism mainly as a sort of peg on which to hang certain curiously-conceived and delicately-executed character-paintings of his own particular *genre*. Possibly that is all that he wanted it for.

Note

1 Sir Charles Warren (1840–1927), general and archaeologist, served as chief commissioner of the London Metropolitan Police, 1886–88 (*DNB*).

"A 'Slumming' Romance." New York *Times,* 21 November 1886, p. 12.

Some half century ago there was a stupid fashion in Europe which engrossed the attention of well-to-do people. Under the guise of charity in order to find means for the doing of good works rich people picked to pieces old stuffs and fringes containing threads of gold. By the sale of the precious metal thus extracted they contributed means to the needy. From taking long cast away frippery and subjecting it to the picking process, after a while old material became difficult to procure, so in order to keep on picking recourse was had to new. In England for the last few years,

not all fashionable society, but a portion of it, has devoted itself to what was called "slumming." By "slumming" was meant the visiting of such scenes of misery in London as Mr. Arnold White describes in his "Perils of a Great City." English charity is munificent, and if we are not in error private subscriptions in London alone, devoted to the relief of the indigent, are larger than the whole Government income of Sweden. From the visitations of the lady, mistress of the manor, who saw with her own eyes who among her poor tenantry wanted coals or blankets, the habit of directly administering to the needy may have had its origin. If we are to believe such notices as may have found their way into the public prints, slumming became somewhat of a mania among a certain set in London. Balls, parties, and festivities were not neglected, but from the scenes of high revelry the leaders of the dance would make it a business to give one another a rendezvous afterward in some wretched quarter of London, and there stand face to face with misery and vice.

Was it simply for contrast that such extremes of life were sought? Did a close contact with all that was low, base, and degrading act as an agreeable fillip? Let us by no means look askance at the motives which thus actuated well-to-do men and women, for "charity shall cover a multitude of sins." Perhaps there was occasionally a little bit of an approach at a masquerade in such visits. The Worth dresses were cast aside and strange and incongruous attempts were made by the leaders of London society to assimilate themselves at least in their garb to wretched surroundings. The scullery maid's cast-off frock or the groom's clothes were borrowed and sometimes, when the visitors were clever, the London jargon, the true slang of St. Giles, the argot of the metropolis, was adopted. It is not worth while for us to moralize on the motives of the slummers or to weigh the actual benefits. Granting that the desire existed to ameliorate the conditions of starving London, for the solid quantity of good done it must have been inappreciable and perhaps more conducive to harm than otherwise. Providence appearing to a starving man or woman in a Haroun el Raschid guise rarely if ever brings lasting benefit. All we wish to do in explaining what is slumming is to show how it has found its place in English romance literature, for Mr. Lang's last story is tinged somewhat with slumming.

Mr. James's "Princess Casamassima" is the novel of slumming, and the type of the aristocratic slummer is Lady Aurora Langrish, of Inglefield, who is the daughter of an Earl. With her charity is a passion, Lady Aurora says: "I don't know whether it's charity—I don't mean that. But whatever it is it's a passion—it's my life—it's all I care for." But besides this visiting of the poor, Mr. James takes up another subject, that of the London Socialists, Nihilists, and Anarchists, and to these he devotes no small portion of his pages.

"The Princess Casamassima" is a sinister romance, and we have no hesitation in calling it a singularly unpleasant one. Having had allotted to him as the maker of an English novel the amplest space, Mr. James has fabricated a tiresome story of 596 pages. With his peculiar tendencies to be retrospective and introspective, he indulges in these qualities *ad nauseum*. That want of virility with which Mr. James has been taxed certainly becomes a distinguishing trait in "The Princess Casamassima." In order to be nice and elegant whenever he can he sprays his subject as with a perfumed atomizer. Mr. James dawdles and lingers, postpones and prolongs, saunters backward and forward, and staves off as long as he can the tragic dénouement, the suicide of Hyacinth Robinson, although the merest tyro in romance reading knows it must come.

On page 454 we have, for a wonder, concisely told who is Hyacinth Robinson, and we feel grateful for the incisive way in which Mr. James puts it. He is "the bastard of a murderess, spawned in a gutter, out of which he has been picked by a sewing girl." The reader having understood this much, the plot of the story can be followed. Hyacinth is the son of a French sewing woman, and Lord Purvis, the father, being some dissipated lordling. In a moment of jealousy Florentine Vivier stabs Lord Purvis, and Florentine spends the rest of her life in prison. Miss Amanda Pynsent, a London dressmaker, takes charge of the child, Hyacinth Robinson, who is of course ignorant of his parentage. When Florentine is at her last gasp in prison she begs to see her child, and Hyacinth is taken to her. In after-life the accident of his unfortunate parentage ruins Hyacinth, for he goes to the British Museum and there reads the whole story of his mother's crime, his father's baseness. His is a mixed nature. Amanda cares for him, and the lad is apprenticed to a bookbinder, Crookenden, and, having strong artistic taste, Hyacinth becomes a master workman. Melicent [*sic*] Henning is the type of the London girl who has "a showroom laugh." Her physical structure is of the opulent kind, and her bodice hardly restrains her bouncing charms. She is a plebeian, and if London ever went republican and a Goddess of Reason were wanted to grace in a procession the British metropolis, providing Mellicent Henning had plenty of shrimps, she would have figured for a heroine in the most statuesque manner. When Hyacinth was a little lad in Lissom Grove, the shabby London quarters where Miss Pynsent lived, Melicent had a fondness for kissing him. As the two grow up Melicent loves Hyacinth in a sensuous manner, though he is always in a spiritual atmosphere which bewilders her.

Eustache Poupin, a French republican

179

and exile, is a clever bookbinder, and from him Hyacinth acquires Socialists' doctrines. If Paul Muniment, an advanced Nihilist, is rather difficult to understand, Poupin is not. We think that Poupin, as Mr. James describes him, is the only natural character in the book. Unfortunately for Hyacinth he meets the Princess Casamassima. She is a nondescript. Mr. James has tried to write of a woman full of the strangest freaks and vagaries, and the Princess is a muddled production. Octave Feuillet at his worst has written up a woman something of this kind—a sphynx in petticoats, a meretricious enigma. The Princess has left her husband, a blundering Italian, and seeking novel sensations, considers slumming in the same guise as she would picnicking. Hyacinth fascinates her, for she wants to know about Socialism, and one night at a theatre, where the young man has gone with Melicent, the Princess sends her go-between, Major Sholto, to invite Hyacinth to her box. The power the Princess exercises over "the bastard of a murderess," recalls an episode in a romance of George Sand. In time this Circe tires of the bookbinder, and tries to get Paul Muniment in her coils, but he is far too clever for her. Diedrich Hoffendahl is the secret spring of the whole Nihilistic movement. He decides who among the great potentates of the earth shall or shall not live. A willing instrument to execute his commands is wanted. Hyacinth at a Socialistic meeting offers himself to do anything required, and he is after a great many demarches put face to face with Hoffendahl, and he takes the oath of implicit obedience. Miss Pynsent dies and leaves Hyacinth a small legacy, and the young man pays Paris and Venice a short visit. Life before this, struggling as he was, surrounded by a world which disgusted him, has been bitter. Now he tastes for the first time all the joys of existence. He revels in the works of art and writes from Venice pretty letters to the Princess, giving her his virgin impressions. He longs to see her again. The terrible vow he has taken occasionally disturbs him. It may, he hopes, never have to be carried out. When he returns to England and is thrown in with coarse workmen in the bookbindery, his spirit revolts for a time, but he after a while becomes happy with his work because he thinks that then he can display his artistic skill. It is bitterness to find, however, that he is no longer on the same footing with the Princess. Melicent is still true to him, and he inclined to seek relief in her protecting power, for with her strong arms she would even fight for him. But Hyacinth is called. All the mysterious clap-trap of a messenger who brings the fatal order of the Nihilistic chief Mr. James writes up. Hyacinth must do the bloody work. It is true the Princess and an old friend of his, Vetch, a fiddler in a theatre, dread that Hyacinth may be Hoffendahl's instrument. Paul Muniment, who has egged on Hyacinth, is as cool and indifferent about his tool as if Hyacinth were a machine.

There is to be some grand festivity where a royal personage is to be present, and it is evident that the removal of this royal personage is on the Nihilistic programme. As Paul Muniment remarked, "This kind of work will help the democracy to get possession that the classes that keep them down shall be admonished from time to time that they have a very definite and very determined intention of doing so. An immense deal will depend on that. Hoffendahl is a capital admonisher." Hyacinth's warmth for the cause is doubted. Even Poupin and his wife are suspicious of him. The day, however, comes. The note Hyacinth has drawn falls due. There must be offered in payment a life—some life, but whose? Schinkle, the slow phlegmatic German, who plods in Nihilism, is as inexorable as fate. Were the gutters running with blood he would calmly puff his pipe. Accompanied by the Princess Casamassima, he hastens to Hyacinth's poor lodgings. They knock at the door, and there is no response. Schinkle bursts the hinges of the door, and finds Hyacinth dead. He has shot himself through the heart. Schinkle picked up the pistol "and carefully placed it on the mantel shelf, keeping, equally carefully to himself, the reflection that it would certainly have served much better for the Duke."

To compare "The Princess Casamassima" with the other works of Mr. James, taking the products of a man's brains and assorting material objects to them, we would say that Mr. James has made before this many nice literary sachets. To do this well calls on the best abilities of a capital perfumer. All sweet-smelling roots must be carefully ground, triturated, mixed, and no scent be too much in prominence. "The Princess Casamassima" is not precisely of this kind. Rather a pomander, or belike a vinaigrette. The case, a perfection of neatness, shows sharp chiselings, is worked up *ad unguam*, but from the inside comes whiffs redolent with the acrid sharpness of thieves' vinegar.

The decadence of a literary art, once most distinguished, we think is appreciable in "The Princess Casamassima."

London *Times,* 26 November 1886, p. 13.

Voltaire said of the prophet Habakkuk that a man with a name like that was capable of anything; and we are equally prepared to find this princess either at the top or the bottom of the scale—either an angel of light or a princess of darkness. It is with surprise, therefore, that we find her remarkably mediocre. True, she dabbles in anarchist plots, lives apart from her husband, and exchanges her palace in Mayfair for a two-storied stucco-fronted house in Pentonville, in order to make acquaintance with the life of the people. But, like most of Mr. James's characters, she is of the *dilettante* sort. And, after all, she is almost an interpolation in this story, which is concerned not so much with the Princess Casamassima as with Hyacinth Robinson. There is, no doubt, an artistic contrast in the tale of this amiable, easygoing, clever little bookbinder, with aristocratic instincts inherited from a putative father, becoming entangled in secret societies, and singled out to do a deed of blood. Such a mission, suited only to society's malcontents, is by the irony of fate forced upon one who is petted by all with whom he is brought in contact; by persons so various as, among others, an orchestral fiddler, a milliner's buxom young lady, a French anarchist, the gawky daughter of a peer, a Socialist *employé* at chemical works, and, not least, by the Princess herself. Perhaps, if the Princess had not taken him up, tired of him, and then dropped him for some other Socialist curiosity, Hyacinth's end would not have been so tragic. But to evolve this connexion of the Princess with Hyacinth's fate requires considerable ingenuity; and, even granting the hypothesis to be true, the plot is fearfully stationary, and the reader is kept waiting while the medley of characters converse with one another with amused curiosity, as though they were so many psychological specimens engaged in a microscopic examination of each other. Mr. James is a master of catching faint *nuances* of feeling, and stereotyping them in dialogue. A small display of this capacity goes a long way in a novel. In "The Princess Casamassima" most people will be of opinion that the author has entirely sacrificed effect to detail; and that this is, on the whole, a monotonous book.

Saturday Review [England] 62 (27 November 1886), 728–29.

In *The Princess Casamassima* Mr. Henry James has broken what is for him new ground, and taken a fresh departure. Hitherto he has been the poet of the Fine Shades, the artist in emotions reduced to vanishing point and situations whittled away to the small end of nothing. It was his function (self-imposed) to demonstrate that immense capacity of being futile which is the peculiar attribute of latter-day humanity. For years, indeed, he has been labouring with all his might, and with uncommon success, to extract sunbeams from cucumbers. Or he might be compared with that other philosopher whose aim it was to bring his horse to live upon a straw *per diem*. He succeeded, it is told, but the animal died in his hour of triumph. Mr. James did likewise. He reduced his readers to a straw (of incident) per volume, and the novel expired—or went near to expiring—in his hands. He is now a changed man. He has taken a nearer view of his art, and has found that the good novelist with decency may comprehend in his scheme such qualities as action, vigorous emotion, brave incident, and even romance. Surprising as it seems, it is none the less a positive fact that he has made a real story, and invented a number of characters in whom it is possible for the common carnal-minded reader—the poor, gross, brutish creature who delights in Scott and Dickens and Marryat—to be sincerely interested. To say that his achievement is complete would be to say

that which is not. There is a great amount of superfluous analysis; much of the dialogue is far too subtle in intention and impalpable in effect; while the heroine is more enigmatic and peculiar than a lady of romance should be. But, considered as a first attempt, the book is wonderfully good. It was scarce to be expected that, after years of refining upon refinement, and "the futilization of futility," Mr. James should bound upon the world as a common downright story-teller, in the manner of Scrooge announcing his conversation to the theory of Christmas. There is no such zealot as your new apostate; and such brilliant and taking melodrama may well have been included in his ambition. But to succeed was beyond his strength; and though he must be credited for a vast deal more than good intentions, it is obvious that the old Adam has been somewhat too much for him. In his new story there is no young woman of Boston who "refuses a duke for psychological reasons." But the personages behave too often as if they had the honour of her acquaintance, and were none the better for it.

All this to the contrary, Mr. James has made an immense advance upon himself, in ambition and material alike. His scene is laid in lower London, his personages are mostly workmen and shop-girls; the stuff of his intrigues is that desperate and far-reaching conspiracy against society, the signs of which were seen in Chicago of late, and but the other day in Vienna. His hero, Hyacinth Robinson, is the offspring of an English nobleman and a French courtesan; and years before the story opens his mother has killed his father, and been sent into penal servitude for life. He is adopted by a kindly little dressmaker and a friend of hers, a Mr. Vetch, who is a fiddler at one of the minor theatres (both characters are admirably observed, and scarce less admirably conveyed); and, with our first glimpse of him, he is hurried off to the infirmary at Millbank, where his mother, whom he does not know, is dying. When next we hear of him, he is a man grown, he works in a bookbinder's shop in Soho, he is an artist in his way, he has learned French, and read much, and is possessed of ideas above his years and tastes beyond his station. He indulges in a pleasant and very reasonable flirtation with an old friend, a certain Millicent Henning, who is employed in the showroom of a great West-End house; in the natural course of things (the girl, a cockney *pur sang*, is a capital study, and Hyacinth's relations with her are touched with singular adroitness and intelligence) he takes her to a theatre. There he is accosted by an acquaintance of his, a Captain Sholto, whom he has encountered vaguely at a political club, and by Captain Sholto he is whisked off to a box, and introduced, as a genuine working-man, to the Princess Casamassima and her companion Mme. Grandoni. The Princess, who is none other than the Christina Light of *Roderick Hudson*, is enchantingly beautiful and very greedy of experience. She has parted with the Prince, has dabbled in politics, and now it is her fancy to know the truth about democracy, and to study the lower strata of civilization from the life. She begins the experiment upon Hyacinth Robinson, who, by the agency of some friends of his, and especially a certain Paul Muniment, has become affiliated to, and at the orders of, a dreadful secret society. The Princess's curiosity takes a good deal of satisfying, and when it is ended as far as Hyacinth is concerned, it centres itself at once upon Paul Muniment and the Brotherhood. Of the extent to which it is gratified, and of the price which the Princess pays, nothing definite is told. The one thing certain is that Hyacinth is commissioned to do murder in the service of the society; that he finds the Princess completely indifferent to him; that he comes

upon Millicent in the act of flirting with Sholto; and that, like the Nejdanoff of *Virgin Soil*, with which book his story has more than one point of resemblance, he solves the problem by killing himself.[1] The world is too much for him, as it was for Hamlet; and, having lost his chance and taken the wrong turning, he escapes the difficulty as best he may, and goes out of life, a failure, but an honest man.

This dark and melancholy history it is which has persuaded Mr. James to break with his past, and essay himself in genuine fiction. He has succeeded, as we have said, imperfectly; but upon his success, imperfect as it is, he deserves, and should receive, the warmest congratulations. The defects of his work, as we have noted, are a superabundance of analysis and an excess of talk. The analysis is always intelligent, the talk is always pointed and apt; but there is too much of both, and the story suffers in proportion. Mr. James has halted between the author of *The Brigadier* and *The Roadside Inn* and the author of *Washington Square* and *The Portrait of a Lady*. His material is excellent, his method is the wrong one; and it speaks volumes for his talent and intelligence that he should have gone so near as he has to reconciling and ordering a set of elements essentially conflicting and diverse. In his next romance—for, of course, he must go on in his new path; one *Princess Casamassima*, with all its imperfections, is worth a wilderness of *Washington Squares*—he must widen the breach between his present and his former self, resist the devil of analysis, face his situations boldly, and content himself with talk that may not be witty, but that is inevitably direct and useful. The vigorous way in which he has handled his characters in the present story—Robinson, Millicent, Vetch, Pynsent, Florentine, the Poupins, Muniment, Grandoni, Schinkel, Lady Aurora—the energy and understanding with which he has touched the more violent of his incidents, the freshness and the romance he has imparted to his feeling for London and its innumerable mysteries—all this bears witness to the wisdom of his choice, and is earnest of much good and taking work to be done in the same field. He has but to follow his own lead in *The Princess Casamassima* not only to do well, but to command the great general public.

Note

1 A work by Turgenev. The two works the reviewer mentions in the next paragraph, "The Brigadier" and "The Roadside Inn," are also by Turgenev.

Graphic [England] 35 (18 December 1886), 646.

Mr. Henry James has hitherto been credited with his admirers for refraining from writing stories on the ground, not that he could not, but that he would not—that he regards the methods of Scott, of Dumas, of Dickens, and of Balzac as artistic degradation. On what ground, therefore, they will defend his publication of "The Princess Casamassima" (3 vols.: Macmillan and Co.) we are at a loss to surmise, seeing that he has evidently done his utmost to write a novel with a story in it, and has, to put the case as mildly as possible, not succeeded. No doubt, however, the style which he has made his own does not lend itself to decided character and dramatic situations without a very decided strain, and the mannerisms of the microscopic analyst of infinitesimal trifles are not to be lightly thrown aside. It may be that Mr. James is deeply versed in human nature and in the physiology of socialistic conspiracy; but he assuredly does not succeed in making anybody believe in his characters. It is not even evident that he himself understands them. The Princess has the air of being a factitious bundle of incompatibilities put together for the purpose of making people wonder at the profundity of her creator, and of tempting them to express admiration for fear of being suspected of lacking intelligence. Anybody, with a little tact, can construct a machine that looks wonderfully complicated, but that means nothing; and nine people out of ten will be ashamed to admit their inability to see the meaning of anything, even to themselves. In this sort of tact, and in the setting of traps to catch the superior people, we have always held that the art of Mr. James consists mainly, if not wholly; and "The Princess Casamassima" is eminently calculated to bear out our opinion, which we must here content ourselves with restating. The novel contains, however, one portrait in which he has very nearly succeeded—his type of the *plebs* at its best and worst, its most honest and its most vulgar, which he studies under the name of Millicent Henning. She is by far the finest creation that has ever come from his pen, and would have been as entirely successful as she is original were it not for her being held too obtrusively under the lens. As for the story itself, not the most scornfully plotless of all his works has ever been so vapid or so dull. Mr. James has obviously known better than his admirers why he has preferred the disquisition to the story; and he is unlikely, we should imagine, to descend from his Olympian heights for a second time.

In the *Princess Casamassima*, Mr. Henry James, without relinquishing that persistent attention to detail which has militated against the success of his later novels, has really written with more breadth and virility than one has come to expect. There are scenes of actual distinctness, almost robustness of treatment, not a few of them being, in common with most of the characters, particularly unpleasant. The final tragedy is graphic with all the sensationalism of a serial in illustrated weeklies of a certain order. The book, however, is so intolerably provoking in involved phraseology; its wordiness, everlasting wordiness is so terrific; and the sentences and paragraphs are frequently put together in Mr. James's most slipshod, slovenly manner that getting at the force of the story is a confusing process. Mr. James's love of singularity and elaborateness runs riot now and then. The plot is not completely worked out—as usual; the reader closing the book with the notion that a great deal more in the way of a winding-up is certainly due to him. The moral philosophy Mr. James seems inclined to inculcate in *The Princess Casamassima* is a trifle elusive. It appears to tend toward a profound, heartless indifferentism toward life, death and everything which concerns the human species, bad or good.

The Princess Casamassima is at once exceedingly tedious and very interesting. The paradox is less startling than it sounds. The fault which results in a tediousness that we will venture to affirm will make it very difficult for a large percentage of readers to get through the book at all, is that—we borrow the phrase—'minute stippling' which while it renders Mr. James's short studies wonderfully effective, is destructive when laboriously carried through three rather closely printed volumes; the interest lies in the number of ideas well worth consideration which will be the reward of any intelligent reader who goes carefully through the book. Whether consciously, or unconsciously, Mr. James has worked out much the same result as the author of *Demos*.[1] He has shown what an utter sham socialism, so called, is. These fiery champions of the starving, oppressed, down-trodden working class, rant, denounce, and are always going to begin, no one seems to know exactly what, but very evidently something which is really to place them in the position of the class they intend to pull down. Meantime they touch not the burdens of the sufferers with one of their fingers. They leave all practical effort to lighten that load to a Lady Aurora, or a Princess Casamassima. We cannot profess much admiration for this half American, half Italian adventuress. She is after all largely a sham, and shams are always vulgar; while Lady Aurora is too blurred an outline to be very interesting. Still, there is a vein of subtle irony in the contrast presented—the two women, reared in luxury, practising the socialism that gives to those who have not; the two artizans capable only of the socialism which takes away from those who have. To any intending reader of *The Princess Casamassima,* we would suggest to keep in his head two ideas—one, that not genuine sympathy with suffering is required to make a socialist—that makes a Shaftesbury—but a strongly developed sense, on the part of the individual, of the horrible iniquity involved in his not being personally exempt from the suffering which is more or less the fate of all humanity. The other, that a beautiful and fascinating woman, playing at socialism, is likely to prove an interesting study, as tending more in the direction of havoc among promising socialists, than in that of advancing the cause. Was Samson a socialist? Whosoever will expand these ideas for himself will, we think, find the tediousness of Mr. James's story overridden by its interest. But why should three different writers produce three different socialists, and call them respectively, Mutimer, Monument, and Muniment? It makes it hard for a critic to avoid getting a little mixed.

Note

1   George Gissing, *Demos: A Story of English Socialism* (1886).

[R. H. Hutton].
"*The Princess Casamassima.*"
Spectator [England] 3053
(1 January 1887), 14–16.

Perhaps this remarkable book has more title to be classed as a "novel" than as any other literary creation. It certainly is still less of a romance than of a novel, and less of a story than of a romance. But if it is a novel, it is one of a very unique kind. It has hardly any incident, unless the tendency of the whole network of circumstance and character to the tragedy with which the third volume abruptly closes, may be regarded as in itself constituting a single massive incident. But strange and unsatisfactory as the book is from every point of view but one, Mr. Henry James has never shown his extraordinary subtlety and strength to greater advantage. One reason of this is that what he loves best to draw, and draws with most success, because there is something in him which this kind of fiction best expresses, is character adrift from all its natural moorings,—character not fitting kindly to its circumstances. And since this story concerning the aspirations of the Nihilists enables him to present us with a whole group of characters which are thus adrift, men who, however well they may discharge their ordinary duties, are deeply convinced that instead of discharging them, they ought to be turning society upside down, and to be despisers of the modest routine by which they earn their bread, it gives him just the sort of field of which he is prepared to make the best use. The hero is one Hyacinth Robinson, the natural son of a young English nobleman, murdered by his light French mistress in a fit of rage and jealousy. He is brought up by a most excellent little dressmaker, who had once been his mother's friend, and whose habitually conventional romance and personal meekness are the last qualities in the world that would exert any moulding influence over his nature. Miss Pynsent is one of Mr. Henry James's foils to the Nihilists of his picture. And for that purpose her character is very happily chosen. She "could not embrace the state of mind of people who didn't apologise, though she vaguely envied and admired it, she herself spending much of her time in making excuses for obnoxious acts she had not committed." Again, Millicent Henning, the vulgar beauty who in her childhood dirties the little Hyacinth's face, as he himself had shrewdly conjectured, by kissing him against his will, and whose vitality and beauty, in spite of her coarse hands, her execrable taste, her restlessness and chattering, her wonderful stories, her bad grammar, her insatiable thirst, and her grotesque opinions, become indispensable to Hyacinth, is a still more admirable foil to the Nihilists of Mr. Henry James's fiction; indeed, no portrait could easily be more vigorous. Hyacinth Robinson himself is intended to represent the struggle between the inherited feelings of an aristocratic father with all kinds of refined tastes and insights, and the light rebellious nature of his French mother, the combination having resulted in his case in a singularly fine artistic faculty, which ultimately renders him at heart very disloyal to the destructive work in which, in his raw enthusiasm for the revolutionary party, he had hastily embarked. The picture of his devotion to all that is beautiful and all that indicates the delicacy of slowly selected hereditary tastes in the Princess Casamassima, and the pang with which he finds her conspiring to upset all that he has learnt to delight in, and discovers that he is really being divided from her by her readiness to sacrifice to the Revolution just that in her which had weaned him from his own enthusiasm for the Revolution, is painted with extraordinary power. And not the least happy touch in Mr. James's picture is that which makes the very genuineness of Hyacinth Robinson's early zeal for the Revolution produce the ultimate undermining of that zeal. When once he has sworn to do the bidding of the chief of the Revolution whenever he shall be called upon to do so, even though his life should be forfeited, he begins immediately to value far more highly those features in the existing state of society which

the Revolution is expected to obliterate. He writes to the Princess from Venice:—

"Dear Princess, there are things which I shall be sorry to see you touch, even you with your hands divine; and— shall I tell you *le fond de ma pensée,* as you used to say? . . . I don't know what it comes from, but during the last three months there has crept over me a deep mistrust of that same grudging attitude—the intolerance of positions and fortunes that are higher and brighter than one's own; a fear, moreover, that I may, in the past, have been actuated by such motives, and a devout hope that if I am to pass away while I am yet young it may not be with that odious stain upon my soul." [*Novels 1886–1890,* pp. 353–54]

But except that Hyacinth Robinson learns to love the great products of the artistic spirit in all ages with a genuine ardour, and that he recognises how little of clear method or principle the revolutionaries have in their destructive designs, his mind is as much adrift as to the true ideal of human life as the minds of all the other persons, not slaves of convention, painted in this book; nor is there one gleam of light that tends to make him think one course rather than another right or wrong. He evidently thinks the Conservatives and the Destructives alike the mere victims of prejudice; and if he learns to dislike the attack on civilisation, it is only because he feels more and more deeply that there is nothing proposed by the revolutionists which could be set up in its place. With the Princess Casamassima herself it is not much better. The glamour of her beauty is admirably described by Mr. James, and her love of emotion for the sake of emotion, too. But as for her principles, she has none except a principle of revolt against things as they are. She believes herself to be so horrified at the miseries of the poor that she would prefer an earthquake of the most destructive character to leaving things as they are; but neither she nor any of her friends pretends to have the smallest notion of the reconstructive principles which are to restore order when once the existing order receives its death-blow.

Even Lady Aurora, the only really noble character in the book, the plain, *gauche,* shy, ill-dressed, noble-minded spinster who devotes herself to alleviating the misery of the poor, partly because she finds the conventional life of the aristocracy so extremely dull and wearisome, but still more from innate goodness, has a kindness for the revolutionary party only because she is half in love with one of the pillars of that party, and has the deepest possible belief that if no one else sees his way, he does. Yet, so far as Mr. Henry James permits us to judge of his characters, no one of them is more completely adrift, no one of them knows less what he intends to do by way of revolutionising society, or how it can be so done as to substitute a more tolerable system for the existing system of *laissez faire,* than this same hero of the revolutionary party, Paul Muniment. He is extremely well described so far as his exterior nature goes. His good-humoured contempt for the vapouring democrats, his advice to the rich and the powerful to enjoy themselves while they can, and not to be so weak as to come half-way to meet those who wish to overturn the existing system, his perfect consciousness of the selfishness and weakness of his comrades, his complete willingness to lead an old friend into imminent peril of his neck without any evidence that the gain to the cause of revolution which will result from the assassination ordered, will be great, his candour in letting the Princess Casamassima know that while he admires her beauty, he avails himself of her friendship chiefly for the money she can give to the cause, and the complacency with which he recommends her to go back to her jealous Italian husband the moment he finds that these supplies of money will be stopped, make up a remarkably vivid picture of a half-educated, strong, passionless, self-reliant, and apparently selfish man. But that of which Mr. James does not contrive to give us even the faintest notion, and which yet would be necessary to complete the picture, is the ground on which Paul Muniment had persuaded himself that it was worth the while of any strong, sane man to upset all existing institutions, if he could. The bare chance that he himself and the abler leaders of the anarchists might be able to build up something stable in the place of what they intended to upset, would certainly not be a sufficient ground to such a man as Muniment. He is described as a man who knows his own mind, and who would not willingly go into captivity to any one. He sees vividly the weakness of the frothy revolutionary party. He is not represented as having any unmeasured faith in the strong and disinterested doctrinaires of the party. He is just such a man, if we understand Mr. James's sketch aright, as would leave political dreams alone, and make his way up the ladder by steady thrift and industry. The great blot on the novel is that the novelist does not contrive even to hint which side of the man it was that made him a revolutionist; hardly even to make us feel quite sure that he is one at all except in appearance. Mr. James does not show us either the strong point in the policy of the party of action which had laid hold of Muniment, or the weak point in Muniment which laid him open to the seductions of an anarchical theory destitute of any strong point. In Mr. James's novel as it stands, Muniment is almost unintelligible—hard, clear, confident, capable, yet in alliance with men who are dreamers of dangerous, sanguinary, and impracticable dreams. All his other characters might be what they are in real life. Paul Muniment, while one of the most lifelike in mere appearance, is—at least without the exhibition of links which Mr. Henry James has suppressed—out of place and out of rotation to the Nihilism of the story.

Nothing, however, is more wonderful than the interest which Mr. James has, to the mind of the present writer, contrived to build up out of a story almost without incident, except the incident of the tragic close—out of descriptions, conversations, letters, sketches which contain no real action, though all of them point to the tragedy which is coming. It is one of those cases in which one almost excuses Mr. Henry James for his habit of leaving everything at the end of what he is pleased to call his novel, almost as unfinished as it was at the opening, though he certainly does finish for us poor Hyacinth Robinson's career. As for the other conspirators who deserved such an end much better than he did, we are hardly enough interested in them, unless it be the Princess, to care at all how their career ended. Nor, indeed, to tell the truth, do we care very seriously about the Princess herself. One has had enough of her beauty, and her contempt for the conventions, and her vague enthusiasm, and her willingness to sacrifice herself for no sufficient end, and is not sorry to let her disappear without hearing what became of her. With all its extraordinary interest, this sort of novel is the novel of a writer who thinks all the world aimless, and loves to exaggerate that aimlessness in his own descriptions of it. The world is not an easy matter to understand; but we can at least see more of a clue and a plan in the world as it is, than in Mr. Henry James's pictures of it, in which the tangles are made more conspicuous than they are in real life, and the helplessness much more universal.

"*The Princess Casamassima*." *Literary World* [Boston] 18 (8 January 1887), 5.

It is safe to say that Mr. James has never given us stronger work than he has put into this story of *The Princess Casamassima*. There is more flesh and blood in it than one finds in any of his foregoing novels, with the possible exception of *Roderick Hudson;* and the field is broader, the characters are more diversified, the central theme is more clearly defined, than one is wont to look for in Mr. James's essays in fiction. As a result, we have now a firmly outlined and well-rounded narrative, supplied with abundant motives for action and moving steadily, if not always swiftly, on to a distinct climax.

There is still enough to say with regard to Mr. James's method, which remains in general hard and dry, like a deftly executed etching by an artist not wholly in sympathy with his material. But the aim of Mr. James, we may suppose, is to record his impressions of life with as little as possible of modifying sentiments and emotions; his realism, even when most aggressive, is always delicate, and we are all the time conscious that he is not giving us the whole picture, although it by no means follows that this is a source of regret. The artist's duty is to select; to suppress some details and to emphasize others. Mr. James chooses to suppress the coarse and brutal elements of nature, and to occupy himself with subsidiary emotions, sentiments, and ideas. With him refined suggestions go farther than naked actualities.

In the story of *The Princess Casamassima,* he takes us into the slums of London, and unveils some of the actors in that human fermentation known as socialism, yet in no instance does he attempt any revelation of the conditions whence socialism takes its rise. With socialistic ideas he is concerned very much, and he studies them chiefly in their action on individuals, but with socialism in the mass he has nothing whatever to do. Strictly speaking, the story is not so much the story of the Princess Casamassima, as it is of little Hyacinth Robinson, whose career is closely traced from his precocious boyhood to the tragic ending with which the book closes. The Princess is, however, the leading personage in the sense of being the most significant character. She is the Christina Light of *Roderick Hudson,* and she retains all the enigmatic qualities that lent so much fascination to her first appearance. She bears a certain likeness to Mr. George Meredith's Diana of the Crossways, and is not a creation easily to be analyzed.[1] The two ruling influences of her nature are an insatiable curiosity as to life, and a mortal terror of ennui. These motives carry her to great lengths, and men are toys in her hands. Little Robinson, the illegitimate son of an English nobleman and a French light-o'-love, grows up to manhood under the care of his foster-mother, a cockney dressmaker, and there takes place in him a struggle of hereditary tendencies. He is, in a certain sense, the victim of circumstances; no attempt is made to heighten the pathos of his fate, but the pathos is only too perceptible, and the inevitable sequence is a triumph of artistic comprehension. Perhaps the most real character in the book is Millicent Henning, a delightful type of the blooming cockney girl, a "magnificent plebeian," and the author spares no pains in making the portrait "as large as life."

It would be useless to attempt to unravel the threads of the story, and to enumerate every personage; if not useless, at least impossible, within reasonable limits.

The book is one to be read slowly; to be put down now and then, and to be taken up again with a pleasant sense of intellectual recreation. There are fine touches of wit on every page, and every page is worth reading.

Note

1 George Meredith, *Diana of the Crossways* (1885).

"The Princess Casamassima." Critic 10 (29 January 1887), 51–52.

The naming of novels is certainly a mystery beyond fathoming. Like the doorplate on a fashionable door in a fashionable street, the name of a novel either signifies nothing, or in a vague, incomprehensive way, indicates that So-and-So lives here— So-and-So being often a very multitudinous individual. Even so it is with Henry James's last accomplishment in the realm of fiction, full of rare figures as it is. The reader traverses 134 pages—close, compact, unparagraphed—a snarl of interminable analysis—before the 'Princess Casamassima,' of whom the book is an eponym, comes to the light, lost as she is, so to speak, in the windings of a palatial labyrinth. When she does emerge, she is found not to be the heroine of the superscription. The doorplate is treacherous: 'Mr. Hyacinth Robinson lives here' (like the 'Ici on parle Anglais' of a Parisian shop-window), is the discovery which the puzzled reader makes soon after opening the door, or beginning the book, and if Hyacinth is first, so Hyacinth is last in the affections of the author, and the 'Princess' is a mere foil, a fringe, an embellishment to this rare and charming young man. And if this peculiarity is puzzling in the volume, as we have it complete, it was infinitely more so in serial form, as it meandered through the monthly coils of *The Atlantic*.[1] And to the serial form, no less than to the essential inconsequence and inconclusiveness of the *denouement,* is due the failure of this socialistic drama, endlessly delightful as it is to the lover of interpretations, of emotions analytically examined of hairs radiantly split, of spectroscopic gratings capable of dividing a ray of light into 32,000 lines to the square inch, or of intellectual engines describing 150,000 sensations to the twenty pages. For to this serial form is due the jerkiness of the narrative, the obligation to make each chapter or book end with a snap or a sensation, to keep the interest of the reader alive till the next installment. This artistic fault comes out rather glaringly when the book is read in continuous form, and one is successively bumped up and down, at regular intervals, by successive sensational incidents. Apart from these defects, 'The Princess Casamassima' is an entrancing bundle of emotions and conversations, of eccentric freaks of the analytical imagination, of London people 'done to a turn' and conspirators realistically handled. Hyacinth Robinson is a *mosca bianca,* as the Italians say: a poetic and exquisite manikin placed in brilliant juxtaposition to the splendid and eccentric Princess and the livid knot of socialist assassins who breed and hiss in the out-of-the-way corners of the book. On him there is a line of him, soul and body, however microcosmically small, that he does not describe and spin out to an infinity of fine gold threads, we have missed the purpose of the book; while Paul Muniment and his bedridden sister, Lady Aurora and Madame Grandone, Pinnie and the Ponpins

are minute bits of realism as luminous and distinct as the microscopic specs which enter into a piece of Florentine mosaic. In this book Mr. James apparently bids definitive farewell to America, for the only hint of *la misère transatlantique* is the single concession that the mother of the Princess was an American. The book is quite characteristically British in its slang, its diction, its allusions, its evident holding of the eye on the 'h'aristocracy.'

Note

1 "*The Princess Casamassima,*" *Atlantic Monthly* 56 (September–December 1885), 289–311, 433–59, 577–602, 721–38; 57 (January–June 1886), 66–90, 145–78, 326–51, 485–507, 645–68, 789–813; 58 (July–October 1886), 58–76, 209–28, 349–75, 433–48.

[Annie R. M. Logan]. *Nation* 44 (10 February 1887), 123–24.

'The Princess Casamassima' disturbs the conviction that Mr. James is the chief apostle of that restricted realism which ignores extraordinary events and unusual characters, and denies the influence of the apparently accidental on the general current of life, and of exceptional individuals on the history of humanity. It fits an empirical yet generally accepted definition of realistic fiction about as neatly as does 'Aladdin and the Wonderful Lamp.' One hardly stretches a point in drawing a parallel of improbability between the adventures of Aladdin with his Princess and the adventures of Hyacinth, bookbinder of Soho, with his Princess, the "most wonderful woman in Europe." Let it not be supposed that Mr. James has gone over to romance and magic; he has only selected people whom very few of us are likely ever to know, placed them in circumstances best suited to develop them, and dispassionately told the whole truth about them. His persistent desire to see the truth, and his marvelous ability for telling it, whether the case under consideration be special or typical, prove that he has become a "realist" in the only significant or, indeed, intelligent sense of the word. Though, as a rule, the value of a study of types is, of course, greater than that of exceptions, the exceptional, if well chosen, almost certainly gives the author the best chance to show his greatest strength. In this series of studies of exceptions Mr. James shows a versatility and power hardly hinted at in his former work. Such complex and high-strung natures as Hyacinth and the Princess call out reserves of keenness and intellectual refinement unexpected even in him; and in the score of uncommon people temporarily united by common interest in a great question, his wit and sarcasm are agreeably tempered by a tenderness and even intensity of feeling which he has hitherto carefully repressed. The gain to the reader in interest is enormous, for, if a novelist will not give us a dramatic plot or thrilling scenes, and will leave off just when he has prepared us for a splendid finish, we are more than compensated for emotional disappointment by the intellectual pleasure of thought directed towards aims and objects not circumscribed by personal desire or local predisposition and habit. Throughout the novel we are carried far away from the average man and his motives in the ordinary conditions of life, but we are not invited to step outside of humanity; on the contrary, our understanding of humanity and sympathy with it are very materially extended and stimulated.

The Princess is an enigma, brilliant and inscrutable. All her frank and illogical talk, all her eccentric behavior, all the author's analysis, fail to make her comprehensible, but they accomplish his intention to portray a woman beyond shadow of doubt dazzlingly incomprehensible. Her personality smacks as little of the respectable aristocracy as of the middle class or the mob. She is a product of high fashion, of the great world, sick to death of all that goes to produce her. She is irresponsible, elusive, incalculable. She is never in the highest sense spiritual, never basely sensual. Her passions are only caprices, and her caprices have for the moment the active force of a great passion. While we know her, her dominant whim is to identify herself with the people, to clap the great democracy on the back, to imagine herself an intimate counsellor of the darkest conspirators, to believe, as she likes to say, that she is head and shoulders "in it." The Princess, as nearly as we can get at her, is a monument of sincere insincerity, and it was well for poor little Hyacinth, who long supplied her imagination with a concrete representative of her caprice, that the end came before he wholly realized the truth.

Little Hyacinth, born in a slum, bred on a poor dressmaker's charity, doomed to bear the burden of a parentage doubtful in all but its shame, is the great figure of the book. His organization is most sensitive and exquisite, and in him all the author's intellectual subtlety and distinction find expression. He is no easier to classify or label than the Princess. He is specifically of the unhappy only—the most unhappy, for his case is not so much that of a nature at war with circumstances as of a nature made up of incongruous, irreconcilable elements—a nature for ever arrayed against itself. At his worst, Hyacinth is never sordid or grudging or snobbish; at his best he is aflame with nobility, not heroic, romantic, and impossible, but entirely consistent with modern sentiment and the aspiration that is permissible or possible to us. Always, in his enthusiasms and dejection, in the light, ironical mood which is most frequent, Hyacinth is indefinably sad. The people whose lives touch Hyacinth's are each in his way as exactly and vividly drawn. No English novelist has given us such a Frenchman as Poupin, such a German as Shinkel, such an Italian as Prince Casamassima. The London shop-girl Milicent Henning—who, by the way, is typical—is perfect in her superabundant health and slang, her scrupulous care for her virtue, and her hopeless, unconscious vulgarity.

It is rash to venture any conclusions about the author's personal attitude towards the Socialistic movement which agitates and colors the lives of his characters. He may be accused of using a serious movement simply for literary purposes, of scoffing at its intensity, playing with its passion, treating it often as frivolously as if it were a question of woman's-dress reform. But there is an undertone of earnestness suggesting that he, like Hyacinth after his eyes began to open, sees most clearly, at the bottom of the cry about elevating the people, the "ulcer of envy, the passion of a party hanging together for the purpose of despoiling another to its advantage.

It is hardly fair to leave this novel without a word about its literary manner and style. There is, of course, very little plot, and that little is immaterial. There is a mass of what, from a hasty reading, may be stigmatized as super-subtle analyses, ultra-refined phrases, fine-spun nothings. But a careful reading—and for the dimmest appreciation that is necessary—will pretty surely acquit the author of such sins, and compel the recognition that, putting aside his skill as a novelist, he has written a book remarkable for the precision, elegance, and distinction of its style.

William Dean Howells. "Editor's Study." *Harper's New Monthly Magazine* 74 (April 1887), 829.

We find *no* fault with Mr. Henry James's *Princess Casamassima*: it is a great novel; it is his greatest, and it is incomparably the greatest novel of the year in our language. It has to do with socialism and the question of richer and poorer, which grows ever more burning in our day, and the scene is contemporary London. Its people are the types which the vast range of London life affords, and they are drawn not only from the highest and the lowest, but from the intermediate classes, who are so much more difficult to take alive. The Princess Casamassima is our old acquaintance Miss Light, of *Roderick Hudson* fame, come with her beauty and splendor to forget her hated husband in semi-sincere sympathy with the London socialists, and semi-personal lovemaking with two of the handsomest. The hero is the little, morbid, manly, aesthetic bookbinder Hyacinth Robinson, son of an English lord and a French girl, who kills her betrayer. For the climax, Robinson, remembering his mother, kills himself—inevitably, not exemplarily—rather than shoot the political enemy whom the socialists have devoted to death at his hand. A striking figure is the plain, good, simple, romantic Lady Aurora, who goes about among the poor, and loves the tough-hearted chemist's assistant, Paul Muniment, and devotes herself to his sister, the unconsciously selfish little cripple. Another is Pynsent, the old dress-maker, who has brought Robinson up, and who lives and dies in awe of him as an offshoot of the aristocracy; another is Captain Sholto, the big, handsome, aimless swell, *dilettante* socialist, and hopeless lover of the Princess; another the Prince, with his passion for his wife and his coarse primitive jealousy of her; others yet are the real socialists—English, French, and German; and the ferment of the ideals and interests of all these is the story. From first to last we find no weakness in the book; the drama works simply and naturally; the causes and effects are logically related; the theme is made literature without ceasing to be life. There is an easy breadth of view and a generous scope which recall the best Russian work; and there is a sympathy for the suffering and aspiration in the book which should be apparent even to the critical groundlings, though Mr. James forbears, as ever, to pat his people on the back, to weep upon their necks, or to caress them with endearing and compassionate epithets and pet names. A mighty good figure, which we had almost failed to speak of, is the great handsome shop-girl Millicent Henning, in whose vulgar good sense and vulgar good heart the troubled soul of Hyacinth Robinson finds what little repose it knows.

Mr. James's knowledge of London is one of the things that strike the reader most vividly, but the management of his knowledge is vastly more important. If any one would see plainly the difference between the novelist's work and the partisan's work, let him compare *The Princess Casamassima* and Mr. W. H. Mallock's last tract, which he calls *The Old Order Changes,* and which also deals with socialism. No one can read it and deny Mr. Mallock's extraordinary cleverness, or its futility. His people are apparently real people till he gets them into his book, and then they turn into stalking-horses for his opinions, those who would naturally disagree with him coming helplessly forward

to be overthrown by those wonderful Roman Catholics of his—so very, very fine; so very, very wise; so very, very rich; so very, very good; so very, very proud and well-born. We have some glimpses of an American girl, who seems at first a reality; but she ends by turning into an impossibility to oblige the author.

Checklist of Additional Reviews

Boston *Evening Transcript,* 3 November 1886, p. 6.

Boston *Beacon,* 6 November 1886, p. 3.

Academy [England] 30 (13 November 1886), 323. Reprinted in James W. Gargano, ed., *Critical Essays on Henry James: The Early Novels* (Boston: G. K. Hall, 1987), pp. 62–63.

Charleston *News and Courier,* 14 November 1886, p. 5.

New York *Tribune,* 14 November 1886, p. 10.

Atlanta *Constitution,* 21 November 1886, p. 13.

Cleveland *Plain Dealer,* 21 November 1886, p. 12.

Detroit *Evening News,* 28 November 1886, p. 2.

New Orleans *Daily Picayune,* 28 November 1886, p. 7.

Portland *Morning Oregonian,* 28 November 1886, p. 2.

St. Paul *Daily Pioneer Press,* 28 November 1886, p. 12.

[Margaret Oliphant]. *Blackwood's Magazine* 140 (December 1886), 786.

Julia Wedgwood. *Contemporary Review* [England] 50 (December 1886), 899–901. Reprinted in Roger Gard, ed., *Henry James: The Critical*

Heritage (London: Routledge & Kegan Paul, 1968), pp. 173–74.

William Morton Payne. *Dial* 7 (December 1886), 189.

Cincinnati *Commercial Gazette*, 4 December 1886, p. 13.

San Francisco *Chronicle*, 5 December 1886, p. 11.

Indianapolis *Journal*, 6 December 1886, p. 3.

Chicago *Times*, 18 December 1886, p. 10.

St. Louis *Missouri Republican*, 18 December 1886, p. 10.

Albany *Evening Journal*, 23 December 1886, p. 3.

Maurice F. Egan. *Catholic World* 44 (January 1887), 559.

Dublin Review 17 (January 1887), 197–98.

Westminster Review [England] 127 (January 1887), 264.

Epoch 1 (11 February 1887), 19.

Lippincott's Monthly Magazine 39 (March 1887), 359. Reprinted in Gargano, pp. 63–64.

THE REVERBERATOR

London *Graphic* 37 (14 June 1888), 46.

Possibly thorough-going admirers of Mr. Henry James (there certainly are such people) will not be disposed to set very much store by his "The Reverberator" (2 vols.: Macmillan and Co.). But there is also a very considerable number of persons whose admiration for the author of "The Portrait of a Lady" is anything but ardent, and to these the novel in question may be recommended. They will regard it as by far the best of all his novels, and will be able to fortify their preference by a long list of reasons. Among these are that it has a story—a vertebrate story—with a beginning, a middle, and very nearly with an end; it contains very little analysis, and none of which even the most imaginative readers between lines can contrive to call subtle; the characters are thoroughly lifelike and—it is an actual, positive fact—amusing. In short, Mr. Henry James comes for once before the public as unlike his natural self as is presumably within his capacity. His American family, the father and the two daughters, are of a type not hitherto described, but eminently worth describing, and recognisable by most people; and Mr. Flack, European representative of "The Reverberator," is only too lifelike, too recognisable, and too eminently worth gibbeting by means of plain portraiture. Simple and unconscious vulgarity, so simple and unconscious as to excite a certain humorous sympathy, has seldom been better illustrated. Its contrast, in another form of vulgarity, is almost equally well rendered in the Franco-American family of the Proberts, who also represent a type as well as their own individualities. In short, the story is a thoroughly good piece of comedy, worth all its author's ponderous investigations into the recondite psychology of nonentities put together.

London *Daily Telegraph*, 18 June 1888, p. 2.

Admirers of Mr. Henry James will find something to please them in "The Reverberator." The novelist in this instance is frankly and openly playful, he makes no pretence at plot, exerts no powers of eloquence or pathos, and contents himself with drawing upon the superficial everyday characteristics of humanity for the motives which move his puppets. The very name of his two volumes—the nonsensical appelation of a journal whose editor is the cause of all the easily-dried tears of the story—and the designation of the house where the chief incidents are enacted, the Hôtel de l'Univers et de Cheltenham, illustrate the light and bantering tone of his work. As in other of his books, his scheme lies in the social friction which recent novelists delight to discover in the relations between Americans and "exclusive" English. Here we have a young girl of by no means pronounced characteristics beloved by an ardent youth of aristocratic connections, and a pushing young gentleman, whose time is pretty equally divided between love-making and the preparation of piquant paragraphs for his eccentrically christened journal. When, in furtherance of deep-laid schemes, the paragraphist falls foul of the select circle into which Francie Dosson, the fair American, is about to be admitted, and is proved to have been abetted by her, the lady nearly loses her lover Gaston. The latter has in the end to choose between friends on the one hand and sweetheart on the other. Mr.

Henry James's amusing skill in the portraiture of wealthy snobbery versus the rough uncultured virtues of the West comes out strongly in these pages, while his witty dialogues and touches of racy humour cover and excuse the extreme thinness of his work in every other respect.

Westminster Review [England] 130 (July 1888), 251.

"The Reverberator" is a charming little comedy. It turns upon the infinite difference between the American and the French ideals of social and family life. In the United States, individual independence of anything like family dictation is carried to a pitch unknown even in England, and the publication in the newspapers of the most intimate details of private life is taken as a matter of course. In not a few instances the notice of the press is courted rather than resented. In France, the state of feeling and opinion, both as to family life and newspaper indiscretions, is just the reverse, especially in the exclusive ranks of the old French *noblesse*. There the *solidarité* of the family is a sacred dogma, and the tattling revelations of society papers are an offence and a pollution. In "The Reverberator" Mr. Henry James has exhibited these opposed conditions of social sentiment in action, and brought them face to face with admirable skill and insight. The prevailing note of the story is delicate, subtle humour; but here and there, there is, as in all genuine comedy, a touch of pathos.

Richard F. Littledale. *Academy* [England] 844 (7 July 1888), 6–7.

The Reverberator is a New York society newspaper; and the doings of Mr. George Flack, its correspondent in Paris, form the subject of the story. The Dosson family, consisting of a father and two daughters—one shrewd and plain, even a little common; the other ravishingly pretty and simple—came over to Europe in a Cunarder with Mr. Flack, who strikes up an intimacy with the father, having ulterior views on Francina, the pretty daughter. Among other services he renders them in Paris is an introduction to an artist who is to paint the younger girl's portrait. At the studio she meets with a friend of the artist, one Gaston Probert, a member of a Gallicised American family, whose other elements are a refined, fastidious, invalid father, and three daughters married to French nobles. She refuses Flack, and accepts Probert, whose people, however, are not delighted with the engagement, and accept her rather on sufferance. Flack persuades her to supply him with materials for a paragraph in the "Reverberator" concerning her portrait, her intended, and all his family; and she tells him everything about them, even of the most private nature (such as the kleptomania of one member, the enforced economies of others, and the relations of married couples to each other), which she has learnt from them since her engagement. All this is dished up by Flack in a coarse, vulgar fashion in the paper, to the intense disgust and torture of the Proberts, who are one and all supersensitive and thin-skinned, and find their acquaintances all over Paris accurately posted in the article. They learn from

Francie's admissions that she is the remote cause of the scandal, and they break with her in a row royal accordingly, though her betrothed does so with extreme reluctance, and only because dominated by strong family affections and associations. But though the "Reverberator" is of the same type as the journals which Martin Chuzzlewit encountered on landing in New York—the "Sewer," the "Stabber," the "Keyhole Reporter," and all the rest of them, far beneath even the *labefacia veritas* of the low-type London society paper—none of the Dossons see any particular objection to the article which has driven the Proberts nearly to frenzy; and Francina Dosson especially does not appear to have the slightest idea that she has grossly violated trust and disclosed an incurable vulgarity of nature. Mr. James makes his readers doubt what is his own attitude towards the question by the views he ascribes to his characters and by the close he puts to his story. Delia Dosson, when she hears of the affair from her sister, at first thinks that the whole thing has been a plot of Flack's to break off her engagement, and to put himself in Probert's place; but when the article comes to hand, and the family read it, none of them sees any particular harm in it: Mr. Dosson, because so much worse has been commonly said in its columns of people who took the abuse simply as one of the ordinary accidents of public life; Delia Dosson, because the article is some weeks old, and she thinks must be already forgotten; Francina, because she likes the praise of her own portrait, and fails to see the stings in the remainder. Of course, this may be all very subtle satire and irony on Mr. James's part, and he may intend to read a lesson to his countrymen on the coarsening of moral fibre and the loss of delicacy and self-respect which a low-class press is apt to generate and foster; but as he makes Gaston Probert come round to the Dos-

sons' view of the situation, and prepare to go with them to America, abandoning his own people thenceforward, this interpretation is scarcely plausible, and no other is creditable.

"A Study of Foreign Americans." New York *Times*, 15 July 1888, p. 12.

From the Americans that frequent Europe for longer or shorter periods Mr. Henry James manages to pick up curious specimens, curious not only to Europeans but to their fellow-countrymen. Are there many American fathers of young girls quite so characteristic as Mr. Dosson? Or is it that Mr. James has observed that the influence of Europe on the average American father is to reduce him to a state of imbecility? It would be risky to criticise an author who has made for years a study of Americans under the special influence of travel and residence abroad when he deals with his pet puppets. Moreover, from this broad continent there must be streaming across the ocean all sorts and conditions of men and women, the like of whom it is permitted but few in this land to know and appreciate. Perhaps under the stress of alien customs and a foreign sky characteristics that were dormant at home begin to display themselves. If this be so, how fortunate that there is so clever an observer as Mr. James on hand to fix these oddities in print before the influence of Europe shall penetrate too far and reduce (or shall we say raise?) them to the standard of European commonplace.

Mr. Flack, the young journalist who tries to break Francie Dosson's engagement to the French-educated American, Probert, is another character that approaches caricature. He and "old man" Dosson understand each other by reason of the lack of refinement common to average citizens of the United States. The latter is not angry when Flack prints in *The Reverberator* much fulsome praise of his daughter, together with a mass of vile scandals about the family of her betrothed. Francie herself is a character hard to realize as American, save in her superficial ways and speeches; she has too little individuality, too poor a spirit to be taken as a type. Where Mr. James does best is in the drawing of old Mr. Probert, Gaston Probert, and his sisters married to French noblemen. The satire is none the less keen because veiled. Gaston Probert's family exemplifies a truth seen constantly in Europe—that Americans, though they never lose their national traits entirely, are apt to assimilate the bad qualities of the foreign community in which they dwell. The moral obliquities into which old Probert has fallen while failing to become a Frenchman are hardly offset by certain gains in urbanity and charm of manner. Mr. James has brought this out in a very artistic manner, as well as the miseries of the daughters married to Frenchmen. Gaston is the turning point of the novelette. Will he have the courage to brave his family, or will the layer of French habits and customs prove too incrusted to allow his love for Francie to triumph? He is a weak character but Mr. James has made the trial a serious one by showing the enormity of Francie's fault. It is she, the fiancée of Gaston Probert, who gives to the enterprising Mr. Flack most of the hints concerning the scandals in the Probert circle, which hints he "works up" with the aid of a Parisian woman and publishes in *The Reverberator*. All this has its moral, too, directed against the pernicious "society journals," for Mr. James shows the wide swath that

such an article as that in *The Reverberator* cuts, doing, in fact, more harm to the innocent and sensitive than to the wicked and callous. The novel is able, though longwinded, sufficiently interesting, without having great sustained interest. It is not very pleasing. Even Gaston forfeits the respect of readers by his finical ways and hesitations with regard to his betrothed. Even Francie is made ignorant, listless, and obtuse to a degree most rare in American girls.

London *Times*, 18 July 1888, p. 16.

Plagiarism of one's own work is no serious offence, but it is difficult to avoid remarking that "The Reverberator" (by Henry James, 2 vols., Macmillan and Co.) moves on the same parallels as "The American." In "The American" was related the attempt of one of nature's gentlemen (who, however, had made his pile out of oil or hides or something nasty) to enter as a bridegroom within the charmed circle of the old French *noblesse*. Here we have almost the converse case, except that it is complicated by the affair of the *Reverberator*. An American father and his two daughters, more remarkable for their good nature than their constant attention to good form, have pitched their camp in "Parus." There they are taken in tow by a well-meaning but vulgar young man, who supplies Parisian scandal to an American society organ, the *Reverberator*. In spite of this damaging introduction the younger daughter meets and is adored by a gentleman whose family are very "high-toned" indeed. American on his father's side and French on his mother's, he has adopted all the superstitions of his mother's caste, including the principle that a young man ought to be the devoted bondsman of his sisters, his cousins, and his aunts. Their prejudices against his proposed match are formidable. But Francie is so beautiful and so lovable that he has as good as enlisted his relatives on her side when the affair of the *Reverberator* happens. That journal comes out with a column, half of it libel, half of it truth, befouling the sanctuary of the Proberts' private life and filling them with shame and mortification. Worse still, the raw material for these calumnies was furnished by Francie herself (innocently, as the readers knows, but as the Proberts do not know) to her journalist friend. Even this they would forgive her if she would explain or ascribe it to her inadvertence. But—and here Mr. James succeeds in warming our hearts towards his somewhat colourless heroine—Francie admits, and even asserts, her responsibility for the whole thing, and there stubbornly entrenches herself. They put it down as *un sens qui lui manque*. Even those who are behind the scenes might suspect the same thing; but we take it, as Mr. James evidently means it, for a flash of chivalry. How the *impasse* is to be pierced we leave the reader to discover. It is a clever story, but we confess to a disability to get up much human interest in the Parisian American—who, as the journalist says, is rather a poor creature if his own country is not good enough for him—and still less in the petty social ambitions with which his world is agitated. "The Reverberator" shows us love brushing away social cobwebs. But love, in Mr. James's pages, is such a pallid thing—platonic admiration on one side and acquiescence on the other—that we are rather surprised to find it emerging the conqueror.

"Droch" [Robert Bridges]. *Life* 12 (26 July 1888), 48.

After an almost unanimous verdict as to the disagreeableness of Henry James's story "The Reverberator" (Macmillan), a reader, with even tolerably acute perception, will be surprised to discover that it is an enjoyable piece of work. It is true that *Flack,* the American society-paper correspondent in Paris, is not an attractive character. Nor was *Bartley Hubbard*.[1] Still they represent a phase of "journalism" which, however, neither Mr. James nor Mr. Howells would claim to be the prevailing one.

Perhaps the severe criticisms of the press were not a little prompted by the prickings of the editorial conscience, which in its rare moments of introspection discovers how hard it is for the man of best intentions to publish a wide-awake newspaper and not violate some of the conventions by "invading the sanctities of the home." Even to be a perfectly fair and just critic of political affairs involves a certain amount of pointed reproof, which must be galling to the circle who are bound to the offending man by love and friendship. The journalist with a conscience is constantly brought face to face with this necessity for sacrificing personal feelings to the public good.

There is no such excuse for *Flack*. He is one of the guerillas of the press, who are perfectly insensible to the feelings of others. The only thing admirable about them is their enthusiasm for their profession. The same praise could be given an expert highwayman.

But, accepting *Flack* as an ugly fact,

what a charming lot of people Mr. James has introduced! The *Dosson* family are satirized only good-humoredly. One knows that the author has a good deal of admiration for their sincerity and honest simplicity. Old *Mr. Dosson* moves through the pages as a perfect delight. "He was fair and spare and had no figure; you would have seen in a moment that the question of how he should hold himself had never in his life occurred to him. He never held himself at all; providence held him rather (and very loosely), by an invisible string, at the end of which he seemed gently to dangle and waver."

Through the wonderful precision and flexibility with which Mr. James uses phrases, he has acquired the dexterity to bring a character into your mental vision with very few words. His beautiful heroine *Francie* is "as straight as a wand and as fine as a gem; her neck was long and her gray eyes had color; and from the ripple of her dark brown hair to the curve of her unaffirmative chin, every line in her face was happy and pure."

Her aggressive and hardly lovable sister, *Delia*, has "a plain, blank face, not only without movement, but with a suggestion of obstinacy in its repose; and yet with its limitations, it was neither stupid nor displeasing. It had an air of intelligent calm."

Waterlow, the artist, is happily hit off in one phrase, as "combining in an odd manner many of the forms of the Parisian studio with the moral and social ideas of Brooklyn, Long Island, where his first seeds had been planted."

And *Probert* gives you the clue to his entire nature when he says that "the most important things that have happened to me in this world have been simply half a dozen impressions—impressions of the eye."

The author speaks for himself in these few sentences, and the fair-minded reader will have no trouble in deciding that this group of characters is well worth knowing.

Moreover, this story arrives at what is, sentimentally, a most satisfactory conclusion. Mr. James has for once given his readers a surprise by not inflicting them with a wholly surprising ending to his tale.

Note

1 A character in William Dean Howells's *A Modern Instance* (1882) and *The Rise of Silas Lapham* (1885).

Christian Union 38 (2 August 1888), 130.

Here, as in so many other of Mr. James's short novels—of which, by the way, he seems to be remarkably productive of late—one recognizes the close social study, the clever contrast of character, the faithful realism, and yet wishes the writer would infuse into his work a warmer human interest and a brighter humor. There is a sense of dissatisfaction as one lays down the book—which he is, however, pretty sure not to lay down till he has finished reading—a feeling that the author has subtly imposed on his readers as types characters that are not types. The American girl in this story, for instance, calmly tells all sorts of disreputable stories about the French family into which she is about to marry to a newspaper correspondent, *knowing* that he means to print the stuff; and she is much astonished when fault is found with her conduct. And though the author doesn't say so plainly, the reader feels that he implies, "This is the daughter of one of the American *nouveaux riches*. Why should she know better?" But this, dear Mr. James, was a question of decency, not one of breeding. Many a girl in the backwoods, in calico gown and without a symptom of "sweetness and light," would have instinctively avoided such a thing. So of the correspondent of "The Reverberator" himself. The satire is very keen, and, no doubt, there is a fair chance to attack personalities in journalism; but, in point of fact, can Mr. James, or can any reader of this, think of the name of *one* weekly paper in this country which keeps two correspondents on salary in Paris, and allows them to take columns of space in recounting the most common-place scandal about quite unknown persons? The thing simply does not exist. Yet Mr. James clearly means his "Reverberator," and its style of Paris correspondence, to stand as fairly representative of a whole class of journals. But perhaps this is hypercritical. At all events, the story has the fineness of touch and delicacy of workmanship that characterize all Mr. James's stories.

"*The Reverberator.*" *Literary World* [Boston] 19 (29 September 1888), 313.

If Mr. James must choose a disagreeable subject—and it seems inevitable—it is greatly to be desired that he do as skilled and well-proportioned a piece of work upon it as in the present case. The individuals who figure in *The Reverberator* are certainly consistent with themselves. A very good bit of characterization is that which represents Mr. George Flack, the journalist and interviewer, as belonging to a "group," with nothing in especial to remember him by. "He was not a particular person, but a sample or memento—reminding one of certain 'goods' for which there is a steady popular demand." Equally good in its way is the sketch which brings Mr. Dosson before the reader—"a man of the simplest composition, a character as cipherable as a sum with two figures."

Nowhere has Mr. James been more successful in carrying out a certain purpose than in this compact, crystallized story. The "interviewer," in the exercise of his legitimate business, as he regards it, makes use of the deliciously guileless Francie, to search into the antecedents of the stately French family, into the privacy of whose sacred home life she is reluctantly admitted because of her betrothal to the infatuated heir, Gaston. Given these conditions, and such an inimitable (but unfortunately possible) girl as Francie, with her utter unconsciousness of the existence of such a thing as honor, what would the ordinary author do with her? Fortunately for the unique completing of the story, Mr. James is not an ordinary author. It is the unexpected that happens; and Mr. Flack is left with a dubious sort of triumph, while Francie and her lover violate all the traditions, and the world goes on as usual except to the defrauded Properts, who are left aghast at the apostasy of their son. Francie is both better and worse than Daisy Miller. Must we accept her also as a type of the American girl, and will our journalists fraternize with Mr. George Flack, or shall we set these two irrepressible and pushing beings down as atrocious caricatures? We will at least give Mr. James the credit of having filled in his canvas with rare skill, disposing his figures in just the right light. No one is too prominent, no one too much in shadow. It is an exceedingly careful and artistic piece of work, and is better worth the hours one can spend over it than most that this author has recently given us.

Dublin Review 103 (October 1888), 431–32.

Mr. James's incisive style gives vitality to his slight sketches of life and manners, enabling the reader to take interest in the faithfully limned but shadowy personages who flit across his pages like the bodiless reflections in a mirror. Their outward form and semblance is accurately reproduced for us, the trick of manner or trait of countenance is vividly brought before us, but superficial intimacy never grows into sympathetic comprehension, and we come no nearer to their inner selves at the end of the concluding volume than at the moment of our first introduction. The fortunes of an American trio, father and two daughters, sojourning at an hotel in Paris, are the subject of the present tale, and the aimless, yet contented vacuity of their lives under these circumstances is doubtless a veracious presentment of those of many of their fellow-countrymen. The group here portrayed are, however, redeemed from inanity by their utter amiability and innocence of guile. The heroine, the pretty and petted Francie, is a pale but exquisite silhouette, and her unflawed sweetness, loyal sincerity, and absolute transparency of character atone for what we cannot but feel to be a total absence of mind. The necessary complication in her destiny is brought about by the treachery of a compatriot, the Paris correspondent of an American society paper, *The Reverberator,* who takes advantage of her simplicity to draw her out on the secrets and scandals of her *fiancé's* family, in order to break off her engagement by their publication. Much turmoil is naturally created among the various sisters and brothers-in-law of the noble French connection into which she is going to marry, and she nobly prefers risking the loss of her lover to clearing herself of complicity by a falsehood. Her beauty and *naïveté* however triumph in the end, and we leave her restored to happiness.

[Annie R. M. Logan]. *Nation* 47 (4 October 1888), 273.

It has long been taken for granted that the elements of Mr. James's novels shall be few and simple, the characters and phases of life typical. Nobody expects anything to happen, or anticipates emotional excitement. Perhaps his strongest book, 'The Princess Casamassima,' missed general appreciation because its strange incidents and deep feeling offend preconceived opinions, and exhibit an art less circumscribed than public wisdom permits to the author. If that wisdom was disturbed ever so slightly by the exceptional novel, 'The Reverberator' will reëstablish it triumphantly. The manuscript of the plot could be packed neatly in a nutshell, or a summary thereof engraved by an ingenious person on a dime. The subject, too, is that which the making his has made the author's fame, viz., the hopeless difference in social point of view between a certain class of Americans and another class, not so certain, but not American. The difference on which the argument rests will doubtless appear to individuals of that certain American class, if by any chance they read Mr. James, to be a flimsy and ridiculous pretext for a story. They will pronounce this judgment, not because they count themselves in that class, but because they know that the author is a finical, snobbish fellow, whose soul is dead to the glories of his own, his native land, and who is always nosing about for a chance to have a fling at it. The question is simply whether you like to have your private affairs set forth in a "society journal"—set forth, either with flattery or disparagement, always mendaciously—or whether you don't. On one side of the question stand the Dossons of America, newly arrived in Paris, and Mr. Flack, George M. Flack, correspondent of the *Reverberator;* on the other are arrayed the Proberts, originally of South Carolina, now in the second generation of denationalization. The Dossons are new-rich, yet not on that account offensively aggressive; on the contrary, of the lowest degree of humility consistent with self-respect and free-born Americanism. The treatment of the Dossons is most admirable. They have so little marked individuality that they are almost characterless, yet the author manages to characterize them perfectly. One cannot decide which is the more wonderful, his power of divination or of apparently effortless expression.

No people were ever more helplessly what nature made them than the Dossons; therefore, no people could be for themselves a fuller explanation and more cordially acceptable apology. They deserve all the sympathy that people so ingenuous as never to have thought of being pretentious can get. They thought an editor, by virtue of this office, was a great man, and George M. Flack, commanding as he did the ear and time of princes and potentates, the greatest of his guild. His explanation that he was "only a correspondent" served only to exalt him; for how much greater an editor free to roam abroad than an editor doomed to stay at home! There was only one position in life which he was not fitted to adorn, and that the position of husband to Miss Francie Dosson. Then it was really Miss Dosson who created this limitation, and she was moved thereto not so much by a doubt of Mr. Flack's greatness as by the knowledge gathered from *Reverberators* at home, that the grandest matches were made by American girls "over there," which knowledge had fired her with vaulting ambition for her beautiful sister, Francie. Thinking Mr. Flack great, they thought, in natural sequence, that it was a splendid thing to have a column in the *Reverberator* all about Francie and her portrait, with the skeletons in the closets of her Franco-American *fiancé's* family, exposed in cold type to a gaping world. It was distinction! It was fame! They were obliged to see that the three demoiselles Probert, by marriage ennobled, took a different view of it. Miss Dosson was "mad" with Flack because he had apparently broken off the grand match, but, to save their collective lives, they couldn't see why the Proberts should go on so, and to the end of time they never would. Francie herself never knew that these family secrets had been confided to her chiefly with kind intention to make her feel herself one of them. She got no nearer to the heart of the disturbance than to perceive a fulfilment of her prediction when she had become engaged to Gaston Probert—that "she knew she would do something," and "now she had." As for the assassin, Flack, what could he have but contempt for antediluvian frumps, who made a row because their doors had been forced, their shrines desecrated, for the increase of the *Reverberator's* circulation, and incidentally for the enlightenment of mankind?

Mr. Flack is a monster, and more monstrous still is the fact that he had excellent grounds for the assumption on which he plied his disgraceful trade. He said, in all sincerity, that he knew "what the people want," and he did. By hook or by crook he proposed to supply that want. Mr. James, holding himself aloof from the controversy, neither preaching nor scolding, simply narrates the effect of Flack's most brilliant stroke on a family whom Flack would not have counted among the people. The Proberts are shocked and furious, and each manifests rage in characteristic fashion. Francie, brought to the family bar, is bewildered. It doesn't occur to her to deny innocent complicity with Flack nor to feign sympathy; and it doesn't occur to the Proberts to admire her honesty. To the Gallic mind, that was shameless avowal of shame. One word of exaggeration here would convert a serious scene into a farce, but that word is not written. Francie, whose fascination for Gaston Probert is a matter of fine lines and color, is endeared to the Anglo-Saxon reader by this splendid exhibition, not of courage, but of natural-born incapacity for lying. It makes her worth Probert's reluctant sacrifice, and worth, too, the incomparable ease, grace, and brilliancy with which her fortunes are narrated.

Checklist of Additional Reviews

Athenaeum [England] 3164 (16 June 1888), 759.

Murray's Magazine [England] 4 (July 1888), 144.

Boston *Daily Advertiser,* 3 July 1888, p. 2.

New York *Sun,* 8 July 1888, p. 4.

"Henry James' New Story." St. Louis *Globe Democrat,* 8 July 1888, p. 22.

Chicago *Times,* 14 July 1888, p. 12.

Hartford *Daily Courant,* 18 July 1888, p. 2.

American 16 (21 July 1888), 217–18.

Boston *Beacon,* 28 July 1888, p. 3.

Cincinnati *Commercial Gazette,* 28 July 1888, p. 6.

[R. H. Hutton]. *Spectator* [England] (4 August 1888), 1066–67. Reprinted in Roger Gard, ed., *Henry James: The Critical Heritage* (London: Routledge & Kegan Paul, 1968), pp. 185–86.

Churchman 58 (11 August 1888), 173.

Epoch 4 (24 August 1888), 55.

San Francisco *Chronicle,* 26 August 1888, p. 7.

Critic 13 (15 September 1888), 123.

Harper's New Monthly Magazine 77 (October 1888), 802.

Scottish Review 12 (October 1888), 414–15.

North American Review 147 (November 1888), 599.

Catholic World 48 (December 1888), 402–5.

Independent 40 (13 December 1888), 1609.

THE ASPERN PAPERS

Saturday Review
[England] 66 (3 November
1888), 527.

Lovers of Venice will find a charm in the first of Mr. James's three little stories, though perhaps only literary people can be expected to feel its real fascination. It is, more even, than is usual with Mr. James, a duel of wits; and, though readers who have followed his past career will know what awaits them at the end of the story, there is still an interest in watching the passes of the swords. The combatants are the storytellers—an American, whose name is not given, but whose master-passion is admiration for a dead and gone poet, Jeffrey Aspern, and one Miss Borde-reau, now verging on her hundred, but who was in early youth the friend of the poet, and perhaps something more. She is believed to be in possession of large numbers of his letters and papers, which it is the object of the poet's adherents—unwarned by the fate of Shelley—to get into their own hands for publication. From the first we back the old lady, but Mr. James has managed the give and take with great skill, and the little sketch is one of much delicacy, while glimpses of the vivid Venetian life serve to heighten the gloom of the still isolated Palazzo, which is the casket of coveted treasure. "Louisa Pallant," the second story, is much in his usual strain, which is merely to say that it is full of clever touches and unexpected turns. The remaining tale, "A Modern Warning," will or will not be classed among Mr. James's successes according to the view which is entertained of the antagonism between the English and American races as a subject for books. Some readers do not want to have this fact continually harped upon; others find much fun in it; and these last will certainly find immense diversion in Macarthy Grice. They will scarcely so much relish the end, where the hapless heroine takes poison and dies. This conclusion seems wholly lacking in reason, and is unworthy of Mr. James, whose readers feel wounded that they cannot follow the subtle workings of his mind. This is a sentiment which every successful author should carefully avoid creating.

George Saintsbury.
Academy [England] 862
(10 November 1888), 302.

It is well known to the initiated, though the story has for obvious reasons not got into the papers, that a conspiracy has long existed in America for the purpose of buying a stout keeled yacht (none of your centreboard toys that are good to dodge the Britisher round New York harbour), manning it with stalwart patriots, kidnapping Mr. Henry James from whatsoever foul European Capua he may be haunting, conveying him to a desert island, and there giving him the choice of death by awful tortures or of swearing on his bended knees and the bones of Washington that he will never more make fun of the American man or woman. The execution of the project has, we understand, only been postponed owing to a patriotic sense of the horrid gap in the ranks of "our gifted and incisive writers" (as an American print had it the other day) should Mr. James prove staunch and prefer art to life. But whether this reluctance will be proof against the last provocation—the third of the tales in *The Aspern Papers*—we tremble to think. All the *portraits-charges* ever drawn of Yankees by Englishmen from Miss Ferrier's impossible Lewiston through the works of Dickens and Mrs. Trollope downwards are mild compared to the dreadful fidelity of Macarthy Grice in "A Modern Warning." The personages of the story are few—Macarthy and Agatha Grice, brother and sister, the usual helpless mother of American fiction, and a masterful Englishman, Sir Rufus Chasemore, who carries Agatha off under the nose, so to speak, of the Briton-detesting Macarthy. The story is extremely clever; but Mr. James neither need nor should have ended it by the suicide of the luckless Agatha, distracted between wifely and sisterly love. Tragedy interspersed with comedy is good literature; comedy ending in tragedy, though unfortunately only too true to life, is not good literature, or very rarely so. The longer "Aspern Papers" proper is also a very good story, though perhaps a trifle spun out. But "Louisa Pallant," which comes between, is good for much less.

New York *Tribune,* 13 November 1888, p. 8.

In the "Aspern Papers" Mr. James exhibits an unequalled skill in evolving interest out of the minimum of material. It is true that this episode has a foundation in fact, but so small a modicum of fact that perhaps it might never have suggested to another than Mr. James the possibility of making a literary use of it. The nucleus upon which the story—if it can be called a story—is erected, amounts simply to this: An old lady living with an elderly niece in an Italian city (Mr. James calls it Venice) was the sole surviving link between the new generation and a once famous poet and prose writer, who passes in the book

under the name of Jeffrey Aspern. This old lady is believed to possess precious memorials of Aspern, who had held very tender and intimate relations to her. An enthusiastic Aspern editor who is gathering material for a new book about his idol learns of the existence of this important literary deposit, and determines to lay siege to the treasure. He succeeds in gaining a foothold in the venerable guardian's house as a lodger, and the whole of the story consists in a minute chronicle of the laborious processes by which in the end he failed to secure the prize. Nothing could be more absolutely unexciting. There is scarcely any action, the dialogue is almost monotonous, and the object of the difficult quest is not of a generally or deeply interesting character. Three people only appear; one is the narrator, and of the others the first is the venerable old custodian of the letters and the other is her niece, a curious, colorless, almost soulless creature, simple to the bounds of imbecility. Yet out of these scanty materials Mr. James has contrived to weave a story which is full of a light and delicate interest, which gives pleasure by the refined and subtle dissection of almost infinitely little things; which is marked by quiet humor; and which contains a great deal of admirable psychical analysis.

"Louisa Pallant," the second tale in Mr. James's volume, is a curious social study, a good deal in outline. The heroine is a woman who in early life jilted the narrator, and who, meeting him on the continent, where she is roaming with her lovely daughter, is affected by an odd kind of remorse which leads her to break off a growing attachment between her daughter and the supposed story-teller's rich young nephew. This strange mother, under a passionate impulse, confides to her former lover the failure of her own life. She sacrificed love for worldly advantage, and was disappointed. She had educated her daughter in all the craft of a mondaine, and had finally discovered that the girl was ambitious, false and heartless. But Mr. James throws a cloud of doubt over these self-revealings, and leaves it undecided whether the mother's confession was after all not part of a plot deliberately devised by that too-clever lady. In the same way the real character of Linda Pallant, the daughter, is undetermined at the last, and the reader is apt to suspect that possibly the author's own mind was not made up concerning these two practically inscrutable women.

"The Modern Warning" is not a pleasing story, and in more than one respect is less artistic than the preceding tales. Macarthy Brice, the distinguished young American lawyer who cherishes so rabid and unreasoning a hatred of the English, is an anomaly. He is, in fact, an unnatural combination of the genuine Yankee and the Irish-American. The education he is credited with is inconsistent with the character and extent of his Anglophobia, which is, in short, nothing less than monomania. The drift of the story is the exploitation of a possible danger in international marriage; the danger, namely, that patriotic sentiment on either side may at some time interfere with domestic felicity. An American girl marries an English Tory official, who presently visits the United States, gathers material, and writes a book in which he records many unflattering opinions. His wife, reading some early proof-sheets of his book, is seized with a decidedly uncharacteristic fit of indignation at the things said about her country. She makes a scene thereupon, and Sir Rufus, her husband, acts with imperturbable kindness, promises not to publish, and frankly declares his entire willingness to sacrifice his ambition to his wife's happiness. For a time all is well. Then the wife begins to harbor morbid ideas to the effect that she has spoiled her husband's career. After long brooding she begs him to pub-

lish; and when he goes on with the printing she suddenly, and without rhyme or reason, kills herself. The catastrophe is led up to by nothing. It is quite impossible to explain it, save on the theory of insanity, and that Mr. James does not once hint at. Thus the impression produced is disagreeable, and there is nothing to show that this unpleasant and abrupt ending was, artistically or otherwise, necessary.

"Droch" [Robert Bridges]. *Life* 12 (29 November 1888), 302–3.

"The Aspern Papers" give the title to a volume made of three recent magazine stories by Henry James, the two others being "Louisa Pallant" and "A Modern Warning." Each is the unemotional study of a disagreeable phase of character. If worth doing at all, they could hardly be done with more skill. Any one sensitive to fine literary form will find in them pleasure enough to counterbalance the unsympathetic qualities. It is akin to the exhilaration one feels when watching a daring and graceful skater. The swing is regular, sinuous, rhythmic; the unexpected and brilliant variations of it are exhibitions of agility; the steel rings clear and musical, and flashes now and then in the sunlight among the minute crystals of splintered ice. The spectator may be chilled, but never bored.

As "The Reverberator" was a satire on the violation of the finer feelings by a type of modern journalist, so "The Aspern Papers" is a satire on the inhuman quality of one phase of literary industry. The delicate force of this study lies in the skill with which the reader is entrapped into a keen interest in the hunt for the love-letters of the poet *Aspern*. When the indelicacy and even cruelty of the whole plot are suddenly flashed upon you, you feel something of the shame and humility which at last overtook the literary ghoul. You are to a degree *particeps criminis,* and understand the weak point in human nature which has led to so many unpardonable literary sins.

"*The Aspern Papers.*" *Literary World* [Boston] 19 (8 December 1888), 451.

This volume contains three long stories from Mr. James's indefatigable hand. They have that air of high breeding which belongs to all his work and which lends attraction to books which have very little substance, the manner being nearly everything and the matter almost nothing. *The Aspern Papers,* for instance, is a delicate, refined and long-drawn-out narrative of the way in which the narrator, a lover of Jeffrey Aspern (represented as a young American poet of the early part of this century), failed to get possession of a collection of letters in the hands of the Misses Bordereau of Venice. The incident is slight, but the *finesse* with which the plot is developed and the delicacy with which the characters of the Misses Bordereau are set forth are traits of a master-hand. But in the name of all probability we must protest against Mr. James's needless slaughter of Lady Chasemore in the third story. It is not characteristic of such women as she is described to be to poison herself under such absence of provocation; her suicide comes upon the reader with a shock of

surprise which immediately turns to indignation at the author for perpetrating such wanton murder!

London *Daily Telegraph,* 25 December 1888, p. 7.

Mr. Henry James is another of our popular writers whose style is always light and graceful. No one can fail to miss the charm of his dialogues with their semi-American tone—an Americanism, however, always distinctive, purged of its crudeness, and at times so whimsical that we hardly know whether the sweet or the bitter flavour predominates in the intellectual food he lays before us. Here in these "Aspern Papers" (Macmillan) if they are not so good as much that he has written before, there will still be plenty who will like the strange conception of the plot, and his manner of handling it, so different from the general run of modern fiction. His appreciators will like the unworldly Tita, "whose attitude was perpetually a sort of prayer for assistance, for explanation," who, "from the moment you were kind to her, depended on you absolutely, with an innocent intimacy which was the only thing she could conceive," and the pleasant excursions she and her literary cicerone took down the classic, picturesque waterways of Venice. They will take no serious exception to the quaint pursuit of the mystic papers, the final stipulation by which only they are to be obtained, and the rather ludicrous conclusion of the story. The chief thing Mr. Henry James has to fear is that his subtle fun will fail in the main to be appreciated by a public which has had a considerable experience of late of the loudest and most pronounced schools of humour that English literature knows.

"Mr. James's *Aspern Papers*." *Critic* 14 (9 February 1889), 61–62.

The creations of Henry James always remind us of a procession of Grecian masks: There is a mask for tragedy, a mask for comedy, one for pathos, another for satire, and so on to the end of the list. The properties never vary, and in each drama we have the same set visages, rigid with horror, dimpled with humor, drawn in sadness, or pursed in irony. They shift about the boards like automatons, but every movement has a studied effectiveness, every pose is statuesque; they are made to speak their lines always in the same voice, but always in the choicest diction; and the harmony of their relations is perfect. And behind these semblances, directing them and informing them, is the mummer, of whose own face we never catch a glimpse. While this characterization holds good of two of the three sketches in the volume before us, one is forced to make an exception of one of them, 'The Aspern Papers,' which lends its title to the book. To the trio of actors in this slight Venetian pastoral has been imparted such vitality that they haunt us after we have bidden them good-by, in a way that people of flesh and blood often fail to do. A correspondent has already called attention in these columns to the closeness with which Mr. James has followed out a portion of Claire Clairmont's unfortunate early career in fashioning his tale, although the events

therein described take place long years after Jeffrey Aspern's prototype is dust and ashes, and the fragile plaything of a summer's pastime has become—well, her niece is somewhere in the shady vicinity of seventy! The half-serious banter of the author borders at times upon grotesquerie, from which it could be saved by no less masterly a hand. And it is from this fantastic borderland in which the story passes, with Venice as its background, where the improbable is always real, that it derives its *naïveté* and charm.

In the whole range of portraiture that bears the mark, 'H. James, pinxit," we are strongly disposed to give the first place to Miss Bordereau; and when we consider by what negative methods this creature is put before us, we wonder at the perfection of the portrait. For it is almost by what is left unsaid, rather than by actual recital and delineation, that this figure, with the basilisk eyes that are never seen yet always felt, is projected against the canvas. And as for Miss Tita—poor, pathetic, ridiculous Miss Tita—she is etched with hardly less firmness than her aunt, and captivates us from the first, as in her pale, ineffectual way she tried to captivate the editor of Jeffrey Aspern's papers. Did Mr. James ever give us a more lambent bit of humor than in the *tête-à-tête* in the Piazza, where her companion is endeavoring to worm from Miss Tita the hiding-place of the dead poet's relics? Miss Tita, who for half a century has grown gray and musty like the old palace in which she lived, and has scarcely ventured from beneath its portals during that period, is ravished like a child by the lights, the music and the laughter. " 'Compromising?' Miss Tita repeated,' in echo to her escort's remark, 'as if she were ignorant of the meaning of the word. I felt almost as one who corrupts the innocence of youth.' Mr. James takes to the old courses of the Doge's city as naturally as a duck to water; even the clubs and drawing-rooms of London have not quite weaned him from them; and in this little idyl we catch many a glimpse of its stately old *palazzi*, as that in which the two old ladies lived, with its 'air not so much of decay as of quiet discouragement,' while through its pages there is a shimmering of the lagoons as through a glass, and the constant lisping of their quiet waters.

The second sketch in the volume, a study of the *emigrée,* causes us to wonder how out of such meagre material Mr. James can erect such graceful structures. The character of Louisa Pallant is a brilliant bit of drawing in the author's best vein, and the other figures in the story are modelled after the pattern we know so well, but which is seldom tiresome. 'A Modern Warning' is another 'international episode,' not so well sustained as its companion-piece; at the end it is melodramatic and unnatural. But then the plot—if we can accuse Mr. James of perpetrating such a thing as a plot—is of little consequence in any of his tales, and one can hardly be otherwise than content with miniatures painted with the exquisite grace of a Fragonard.[1]

Note

1 Jean Honoré Fragonard (1732–1806).

Universal Review
[England] 3 (March
1889), 427–28.

Mr. Henry James' collection of studies, entitled the 'Aspern Papers,' should have been reviewed before, as the book appeared in the early autumn of last year. We are glad, however, to take the opportunity of noticing it and saying what scant justice is, in our opinion, dealt out to this author in the unduly scornful estimate of his writing which appears in another portion of our present number.[1] The book in question shows Mr. James at his best: the tales do not pretend to be of any serious importance, but the workmanship of the writing is throughout exquisite. The story which gives the title to these two volumes is absolutely without incident of any kind or shape, and is simply the record of how a man spent some weeks in a Venetian palace with an old and an elderly lady in the endeavour to obtain from them some papers relating to the history of Jeffrey Aspern, who was, we are told, a famous littérateur, and of whom at the time at which the study opens the narrator was writing the biography. Of course this is mosaic work of Mr. James'; it *is* over-refined, not to use Mr. Buchanan's more unpleasant adjective; but it has also qualities which are alike rare and admirable. The author creates an atmosphere, relative to both feeling and objective fact, as subtle as it is powerful; he enters into the lives of his characters not only through the easy portals of superficial speech, appearance, and plain label description, but by carefully thought out dialogue and analysis of motive, which do, in the course of the story, build up before us a character whom we can understand and believe in, though we feel, in contradistinction to the work of our greater English novelists, that we might pass the *dramatis personae* of any of Mr. James' books a hundred times in the street and never say to ourselves, 'There goes So and So.' We fancy rather that after a long dinner, when the conversation had been general and discursive, and after some hours of subsequent talk by the fire, we might possibly say about midnight, 'Ah! I know you now; you are Jeffrey Aspern,' or any other character of whom Mr. James has written.

216

1 The reviewer refers to Robert Buchanan's "The Modern Young Man as Critic," pp. 353–72, which included a scathing critique of James's abilities as a critic.

Scottish Review 13 (April 1889), 448.

The Aspern Papers (Macmillan), the first of the three stories contained in these two volumes, is a very happy effort in Mr. James' peculiar style; and shows to great advantage his marvellous power of manipulating the slenderest materials. The way in which the man, so to speak, sinks the biographer, actually in port, is delightful; though it is disappointing to lose in consequence all knowledge of what the papers contained. *Louisa Pallant* is too vague and incomplete to be anything save irritating. In *The Modern Warning*, we find the American Eagle screeching anew, and disposed to wave aloft the Star Spangled Banner, while he dances on the faded worn-out Union Jack, and we feel inclined to say, 'My dear bird, do not screech so loud. Nobody denies the glories of the Great American Nation! and at any rate, be logical. If Great Britain is the home of a worn-out despised nation, be not so exuberantly exultant over every American girl who contrives to get herself chosen as a wife by a son of that degenerate race.' In truth, the excessive delight of our American cousins over these transactions seems a little uncomplimentary to their women, very much so to their *men*. But if we are to accept Agatha Grice as a fair representation of the sort of treasure an Englishman secures when he takes unto himself an American wife, why, we can only say the wrongs of his neglected country-women are amply avenged; and *The Modern Warning* is a very emphatic 'Englishmen beware' indeed!

Checklist of Additional Reviews

New York *Sun*, 11 November 1888, p. 4.
Boston *Evening Journal*, 16 November 1888, Supp., p. 2.
Athenaeum [England], 3186 (17 November 1888), 659–60.
Boston *Herald*, 19 November 1888, p. 3.
Epoch 4 (23 November 1888), 290–91.
Chicago *Inter-Ocean*, 24 November 1888, p. 11.
Churchman 58 (24 November 1888), 643.
Literary World [England] 38 (30 November 1888), 445–46.
Graphic [England] 39 (1 December 1888), 586.
Detroit *Free Press*, 8 December 1888, p. 3.
William Morton Fullerton. Boston *Daily Advertiser*, 10 December 1888, p. 5.
New York *Times*, 16 December 1888, p. 19.
Indianapolis *Journal*, 17 December 1888, p. 3.
Hartford *Courant*, 18 December 1888, p. 2.
Christian Union 38 (20 December 1888), 737.
Cambridge Review 10 (1888–89), 126–27. Reprinted in Arthur Sherbo, "Jamesian Gleanings," *Henry James Review* 11 (1990), 50–51.
[Annie R. M. Logan]. *Nation* 48 (25 April 1889), 353.

THE TRAGIC MUSE

"*The Tragic Muse.*" San Francisco *Chronicle,* 22 June 1890, p. 10.

It is a late day to describe or even comment upon the literary art of Henry James. His latest novel, "The Tragic Muse," contains the very quintescence of his style, in that it is analytic, introspective and philosophical to a degree. Withal, however, his portraits are those of real people, and there is a thread of story telling running through the book which assimilates it to a novel in the common acceptation of the term. Mr. James has bestowed much pains upon his portraiture of Miriam Booth, [*sic*] his "Tragic Muse," with the result of having created a character which is clearly individualized and possessed of much originality. The portrait, too, of Gabriel Nash, whose only object in life was to be natural, and yet who left the general impression of being tremendously affected, has the air of being taken from life, so clearly outlined is it, and were it a few years back it might have been surmised to be a clever sketch of Oscar Wilde. The admirers of Henry James—and they are by no means few—will find in the "Tragic Muse" fresh evidence of the genius of their favorite author, for it is the very perfection of the style which is characteristic of James.

Christian Union 41 (26 June 1890), 913.

It is an interesting fact that both Mr. Howells and Mr. James seem to have recovered a good degree of their former freshness and hold upon life in their recent stories.

"A Hazard of New Fortunes" registered a very perceptible inflow of vitality and power,[1] and Mr. James's latest story, *The Tragic Muse,* which appeared serially in the "Atlantic Monthly,"[2] and has now come from the press of Houghton, Mifflin & Co. (Boston) in two handsome volumes, shows a similar gain in freshness of feeling and vigor of treatment. When Mr. James published "The Bostonians," it seemed to many people as if he had parted not so much with his art as with that vitality which alone makes art valuable. "A London Life," although a very disagreeable story, indicated a return to his earlier methods, and "The Tragic Muse" seems to us stronger and better in every way than "A London Life."[3] It is in many respects the best story Mr. James has written. It deals almost exclusively with English life, and sets in fine contrast the artistic interests and ideals, as illustrated in painting and on the stage, with the standards and ideals of conventional English public life and society. This contrast gives the story its deepest interest, and it is indicated with all the subtlety and delicate discrimination characteristic of Mr. James. There is probably no American who could convey with such delicacy and refinement the various shades of feeling, the nice gradations of difference and distinction, which are part of the artistic temperament. In fact, Mr. James's natural aptitude for the comprehension of these things, and his remarkable facility and felicity in expressing them, exposes him to the danger of interpreting the artistic temperament too largely on the side of its weakness—that is, on the side of its extreme sensitiveness and receptivity, rather than on its creative side. It is this side of artistic life which one feels continually in Nicholas Dormer and Miriam Rooth; but it must be said that this is a side of life which is generally missed both by English and American observers. The French understand it, and it is beautifully expressed by the old French actress who appears on the scene as Miriam's unwilling teacher. The intellectual quality of "The Tragic Muse" is very high. There is so much subtlety of observation and reflection, so much brilliancy of discrimination, so many ideas advanced, that one often stops and asks whether, after all, Mr. James is primarily a novelist. That he is a man of letters of very great talent and uncommon training goes without saying; but one is often too conscious of his style, too frequently interrupted and checked in reading the story by the presentation of some striking idea or some brilliant bit of characterization. The impression that one receives is that the story is a *tour de force* of a very accomplished and brilliant man, rather than the natural expression of a supreme talent for fiction. Mr. James tells his story with too much brilliancy; one is often more interested in the narrator than in the narration. And yet it is admirable as a story!

Notes

1 William Dean Howells, *A Hazard of New Fortunes* (1890).
2 "The Tragic Muse," *Atlantic Monthly* 63 (January–June 1889); 1–20, 184–205, 289–309, 509–28, 629–48, 764–85; 64 (July—December 1889), 44–64, 245–65, 389–410, 537–56, 652–69, 735–52; 65 (January–May 1890), 54–70, 208–24, 320–37, 444–65, 588–604.
3 "A London Life," *Scribner's Magazine* 3 (June 1888), 671–88; 4 (July–September 1888), 64–82, 238–49, 319–30.

"Art in Romance." New York *Times,* 29 June 1890, p. 11.

"The perfect presence of mind, unconfused, unhurried by emotion, that any artistic performance requires, and that all, whatever the instrument, require in exactly the same degree; the application, in other words, clear and calculated, crystal firm, as it were, of the idea conceived in the glow of experience, of suffering, of joy."

This compact formula, which Mr. James lets fall in discussion of the actress who gives this book its name, renders fairly the impression made by "The Tragic Muse." The characters live and move in an art atmosphere. Mr. James deals with art artfully, taking the word in a double sense and in a much broader sense than it is often possible to use it. The very obvious purpose in the book has the unusual effect of extending rather than contracting its limits. It is not so much that Mr. James has shown art in many phases of result, but he has shown the part it plays in many natures dedicated to it in some cases with more or less unwillingness. Mr. James's work generally gives the feeling that, he is personally acquainted with the facts—he is at times faithful to weariness, as in "Washington Square"—only the compensating satisfaction of hearing the absolute truth can atone for its barrenness of fancy. In nothing except, perhaps, "Princess Cassamassima" has he seemed to work without dwelling among his material. There is a fidelity about it all that makes each topic, each phase, that he treats particularly interesting to the reader previously interested in that particular phase, as Custom House reports are interesting to tariff reformers; he gives intellectual information and in a very fair and accurate fashion, but if we say that he is at home in "The Tragic Muse" it seems to mean something quite different and more literal than this. He is at home—there is familiarity, ease of handling, intimate knowledge such as a good patriot shows in speaking of his country. It is, or appears, more evident than in any previous book that Mr. James is interested right through. The plot or connection is not difficult to follow. "The Tragic Muse," is Miriam Rooth; an actress and an artist, so thoroughly the former that one is a little at a loss to lay hold of her womanhood, though it is continually suggested and Miriam herself by no means ignores it. She is still more artist than actress, ready to give herself up and renounce every more individual satisfaction for that of reaching after her ideal. It would be truer to the spirit of her character to say that this is her individual satisfaction, the only one worth mentioning in her fervent life. Mr. James subtly indicates the attraction that the "artistic temperament" has for itself by letting the flame of Miriam's loyalty to her aim swerve a little and flicker in the direction of Nick Dormer, who is also an artist "in oils," without a suggestion of intensity in any other direction. He is a wonderful drawing from life; a young Englishman who is made M. P. and tosses over his place, together with the sanctity of his inheritance, the British pride of doing what his father, and presumably his grandfather, did before him, and, most of all, the combined influence of his mother and the woman he wants to love—all these he lets go to paint portraits in his happy, disordered studio. Of course there is a certain base selfishness in his sweet-tempered, conscious absorption, and equally, of course, there is a certain high-minded self-abnegation, a noble fervor of appreciation of all that is great in his choice, and of its distance above him and its absolute claim upon him. It is this that Miriam feels and glows over as he paints her portrait.

In Nick Dormer's character more perhaps than in any other Mr. James displays his startling capacity for absorbing and giving out the truth. It is so much more difficult and so much more impressive to show things veritably than to say that they are so. The most possessed lover of art for art's sake or for his own sake, or for the sake of anything, could not fail to be stirred and wakened and lifted up by Mr. James's tributes to the sacred fire which in his hands burns largely, steadily, and with a great, still flame. He makes Nick say just after he has been elected member for Harsh and before he resigns:

> "There it is; there's the naked, preposterous truth; that if I were to do exactly as I liked, I should spend my years copying the more or less vacuous countenances of my fellow-mortals. I should find peace, and pleasure, and wisdom, and worth, I should find fascination and a measure of success, in it— out of the din and the dust and the scramble, the world of party labels, party cries, party bargains, and party treacheries, of humbuggery, hypocrisy, and cant. The cleanness and quietness of it, the independent effort to do something, to leave something which shall give joy to man long after the howling dies away to the last ghost of an echo—such a vision solicits me at certain hours with an almost irresistible force."

Yet with these two supremely artistic natures we see, together with their fine devotion to their idea, a marvelously-perfect representation of the other side of it, the attendant self-indulgence, the streaks of hardness, the riding rough-shod or velvet-shod, according to their differing susceptibilities, over the passions, the ambitions, the loves, the hopes, the prejudices of those outside their hallowed world.

He is capable of inspiring the strongest affection, to which he responds gently, sweetly, demonstratively; and at the same time, in the interest of his art, he is capable of dealing a leveling blow at the pride that is almost stronger than life with his mother, he is capable of wounding, in a way unwittingly, the deepest beliefs of his affianced wife, he is capable—and yet this comes about through an awkward, admirable honesty—of contending for his "idea" at the deathbed of his oldest and most generous friend.

It is something the same way with Miriam. Her renunciations creep by the side of her gains. Her mother is a weariness, but she uses her. She grasps at everything that will help her build her career more solidly. She gives up the social position offered her by Peter Sherringham's infatuation somewhat more gloriously and scornfully than Nick lays aside his honors. She burns with a half-lurid light that changes the aspect of things around her. She follows the law of development so grandly that to make comparisons in the attempt to prove her unnatural would be crude and foolish. There is no brutality—only his inevitable fidelity—in the way. Mr. James insists on the actress's place in the social world, but there is something like brutality in Miriam's own splendid, uncompromising recognition of it characteristic of her whose refinements are spent on her representation of natures not her own. Her character, multiform and harmonious, at once unique and common, gives an opportunity which Mr. James has made use of to produce the purest strain we have known from him. Among all these throbbing pulses and fevered minds he has set Nick Dormer's little sister Biddy, blooming and fresh as a flower of the field, with her sweet devotions, her young dignity, and her pretty wisdom of innocence.

When, at the end of the book, we see her walking on the road to happiness with shining eyes it cools the scene and gives a dewy morning aspect to our last impression.

"The Tragic Muse," quite unlike Mr. James's typical choice of composition, is a story full of movement. They're all struggling, all aspiring, all contending, they are pulled this way and that. It would seem that after cautious advance guards have been sent out Mr. James is suddenly in the midst of the fray. With the exception of "The Princess Casamassima," in which, as we have said, Mr. James seems almost too aloof from his subject, he has presented no such spectacle of conflicting forces. It is thrown into bold relief by the introduction of Gabriel Nash, the apostle of being in opposition to doing. With him Mr. James has seemed to let himself go in a wild revel of the imagination. Nick Dormer's description to Biddy of the flitting of this metaphysical person condenses the reader's impression of him.

"He has melted back into the elements—he is part of the ambient air."

Mr. James's former work appears to have been a schooling for this latest book, which takes its place, for the present at least, as a masterpiece. In it one does not think of the author as a disinterested observer, but he equally avoids the great danger of personal bias. It teems with individuality, but a composite individuality, made up of the various consciences and temperaments included in it, which does not force itself upon us, but is pervasive and elusive—the spirit animating the body. The book is valuable not only as a production but as an inspiration.

As an analytical observer of society Mr. James has few rivals. He knows his Paris and his London thoroughly, and yet, being an American, he never loses his place as an observer. This power of brilliant rendering of the kaleidoscope effects which play on the surface of society life in France and England is as conspicuous as ever in Mr. James's new story, *The Tragic Muse* (London: Macmillan, 8vo, 3 vols.). The paramount importance of political life to the upper classes in England must strike an American strangely. Mr. James knows London too well not to grasp the fact, but perhaps no American can perceive how absorbing a pursuit politics become even to those who have little enthusiasm for higher ideas. Mr. James shows us two persons who cast aside all hindrances, who sacrifice everything, to follow art, and yet neither of them is an enthusiast. The "Tragic Muse" is at first an ignorant, clumsy, handsome girl with a strong will; she works through her disadvantages, and by sheer determination to reach the top of her profession she strides on to perfection. She remains sordid to the end. She tramples down her own and other people's feelings, allowing nothing to stand in the way of her chosen career. She is not brutal; she is only business-like, and when she marries it is with a single eye to her professional interests. The cruel struggles which her diplomatist adorer goes through are well described. Mr. James and the reader watch him as he writhes, with pity but not with sympathy. What they do sympathise with is the threatened destruction of his promising career if he takes to himself an "impossible" wife. Nick Dormer, on the other hand, spoils his career for the sake, not of art, but of an artistic life. He gives up politics, for which he is singularly adapted, for he is eloquent and popular both at the hustings and in the House, and this involves for him probably the sacrifice also of his marriage with a rich and ambitious woman, who has already got him into Parliament by her interest and efforts, and certainly a fortune from an old cousin. All this he gives up to follow his artistic bent. He is not a youth, and no mention is made of the severe training which every man must go through if he is in earnest. He takes the attitude of a dilettante, having too little belief in his own powers and too little devotion to art for art's sake. He has a strange, shadowy, fantastic friend whose rank in the writer's estimation it is hard to fix. The talk between these two is so vague, so ineffective that we can only hope he is not intended to show us what life should be. He merely flits about urging others to do, while he does nothing himself. Life is easy in Mr. James's world if you will only have it so. When the actress is married and the diplomatist's struggles are over he turns to the little girl who has always been in love with him, and she sweetly accepts him. And we are given to understand that after all the beautiful Julia Dallow, with her riches and her ambitions, will at least forgive Nick Dormer and restore him to favour. The subordinate people of the story are imagined and finished with Mr. James's usual happy touches. There is little description of scenery, but one deserves notice—the view of Notre Dame by night—as an instance of the author's singular power of making city scenes vivid and exquisitely picturesque.

Speaker [England] 2 (19 July 1890), 83.

It is frequently said that Mr. Henry James always avoids the use of sensational incidents. This is not just. It should never be forgotten that he has written a ghost story, and that more than one of his characters have committed suicide. The bookbinder in "Princess Casamassima" killed himself in the most interesting way. Consequently, when we find, as in "The Tragic Muse," a very little incident made to go a very long way, we feel that this is due not to any want of the inventive faculty in the author, but to the deliberate choice of the other method, of which he is, perhaps, the best living exponent. He could give us incidents—sensational incidents—if he thought they were good for us, but he knows a better way. We have, it is true, a Parliamentary election in these volumes, but it is not exciting, nor is it intended to be exciting. We have several love-scenes, but they are rather pretty than passionate; and the lovers are never so fervid as to forget to be rather extraordinary. We have, too, the story of a tragic actress, but the reader is to be interested in the study of her character far more than in the incidents of her career; and, undoubtedly, the sketch of Miriam Rooth is the strongest and most original thing in the book. For the rest, there are many pages of small talk, with a careful notice of tone and gesture, much that is brilliant and bitter, a close insight into the most minute characters, and a careful and self-conscious style.

There is something to be said for the method. But one may admire an etching, and yet consider that there are certain limits to the proper use of the etching needle. Mr. James's shorter stories have the deli-cacy of an etching, and in them he shows a clear sense of the right relations of his subject to the length and manner of treatment. But he must have been wanting in that sense when, in "The Tragic Muse," he extended his little delicacies, refinements, and epigrams over more than seven hundred pages. We must notice, too, the undue prolixity of a part of the book, and the confused hurry of its conclusion.

There is little warm, genial humanity in the story. Each little perversity, or whimsicality, or meanness in the author's characters—they are mostly ignoble characters—is brought out, mounted in an epigram, and slid beneath the author's merciless microscope. And there are things in the book which are rather tricky than artistic. One, at least, of the characters is an unsolved problem; this is a pretty trick, and easy of execution. You sketch an ordinary character and then write a few inconsistencies into it, make it quite clear that you know they are inconsistencies, and that they have not slipped in by mistake. Either give no explanation, or give several explanations; hint that you know all about it, but avoid being in any way satisfactory on the subject. Another pretty trick is to anticipate a criticism by putting it in the mouth of one of your characters. "You talk like an American novel," says Nicholas Dormer to Gabriel Nash in the third volume. It is precisely what Gabriel Nash has been doing, not only on this occasion, but all through the book. Moreover, two of the characters are accused by a third of imitating Gabriel Nash. It is a just accusation. They do talk like Gabriel Nash, and he talks exactly like an American novel. Of course the humble reader thinks that Mr. James has only noted the similarity in order to mark some peculiarly subtle distinction. We prefer to think that Mr. James is even a better critic than a novelist; and that when he has unconsciously allowed one character to resemble another too closely, he subsequently discovers the mistake.

In all probability the author looks upon "The Tragic Muse" more as a literary performance than as a mere story. Keen interest and excitement are the demands of a vulgar crowd; the exquisite appreciation of witty subtleties is a higher gift. But may we point out that few things are more dull than persistent brilliance? Mr. Henry James is very much afraid of being dull, and the fear hampers him. Less carefulness and more freedom of movement would have made a better and more artistic work. As it is, the writing is frequently thin, frigid, and artificial. It wants vigor and variety; much of it is a vain repetition of the author's previous work. Had the book been the work of a previously unknown writer, we might have greeted it with more enthusiastic praise. But Mr. James has fairly earned the right to be judged by a high standard, a standard to which we cannot think that "The Tragic Muse" attains.

Athenaeum 3274 (26 July 1890), 124.

Mr. James and Mr. Meredith have one point of contact: books by either may not be dipped into with enjoyment, or even comprehension; it is all or nothing with them; every word or none must be read. Whether (as with Mr. Meredith's) a book of Mr. James's may be returned to with renewed interest is another question, and has nothing to do with the book before us. 'The Tragic Muse' has a good deal of the ingenuity and careful accomplishment which one expects from him, but little or none of the keenness of perception and discernment, the delicacy and distinction of touch, which marked 'Daisy Miller' and 'A Bundle of Letters,' and made them famous. The handling is ill assured and tentative, as well as too heavily laboured for the issues and interests at stake, which are slight, not to say trivial, in essence, or postponed and attenuated to the merest nothingness. Mr. James still shows himself fond of working round a situation, of circling and wheeling about it, but always receding without even carrying away the barriers, yet returning to it again and again from another direction or from another vantage, but never, so to speak, vaulting it triumphantly. The story, if we may say so, is for the most part negative—a history of occurrences that do not occur, unions that perpetually hang fire, passions that come to nothing, aspirations—political and intellectual—that have no fruition, with other episodes of a clever but barren quality. There is, too, more French than one cares for in an English novel. Mr. James, as we know, has lately had much to say about the canons of art in general, and of the drama in particular. The part relating to it and the theatrical *débuts* of the young person of Jewish antecedents is, perhaps, more interesting and better presented than the rest. There is also a good deal about painting, mostly of the contemporary and actual chatter of the studios, but given with an air of some gravity and conviction—the sort of talk that is so much with us just now; the "art for art's sake" point of view, which the British public is struggling to grasp. There are three or four personages (male and female), society people mostly, and the actress, with her mother, who has some of Mr. James's familiar but good touches. In Lady Agnes and her surroundings we have a picture that is characteristic of life as it is in London drawing-rooms, or at any rate in Mr. James's conception of them, which perhaps comes to much the same thing. There is the suspicion of a male snob somewhere about—we will not say where, but he is present. It is the actress who has the most body—and soul, too—who is, in fact, the most human of the party. She has some force, and above all, some directness, which is not given to the others. All more or less produce the feeling of people playing at a game called life, the deeper issues and the more significant moves of which Mr. James may manage to suggest with some cleverness, but which one shrewdly suspects he could not really "tackle" if he would. One young man is burdened with the feeling "of that complexity of things of which the sense had lately increased with him, and to which it was owing that any thread one might take hold of would probably lead one to something discomfortable"; also with "an acute mistrust of the superficiality of performance into which the desire to justify himself might hurry him." There is a good deal of this sort of thing about the story, of course interspersed with many and sundry good things. Altogether those who know Mr. James's writing well are principally struck by the sense of flatness and absence of relief, and the undeniable cleverness of what is, however, after all, much more like studio work than work that is the result of direct contact with nature.

Godey's Lady's Book 121 (August 1890), 172.

The readers of the "Tragic Muse," which has just been published in two volumes, after running as a serial through the pages of the *Atlantic Monthly,* will be well rewarded for their patience. The contest between artistic genius on the one side and influence of love and political ambition on the other, is twice illustrated in the "Tragic Muse" by different sets of people. Nick Dormer, the son of a deceased member of Parliament, loved by a beautiful, rich, and politically ambitious woman, urged by every family tradition and influence, as well as by natural facility towards a political life, throws up the seat in Parliament, to which he has just been returned, and his chances and wealth, and breaks with the woman who loves him, in order to take up portrait painting. In the other contest Peter Sherringham, loving the theatre as Dormer loves painting, with the knowledge and taste to make him a manager, if not an actor, more in love with the great actress, Miriam Rooth, than Dormer is in love with Julia Dallow, cannot bring himself to propose marriage to this splendid woman of genius until it is too late, except on condition that she shall give up the stage. She clings to her art, of course, with even less wavering than Dormer took to portrait painting, from which results the artistic temperament might draw the inference that it is stronger than any other worldly influence, and that as it can resist such temptations as love, wealth, and worldly position, so it can overcome all unfavorable surroundings.

If one is tempted to say that Mr. James has the making of a great essayist, and to wonder why he selects the cumbersome machinery of the novel for the expression of his thought, why he sacrifices so little to popularity and should yet sacrifice so much, the wonder dies away in the deep impression made by the strongly dramatic scene between Miriam Rooth and Peter Sherringham, where the diplomat, on the eve of his departure for America, makes his last appeal to the actress to leave the stage and become his wife, and the actress caps his reasoning with a better logic, springing from a depth of feeling which he has not yet sounded. Such a scene is only found in a strong novel, which this one undoubtedly is. It is one that seaside and mountain coteries would do well to add to their collection for summer reading, when they want intellectual food worth digesting.

"Henry James's *Tragic Muse*." *Critic* 17 (2 August 1890), 55.

One sits down in a shady veranda looking over blue waves at bluer mountains far away, to match the sparkle of a perfect atmosphere with the kindred quality in Henry James's new book, justly confident that from such exercise will result no sense of disappointment. In the two long volumes of 'The Tragic Muse,' the familiar facets of this author's wit display an undiminished glitter. His rare and exquisitely polished skill as an essayist—by many of his admirers held in greater esteem than his power as a writer of stories meant to fascinate or to amuse—has in no one of his novels been more vividly *en évidence.* Each chapter, barren though it may be of incident, hanging to that preceding it by the merest film of plot, is shaped with such nicety, and sprinkled with such a prodigality of witty sayings, and (to quote his own phrase) 'supersubtle' analysis of men, women and things, as to fit it to stand alone as an example of a unique personality in American literature.

Our first glimpse at the *dramatis personæ,* the two couples, *et al.,* composing the little group of English folk around whom the action of the tale revolves, sees them in Paris in the galleries of the Salon, lunching at a restaurant, while indulging in a discussion of seventy-seven printed pages in length intended to set before the reader the conditions and relations, each to the other and to the world, of the clever, or vague, or sketchy, or paradoxical persons to whom he is thus introduced. And just here let us remark upon the close attention needful at times, to disentangle the thread of this elusive variety of talk, with which the followers of Mr. James's writings are so well acquainted. It is always a little exasperating to the average member of society to stand craning his neck, as it were, and striving to follow such 'somersaults in the blue' of a gifted imagination. Mr. James reminds us of a person in ambush behind a window-shutter, amusing himself with casting the reflections of a hand-mirror in the eyes of the passers by. It is difficult not to have the impression that he is enjoying a laugh in his sleeve at the commonplace people who for the life of them cannot help winking and blinking, in face of an intellectual divertisement in which philosophy and speculation are conveyed by these dazzling flashes. All this displays his enormous resource in clothing original thought with unexpected phrases; but it does not teach, comfort, or enlighten, like the plain-sailing prose of Thackeray, Tourguéneff, or Daudet, and with our foremost living writer of fiction, Americans would like to have sympathy as well as admiration. The reader lays down Vol. II. of 'The Tragic Muse' feeling—to make use of one of the author's rare allusions to his fellow-countrymen—'kind of lonely, as the Americans say.'

Nicholas Dormer, born in the gyves of English aristocratic conventionalism, and yearning to escape into the free fields of self-supporting art; Peter Sherringham, the diplomat, who discovers, financially develops, and falls madly in love with Miriam, the 'Tragic Muse'—and whose fencing with that young woman on the subject of his inconvenient passion is, by the way, so admirably done; Basil Dashwood, the young man of good society who goes on the stage for love of Art, and settles down to 'drawing patterns, hunting up stuffs, bristling with ideas and pins,' in the service of the star; Gabriel Nash, the business of whose life is to talk about the reason and essence of things, who belongs to the Anonymous Club of which he is suspected by his friends of being the only member—who effects, in the end, a 'Hawthorne-like disappearance' from the scene, entirely compatible with his performance when before it—these are the chief men-folk of the tale. Of the women, Miriam, in her ascent from the bare asphalte of crude beginnings to the empyrean of dramatic fame, is to us less delicately pictured than Julia Dallow. Spite of the name gained by her first marriage (with a man on whom her own cousin comments thus unpleasantly: 'He used to look greasy—his name ought to have been Tallow'), this heroine is 'a beautiful specimen of the English garden flower, the product of high cultivation and much tending,' a 'perfect type of the object *raised,* or bred, and everything about her is homogeneous, from the angle of her elbow to the way she drops that vague, conventional, dry little "Oh!" which dispenses with all further performance. That sort of completeness is always satisfying.'

Lady Agnes Dormer—the British matron, whose widowed path through life is attended by the 'strenuous shade' of the deceased Sir Nicholas—is well described as 'the high executive woman, the mother of children, the daughter of earls, the consort of an official, the dispenser of hospitality, looking back upon a life-time of luncheons.' It is Lady Agnes who, impressed against her will into a hearing of recitations from the explosive Miss Rooth, wears, 'much of the time, the countenance she might have worn at the theatre during a play in which pistols were fired.' One of the two daughters of this conservative dame is a delightful Biddy, ultimately mated with her handsome cousin Peter, by the time the fires of that young gentleman's love for Miriam had died down and he has become the resigned 'Minister to the smallest of Central American republics.' And then, could anything be better than Mme. Honorine Carré, 'the Balzac of actresses, the miniaturist of white-washers'?

No hasty finger-tip, laid here and there upon its salient points, can do justice to this studied and spirited romance—for romance it is, in the teeth of the choice for his personages, by the creator of Dr. Jackson Lemon, of such titles as 'Nick,' 'Bid,' Gabriel Nash, Peter Sherringham, Julia Dallow, and Miriam Rooth. As Gabriel himself observed about the defunct Mr. Pinks of Harsh, 'What names, to be sure!'

Saturday Review [England] 70 (2 August 1890), 141.

The Tragic Muse will have a special interest for Mr. Henry James's English readers, as in it for the first time he shakes himself free of the toils imposed by his nationality, and gives to the world a novel which does not contain even one American. Not one *soi-disant* American, that is; for it must be confessed that Miriam Rooth, the Tragic Muse herself, and her friend, Gabriel Nash, are much more like certain types of Americans with whom fiction has made us familiar (does not Miriam even talk of "once in a while"?) than any known form of English development. It is quite possible, indeed highly probable, that such Americans do not really exist; but their presentment is fondly cherished by a particular class of popular author, who delights in them as the most complex and subtle productions of which his brain is capable. The story is mainly concerned with the career of Miriam Rooth, from her first appearance as a handsome, awkward, tactless, self-confident girl, with a real, though very dormant, talent for acting, and a passion for the stage, to the moment in which she makes her bow as the elegant, successful actress whose belief in herself and love for her profession are the strongest things about her. One of the best scenes in the book is the early one where Miriam, accompanied by her adoring mother, proceeds to give recitations to an old French actress, with the irrepressible Gabriel Nash and two other young Englishmen, Dormer and Sherringham by name, for audience. The impartiality of the Frenchwoman's attitude towards the apparently stolid and hopeless performer, her practical questions and suggestions, and the determination with which she declines to be led from the point by the maternal garrulity of Mrs. Rooth, are admirably rendered, and, as afar as we are aware, are a new "note" in fiction. No less effective is the description of Miriam's recitations before a company of English ladies in the rooms of Peter Sherringham, one of the secretaries at the British Embassy. At that time Miriam's powers of conception and execution were as limited as her self-confidence was great. Once started, she went on like a barrel-organ, till the nervous host had a hint conveyed to her that she would do well to stop. The episode reminds us of one in *Pride and Prejudice,* where Mary Bennett, on being asked politely by her host at supper to give them a song, continues to warble, till her father mildly remarks that "she has delighted the company long enough," and that they had better be going. We are not told what the sensations of Miss Bennett's hearers were on this occasion; but Mr.

James has sketched for us (not without some malice) those of the cultivated beings who listened to Miss Rooth. All were deeply impressed. Shrieking they took for power, squeaking for pathos; and Sherringham's cousin, Biddy Dormer, was so deeply moved that she came forward to thank the heroine of the exhibition, and to tell her how beautiful she thought it. In the picture of Biddy Dormer as the best type of English girl Mr. James has achieved a triumphant success. It is not an easy thing to convey on paper the charm of a young girl (in the English, not the American, sense of the term) who is modest, yet not shy or silly; able to take care of herself when necessary, but always preferring to be looked after by somebody else. We feel all the fascination of Biddy and are even prepared to forgive her her horrible name. The other characters are less true to nature and less agreeable to contemplate. Biddy's mother, Lady Agnes Dormer, mother likewise of Nick and Grace, is intended to be a good, narrow-minded, hardworking Englishwoman; but she is likewise intended to be a lady, and surely it is not the custom of ladies to talk so very plainly as Lady Agnes does about the desirability of Nick proposing to his rich cousin Mrs. Dallow, or to allow eligible suitors to see as clearly into their hearts as she allows Peter Sherringham to see into hers? However, every one is so odd on this same question of love affairs, that perhaps Lady Agnes may only have accommodated herself to the prevailing spirit. Peter Sherringham passes by Biddy's secret devotion and falls gradually more and more in love with Miriam, to whom he is perpetually offering his hand; yet somehow there is a sense of reality lacking in his declarations which convey more of pique than passion, and we are not as surprised as we ought to be that Miriam sustained "the rummage of his gaze." Nick Dormer, the person whom Miriam really prefers, though she marries a useful all-round young actor, suffers the beautiful actress to make him her confidant while he is taking her portrait; and even discusses his mother and sisters with her and Gabriel Nash. Indeed, the want of reticence observable in all the characters is remarkable in English people with whom it is, mercifully, the exception either to talk about their feelings or to plunge into analysis, as both Dormer and Sherringham have a trick of doing. In Miriam Rooth Mr. James has attempted to show a woman whose personal gifts can only be developed by long and hard labour, and whose gifts become graces under the sun of prosperity. But, though he contrives to realize well enough the glittering, unrestful, self-absorbed personality that is the almost necessary outcome of an actress's life, he has not been able to make her lovable, or to gloss over the vulgarity or want of humour that so often degenerates into pertness. Gabriel Nash is a superfluous figure altogether, and only serves the purpose of perpetually admiring Miriam, and exclaiming "Isn't she wonderful?" There is some excellent talk about acting; and lovers of the Français will linger round the pages that deal with that shrine, and with the pictures of Rachel in the foyer. Mr. James is thoroughly at home here, and his criticisms are always worth attending to. It is a pity the book was not compressed a little, as the story would gain much, and that the characters do not confine themselves either to French or English, and not converse in a medley of both. It is likewise a mistake to allow the Dormer family to talk for nearly eighty pages—off and on— about one "Julia," without any explanation being given as to who "Julia" may be. This has exactly the same effect on the reader as listening to two people discussing an intimate friend who is unknown to the third, and conveys the sense of ill-breeding. In short, *The Tragic Muse*

is full of Mr. James's usual excellences and defects; and those members of the public who have once got over the "Julia" difficulty will find a great deal to reward them.

"Tragic Amusement." *Scots Observer* 4 (2 August 1890), 282–83.

Nicholas—who is also called Nick—Dormer, the hero of Mr. Henry James's new novel, was from time to time a member of Parliament. He was reasonably well-bred and well-behaved, and if one had known him one would without hesitation have asked him to dinner, lent him a sovereign, or believed any statement he might have made upon a simple matter of fact within his own knowledge as to which he had no apparent interest in telling a lie. He was not at all mad. And he was a Liberal. This anachronism is probably due to the fact that when Mr. Henry James began *The Tragic Muse* there was no violent inconsistency in the conjunction of qualities just enumerated. Certainly if it took Mr. James as long in proportion to write the story as it takes a conscientious reviewer to read it, he must have commenced the task at some time long before the end of the remote epoch when such a thing was possible. Length is the dominant characteristic of the romance. The number of pages is by no means excessive; and though there is a good deal in each, the number of words is probably not greater than in many a commonplace three-volume novel. But the stodginess of it! the complacent reeling off of paragraph after paragraph pages long, made up of sentences like this: 'Imitation is a fortunate homage only in proportion as it is delicate, and there was an indefinable something in Nash's doctrine that would have been discredited by exaggeration or by zeal'! Of course the author occasionally permits the characters to speak to each other, but when they do they are as fluent, as refined, as circuitous, and as cryptic, if not quite as long-winded, as Mr. James himself.

There was a vulgar girl called Miriam Rooth, who wanted to be an actress, and became one, and immediately had an extravagantly brilliant success, and is left at the end of the story playing Juliet in a blaze of popularity, and married to a fool who was also an actor. There was Nick Dormer, whose friends made him a member of Parliament, and who, after thinking and talking over the question as if he had all eternity to do it in and nothing else to do in eternity, abandoned politics for portrait-painting. There was Mrs. Dallow, a rich young widow, who loved Nick and whom Nick sometimes wanted to marry, and first she would and then she wouldn't and then she was inclined to think perhaps after all she should (at which stage we leave her, thankful to be permitted to do so on any terms). There was Mrs. Dallow's brother Peter, a secretary of embassy and presently minister to a Central American republic, who had a most consuming passion for Miriam, and when she married the actor promptly consoled himself as well as he could with Nick's sister—the only person in the book who is at all pleasant or natural. Then there is one Nash, a partly crazy little philosopher given to uttering paradoxes, whom Nick thought extremely amusing and whom Nick's friends thought rather offensive, whose philosophy was that no one should ever do anything except lounge and gratify his sense of the beautiful. And that is all: at least, none of the four or five other personages is of any importance.

The events, therefore, are one successful parliamentary candidature, one resignation of a seat, the commencement of three portraits (none of them ever finished) and the painting and exhibition of a fourth (in the valedictory paragraphs), one marriage, (about) six offers of marriage (four of them Peter to Miriam), two resulting engagements (Nick and Peter), one subsequent breach of promise (Nick—at least he was the victim of it), three successful dramatic productions (Miriam); and one change of vocation (Nick). About which episodes they all talk on, and on; and on, and on, especially Mr. Henry James. None of them, except occasionally the crushed Nash, says anything that seems to have been really worth the trouble of printing, and the impression one gathers from the whole is that Mr. James is a nightingale or some other bird of a poetic character who 'does but yarn because he must,' or, to put it another way, because he enjoys yarning. The practical conclusion arrived at and acted upon by Mr. Dormer, that a man with a considerable taste and some ability for portrait-painting, and no taste at all for parliamentary life, will probably enjoy himself more as a fairly good portrait-painter than as a Liberal member of Parliament, will command general assent, but cannot honestly be hailed as an important discovery.

Mr. James writes much better grammar and uses many fewer strained and fantastic locutions than his compatriot Mr. Howells, but he is nearly as dull (duller than *The Shadow of a Dream*) and much longer. He ambles equably through his unending paragraphs, but there is nothing violent about him, only a few little sloppy inaccuracies. Several of the chief characters have lived more or less in Paris, and introduce French tags into their talk with exasperating frequency. Otherwise there is nothing about them that can be called offensive except their existence; and they need not exist for any one who does not want them.

William Dean Howells. "Editor's Study." *Harper's New Monthly Magazine* 81 (September 1890), 639–41.

We fancy him [John Hay] in company there with another American who is chiefly recognizable as American because he is not recognizable as anything else, and who must be called a novelist because there is yet no name for the literary kind he has invented, and so none for the inventory. The fatuity of the story as a story is something that must early impress the storyteller who does not live in the stone age of fiction and criticism. To spin a yarn for the yarn's sake, that is an ideal worthy of a nineteenth-century Englishman, doting in forgetfulness of the English masters and grovelling in ignorance of the Continental masters: but wholly impossible to an American of Mr. Henry James's modernity. To him it must seem like the lies swapped between men after the ladies have left the table and they are sinking deeper and deeper into their cups and growing dimmer and dimmer behind their cigars. To such a mind as his the story could never have value except as a means; it could not exist for him as an end; it could be used only illustratively; it could be the frame, not possibly the picture. But in the mean time the kind of thing he wished to do, and began to do, and has always done, amidst a stupid clamor, which still lasts, that it was not a story (of *course,* it was not a story!), had to be called a novel; and the wretched victim of the novel-habit (only a little less intellectually degraded than the still more miserable slave of the theatre-habit), who wished neither to perceive nor to reflect, but only to be acted upon by plot and incident, was lost in an endless trouble about it. Here was a thing called a novel, written with extraordinary charm; interesting by the vigor and vivacity with which phases and situations and persons were handled in it; inviting him to the intimacy of characters divined with creative insight; making him witness of motives and emotions and experiences of the finest import; and then suddenly requiring him to be man enough to cope with the question itself; not solving it for him by a marriage or a murder, and not spoon-victualling him with a moral minced small and then thinned with milk and water, and familiarly flavored with sentimentality or religiosity. We can imagine the sort of shame with which such a writer, so original and so clear-sighted, may sometimes have been tempted by the outcry of the nurslings of fable, to give them of the diet on which they had been pampered to imbecility; or to call together his characters for a sort of round-up in the last chapter.

The round-up was once the necessary close of every novel, as it is of every season on a Western cattle ranch; and each personage was summoned to be distinctly branded with his appropriate destiny so that the reader need be in no doubt about him evermore. The formality received its most typical observance in *The Vicar of Wakefield,* perhaps, where the modern lover of that loveliest prospect of eighteenth-century life is amused by the conscientiousness with which fate is distributed, and vice punished and virtue rewarded. It is most distinctly honored in the breach in that charming prospect of nineteenth-century life, *The Tragic Muse,* a novel which marks the farthest departure from the old ideal of the novel. No one is obviously led to the altar; no one is relaxed to the secular arm and burnt at the stake. Vice is disposed of with a gay shrug; virtue is rewarded by innuendo. All this leaves us pleasantly thinking of all that has happened before, and asking, Was Gabriel Nash vice? Was Mrs. Dallow virtue? Or was neither either? In the nineteenth century, especially now toward the close of it, one is never quite sure about vice and virtue: they fade wonderfully into and out of each other: they mix, and seem to stay mixed at least around the edges.

Mr. James owns that he is himself puzzled by the extreme actuality of his facts; fate is still in solution, destiny is not precipitated; the people are still going uncertainly on as we find people going on in the world about us all the time. But that does not prevent our being satisfied with the study of each as we find it in the atelier of a master. Why in the world should it? What can it possibly matter that Nick Dormer and Mrs. Dormer are not certainly married, or that Biddy Dormer and Sherringham certainly are? The marriage or the non-marriage cannot throw any new light on their characters; and the question never was what they were going to do, but what they were. This is the question that is most sufficiently if not distinctly answered. They never wholly emerge from the background which is a condition of their form and color; and it is childish, it is Central African, to demand that they shall do so. It is still more Central African to demand such a thing in the case of such a wonderful creature as Gabriel Nash, whose very essence is elusiveness; the lightest, slightest, airiest film of personality whose insubstantiality was ever caught by art; and yet so strictly of his time, his country, his kind. He is one sort of modern Englishman: you are as sure of that as you are of the histrionic type, the histrionic character, realized in the magnificent full-length of Miriam Rooth.

There is mastery for you! There is the woman of the theatre, destined to the stage from her cradle: touched by family, by society, by love, by friendship, but never swayed for a moment from her destiny, such as it is, the tinsel glory of triumphing for a hundred nights in the same part. An honest creature, most thoroughly honest in heart and act, and most herself when her whole nature is straining toward the realization of some one else; vulgar, sublime; ready to make any sacrifice for her art, to "toil terribly," to suffer everything for it, but perfectly aware of its limitations at its best while she provisionally contents herself with its second-best, she is by all odds so much more perfectly presented in *The Tragic Muse* than any other like woman in fiction, that she seems the only woman of the kind ever presented in fiction.

As we think back over our year's pleasure, in the story (for we will own we read it serially as it was first printed), we have rather a dismaying sense of its manifold excellence; dismaying, that is, for a reviewer still haunted by the ghost of the duty of cataloguing a book's merits. While this ghost walks the Study, we call to mind that admirable old French actress of whom Miriam gets her first lessons; we call to mind Mrs. Rooth, with her tawdry scruples; Lady Dormer, with her honest English selfishness; Mrs. Dallow, with her awful good sense and narrow high life and relentless will; Nick's lovely sister Biddy and unlovely sister Grace; Nick himself, with his self-devotion to his indefinite future; Sherringham so good and brave and sensible and martyred; Dashwood, the born man of the theatre, as Miriam is the born woman; and we find nothing caricatured or overcharged, nothing feebly touched or falsely stated. As for the literature, what grace what strength! The style is a sweetness on the tongue, a music in the ear. The whole picture of life is a vision of London aspects such as no Englishman has yet been able to give: so fine, so broad, so absolute, so freed from all necessities of reserve or falsity.

Murray's Magazine [England] 8 (September 1890), 431–32.

It is not at all easy to judge a novel of Mr. Henry James's, because it always seems to need a special standard of criticism. When we hear that a lady "supremely syllabled" a very ordinary remark, we feel inclined to speak slightingly of the writer's intellect; but then, lo and behold! we come across some suggestive epithet, some delicately-turned phrase which we feel to be worthy of the author of 'Daisy Miller' and 'The Portrait of a Lady.' But perhaps to mention this difficulty is only to say that Mr. James occupies a unique place in contemporary literature. His books must be judged as a whole, and any criticism which selects special phrases and episodes will shoot very wide of the mark. 'The Tragic Muse' is concerned with the fortunes of several people, who all in their various ways are occupied in trying to define the right place of Art in their lives. We have a great actress uncertain how far she must also be a woman; a secretary of legation unable to reconcile diplomacy with a passion for acting and for this particular actress; a member of Parliament forsaking politics for portrait painting, a fantastic friend aiding and abetting him, and a number of relations breaking their hearts over his defection. It is the doubts and delays of these half-hearted lovers of art that we are called upon to follow through three very long volumes, and only the consummate skill with which the characters are

made to grow before our eyes could bring us to the end without more than a half-suppressed yawn. For, indeed, the story is very long drawn out, and perhaps Miriam Rooth, interesting as she is, would have been rather more interesting if her interviews with Peter, her wavering lover, had been somewhat curtailed. It is she who most engages our affection; but Nick Dormer, the M.P. turned painter, is a very clever piece of portraiture. In Gabriel Nash's extravagant æstheticism there is an element of caricature which detracts from its life-likeness, and Mrs. Dallow is rather shadowy and eludes our grasp as she eluded Nick's. For the comfort of those who fail to appreciate a story without an end, we may mention that in this book at least Mr. James so far condescends to the popular level as to give us a very clear hint of the way in which his *dramatis personæ* finally solve the problem set before them.

Spectator [England] 3248 (27 September 1890), 1109–10.

When any person acquires a taste for an article of diet which is not attractive to the unsophisticated palate—say, caviare or truffles—he will notice, should he be in the habit of examining his sensations, that his pleasure is derived from the very quality of flavour which in the first instance most strongly repelled him. In this respect, there is an exact correspondence between taste dietetic and taste artistic or literary. For example, there is probably no known instance of the "natural mind" having been drawn by instinctive admiration to the pictures of Mr. Whistler or the books of Mr. Henry James; for the natural mind the former are meaningless, and the latter dull. When, however, a certain educational process has been gone through, the cultured person who has been subjected to it finds not merely that he has gained a new pleasure, but that the new pleasure consists in exquisite appreciation of the quality that he once called meaninglessness or dullness. What to the outsider is the marring defect, is to him the making virtue of the master's work, and therefore the more prominently it betrays itself, the warmer will be his enthusiasm. This being so, it seems highly probable that the little company of superior persons who regard the novels of Mr. Henry James as especially admirable and enjoyable works of art, will attach a peculiar value to his latest book, *The Tragic Muse,* which is, we think, stronger than any of its predecessors in those Jamesian peculiarities by which they are charmed and the profane crowd repelled. Though the book is a very long one, there is even less of that vulgar element known as "the story" than usual; indeed, were the narrative summarised, it would be seen that Mr. James has all but realised that noble but perhaps unattainable ideal,—a novel without any story at all. Even that surely less vulgar kind of interest which is secured by the lively and lifelike presentation of character, is minimised to the utmost, for Mr. James cannot be said to *present* his men and women at all; what he does present is a thin solution of talk, in which they are, so to speak, dissolved, and from which we have to extract them by a mental process of precipitation. Considering that the flow of talk is perpetual, and that all the people in the book are fond of talking about themselves, it is absolutely astonishing how much Mr. James manages to write without giving a single revealing hint. The secret of this density of the conversational medium, which makes his characters appear like men and women seen through a mist, is to be found in his persistent refusal to employ the method of characteristic selection. Open a novel of Jane Austen at any page (and we name her because she, like Mr. James, is a realist who loves the commonplace) and you cannot read a couple of pages without forming a fairly clear idea of the situation and of the attitudes of the actors, because the talk, both in its matter and in its tone, is not merely talk which would have been natural at any time, but talk which would have been inevitable at that special time to those special talkers. In *The Tragic Muse,* on the contrary, the chatter hardly ever bears any recognisable impress of character of a situation; it is external, automatic talk *pour passer le temps,* that is heard in the club smoking-room, or in a drawing-room while afternoon tea is being handed round, or in a railway carriage during a long journey, when a common boredom inspires a mechanical sociability. We do not learn to know people in these places, because only the outer shell of their nature is in evidence; and we do not learn to know the people in Mr. James's novel, for the same reason. "That's the delightful thing about art," says Mr. Gabriel Nash, "that there is always more to learn and more to do; one can polish and polish, and refine and refine." Well, that is true; but there must be something to which these processes can be applied, and it is this something that we miss in *The Tragic Muse.* If Mr. James had made Miriam Rooth and Peter Sherringham and Nick Dormer sufficiently substantial to bear it, he might have polished and refined them at pleasure: as it is, so far from possessing substance, they have hardly recognisable outline.

Dublin Review 3d series 24 (October 1890), 466–67.

The "Tragic Muse" of the title-page is an underbred girl with a strong vocation for the stage, and an unlimited supply of the pushing egotism which so often accompanies that and other forms of genius. Beauty is at first her only apparent qualification for her profession, but being a heroine she develops the remaining ones in process of time, and becomes a famous actress, whose success, however, fails to interest the reader in any degree. The other characters are almost equally out of the range of sympathy. The hero, "Nick" Dormer, is a contemptible creature with æsthetic proclivities, who throws up a promising parliamentary career to potter over an easel, and alienates by his half-hearted courtship, the beautiful and wealthy woman who is willing to bestow her heart and fortune on him. The book is, as a matter of course, rich in clever satire of minute points of character, but shows total inability to grasp or present any one as a whole. Mr. James's artistic vision is microscopic, and consists entirely of analysis of detail without the synthetic power of combining the magnified minutiæ on which our whole attention is concentrated. He is consequently best as a satirist, or in the lighter sketches, where a caricature likeness of character will suffice. On a large canvas his vagueness becomes blottesque rather than suggestive, and the attempt to fill in his outlines only makes them more unreal. In the present work the story is of the slenderest, and stagnates through three closely printed volumes of prolix conversations, varied by tedious dissection of motive in commonplace characters. The author's sarcastic vein finds a butt in the portraiture of the professional æsthete, Gabriel Nash, whose artistic epicureanism is scarcely an exaggeration of the inanities indulged in by this modern type of humanity.

Overland Monthly 2d series 16 (October 1890), 437.

By far the most notable work of fiction now to be reviewed is Henry James's *The Tragic Muse*. Its publication as a serial in the *Atlantic* has already won for it many readers, and if we mistake not, as many admirers; for no work of Mr. James for many years is as attractive as this. "The Princess Casamassima" opens in a more interesting way, perhaps, and yet many readers fell by the wayside in the long progress of that story as a serial. This book, on the other hand, opens with chapters not likely to please any but the most ardent lover of the naturalistic and plotless novel. It requires seventy-five pages at the start to relate the small talk of a tour of an art gallery and a restaurant dinner. This talk goes far, it is true, in revealing the characteristics of some of the principal characters, and serves as a fore-scene that gives the "tragic muse" herself a chance to make a good entrance in a following scene. It is admirable, too, as the whole book is, and as all Mr. James's works are, for its perfect polish and consummate naturalness. But these intellectual pleasures require for their enjoyment a trained literary ear, and even those of some pretensions to such training are apt to long at times for a little more "air,"—something that can be whistled.

But Mr. James makes some concessions

to this desire for "story," and almost goes so far in this book as to bring it to the definite conclusion of marrying and living happy ever after. The principal characters are all paired off at the end in true romantic style,—except the one incongruity that the leading lady marries only a walking gentleman. It is the story of a young lady of dubious extraction and vulgar surroundings, who yet possesses the true artistic temperament so strongly that she pursues the rocky way to professional eminence. She is aided much in this by a young diplomat, who struggles long between his love for her and his ambitions.

The artistic moral of the story is further enforced by the introduction of an ambitious young politician, who resigns a seat in Parliament in spite of the pressure exerted on him by his political sweetheart, to pursue the divinely inspired calling of a portrait painter. His noble combat with himself, and his shame-faced attitude toward the sacrifice after it is made, are admirably drawn.

It goes without saying in a James story that all the minor characters are worked out with great faithfulness,—the best of them being, perhaps, the æsthete, Gabriel Nash, with his settled determination to *be* rather than to do.

All these characters discourse much and admirably on art, dramatic, pictorial, and general, and an interest in these subjects is necessary for full delight in the book. Possibly it is this artistic tone, of which James is surely a master, that makes *The Tragic Muse* of special interest.

[Annie R. M. Logan].
Nation 51 (25 December 1890), 505–6.

If Mr. James were, like his only English rival in the art of fiction, Mr. Stevenson, naturally impelled to write chiefly stories of adventure, he would get more applause than he does for his beautiful manner and exquisite style. Many instinctive censors of literature believe that Stevenson's stories are all action, therefore great; that James's stories are all rest, therefore fine-spun inanity. This sort of comment leads one to suppose that people who are not continually rolling down stairs must not consider the charge of torpidity an aspersion, and that nothing ever is accomplished in life by less violent methods. Most of the people in 'The Tragic Muse' are exceedingly careful of their steps, and yet they achieve a good deal. Nicholas Dormer gives up fine political prospects and a great marriage for the sake of a beggarly art; Peter Sherringham, after much vacillation, is ready to fling over diplomacy and the star of an ambassador for love of the Tragic Muse; the Tragic Muse herself, Miriam Rooth, never dreams of giving up anything, but holds fast to her one idea, much to her worldly advantage. It is true that the two men and most of the subordinate characters are less interesting for what they do than for what they think, for mental activity preliminary and subsequent to physical. Mr. James is, in fact, guilty of selecting complex creatures—creatures who are centuries away from savage simplicity—and of devoting his greatest energy to the exhibition of the storehouse of their complexities, the mind. He finds an infinite variety of mind, and its tricks are vastly more surprising and entertaining than a conjurer's tricks, which we see but do not in the least understand. There is the dull, ponderous, prejudiced mind of Lady Agnes; the naïve mind of her daughter Biddy, its ingenuousness crossed by inherited worldliness; the worldly mind of Mrs. Dallow, with innumerable shades, refinements, and even contradictions of worldliness; the mind of Peter Sherringham, her brother, very like hers, but the contradictions heightened by greater possibility of passion; the mind of Nicholas Dormer, slow like his mother's, but much less under control, capable of no end of fantastic flights; last, the mind of Gabriel Nash, serenely philosophical, but nebulous, unreliable, elusive.

Nash is nothing but a mind, a sort of incarnation of wisdom gathered through observation, the sharpness and justice of which have never been impaired by feeling. The other minds are only parts of substantial beings—far the most important parts, most subtle and intricate, altogether most worthy of one whose avowed profession is the complete representation of men and women. But Mr. James realizes that approximately primitive people, people who do more and better than they think, are still to be found in the world, often making great bustle and exciting wild curiosity. The Tragic Muse is one of these. Of mixed race, with a not distant Jewish strain, vagabond from her birth, beautiful, polyglot, and poor, she turns instinctively to the stage, where her natural advantages can be most brilliantly utilized and the disadvantages of circumstance most speedily conquered. Enormously vain, with imperturbable self-assurance, showy, hard, not ungenerous, capable of assuming every emotion and incapable of feeling any not connected with public applause and the receipts of the box-office—such is the Tragic Muse, by far the most brilliant and faithful representation of the successful modern actress than has ever been achieved in English fiction.

Checklist of Additional Reviews

Critic 16 (n.s. 13) (17 May 1890), 250.

Boston *Daily Advertiser,* 14 June 1890, p. 5.

Boston *Evening Journal,* 14 June 1890, Supp., p. 4.

Chicago *Times,* 21 June 1890, p. 10.

Chicago *Tribune,* 21 June 1890, p. 13.

New York *Tribune,* 22 June 1890, p. 14.

G.W.A. *American* 20 (28 June 1890), 213.

Chicago *Inter-Ocean,* 28 June 1890, p. 12.

St. Louis *Republic,* 28 June 1890, p. 10.

Portland *Morning Oregonian,* 29 June 1890, p. 14.

Cincinnati *Commercial Gazette,* 12 July 1890, p. 10.

New York *Sun,* 12 July 1890, p. 5.

Cleveland *Plain Dealer,* 13 July 1890, p. 5.

Literary World [Boston] 21 (19 July 1890), 231–32. Reprinted in Roger Gard, ed., *Henry James: The Critical Heritage* (London: Routledge & Kegan Paul, 1968), p. 208.

Indianapolis *Journal,* 25 July 1890, p. 3.

Churchman 62 (26 July 1890), 109.

Book Buyer 7 (August 1890), 289.

Chautauquan 11 (August 1890), 649.

[William M. Payne]. *Dial* 11 (August 1890), 92–93. Reprinted in Gard, p. 209.

"*The Tragic Muse.*" Louisville *Courier-Journal,* 9 August 1890, p. 7.

Literary World [England] 42 (15 August 1890), 123–25.

Graphic [England] 42 (16 August 1890), 175. Reprinted in Gard, p. 200.

George Saintsbury. *Academy* [England] 38 (23 August 1890), 148. Reprinted in Gard, pp. 201–2; James W. Gargano, ed., *Critical Essays on Henry James: The Early Novels* (Boston: G. K. Hall, 1987), pp. 65–66.

Horace E. Scudder. *Atlantic Monthly* 66 (September 1890), 419–22. Reprinted in Gard, pp. 213–17; J. Don Vann, *Critics on Henry James* (Coral Gables: University of Miami Press, 1972), pp. 19–22.

Cottage Hearth 16 (September 1890), 294.

Lippincott's Monthly Magazine 46 (September 1890), 423.

Public Opinion 9 (September 1890), 539.

Kate Upson Clark. *Epoch* 8 (5 September 1890), 77.

THE OTHER HOUSE

New York *Tribune*, 27 September 1896, sec. 3, p. 2.

Mr. James has written in "The Other House" a story which probably could never be put on the stage, yet it incessantly recalls the bustle of those French comedies which keep the curiosity of the spectator at concert pitch through innumerable changes of scene. His drama is unlike Mrs. Ward's [*Sir George Tressady,* reviewed in the same column] profoundly complicated. He presents a man as vowing to his dying wife that he will never remarry, at least during the lifetime of their child. He later places the widower between two women who both love him, though he loves only one. The unloved woman murders the child, who is an obstruction to them all, and does so, not that she may marry Tony Bream herself, since that looks impossible, but in order to incriminate her rival. Tony, moved by a curious loyalty to the woman who, though the murderess of his own child, has loved him, assumes the guilt of the tragedy. Mr. James leaves him on the brink of the consequences of this grisly affair. Is it an affair of nature? Perhaps, though an air of improbability hangs over the book. Yet the author excites interest through the protest which he makes, the protest to which reference has already been made, and he amuses—though the epithet might seem hardly to fit so sombre a book—through the ingenuity of his narrative. It is as full of interruptions as a melodrama, as full of moments in which the reading of a letter, the entrance of a third person, changes the course of things, as one of those plays in which the audience is hurried from one surprise to another, while the mystery grows ever deeper and deeper. Where "The Other House" invalidates its purely theatrical quality and becomes the strictly analytical essay which so many of the author's works become, is in being a conversational novel, a volume of dialogue which drives the brain almost frantic in its splitting of an infinite number of hairs. Here again, as in "Sir George Tressady," the reader is obliged to forego the attraction of a normally unfolded episode or series of episodes in actual life, for the less impressive exhibition of what a writer of intellect can find to say about the idiosyncrasies of individuals. The range of "The Other House" is narrower than that of Mrs. Ward's novel. But the analytical turn of mind illustrated by the former book is about the same as that revealed in the latter. Both writers are excellent talkers, and to listen to their talk is, if not an inspiration, at least a stimulus and a pleasure.

New York *Herald*, 17 October 1896, p. 14.

Very clever is Henry James' new book, entitled "The Other House," published by Macmillan & Co. Of most careful workmanship there is abundant evidence, and to many this will prove the chief charm of the work. Unlike Homer, who, we are told, nods sometimes, Mr. James is ever wide awake and would evidently as soon be found guilty of committing sacrilege as of writing a slovenly sentence. There are those who think that such extreme attention to details is apt to damp an author's enthusiasm and to cast an air of frigidity about his work. They do not hold with Horace that a literary work should be pruned and repruned many times before it is given to the public, and they are perpetually reminding us that some of the best things in the English language have been struck off at white heat. Doubtless, the via media is the best. We cannot fancy Mr. James striking off anything at white heat; on the other hand, human life being short and readers clamorous for fresh food, he cannot take Horace's advice literally. He is simply an artist whom long practice has made eminently skilled in the use of words. "The Other House" is a simple and attractive story. The characters are original and well drawn. The incidents are natural and clearly described. The dialogues are crisp and to the point. Neither of "padding" nor of vulgar sensationalism is there any trace. A most meritorious work, then, and one which can hardly fail to add to the author's reputation. If we miss in it some of those qualities which seem to us to go to the making of a first class work of fiction, we should remember that we find in it many other qualities which may be quite as desirable. The author does not inflame us with enthusiasm or take us off our feet by bursts of passion or vivid descriptions of stirring scenes, neither does he enchain our attention as many a less talented writer can enchain it; but, on the other hand, he gives us many a jewelled sentence and happy thought; he charms, though he never stimulates, us; he shows us many a hidden chamber of the human heart; he delights us by his deft handling of the English tongue—in a word, he constrains even those who do not admire him to admit that in the art of writing fiction, as he conceives it, no one can surpass him. We enjoy "The Other House" as we enjoy a calm, summer sunset or a quiet bit of country scenery. There are times when disturbance of any kind is abhorrent to us, and then the well bred placidity of Henry James is welcome.

"Henry James's Latest Work."
New York Times Saturday Review of Books and Art 1 (31 October 1896), 4.

Mr. James is without doubt an enviable author, in that whatever else a new book of his shows, it is sure to show his unflagging interest in his craft and the allurement to him of each new problem or predicament that presents itself. This is the case equally with his failures and his successes. The populace may sibilate him, but he applauds himself when he has produced something that defies general appreciation. The populace may even attribute its want of appreciation to the flagging of the author's own interest in his work. The experienced reader, however, will be very wary of doing this, for the experienced reader is aware that the author is liable to follow a flat failure with a distinguished success, a book which he wrote for his own exclusive enjoyment with a book his satisfaction in which he is willing to share with the public, without fear of vulgarizing his own enjoyment. There are signs that he himself is perfectly aware of the difference. At one time this seemed to be indicated by the infallibility with which he unloaded works foredoomed to unpopularity upon one publisher, reserving for another works in which there was for the publisher a fair prospect of recoupment. This sign seems now to have failed, for the last work of Mr. James's which we had occasion to notice, the collection of "Embarrassments," which could not have been even meant to be understood of the people, bore the same imprint with the present volume, which has already achieved its success in England and carries inherent assurance of success in this country.

In noticing "Embarrassments" we took occasion, we believe, to liken Mr. James to a musical virtuoso who should produce at a public performance the exercises with which he limbered his fingers in solitude, and, if he were considerate, within deadened walls. The interest of these things is not in the least, or is in the very least, human, but almost entirely technical. Their purpose is to enable the performer to do something else, say to write "The Other House." To continue the figure, Mr. James has a wonderful execution; he knows his double counterpoint to the bottom, but there is a scantiness of what the musical critics call "thematic material." In plainer words, good tunes do not very often occur to him, to be developed with the resources of this accumulated art. When he does get a good tune, he knows so well what to do with it that the result is apt to be a masterpiece. And we have no hesitation in calling "The Other House" a masterpiece.

It is understood all the while that the reader of Mr. James, of, to recur to our illustration, the listener at him, must be ready to do his full share of the work, and the reader most solicitous to be sympathetic must often be moved to complain that he is overworked. When the involution of the statement comes from the involution of the thought, and its complexity from the purpose to represent a complication in its fullness, there is nothing for it but industry on the part of the reader—an industry which is likely to be rewarded. But when the question is of a statement of perfectly commonplace facts, the reader has a right to demand that the statement be so plain that he can take it in at one reading, and to complain when the writer spares himself trouble at the reader's expense. Take the second sentence in "The Other House":

A great deal more went on there, naturally, than in the great, clean, square solitude in which she had practically lived since the death of Mr. Beener, who had predeceased by three years his friend and partner, the late Paul Bream of Bounds, leaving to his only son, the little godson of that trusted associate, the substantial share of the business in which his wonderful widow—she knew and rejoiced that she was wonderful—now had a distinct voice.

The humblest-minded reader cannot be expected to think of such a preliminary explanation that, if he does not like it, it is because he is not worthy of it. He has, in fact, a clear grievance. It is hard reading, because it is bad writing. And there are a great many of such willfully or carelessly, in either case unnecessarily, difficult passages in the book.

And yet no discerning reader is likely to dispute that it is a great book, one of the best of its author's works, one of the best of modern novels. The London correspondent of *The Times* touched the point of its excellence when he pointed out that it was a tragedy told in polite comedy. It is more than that, because, in fact, the tragic note is struck very early, almost at the outset, and the note, a note of suspense and warning, is repeated with increasing frequency up to the final catastrophe. The author's method, the method of slow and patient accumulation of detail and circumstance to make that credible which, stated baldly and crudely, would be incredible, has never been employed to better advantage nor to a more impressive result. The characters are built up before us under the increasing stress of the situation, until at last it becomes not only natural but inevitable that a young English lady shall detestably murder a harmless child, and that the witnesses of her crime shall combine to shield her from its punishment. The processes by which the work attains its end are "artificial" in the old and good sense. The highest technical skill is needed to make such a story plausible. But the end itself is much beyond an exhibition of technique. It is to present, forcibly and movingly, a human tragedy, and it is attained.

Athenaeum [England] 3601 (31 October 1896), 597.

Who runs should, yet possibly may not, read between the lines in Mr. James's new novel—may not see that it not only contains dramatic situations, but is a play in all save name and externals. Instead of acts it is divided into three books, and the interest continues to deepen steadily till the final crisis. It reads as though the author had at first conceived it in no other light than a play, but had afterwards, as it were, recoiled from the ineptitudes and vulgarities that on the stage are often the ruin of the best dialogue, action, and incident. Considering the state of the drama in spite of many important improvements, we cannot blame him for eschewing the ordeal. In leaving 'The Other House' as a very notable and distinguished piece of work, he may even be congratulated on having chosen the better part. Those who best know Mr. James's qualities and the short-comings of theatrical impersonation may agree that he has not improbably saved much that is supremely delicate in touch, much that shows the most sensitive care for the right distribution of light and shade, and many fine distinctions in tones and manners, which would have lost focus and significance in the glare of the footlights, from possible misapprehension and misinterpretation. Short of being actually witnessed with the bodily eyesight, 'The Other House' (by the skilful arrangement of its events and figures) should become, by a mental adjustment on the part of readers, equivalent to a dramatic performance. In it Mr. James has actually touched the heart of life more closely and more persistently than in his recent works. Where the action sweeps relentlessly forward to the tragic conclusion—which on this occasion he makes no attempt to blink—there can be but few digressions and hesitations. Quiet and restrained as are almost all the scenes, the thing palpitates with the emotion belonging to a work of art that has been cast and fused in one supreme effort. Mr. James has abandoned his ordinary method of working about and around an idea; his actors by their every word and gesture advance instead of retarding the action and interest. There are three men, three women, and a child—the last a most important, though passive instrument in their hands. On this child hinge, directly or indirectly, the fates of the rest of the group. The first book contains, as it were, the prologue, and subtly suggests the coming clash of interests and affections. A necessary interval of a few years does not interfere with the sense of unity in the piece. The second book again discovers the same characters in the same place, under slightly altered conditions, but intensified and dominated by the same impulses. In the third the catastrophe and its consequences untie the knot and scatter the actors. We have said that it is a story of human interest and passion, but at the same time we may add that a feeling of artificiality is present in the play of repartee, the verbal parryings, the purposes and cross purposes. Mr. James has been very ingenious, very admirable in the intensity he has thrown into many of the scenes and situations. It is a grim drama indeed that, in spite of this masquerading, is played out in the small provincial town. The end of the child, the fashion of its taking off, is horribly realistic. More obscure and less tangible are the workings of Rose Armiger's mind, and yet in a manner but too clear and definite.

"Mr. Henry James' Latest Novel."
Saturday Review [England] 82 (31 October 1896), 474–75.

Within the past few years Mr. Henry James has produced a number of relatively short stories, each having for its central figure a novelist, which taken together exhibit, as perhaps no other work of his does, all the choicest qualities of his art. It is to be hoped that in some future edition of the author's writings it may be found possible to bring them all together in a single volume. Thus combined, they would present a study of contemporary bookmaking such as no other language but our own contains. It is never quite fair to identify a novelist with any given point of view in his work; but it is impossible to ignore the note of pained contempt for the kind of fiction the crowd runs after nowadays which is sounded in all these tales. It rings out loudest in "The Next Time."[1] Here we have the novelist who is, from the commercial standpoint, an "exquisite failure." He tries deliberately to write novels which shall be bad enough to be popular, and at each attempt he and his connexions are confident of success. Blank failure comes each time instead. The book is still too good, and amid increasing poverty and depression, the hapless man of letters begins the task again, hoping against hope for "the next time." He breaks down at

last under the struggle and dies while at work upon a novel which "is a splendid fragment; it evidently would have been one of his high successes. How far it would have waked up the libraries," Mr. James cynically concludes, "is, of course, a very different question."

We hasten to deprecate any direct application of what we have quoted to the case of this new novel by Mr. Henry James. During all the twenty years and more of his writing life, the author has produced nothing which makes more incessant demands upon those peculiar faculties of perception and swift yet delicate analysis that he has himself developed in his admirers. None the less, "The Other House" is clearly the product of a determination on the part of the writer to open a new vein—to assume, in the words of the poor hero of "The Next Time," a "second manner." The change has no reference, it is true, to what are imagined to be the tastes of the circulating libraries, although, oddly enough, it happens that the book furnishes one of the few exceptions of the year to the new rule of single-volume novels. It may be put down instead to the increasing hold which the idea of writing for the stage has fastened upon Mr. James's fancy.

"The Other House" is conceived in a purely dramatic spirit, and worked out with a scrupulous regard for the conventions and limitations of the theatre. Although it contains 500 pages, it concerns itself solely with the events of two days, and divides itself into three parts, each of which has a set scene provided for its action, so finite and circumscribed that the reader has a sense of missing the stage directions. Act I., if we may so call it, passes in the hall of the semi-rural residence of a young banker, Mr. Tony Bream. It is the luncheon hour, and reference is frequently made to the table spread in an adjoining room, but we never see it. Upstairs the banker's young wife is in a state of collapse after the birth of her first child, but we know of her only from the bulletins which the doctor imparts to the characters who pass in and out of this hall. So faithfully are the possibilities of stage-carpentering kept in view, that the observant reader soon gets a mental picture of this "hall," with its glass doors opening upon the verandah, its writing-table on the prompt side, its chimney-piece with the French clock, and its convenient minor doors at the wings. The scene of Act II. (four years have elapsed) is on a shaded lawn, from which is obtained a view in the distance of the banker's residence—that is to say, "The Other House." In the middle distance there is a beautiful little stone footbridge, crossing the river to his grounds. In the foreground we see a tea-table with chairs on one side, a hammock on the other. Here passes, apparently within a couple of hours, the principal action of the book, the narration of which occupies 300 pages. Then the lights are lowered, and the scene changes to a drawing-room. It is twilight, with "the glow of the western sky faintly discernible through the wide high window that was still open to the garden." The servants bring in the lamp, and close this window, but later it is opened again to serve as an exit. There is a central door which is said to open into the library, and another entrance at one side, from the hall. Here, in semi-darkness, the very powerful though brief Third Act goes forward in rapid strenuous dialogue and vivid situations to an eminently dramatic curtain.

The most obvious drawback to this method of construction is that it sacrifices almost entirely that side of Mr. James's art in which he is most nearly without rivals; there is room for very little of the daintily whimsical commentary upon his characters, their looks and thoughts and motives and amiable absurdities, which he knows how to make so delightful. When he is not putting dialogue into the mouths of these characters, he is engaged almost wholly in providing that necessary description of their movements, their smiles and sighs and general stage-business, which in the theatre the spectator would see with his own eyes. One cannot escape the feeling that this latter is work which other and much lesser men do with more facility than Mr. James. The cultivated indirection of his style, so charming when it has a subject to match, gets in his way when it is merely a question of supplying the physical links in a chain of earnest and momentous dramatic dialogue. At the critical moment in an interview between the two people who have the chief burden of the tragedy on their shoulders, for instance, this is given in explanation of a pause: "She spoke without discernible excitement, and Tony had already become aware that the face she actually showed him was not a thing to make him estimate directly the effect wrought in her by the incongruous result of the influence he had put forth under pressure of her ardour. . . . What he most felt was a lively, unreasoning hope that for the hour at least, and until he should have time to turn round and see what his own situation exactly contained for him, her mere incontestable cleverness would achieve a revolution during which he might take breath." Of another character who finds himself under a cross-fire of feminine innuendos, it is said: "Smiled at in alternation by two clever young women, he had yet not sufficiently to achieve a jocose manner shaken off his sense of the strange climax of his conversation with the elder of them." These are, of course, aggravated examples of what we mean: there is, perhaps, nothing else in the book quite so difficult as either of them; but they illustrate the tendency to make hard work of what should be simple plain sailing, which is the chief obstacle in Mr. James's path as a writer of drama.

At the risk of seeming captious, we have dwelt upon this less welcome aspect of "The Other House," for the reasons that whatever Mr. Henry James does is of importance to literature, and that any display of his craftsmanship employed under new conditions, or upon novel materials, must be of great interest to other writers. The means by which he arrives at his final effect are open, it seems to us, to a good deal of criticism. As has been said, men who are not to be compared with him, artistically, would handle the merely conventional machinery of narration with much more simplicity and effectiveness than he has been able to command. The reader preserves an annoying sense of this almost to the end of the book. But one admits, on the other hand, that when this end is reached, the grim force and power of it are truly remarkable. The story itself cannot be said to present mysteries at any point; as if in obedience to the stage-dogma that there must be no secrets kept from the audience, the *motif* of the work is exposed at the outset. A dying woman whose girlhood had been embittered by the cruelties of a stepmother secures the infant daughter she is leaving behind from a like experience by getting her husband to swear that he will not wed again so long as the child lives. Her dearest school-friend is a guest in the house, and it is apparent from the beginning that she is resolved to marry the husband, and will not scruple to kill the child. With this potential tragedy in the air, the story proceeds for the greater part on lines of comedy. The interest is so slowly concentrated upon the young lady who is to do the murder that one finds himself well into the middle of the crime without realizing that the affable game of conversational cross-purposes over the tea-table is finished. The child who is foredoomed to death, moreover, has been kept, no doubt by design, as conventionalized a dummy as any stage-baby; the killing of it seems for the moment rather a relief than otherwise. But here a curious thing happens. The reader unexpectedly finds upon reflection that the printed page has faded away; he looks in retrospect over the footlights instead, and the murderess of "The Other House" becomes a great *tragédienne,* the central figure in a dramatic situation of commanding intensity of force. There is no gainsaying the grip of the effect which Mr. James secures at the finish.

Note

1 "The Next Time," *The Yellow Book* 6 (July 1895), 11–59. Reprinted in *Embarrassments* (1896).

"Henry James' Latest Novel Is a Stirring Tragedy." Chicago *Tribune,* 10 November 1896, p. 3.

Henry James has been caught doing things in his latest novel, "The Other House" (Macmillan), which are the rankest heresy—for him. Can it be that he has fallen a victim to the hypnotic power of his own puppets? Since John Kendrick Bangs[1] has revealed what miseries a rebellious heroine can inflict upon a realistic author one trembles for Mr. James. When so painfully peaceful a novelist as he suddenly murders a little 4-year-old girl it is time to begin looking for the Svengali in the case.

The characters in the book are strong—so strong that perhaps they have arisen and overpowered their creator. They actually do things. This violation of all the James precedents, one suspects, has been flagrantly committed despite the helpless and horrified protest of the author. But one cannot be sorry it has happened.

Rose Armiger is at times less than human, but her character is reasonably consistent as the author has conceived it. The story of her love and of the crime to which it led is at times repellent, but faultless in unity and fascinating in interest. Henry James is a literary painter of miniatures, a critic, and a creator, but, above all, an artist. There may be flaws in the materials and the situations he creates, but none in his artistic treatment of them. One may not like the characters in "The Other House," but it cannot be denied that they live and breathe in a style quite unusual for the figures of a realistic cameo.

The banking house of Beever & Bream rested on two solid ancestral piers. One consisted of Mrs. Beever, her son Paul, and her prospective daughter-in-law, Jean Martle. The other house was composed of Tony Bream, his wife, and his wife's school friend, Rose Armiger. At the time when the curtain rises Tony's wife is dying, after giving birth to a daughter. Before departing she solemnly binds Tony, in the presence of witnesses, never to marry again during the life of the child.

At this same critical moment Rose Armiger's betrothed arrives from the antipodes to claim his bride. But Dennis Vidal finds Rose more interested in Tony's tragedy than in her lover's plans. Things move rapidly, until Rose suddenly casts off Vidal. The subtlety with which the girl's real hopes are shown to center now in Tony is the highest form of art.

After portraying this crisis in exquisite detail the author suddenly shifts the scene to four years later. Here matrimonial affairs are soon found to be in a most alarming tangle. Rose still loves Tony, Tony is keeping his promise to remain single, but is in love with Jean Martle. And, worst of all, Jean loves him, instead of Paul Beever, for whom she is intended. And Paul hankers for Rose. The game of cross purposes is brilliant, and Mr. James treats the situation as an artist should. The drama develops rapidly, and attention becomes almost insensibly concentrated on the baby girl, who is all that stands between Tony and marriage.

The second grand dramatic climax of the book comes when all the acting characters are together at Mrs. Beever's, and when the news suddenly comes that the child has been drowned. The blame falls between Jean and Rose. Tony, the father, suddenly declares he is the guilty one. The interest is intense through the following chapters, in which it gradually comes to light that Rose Armiger deliberately drowned the child in a last insane hope that she might throw the blame on her rival, Jean, and satisfy her life's passion for Tony.

The author handles his motives well, and the final departure of Rose into the night and exile is dramatically, if not morally, satisfying. But even Mr. James cannot create a feminine character that can commit child-murder under such circumstances and still be human.

Note

1 John Kendrick Bangs (1862–1922), American humorist, editor, and lecturer, is best known for *Three Weeks in Politics* (1894) and *A Houseboat on the Styx* (1895) (*Dictionary of American Biography*).

Academy [England] 1280 (14 November 1896), 385–86.

After a considerable interval, devoted to experiments in other forms of imaginative literature, the short story, and the play, Mr. Henry James gives us a new novel. We can but open it in some trepidation. Will devouring time have robbed nothing of the keen psychology, the subtle portraiture, the cunning evolution that have delighted us so often? A very early scene dispels such a fear. The sweet Roman hand is at work in the first interview between Rose Armiger and Dennis Vidal, with its delicate sword-play, its exquisite indication of cross-purposes, and the clash of standpoints. Like Mr. Meredith, Mr. James has always before him the problem of rendering, through the medium of mere words, more than the mere words of a dialogue. To put its very intonation, the atmosphere of it, on the page—this is the ideal which he often comes so near achieving. Like Mr. Meredith, and yet with how great a difference, as a rule, in the solution. But is it a mere fancy to perceive in the present novel the influence of the one living master of English fiction who could have taught anything to Mr. James? Do not some flashes of Meredithian intensity break the unruffled lucid calm of Mr. James's familiar manner? Does not Tony Bream owe something, in conception at least, to Victor Durance? *The Other House* compels admiration, but it also strongly compels protest—the very protest itself, perhaps, only another tribute to the vitality and persuasiveness of Mr. James's puppets. But surely in the figure of Rose Armiger subtlety has been pushed beyond the borders of enigma. We are accustomed to the impassive masks of Mr. James's heroines; when we get the keynote, the inexplicabilities generally arrange themselves into a sufficiently logical whole. But we submit that in Rose Armiger the burden of interpretation laid upon the reader is too heavy for him to bear; it is to make bricks without straw. Even after the *dénouement*, going back over the earlier scenes with perhaps more patient analysis than a novel may fairly claim, we are still unable, at certain points, to see what, in homely phrase, the woman is dying at. There is one passage which we can only make intelligible to ourselves by the somewhat bold process of emending the text. We should be gratified to Mr. James if he would tell us whether we ought not, on the eighth line from the bottom of p. 196 of vol. ii., to read "hate her" for "take her." Of course, the change inverts the meaning of the sentence. It is possibly because we frankly find Rose Armiger such a puzzle that the *dénouement* itself, with its sudden revelation of the resourceful triumphal woman as a criminal of an especially revolting and not even very plausible kind, fails to convince us, almost offends us. We cry out against it, "It could not be so!" We feel that Mr. James had no right to enlist our sympathies, even in error, for the woman; to give us no hint; and then at the end to submit us to such outrage. We close the book with something of emotional disturbance, as well as of intellectual perplexity. But it is an astonishingly clever and interesting book, for all that.

"The Other House." Critic 29 (28 November 1896), 335.

The appearance of a new book by Mr. Henry James is always an event to the connoisseur of letters. It cannot be stated too explicitly or published too widely that "The Other House" is an event of the first order. In a small way it is a revolution. Mr. James has done something new. His name has been for long a synonym for cleverness and conscious skill, but on laying down this volume the reader is forced to confess that henceforth, if the writer so wills, it is also a synonym for power. The book has grip. Up to this time Mr. James's grip has apparently been nothing more than an exquisite sense of touch. The plot is compact of passion, terror, tragedy. Heretofore the author has avoided all but the decorous intellectual tragedies comprehended only by the elect, and has ignored the passions—perhaps because they are not well-bred—in favor of the perceptions. Here for the first time he permits himself a hand-to-hand bout with those elements of human nature and life which he has previously handled with gloves. The result is a book in which for once the crowning impression is not "What a clever writer!" but "What a powerful tale!" In literature, also, he who loses his life shall find it. Mr. James's reward for the perceptible amount of self-repression involved in the situation and handling of the story will be a wider, more diffused appreciation of its merits.

Briefly, the story deals with the predicament of Anthony Bream, who promises his wife on her deathbed not to re-marry during the lifetime of their child. As he subsequently loves a very beautiful and charming young woman, the promise, which he does not contemplate breaking, grows irksome to him. It also affects Rose Armiger, his wife's dearest friend, whose passion for him antedates Mrs. Bream's death and is practically a mania, but while it stands in her own way, it is also from her point of view a safeguard, though not an absolute one, against his making another marriage. Disappointed in her attempts to ensure the marriage of Jean Martle, the other woman, to another man, and losing faith in the strength of Tony's honor as against his emotion, Miss Armiger murders the child in such a way that she believes suspicion will fall upon Jean, thus, at least, preventing forever any union between her and the child's father. In the brief time when it seems that Jean may really be responsible for the crime, Tony, to shield her, declares that he did it himself to recover his freedom, but the truth is made clear through the agency of Dennis Vidal, for years a suitor for Rose's hand, and accepted by her, by implication, on the afternoon of the tragedy, in order to protect herself.

Stated thus, in bald outline, the story sounds crudely sensational, but when the search-light of Mr. James's intuition is turned across the situation, it is seen to be anything but crude, though it still remains immensely striking. In the way of subtle linking of motive with event and the interaction of character upon character, Mr. James has never done anything stronger or more artful. Granting the character of Rose Armiger—it is a good deal to grant, but we readily make the concession of her possibility for the sake of the result—the argument of the whole thing is absolutely flawless. It is complicated, but its complexity is as coherent as that of some living organism. In all points of technique the book is really marvellous. Up to this time, the writer's most ardent admirers have never claimed for him a constructive ability of the first order as a novelist. When, some six or eight years ago, he abandoned the form of the novel and devoted himself to the study of the short story, it presently became apparent that he had the power of presenting a single situation, a detached phase of life, more completely and significantly than anyone else has ever done. It seemed that he had found for the first time his *métier,* the work for which his rare talent was designed. The present volume overturns completely this theory of the ultimate use of Mr. James in literature, for in it he has applied his perfected method of the short story to the problem of the novel with an almost startling success. The entire action of the book takes place in two half days; a morning at Bounds, the house of Anthony Bream, and an afternoon at Eastmead, the home of Mrs. Beever. To so arrange the stage that in these two scant scenes the characters, motives and relations of the six personages who play leading parts, become obvious and their destinies clear, is a feat of dramatic construction beside which Sardou's most compact bits of craft[s]manship seem clumsy and badly done.[1] The accusation of artificiality, which might well have been brought against such a marvel of structure had the theme been one of Mr. James's customary intellectual motives, can hardly be sustained against a book so full of "pity and terror," so vibrant with the true tragic note, that the general reader is likely to overlook construction altogether in favor of more absorbing qualities.

Better and more exciting than the discovery of a new force in letters is the revelation of a fresh power in an old friend. Mr. James has written for nearly thirty years to the delight of an audience fit though few. He now comes forward exhibiting qualities adapted to the subjugation of the many. Has he had them up his sleeve these three decades? Have life and art revealed themselves afresh to him in

the "middle years"? Or is it only that he has resolved to conquer the populace? Readers of "Embarrassments" will remember the history of Ray Limbert, an exquisite literary artist whose productions did not sell, though he was continually making more tremendous efforts to be obvious and popular, more desperate bids for general acceptance. Each time he only succeeded in producing "a more shameless, merciless masterpiece." The temptation to compare Limbert and his creator is strong, but the latter will have the happier fate. If "The Other House" is in any sense a bid for popularity, it is preordained to be a successful one. The thrill of the story naturally is not for the readers of "shilling shockers," but it will appeal to many whom even the art of his short stories left cold. No one could have predicted that Mr. James would have undertaken the apotheosis of the police gazette, but this is practically what he has done, and he has made its footing firm upon Olympus. The book is a masterpiece, and we predict that the hour of the author's universality is at hand.

Note

1 Victorien Sardou (1831–1908).

Edith Baker Brown. *"The Other House."* Bookman [New York] 4 (December 1896), 359–60.

Tony Bream's wife dies at child-birth; but, before death, mindful of her own tragic youth under a stepmother, she binds him by a promise not to marry again during the lifetime of her child. The facile Tony, who hardly will admit the seriousness of his wife's condition, ardently takes the pledge. Then he is left, a man easily pleasing to women and easily pleased by them—so that even before his wife's end he has guilelessly committed himself to the interest of two of them—yet intending to be chivalrous to his wife's memory and quite unconscious of his real situation. The story opens with studied cynicism; it continues to follow the lead of subtle character motives, and a subtle irony too gay to be called humour, with so trifling a manner that we are hardly prepared for the culminating tragedy. The child is the central figure of it. In their opposing attitudes to her, the two women who have come to love Tony Bream and have a place in his destiny embody the dramatic contrast which is a part of Mr. James's character study. The growth of their passion furnishes him with a story to his purpose. Jean Martle loves the child because it belongs to the man she cannot marry. Rose Armiger hates it while it stands between her and the possibility of her union with its father. When she finds that the real obstruction to that is Tony's love for Jean, she kills the child to incriminate her rival and destroy the love that she cannot herself win. This plot is the plot of strong tragedy; but it seems better fitted to the world of crude and elemental passions than to the sophistications and refinements of Mr. James's art. The essential inhumanity of the story is less its subject than its author's handling.

Those who have watched what one can only call the decline of Mr. James's art during the last few years must have been more and more painfully conscious of its steady retreat from life. His original humour was not only so penetrating but so delightful, his work was so poetic at its best, that one overlooked the excess of refinement that threatened an art otherwise

perfect. His early books, too, had a vigour that belonged to life rather than to the artist's studio, and that removed their author as a critic far from the aesthetic dilettante. But the dreary stories which have been appearing within the last few years under Mr. James's name, and now this last novel from his pen, lack the vital spring of art. Merely in point of construction, *The Other House* is as artificial as the stage. Indeed, in its abandonment of narrative and comment, its paucity of scene, its complete dependence on the dialogue, it seems, until its closing chapters, like a play without the necessary excitement of action or the direct and speaking passion that alone carries conviction from the boards. It is like a drawing-room farce interminably and dully prolonged until the last scene. Then, with an artistic shock that is hard to bear, it becomes a tragedy of awful proportions.

In the chapter next the last, one hears the first real note of life that has not yet sounded through all the course of the story. Before the reader seems to walk with abstractions of personality and the embodiments of Mr. James's critical observations. There are no Isabel Archers or Christina Lights, no Hyacinths or Roderick Hudsons in the dramatic list; and he stumbles toward a purpose through a style that extenuates until it blinds one to the author's intention.

> "She spoke without discernible excitement, and Tony had already become aware that the face she actually showed him was not a thing to make him estimate directly the effect wrought in her by the incongruous result of the influence he had put forth under the pressure of her ardour."

Sentences like this have to be read more than once to get a hold on the understanding. But there is a chapter of redeeming passion and directness before the story goes out, which seems to rise to the demands of Mr. James's subject. We are glad to quote it as proof of his possible power.

> "In an instant he had met her; in a flash the gulf was bridged; his arms had opened wide to her and she had thrown herself into them. . . . Their long embrace was the extinction of all limits, all questions—swept away in a flood which tossed them over the years, and in which nothing remained erect but the sense and the need of each other." [1896 Macmillan ed., pp. 365–66]

This recalls May Garland as she flings herself on Roderick's body, or Isabel Archer at Ralph's death-bed. It is supremely beautiful. It is the one moving passage in the book, unless we count as moving the moral shock that the reader sustains in coming upon a tragedy so awful as the *dénouement* of a book apparently so cool and so little serious. *The Other House* has the virtues of Mr. James's usual conscientious work and his subtle dealing with character—the last most happily illustrated in the study of Tony Bream. But it trifles with its theme; it does not hold the sympathies with the conviction of life. Its general failure in emotion has spoiled a conception which might have been poetic, and made it artistically unpleasurable.

Current Literature 20 (December 1896), 486–87.

The half-dozen individuals who appear prominently in this story are perhaps as odd a collection as were ever assembled by a writer of fiction, from Tony Bream the banker who is as unlike one's preconceived notions of a man of finance as say Will Ladislaw of Middlemarch, to Dennis Videll, the young man from China, all are drawn with such careful avoidance of the conventional and commonplace point of view that the result attained seems strained, and not wholly satisfactory to the reader.[1] A constant suggestion of unreality and stagecraft pervades the story, while the hand of the playwright is plainly visible in the carefully worked-up-to climax wherein a lovely and innocent child is ruthlessly and most unnecessarily murdered. The dialogue is perhaps more disjointed and heavily burdened with epigram and repartee than is usual in Henry James's stories, which tends to the development of a curious nettled feeling on the part of the reader at his own obtuseness in not readily deciphering its meaning which is so obvious and clear to the interlocutor that he or she seldom fails to make an even more "difficult" verbal return.

So carefully subdued in tone is the story that at times the figures before us seem to lose their firmness of outline, as though moving in the dusk, and then the influence of writers of the Dutch school, more especially Maeterlinck, is suggested; a likeness increased, perhaps, by the monotonous repetition, like a refrain, of the last speakers' words.

To say that The Other House lacks interest would be untrue. In fact, it is surprisingly and absorbingly interesting, considering the blemishes indicated, and this result goes to show that a writer of Henry James's cleverness and artistic skill can take an unpromising plot, and make it seem at least probable; can draw for us men and women not essentially true to life, and yet successfully impose them on us as such. But after all, does not this story partake somewhat of the nature of a tour de force on Mr. James's part? And can we help involuntarily longing for other days, when possibly the skill was less, when such beautiful stories as The Portrait of a

Lady were not only possible, but were ours to have and delight in.

Note

1 George Eliot, *Middlemarch* (1871–72).

Literary World [Boston] 27 (26 December 1896), 476.

Mr. Henry James as a portrayer of the mild emotions is all very well, but when, as in *The Other House,* he endeavors to depict overwhelming passions, heaven save his readers. The rather common and boisterous Tony, who is a conquering hero with the fair sex, is so poorly drawn that it seems inconceivable that Rose should fall in love with him, much less adore him to the point of drowning his only child because he is under a solemn vow not to remarry during the lifetime of his daughter. The plot of *The Other House* is really revolting in its cold-blooded lack of moral sense, and even Jean, the only respectable character in the book, has a lack of self-respect and ordinary propriety in speech and action. Here and there in this book are clever descriptions and well-cut phrases, but in it as a whole, as in all Mr. James's later works, the author reminds us of a juggler who is trying to see how many brightly colored balls he can keep going in the air at once, only this literary juggler substitutes highly colored impressions for balls.

"Henry James's Last Novel." *Overland Monthly* 29 (January 1897), 106.

The Other House is so little like "Daisy Miller" that one would never have ascribed it to the same author. In it Mr. James has sacrificed interest to literary finish and its readers feel its unreality from start to finish. It reminds one of a play on the stage and as such it would make a hit. Its sentiment, passion, and climax, are the incidents of a stage plot. Moreover, its life is the life of its conversations. In fact it is nothing more than a bundle of clever talk between a lot of clever people.

Rose Armiger, the pretty villain, is a bit too artificial to command either the admiration or the hatred of the reader, while the character of Tony Bream is far too weak to make anyone but James's heroines fall in love with him. Withal the story is bright, light, and artistic, which is a sufficient excuse for its perusal.

Checklist of Additional Reviews

New York *Sun,* 17 October 1896, p. 7.
Salt Lake [City] *Tribune,* 18 October 1896, p. 11.
National Observer [London], 16 (24 October 1896), 681–82.
Chicago *Inter-Ocean,* 31 October 1896, p. 11.
Bookman [England] 11 (November 1896), 49.

Chicago *Evening Post*, 7 November 1896, p. 5.

Congregationalist 81 (12 November 1896), 725.

New York Observer 74 (12 November 1896), 756.

London *Times*, 14 November 1896, p. 15.

San Francisco *Call*, 15 November 1896, p. 21.

American 25 (21 November 1896), 315.

San Francisco *Chronicle*, 22 November 1896, p. 4.

Independent 48 (10 December 1896), 1693.

Atlantic Monthly 79 (January 1897), 137.

Andrew Lang, *Cosmopolis* (January 1897), 69–70.

Nation 64 (28 January 1897), 71.

Graphic [England] 55 (30 January 1897), 134.

Chautauquan 24 (February 1897), 630–31.

THE SPOILS OF POYNTON

To project a soul into inanimate things, and thereby to make the latter tremendous factors in the development of a story touching the entanglements of a man and some women—that is a feat of no mean significance. It is the feat which Mr. James has accomplished in "The Spoils of Poynton." When he first published that novel, in the pages of "The Atlantic Monthly," he called it "The Old Things."[1] The title now employed is a better one, inasmuch as it indicates more exactly and more subtly the part which Mrs. Gereth's treasures play in the drama of her life and of her son's love affairs. Conceive of the artistic treasures at Poynton as merely "old things," merely a collection of bric-à-brac, and no matter how precious they are shown to be in the eyes of the possessor, they do not rise to the level of passion. Regard them as "spoils"; regard them as objects exciting strong antagonism between individuals; regard them, in short, as forming a bone of contention, and they immediately stand, as has been said, in full possession of a soul. Mr. James has not often acquitted himself so well as upon this occasion. "The Other House," published two or three months ago, had more dramatic force in it than "The Spoils of Poynton," but the latter is a much more substantial book, one that promises to last much longer. It can afford to be without the brilliant patches that marked the tour de force to which we have just referred. It is the better book for showing power well sustained from the first page to the last. This observation should not be applied, perhaps, to the working out of the climax in the concluding chapter. There is a hint here of the god from the machine. But it must be acknowledged that there is only a hint of artificiality, and that, probability aside, the terminating episode has a certain poetic fitness.

In fact, the whole story has a suggestion of poetry about it which is not common in Mr. James's work. It springs from the character of his mutely eloquent bric-à-brac at Poynton. Those snuffboxes and carvings bring into the novel an element of color and quaintness which is never still. Like rich tapestries waving and glimmering in some old-fashioned mansion, they figure now in the distance, now in the foreground of "The Spoils of Poynton," until every page is suffused with the atmosphere of a beautiful scene. The book is one of conversations, as is invariably the case with Mr. James, but he has repeated in his dialogue the quality of his allusions to Poynton's adornments. One may not find in the speech of Mrs. Gereth or of Fleda the touch of art which distinguishes the house that causes them both so much difficulty, but the influence of that aesthetic haven is implicit in all they do. The narrative deals with several poignant situations, with scenes of comedy that have a tragic element in them, yet the key never changes; it is derived from Poynton and from nowhere else. It shows the more vividly the consummate skill which Mr. James has exercised that his unity of design has not confined him, as it so often has confined him in other stories, to an excessively narrow sequence of episodes. On the contrary, there is considerable incident in the narrative, and a play of character which extends over a fairly wide scale. What is perhaps most alluring in the novel is the really unconstrained spirit of vivacity which pervades it. The stream of Mr. James's humor does not always run smoothly. It is apt to be intermittent, and, indeed, the whole progression of his narrative is often jerky and obscure. In "The Spoils of Poynton" he moves with effortless and unfailing ease, the attack never falters, the little play unfolds from one scene to the next without a single hitch. Altogether, "The Spoils of Poynton" is a joy to read. Mr. James reveals himself in it the absolute master of his material and his style.

Note

1 "The Old Things," *Atlantic Monthly* 77 (April–June 1896), 433–50, 631–40, 721–37; 78 (July–October), 58–74, 201–18, 376–90, 518–30.

Chicago *Evening Post*, 20 February 1897, p. 5.

Mrs. Gereth's son falls in love with a young woman named Mona Brigstock, declares his intention of marrying her and incidentally announces that he will take possession of Poynton, together with all its art treasures. Mrs. Gereth objects to Mona Brigstock and asserts that she will not only leave Poynton, but will take with her all the valuable bric-a-brac, robbing the ancestral home of its chief charm, and thereby hangs a long, turgid, inexpressibly dreary tale.

The story is Henry James' latest, and the title of it is "The Spoils of Poynton." Considering the source, we are not surprised at the unrelieved monotony of it; but surely in this effort Mr. James outstrips his reputation, for never was there written a story wherein an author displays such a paucity of ideas, such a woeful lack of imagination as one finds in this colorless romance.

In "The Other House" Mr. James seemed to rouse himself and actually indulge in a situation or so, but his relapse in this instance has been complete, and in "The Spoils of Poynton" one chapter melts into another without the ripple of an event to mar the perfect sameness of the recital. It may be said that this dead level of inaction is just the kind of fiction the author prides himself upon writing; that this effect is precisely the consummation devoutly to be wished, but the sense of poverty it brings with it certainly no artist, and Mr. James least of all, would knowingly applaud. Say we excuse the characters from active parts and from all conversation, there is nothing left for them to do but think, but Mr. James does not encourage them in this to any great extent. If they think at all it must be in one direction only; he strikes the keynote and everybody must follow one note and never stray from it. In "The Spoils of Poynton" the subject is the moving of Mrs. Gereth from Poynton and the removal of the bric-a-brac from that place. Mona objects to this and declares she will not marry Owen Gereth unless the ornaments remain intact. Mrs. Gereth outwits the young lady and her son by removing the desired objects between two days and fits up a distant country house with them. A fourth person, a girl with the painful name of Fleda Vetch, is given the role of peacemaker, and when the irate son swoops down on his grasping parent and demands the return of his blue dishes and things, Fleda sees him with the fell purpose of mollifying him. She performs her task not wisely, but too well, and Owen, smarting from the various scenes he has had with Mona, falls desperately in love with Miss Vetch in spite of her name.

Having experienced a change of heart the next question is to break his engagement with Mona. He tells the young lady's mother that he does not love the daughter and she in turn carries the tiding to Mrs.

Gereth. That good but blundering woman now sees the way clear for Owen to marry Fleda, whom she sincerely loves, and post-haste sends her purloined collections of beautiful things back to Poynton. Unfortunately, Owen goes to see Mona for a last interview and she in some way not explained succeeds in making up the quarrel and a few days later they are married, notwithstanding the fact that he has proposed and has been accepted by the all-too-confiding Fleda.

When the news is broken to the mother and girl we are disappointed if we imagine their grief will make them voluble. Fleda still worships the false Owen and with some meager sobs from these baffled ladies the book ends.

Such is the length, breadth and thickness of Mr. James' latest offering. Throughout the story there is nothing talked of or thought of but the small differences arising between mother and son regarding the possessing of the "spoils" of Poynton. The question is presented in four different ways by the number of men and women in the romance; it is gone over and over again, it is analyzed, it is discussed to threadbareness by the author independently and by the characters alone and ensemble. It does not require any great straining of the imagination to sympathize thoroughly with Mrs. Gereth; her daughter-in-law is plainly coarse and unappreciative and Fleda Vetch is just as plainly refined and appreciative and would have made the better wife of the two for the very stupid son, but all the circumstances put together are no excuse for over three hundred pages of solid reading matter apropos of them. With the world teeming with rich subjects it seems inexcusable for an author to spend his time with such unresponsive trifles and to inflict on a kind public such a dreary waste of words describing them.

"Henry James: His New Novel That Shows He Is Still Spinning His Work Out Fine."
New York Times Saturday Review of Books and Art, 20 February 1897, p. 1.

Mr. James, in these later years, is spinning finer than ever. It is not only that his material in this novel is scant. Trollope, Crawford, and a dozen others have wrought skillfully with as little matter. But in the treatment of his subject Mr. James absolutely neglects all the opportunities any other novelist would seize upon. In the present case we have a mother, a son, and two young women, all of the "upper middle class," and in all the book not more than half a dozen other sketches of character for relief. Speaking broadly, the mother wants the son to marry one of the young women, and he intends to marry the other, and does. There, with another deserving hero, or even without one, would be material enough and to spare for the sentimental novelist.

But Mr. James makes nothing at all of the situation that he might be expected to make. He has few turns in the generally straight course of his narrative, and not one of them is obvious. He allows nothing for the romantic taste that is in us all. The study of character is his single aim, but it is invariably study pursued with no idea of giving the shallow entertainment; with no dwelling upon eccentric traits humorously, with no tenderness for the weak, with no appeal either for laughter or for tears, and, it must be confessed, with a result which, if pleasing to one's finer senses, is yet scarcely tangible.

The most appreciative reader of this volume of exquisite English, (always the only right word in the only proper place,) will lay it down with no definite idea in his mind of the identity of Mrs. Gereth, Owen, Fleda Vetch, or Mona Brigstock. Once in a while, in his earlier novels, Mr. James so presented a personage that one felt, for a time, one knew him or her; as, for example, the protagonist of "The American," the girl in "The Tragic Muse," and that horrid brother and sister in "The Princess Casamassima." But who remembers their names now? In his later books his aim has surely been far from making us care much for the creatures of his imagination.

Mrs. Gereth is the type of good taste so highly developed that it has become almost a malady. So exquisite is her sensibility, so exacting her fastidiousness, that nearly every other woman she meets seems a "frump," and the popular literature and art, decorative, plastic, and graphic, of England at the close of the nineteenth century is to her unbearable. Yet, when her son marries, she must give up Poynton, which is all perfect, without a false note, every room representing a lifetime of joyful labor in selection; and her son will marry Mona Brigstock, who will care for nothing there, and will desecrate the house with "bric-à-brac," things from Liberty's, and anti-macassars. As it turns out, Mona does "care" in a sort of animal way, without a touch of real appreciation; and that lends to the situation, as Mr. James treats it, an almost tragic tone.

The irony is appreciable, of course, but while Mr. James is bound to treat of Mrs. Gereth with a touch of irony, his sympathy with her, in all her trials, is sufficiently evident. It is sad to think that not one novel reader in ten thousand, probably, will be able to comprehend his and Mrs. Gereth's

and Fleda Vetch's views of life, art, and conduct, leaving sympathy out of the question. But the appreciation of the one in ten thousand is worth working for, and the knowledge Mr. James must have that his delight in the book's subtlety and refinement, the grave, thoughtful piquancy which is its substitute for humor, will be keen while it lasts, is, perhaps, a sufficient reward. And counting all the tens of thousands of novel readers in the English speaking world, one from each of the tens of thousands will make up a company that is worth while. So that we need not grieve for Henry James.

"*The Spoils of Poynton* Is Typical of Henry James." Chicago *Tribune*, 22 February 1897, p. 3.

All the good and bad points of Henry James' style are typified in his new novel, "The Spoils of Poynton" (Houghton, Mifflin, & Co.). In it we have Henry James at his best—and worst. Those who like his perfect literary miniatures, his infinitely clever women and his gawkish men, his dearth of action and his deluge of analysis, with all the appurtenances of the subjective novel, will find pleasure in "The Spoils of Poynton." But the others—and they are the vast majority—will not find this as interesting a novel as the less typical "The Other House," which preceded it from Mr. James' pen.

The scenes are laid in several English country houses, one of which is Poynton, the sumptuously adorned home of Mrs. Gereth and her son Owen. But for the most part it matters little whether the action takes place in England or in Oude.

For the story is chiefly subjective, not objective. It deals with the mind and feelings, not with things or acts. It has to do with the inside rather than with the outside. It used to be that the inside of a fiction character was as dark as the inside of a cow, and we had to depend upon the character's words and acts to discover his secret motives and to make up our minds whether he was thinking or suffering or deteriorating. But Mr. James has changed all that. Like the up-to-date doctor who makes his patients swallow an electric light bulb and turns the X rays on them to boot, Mr. James illumines the whole interior of his characters and calmly dissects their thoughts while you wait. It is a curious process and done with marvelous skill. But it depends upon one's taste for clinics whether the book bores or interests him.

Mrs. Gereth is a remarkable woman— only less remarkable than Miss Fleda Vetch, the young woman whom she wishes to marry to her son Owen. But Mr. James' women are all remarkable. Between Providence and Mr. James as creators it must be admitted that Mr. James has the more uniform record in this regard. The remarkable characteristic of both Fleda and Mrs. Gereth is the almost superhuman delicacy of their esthetic sense. It comes to light in the first chapter, on the morning after Mrs. Gereth has been kept awake most of the night by the wallpaper in her room at Waterbath. Mrs. Gereth flees from the painful ill-taste of the house in which she has been a guest, and meets Fleda likewise fleeing. "Isn't it dreadful?" "Horrible! horrible!" That was the beginning of the long and close friendship between these two kindred spirits.

The thing that had caused Mrs. Gereth to tear herself away for a day from her beloved Poynton, with its symphony of art decorations and collected treasures, was nothing less than the suspicion that her son Owen was thinking of marrying Mona Brigstock, one of the inmates of Waterbath. Of course she can see from a glimpse of Waterbath that Mona is a frump. The thought of such a girl becoming mistress of Poynton sets her wild. If the subject did not forbid of levity we might say that from that moment she became a Mona-maniac. It becomes her fixed intention to switch off Owen's affection from Mona to Miss Vetch, and the book is made up of the futile struggle thereto in the interval between the engagement and the marriage of Owen and Mona.

Technically the book is a perfect piece of literary art. Using scarcely any but these four characters, and confining itself to one locality and to but a few months' time, it portrays vividly the mental and moral struggles that went on about the art treasures—the spoils of Poynton. Mrs. Gereth has put her life's work into the collecting and arranging of these treasures. By her husband's will the place has been left to Owen, and now she must relinquish the whole into impious hands. She calls Fleda to visit her, and the fact that Fleda secretly loves Owen complicates the plot. When Owen's marriage day is set and he gives his mother notice to quit there comes a pretty little climax in which Mrs. Gereth suddenly leaves the house, but illegally takes along all its accumulated treasures.

The result of this coup d'état is to put Owen into a dilemma. His betrothed refuses to marry him if she has to go into a despoiled house. He must either set the lawyers and police at his mother or lose his bride. In this dilemma Fleda serves as a medium of intercommunication, and presently the susceptible youth is in love with Fleda, having become disgusted with the grasping demands of his betrothed. But Fleda, who is quite an admirable character in spite of her cleverness and ultra-estheticism, holds Owen off until he shall have extricated himself honorably from the other alliance.

The situation is tense when the various motives of the story converge upon Fleda. Her own love, Owen's appeals, and finally Mrs. Gereth's offer to send all her treasures back to Poynton if Fleda will be its appreciative mistress, all tend to pull her off her feet. But she insists on her conditions. Suddenly Mrs. Gereth sends word that she has sent back everything to Poynton for her. This is the climax of the book—the psychological tragedy that occurs when Mrs. Gereth discovers that she has been premature—that the hated Mona now has her condition fulfilled, and that Owen has married her in spite of all he had said to Fleda.

It was scarcely necessary for Mr. James to burn down Poynton and reduce all its tapestries and statues to smoke and ashes. The impression of a futile and disappointing denouement was sufficient without that. The abortive love affair between Owen and Fleda would be a quite sufficient damper upon the reader's enthusiasm. But in thus discouraging the obtrusive optimism of the reading public Mr. James is no doubt true to his creed of realism.

Yet for the sheer honor of the masculine half of humanity it must be contended that Mr. James is no realist. The crass stupidity of all Mr. James' male characters is impious. In the presence of these creatures we are not bound to bow before the decree, "God made them, therefore let them pass for men." Mr. James has made them, and we refuse to let them pass for anything but scarecrows, created to set off the superhuman cleverness of his women.

"Comedy and Tragedy." *Pall Mall Gazette* [England], 22 February 1897, p. 4.

With the memory of Mr. Henry James's last book, "The Other House," present in our minds, we read this one with some misgivings. In "The Other House," without any adequate warning—or we were abnormally dense—Mr. James suddenly sprung upon us, as we smiled over a pleasant little cup-and-saucer comedy, a most ghastly tragedy. When, therefore, we found that the point of departure in this book was a collection of objects of art in a country house, and that such human emotions as entered into the story were occupied entirely with desire of this collection—we speak of the first half or so of the book—we scented murder in the air. We thought it probable that in the middle of some subtly humorous conversation about an old vase a footman would enter with the proprietor's head on a charger. We are glad to say that nothing of this sort happens. It is true that the comedy is resolved into tragedy at the end, but it is tragedy of a reasonably mild description, the tragedy merely of futile love, of hearts which would some day patch themselves up comfortably.

The motive of the story is really, we think, the futility of delicacy in its dealings with rougher things. There is superimposed on this the plain comedy of two women fighting for the collection of curios—for the spoils of Poynton—still the other, as we take it, was Mr. James's goal. But we must give an outline of the story to make plain our meaning. Mrs. Gereth, then, was a woman of rare culture and knowledge of treasures of art, and she and her husband had made at Poynton a unique collection of these treasures. When the story begins her husband was dead and had left Poynton and its treasures, not to his wife, but to their ordinary son, who did not value them. The son became engaged to be married to Mona Brigstock, a hopelessly inartistic young woman. Mrs. Gereth was told to retire from Poynton to a house belonging to her at Wicks, whereupon, in artistic frenzy, she defied the law and carried away with her the unique collection. Then Mona refused to marry the son until it was restored. Meanwhile Mrs. Gereth had made a familiar of Freda Vetch, an artistic young woman, who fell in love with the son. He, disgusted with Mona, returned Freda's love. And here is the point of comedy and tragedy: the mother and son would not speak, and Freda was their intermediary; now, if Mrs. Gereth stood firm the hated marriage would not take place (since her son, who did not really wish it, would not use the law to compel her), but Freda's delicacy would not let her take advantage of this; she did not tell Mrs. Gereth that her best course was to stand firm and disappoint the greedy Mona, or that the son loved herself. Eventually, however, Mrs. Gereth discovered the latter fact, and never doubting that her son would be man enough to marry his new love, sent back the collection to Poynton, being willing to give it up to Freda. But Mona, using means (as Mrs. Gereth said) which a modest girl would not, or showing (as Freda said) to better advantage now that she had her way, kept Owen to herself, and married him, leaving the two other women to console themselves as they might at Wicks. Owen wrote to Freda asking her to take a keepsake from Poynton, and when she went to take it she found Poynton, with its collection, in process of being burned. And that is the end. Such a crude summary, of course, does not convey, even

in little, a just idea of a story by so finished a writer as Mr. James. We have given it because in showing the material scheme it enables us to justify our foregoing description, and to make clearer our primary objection to the book. It seems to us that here, again, Mr. James has mingled comedy with tragedy in a manner of which the justification is not obvious. His background, the struggle for an artistic collection, is one of comedy, his dialogue and his manner throughout are of comedy; his leading idea, the desertion of the finer for the coarser, and the worldly futility of the finer, that is tragedy. And there is no balance of comedy in Mona; she is merely an undeveloped idea of successful self-aggrandizement. A further objection we have is that when the interest of a theme is psychological the catastrophe should not be left to material chance. It is so left here, in essentials; it was the act of sending back the treasures to Poynton that gave Mona her chance, and the sending of them was not in the order of psychological development: it was a whim, and we think an unlikely whim, of Mrs. Gereth. But these objections are tentative; we have no wish to dogmatize on the matter, and our praise may be positive. The merit of an acute and subtle intelligence, and of a psychologically active imagination is here, as in the author's other work. The book is sometimes bold in its triviality, and it justifies its boldness, for you cannot help being interested in it.

Manchester *Guardian*, 23 February 1897, p. 4.

Mr. Henry James has done a bold thing in his new novel *The Spoils of Poynton* (W. Heinemann, 8vo., pp. 286, 6s.). He has made the interest of the book—dramatic, romantic, and tragic—centre not in a man, nor in a woman, nor, indeed, in any living being, but in a collection of inanimate objects. This is of course not the first time that the thing has been done even by Mr. James himself. The true hero or heroine (it is difficult to determine the sex in such a case) of "The Coxon Fund" in "Terminations" was Mr. Coxon's genius for conversation, Coxon himself even being a mere appendage to his powers of talk.[1] Mrs. Gereth, a woman possessed of an exquisite taste for *bibelots,* is left a widow with an only son, to whom Poynton, the home of her married life, and all its inestimable treasures, which owe their very existence there to her, are left, with that absoluteness which characterizes our English law of primogeniture. Everything, so far as poor Mrs. Gereth is concerned, depends upon whom Owen marries. He proposes, of course, to the wrong woman. The right woman has meanwhile been discovered by Mrs. Gereth in Miss Fleda Vetch, whose aesthetic susceptibilities are, if possible, as keen-edged as those of Mrs. Gereth, and who possesses, besides, a character of great depth, strength, and sweetness. But, neither the son nor Miss Vetch seeming to see the matter in the same light, poor Mrs. Gereth resolves upon a *coup de main.* After packing stealthily for several days, she retires to her little dower-house in the dead of the night, taking *all* the contents of Poynton with her, and, installed once more in the midst of her treasures, bids defiance to the world. At this the gorge of Owen's *fiancée* naturally rises, and she flatly refuses to marry him until the glories of Poynton are returned. How the crisis terminates readers may discover for themselves. But that there is a fund of rich humour in the situation is undeniable, and in parts where Mr. James seems to give himself up to the hu-

morous side of it, it is delightful reading. At times, however, he is inclined to take it too seriously, and then it is that a sense of unreality creeps in. But the old felicity of phrase and epithet, the quick, subtle flashes of insight, the fastidious liking for the best in character and art, which have given Mr. James his peculiar place in modern literature, are as marked as ever, and give one an intellectual pleasure for which one cannot be too grateful.

Note

1 *Terminations* (London: William Heinemann, 1895).

[Arnold Bennett]. *Academy* [England] 1295 (27 February 1897), 256.

The works of Mr. Henry James are a series of exquisite disappointments. To say that they are exquisite is to say what all know. Each phrase is sought out, and each shade of character finely observed—have not many reviewers said it? He is admirable in his cleverness, his conscientiousness, and his right self-respect. He seeks the phrase, but he is never the fool of the phrase; no bright and alluring collocation of words, like some dancing light, has ever misled him. He does not go out with his gun potting at the general public—has never brought down his brace of tall curates with the two volumes fired in rapid succession—and they make bigger bags in the Crockett cabbage-plot. Mr. Henry James writes for the few, and belongs to the very few. It is, indeed, almost a pity that so many dunces have been banged, bullied, and frightened into saying that they like the work of Mr. Henry James, but that he is really too subtle. It is a pity, because, in the first place, no dunce ever liked the work of Mr. Henry James; and, in the second place, because the trouble with Mr. Henry James is, that he is not subtle enough. For instance, he seems to have feared at times that his style wanted warmth, geniality, spontaneity; and, thus fearing, he gives us an occasional "didn't" for "did not." This is not subtle, and it misses its effect. His heroes and heroines, again, take that course of action which best satisfies good taste and feeling. But, though rejected, the other course is considered. They deliberate. They choose. They are painfully anxious to have the good approval of everybody. Their most spirited action is discounted by nervousness and long self-communion. We find ourselves liking them less than we ought to like them; they are all right, but they have to take so much trouble to be all right. Mr. Henry James is subtle enough to work out the difficult sum correctly; but not subtle enough to rub out the working on his slate, and leave only the effective answer. His characters are not marionettes; they do live, and move, and have their being, but they know all the time that Mr. Henry James is looking; they are not sufficiently disengaged and projected.

If he were half as good nobody would mind, and six lines of stereotyped approval (for he would still be good) would be his portion. But he has a point of view, an insight, a right judgment, a hatred of the common, a style; he makes and uses his phrase like a master, and he takes care. Were his gifts and his conscientiousness less, he would disappoint less; as it is, one cannot forgive him the least thing—such forgiveness would be an insult. It is, perhaps, possible that his creative faculty and his critical faculty work simultaneously, each to the prejudice of the other; and that

it would be better if he first made and then corrected. However that may be, his work is always exquisite, and yet always something of a disappointment.

"The Spoils of Poynton" are furniture—objects of art. They have been collected through long years, with love and knowledge, by Mrs. Gereth and her husband. Poynton is a beautiful treasure-house, a little heaven. Mrs. Gereth is now a widow; when her son Owen marries she will have to give up Poynton and all that therein is to him and his bride, and to retire to Ricks—a lesser place, formerly the residence of an aunt, and furnished as all aunts always furnish. Now Mrs. Gereth is the real collector; these spoils are almost her reason for living; she loves them, understands them, respects them. To one who could equal her affection and appreciation, to one worthy of these beautiful things, she could surrender them. Her haunting horror is, that she will have to surrender to Mona Brigstock of the Brigstocks of Waterbath, of whom Owen appears to be becoming fond. If Poynton is a little heaven, Waterbath (so far as the house is concerned) is simply Hades without the picturesqueness—cheap, tasteless, full of gimcracks. Mona is beautiful, wooden, expressionless, grasping, knows that the spoils are very valuable, and is incapable of considering them, or anything else, otherwise than commercially. Owen is a handsome, heavy, honest fool, of "ponderous probity," but also of an almost incredible weakness. And Fleda is the other girl, worthy (as Mrs. Gereth knew) of the spoils, and worthy of far more. There is the germ of the book—most of the people and some of the motives.

When Mr. Henry James makes out a little list of his achievements (and it would be difficult to imagine anything more unlikely) he must not omit Mrs. Gereth. He has seldom, if ever, given us anything better. The character is clear, objective, original. She is a woman of refined taste, and is sometimes almost slangy; she is capable of great sacrifices, and is guilty of conduct that—well, "the Brigstocks say it's simply stealing," says Owen plaintively; and we are inclined to agree with the Brigstocks. Yet only at the end do we remember that there are things in her which, baldly stated and at first sight, might appear paradoxical. Throughout she has been quite true and convincing. It is the misfortune of Mr. Henry James that he draws those people best whom he does not quite like. There is much that is good in the delineation of Owen and Fleda, but they do not convince as Mrs. Gereth convinces. The story contains at least two strong dramatic situations: the humour is delightful; the style is Mr. Henry James. If it disappoints, it is for want of a little more warmth and humanity, because the reader cries out for someone who shall be admirable without being nervous and hesitating, and never finds that person. . . .

Athenaeum [England] 3619 (6 March 1897), 308–9.

The first impression produced on the reader by Mr. James's latest novel is that he is looking at things through glasses not quite suited to his focus; the next, that it must have cost the author a deal of trouble to write. If you debar yourself from the use of "spade," "implement of husbandry," or "adjective shovel," it is not always easy to find an English phrase that will legitimately denote the article, and when you do find one the chances are that your reader will not be sufficiently in the habit of associating it with the object indicated to be able, without conscious effort, to proceed from it to the idea of that object. And conscious effort is just what the novel-reader does not want. The odd thing is that the story is really simple enough. Mrs. Gereth is a widow who has spent her married life in making a palace of art at Poynton. The house and all the pretty things in it have become her only son's property, and the question that torments her is whether he will marry some one not only capable of appreciating her "lordly pleasure-house," but also willing to allow its creator to continue in undisturbed enjoyment of it. Unfortunately he, being a person of dull perceptions, settles upon a girl who has been brought up in an atmosphere of opulent bad taste, but is sharp enough to see that Mrs. Gereth's *bric-à-brac* is worth holding fast to. Mean time that lady had pitched upon a damsel who combines the qualifications which she requires in a daughter-in-law, and the story amounts practically to a narrative of the contest (for the spoils of Poynton) between Mona Brigstocke and Mrs. Gereth, fighting behind her *protégée*, Fleda Vetch. We cannot exactly congratulate Mr. James this time on his taste in nomenclature. The situation is further complicated by the fact that the elder lady, when retiring from the house in consequence of her son's engagement, carries off a "large and important" selection from the portable property contained in it. The struggle is well balanced, and the reader is never justified till it is over in anticipating one end or the other to it. The more obvious characters, Owen Gereth and Mona, are concrete enough, if not very interesting—they are the *matter*. Mrs. Gereth, the *force*, is decidedly more of an abstraction, and not wholly a pleasant one, if we rightly decipher the plan of campaign which she enjoins upon Fleda. As for Fleda herself—well, the mind and heart of a girl such as Mr. James seems to have in his eye is an unexplored region to any man, so anything may be put there, and no one has any right to say it cannot be there. The only real fault in the construction of the book is the fire at the end. A catastrophe of that kind has no business in a novel unless it be either cause or effect. Now here, so far as the story goes, it is neither.

be found developing the countless mannerisms and affectations of his latest work. "The Spoils of Poynton" is not so unpleasantly marked in this respect as "The Other House," but it is full of strain and effort, of words employed in forced and unnatural meanings, of artificiality. In this case we have to modify the familiar saying, hard writing for once makes very hard reading as well.

"Henry James' Latest Novel."
San Francisco *Chronicle*, 14 March 1897, p. 4.

"The Spoils of Poynton," as Henry James' latest novel is somewhat oddly called, is likely to confirm many readers in their belief that the author is never now to be expected to repeat the brilliant successes of his earlier work. The book, like its immediate predecessor, "The Other House," has undoubted cleverness; in parts it is very clever indeed; but it is overwrought, often tiresome and withal unconvincing. It suffers throughout from unnecessary analysis and amplification; the most commonplace incidents are elaborated with wearisome prolixity; the characters constantly try the patience of even the closest reader. Here and there the author rises to an occasion, and a few thoroughly interesting pages are the result; now and then, too, an epigrammatic sentence or the neat turn of a phrase comes like a glimpse of sunshine in a gray day. But as a whole the story drags, and, though the close is effective, the general feeling left is one of depression.

It is to be regretted that a writer with so admirable a sense of style as Mr. James has often shown that he possesses should

Mervin Erie.
"*The Spoils of Poynton*." *Bookman* [New York] 5 (May 1897), 258–59.

The spoils were a legacy of curios which the son might possess at his marriage. Poynton was the great house, in England, where they were religiously kept by his mother. So long as Poynton was not despoiled, the son's marriage was possible. The mother surreptitiously removed the curios. How, then, were these twain, wilful maiden and artless youth, to be united without breaking the father's or the maiden's will? Suffice it that for a time bric-à-brac, like Alcibiades's son, ruled the world. The book is no trifle; read it, and then prate of "real sorrows" if you will! Of all things prolific of woe—and it is amazing how many woes begin and end with things—bric-à-brac is easily proved to be the worst. Mr. James deserves infinite credit for seeing life in its true relations.

Fleda, who is the hub of this story, from whom the other characters radiate like spokes, underwent a curious psychological development. At the start she was exemplary, and assumed that every tribute was paid to her insignificance. Her woman friend, however, was a mirror in whom she soon beheld her truer and less sophisticated self. The moment came when, enamoured of the reflection, she "pulled herself together," as young women do when they think the future is theirs, and went forth to conquer the world. Her insight became phenomenal. It bewildered her lover, obfuscated her lover's mother, and finally outwitted Mrs. Gereth, her mentor, under whose wide wing she had taken refuge. Her moods and tenses are carefully differentiated as the story progresses, and one sympathises with her acutely when she says:

"I haven't a rag of pride. I used to have, but it's gone. I used to have a secret, but every one knows it now; and any one who looks at me can say, I think, what's the matter with me."

The trouble was that Mrs. Gereth was incessantly at her post, attaching a "tinkling bell" to every word, look, and action of her *protégé*.

Mrs. Gereth is a better rounded character, because simpler. There was nothing mystic or elusive about her. She was somewhat of a termagant, or, as she expressed it, she lacked reserve. She would have loved you for doing justice to her "deep morality," but have wished, herself, to tell of the quickness and quietness with which she operated. Sentences beginning "Why the devil," and "I'll be hanged," addressed to her intimate, indicate intensity rather than vulgarity; and those words hastily penned to her boy, "Go to see her, and try, for God's sake, to cultivate a glimmer of intelligence," leave the impression that she was a force as well as an influence. How far she went in making Fleda's way straight before her appears in the following:

"Do you mean to say that, Mona or no Mona, he could see you that way, day after day, and not have the ordinary feelings of a man? . . . Do you mean to say that when, the other day, one had quite made you over to him, the great gawk, and he was, on this very spot, utterly alone with you? . . ."

It is wonderful how these two women—Mrs. Gereth and Fleda—got along together. They never quarreled; they just diverged and became parallel again. In the end the elder was appalled at her dependence upon the other. And Fleda, like many another feminine soul, was inspired by the very clumsiness and indecision of her lover. Indeed, "her desire to serve him was too passionate, the sense that he counted upon her too sweet" for ordinary comprehension. With such a person she felt that she could be "exceptionally human." That she is human with him, or at all, may be questioned. The crass stupidity of Owen and the utter conventionality of Mrs. Brigstock are a screen on which the eyes linger till, drab becoming the prevalent mental colour, Mrs. Gereth is declared a monstrosity and Fleda a screaming upstart! Nothing needs to be said for Mrs. Gereth; she would galvanise a toad. In accounting for Fleda, however, one must not ignore the velocity of her propulsion from Mrs. Gereth's catapult. Her environment gave her a fine twist. She is neither superhuman nor degenerate, but normally complex.

If need were, it might be added that the details of Mr. James's workmanship deserve close scrutiny. Each situation is a miniature, each sentence a piece of thread lace. With what delicate incisions he approximates to his meaning! As he said of Abbey, "Everything is so human, so humorous and so caught in the act, so buttoned and petticoated and gartered, that it might be round the corner; so it is, but the corner is the corner of another world." The analyst must ever be open to the accusation of other-worldliness. This, because he keeps both eyes on the object, and does not drop his tools now and then to tickle his readers between the ribs. He is usually too interested to think of anybody's self-love. The real question is, Can one be true to his constituency when merely true to his subject?

"Mr. James's New Novel." *Bookman* [England] 12 (May 1897), 42–43.

Mr. James's success here defies clear explanation. It seems far more individual, as well as more striking, than his art. Another might rival him in the production of something costly and fine out of materials few and meager. But his temperament, which is ever hovering between its kinship with the solid and the light, counts for much; and this story, which in any other hands could only have been clever and amusing, turns unexpectedly into something substantial and permanent. Our one discontent with it must express itself as a desire that Mr. James, who has at his command so perfect and limpid a style for analytical narrative, would not cultivate his tendency to rival Mr. Meredith in the avoidance of obvious constructions.

One almost maligns the worth of "The Spoils of Poynton" in mentioning the frivolous structure on which it supports nearly three hundred pages. A woman of supreme good taste, with a genius for making a house a haven of harmony, finds herself face to face with the ugly fact that her son is about to marry an arch-Philistine, for whom she must give way. She is a woman of spirit and will, and the situation is intolerable. Red rioting revolt is her weapon; she walks off with the pick of the collection, and with her born genius for arrangement, creates another haven of harmony in the small dower-house at Ricks. The negotiations between her and her son—a stupid, inarticulate, handsome, and charming young man—make inimitable comedy. His enthusiasm for Poynton had not been wild, as it had never been intelligent; he was a most gentlemanly, if not a tender, son; but he is being prodded by the Philistine fiancée, who has no loving eye for the things, but smells their value, and is of the order that will fight to the death for material rights. His sense of fair-play to her mingles with a desire to respect his mother, even though she is a bold marauder; his disgust at Philistine greed is aided by his new-awakened love and admiration for the girl of finer fibre, the beloved of his mother, to whom Poynton and its spoils would have been surrendered with the best grace in the world, and again hindered by the fine-souled girl's hurling him back on his fair-play instincts. The result is that decorous farce, in which Mr. James is unsurpassable. The vigorous shoving onslaught of the Philistine family, the brave holding out of the bold marauder, are a joy to witness. We back the Philistines all through; for the marauder has but a poor ally in Fleda. She is not even an ally in the marauding, only in artistic appreciation, and in a secret adoration of the stupid and charming young man; and the strength from these is undermined by a terribly active conscience and a sense of refinement which inconveniently goes far beyond the aesthetic region, and pervades her whole being. The Philistines rollick into victory, of course; and after all one cannot feel a very keen regret for the stupid Owen's fate.

But otherwise, too, the day is theirs—till we look back on the story. The Brigstock family, Mona in particular, and Owen, the distressed owner of Poynton, are triumphs. Mrs. Gereth is a perfect embodiment of a point of view, the point of view that intelligent appreciation should give proprietary rights, but rather shadowy, more humanly considered. Fleda fades a little dimly into the finenesses of her soul. But Mona and Owen are as living as they are loud and fresh coloured. They both impressed Fleda with their abounding vitality, on which brains had never made one exhausting demand; she regarded them with no intolerance, even while she rehearsed their graceless confidence, and could "hear, with all vividness, the pretty passage between the pair [regarding the priceless treasures, the inimitable harmonies of the most perfect house in England]. 'Don't you think it's rather jolly, the old shop?' 'Oh, it's all right!' Mona had graciously remarked; and then they had probably, with a slap on a back, run another race up or down a green bank."

Perhaps another would have left it all comedy, and he would probably have been right. But Mr. James's human sympathies, if rather shy, are unconquerably strong. And here comes in his individual power, that in a story, the fun of which makes our eyes glisten, and with whose finer heroine we almost lose patience for a subtle virtue and refinement so much beyond the needs of the case, our last thought is still with her. Her little tragedy, in this setting, comes perilously near to spoiling the story; and yet, after all, we do not resent its stopping our fun, for it gives permanence and the element of the substantial to the graceful, trivial farce.

"The Spoils of Poynton." Critic 30 (1 May 1897), 301.

It is hard for the appreciative reader to pay adequate tribute to a book which has given him such keen pleasure as "The Spoils of Poynton" must give. It is more than a novel, it is a piece of decorative art. It has all the author's chronic merits, and some others which are fresh and acute. Its theme, for instance, is new. It contains the only wholly adequate and sympathetic study of the collector's passion that we know in fiction. Everybody who has ever loved "old things" and collected them, however modestly, is bound to thrill in response to the motive of the book. Its audience ought to include all that inner circle of devotees of the exquisite who find their solace for living in a cheap, hideous, machine made world, in owning and doting upon a few good examples of the craftsmanship of more leisurely and more artistic generations. The rapture of the collector, or of the man who only collects yearnings for specimens he may not own, is a thing apart. It springs from a special sensibility to beauty as applied to decoration, and it cannot be described by those who have not known it. How intimately Mr. James must know it, the book testifies.

The story opens with the meeting at Waterbath, the house of the Brigstocks, of Fleda Vetch and Mrs. Gereth. The latter's home in the south of England, Poynton, is famous for its rare perfection. The house itself, an exquisite specimen of early Jacobean domestic architecture, forms "a matchless canvas for the picture" which Mrs. Gereth, with the collector's "almost infernal cunning," has been able to make.

For twenty-six happy years she and her husband have collected objects of beauty. Their things have come from every corner of Europe, and, although they have not very much money, they have succeeded in getting only the best. Mrs. Gereth "had waited for them, worked for them, picked them over, made them worthy of each other and the house, watched them, loved them, lived with them." Nevertheless, on her husband's death the house and its rich apparel go to the son, Owen, whose pride in it is vague and uninitiated.

The principle of taste had been omitted from the composition of the Brigstocks of Waterbath, and their house is a horror to more happily endowed persons. Fleda Vetch, a girl who has no money but possesses a direct and heaven-sent apprehension of good things, is naturally drawn to Mrs. Gereth by their common distaste for their surroundings, and the woman takes an immense fancy to the girl. Owen Gereth, however, attaches himself to Mona, the eldest daughter of the Brigstocks, and presently brings her down to Poynton, which she inspects without comprehension, but ultimately signifies her willingness to marry Owen. The prospect, not only of being separated from her treasures, but of resigning them to a perfectly unworthy and unsympathetic wardenship, is unendurable to Mrs. Gereth. She hysterically flings Fleda at Owen's head, and at first refuses to leave Poynton, then consents to go to Ricks, the dower-house that is her portion, if she is allowed to take "what she requires" of the glories of Poynton. Owen's notion is that she shall take a dozen of the best pieces, but Mrs. Gereth's requirements are large, and, like a thief in the night, she swiftly and silently removes to Ricks practically everything the house contains. Mona becomes sulky, holds Owen responsible for the despoiled house, and declines to marry him until the things are restored. Her behavior alienates him,

especially as he has allowed himself to be deeply attracted by Fleda, who becomes the intermediary between him and his mother in the negotiations about the things. Fleda, who has loved Owen from the first, finds herself arbiter of her own fate and his. If she tells his mother what Owen has told her—namely, that Mona will not marry him until the things are restored—Mrs. Gereth will assuredly never give them up without violence which Owen will not use. The marriage will then be "off" and Owen free. What she does in this delicate dilemma must be learned from the book; and the fate of the "old things" is too dramatic and exciting to be told except in the author's words.

The character of Fleda is one of the finest of the author's conceptions. She carries her love of ideal beauty over from the department of appreciation into that of action, and seeks to apply to conduct the tests for art. Whether one agrees with her notions of duty or not, he must recognize the delicacy and fidelity with which she is drawn. Here is "the portrait of a lady" beside which even Isabel Archer's presentment seems crude and unfinished. In her character, and, indeed, throughout the book, the writer comes so near truth that he attains absolute beauty. The love passages—and when did Mr. James ever do actual love-scenes before?—are of an extraordinary force and fire; the lovers are human and real. In short, the cleverer Mr. James becomes, the more convincing he grows. One gets from his work at its best an intimation of perfection, a deep consciousness that here is something so fine that it could not be bettered; and this consciousness becomes almost overwhelming to the reader of "The Spoils of Poynton."

[Annie R. M. Logan].
Nation 65 (1 July 1897), 18.

A certain degree of responsive sympathy with the collector's passion is absolutely necessary for enjoyment of 'The Spoils of Poynton.' Given that sensibility, however slight, Mrs. Gereth is an impressively tragic figure; without it, she appears as a quarrelsome person, probably mad, bent on depriving her son of property allowed him by law because she doesn't like the girl he wishes to marry. Fortunately for Mr. James, it is fashionable to care for things, old things, artistic things; and as fashion often serves as well as genuine feeling, he may be pretty sure of a large and appreciative audience. The lioness defending her cubs is a poor figure for ferocity compared with Mrs. Gereth beating off swine (particularly named Brigstock) from her pearls, the treasures of Poynton. She and her things are one, and whatever may have survived after the elements took a hand in the fray and swept Poynton from the face of the earth, it could be but a pale and soulless image of that ingenious, unscrupulous, and vindictive apostle of æstheticism. Her defeat by the terrible Brigstocks calls for tears much more peremptorily than does the defeat of her astute confidante and go-between, Fleda Vetch, by the chief of those children of darkness, Miss Mona Brigstock. Up to the point where Owen Gereth declares that he is free to rid himself of Mona, her bad taste, and sordid soul, free to love Fleda and happily end the tiresome squabble with his mother, one accepts the possibility of her consuming secret love for Owen. But at this point, loving Owen, loving his mother, loving the things, and having the whole game in her hands, it is difficult to believe that any girl, however subtle and high-minded, ever so deliberately surrendered everything to the enemy. The serious passion of the tale, however, is that of Mrs. Gereth for her things, and the expression of that passion is so perfect that it makes very little difference whether Fleda is a natural, human girl, or an incredible figure woven of whimsical fancy and subtle phrases. The fancy is fine enough and the phrases are good enough to afford a rare pleasure, of a kind which the author alone is able to give us in perfection.

Checklist of Additional Reviews

Boston *Evening Journal,* 20 February 1897, p. 7.

Chicago *Inter-ocean,* 20 February 1897, p. 10.

New York *Sun,* 20 February 1897, p. 7.

E.F. *Providence Sunday Journal,* 21 February 1897, p. 15.

Springfield [Mass.] *Republican,* 21 February 1897, p. 13.

Outlook 55 (27 February 1897), 610.

Spectator [England] 78 (27 February 1897), 309.

Brooklyn *Daily Eagle,* 28 February 1897, p. 10.

Cleveland *Plain Dealer,* 28 February 1897, p. 13.

Indianapolis *Journal,* 28 February 1897, p. 12.

Boston *Evening Transcript,* 10 March 1897, p. 9.

Public Opinion 22 (11 March 1897), 312.

Literary Review 1 (15 March 1897), 41.

Annie W. Sanborn. St. Paul *Daily Pioneer Press,* 21 March 1897, p. 15.

Literary World [England] 55 (26 March 1897), 289–90.

Book Buyer 14 (April 1897), 303–5.

Talcott Williams. *Book News* 15 (April 1897), 389.

Churchman 75 (17 April 1897), 608.

Literary World [Boston] 28 (17 April 1897), 126–27.

Academy, [England] no. 1305 (8 May 1897), 506.

[William Morton Payne]. *Dial* 22 (16 May 1897), 311.

Independent 49 (29 July 1897), 980.

WHAT MAISIE KNEW

Manchester *Guardian*, 28 September 1897, p. 9.

The problem of the possible aspects which life might take for a small girl-child whose parents have found in divorce only a wider licence for temper and vice, though probably repellent to most people, is sufficiently complex to attract a mental analyst of the stamp of Mr. Henry James. In *What Maisie Knew* (W. Heinemann, pp. 304, 6s.) Mr. James has so far triumphed over the difficulties of the subject as to present us with a credible picture of childish innocence, preserved in the midst of glaring evil by means, not of stupid obtuseness, but of a rare sensibility, tact, and sweet power of devotion. This is indeed a victory, and one of no mean order, for, although largely due to the author's unrivalled skill in the art of allusiveness and skating over thin ice, we are yet conscious that verbal dialectics alone could not have saved from besmirchment the small figure of this helpless toy of chance and evil passions. From other points of view, such, for instance, as the enjoyment of the reader, success is more questionable. More even than in some of his other works are we haunted here by the impression that it is the thorny setting of the fruit rather than its succulence which has tempted the author to lay hands on it. It is a study, not a story or drama. The portion of Maisie's life which it covers is only a few years of childhood, and they may be described roughly as a duel for the possession of her person. On one side the forces of respectability are represented by Mrs. Wix, an elderly and outwardly grotesque but wholly devoted governess, and by Sir Claude, the second husband of Maisie's mother, who is resolved to put the child outside an atmosphere from which he has no moral strength himself to escape; on the other are arrayed (though in succession rather than side by side) Maisie's father and mother, and the woman who has become first her step-mother and then the lover of Sir Claude. These persons, hostile in everything else, are at one in using Maisie simply as a tool to be picked up or dropped to suit their own needs. The crucial point of the complication arises from the *liaison* between two members of the opposing parties—the step-mother and step-father—of which the child herself, in her lively affection for both, has been the innocent instrument. The battle and the book close with Mrs. Wix bearing Maisie across the Channel in triumphant flight, but the horizon of the future is left veiled in cloud. From the nature of the case the book is monotonous, and, in spite of the changeful dialogue and the delicious insight into childish character with which every page is full, this monotony presses hard on the reader before the close. We feel that the author has performed his task as perhaps no other man could. Only, whatever entertainment or admiration the book may call forth, we cannot imagine anyone reading it a second time. It is undoubtedly a work of art, but hardly one which we wish to hang on our walls.

"High Water."
Pall Mall Gazette [England], 11 October 1897, p. 10.

Mr. Henry James has now been writing for a long period in years. He began in America, and has slowly worked his way by the Continental route to England. All that time he has also been growing steadily in the favour of the appreciative, if not in popularity, until to-day he holds a high and distinctive position among novelists of the English-writing races. He stands in the van with one or two compeers, and no more. Bit by bit, piece by piece, he has accumulated his dignity, as absolutely undeterred by the threat of popular coldness as he has been indifferent to the lure of popular approval. Mr. James once wrote a short tale in which a novelist failed because he was too good to be popular. He swore regularly to do "better" (that is, worse) next time, but with punctual precision each next time he was found to have fulfilled his artistic conscience. No one would venture to say that Mr. James ever contemplated so gross a breach of morals, merely because he is utterly incapable of the feat. He may have one reader (audience fit, though few!), and he will still be writing, turning his phases with the old gusto, probing emotions with the accustomed delicacy, exercising the familiar humour. The rewards of popularity affect no writer of Mr. James's temperament; he is not tempted into despair, but cleaves to his taste, such as he has conceived it. And in the end the reward may not fall so far away as those generations of posterity which shall judge us, and set us up in our niche, or cast us down among the shards.

This latest novel from Mr. James's pen seems, beyond doubt, to touch his highest point. It is a work very difficult to criticise, very perplexing to appraise. But beyond and above all the one fact of its astounding cleverness stands forth. It is quite impossible to ignore that, if the word have any significance, and is ever to be used at all, we are here dealing with genius. This is a work of genius, as much as Mr. Meredith's best work, though on quite other human lines, as the readers of both need not be reminded. And the next point which may occur to a reader, as he lays down the book, is that the author has generously,

willfully, almost wantonly handicapped himself. He had selected a strange medley of sordid intrigue, in which some vivid and curious characters perform the antics of that human comedy on which Mr. James loves to dwell as much as his great contemporary. It was a *partie carrée,* a group hard enough in itself to conceive, set forth, and illumine in the subtle manner to which the author has accustomed us. But conceive that this medley, these intricacies of motive, this tangle and confusion of emotion, are all transmuted, reflected, determined through the mind of a little girl of eight years! The thing, one would say, was preposterous. What on earth, indeed, *did* Maisie know of all this terrible human imbroglio? She knew nothing—that is obviously the answer which Mr. James desires us to take from his story; and that very fact that she knew nothing, was really aware of nothing, stared on life through childish and innocent eyes, surveyed the dustheap and the dungheap with her incomplete and wondering vision—that fact composes the amazing difficulty of Mr. James's task. To render the action and the motives through Maisie's mind to the reader, and yet leave upon that virginal spirit the stain or shadow of no comprehension—such has been the author's work. His success is commensurate with the difficulty. Of all the figures that tread the mazes of the story—Farange, her father, Mrs. Beale, Sir Claude, even Ida herself—none is fixed so indelibly and marked with such personality as the child. Mr. James's plots do not bear the bald analysis of a review; they must be taken in the context. To any one who will drop his Hall Caines and Marie Corellis for a time and take the trouble to read through this book, every single act and feeling of the child will be pathetically convincing. The grime and squalor of the life of these characters make an impression upon the reader. But they never touch Maisie. She is no heroine, of course; she is what her unnatural life made her—weak, yielding, a little deceitful, feebly affectionate, but above all ignorant, peace-loving, and possessed of that weary craving for rest and home and some one to cling to. To the last she is defeated, and even when Mrs. Wix carries her off in triumph, we are not quite certain if she has gained what was the desire of her heart.

What did Maisie know? There was little that she had not heard. Every vain, selfish, or cowardly character in the book pours confidences into her ears. She herself boasted to her father that she knew everything; she liked to know. The pathetic part of it, and yet the best part of it also, was that, as we have said, she knew nothing. We have remarked upon the surprising difficulties which Mr. James has thrown in his own way; and yet we should not be astonished to learn that Mr. James had conceived the book entirely for the sake of that central figure with its distressing problem. He is used to set himself hard tasks, and executes them whether any one cares or not. This time we venture to think that he has achieved something which must strike even that mysterious and loose-headed person, the general reader. And yet, perhaps not; and, if not, at least he has enriched the heritage of our descendants.

Spectator [England] 3618 (30 October 1897), 603.

In *What Maissie Knew* Mr. Henry James presents the unedifying spectacle of a man of great talent and subtlety, whose sympathies are obviously on the side of the angels, toiling with unflagging persistence and desperate attention to detail over the portraiture of half a dozen as unlovely and squalid souls—spite of their fashionable surroundings and showy exteriors—as it has been our misfortune to encounter in the range of modern fiction. It reminds us of nothing so much as a beautifully dressed child making an elaborate mud-pie in the gutter. The mud-pie is a regular work of art, and the child continues to keep its own hands and dress unsoiled. But when all is said and done, the result is only a mud-pie and nothing more. Maisie is the only child of thoroughly disreputable parents, who have just been divorced at the opening of the tale. According to the arrangement, Maisie spends her time alternately with her father and mother. Governesses are provided, and her father marries the younger, handsomer, and incomparably more worthless of the two. The mother also marries again, her second husband being a feeble, invertebrate creature called Sir Claude. Then Maisie, who all the time is tossed about like a shuttlecock between this disreputable quartet, is the innocent means of bringing her new stepmother and stepfather together, with results that can be easily imagined from their antecedents. Mr. James, it is true, refrains from the crowning feat of making the father and mother marry each other again. That would have exposed him to the charge of attempting to enter into rivalry with the hideous finale of *Jude the Obscure*. But it could not have rendered the book more disagreeable than it is. The elaborate ingenuity with which this wretched little child is hemmed round with undesirable relatives in our opinion entirely robs the figure of its intended pathos. Maisie escapes in the end, thanks chiefly to the dogged determination of the ugly governess, and to the gradual emergence in the child of a moral sense. There are a great many passages in the book which are evidently meant to be humorous. This, for example, from the description of the divorce proceedings—"The father, who, though bespattered from head to foot, had made good his case, was, in pursuance of this triumph, appointed to keep her; it was not so much that the mother's character had been more absolutely damaged as that the brilliancy of a lady's complexion (and this lady's in court, was immensely remarked) might be more regarded as showing the spots." For the life of us we fail to see where the fun comes in, though no doubt this strenuous facetiousness has its admirers. We note, in conclusion, that some of the names—Wix and Moddle, for example—remind one of Dickens. But we hasten to add, in justice to Mr. Henry James, that there is absolutely nothing else in the book which the most fanatical plagiary-hunter could indicate as recalling in the faintest way the manner or matter of the immortal "Boz."

Indianapolis *News,* 3 November 1897, p. 5.

There are some stories that lend themselves admirably to purposes of serial publication and others that do not. A serial story, to be really successful, must be at least slightly sensational, and the public will receive it better if each installment ends with a thrilling incident "to be continued in our next." "What Maisie Knew," the latest work of Mr. Henry James, is not a story adapted to this sort of publication. The book contains not a single sensation in the ordinary meaning of the term; there is little incident, a paucity of conversation. Indeed, the story lacks all of the requirements of the modern devourers of fiction, who, reading to be amused, seize on a book as a beast does on its prey, gnaw out the sensational incidents, gloat over the

juicy places and gallop over the conversational pages, delighted at the "easy reading." "What Maisie Knew" is a study of child-life, an analysis of the conscience and mind of a child whose position in life is anomalous, unique; one is tempted to say, impossible. The story is simple, yet complex.

To tell the story without stopping to analyze the feelings, the thoughts of the characters, a newspaper writer, used to be sparing of his words, would take no more than a column of a newspaper to tell "what Maisie knew," but then the reader would simply learn the hard conditions under which Maisie Farrange lived, without receiving any of the secrets of the child's soul. One would miss the sympathy, the tenderness, the fine insight, the clear understanding of Mr. James. This soul of a little girl is a spirit that can not be seized upon, catalogued and spread upon paper by the ordinary methods of the novelist. It has to be approached reverently, gently, lovingly. There are those who, reading chapters of this story in the Chap-Book, where it appeared serially, could see only a strange confusion of words, and even before the story was brought to a conclusion we had essays on Mr. James in which the essayists tried to tell us that the author, having cultivated for years a curious, indirect style of writing, had at last found himself captured by his style which had run him off into the by-paths of obscurity.[1] It is true, indeed, that Mr. James uses many words, sometimes pages of words, just to portray one little thought of a little child, but he uses his words—he is not used by them. This is not a book to be read hastily, with skipping of passages, with a cloudy mind; it is a story that demands keen intelligence, alert brain, perceptions, fresh and eager. For those who do not care to take time to read this book, the book has no message; for those who are willing to give attention, to look at the lights and shadows, not to con words, but to read them, the book will reveal beautifully the soul of a little child, sensitive and shy.

What Maisie knew was pitiable enough in its tragedy and its perplexing responsibilities. She knew that her father and mother were divorced, that each had married again, and that the second wife and the second husband were lovers. She knows, the knowledge coming painfully bit by bit, that her father is a scoundrel, that her mother has many lovers, that her step-father and her step-mother are not nice persons. She knows, too, that all these people use her and her innocence for the most vile ends, hiding behind the respectability of her childhood. "She was the little feathered shuttlecock that they fiercely kept flying between them. The evil they had the gift of thinking or pretending to think of each other they poured into her little gravely-gazing soul as into a boundless receptacle; and each of them had doubtless the best conscience in the world as to the duty of teaching her the stern truth that should be her safeguard against the other."

Out of this material Mr. James builds up his story, or rather, having built the story and seeing the wretchedness and the tragedy, he has with great pains extracted the soul of the little girl and presented it to his readers. If one reads the book understandingly and with intelligence, the humor of the grim tragedy will disclose itself and the pathos will become apparent, and as one sees that the artist is leaving not even the smallest necessary details out of the picture, one becomes convinced that this is not simply a story, that it is a picture of life, pathetic, sad, forlorn. No one of the characters is drawn positively in any part of the book; they appear first as shadows, and as the light shines upon them they become more and more distinct, and, when one having made an end of reading

lays down the book, there appears in the mind, a clear, coherent picture of Maisie's mother, Ida Farrange, with her pretty, vapid face, her hard eyes, her temper, her infidelity; there is Maisie's father, a tall man with russet beard and teeth of which he is proud; there is Sir Claude, Maisie's step-father, weak but generous, vicious, but good-natured, there is Mrs. Beale, the step-mother, bold, handsome and unscrupulous, and there is poor old Mrs. Wix, with her love for Maisie and her "straighteners." Shadows still remain the baron and the count and the captain and the host of Ida's lovers who flit across the page, all of whom try to use poor Maisie for their own selfish ends and who bribe her with chocolate creams to be blind to their sins.

Through all this Maisie lives clean and unspotted. The book is an admirable study of life, not a "realistic" picture of life, but life felt and interpreted by a rich imagination. The book should add largely to the reputation of Mr. James.

Note

1 "What Maisie Knew," *Chap Book* 6 (15 January—1 May 1897), 214–19, 253–60, 289–95, 326–31, 361–67, 395–401, 428–34, 478–85; 7 (15 May—1 August 1897), 16–25, 57–62, 90–97, 125–31, 162–68, 198–209.

Athenaeum [England] 3654 (6 November 1897), 629.

Considering their nature and workmanship, Mr. James's novels appear with a frequency that is little short of surprising; yet 'What Maisie Knew' is in some respects as remarkable as anything he has written. Its importance, if not its pleasantness, must be certainly apparent to those on whom analysis of the finest quality and delicate delineation are not thrown away. The way in which Mr. James manages to preserve his poor little heroine, and yet to plunge her into a more than tainted atmosphere, is quite a masterly performance. Yet this constant approximation of a child-mind, especially such a one as Maisie's, to the doings of the horrid quartet of persons who principally dominate her fate, is to the reader oppressive and painful. So much is this the case that one questions whether Mr. James, with all his discrimination and power of selection, was happily inspired, even artistically, in choosing such ground. The situation may be in many respects but too real. One shrinks all the more from the lengthy view of the grimy channel in which the child's young life runs. It is as though one were forced to watch a flower caught in the eddies of a sewer, whirled back and forth, and round and round, on its turbid waves. The impulse to pluck it out may be inartistic, but it is there, and it occasionally spoils one's reading. It seems almost incredible that in the story there should be none to retrieve the child from her surroundings. And yet the sordid details are more suggested than described. The central idea is managed as only Mr. James, perhaps, can manage a difficult individual or social problem. His treatment of the mind of Maisie itself is constantly beyond praise in spite of the circumstances in which he has set her: the saddest, the most poignantly melancholy position, morally if not materially, in which a forlorn childhood can be placed. And what is more, he has left her there, not mitigating nor abating one jot of the evils. Yet in a sense he brings her forth unscathed and triumphantly through the ordeal. Maisie is redeemed by no outside influence, but only by the force of a singularly buoyant and innate grace of nature. Mr. James's remarkable sleight of hand or thought appears in the way he first penetrates, then reveals, the child-mind. For, in spite of all her sad half-knowledge of some of the ugliest and meanest phases of life, she retains a child's heart and mind at their sweetest. What Maisie knew, or in spite of her undesirable opportunities did not know, is the real subject of this astonishing drama. The cleverness is cleverness of treatment more than cleverness of conception. The people who are her parents and those others who develop into step-parents are more or less of the pot-and-kettle type, if one may use so homely an expression. Wherever they may be gathered together there an ignoble and vulgar atmosphere is at once created. From first to last the child plays the part of shuttlecock in the sordid game in which they are engaged. Yet of their miserable cross-purposes we in fact see only as much as Maisie with her innocent vision perceived. She is not the angel type of child, but only a human child of generous temperament and instinctively fine breeding. How with her parents she comes by such qualities let writers on heredity decide. One thing we ask ourselves: Has Mr. James sufficiently allowed for the restraining influence of public opinion? Surely no people ever gave themselves away so completely as the wretched Beale and the monstrous Ida. Mr. James knows so very well what he is about that we are probably in error in holding the belief that the mother must for her own sake have occasionally made some slight attempt to what is called draw a veil. She is almost too crude to be true, and we find no suspicion of the occasional charm with which she is credited. And yet we know that Idas exist and are in our midst in a slightly modified form. The other members of the unengaging quartet are in sundry ways less obnoxious. The false positions, socially speaking, in which they all stand with regard to one another and to Maisie are so extraordinary as to be almost farcical. But all this is not what really exercises Mr. James's powers. It is simply, as it were, the mind of Maisie, and it alone, moving in worlds fortunately not realized.

Saturday Review [England] 84 (20 November 1897), 537–38.

Mr. James is a brilliant skater on thin ice; and this story gives his accomplishment full play. A little girl lives by turns with either of her divorced parents: her father a selfish scoundrel, her mother a no less unamiable creature. Both marry again: her mother marries a weak, good-natured man about town; her father marries his mistress, the child's governess, "a person superior to any confusion." Maisie lives in these new households by turns, and plays a part in the extraordinary drama of the falling asunder of these well-assorted couples. She receives amazing confidences; witnesses amazing meetings, amazing interviews in which wives, husbands, lovers, and mistresses mingle in an amazing confusion; and in the end sees her stepparents drifted into the relation of lover and mistress. It would seem almost impossible to treat of a child in such malodorous surroundings; but though, as Mr. James says of his child heroine, "only a drummer-boy in a ballad or a story could have been so in the thick of the fight," thanks to his skill, and a girl-child's natural disposition to keep such matters on the sentimental plane, we are never shocked. Most of his obtuse readers will believe Mr. James to be reticent: he is not. The "i's" are dotted; but the dots are very small ones: once, for example, a lady shows "a deficiency in the air of a honeymoon," once a gentleman forgets his stick. Such a book must needs wear the air of a *tour de force;* and Mr. James's fault, a straining to be always subtle, even where plainness would be more effective, accentuates that air. But, in spite of this not rare sense of strain, it is an excellent book. The vulgar, selfish, beautiful people are presented with an amazing realness: now they themselves reveal their depths, in wonderful phrases that ring with the cold truth, in actions of an astounding meanness; now the ironic humour of the writer flashes its light into the slimy crannies of their souls; they are in perpetual vivid contrast to the finer natures who suffer by them. The sophisticated Maisie, with her selfishness and her generosities, with her passion for peace-bringing compromise, ever meeting the shock of the unsavoury loves and hates of her elders, ever craving the natural affection her due, and ever starved, is one of the most pathetic figures of a child in fiction. She is the creation of a fine imagination and a fine sympathetic insight, treated with a fine subtlety. It is hard to say whether she is more pathetic in her joys or her sorrows; for Mr. James is a master of pathos, ever impressing on us that the happiness of the humble is even more pathetic than their grief; and under his treatment Maisie sobbing "Oh mother, mother, mother!" is no more pathetic than the wonderful Mrs. Wix rejoicing at the courtesy of Sir Claude, "Even to the hard heart of childhood there was something tragic in such elation at such humanities; it brought home to Maisie the way her humble companion had sidled and ducked through life."

"Henry James' Study of the Moral Effects of Divorce."
Chicago *Tribune*, 22 November 1897, p. 8.

After tossing about in the trough of the sea of fiction, such a ride on the crest of the wave as Henry James' "What Maisie Knew" gives the reader is apt to bewilder him for a moment. Certainly it leaves him so thankful for its negative virtues—so many things which the other books are and this is not—that its varied positive excellences come as an afterthought. And this, reflection will convince him, was the exact intention of the author.

Mr. James can write fiction which is instructive as well as entertaining; but he differs from most of his fellows in telling a story which is humanly interesting and letting the rest take care of itself—quite a different matter from catching an unfortunate reader and making him sit through page after page of preachments. Nor is the moral a logical deduction from a series of texts—it is an impression none the less strong from not being set in words of a philosophy of life—in Maisie's case as strange and untoward a one as can be derived from Arthur Morrison's "Children of the Jago." [1]

Beale and Ida Farange, father and mother respectively to Maisie, are so mutually unworthy that her obtaining a divorce is regarded as a wonder. The story is an English story with hardly a soupçon of America in it. It is, furthermore, a straw to point the wind in being the second English divorce novel of the year, Leonard Merrick's "One Man's View" being the other.

The divorce obtained, a difficulty over money divides the time of the little girl between the parents, six months of every years with each. Thereupon the childish brain is filled and the childish memory taxed with all the blame and opprobrium each can heap on the other, until Maisie discovers, with the inscrutable and savage cunning of childhood, that by feigning stupidity she may bring an immediate punishment upon herself, but one which is incomparably less than the burden of the vile messages which would otherwise be laid upon her. It is not the indecency of these communications which bothers Maisie—she is too young—nor yet the sorrow which she inflicts upon the one on whom the scurrility is unladen; it is simply the mental strain of having to remember. For her parents, from beginning to end of the book, she shows such love as is meted out to her, neither more nor less—a moral which is none the less plain from its lack of obviousness. In fact, there is a curious moral torpor in the atmosphere throughout, and the child is little affected by anything said within her own circle, another inevitable result of the instructions which were poured out upon her devoted head before she bethought herself of being stupid.

A Miss Overmore is engaged by Mr. Farange as governess to Maisie. She is a delicately vulgar person with that nice blending of vulgarity through inadvertence and vulgarity through design which is one of Mr. James' favorite and most successful shadings. Mrs. Farange has a Mrs. Wix, who is a delightful personality, to perform the same necessary office. "She wore glasses, which, in humble reference to a divergent obliquity of vision, she called her straighteners, she explained to Maisie as put on for the sake of others, whom, as she believed, they helped to recognize the direction, otherwise misleading, of her glance." She is almost the only person in the book who gives the child any tenderness, and the result is curious in more than one sense, at the dénouement.

The parents being what they are, and leave to remarry not having been withheld by the court, it is not long before Beale Farange has made the pretty Miss Overmore his wife, while Mrs. Ida is led to the altar by Sir Claude. The complications, bad enough in all conscience, are given an element that is comic almost to the straining point by Sir Claude's meeting with the second Mrs. Farange through his desire to know Maisie, and the prompt manner in which they fall in love with one another. As little or nothing is concealed from the child's observation, she soon has abundant opportunity for perceiving, as the story progresses, that her real papa is interested in an "American" Countess who supports him; while her real mamma is so variously engaged that she is never sure what the name of the favorite of the hour may be. Under these circumstances it is seemingly difficult to tell what Maisie did not know—seemingly rather than actually, for the author never forgets the blessed innocence of young maidenhood, which, even when carried to the lengths it assumes in "The Mysteries of Paris," is felt to be in accord with reality.

There are no tragic notes. Beale flees with his Countess and leaves his wife free. Ida goes away and leaves Sir Claude unhampered. Mrs. Wix stays with Maisie— all the more, to do her credit, because she knows that the two step-parents are making an interest in Maisie the pretext for more open communication. It is Mrs. Wix who, in despair, tries to cultivate in the child what she calls a moral sense. In doing it, she even discovers herself as a sort of mild Germinie Lascerteux. But it is all to the same end—What Maisie knew neither father nor mother, pretty governess

nor homely, was ever able to ascertain. And in this lies the climax of the story, wrought, like its details, convincingly from the soiled and blotted human documents in hand.

Mr. James has achieved a success; and his book, which is published by Herbert S. Stone & Co., is rightly described as "important." So long as parents are to be divorced, so long will it remain a problem what it is that the Maisies are to know.

Note

1   Arthur Morrison, *Child of the Jago* (1896).

"Henry James's New Work, *What Maisie Knew.*" *New York Times Saturday Review of Books and Art* 2 (27 November 1897), 9.

To read "What Maisie Knew," the latest contribution of Henry James to the curiosities of modern literature, is to go through an experience almost or quite as remarkable as that of his unfortunate little heroine. That non-existent being, the average reader, on completing the task of perusal—if he or she does complete it—is more than likely to transmute the bewilderment into irritation, and to condemn the book in a few vague but emphatic remarks about the obscurity of its style, the moral squalor of its characters, and the author's cynical refusal to answer the conundrum in the propounding of which he has used up every one of his 470 pages. The more or less professional commentator on books, though he may envy the person who can make this summary disposition of Maisie, her knowledge, and her inventor, has too much conscience (if it isn't too little courage) and too much appreciation of "art," (if it isn't appreciation of the necessity for a pretense of such appreciation) to put the confession of his disappointment in a form so brief.

And therein is the commentator fortunate, because just a little of the preliminary reflection that is required for writing about a book—as distinguished from talking about one—will reveal to him that the vague but emphatic remarks which he longed to echo were inaccurate as well, and unjust to a degree really ridiculous. Then, alas! he is in danger of rushing to the opposite extreme, and, saved from the crime of indefensible condemnation, of falling into that of superheated praise. Curiously enough, too, even though the critic of "What Maisie Knew" goes to work very deliberately indeed, the result may seem to be made up of contradictions, a fact due to the widely differing emotions with which he read the first and second halves of the book.

This last statement, it is to be hoped, will not be taken as expressing the opinion that the first half is good and the last half bad. Such is by no means the case, for each is a piece of marvelously skillful manipulation of words, or, to be exact, the skill shown in the first chapter is maintained to and through the concluding one. Not the manipulator's adroitness, but the observer's attention, is what weakened as the performance went on. Hence comes the pleasant necessity for laudations thoroughly sincere, and the painful necessity for that savagest of detraction, the question, "Was it quite worth while?"

It is like this: Mr. James evidently began and ended the book under the influence of a determination to see what would happen if he filled a volume with those peculiarities of thought and diction over which his devotees have hitherto waxed so enthusiastic; if he did not distract their attention with anything whatever in the shape of a story, of incidents, or the usual literary machinery. Well, he has filled the book, and now, doubtless, with hand to ear, is listening intently.

Of course, the style of "What Maisie Knew" is not obscure at all; that is, there is no sentence in it whose meaning does not become clear and whose perfection is not obvious when you read it over the second time and get the accents and inflections properly adjusted. Difficulty, not obscurity, is the term to use, and the thing itself is highly enjoyable—for a hundred pages or so and for those who are not "average readers." After a while, however, the reviewing of sentences begins to pall upon one, and into one's mind creeps an inquiry whether lucidity of style is not a quality so precious that its voluntary abandonment by an author is unpardonable. And, as if to lend vigor to this problem, Mr. James has maliciously used short words almost exclusively, has fairly rioted in monosyllables. "If you can't catch my idea at a glance you must be stupid indeed," he seems to say—which is most aggravating, as he doubtless knows, and not the less so because here and there, thickly, he has sprinkled gems of simplicity, flashing with wit, with truth, or with the radiance of absolute newness. Surely much can be, must be, forgiven the man who, at this late day, invents a simile so supernaturally apt as that by which Mr. James makes clear Maisie's position: "Only a drummer boy in a ballad or a story could have been so in the thick of the fight." The wonder of that achievement lies in what now looks like its inevitability. Anybody could have written it—and nobody ever did! Lines almost as good can be found in the book by the hundred, and yet the hint of weariness made some paragraphs ago shall not be withdrawn.

Now, as to the people whom Mr. James introduces. They are a queer lot, certainly, and about their high average of "horridness" there can be no doubt. Maisie herself is an innocent enough small monster, but still a monster; the four or five others—barring one old woman who may be decent, but none the less is grotesque—pair, unpair, and pair again with the calm unmorality characteristic of the barnyard. They would excite general disapprobation in a Sixth Avenue restaurant at 2 A.M. Still, the repeatedly mentioned average reader will, as ever, be mistaken in calling the book morally squalid. Exquisite workmanship is never that, and "What Maisie Knew" is perfect in every detail. As Mr. James did not concern himself about anything except details, it is rather absurd to find fault with his product as a whole.

He has deigned to perform for an evening as a literary juggler, and he has played the rôle with artistic realization and observance of its natural limits. There is no "lesson" in his divertissement, no information, no edification; only deftness, productive of "Ah's" and "Oh's." He can afford to do this once in a way, because we all know that he is capable of real writing; that he can demonstrate the possession of other and higher powers than ingenuity. It will be well, however, for him to resist hereafter the temptation that lies in the consciousness of his virtuosity. His graver admirers long ago learned to take his mastery of means and method for granted, and prefer that he should elicit from them something else than exclamations.

"What Maisie Knew." Literary World [Boston] 28 (11 December 1897), 454–55.

Mr. Henry James, it is reported, remarked lately to a friend that he had reached that point in his literary career when he could write exactly what he liked. The first uses to which he has put this newly attained freedom seem to us regrettable; being, firstly, his paper on Du Maurier,[1] an orphic utterance, unintelligible except to the initiated, and secondly, the novel whose name heads this paper.

What Maisie Knew is of a quality incredible in a writer whose work has heretofore been, morally, beyond reproach. In what it says, still more in what it suggests, it ranks, except for a terrible underlying dullness, with the worst schools of French fiction. Maisie is a little child, not more than five or six years old, when her parents obtain a mutual divorce with an agreement that she shall divide her year equally between them. In the six months spent with her worthless father she hears her mother's name daily mentioned with oaths and foulest reproach. Going thence to an equally worthless mother, she learns, in language only less profane and foul, that her father is a profligate wretch. Neither spares one detail of coarse objurgation for pity at her helpless babyhood. Presently, the pretty governess, hired by the mother, follows Maisie to the home of the father and becomes that father's mistress. A little later the mother makes a second marriage. Husband No. 2, a goodnatured person, as weak and dissipated as, but less violent than, his predecessor, takes a fancy to the little girl, and she learns to adore him. She also adores the ex-governess, her father's mistress and later his wife. When, therefore, father No. 1 deserts wife No. 2, and goes to live with (and on) a third lady, and mother No. 1, having tried a variety of lovers (all with Maisie's knowledge and connivance), elopes with the latest, and father No. 2 and mother No. 2 form a connection, Maisie, by this time nine years old or so, sees no harm in the arrangement. She talks the situation over with her governess, and is prepared to accept it happily.

Such a plot seems inconceivable. Its author exhibits not one ray of pity or dismay at this spectacle of a child with the pure current of its life thus poisoned at its source. To him she is merely the *raison d'être* of a curiously complicated situation, which he can twist and untwist for purposes of fiction. One feels in the reading that every manly feeling, every possibility of generous sympathy, every comprehension of the higher standards, has become atrophied in Mr. James's nature from long disuse, and that all relation between him and his kind has perished except to serve him coldly by way of "material."

It goes without saying that the style of the book is jerkily incoherent. The characters, Maisie included, converse in vague inuendoes, and, as no answer is promised "in the next number," the readers of the story—may they be few—will probably never understand exactly what any one concerned said or did or meant. This is just as well, for what little one is able to understand is alike repellent to taste and feeling, to law and gospel.

Note

1 "George Du Maurier," *Harper's New Monthly Magazine* 95 (September 1897), 594–609.

Illustrated London News 111 (25 December 1897), 924.

In his latest fiction, which appeared originally in the *New Review*, Mr. Henry James seems to have been trying an experiment which cannot be pronounced successful.[1] It may be described as an attempt to make very uninteresting persons interesting by the sheer force of the novelist's will. The heroine, Maisie, who in the course of the story never emerges from comparatively early girlhood, is the only child of "Society" parents, who are no better than they should be, and who are divorced in the first chapter. Husband and wife marry again, but each is faithless to the new spouse, though without a second scandal in the Divorce Court. At first Maisie leads a neglected life, one half of the year with her father and the other with her mother, both of them equally worthless. When they marry again she is bandied about between her step-father, her mother's second husband, and her step-mother, her father's second wife, also a worthless pair. The step-father is kind to her after a fashion, and at last a tender feeling towards him grows up in Maisie's youthful breast, but only for her to discover at the end of the volume that he is resolved to throw her overboard and to cling to her step-mother, whose husband has deserted her, and with whom her step-father has been flirting desperately. This is all the story, which is without anything that can be called incident or plot. The volume consists mainly of a chronicle of the unedifying sayings and doings of Maisie's parents and of her step-father and step-mother, diversified by endless dialogues between her and a vulgar *gouvernante* respecting the sayings and doings aforesaid. The heroine herself is by no means a striking or interesting young person. "What Maisie Knew" at the end of the book more than at the beginning was that her relatives were disreputable people, and that a dissipated young man preferred the society of a handsome, artful, and experienced woman of the world to that of a chit of a girl, with nothing but prettiness and simplicity to make her attractive. And it is for such an insignificant result that a man of Mr. James's long-acknowledged ability as a writer of fiction and reputation for skill in "psychological analysis" has taken the trouble to write an elaborately tedious book.

Note

1 *New Review* 16 (February–June 1897), 113–28, 241–63, 352–72, 469–90, 581–602; 17 (July–September 1897), 1–20, 216–40, 334–56. Leon Edel and Dan H. Laurence, *A Bibliography of Henry James, Third Edition* (Oxford: Clarendon Press, 1982), no. D480, explain that the *New Review* text differs significantly from the *Chap Book* version of *What Maisie Knew.*

"*What Maisie Knew.*" *Critic* 32 (8 January 1898), 21.

The lids of this harmless-looking volume, sober in gray and gold, inclose one of the most astonishing literary *tours de force* the present generation has been privileged to behold. Mr. James has occupied himself for the two years past with some remarkable experiments in themes and methods, but his latest achievement is also his most startling. With the greatest respect for Mr.

James and for the heroine of his new volume, it may be added that he has done other things better calculated to add to the gayety of nations than this curious and wonderful study of the mental processes of a sadly-wronged but exquisitely right-minded child.

The book is a piece of alchemy rather than a novel. If the author does not exactly turn dross into gold, he performs the equally extraordinary feat of transmuting the waste material of society into something hard and clean and brilliant. Four of the chief characters are impossible persons of incredibly abandoned conduct, but by the simple expedient of filtering their complicated and corrupt story through the mind of a child, who apprehends neither morality nor immorality, but only kindness or cruelty, vulgarity or refinement, it is presented to the reader who is wiser than Maisie, as void of offence as it came to her. One veteran novel-consumer was heard to complain that in the process of passing through Maisie's brain the offending personages lost all the interest attaching to wickedness, and it is certain that they move before one flatly and jerkily, like a procession of shadow pictures thrown upon a screen. They are Punch and Judy figures in two dimensions only, not rounded sinners of flesh and blood, but this appearance is only one tribute the more to the marvellous success of the psychological feat Mr. James has performed in inclosing himself in the child's mind and ascertaining her point of view of the tragic comedy of Beale and Ida Farange.

When we meet Maisie first, as a child of six, her parents have been separated after resounding proceedings in the divorce court. Subsequent litigation to determine the custody of the child has resulted in a division of her year between them, six months to each, apparently because neither is fit for the entire charge of a child. They want her "for the harm they could with her unconscious aid do each other," and the fact that Maisie passes from one to the other unscathed is eloquent as to the quality of the clay of which she is illogically wrought. The first important discovery of her abused little life is that she is not obliged to repeat to one parent the revilings the other has poured into her ears.

She encounters affection for the first time in her life in the person of a beautiful governess, Miss Overmore. Unfortunately, Miss Overmore later also encounters affection in the person of Beale Farange, whom she meets when walking with Maisie. Ultimately these two marry, while Maisie's mother unites herself with a certain splendid and fascinating Sir Claude, a man who has a vocation for the family life which his wife does not encourage. Sir Claude, who calls upon his step-daughter at her father's house, wins her heart at once, as she does his. Unfortunately, also, a similar exchange takes place between himself and the resplendent Mrs. Beale Farange, née Overmore. Ultimately Beale Farange "bolts" to America with a third woman; Ida "bolts" to South Africa, and Maisie is left to choose between her step-parents, whose connection the exigency of English law condemns to remain irregular, and her incompetent, ludicrous, but devoted and absolutely respectable governess, Mrs. Wix, who has labored heroically to save Sir Claude's soul and inspire Maisie with a "moral sense." And Maisie, who has taken for granted all the horrors through which she has passed, and with whom the judgments of the world have no weight, Maisie, wise and innocent, chooses with wrenching of the heart-strings to go with Mrs. Wix. In other words, she knows, by what amounts to inspiration, that the conventions of which she has only heard in their transgressions, are necessary, inevitable, right, the one appropriate shelter for a woman-child's life.

This is the supreme and final thing that Maisie knows. And, certainly, it is the end of wisdom.

The skill and tenderness with which Mr. James has handled this unheard-of plot go far toward winning his pardon for the atrocity of having devised it. He does not lose one of its numberless opportunities for humor or pathos. The book is one more master-piece from a pen that produces little else. If at moments it becomes a slightly tedious master-piece, that is only another proof of its perfection. Maisie's parents are naturally tiresome, and her step-parents are not exempt from the same curse. To be wicked is generally to be vulgar, and it is also at times to be interesting—but not in the eyes of the Maisies. The preservation of Maisie's point of view necessarily involves the occasional weariness of the reader, but this is a price that he pays gladly. It is not much to give for the pleasure of beholding Mr. James's marvelous feats of skill.

But the book has a value beyond its wonderful technical worth. The unconscious moral sanity of childhood needs no justification, and the basic principles of society are amply able to defend themselves. Mr. James means nothing so impertinent or inartistic as to justify the one directly or to defend the other by implication, and it would be impertinent too, in a critic, to commend such a piece of art on the assumption that it was obviously designed to be ethically instructive. Nevertheless the satisfying fact remains that this master-piece, like all others, must, by the eternal law of art, exalt, in its last analysis, the sanities and delicacies of our life.

[Annie R. M. Logan].
Nation 66 (17 February
1898), 135.

Mr. James's 'What Maisie Knew,' if told directly, might be entitled 'What Maisie Didn't Know,' and would be no more fit for publication than is the evidence given before divorce courts sitting in camera. The device of unfolding a tale, not only without a moral, but without morals, through analysis of impressions made on the mind and character of a child, thrusts the burden of impropriety on the mind of the reader. For, however wide awake a child may be, it is blind as a bat to the cause of certain effects, such as a constant change and exchange of presumptive and ostensible fathers and mothers, coming about without a death in the family. The gross facts of the relations between the men and women who assume the parental attitude towards Maisie have no sort of attraction for Mr. James, and he rigorously confines himself to Maisie's point of view, her observations of and reflections upon the rather monstrous persons for whom, at a very tender age, she perceives herself to be "a centre of hatred and messenger of insult." Whether it is natural or probable for a child to have accepted and used such circumstances in the way that Maisie did, no one can say with any positiveness. To maintain any respect for humanity, her case must be considered as unique, with nothing in the records of the race to select for comparison. The fact that she never excites an emotion of compassion or pity, may be taken as an indication that she is neither natural nor probable. As we follow her interpretations of marriage and divorce, and of connections demanding one or the other or both, we get to feel that she is an arbitrary, artificial construction, and that the author, fascinated by an experiment, did not realize that he was being beaten.

The method is experimental, and, considering its very great difficulties, cannot be called a failure. The passive Maisie is the centre of action, the bone of contention, and the innocent, confidential agent through whom alone her abandoned guardians reveal themselves to each other and to the public. So far as the guardians are concerned, the revelation is complete, and it is their vivid presentation in this indirect fashion that justifies the experiment. In phrase and comparison, Mr. James is even unusually brilliant, but falls too often into alarming passages, through whose clauses and parentheses few are gifted enough to find a way. It is a sad moment for a writer when he mistakes obscure diction for subtle thought, and Mr. James is confronted with this moment more than once in 'What Maisie Knew.'

Checklist of Additional Reviews

Bookman [England] 13 (October 1897), 22.

"Fiction Supplement." *Academy* [England] (16 October 1897), 89. Reprinted in Roger Gard, ed., *Henry James: The Critical Heritage* (London: Routledge & Kegan Paul, 1968), p. 269.

"Book Reviews Reviewed." *Academy* [England] (23 October 1897), 332.

Literature [England] 1 (23 October 1897), 19. Partially reprinted in Arthur Sherbo, "Still More on James," *Henry James Review* 12 (1991), 101–2.

Chicago *Times-Herald,* 30 October 1897, p. 9.

Brooklyn *Daily Eagle,* 31 October 1897, p. 16.

Providence *Sunday Journal,* 31 October 1897, p. 15.

New York *Commercial Advertiser,* 6 November 1897, p. 12.

New York *Sun,* 6 November 1897, p. 6.

Portland *Morning Oregonian,* 7 November 1897, p. 12.

New York *Tribune,* 7 November 1897, Supp., p. 9.

Annie W. Sanborn. St. Paul *Daily Pioneer Press,* 7 November 1897, p. 18.

San Francisco *Call,* 7 November 1897, p. 23.

Outlook 57 (13 November 1897), 670.

St. Louis *Republic,* 13 November 1897, p. 4.

New Orleans *Daily Picayune,* 17 November 1897, p. 6.

Hartford *Courant,* 25 November 1897, p. 13.

Literary World [England] 56 (26 November 1897), 420–21.

Louisville *Courier-Journal,* 27 November 1897, p. 7.

Everard J. Appleton. Cincinnati *Commercial Tribune,* 28 November 1897, p. 27.

"*What Maisie Knew.*" San Francisco *Chronicle,* 28 November 1897, p. 4.

Book News 16 (December 1897), 289.

Review of Reviews 16 (December 1897), 727.

Congregationalist, 82 (2 December 1897), 860.

"Droch" [Robert Bridges]. *Life* 30 (9 December 1897), 518.

Independent 49 (16 December 1897), 1660.

London *Times,* 25 December 1897, p. 6.

Public Opinion 23 (30 December 1897), 855.

London *Echo,* 31 December 1897, p. 1.

Book Buyer 16 (February 1898), 66–68.

Bookman [New York] 6 (February 1898), 562.

THE TWO MAGICS

Literature [England] 52
(15 October 1898), 351.

It is not our fault if we fail to understand Mr. James' new book. He leaves everything unexplained. We cannot say with any confidence why the volume, which contains in one cover two generically dissimilar stories, should be called, as a whole. "The Two Magics," or why one half of it should be entitled "The Turn of the Screw." Nor are we sure whether these two stories are thus associated fortuitously or from design. All we know is that while "The Turn of the Screw" supplies the author with a most recondite subject, and exhibits his subtlest powers, the second story, "Covering End," is as conventional as an ordinary stage comedy.

The first half of the book, "The Turn of the Screw," is so astonishing a piece of art that it can hardly be described. It is fiction . . . but it is not a novel; it is full of apparitions, generally in broad daylight, but it is not a ghost story. Its subject, we hope, will not become a common motive with novelists, for it is nothing less than the demoniac possession of two young and otherwise delightful children, a boy and a girl, the elder of them barely ten years old. About a year ago we noticed Mr. James' other remarkable study of abnormal childhood; but "What Maisie Knew" was a trifle compared to the weird knowledge of little Miles and Flora. The tale is told by the new governess, a girl of twenty. She is employed by the children's uncle, who lives in London, taking no interest in them whatever, to superintend them and manage the large old house in Essex in which they live. A stolid, middle-aged housekeeper is the young lady's only ally. She finds both the children exceptionally charming. But they are haunted and possessed by the ghosts, demons, or visible presence of an infamous former valet of their father's, and an infamous former governess of their own, in horrible cooperation; and these familiar appearances do not appal either the children themselves or their new governess. So far as there is a story, the trials of the new governess (she has no name) form the story. Its end seems, as regards the boy, tragical; and, as regards the girl, inconclusive. The boy dies, after a striking scene in which the new governess rids him of the demon; the girl is merely taken away in a carriage by the housekeeper, and it is uncertain whether her end, logically, is peace. We cannot enter into the morbid psychology of such a work as this. The question is whether, given the impossible circumstances, the action and reaction of good and evil in childhood, for that, perhaps, is what it all comes to in the last resort, is well described. Yet we are doubtful whether this is really the problem, partly because the subject does not admit of any plain statement of it, and partly because Mr. James, though one of the most interesting of writers, is not also the most lucid.

But what of the Two Magics? The second story, "Covering End" (the name of a country house), bears all the marks of Mr. James' style and is, therefore, literature, like the rest of his work. All the same, it is just such a story as an inferior writer might tell with almost equal effect. In fact, it is impossible not to see that twenty-five years ago it would have been played admirably at the Haymarket Theatre, with Buckstone, Howe, and Mr. and Mrs. Kendal in the four principal parts. Why has Mr. James, the artist, suddenly summoned to his artistic stage these old dramatic friends of ours—the embarrassed heir, the American widow, the old family servant, and the vulgar creditor? We look dubiously for the magic asserted by implication on the title-page. The thing at least is an antidote to the gloom and gruesomeness of "The Turn of the Screw." Shall we say, then, that it has a magic of its own, the magic of the possible, the human, the sane, and the commonplace, the magical attraction of that which is no magic at all?

"Mr. James's New Stories."
Athenaeum [England] 3704 (22 October 1898), 564–65.

The variety even more than the fertility of Mr. Henry James's imaginative power is sufficiently attested by the publication, within a month or two of one another, of these two books.[1] Except for one or two common characteristics, of which we shall speak, it is difficult to believe that the two volumes are by the same hand. In the first the story, thin as it is to begin with, is almost lost in the subtle research of phrasing and the torturing of sentiment which seem good to the author; whereas in the two stories contained in the other volume the crisp, definite outlines of the plot are never blurred, but stand out distinct in the masterly narratives. It is not at all that one book is bad as compared with the other; they are so different they can hardly be compared, but the one might almost be called a most laborious analysis of a suggestion, while the other contains two most vividly presented creations.

It has become almost hackneyed to talk of Mr. Henry James's subtlety; but there is no other word which so adequately expresses a constant quality in his work, and his use of this common quality in the two volumes before us illustrates better than anything else their real diversity. 'In the Cage' is an account of a telegraph girl's interest in two people's love story, which she guesses at from the telegrams she has to dispatch for them; she naturally falls half in love with the hero of the episode, but nothing comes of that except a charming conversation on a seat in Hyde Park. But the girl has to use the most extraordinary ingenuity to discover whatever she does of the story, and in her efforts she almost gets to talk and split logic as if she were the author himself. The fault of the story is that there is no adequate return for all the torturings of inquiry and expectation in it. The girl herself is charming; the greatest admiration is due to the author for the accumulation of delicate touches by which he shows her hunger for romance, her delight in knowledge, her perfect natural good taste joined to certain slight faults in breeding due to her surroundings, and her rigid command over her self-respect, even when venturing on a certain extravagance of conduct. But admitting all the charm of her character, one is inclined to think her too good to be squandered on the subtleties of a mystery which is never really cleared up. The whole story is set out with too vast an appendage of nods and hints and things kept back; and it ends in fizzle. What all the telegrams were about and what all the difficulties were we are no clearer at the end than at the beginning. As the author himself most excellently puts it,

> "She still seemed to wait for something—something in the key of the immense discussions that had mapped out their little week of idleness on the scale of a world atlas. Something came at last, but without perhaps appearing quite adequately to crown the monument."

It would be difficult to criticize the book better in a few words. The fact is that in such stories as these Mr. Henry James takes himself much too seriously. He has been interested in seeing telegraph clerks at work, he wonders what they know or guess of the secrets of which they have a glimpse, and so he sets to work to write a book in which he will pick one to pieces. It is true that he shows us the telegraph clerk, but with such an apparatus of confused plot and counterplot that her real charm is almost lost sight of; it is like using a steam-hammer to crack a nut. The very style reflects the difficulty; all through the book the phrases are tortured and obscure, parentheses abound, and it almost looks as if an attempt were being made to conceal the poverty of the idea in vast swaddling-clothes of verbiage. Take this sentence, from the very first page:—

> "That made it an emotion the more lively—though singularly rare and always, even then, with opportunity very much smothered—to see any one come in whom she knew, as she called it, outside, and who could add something to the poor identity of her function."

The idea intended to be conveyed is not particularly elaborate; but it would be hard to imagine a more involved and unemphatic way of conveying it.

But 'The Two Magics' is a very different sort of book. The first tale, 'The Turn of the Screw,' is one of the most engrossing and terrifying ghost stories we have ever read. It is a real creation, and the idea of it is quite novel. Briefly, it is about the influence which two evil ghosts have on the lives of two young children, and about the efforts made by their governess to overcome the sinister attacks. Here the author makes triumphant use of his subtlety; instead of obscuring, he only adds to the horror of his conception by occasion-

ally withholding the actual facts and just indicating them without unnecessarily ample details. A touch where a coarser hand would write a full-page description, a hint at unknown terrors where another would talk of bloody hands or dreadful crimes, and the impression is heightened in a way which would have made even Hawthorne envious on his own ground. And here, too, the style—braced up, as it were, to the task of not missing a detail of the author's effects—loses its flabbiness and indistinctness, and only gains in stimulating power where a curious turn of phrase is substituted for a more hackneyed expression.

The other story in the book, 'Covering End,' though not so striking as the first, is in its way excellently told. Here the vein is light. It is an account of how one of those ever-charming American women swoops down on an old family mansion, conquers it and its owner for her delightful self, and puts to rout the swelling vulgarity personified in the portentous solicitor Prodmore. The whole thing is almost a farce, even to the very names of the characters. Mr. Henry James condescends to paint-in his effects with the thickest of brushes; but it seems to do him good for once to kick over the traces of his over-anxious analyzing, and to indulge in a real frolic. And even in this his horror of the too much, which in his bad moments subtilizes away his effects to nothing, prevents the slightest touch of vulgarity: it is a charming piece, made all the more piquant by the occasional lapse into the elaborate style which he can never quite shake off.

Mr. Henry James has been publishing a great deal lately. This last book almost makes one hope that with an absence of too great deliberation in writing will come out more of the natural man, and less of the intricate criticism and of the excessive sense of the importance of his subject that have marred several of his later books.

Note

1 *In the Cage* (London: Duckworth, 1898) and *The Two Magics* (London: William Heinemann, 1898).

"Mr. James's New Book." *Bookman* [England] 15 (November 1898), 54.

Mr. James is in a queer mood. Nearly all his later stories have been tending to the horrible, have been stories of evil, beneath the surface mostly, and of corruption. His genius is essentially a healthy one, we have always felt, and he has had great respect in times past for the *convenances*. He does not outrage them now; his manners are perfect, even in his late studies of the putrescence of human existence. "What Maisie Knew" was one of these; but the story was a triumph of beauty in the end. Its theme was that purity and candour and joy could be strong enough in the heart of a young creature to counteract the miasma of the evil amid which she lived, not all unconscious either. His purpose was abundantly fulfilled. The first of the two stories here—the other hardly counts, though it is a readable enough extravaganza—is another study of the same unpleasant kind of fact, but so much more horrible, that it surely marks the climax of this darker mood, out of which Mr. James may emerge with a profounder, or perhaps only a bitterer strain. The situation of Maisie is reversed. The circumstances, the conditions, in "The Turn of the Screw," all make for purity, beauty, and joy; and on the surface these are resplendent. But underneath is a sink of corruption, never uncovered, but darkly, potently hinted. One's heart cries out against the picture of the terrible possibility; for the corrupted are children of tender years. Every inch of the picture seems an outrage in our first heat. Even in colder moments, if we admit the fact of infant depravity, if we own that children are supreme actors, and can bar doors on their elders most effectually, we must deny the continuity and the extent of the corruption as suggested here. Mr. James has used symbolism to help him out with his theme; so, at least, we may speak of the two ghosts—one of a rascally valet, the other of an iniquitous governess—the origins of the evil in their lifetime, who haunt the children after their death. Their horrible invitations to evil are joyfully responded to. We have never read a more sickening, a more gratuitously melancholy tale. It has all Mr. James's cleverness, even his grace. The plottings of the good governess and the faithful Mrs. Grose to combat the evil, very gradually discovered, are marvellously real. You cannot help but assist at their interviews, and throb with their anxiety. You are amply convinced of the extraordinary charm of the children, of the fascination they exercise over all with whom they come in contact. The symbolism is clumsy; but only there in the story has Mr. James actually failed. It is not so much from a misunderstanding of child nature that he has plunged into the deep mistake of writing the story at all. Here, as elsewhere in his work, there are unmistakable signs of a close watchfulness and a loving admiration of children of the more distinguished order. A theory has run away with him. It is flimsily built on a few dark facts, so scattered and uncertain that they cannot support a theory at all. He has used his amiable knowledge of child life in its brighter phases to give a brilliant setting to this theory. His marvellous subtlety lends his examination of the situation an air of scientific precision. But the clever result is very cruel and untrue.

"*The Two Magics.*" *Overland Monthly* 32 (November 1898), 493.

Those who like the weird will be fascinated by the *Turn of the Screw,* one of the two stories just published by Henry James through the Macmillan Company. The reader's hair will rise at the beginning of this remarkable tale, and it will not settle down comfortably even when the end is reached. Mr. James's style has become as interesting as a Chinese puzzle. It reminds one of George Meredith—with a difference. With the riveting of the reader's attention on every sentence on the one side, while the sensationalism of the story holds absorbingly on the other, Mr. James has reached a combination which is unique among story-tellers. The second story, "Covering End," is a faint reminder of "Daisy Miller"; but Mr. James's characters, in both ways and speech, have grown more intricate since Daisy Miller's time.

"*The Two Magics.*" Indianapolis *News,* 9 November 1898, p. 5.

The title of Henry James's recent volume is something of a puzzle; "The Two Magics" it is called, and it contains two stories, "The Turn of the Screw" and "Covering End." The first is a gruesome tale of a girl and a boy, possessed by the spirits of their governess and their uncle's valet, under whose care the children had been left, and of whose crime they had been dimly conscious, though wholly reticent. "Covering End" is the name of a beautiful, famous English country house, which is saved to its impoverished and indifferent owner by the money, shrewdness and tact of an American widow from "Missoura Top." There are two love stories mixed with the account of the widow's enthusiasm for the house and its treasures; one of which is begun and both are happily ended in half a dozen hours. What are "The Two Magics?" It does not much matter, since James retains his own magic, as this book is ample evidence that he does. There are people who are not susceptible to the influence of this magic, but that is their misfortune; the fault of no one. Those, however, who enjoy searching delicate humor, subtle analysis of emotion and motive, together with vivid portrayal of character and invariable good temper, will miss from "The Two Magics" none of Henry James's charm.

"Henry James as a Ghost Raiser." *Life* 32 (10 November 1898), 368.

Henry James has frequently given his readers shivers by the coldness with which he treats intense emotions. But it is a new thing for him to create a semblance of terror by a genuine story of "uncanny ugliness and horror and pain." In his latest volume, "The Two Magics" (Macmillan), he has shown what he can do with a tale of the Poe sort—and he does it extremely well. He calls the story "The Turn of the Screw," and he does not hesitate to give it the extra twist that makes the reader writhe under it. And when you sift the terror to its essential facts, there does not seem to be anything in it to make a fuss about. That two supremely beautiful children should be under the evil spell of the ghosts of a dead governess and a wicked valet is not, on the face of it, a very awe-inspiring situation. Indeed, the ludicrousness of it, in these enlightened days, is always in danger of breaking through the hedge which the author has ingeniously constructed around it.

But right there is the place for the literary artist to show what he can do—and Henry James does it in a way to raise goose-flesh! He creates the atmosphere of the tale with those slow, deliberate phrases which seem fitted only to differentiate the odors of rare flowers. Seldom does he make a direct assertion, but qualifies and negatives and double negatives, and then throws in a handful of adverbs, until the image floats away upon a verbal smoke. But while the image lasts, it is, artistically, a thing of beauty. When he seems to be vague he is by elimination creating an effect of terror, of unimaginable horrors.

While his art is present in every sentence, the artist is absolutely obliterated. His personality counts for nothing in the effect. He is like a perfect lens which focuses light, but is itself absolutely colorless.

"The Two Magics." Literary World [Boston] 29 (12 November 1898), 367–68.

It is seldom that one finds within the same covers two stories so widely different as these which make up Mr. James's last volume, with a difference which lies not in skill but in the very essence and spirit which make one a haunting horror and the other a delicately sweet memory. Like many of Mr. James's titles this one is suggestive rather than descriptive, but one reading proves the suggestion excellent, and the "Two Magics" are indeed two with a world between them and the two stories, "The Turn of the Screw" and "Covering End," which exemplify them.

We began the former tale in the early afternoon twilight, almost at the first page answering with a shudder and a creepiness to the hint of the gruesome to whose contemplation we were invited—a hint that had its fulfillment in such vividness that we were glad of circumstances that led us to finish the reading in the obtrusively human companionship of a crowded trolley car. However we may depreciate the art which does not permit happiness in its enjoyment, however strong may be our wish that the "society with the long name" should protect children from abuse in fiction as well as in life, we can nevertheless feel only admiration for the touch with which in this and an earlier instance Mr. James has depicted the child life and the child mind. If we can call "What Maisie Knew" a picture of purity in the midst of pollution, so we might call this story of poor little Miles and his sister Flora a picture of corruption in the midst of rare loveliness. The story is simple enough when you state the plot—two orphaned children with outward show of more than human perfection, who are in communication with two apparitions or rather familiar spirits; a homely, dear, old, English nurse; and a devoted governess whose love for her pupils strengthens her to shield them and to crush down her own fear. So stated, one will acknowledge the simplicity, but the horror and the ingenuity lie behind this simple outline. The spirit of the man who attacks the boy as that of the woman who visits the little sister is evil undiluted; in life they were in guilty association, guilty in their relations with each other and in their damnable and successful efforts to pervert in ways inexpressible the child minds intrusted to their care, and after their tragic deaths they were still united in their hellish endeavor to maintain their vile influence and to add to their own damnation that of the two child souls. And the subtle crowning horror is the joy with which the two children, supernaturally trained in deceit and hypocrisy, welcome their evil spirits, a joy so depraved in its suggestiveness as to be more gruesome than the most vividly imagined physical fear.

So much for one magic power, evil, destructive, hellish, and yet so skillfully, so moderately expressed that the art is still fine; and then in sharp and sudden contrast we feel the second, the magic charm of love at first sight. This plot, like the other, is simple, but here there is only sunshine with just enough shade to throw out the brightness; only a masterly raconteur could make a plain tale and an old one so charming as this. The setting is an ancient English "show" house, mortgaged to the last farthing of its value; the chief players are the penniless soldier-owner and a young and rich and charming American widow; the man and woman meet one afternoon as perfect strangers in the magnificent old hall of the manor; in scarce an hour they part as plighted lovers and the future of the old house is saved. Impossibly simple it sounds in our telling, but in Mr. James's it seems an inevitable "game of consequences" most charmingly related.

We often hear it is not so much what one says as how one says it that counts; although we cannot follow this statement to its length, we find our great enjoyment in Mr. James's book, and a genuine one,

more in the fashion of telling than in the story told. That one tale is horrible and repellent in its conception, and the other almost hackneyed in its familiarity, are facts not to be denied, but knowledge and power control alike the horrible and the commonplace, justifying each with a beauty of style that can bring unquestioned into close comparison and one judgment pictures that are as far separated as the powers of darkness and the powers of light.

H. W. Lanier. "Two Volumes from Henry James." *American Monthly Review of Reviews* 18 (December 1898), 732–33.

Mr. Henry James is represented this year by two volumes, exhibiting the extremes of his art. *In the Cage* (Stone), if any name less well known appeared on the title-page, might be pronounced stupid, strained, and overdrawn without much compunction. In the light of Mr. James' former work one can recognize some of its subtlety, some of its laboriously intricate analysis and complex psychology.

What a relief is it to turn from this dreary monotone to *The Two Magics!* This astonishing book contains two stories, "The Turn of the Screw" and "Covering End," and the present reviewer must confess to no little racking of brains in the search for the author's meaning in classing them together. Apparently the first shows the mysterious legacy of evil that may continue in force after death; the second that peculiar, manifold, and irresistible influence which breathes from a dwelling for many generations the habitation of a line of sturdy ancestors—or is it the "magic" of a charming woman's personality? Although, if either happen to be the right guess, the general title is not at all felicitous, and the two tales might far better go merely as a couple of stories; although the introduction to "The Turn of the Screw" seems a needlessly awkward method of starting the story. In spite of any criticisms that may be made, it is impossible to read this horribly absorbing narrative without recognizing that it is a notable achievement. It is in an entirely new vein for Mr. James and one in which his delicate, subtle psychology shows to best advantage, for the foul breath of the bottomless pit itself, which strikes the reader full in the face as he follows the plot, puts to shame by its penetrating force and quiet ghastliness the commonplace, unreal "horrors" of the ordinary ghost-story; it does indeed give an extra "turn of the screw" beyond anything of the sort that fiction has yet provided. There is something peculiarly against nature, something indescribably hellish in the thought of the beautiful little children holding unholy communion with the wraiths of two vile servants who had, when alive, corrupted them; and it would be difficult to find anything so unpretentious capable of producing such a living, vivid, indelible impression upon the mind. Let us hope that Mr. James will soon again give his unique gifts another chance in a field so congenial. To my mind it is the finest work he has ever done: there is a completeness, a finish, a sense of easy mastery and boundless reserve force about this story which are entirely fascinating. Looking back upon the tale when one has finished it, one instinctively compares it to a beautiful pearl: something perfect, rounded, calm, unforgettable. It would not require a rash prophet to predict that

The Two Magics (Macmillan) will outweigh a score of such books as *In the Cage* in the future estimate of later nineteenth-century literature.

Illustrated London News 113 (3 December 1898), 834.

Of "Covering End," the second tale in "The Two Magics," one can but say it is an agreeable, sentimental farce, not in Mr. James's best manner, yet amusing enough. The first one, "The Turn of the Screw," is quite in his best manner. He has rarely written anything so subtle, so delicate in workmanship, so intense in feeling, so entirely artistic. And what a subject has he chosen to spend all this art and emotion upon! There are readers, we believe, who have faced the horrible in several literatures, and who will come to the conclusion that Mr. James has capped it all. The subject will outrage many minds far from prudish, with its sickening suggestion of evil nestling in the fairest of all fair places, the souls of little children. To us it appears gratuitously painful. But the land of art is wide and free, and we cannot say it excludes studies of morbidity and of demoniac possession. As such must we describe this story to ourselves, if we are to tolerate it at all. The children, a gifted, beautiful, fascinating pair, are in the thrall of a dead man and woman, whose lives were loathsome. They act their pretty parts of innocent babes to perfection; but the love of two good women probes beneath their beauty, and finds the sink of corruption. When one fair witch is discovered (in a scene as haunting as any medieval tale of devilry) her beauty fades; the evil within looks out boldly at the world. Her brother's little soul becomes a battle-field of struggling forces, good and bad. The malignant spirit is worsted, but the price of victory is death. There is something really great in the story, and assuredly the skill is superb. But surely we are not merely sentimentalists in our protest against children being made the pawns in this horrible contest.

T.S.
"The Two Magics."
London *Review*, 3 December 1898, pp. 17–18.

Now and then the tired and jaded reviewer strikes an oasis in the vast desert of modern literary fiction-making; when he does, he sighs contentedly and sits down to enjoy the cool shade, and abandons himself to the delight born of the new surroundings. He cools his mouth with the fresh waters of the spring, and the clean palate recovers its natural taste. This, perhaps, may suggest the effect made upon us by reading and re-reading Mr. Henry James's latest work.

The volume consists of two tales. The first—"The Turn of the Screw"—may be described as a fascinating ghost story. The second—"Covering End"—is best characterised as a one-act play in narrative form. But why "The Two Magics"? The title seems to have puzzled not a few readers. We take it, however, that Mr. James, in his first tale, has attempted to show the working of that spiritual and incomprehensible influence, which is the outcome of our real or ideal relations with what, for want of a better name, we call "spirits." It is a story of that magic which comes to us from across the "borderland"—from "the dead," as we say. The second tale, on the other hand, deals with the living magic, just as spiritual and just as incomprehensible, which radiates from the activity of a gifted, beautiful, and great-hearted woman. That is our explanation of the title; and be it the writer's or not, it will suffice for a clear enjoyment of these two almost perfect pieces of storytelling.

"The Turn of the Screw" tells of a governess who is left in sole charge of two very beautiful children—a boy and a girl. Miles and Flora are not common children; but then they are placed in uncommon circumstances, and live in uncommon relationships. A previous governess and a valet who had lived in the house with these children had both died in strange ways—how, no one knows. They had lived unholy lives together, even while they could affect the natures of the two children; and in the midst of their wickedness had been taken from this earth. Thus the evil influence they exerted when alive they continue to exercise after their death—they haunt the house both by day and night. The children seem gifted with quite a devilish ingenuity for smoothing the way for clandestine meetings with these "ghosts," and calmly, fearlessly, and innocently evade giving any information. The new governess suffers very tragedy in the knowledge that Miles and Flora are actually lying and scheming to hoodwink her. She has herself seen both the "ghosts," and even caught the children in their company; but she is at a loss how to right matters for them and herself. For "saying things" the boy had been sent home from school; and yet she cannot believe that a child with so innocent a face could be wicked. A clue to the truth comes to her at last; but how to make Miles confess to the truth? The confession, however, comes, and with it the governess suddenly realises, as if by an inspiration, what it is from which the boy suffers. Mr. James's expression of this realisation is a wonderful piece of work, forming a brave climax to a brave story.

To turn from this to the tale of the charming old house, "Covering End," is to awaken from the spell of the black wand of a wizard only to be entranced by a fairy's touch. Captain Yule, the nominal owner of his ancestral home, "Covering End," comes into his estate to find it mortgaged up to the hilt to Mr. Podmore, a gentleman with a commercial soul and social ambitions. To realise these ambitions without doing hurt to his instincts, Mr. Podmore asks the Captain to meet him at "Covering End," for the purpose, as it transpires, of arranging a marriage between him and his daughter Cora. The daughter is also invited by the father to come, but she is delayed a little owing to an appointment which she keeps with her sweetheart. On her way to the house she meets, in the train, a young American widow who has a passion for visiting "the stately homes of England"; but she turns up in time to receive from her father his plans for her future. Then come the scenes between Mr. Podmore and Captain Yule, between Mr. Podmore and his daughter, and between Miss Podmore and Captain Yule—all excellently well-staged and charged with delightful dialogue. One can understand the play and stress of the emotions between a money-grabbing, overriding, and ambitious father and unwilling daughter, and a clean-hearted but helpless English gentleman. Right into this atmospheric disturbance shoots the one ray of sunlight in the person of Mrs. Gracedew, the young American widow, and wherever she moves she transfigures. She is the gracious influence by which, finally, all is rightly placed and happily settled "for ever and a day." If our readers wish to enjoy a genuine play at home and by their own firesides they should read "Covering End."

Now, apart from these stories as stories, "The Two Magics" stands witness to the power of a great artist. If the elaboration of their plot-schemes has the effect of gradually but surely overpowering us in ever-progressing interest, they produce a yet more convincing proof of Mr. James's mastership in the literary craft by the persuasive charm and perfect fitness of their form-expressions. Nothing could be subtler than the way in which Mr. James identifies the objects say, in a room, with the emotions of the person who is looking at them. Dead things are made living by means of the relations in which these stand to personalities, and take on themselves the moods of the thinking men and women, and so contributing their quota to the "atmosphere" of the story. The simplicity of this portrait of Chivers, the family servant at "Covering End," following a description of his surroundings, is exquisite:—

His re-appearance interrupts, and yet in a manner, after all, quickens our intense impression; Chivers on the spot, and in this severe but spacious setting, was so perfect an image of immemorial domesticity . . . Considerably shrunken and completely silvered, he had perpetual agreement in the droop of his kind white head, and perpetual inquiry in the jerk of the idle old hands, now almost covered by the sleeves of the black dress-coat which, twenty years before, must have been by a century or two the newest thing in the house, and into which his years appeared to have declined very much as a shrunken family moves into a part of its habitation. [1898 Macmillan ed., pp. 221–22]

We get Chivers complete if we couple that with this:

Chivers seemed to scan impartially the whole field. "If you could just only *tell* me, sir! I quite seem to waste away—for some one to take an order of."

Clement Yule by this time had become aware he was amusing. "Who pays your wages?"

"No one at all, sir," said the old man, very simply. . . . "I think it does, old boy." [1898 Macmillan ed., pp. 260–61]

Every touch gives just the very message it was intended it should. Mr. James's fine taste for effect is only equalled by the fine quality with which it is charged. The seeming complexity is, in reality, a deft arrangement of the very simplest elements, leaving the impressing of a satisfying harmony.

Mr. James's title for this book is, after all, a modest one. Instead of "The Two" he might have said "The Three Magics"; for above that of "spirits" and above that of woman is the magic of the artist who fashions both "spirit" and woman.

London *Times,* 28 December 1898, p. 10.

A ghost story ought to be short, persuasive, and in harmony, nowadays, with the provisional conclusions of psychical science. The best fictitious ghost stories, like Lord Lytton's "The Haunters and the Haunted" and Mrs. Oliphant's "Old Lady Mary," fulfill these conditions, as does Scott's "Tapestried Chamber." A ghost, of all things, ought to avoid making himself too cheap. Now, Mr. Henry James's tale, "The Turn of the Screw," in his newest volume, THE TWO MAGICS, is not short (169 pages), is not persuasive (we could

read it unmoved at midnight in a haunted house), it is not in conformity with the results of science, and the ghosts are too punctual and frequent. Out of the vast collections of phantasms brought together by the S.P.R., almost no sign of purpose on the ghost's side is offered, and when he may be suspected of a purpose he scarcely ever manages to make its nature intelligible. He somnambulizes, so to speak, in a restless, incoherent dream. On the other hand Mr. James's two phantasms have their purpose sun-clear before them and are most pertinacious. Their idea is to corrupt two very nice children, brother and sister. The male ghost is that of Peter Quint, a bad menial; the lady ghost is that of his mistress, recently governess to the children. These are pretty ideas for a fable! The narrative is supposed to be written, many years ago, by another governess, who had developed Mr. James's style, down to an occasional Americanism. She can, and often does, see both ghosts, and the interest of the tale lies in the cunning with which the children (attached to the ghosts) battle her efforts to separate them from "the hideous author of our woe, the white face of damnation." Quint has already caused the expulsion of the boy from his private school, where his conversation was undesirable. Alas, little boys need no Quint to make them talk in a style that would disgust an Apache. The narrative concludes with the death of the poor little boy and the removal of his sister from home. But are ghosts purely local? One is recorded to have followed a family from Brompton to Bayswater, and the banshee of an Irish house has turned up in Barbados and India. If the defunct governess was not purely local there would be no use in removing the little girl. In short, a ghost story does not seem to be within Mr. James's artistic resources. If Mr. James's friend, mentioned at the opening to the story, knows only one case of a child seeing a phantasm, he must be inexpert in these matters. The other story in the book, "Covering End," tells how the irresistible American lady of fiction prevents an old and beautiful English country seat from going out of the family into the possession of a Mr. Prodmore. This personage is not unlike Dickens's Mr. Bounderby, and other characters of that blatant species. He is not, in his conversational style, very like any known type of Briton. The tale aims at rather broad-blown effects, and, like its companion, is unpersuasive, and *difficile à croire.*

Munsey's Magazine 20 (February 1899), 823.

Henry James has made a tenstrike with his new book, "The Two Magics." And yet only half of the book can be called good, for it consists of two long stories, one of which is woefully dull. The other, entitled "The Turn of the Screw," is one of the most original ghost stories ever written, and absolutely the most modern. The style is involved, for Henry James has lost his former clarity and simplicity, and the ending, as is the case with so many of his tales, is exasperating; nevertheless, the story is brilliantly entertaining, and it has set the critics in both England and our country to renewing their praises of this expatriated American novelist. Mr. James is a writer of whom it is probably true to say that he has always been more popular with the critics than with the public at large.

Chautauquan [Buffalo] 28 (March 1899), 630.

In a volume entitled "The Two Magics" are two tales very unlike in character. The first one is "The Turn of the Screw," in which the author, Henry James, again displays his skill as a delineator of psychic phenomena. In this particular story the theme is the continued influence on two children of a disreputable governess and her accomplice after their disappearance and the discovery of this influence by another governess who is keenly sensitive to psychic impulses. The intangible is here painted with a skill little short of the supernatural, and in dealing with these subtleties of the mind the author has produced a tale whose suggestiveness makes the blood bound through the veins with unusual rapidity. In the second story, which, in comparison with the first, takes on a farcical character, Mr. James has employed a clearer, less complicated syntax, and, improbable as the story is, the reader enjoys the sensation of easily comprehending the meaning the author wishes to convey.

Checklist of Additional Reviews

Manchester *Guardian*, 11 October 1898, p. 4.
New York *Tribune*, 23 October 1898, supp., p. 14.
Detroit *Free Press*, 24 October 1898, p. 7.
Outlook 60 (29 October 1898), 537.
  Reprinted in Robert Kimbrough, ed.,

The Turn of the Screw: Norton Critical Edition (New York: W. W. Norton), pp. 171–72.

Springfield [Mass.] *Republican,* 30 October 1898, p. 8.

Book Notes [New York] 1 (November 1898), 331.

Annie W. Sanborn. St. Paul *Daily Pioneer Press,* 6 November 1898, 26.

Portland *Morning Oregonian,* 13 November 1898, p. 22.

New Orleans *Daily Picayune,* 27 November 1898, p. 10.

Sketch [England] 24 (30 November 1898), 220.

Ainslee's Magazine 2 (December 1898), 516–19. Reprinted in Kimbrough, p. 173.

Hamilton W. Mabie. *Book Buyer* 17 (December 1898), 437.

Critic 33 (December 1898), 523–24.

Reprinted in Roger Gard, ed., *Henry James: The Critical Heritage* (London: Routledge & Kegan Paul, 1968), p. 276; Kimbrough, pp. 173–74.

[Annie R. M. Logan]. *Nation* 67 (8 December 1898), 432.

Literary World [England] 58 (9 December 1898), 456.

Graphic [England] 58 (10 December 1898), 756.

"Book Reviews Reviewed." *Academy* [England] 1391 (31 December 1898), 561.

Edward Ackermann. *Book Notes* 2 (January 1899), 48–49.

Dixie (January 1899), 59–60.

Sewanee Review 7 (January 1899), 124.

Independent 51 (5 January 1899), 73. Reprinted in Kimbrough, p. 175.

Ainslee's Magazine 3 (February 1899), 112.

THE AWKWARD AGE

Manchester *Guardian*, 2
May 1899, p. 4.

Mr. Henry James once wrote a highly ingenious and wholly delightful short story
called, if we remember rightly, "The Pattern on the Carpet." [1] It was the story of a
great master of fiction, such a master as
occurs more than once in Mr. James's
work, who was frank enough and uncau-
tious enough to inform his most ardent
"appreciator" that neither he nor anyone
else had seized the one important point
that made the real merit of all the novels
that he and the rest pretended to admire.
There was a "secret," a something everywhere patent to the enlightened eye, but
latent, it appeared, for all the world; and
this mysterious something was likened to
the pattern running through all the colours and the splendours of an Eastern carpet. And we must confess that this fable
seems to us to apply to Mr. James's latest
novel, *The Awkward Age* (William Heinemann, 8vo, pp. 414, 6s.). To us it seems
enigma, the very quintessence of riddle;
and yet one has the sense that there is an
answer, that behind all the subtleties, the
questions indicated and not asked, the answers that are to be guessed at but are not
given, the reckoning up of character that
seems "worked" rather by logarithms
than by the common rules—that behind
and beneath all this there is a very definite
meaning, and a purpose that is quite clear
to the author's understanding. "The Awkward Age" is the story of a group of Lon-
doners in "society." The old Mr. Longdon, once the "flame" (he would almost
have used the word) of Lady Julia, mother
of Mrs. "Brook," as the characters call her,
and grandmother of Nanda, returns to the
world after a long retirement in Suffolk,
and he is at once enchanted by the very
striking physical likeness that Nanda
bears to the fine, gracious, and gay lady of
the mid-Victorian period whom he had so
ardently worshipped. But he finds the girl
just emerging from the background where
her mother has kept her into the midst of
the singular coterie which gathers round
Mrs. Brookenham. It is, to put it gently, a
coterie which is continually skating on the
thinnest ice with the keenest enjoyment of
the sport; it is a circle where "revolting"
French novels lie on drawing-room tables,
which has members (of opposite sexes)
who have to be "asked together;" it is a
society which would infinitely prefer anni-
hilation to plain speech on any conceivable subject. Well, Mr. Longdon wishes to
rescue Nanda by means of the epigrammatic but apparently more worthy Vanderbank, but the scheme breaks through;
and the last chapter, the uncertain crown
of many uncertainties, leaves one hesitating whether Mr. Longdon has redeemed
Nanda or whether, perhaps, she has not
rather corrupted him. On this general plan
(always assuming that we have correctly
gathered even so much) Mr. James has
constructed his story, or rather his study,
and from this theme, which might seem
simple enough, he has elaborated his intricate and wonderful composition, much in
the manner of Palestrina elaborating a
whole Mass from the first notes of a
plainsong hymn. It is amazing in its way,
a triumphant exercise in the art of hinting,
but it breeds in the mind of the reader a
wild desire to take a chapter or two of
"Rob Roy" afterwards with a view to correcting the subtlety. The book is written in
a style that strikes one as tiny, delicate, sincere; and if Mr. James really knows the
prototypes of his characters there is one
great consolation that he may lay to his
heart. In the coterie there was a fine of a
five-pound note exacted from anyone who
made an obvious epigram; only one instance of the enforcement of this rule is re-

corded, and certainly the author of "The Awkward Age" need feel himself in no danger of this score.

Note

1 "The Figure in the Carpet," *Cosmopolis* 1 (January–February 1891), 41–59, 373–92. Reprinted in *Embarrassments* (1896).

"Mr. Henry James Exasperates."
Pall Mall Gazette [England], 8 May 1899, p. 4.

Perhaps the surest way to induce a novice to Mr. Henry James's work never to attempt another book of his would be to start the patient with "The Awkward Age." As is always more or less true of Mr. James, the attraction of his style and substance (the two are almost inextricably one) fights a continuous battle with their irritation. And in this case, while attraction wins throughout to the extent of urging persistence in reading, irritation wins the rubber decisively as the book is closed. Both in substance and verbal style he proves himself, as ever, a master of shades and suggestions. A delicate little touch here, a scarcely perceptible change in pressure there, a slight deflection of line not to be detected, except under the microscope, and he has achieved the precise effect that he desired with extraordinary nicety. And the result is so complete that effort does not show in it, save that one is certain that no man could have reached such a degree of elaboration without effort. Mr. James's verbal style is a revelation to the normal slipshod person; for his awkward adverbial inversions of the type of "Do you like so very much little Aggie?" are not an exception, since they are due, not to carelessness, but to some perfectly unintelligible but consistent reason.

But the sense of irritation which inevitably accompanies such non-natural elaboration of style, though there it is mastered by admiration, predominates in regard to the matter of this book. Almost entirely dialogue, it represents the speech and relations of a little set of people who are intensely clever talkers together, and have made a perfect science of their artificiality of talk. The tremendous plainness with which, in real fact, they call a spade a spade in speaking to each other, and canvass the motives and feelings of each other and their nearest, is supreme; but not for one moment would they ever call a spade verbally a spade. They would suggest it with every refinement of word-fencing. One of them is fined five pounds for "cheap paradox," and you feel that they would never let themselves, nor would Mr. James let them, be cheap at any price. But behind their subtlety of talk is the subtlety of mind of many of them, and behind that Mr. James's own subtlety; and what with one subtlety and another, it is really impossible to know where you are. Why did not Vanderbank marry Nanda? Because he did not wish to appear to be bribed by her threatened dowry, or because she wrote his name on that risky book which he lent her mother, or for some other equally vulgar reason? Mr. James is not going to make that too clear. You must work the suggestions and shades of allusions out for yourself. And, in honest truth, life is not long enough to warrant the conscientious working out of a novel. Most of these characters are not meant to be sympathetic; but the influence of the whole overwhelms them all. One cannot feel a permanently complete human interest in Nanda, or in that aggressively maiden person Aggie, or in "Mr. Mitchy," who ought to be very likable, or even in the comparatively simple old Rip van Winkle from Beccles. These people undoubtedly perfectly understood each other as a rule, and Mr. Henry James understands them always; but the reader only by flashes. It has been said of Mr. Disraeli that at one time he became so affected that he positively affected affectation; and here Mr. James has refined refinement, subtilized subtlety, and suggested suggestion to bewilderment. That he continually gives the reader more ideas than can possibly be put in plain words, constitutes his degree of triumph as he proceeds; that he fails to give a complete idea of the whole proves that he has this time smothered himself with elaboration.

"Silver-Point Realism." *Academy* [England] (13 May 1899), 532–33.

Mr. Henry James is the wonderful artistic outcome of our national habit of repression. He has learned how to make repression a factor of art instead of an impediment. To all real things, even those over whose discomforture Sir Francis Jeune presides, belongs an infinite variety of words and gestures whose presence in a publication "there's none to dispute." But they are legible, and, emanating from the things themselves, they witness uncompromisingly to their existence. For the art of Mr. James such words and gestures are enough. Nay, holding aloof as he does, yet without affectation of prudery, from the frank image of an act-in-itself, and dwelling with the thought behind it, he presents a more significant idea of both thinker and doer than were otherwise to be obtained.

The Awkward Age is a complex illustration of his method. It is an urban drama of that fast life which, perhaps as a result of its "fastness," produces an atrophying cleverness that has learned to anticipate naïf opinion of its depravity. The members of the little West-end circle, on whose affinity with US Mr. James seems with astonishing affability to calculate, vie with one another in their appreciation of the old-world chivalrous gentleman who sits like a bewildered stranger at the feasts. They have arrived at the point when everything exists as it is conceived to exist. It is not with the eyes of backbiters, but of psychologists, for instance, that they read elopement in Lady Fanny's eyes. In the anticipatory relish of what, for convenience, we will call "sins" they are such epicures that the sin itself, the act-in-being, would be anti-climax. So we ourselves thought as we read through what the plain but polite Briton will consider a masterpiece of ambiguity. We did not want to know if Lady Fanny eloped with her Captain, or if Vanderbank committed adultery with Mrs. Brookenham. The malaria of their atmosphere was accounted for by that delay in accomplishment which means the incessant re-creation of the same fact on the mental plane. The author gains his effect with the minimum of the kind of information which furnishes a newspaper. He knows it is not necessary for things to happen in the sense of making a noise or a rustle.

The story is a sad one, for it traces the gradual development of a tragic sense of the atrophy of which we spoke in two of the only three generous natures with whom it deals. Mr. Longdon, seeing in Nanda the outward counterpart of the woman he had loved in his youth, would have done anything to unite her with the man she loved. But the latter, Vanderbank—he is a portrait worthy to stand by Sir Claude in *What Maisie Knew*—is incapable of the sacrifice which a combination of futures demands. He has lights and stirrings, he knows what it is to be dissatisfied, but he is too clever to be mastered by impulse. Moreover, he owes allegiance to the girl's mother—that allegiance which may or may not be prejudicial to Mr. Brookenham. With one of those splendid feats of audacity by which Mr. James turns a sudden glare on the lurking badness which he plays the showman to so debonairely, he makes Nanda beseech Vanderbank not to desert her mother.

"Do stick to her. . . . I don't believe you thoroughly know how awfully she likes you. . . . I suppose it *would* be immodest if I were to say that I verily believe she's in love with you. Not, for that matter, that father would mind. . . . That's the only thing I want. When I think of her downstairs there so often nowadays, practically alone, I feel as if I could scarcely bear it. She's so fearfully young."

There are few who dare write such a passage, or venture a pathos so supreme bordering on a vulgarity so abject. In achieving Nanda Mr. James has given us a veritable child of the age. But the "awkward age"? It is not very easy to see where that comes in, except that it was awkward for Mrs. Brookenham to own in public a child of nineteen. As for Mrs. Brookenham she is marvellous; her talk radiates the subtlest shafts of femininity. Not less, however, does she emanate a deadliness to which even the lightest of us may accord a shudder, and incline to accept the last irony which leaves no shelter for Nanda from the miasm of polite corruption, save with one who had loved her grandmother and would fain have married her to another man. Let it be added that the style of this study of life is delicate and incisive as of old. The words are picked, but not with gloves: they hold the distinctive nu-

ances which the refusal to use slang confers on words of ancestry on the lips of ladies and gentlemen. Here and there a wonderful bluntness is allowed. One feels it was heard in the soul—is authentic. Charming bits of landscape, alluring glimpses of a sweeter life, occur as occasion arises. Yes, the book is another "Henry James." Let us thank the proprieties, the conventions of this land, the genius of repression, which have created that need for a new realism, delicate as a silverpoint, to which his works make so satisfying a response.

"Typical Novel by Henry James."
Chicago *Tribune*, 13 May 1899, p. 10.

One would not be far amiss in calling Henry James the Browning of fiction. He delights in the same obscurity of omission and commission and in the same passion for working over a situation from many different standpoints. "The Awkward Age," with its ten "books," reminds one of "The Ring and the Book." Those who profess to enjoy that cryptic and many-jointed poem will doubtless delight in Mr. James' novel. To the rest, "The Awkward Age" will be a thing to be approached with terror rather than with enjoyment.

In this novel Mr. James has given free rein to his passion for analysis and ultra-refinement of phrase. It is a book of 457 closely printed pages, and almost every page is pure dialogue. The volume is made up entirely of the talk of a certain London society set of which the author has made a study, and there is not enough action in the whole to move a butterfly's wing. The book is rather a study of a static situation and of a certain group of ultra-modern English characters than a story.

There are ten characters in the group, and each has a separate division of the book named for him or her. Throughout all the divisions alike these critical-analytical personages chatter and talk by innuendo and dissect each other and themselves without ceasing. It is as if Mr. James had multiplied himself by ten and made a novel of the ten Jameses, masculine and feminine. The art is of the finest and the study of human nature is of the most microscopic, but the most loyal Jamesite surely cannot feel regret at parting company with these people at the close of the book. The uninitiated will cheerfully vote the whole clique intolerable after a brief acquaintance.

The author plunges one into the Buckingham Crescent inner circle without introduction. Mr. Vanderbank, a young clubman, has just discovered Mr. Langdon, an old man who has lived outside of London for a generation and has now come back to study the modern or "awkward age." The cause for Langdon's retirement so many years ago proves to have been his unrequited love for a certain Lady Julia, and in due time he meets Miss Nanda Brookenham, the granddaughter of his former sweetheart, and is moved to tears by the girl's likeness to his lost love. It requires three of the ten books to tell as much as this.

The old-fashioned Mr. Langdon is welcomed to the small and sporty set in question because of his oddness and his money. He studies Vanderbank, Mrs. Brookenham, Mr. Mitchett, little Aggie, and the rest, while they study him and dissect him, as they do themselves, until the small hours of the morning. It requires oceans and desert wastes of conversation to do this, and these will be found in unabridged form in Mr. James' characteristic pages. Every time a character pauses in speaking Mr. James tells you of it. Nanda and her mother "hang fire" until one wearies of the phrase. "Explanations spoil things," Mrs. Brookenham remarks once, but the author goes on explaining and refining. If a character runs out of words he expresses himself "by his silence and his eyeglass." Sometimes even these are too plain, and the characters run along for a page at a time deftly leaving their meaning to be caught from dim hints and occult fragments of unfinished sentences.

As usual the inevitable fogginess of this author is relieved by occasional flashes of style, as in the characterization of Mr. Cashmore, who "would have been red-headed if he had not been bald," or of Nanda's spendthrift brother, who "had as many wants as an advertisement page in the Times." Mrs. Brookenham says she cannot enter into her daughter's life because "you can't get into a railway train while it's on the rush," to which Mr. Cashmore responds: "Do you mean she's so fast?" Mrs. Brookenham has to "hang fire" before replying, but she manages in time to say that Nanda is only a modern daughter—a product of our own time—"and who is one, after all, that one should pretend to decline to go where the time may lead?" Such are some of the grains out of the bushels of chaff.

The static situation that takes the place of action is found in the relations of Nanda and Vanderbank. The old man from the country likes Van and adores the girl because she resembles her grandmother. As Nanda and Van are congenial Mr. Langdon undertakes to make a match between them by telling Van he is going to give Nanda a fortune if Van will marry her. Mitchett has been in love with Nanda, but when he learns of this he generously sacrifices himself on the altar by marrying little

321

Aggie, whom he does not care for. Then Van fumbles and hesitates and "hangs fire" for a year or more, until his inaction has created several hundred pages of close and hard reading and has nearly reduced poor Nanda to spinsterdom. His vacillating character and his lack of love for the girl are well brought out, but the process takes an unconscionable time.

Nanda finally furnishes the climax to the story by consenting to marry the old man himself. Ordinarily a match between a girl of 18 and a man old enough to be her grandfather is not considered a great triumph for literary-matrimonial purposes, but after 400 pages of the actionless Mr. James it is wildly exciting. It would have been more considerate of Nanda if she had done it several hundred pages sooner.

The characterization of Nanda is good, though she is so much like the rest of her clique that only the microscopic differentiations of Mr. James' pen distinguish her. There is a delightful touch in the scene where Van calls on her for the last time and where she appears utterly oblivious of the fact that he is expected to propose, devoting all her eloquence to upbraiding him for his absences on account of the extent to which her mother misses his company. "When I think of my mother down-stairs there so often nowadays, practically alone," says this modern daughter, "I feel as if I could scarcely bear it. She's so fearfully young."

Here we have Henry James, carver of cherry stones, at his appointed task. The cherry stones are often fine and every one has a touch of art. But somehow "The Awkward Age" gives one the impression of an attempt to build a palace of carved cherry stones, and the tout ensemble is neither strong nor pleasing. Mr. James has written better novels than this.

Saturday Review [England] 87 (13 May 1899), 598.

Mr. James will imperil his vogue if he is not careful. We have grown to look upon him as a dainty, dapper, well-groomed author, who, despite some Transatlantic eccentricities, could be introduced to our friends of both sexes. But every year he grows more careless of his literary person, his epigrams are more flashy, his innuendoes are less clean-shaven, until in his present presentation he may almost be denied admittance as shabby-genteel. Were this his first appearance, we would dismiss him as an American intent upon a very serious attempt to depict English society, but possessed of no materials other than those reposing in his inner consciousness. His men, though represented as belonging to a smart set, are neither English nor gentlemen. They exclaim "See here" upon the slightest provocation; we hear of "the perfection of their evening dress and the special smartness of their sleeveless overcoats;" and their behaviour always recalls that of a strolling mummer, who mistakes insolence for ease and rudeness for wit. The ladies are mere caricatures of new women, and the children, of "awkward age," parody the precocity of the most unnatural French creations. Nine-tenths of the book are conversation, and consist of tedious, vain repetition. And yet we feel that the characters are alive, though we can never conjure up any interest in them or come to desire their better acquaintance. The coherence of the style may best be gauged by an extract: "Lord Petherton, a man of five-and-thirty, whose robust but symmetrical proportions gave to his dark-blue double-breasted coat an air of tightness that just failed of compromising his tailor, had for his main facial sign a certain pleasant brutality, the effect partly of a bold, handsome parade of carnivorous teeth, partly of an expression of nose suggesting that this feature had paid a little, in the heat of youth, for some aggression at the time admired and even publicly commemorated." Was there ever such a sentence outside a shilling shocker? As for the story, Mr. James has no more to tell than the needy knife-grinder, and equally little right to an expectation of our sixpences.

Indianapolis *News*, 24 May 1899, p. 5.

We do not want to scare any one away from what might prove an entertaining study, but it is only fair to say that that inextricable confusion in which Mr. Henry James's redundancy of language and ideas has wrapped his later works of fiction has never been worse confounded than it is in his latest novel, "The Awkward Age." It is simply amazing to what lengths Mr. James has gone in elaborating the especial James style of subtle analysis, and the care with which he so thoroughly eliminates anything from his modern work which might savor of human interest. In the old times, James used to create real living people; flesh and blood creatures, like Daisy Miller and some of the people in "The Portrait of a Lady," but he has relegated all that to the rear and his love for refinement and intellectual delicacy has led him into the blackest depths of obscurity. There is rumor that there exists somewhere a class of readers to whom Henry James is a marvel of clearness and sanity—that these readers are in a state of chronic perplexity over the question why everybody should not see the delicate humor, the masterly drawing of character, the subtle analysis, the hidden drama. It may be true that some people can see what Mr. James is driving at, and, perhaps, these people are more fortunate than most of us. "The Awkward Age," a very long story, has ten subdivisions, or "books," each named after one of the characters. The volume is made up almost entirely of dialogue, or chatter, which, to the uninitiated, is vacuous and inane. With every copy of the book might go a guarantee that even the most timid soul should not be excited, for the entire action of the story is never more violently expressed than by some character walking across the drawing room floor.

Without any explanation, Mr. James rings up the curtain, and we see at once into the most sacred and exclusive circle of Buckingham Crescent, London. For the first three acts, or books, the stage is held by Mr. Vanderbank, a young clubman; Mr. Langdon, an old beau, who has lived out of London for many years and who has just returned to study the modern or "awkward" age, and Miss Nanda Brookenham, a young girl. Langdon's retirement from London, we learn, was due to the fact that he had been jilted by a certain Lady Julia, and when in the "awkward" age he meets Miss Brookenham, the granddaughter of his former sweetheart, the resemblance to his old love moves him to mawkish tears. This being established, the play moves on; there is a rush of characters, Mr. Mitchet, little Aggie, Mrs. Brookenham, Mr. Cashmore and a lot of others, all of whom have slang names, which Mr. James uses with the abandon of the young man about town. These people gabble, gabble, gabble through ream after ream of paper; it can't be called conversation; it is only smart talk. The old-fashioned Langdon studies, audibly, the characters of the people he meets, and in turn Mrs. "Brook," "Mitchy," "Tishy" (for these are some of the nicknames which Mr. James's "intellectual delicacy" has led him to adopt), Vanderbank, little Aggie and the rest dissect and pull to pieces the character of Langdon. All this, as may be imagined, is not wildly exciting. The "story" part of the "Awkward Age" has to do with the marrying off of Nanda Brookenham. Mr. Langdon takes to the girl because he had been in love with her grandmother, and he tells Vanderbank that if he marries Nanda he will give the girl a fortune. Vanderbank worries and fumbles, stumbles around in his love-making for several hundred pages of "talk," until he has nearly driven poor Nanda insane and induces somnolence in the reader. Finally, Langdon grows tired of Vanderbank's inaction, as the reader does, and he marries the girl himself.

Now, if it be treason to say that such a trivial plot as this is dull and deadly and uninteresting, then make the most of it. One can not help but admire the fine literary skill of Mr. James, but literary skill, unlike charity, will not cover a multitude of sins. Nor would we be understood as denying that there are occasional cases of wit in this desert of inane gabble; there are gleams of lucidity at intervals, as when we learn that Mr. Cashmore "would have been red-headed if he had not been bald," or when we hear that Nanda's improvident brother "had as many wants as the advertisement page in the Times," but the few Joe Miller jokes scattered through these 457 pages are insufficient to lighten the general gloom. Lest readers should think we have exaggerated the fog which envelops the conversation of these characters, we give the following specimen of a dinner party talk, and ask if it does not resemble, in a marked degree, the chaotic talk of the inmates of a lunatic asylum:

"The sign of Tishy Grendon—as it had been often called in a society in which variety of reference had brought to high perfection, for usual safety, the sense of signs—was a retarded facial glimmer that, in respect to any subject, closed up the rear of the procession. . . . 'Here's Nanda now, who's beautiful,' she vaguely continued, 'and Nanda ———' 'Oh, but, darling, Nanda's clean, too!' the young lady in question interrupted; on which her fellow-guest could only laugh with her as in relief from the antithesis of which her presence of mind had averted the completion, little, indeed, for the most part, as in Mrs. Grendon's talk that element of style was involved." [1899 Harper ed., pp. 326–28]

If the question arises, what is the purpose of "The Awkward Age"? we must reply we have been unable to discover; if one asks, what does it mean? we should be forced to confess that we do not know. If any one wonders whether people will read this book and enjoy it, or pretend to enjoy it, we can only say that we wonder, too.

Athenaeum [England] 3735 (27 May 1899), 651–52.

The sort of people presented in Mr. Henry James's new novel are not met every day. Still, there are factors in them that must be reckoned with, and they have their prototypes in a certain small section of society. The smallness of that section and some other reasons make it improbable that they will appeal very strongly to the sympathy, or perhaps to the understanding, of the majority of readers. Interest they will evoke in a few, but even these will scarcely accord anything in the shape of liking or esteem except to one or two. The real amateur of Mr. James is, however, more concerned with his view and treatment of people than with the people themselves—with his consummate mastery of any material he chooses to work in than with the moral or other aspect of the subject. 'The Awkward Age' is just another concrete expression of his keen observation of social tendencies and phases, and his truly remarkable power of selecting a difficult or uncommon situation or environment and making it his own. He can also make it the reader's, provided the reader be of the right sort—one who knows how to follow his intricate involutions of idea and phrasing. The amount of cleverness dispersed through these pages is amazing, though not amazing in the sense of being unexpected. As book after book appears, only to confirm conclusions long since established, it almost seems that further advance on the old lines is impossible. Yet on these rather than on others his admirers, as a rule, prefer to meet him. He is most truly at home in the chiaroscuro of faintly lit drawing-rooms, when talk is at its subtlest and veiled emotions are exchanged or suggested. There have been interludes when he has attempted life at high tide, or striven to penetrate the dubious regions of the supernatural. The strongly dramatic outlook and action in 'The Other House,' and the strange horizons opened up in 'The Two Magics,' are cases in point. But 'The Awkward Age,' again brings him back to more familiar ground. Needless to say, it is a place where strong incident and violent outbursts are excluded. The scene and theme are one: a late nineteenth-century drawing-room (we had almost said a drawing-room of the future) and the growing difficulty of the parental relation.

The awkward presence of children at the fashionable fireside is the problem. The difficulty is by no means universal, but one more or less felt in a limited stratum of society. It is a fragment of this society that is "conveyed" from the complex mosaic of modern existence by the author's cunning touch.

To guard against giving the story away (the real difficulty would be the converse, since there is no story), reference need not be made to the few events that do occur. Very little of an external kind happens. The action passes for the most part in the brain-cells of a small group of intriguers and observers. Yet we find a life or two unobtrusively blighted by the schemers. The aim—and who shall say it is unsuccessful?—is to set in movement a train of carefully repressed emotions, a bewildering criss-cross of motives and interests (more or less intangible and ephemeral) that make the daily life of a few intensely sophisticated men and women. This extreme sophistication, mingled with not a little bad breeding, is perhaps somewhat forced. The elemental passions, the love of lovers, parents, children, have been so worn down by constant analysis and introspection as to be non-existent. The atmosphere has become so artificial, partaking so little of the quality of real air, that natural healthy breathing seems almost impossible. No outdoor being could thrive when these strange people live and expand. One is conscious of the sense of oppression that broods over the fitful brilliance of the picture. Nanda of the awkward age should have been "a simple child that lightly draws its breath," but is instead a social martyr, a victim to the singularly ambiguous situation of her parents. Hers is not the innocence of ignorance, but the well-tried innocence of a nature too fine to take on ugliness. Her mother, the "wonderful Mrs. Brook," has not so many children as the old woman of the shoe, though more than she can comfortably "do" with, especially Nanda. Buckingham Crescent is the resort of talk and talkers of a very "go ahead" style. It is by talk alone that the book advances: talk or significant silence broken by meaning gestures, marked emphasis, ejaculations, pauses, and a hundred devices of which Mr. James is master. Sometimes the conversation is a verbal fencing match in which thrusts, retorts, and parryings have to be closely watched. A charm, sometimes a snare, of Mr. James's method is that no such thing as explanation is ever vouchsafed either by himself or his characters. You overhear and interpret as you can, but nothing is said for your benefit. Therefore the need for an intelligent attention to every shade and half-shade in intonation and manner. If you have to strain an ear for what is said, you must do it still more for what is only implied. Many people will think that for all this trouble they get no adequate return—that so much careful and long-winded suggestion overbalances the thing suggested. This feeling condemns them as those for whom Mr. James spreads the net of conversational delicacy in vain. Yet with all respect for the sustained ability, adroitness, and suppleness of diction, moments of weariness and a sense as of ineffectual striving with shadows do overcome one. The artificiality—even triviality—of some of the issues at stake strike one, more especially when the coterie plume themselves on their superior smartness and entire absence of all prejudice. So much rarefied psychology, paralysis of will, and general bloodlessness has, after a time, a stultifying effect on the mind. Two contrasting studies of girlhood are full of excellence. Each girl is a drag on the trend of talk, the discussions of life in general, and clique life in particular, which are the order of the day and night with their parents or guardians. Both have elders who philander not only with a group of *habitués,* but with every taste and topic, ancient and modern. Another important study is Mr. Longdon, Nanda's champion and benefactor. We note a stock phrase or two too constantly repeated, a Gallicism or Americanism here and there, unworthy of its setting, of Mr. James, and of a book which he, and he only, could have written.

"Mr. James' *Awkward Age.*" Chicago *Evening Post,* 27 May 1899, p. 5.

Henry James' style has been running away with him for a year or more, and in "The Awkward Age" it has become a barrier between the reader and all the author's characters. Too great an artist to label his creations, here, as in all other work, Mr. James paints delicately and subtly the characteristics of the people who move past you, making their actions speak louder than any words of his. So far all is well and no lapsing from power is to be laid to his pen. But the insistent style in which he has been clothing his narrative now slips away from the leash and tears his conversations to pieces, like the mischievous thing it is. The ideas likely to be in the minds of the various and varied personalities match with their deeds—and so far, again, it is well. But we recall the bright bits of dialogue that Du Maurier used to illustrate for Punch, and the fact that the strong family resemblance existing between the pictured personages was even less strong than the identity of their manner of speech. This is what we now find in Mr. James.

Moreover, the voice is always his voice. Mr. Langdon has the ideas of a Mr. James of a long generation ago—and the language of the Mr. James of the living present. Mr. Mitchett and Mr. Vanderbank and Lord Petherton are, respectively, a man of wealth, a good fellow and a noble man. These phases of man in modern society are admirably differentiated in all essential respects until they begin to talk; then, without exception, they speak with the tongue of Mr. James, whether their hands be the hands of Lord Petherton or of Mr. Mitchett. And the women adopt the same dialect—an Italian duchess, an English woman of fashion, their young married female friends and their two young daughters, all use the Jamesian modulations.

But the studies of humanity in modern British society abate nothing of interest. As in "What Maisie Knew," the story turns upon a study of the girlish mind when brought into contact with the hard facts of a relentless world. The Italian duchess would keep her Aggie from the slanders and scandals of polite society and the forbidden knowledge they imply: she is the convention of continental Europe in this regard duly vivified. Mrs. Brookenham means that her Nanda shall be free as American girls are free, and she comes down to the maternal drawing-room after her seclusion in a school-room, with avid ears. The convention of marriage, too, plays its part. So the little drama unfolds in all its modernness; with the admirable foil of Mr. Langdon of the last generation to see it with eyes so old as to have regained their pristine focus and strength. If Mr. James would only let his people do their own talking!

"Henry James's Latest Novel."
New York Times Saturday Review of Books and Art 4 (27 May 1899), 349.

The stanchest admirer of Henry James must falter sometimes. Here are 457 pages of style and manner—all estimable for what they are—employed to tell a story which is likely to satisfy only the most deeply initiated few, and to interest them principally as another theme which lends itself so well to the master's most painstaking and lingering, if wonderfully facile, "treatment."

Again, in "The Awkward Age," Mr. James devotes himself to studying so patiently as to severely try the ordinary reader's patience, what one of his personages describes as "the more and more extraordinary development of English manners." But there is no reason why one who enjoyed the exquisite subtleties of "In the Cage" should not follow the evolutions and intricacies of expression employed to denote the mental states of the personages in "The Awkward Age" with still greater enjoyment, for there is so much more of the later book than there was of the earlier.

The fineness of the workmanship is not to be disputed, and it is not to be greatly deplored, either, for we who have liked so well the Henry James of "The American" and "Princess Casamassima"; of "The Private Life" (with its delicious irony)[1] and "The Turn of the Screw" (with its shuddering horror) should surely be of vision sufficiently purged to see clearly that the drier, finer, more elusive qualities of this may satisfy a taste in literature even nicer than they appealed to. We may falter in the task of reading, therefore; we may find ourselves vexed by so much minute analysis of character all but characterless, of so much elaboration in picturing merely sordid minds; but if we have ever liked James, we are pretty sure to read to the end, and to feel rather glad we did at the finish.

That is equivalent to saying that any one who has acquired, in some measure, the habit of liking Henry James's writing, because of the ineffable charm of his wit when it is brightest, of his mastery of the very spirit of Comedy, when he is in the right mood; of his comprehension of tragic heights—and depths—may find enjoyable passages, many of them, perhaps, in "The Awkward Age." The wit is not brilliant in this, but it is appreciable; the buoyancy of comedy is missing, the suggested tragedy has neither heights nor depths. But, after all, the work is the outcome of keen observation of modern social life in its fullest development by a master mind. The note-taking, in this instance, has been rather tediously minute, and the particular subject happens to be rather dull.

It has been said, over and over again, that however much one may like James's novels, he vividly remembers few if any of their personages. Even Mr. Howells is more successful in transplanting from society in fiction men and women so full of life that they are not individually forgotten as soon as the reader closes the book. James's characters often interest us very much while we are actually in their company, but we cannot for the life of us remember their names the next day. There may be other reasons for this than mere uncertainty of characterization. Perhaps James in picturing so well the minds of his creatures fails to give them permanent corporeal form. Some of them come back to us from time to time, as vague shadows.

Daisy Miller is almost his only clearly remembered character.

It is not likely that these new folks of "The Awkward Age" will be longer remembered than most of the others. The hero is a Mr. Longdon, aged fifty-five years or more, a kindly, well-bred, fastidious, sentimental gentleman; and the heroine is Nanda, who may be a reincarnation of the soul of her grandmother, Lady Julia. The grandmother Longdon loved, in his extreme and impressible youth, and Nanda he marries nearly forty years later, because of her strong resemblance to Lady Julia, and because that marriage will be the easiest way out for Nanda—out of a set, an environment to which she clearly does not belong.

Nanda at nineteen is grave and self-possessed, knowing many things a girl of her age (in Longdon's opinion) should not know, a terrible problem for her mother, as she emerges from the schoolroom into a little world of vanity, extravagance, frivolity, and adultery. Nanda is reasonably sound-hearted and pure-minded. But it cannot be truthfully said that she is ever charming, or that Longdon, who tries hard in many ways to make her lot happier, to make it possible for her to wed a young and handsome man, is a very taking hero. The situation might have been treated much more "effectively," with less philosophy, with less insistence on manners and the lack of them, even with less cruelty.

As for Nanda's human surroundings, they are described as "simply a collection of natural affinities, meeting perhaps principally in Mrs. Brook's drawing room . . . and governed at any rate everywhere by Mrs. Brook, in our mysterious ebbs and flows, very much as tides are governed by the moon." Mrs. Brook is Mrs. Brookenham, Nanda's mother, a lovely lady, who has "got on" quite mysteriously, and the "set" includes "Mitchy," a wealthy chatterer with a receding chin; Lord Petherton, the Duchess and "Little Aggie," Vanderbank and Tishy Grendon, Nanda's dreadful brother Harold, and a dozen or so more, some of whom are really smart while all of them are open to suspicion. Depravity seems to be their common bond. But not even that shocks us. In fact, nothing in "The Awkward Age" shocks or uplifts one much.

Note

1 "The Private Life," *Atlantic Monthly* 69 (April 1892), 463–83. Reprinted in *The Private Life* (1893).

Detroit *Free Press*, 29 May 1899, p. 7.

Mr. Henry James' new novel, "The Awkward Age," is a satire on all the phases that London society presents to those who understand it. The title is a reference to the present condition of English society. It is an awkward age, brought about by the necessity of reconciling the practical freedom of the American girl which the English girl has now virtually acquired, with a social mixture distinctly opposed to that of the American and much more nearly approaching French customs and ideals.

There are two girls in the story, set as types of what girls become under the two systems of bringing up, and who appear as foils to each other. One is Nanda, brought up under the English custom which excludes the girl from her mother's drawing-room and her friends until she is ready to marry—or more exactly, until her mother sees fit to bring her out. The mother is ambitious, young and charming. The conditions of her drawing-room change with Nanda's coming. Everything thereafter goes toward the protection of the Young Person's innocence. But she hears, guesses, puts together and secretly assimilates a whole order of revelations, allusions and betrayals that are the essence of the world she lives in, and not at all included in what her mother wishes her to know.

The other girl, Agnesina, "Little Aggie," is in direct contrast. Her mind has been kept perfectly pure. She is the type in strongest contrast to Nanda: she is entirely innocent, as ignorant of the world as she is innocent.

The hero is a young Englishman of the better sort and, of course, represented as a superior being, much in request in aristocratic circles. He likes Nanda, but he hesitates about making her his wife because he feels she is too wise, too saturated with worldliness and knowledge of life; he hesitates and watches, and the situation gets beyond him.

The most delightful figure in the book is old Mr. Longdon, who knew Nanda's and Vanderbank's grandmothers, and naturally wishes to see his young friends marry. The story reflects, as intimately as a mirror, the small lights and shadows of daily life; it is characterized by the delicate perception, the microscopic detail and the subtle comedy and tragedy that Mr. James always puts into his writings. But truth to tell, unless one has a keen perception of literary art and style "The Awkward Age" will be voted prosy if not dull.

"Mr. James' New Novel." *Bookman* [England] 16 (June 1899), 81.

The honest reader in search of a story will stare dazedly through perhaps a third of Mr. James's new book, and then shut it with a snort. Serious readers in search of a problem will go along the road a little further, but if they continue too long, their wrath at the end will surely consume the writer. Students of character may complain that too great a burden is put on them. Indeed, everyone has excellent grounds of complaint against "The Awkward Age." The book is extraordinarily clever. Such as have some time on their hands, who are well saturated with Mr. James's later style, and have no particular expectations to be cruelly disappointed, will enjoy a large portion of it, will marvel and chuckle over many pages, and yet think after all it was hardly worth the trouble of writing. In "What Maisie Knew," he suggested the tragic circumstances surrounding a young life, with a delicacy and a restrained pathos that were admirable. In "The Two Magics" he cast off restraint and revealed depths of horror lurking under the fairest surface. His new book is also to some extent a study of degeneration, but the question is dealt with so lightly, and so politely, that you are convicted of priggery if you take it seriously at all. He introduces us to a London set, lively, graceful, perfect in their worldly *role*. It would be the worst of manners to inquire whether at bottom they are very good or very bad. They talk a great deal in a language of their own that has grown out of their constant intercourse with each other. An outsider must listen hard and guess a great deal. The set contains two girls. One of them has been guarded from its influence, the other has sucked in all it had to give, and judged the result, while she was still in pinafores. If you have leisure to study the members of the set in Mr. James's fashion, helped by the example of that other outsider, Mr. Longdon—a gentleman of the old school, who comes back to London after thirty years of retirement, to watch and wonder painfully—you will own that some of them, Mitchy, the Duchess, Mrs. Brookenham, and Nanda, are marvellously worked out. But you must take time and trouble. There is no other living writer who could have written the book, who could so patiently and delicately labour to make a fine point, who could deal so sensitively with fine shades, who could analyse the slight so subtly, so wittily. There is infinite grace in the detail; and there is genuine fun in the observation. But taken as a whole, the effect is clumsy and even wearisome. There is ten times too much good stuff. He works a delicate thing to death.

Critic 35 (August 1899), 754–57.

As Mr. Henry James has no rivals in his own field to overcome, he continues to surpass himself with regularity and ease. "The Awkward Age" is ahead of anything he has yet produced, for subtlety and acute insight. What Mr. James will do next is beyond conjecture, for certainly it would seem that in this particular direction he has reached the utmost limit. The book is a study of certain phases of London society to which other novelists of late years have borne awkward and incomplete testimony. What they have intimated shamefacedly, Mr. James has set forth with his customary lucidity and exhaustiveness. There now remains nothing to be told about the conversation and the complications in those circles where vast moral indifference is united to extreme intellectual acuteness. Such a circle revolves around Mrs. Edward Brookenham. They are brilliant people—though half their brilliance is mere audacity—and it is something of an intellectual exercise to follow the implications of their talk, which is faithfully reproduced at an almost wearisome length. They chatter about everything, and the more impossible the subject the more fervently do they dwell upon it. The question, for instance, of whether Lady Fanny Cashmore, is, or is not, about to "bolt" like Anna Karenina "to one of the smaller Italian towns" contains inexhaustible food for research and discussion.

Given such a society as this, what part in it must the young person play? This is the question which the book proposes. Mrs. Brookenham, the daughter of a lady of the old school of so fine a type that her memory is still an inspiration to the man who had loved her in his youth, has herself a daughter, Nanda, who reproduces the wonderful grandmother, Lady Julia, exactly in her physical aspect, but, greatly to her own regret and that of Mr. Longdon, the delightful elderly gentleman who had loved Lady Julia, it is out of her power to reproduce the mind and manners of that gentlewoman. For Nanda cannot be said to have led the sheltered life. In such a house as her mother's she has been "exposed" to all kinds of information. Although Mrs. Brookenham complains that when Nanda arrives at the age where she must positively sit in the drawing-room and meet people, the tone of the circle is thereby altered to such an extent that its converse is flat and unprofitable, none the less Nanda arrives speedily at a state of enlightenment concerning the miasms of life

which is undesirable for the unformed mind. Vanderbank, whom Nanda attracts, and whom Nanda in turn loves, considers this illumination so undesirable that he makes it the ground of declining her hand when it is offered him by Mr. Longdon, who proposes to dower the girl generously if his young friend will marry her and remove her from her mother's sphere of influence.

Nanda, who knows everything, knows this, too, and her behavior under the circumstances is so wonderful and so exquisite, yet so simple and natural, that the reader's emotions are uncomfortably stirred in her behalf. Nanda is, in fact, Mr. James's supreme creation. He has always been interested in the niceness of the nice girl, and has believed in and set forth, at great length and in many ways, her essential nobility and high-mindedness. Daisy Miller was one illustration of this, and Isabel Archer another. Fleda Vetch demonstrated the same qualities in a different way, and Maisie—poor little Maisie—who clung by instinct to conventions and proprieties which she had known only in their overthrow, seemed, until Nanda appeared, the most convincing proof a novelist could devise of the elemental fineness of girl-nature. But Nanda is a piece of even more absolute, more beautiful evidence. Moreover, she fixes a type and points out the course evolution must needs pursue. She, in fact, supplies the ideal of the form the Nice Girl must take in the next century if society continues to grow more lax in its manners and morals. There always have been nice girls; there will continue to be nice girls, although they may have to develop under circumstances which have hitherto been considered prohibitive. Nanda is prophecy.

On the other hand, Mr. Longdon is history. He is the best of the old school of manners as Nanda is the best of the new, and his sufferings in modern London make very clear the difference between the atmosphere of forty years ago and that of to-day. The fact that it is possible for the polite world as he knew it to have evolved into the contemporary polite world sets him doubting the foundation of things— "The more one thinks of it," he bemoans himself, "the more one seems to see that society—for we're *in* society, are n't we, and that our horizon?—can never have been anything but increasingly vulgar. The point is that in the twilight of time—and I belong you see, to the twilight—it had made out much less how vulgar it *could* be. It did its best, very probably, but there were too many superstitions it had to get rid of. It has been throwing them overboard, one by one, so that now the ship sails uncommonly light. That's the way"— and the old man with his eyes on the golden distance ingeniously followed it out—"I come to feel so the lurching and pitching."

Another question which the book raises is, What part can any distinguished soul play in such a society? There seems to be no room in it for goodness, no formula nor convention to govern the instincts of those who happen by nature to be righteous or refined. It does not provide for such freaks. The adorable Mitchy, little as he looks it, is a distinguished soul, and at the end the reader, like Mr. Longdon and Nanda, is "anxious about Mitchy." He is not provided for in the scheme of things, and, when this is the case, it is only the strongest who can provide for themselves.

Mitchy, Mr. Longdon, and Nanda are delightful acquaintances, but the reader has to pay a high price for meeting them, since to do so he must also meet Mrs. Brookenham, the Duchess, Lord Petherton, Mr. Cashmore, and other odious people. There is a certain satisfaction in observing that even Mr. James's art has a limitation. Although he writes, with equal sympathy, of the righteous and the unrigh-teous, he simply cannot achieve a fellow-feeling for the people who ought to have right feelings, and do not. This limitation is curiously illustrated by the fact that "Mrs. Brook" and Vanderbank are the only characters in the book which do not impress the reader as they seemed to impress their associates. Their vaunted charm is invisible. Vanderbank strikes us as a superior variety of cad, and Mrs. Brookenham's grace is never realized, and her intelligence becomes unspeakably tiresome, as misapplied intelligence usually does. There is nothing quite so stupid as cleverness gone wrong.

The short story of rural New England has become a staple commodity of that region—that is to say, it has grown to be one of the necessary furnishings of our lives, as important in its way as the codfish of Gloucester, the shoes of Lynn, or the prints of Lowell. This is partly, of course, because New England has been blessed with such faithful observers and artistic recorders as Miss Alice Brown, Miss Jewett, and Miss Wilkins,[1] and partly, also, because rural life in New England leads itself to the purposes of literature, in that it has less brutality and more moral elevation, even now, than rural life anywhere else the whole world over. The farther the child of New England roams, and the more of this world he sees, the more he wonders and admires when he thinks of the point of view that is maintained in the land of his nativity, and the more thankful he feels himself for that ineradicable tincture of Puritan blood which, even in the hundredth dilution, enforces its standards upon its inheritors.

Note

1 Alice Brown (1857–1948), Sarah Orne Jewett (1849–1909), and Mary Eleanor Wilkins Freeman (1852–1930)—all three popular and prolific American authors.

Sewanee Review 8
(January 1900), 112–13.

Mr. Henry James's latest novel, "The Awkward Age" (Harpers), is a striking illustration of the danger a brilliant writer runs in giving himself up too exclusively to a particular method of composition. Mr. James's fortes are psychological analysis of character and brilliant management of conversation. These are two of the prime requisites of successful modern fiction, but even modern fiction requires fair narrative ability at the hands of its writers, and Mr. James in the overcultivation of his own special gifts seems to have lost whatever gift of narrative he may have once possessed. "The Awkward Age" is divided into ten parts, named after the leading characters; each part moves the story forward a little, but leaves the reader more and more bewildered in a maze of clever conversations. One learns that one is in the midst of a small section of *fin de siècle* London society, in fact, of a group of decadents who hover around an extremely clever woman, Mrs. Brookenham by name. Their brilliant circle is broken up, however, by the fact that her daughter Nanda can no longer be kept in the nursery, and yet is hardly sophisticated enough to make an unembarrassed inmate of her mother's drawing room. The part of rescuing her from her environment is undertaken by a rejected lover of her grandmother, Mr. Longdon, a delightful representative of bygone days, who is as much puzzled by the oversubtlety of the conversations he hears as we are. He finally succeeds in his philanthropic attempt, and we feel that the attenuated story has at length come to its destined end; but after all we are much more certain that Mr. James is an obscurely brilliant writer than that we have been reading a story at all. We frankly confess that the Brookenham set is too clever for us. If, to be a really fine art, conversation has to be unintelligible to an ordinary mind, and if psychological analysis has to be carried to a point of subtlety considerably beyond any attempted by Shakspere or Balzac, and if conversations and character analysis are the two poles around which the ellipse of modern fiction is to be drawn— we are willing to commend the novels of to-day to the careful attention of students of advanced mathematics, and shall content ourselves hereafter with the simple old novelists who were unsophisticated enough to write straightforward stories.

Checklist of Additional Reviews

Book Notes 2 (May 1899), 314.
Literature [England] 4 (6 May 1899), 475–76. Reprinted in Roger Gard, ed., *Henry James: The Critical Heritage* (London: Routledge & Kegan Paul, 1968), pp. 283–84; Arthur Sherbo, "Still More on James," *Henry James Review* 12 (1991), 105–6.
Spectator [England] 82 (6 May 1899), 647. Reprinted in Gard, p. 282.
Boston *Sunday Post*, 21 May 1899, sec. 2, p. 4.
New York *Tribune*, 21 May 1899, supp., p. 13.
Providence *Sunday Journal*, 21 May 1899, p. 15.
Boston *Evening Transcript*, 31 May 1899, sec. 2, p. 12.
Chicago *Times-Herald*, 1 June 1899, p. 9.
Outlook 62 (3 June 1899), 314.

St. Louis *Post-Dispatch,* 10 June 1899, p. 4.

Lucian L. Knight. Atlanta *Constitution,* 11 June 1899, supplement, p. 9.

Brooklyn *Daily Eagle,* 11 June 1899, p. 19.

St. Paul *Daily Pioneer Press,* 11 June 1899, p. 20.

San Francisco *Chronicle,* 18 June 1899, p. 4.

Literary World [England] 59 (23 June 1899), 575.

New York *World,* 24 June 1899, p. 6.

Bookman [New York] 9 (July 1899), 472. Reprinted in Gard, pp. 292–93.

[William Morton Payne]. *Dial* 27 (1 July 1899), 21. Reprinted in Gard, p. 261.

New York *Sun,* 1 July 1899, pp. 6–7.

Minneapolis *Tribune,* 16 July 1899, section 1, p. 4.

Literary World [Boston] 30 (22 July 1899), 227. Reprinted in Gard, p. 294; James W. Gargano, *Critical Essays on Henry James: The Late Novels* (Boston: G. K. Hall, 1987), pp. 40–41.

Millie W. Carpenter. *New York Times Saturday Review of Books and Art* 4 (12 August 1899), 544.

London *Times,* 15 August 1899, p. 9.

Nation 69 (24 August 1899), 155. Reprinted in Gard, p. 298.

Churchman 80 (2 September 1899), 266.

Springfield [Mass.] *Republican,* 17 September 1899, p. 15.

THE SACRED FOUNT

"Vampires: A Story about Them by Henry James." New York *Tribune*, 9 February 1901, p. 8.

When Mr. James published "The Turn of the Screw," in the fall of 1898, he must have inspired in many a breast the wish that he would trust himself again to the train of speculation so powerfully exploited in that eerie narrative. It carried him, for the moment, away from the trivialities which have too often engrossed him, and enabled him to breathe the spiritual airs of creative imagination. In the following summer came "The Awkward Age," an anti-climax, if ever there was one. "The Soft Side," a book of short stories published last September, suggested that the impulse which gave us "The Turn of the Screw" had had its day, had been sacrificed to the author's predilection for things of sublime inconsequence. But Mr. James has all the time been turning over in his mind the thoughts which had yielded such good fruits in the masterpiece mentioned above, and in "The Sacred Fount" he returns to the treatment of them with renewed interest. In the interval, however, he has had leisure to give his ideas a new twist, the kind of twist, alas! that his peculiar foibles as a writer of fiction might have warned us to expect. He deals, as he dealt then, with conditions bordering on the supernatural. But where he was imaginative he is now as innocent of that quality as it would seem possible for a dabbler in esoteric mysteries to be. Where he thrilled us in "The Turn of the Screw" with a convincing sense of an unreal presence he now clothes his vampires in evening dress; he puts them, with their victims, through the decorous paces suited to an English drawing room, and where he might have made them shapes of dread he leaves them figures of fun.

His vampires are a man and a woman, the latter married, the former a bachelor. She is somewhere in the forties, if not further up the hill, and she was born "plain." He is a handsome man, still in his prime; he was born stupid. Grace Brissenden, the woman, marries a man much younger than herself, and by some subtle process unloads her years and disabilities upon him. She waxes young, beautiful and clever, while "poor Briss" takes on decrepitude of mind and body, grows old, bowed, listless and pathetic. Gilbert Long, the dull Adonis, borrows no physical charms from the lovely Mrs. Server, who is his supposititious providence—he does not need to—but she is almost drained of intellectual brilliancy that he may shine resplendent, a paragon of eloquence. The sacred fount is—but what is it? When you have identified the victims of the two vampires you have, so to say, given a local habitation and a name to each unholy incubus. Guy Brissenden, sacrificing himself that his wife may be aggrandized, stands forth as an image of goodness, weakness, generosity, helplessness, what you will. May Server may be called, like him, a martyr. But here we are only on the outskirts of the situation. How do they do it? Why do they do it? For it is significant that there is no thought in this book of the malignant and obscene vampire of the ancient bestiaries, but a deliberate borrowing, a deliberate lending. It is a compact. A definite game of give and take goes forward. Nothing is held back. The gift is as of a whole intelligence, it involves almost a complete exchange of personalities. What more exciting theme could a novelist desire? With "The Turn of the Screw" in mind, it seems as if Mr. James must certainly rise to his opportunity and produce a great book. But he bids us to a

Barmecide's feast. If he had tried to tell us the secret of the sacred fount and had failed he could have been forgiven. He does not even try.

The thing he does try for is wellnigh unbelievable in its irrelevance. The man into whose hands he puts the unfolding of his story goes down to Newmarch, a great English country house, for the week end. On the way down he travels with Grace Brissenden and Gilbert Long, marvels at the rejuvenation of the one, the intellectual efflorescence of the other, and vaguely suspects that something unprecedented has happened to both. Forthwith, to the extent of some three hundred pages, he is exhibited not as seeking a solution of their bewildering improvement, but as frantically endeavoring to identify the individual by whose loss one of the pair has been enriched! That Brissenden is his wife's salvation is taken for granted. But is Gilbert Long indebted to Lady John or to May Server? That is the question which drives the man half mad. He talks with Mrs. Brissenden. Unconscious of her own significance in the mind of her interlocutor, she becomes deeply interested in applying the theory to Long, and declares for May Server as the probable source of the miraculous change he has experienced. But at the end she is terrified lest her own secret escape her, and she withdraws from the discussion, declaring that the whole business is absurd, and that her analytical friend is simply crazy. He is not altogether baffled. One feels as the tale ends that he sticks to his conviction about both vampires and both victims. The reader, however, is baffled, horribly, and wonders why Mr. James has taken so much trouble to land him in an *impasse*. Mr. James would say, perhaps, that he never intended to land the reader anywhere else; that all he cared to do was to exhibit the analytical mind—which is to say, the Jamesian mind—in operation around a problem

having naught to do with anything so queer as an exchange of individualities, having no spiritual mystery whatever. His problem is one simply of flat, flagrant, and even somewhat vulgar curiosity about trifles. Then why, we are inclined to ask, call this book "The Sacred Fount," as though the fount were the thing which had caused the book to be written?

What is it to us that May Server was or was not the particular person who helped Gilbert Long to be brilliant? The thing worth knowing is the manner of her helping him. We wonder if Mr. James will not wake up some fine day and, after a rereading of this novel, slap his forehead and exclaim with dismay: "Goodness! I forgot to say anything about the fount!" It is more probable, though, that he will smile commiseratingly over the absurdity of those readers who do not appreciate, as he does, the value of an exercise in the juggling of inductive processes, the subject matter around which the processes play being of less than secondary importance. At a pause in the analysis, when everything promises to develop in accordance with his original hypothesis, the teller of the story remembers how, in a childhood haunted with fairy tales, he "moved in a world in which the strange 'came true.'" It was the "coming true," he adds, "that was the proof of the enchantment, which, moreover, was naturally never so great as when such coming was, to such a degree and by the most romantic stroke of all, the fruit of one's own wizardry." He hugs himself as he sees his speculations about May Server "coming true." But we feel too clearly the presence of his own wizardry. Life does not live itself out in these pages. There is nothing but the falling into place of the figures in a pattern which the author has known all along how to put together, but has kept on juggling with in order to make us think him clever. We ought to be impressed. But we keep thinking of

Dr. Johnson's comment on the performance of the trained animal. One recalls the famous description of Shelley, that "beautiful and ineffectual angel, beating in the void his luminous wings in vain." Only there is nothing angelic about Mr. James. Impish is the better word. Nor does he deal in luminosity, but rather in "the palpable obscure."

Joseph Edgar Chamberlin. "Henry James's New Novel."
Boston *Evening Transcript*, 13 February 1901, p. 12.

Mr. Henry James's new "novel" (it never could be called one except in quotation marks), "The Sacred Fount" (Scribner's), is the most extraordinary book I have read for a long time. To sum the matter up, it seems insane. I don't for a moment imagine the author is insane; apparently it has merely pleased his fancy to make an insane book. It is an attempt to apply a high order of mysticism to a series of flirtations at a house party at a country seat in England. The man who is supposed to relate the story goes out to Newmarch with other guests. He is a man of mature years—apparently a bachelor. On the way out he is struck with the curious fact that four of his fellow-guests, a man and his wife and another man and another woman, have undergone a great change. Two of them, one a man and one a woman, have become younger, fresher, more clever and witty, while the other two, the remaining man and woman, have grown preternaturally old and have lost

their wit. He becomes obsessed with the solution of the problem why these changes have taken place. He makes out that the people are in love, and as in love there is always one who takes and one who gives—"one who gives the lips and one who gives the cheek"—the bloom of each of the two who have bloomed has been drawn from another who has been sapped, wrung dry of life. In the case of the married pair it is supposed that it is the wife (who is older than the husband) who has sapped him. Has the man of the other pair bloomed at the expense of the woman who has wilted, or has he sapped some other and possibly unknown party, and has she been sapped by somebody who isn't there? The book deals with the attempt to solve the problem by close observation and analysis. The spring at which the two fortunate personages in the story, the ones who have bloomed, have drunk, is the "sacred fount," naturally—that is easy. The discoverer of the change in these four people communicates his discovery, or a part of it, to two of his fellow-travellers, one of whom is the lady who has bloomed at the supposed expense of her husband; but of course the discoverer communicates to her only his discovery as to the other couple. This introduces a complication which might be pleasing if the author had not committed such indiscretions as devoting four or five chapters to one conversation with her—the dialogue being interrupted, of course, with long studies of the psychological conditions bound up in her own and her interlocutor's utterances.

The house party at Newmarch is a series of elaborate flirtations, in which certain of the more innocent flirtations are used, or are supposed to be used, to screen other and less innocent flirtations; and there is much talk of red herrings drawn across trails to throw the hounds of scandal off the scent. This aristocratic party is certainly a very remarkable and cloudy affair according to the social standards of Mr. James's native country. That there is a difference between the social customs of England and America, to our advantage, must be evident from his picture of this bit of English life; no one could assume that Mr. James has given us a false account. Gentlemen in this country do not make their flirtations the subject of such free and frank discussion as that which prevails at Mr. James's Newmarch; they are hardly accustomed, when rallied on being caught in secluded nooks with certain ladies, to come out flatly, to a mere acquaintance, with such exclamations as this: "You know I decidedly have too much of that dreadful old woman!" In the case in the "Sacred Fount" where this remark is made, the "dreadful old woman" is a certain witty and attractive flirtatious lady of whom—and of another man—the book has just said:

> "Lady John was in love with him [Gilbert Long] and had kicked up, to save her credit, the dust of a fictive relation with another man—the relation one of mere artifice and the man one in her encouragement of whom nobody would believe. . . . Well, the proof I just alluded to was that I had not sat with my friends five minutes before Gilbert Long turned up." [1901 Scribner's ed., pp. 104–5]

The teller of the story, in the course of his watching of Mrs. May Server in the attempt to find out who is her lover, comes very near to falling in love with her himself. He is therefore shocked, stupefied, knocked out of his senses, by the apparent revelation that her love affair is not one of the delicate and pitiful sort that he had supposed, but merely a gross one, and that her change and her nervous condition are not due to the torture of conscience, but simply to the fear that he knows all about the affair and is going to tell. I have said that there is a good deal of mysticism in the book. There certainly must be in any piece of serious work by a man who has Mr. James's inheritance, education and genius. The investigator of the amours of May Server works himself up into a sort of fever of omniscience; by the tense application of his faculties he acquires the mystic's sense of being in with the creation of things; he has drunk of the cup of seership.

> "It appeared then that the more things I fitted together the larger sense, every way, they made—a remark in which I found an extraordinary elation. . . . I had positively encountered nothing to compare with this since the days of fairy-tales and of the childish imagination of the impossible." [1901 Scribner's ed., pp. 127–28]

Doubtless Mr. James's father, who was, I believe, a Swedenborgian minister, would early have taught him to recognize the fact that the application of the gift of seership to the purposes of an analytical society novel would be "disorderly," and, in fact, we are pretty well convinced when we get to this point that we are on the road to madness. I fancy the reader does not care to follow the road any farther. The book is interesting in at least one respect—as an example of Mr. James's style as he writes in the prime of his life. This style is a mingling of the elaborately polished and the colloquial, with a predominance of the colloquial. The author uses in his most serious text—we may assume, of course, that it is a part of the lingo of the supposed narrator of the story, who is presented as an Englishman of extreme cultivation—all the current slang, such as "caught on," "out of it," her "pull," and so on. When a person speaks, he is said to "play up." The book is a curious revelation, to an American, of what seems the tendency of English conversation to develop new and strange verbal combinations derived from the French, new placings of adverbs and the like. Here is one of the expressions of the cleverest woman in the story: "You after all then now don't?" This is another example: "What does he say that's further interesting about that?" Somebody is described as "not feeling free to show for quite as impressed as he was." In another place the text has this extraordinary sentence: "It comes back to me that, the sense thus established of my superior vision may perfectly have gone a little to my head." This is good French, but not good English; indeed the talk of English society seems to become less English every year. "The Sacred Fount" is surely not a well of English undefiled.

Nor can I recommend the book, though it is a study of love and the day the 13th of February, as a valentine for the young person.

"Mr. Henry James." London *Daily News,* 19 February 1901, p. 6.

Mr. Henry James reports of one of his characters in "The Sacred Fount" (Methuen): "He only exclaimed more indulgently, that he didn't know what I was talking about." With every wish to grant the utmost indulgence to Mr. Henry James, because of his undoubted cleverness, we confess that we entirely sympathise with this apparently slow-witted man. In fact, a perusal of "The Fount of Life" has sent us tripping contentedly over to the tents of the Philistines quite unashamed of a desertion which has caused us not a single pang. Captive and quiescent in the camp of the enemy, bounded by

a dimly seen, if somewhat circumscribed, horizon, we may permit ourselves to sit down and ask what it all means. As much as comes within the range of vision of the Philistines is soon told. A party of people spend two days in a country house, to the host and hostess of which we are not introduced. One of the ladies has married a man younger than herself, but while she looks younger than her age, he looks older than both of them put together. One of the men talks cleverly—at least we are told so—whereas he is known to be impenetrably stupid. He is, in fact, the man who didn't know what Mr. James was talking about. And there is a beautiful lady who displays a restless disposition. The rest of the party spend their time in walking about the house and garden discussing the situation. That is all. Some conclusion is probably arrived at in a duologue which occupies the last forty pages of the book, but what that conclusion is is beyond the scope of the Philistine brain to discover. The conversation of Mr. James's characters presents much the same difficulty as a passage from a Greek play to a schoolboy after he has looked up the difficult words in a dictionary, and before he has settled himself down to his construe.

Well, after all the atmosphere of the Philistine camp is not invigorating, and perhaps we shall feel ashamed of deserting to it, if Mr. James will give us another book like "The American" or "The Two Magics." And there are compensating passages even in "The Sacred Fount." We must give ourselves the pleasure of quoting Mr. James in one of his more lucid moments.

"There was a general shade in all the lower reaches—a fine, clear dusk in garden and grove, a thin suffusion of twilight out of which the greater things, the high tree-tops and pinnacles, the long crests of motionless wood and chinnied roof, rose into golden air. The last calls of birds sounded extraordinarily loud; they were like the timed, serious splashes in wide, still water of divers not expecting to rise again. I scarce know what odd consciousness I had of roaming at close of day in the grounds of some castle of enchantment. I had positively encountered nothing to compare with this since the days of fairy-tales and of the childish imagination of the impossible."

Mr. James's characters, alas! walk this enchanted garden with their inevitable "obsessions" and the charm is lost.

Academy [England] 1503 (23 February 1901), 165–66.

Had anyone but Mr. James written this book, his admirers might well have cried: "Oh, 'tis sacrilege." But since Mr. James himself is the author, what can we say but that he has, in his own brilliantly tedious way, with his own inimitable art, and with his own occult knowledge of what the lifting of an eyebrow or the movement of a back *may* mean—succeeded triumphantly in an elaborate satire on himself—that is, on his own obsession? Everybody knows what Mr. James's obsession is, and, after achieving the last page of this volume, it is evident to us that Mr. James also knows. With him, as with the character without a name who tells the story, the vision of life is an obsession. To him, for real excitement, "there are no such adventures as the intellectual ones"; in every word or action of his fellow-creatures he perceives motives that, like the lines on a railway siding, have no beginning and no end. Mr. James has never carried his analysis of the daintily unimportant further than in *The Sacred Fount,* and never before, to our

knowledge, has he, after incredible labour with bricks of gossamer and mortar of sunbeams, blown down the dainty edifice with such a good-humoured series of puffs. The last page brings a vision of Mr. Henry James stepping forward, and saying with a profound obeisance: "You perceive how prodigiously I know myself."

The Sacred Fount, we may say without more ado, is youth. The theme of the book is the hypothesis that youth has the power to rejuvenate and vivify age, but at the cost of the oozing away of the sap of youth from itself. But Mr. James is not a believer in his own theory; or only to a certain extent. He turns tail, he allows his speculations to be derided, and the end is more smoke than fire; or perhaps it would be fairer to say that he uses his hypothesis merely as a means of showing to what prodigious lengths the analytical mind can go. It is as if the Princess in the fairy tale, from the suggestion of the presence of the pea beneath her mattress, had created a market garden of flowering shrubs. The pea represents the cell from which Mr. James, as master nurseryman, has produced his garden of exotics. A day and an evening cover the period of the story, which passes at Newmarch, a country house of "liberal ease" and delightful appurtenances. There a few choice guests are gathered. Among them is the narrator, with his passion for embroidering "on things" and his genius for seeing a hundred complex reasons behind a cursory remark or a chance movement. "The way you get hold of things," says Mrs. Brissenden (sometimes she is called Mrs. Briss), "is positively uncanny." It is. Here is an example of just how much the nameless narrator (we must restrain ourselves from the temptation of identifying him with Mr. James) *sees* in a glance:

Something further had befallen me. Poor Briss had met my eyes just previous to my flight, and it was then I satisfied myself of what had happened to him at the house. He had met his wife; she had in some way dealt with him; he had been with her, however briefly, alone; and the intimacy of their union had been afresh impressed upon him.

We have not space to quote the many things this Röntgenray-eyed guest saw in Mrs. Brissenden's back, but we can assure the reader that a page of the book does not cover them. His awakening is due to Mrs. Brissenden. She patiently refuses to play the part of a pretty fly, refuses to walk into the parlour to put a pretty copingstone to his palace of gossamer. Instead she fires her bright artillery at him, and the concussion shakes down the palace of gossamer. He has been elaborating his theories at infinite length, and her comments are: "How can I tell, please, what you consider you're talking about?" . . . "You see too much." . . . "You talk too much." . . . "You over-estimate the penetration of others. . . ." [Ellipses in original review.]

> "You're carried away—you're abused by a fine fancy: so that, with your art of putting things, one doesn't know where one is—nor, if you'll allow me to say so, do I quite think *you* always do. Of course I don't deny you're awfully clever. But you build up—you build up houses of cards."

Are we extravagant in suggesting that this is Mr. Henry James, in a grimly humorous mood, turning his analytical mind on himself.

The skill of the story is enormous; the triumph of its artistic presentment is indisputable: only Mr. James could have written it. So much we grant willingly; but since an author's power of being able to interest his reader in his story, as story, must depend on the temperament and predilection of the reader, we will give our personal verdict by slightly modifying one

of Mr. James's own locutions. The narrator, in the pause that follows some remarks he has made to Mrs. Brissenden, thus soliloquises: "Oh, how intensely she didn't like such a tone! If she hadn't looked so handsome, I would say she made a wry face over it." We would say—the transposition is slight: Oh, how intensely we didn't like having to read our way to the very end of *The Sacred Fount!* If Mr. James hadn't so handsomely put into it all his delicate talent, and thus illumined the tediousness of the story, we should not only have made a wry face, but yawned ourselves away to the company of—well, of John Silver or Captain Kettle.

L.R.F.O.
Speaker [England] new series 3 (23 February 1901), 580–81.

The Sacred Fount shows Mr. Henry James at his favourite pursuit of building cardhouses. This is an occupation that requires dexterity, patience and a fine quality of nerve, and Mr. James is an adept at it. The most slippery packs have no difficulties for him; under his skilful manipulation goldrimmed edges cling to a surface as of polished ivory. We watch with tense nerves and held breath the flimsy building rise story upon story, and, if we cannot control an occasional desire to go into the street and blow out the gas lamps or wrestle with the pillar-box, we are at least intensely fascinated by the delicacy of his touch and in continual round O's of astonishment at some specially difficult feat of balancing. Time after time the whole structure is saved as by a miracle, or is half demolished to remedy a defective lower story (while all the time—if we may be permitted a low comedy aside—there is a doubt whether the fault is not in an upper one). So the magician builds and we watch with wonder.

Yet if we remember aright our days of building with cards, something more than building entered into the pastime. The great joy was to bring off at the right moment the swift climax of destruction. So we must confess of being sustained through Mr. James' building operations by secretly cherishing the infantile hope that the time will come when it will suddenly collapse, or we shall be allowed to breathe and disperse it, or lay it flat with a generous sweep of the arm. Mr. James, however, gives us no such sudden release. Cramped and suffocated as we have become during the process of building, we must still sit quiet and endure, if our nerves have stood the test, a process not of destruction, but of unbuilding, a slow and deliberate removal of each card, accompanied by the regrets of the builder that anything so fine should have been destroyed. To adapt his own conclusion as to the whole concern, his method is indeed wonderful; what he too fatally lacks is the right tone.

To drop metaphor—though, indeed, we can find nothing in the ordinary threadbare phrases of criticism to express so well the impressions left on the mind by a novel of Mr. James'—this book begins brilliantly, becomes somewhat tedious through over-elaboration, and ends disappointingly with a dialogue filling a quarter of the entire work. The idea is a characteristic one; it may be described as a kind of exercise in psychological dynamics with the following problem: given a body travelling in a new direction with accelerated speed, to find, from a given number of other bodies, one whose impact has produced the new course and whose momentum has been transferred. Thus, when Mr.

and Mrs. Brissenden married, she was twice his age and looked it. When Mr. James meets her on the way, like himself, to spend a day at a country house that is the resort of intellect and beauty, he does not recognize her, she is so young and, consequently, attractive. How has she become so? A glance at "poor Briss," prematurely aged and careworn, discovers the reason at once. Here is an analogy that may be used as a torch to investigate the case of Gilbert Long, once dull of understanding, now a brilliant leader of conversation. The search for his complement, the sacred fount which gushes from him, becomes an irresistible sport for Mr. James. The theory which he seems on the way to discover obsesses him, and the obsession grows in intensity as he ponders over it in solitary walks on Newmarch terraces and through Newmarch glades. Fantastic developments and applications of his views occur, and are described with a wonderful lucidity. Up to a certain point the intellectual excitement of the investigation is kept up to a white heat; then it is unaccountably allowed to cool, and, as we have already expressed in other words, the charred remains, instead of being buried out of sight, are subjected to a minute examination by way of a climax. We can quite understand that a complete vindication of the entertaining theory developed in the constructive part of the book would not have been consistent with Mr. James' realistic method, but we think that the immense pains he is at neither to reject it nor completely to substantiate it are too marked and laborious. There is much to be said to justify an obscure ending for such a novel, and we feel sure that the obscurity, which is the total effect of a conversation that in detail is comparatively lucid, is intentional. The obscurity, however, might well be produced in two or three paragraphs: eighty pages of it make rather an Arctic night.

This book is a *reductio*—almost *ad nauseam*, if we may use such a phrase—of Mr. James' methods. Love occurs in it as a "decent working hypothesis," and his fellow guests at Newmarch are "pieces in my collection." We almost feel the pin piercing the specimens as he fixes them on his setting-board. No doubt he is having a laugh somewhat at his own expense, and we must not admit to having missed the sardonic smile in the conclusion. "I wonder if you'll understand if I make you an explanation," he says, in the course of the tremendous final dialogue, and the answer he gets is "most probably not." *The Sacred Fount* is, in fact, from one point of view (we suspect intentionally), a study in intellectual arrogance. Mr. James judges the emotions of mankind, his own included, drily with a bleak aloofness; if his insight became the omniscience he affects, how carefully we should avoid him! As it is, we cannot repress a shudder even while we admire and laugh.

Athenaeum [England] 3827. (2 March 1901), 272.

Mr. James narrates this story in the first person, so that the experiences and reflections of the narrator appear as if they were Mr. James's own: in order to keep up the dramatic illusion, we shall preserve Mr. James's own name in describing the narrator, though it must not be imagined that we regard his use of the first person singular as anything but a dramatic fiction. "Mr. James," then, one summer day found himself at a London terminus on the way to a country house party, which, we are to believe, was one of the smartest: for example, not only do the husbands pair off as a matter of course with other people's wives, but they do not even take the same trains as their lawful partners; moreover, the food and the pictures and other luxuries of a decadent civilization are all to be found of the very best at this smartly unconventional establishment. Poor "Mr. James," the dramatic character, evidently not being wholly at home in such a smart set, is naturally somewhat impressed and rather shy at the prospect before him; but he very sensibly determines to make the most of a unique occasion by going about with a mental note-book and an inquiring disposition; and he does not lose an instant in beginning. For at the station he sees a Mr. Long, whom he had once or twice before met at the same house, but who had always hitherto consistently cut him at other places. This gentleman he had consequently put down as a fool; but on this occasion Long recognizes him with some warmth, and the change is so remarkable and surprising to "Mr. James," that he immediately assumes that Long has become quite intelligent, and devotes his inquiring mind through the rest of the book trying to find out how such a change has come about. He has not arrived at the end of his train journey before he has elaborated a theory in collaboration with a Mrs. Brissenden, who of course is travelling down without her husband, and who, in the well-known way of smart people, habitually calls this husband "poor Briss." The theory, shadowy as it is, seems to be the chief point of these pages, so we shall leave anybody who is sufficiently interested to find it out for himself. To find confirmation for it "Mr. James" has a merry time of it with all the other characters of the book. He goes about buttonholing all the men, generally opening with "My dear man," to show his intimate knowledge of polite society; and even the ladies of the party have an occasional "my dear woman" tossed to them. He does not impart to any of them his theory—he is far too subtle for that—but he tries to lead them, by the most terribly long-winded conversations, into admissions of a position of which they are supremely unconscious. To do them justice, most of his interlocutors are supremely bored by him, and have very little scruple in telling him so. "You can't be a providence and not be a bore," says one of the "good women" plainly enough to him. But if his interlocutors are bored, what must his readers be? for, not content with writing out all these subtly incoherent conversations at length, he sometimes interrupts them for four or five pages on end to explain the portentous signification which his imagination sees in a droop of the lips or a movement of the hand. The book ends up with a conversation of about one hundred pages with Mrs. Brissenden. It takes place in the drawing-room after twelve, when most of the ladies have gone to bed and the servants have been "squared" (another subtle and characteristic touch of smart society) to leave the lights on. As a result of this terribly improper conference in the full blaze of the electric light, it appears that not only is "Mr. James's" theory incorrect anyhow, but that it is absolutely gratuitous, as the fact which it should have explained is not a fact, for Long turns out to be as great an ass as ever. The whole book is an example of hypochondriacal subtlety run mad. The characters in the book are simple, stupid English people, direct and comparatively uninteresting, and "Mr. James" becomes simply a bore, besides being vulgar, in his absurd attempt to read into them subtle conditions of soul of which they are totally incapable.

"A Puzzle."
Chicago *Tribune*, 5 March 1901, p. 13.

Henry James' new novel "The Sacred Fount," is almost certain to give rise to controversy. In the first place, it justifies to the full every adverse criticism ever passed upon his work by those who do not like his methods; in the second, it has puzzled his friends and admirers until they are not certain that their favorite author is not deliberately mystifying them and so betraying their confidence.

After going over the book with the painstaking minuteness required by any profound psychological treatise, an ardent admirer of all the previous novels from Mr. James' hand finds himself compelled to state that he has little or no notion what it is all about and that he does not believe Mr. James himself can inform him. Moreover, he cannot see that the novelist has written a book to be read at all—certainly those who dislike the man's work will not read, and as those who like it cannot read it, the question is, why was it written? For the fault is not in the style, which is limpidity itself in comparison with some other books from the same hand, but in the fundamental lack of underlying consistency of plan which makes every page a contradiction of its predecessors, and every psychological development in the argument at variance with all that has gone before, as well as with all that comes after.

The first working hypothesis which the interested reader will form of the intention of "The Sacred Fount" is that the author is going to demonstrate with customary subtlety the action of love as a universal solvent of all human barriers and all human incompatibilities. From time to time thereafter the same notion drifts into the brain; but less than nothing of it remains at the close, and, like the man wearied by many conundrums, he has to give up at last. More's the pity!

Manchester *Guardian*, 6 March 1901, p. 3.

In his more recent works Mr. Henry James makes large demands upon the intelligence—we had almost said the patience—of his reader. The psychological problem which always underlay his earlier and happier efforts now dominates his story to such a degree that it has almost entirely banished incident. THE SACRED FOUNT (Methuen and Co., 8vo, pp. 316, 6s.) is hardly to be classed as a novel. The scene, it is true, is laid in a country house, and the plot—what plot there is—turns upon the mutual relations of certain ill-defined men and women, whose individuality almost disappears in the subtle analysis to which they are subjected. The reader's interest is claimed for the causes that have produced certain effects in the demeanour of a man and woman, but the effects are so unimportant to anyone except a society gossip that it is difficult to be concerned for the producing causes. What is the Sacred Fount from which Mr. Long and Mr. Server have drunk that they are so changed? We are not sure that we know, even at the end of the story—and how weary a journey it has been to reach that end!—and we are quite sure that we do not care. What is become of the fresh vitality and human attractiveness that made Mr. James's earlier characters so interesting? He devotes so much labour to the analysis of motive that he no longer leaves any space for incident, forgetting that no character can take a clear individuality until it comes into action or into that sort of inaction which may fairly stand for action. In this book the same problem is set again and again with wearisome iteration in every page, and it is a problem so futile in itself, so barren of any profitable result, that it is difficult to understand that any sane mind could be interested in it. Like other writers, Mr. James has allowed the dominant interest of his own mind to destroy the objectivity of his treatment. Till he can get back to that his work will remain what it has now become—a parody of himself.

"Henry James at His Vaguest: *The Sacred Fount,* His Latest Work, Is Also His Most Characteristic." Louisville *Courier-Journal,* 9 March 1901, p. 5.

It seems strange now to look back only a few years and recall that the American field of fiction was then so barren that new books by James and Howells were annual literary events eagerly awaited and widely discussed. They were dinning the gospel of pseudo-realism into our ears very loudly, these two. The burden of James' preaching was, "character is action and action is plot." And year after year he would set forth a new set of properly drawn, properly tinted, properly grouped, workmanlike characters, who passed their entire time in introspection and positively indecent meddling with their neighbors' inner consciousness. They never, by any chance, did anything or said anything worth re-

347

membering, and nothing ever happened to them, and no one would have cared if it had, for these characters of Mr. James, while very realistic, were always rather uninteresting individuals. But the critics were already busy chanting in chorus the subtlety of Mr. James' analysis, his lucidity of style and his perfection of form—a chorus that they have continued until the present day, presumably from habit.

Meanwhile Mr. Howells was scolding us into the puzzled conviction that, from the view point of the higher intellect, Tolstoi was the only prose writer of the Nineteenth century worth reading—except Howells and James. The man who dared admire Thackeray, Dickens, Dumas or Scott was a votary of the childish, the antiquated and the obvious. And the obvious was supposed to be about the worst thing to be a votary of that could be imagined. The only fiction worth while was this or that example of dissection of the wearisome New England conscience, which, to the untutored Southern Philistine, has always seemed to be in a continual condition of ethical cramp colic. And for light mental diversion we were commended to frolic through the eight volumed "War and Peace" of Tolstoi. Of course, when no one was looking, we would slip out from the shelves the well-worn, well-loved tales of "Esmond" and "Quentin Durward" and "Sidney Carton" and "d'Artagnan." But it was done with an uneasy jam-stealing-from-the-top-shelf-in-the-pantry sort of feeling and a consciousness that we were not at all approved by our leading critics and novelists.

There was indeed a band of Meredith followers and another of Hardyites, but most Americans were partisans of either Howells or James. And the mot of one of the latter was regarded as a stroke of genius, when he said "Mr. James is the greater, because he went to London and read Balzac, while Mr. Howells stayed at home and read James."

But an astounding change was at hand. Stevenson's note of pure romance was heard and Kipling came, the true realist, the typical "votary of the obvious," of "the God of things as they are." And here and there arose young men, like James Lane Allen and Harold Frederic and others, followers of neither of the two masters, but like them scornful of pettiness and trivialities, and telling with beauty of expression and literary form of men and women who actually did things and to whom things actually happened. And as the coming of really fine novels created the proper perspective, the work of Howells and James shrivelled to its true proportions.

Mr. Howells, always a delightful essayist, has passed into editorial work. Mr. James has remained in London, but apparently he has stopped reading Balzac. He has become more English than the English. He parades his intimate acquaintance with all grades of English society and while he puts forth every year one or two sets of new characters, his fame still rests chiefly upon that truthful satire on his new-rich countrywomen, "Daisy Miller," and the fate of Howells is also his. But the critics still praise his subtlety and his style and "The Sacred Fount," his latest novel, will doubtless meet with the customary reception.

"The Sacred Fount" belongs in the class of physiologico-psychical fiction based on the ancient truism that in every love, one is the lover, the other the loved, or as Mr. James quotes one gives the lips the other gives the cheek. He takes Walt Whitman's well-known theory of emanation, that a sort of divine afflatus proceeds from the healthy human body to one in disease when the two are in intimate association, and adapts it in fantastic fashion to the mind. He shows two couples, one married, the other linked in one of those unions which seem to be highly favored in the highest social circles of England. In one case a young man wedded to a woman much his senior becomes prematurely senile, while she shows no trace of the passage of years. In the other a handsome fool becomes surpassingly brilliant—at least the author tells us so, for there is no evidence of wit or wisdom in his utterances. Then come some hundreds of pages devoted to analytical researches to discover what woman has voluntarily bankrupted her mentality in order to furnish the handsome fool with brains and afterward to aid her in her efforts not to be compromised. And that is all there is to "The Sacred Fount." He sums up his theory in this fashion:

"One of the pair has to pay for the other. What ensues is a miracle, and miracles are expensive. What's a greater one than to have your youth twice over? Mrs. Briss had to get her new blood, her extra allowance of time and bloom, somewhere; and from whom could she so conveniently extract them as from Guy himself? She has, by an extraordinary feat of legerdemain, extracted them; and he, on his side, to supply her, has had to tap the sacred fount. But the sacred fount is like the greedy man's description of the turkey as an 'awkward' dinner dish. It may be sometimes too much for a single share, but it's not enough to go round."

The characters meet at a country house which is "the great asylum of the finer wit, more or less expressly giving out that, as invoking hospitality or other countenance, none of the stupid, none even of the votaries of the grossly obvious need apply." As a sample of the finer wit one aristocratic woman remarks of another that she is "on the rush," "on the pounce" and "all over

the place." We also learn that one of the days was "large and hot." But for the finer wit, who could have dreamed of such a thing as a "large" day? And running throughout the tedious drawing of conclusions from a sidelong look or an elevated eyebrow flock the superlatives. "Immense," "magnificent," "sublime," "awful," "frantic," "prodigious" applied to the most trivial thoughts and happenings, while the author dwells complacently upon his own subtlety, his "preposterous acuteness"; his "transcendent intelligence" and like qualities. "Suppressed communication" is one of his favorite topics, which means, if it means anything, what two people think each other is thinking about when they are saying nothing. A thrilling passage is where "I sat straight down on the nearest of our benches, for this struck me as the best way to express the conception with which the sight of Mrs. Server filled me." And then for two pages he goes on to tell what he thought Mrs. Server would think about his sitting down.

But farther criticism on Mr. James is useless. The one critic thoroughly competent to handle his case passed from earth when William Makepeace Thackeray, that keen-eyed lover of true men and true art, closed his eyes.

"Manner."
London *Daily Chronicle*,
11 March 1901, p. 3.

The idea which we have painstakingly disinterred here is that of the parasitic action of some persons upon some other persons. We take no little credit in having got into a phrase what Mr. James, a much cleverer person, has taken a book to express. Everybody knows now what is Mr. James's later manner; we have given up hope of a return to his more charming earlier style; there may have arisen a school of readers who prefer the second to the first, and, if so, they should be happy, for with every book his manner, so to say, gets later and yet more late. We remember the time when, if not spoken to or interrupted in any way, we could "get the hang" of the story in the first chapter or so; now, half-a-dozen chapters must be thoughtfully "construed" (using the word in its public-school sense) before he lets it slip his pen, and a day may be coming when, if we all live, he will succeed in secreting it throughout the entire book. We conceive this to be the bourne towards which Mr. James is travelling.

Here you have a house party—and he gets the feeling of this particular kind of house party wonderfully well—in a big English country house, of which there are only four in England. Mrs. Humphry Ward wrote a novel in which she essayed a description of one of these four. The thing can hardly have much interest for the great reading public, but then, does the great reading public aspire to understand Mr. James? Wouldn't he be rather angry if they did? Anyhow, you have the fascinating study of temperaments reacting upon temperaments to that extent that the very seal of youth itself is transferred from brow to brow. In bare words, you have a man married to a woman older than himself, who ages inexplicably as she grows inexplicably younger, and you have to follow the author as he explains or rather does not explain how it is done. But it is an indiscretion, almost an offence against decency, to put Mr. James's book into bare words, and no wonder we do not succeed in making his purposes clear; we do not deserve to succeed; the attempt is flagrant,

is impious. The story is told in the first person (a system that, in other hands, makes for clarity!). And here is the last sentence but one: "Such a last word—the word that put me altogether nowhere—was too unacceptable not to prescribe afresh that prompt test of escape to other air for which I had earlier in the evening seen so much reason." That is quite one of the easiest sentences in the book too.

"A Mysterious Novel." Independent 53 (14 March 1901), 619–20.

What Mr. Henry James accomplishes is never very impressive, but the manner of his doing is the chief thing. In this particular volume apparently his purpose is to demonstrate a theory of art rather than to relate a story.

No events are recorded, but the development takes place during two days at "Newmarch," where a house party is in progress. Among the guests is a sort of refined Sherlock Holmes with a rat terrier's nose for scandal. He begins his investigations with the impression that certain people present have tapped the "Sacred Founts" of passion and vitality in some other people probably present, but to be identified. The fortunate ones are recognized by their supernatural brilliance and gross selfishness, while the victims are supposed to be in the case of the doomed spirits described in "Vathek," wandering with hearts of quivering flames in terrible silence through the firelit gloom.[1] But without developing these tragic possibilities further than to comment upon them the author unexpectedly presses his people back into normal relations. Everybody, except one man, who has been drained dry, regains the use of his own fountain and is confined to that source. No explanation is ever given of the mystery which underlies the return, tho the Sherlock Holmes wags his tail upon the scent of it throughout the volume.

The situations are in fact merely posts upon which the author hangs his literary decorations. And the question is why he affects a vagueness so reprehensible in the average writer of fiction. He shows Browning's density without having Browning's excuse for being obscure. He kicks up too much literary dust for the size of his caravan. He works with his back to the reader and does not really care whether anybody looks on to admire the performance or not. With him it is like a game of solitaire; he is absorbed in working out his own theory with the little pin point of his genius, and more particularly for his own satisfaction. Usually an author will give the reader the benefit of his "bull's eye" as they advance together through the dark mazes of the plot; but, either because he has no plot to disclose or because he considers a "bull's eye" lantern an East Side vulgarity, Henry James leaves his stumbling reader to follow as best he can. He never gives him a friendly tip in an "aside" when his people fall to discussing important secrets beyond the range of his information. After the way we have enjoyed the confidences of such as Scott and Bulwer Lytton, and of recent writers even, this refusal to recognize us on the part of Mr. James is mortifying.

The story, such as it is, advances more through telepathy than by conversation or narrative forms. The characters sit with their backs to each other while rich glooms intervene, and *feel* what the other thinks. And the author understands too well the pit from which we are digged. Spirituality can never grow above his carnal suspicions. He holds his people remorselessly down to the flesh. Their convictions are social and secular rather than ethical. His men only show their shirt fronts, and once in a long while we may catch a glimpse of a lady's ankles, but of their souls, never a hint. Not having the genius necessary for dealing with these high things, it is consummate art not to call attention to them. He merely bows in graceful acknowledgment when he appropriates our religious paraphernalia to offset the "pagan piety" of his women.

His manner to all his characters is that of the tempter. He consistently appeals to the worse motives in the class of men with which he deals. His art consists in portraying their struggles against his solicitations. Balancing his heroines one at a time anywhere upon a little projecting sentence, he offers them all the kingdoms of the earth to jump off into something guilty. But they have been too well bred to compromise themselves. With their heads on one side they only enjoy the possibilities involved, then bow naïvely and shake an accusing finger at him as they step back and down into the commonplace, which must be provoking after the pains he has been at to arrange the scenic effect for their fall.

In the end the reader is left to his own confusion. And if he has not kept up with the author's rapid process of deduction and elimination he is indeed confused. The truth is, Mr. James has done nearly everything that we condemn in other writers, not stupidly, but gracefully, with the audacity of a man who challenges every standard of excellence that does not conform to his own. But we predict that "The Sacred Fount" will have more purchasers than readers. People are not so much interested in the science relating to the way a story ought to be told as they are in the narrative itself.

Note

1   William Beckford, *Vathek* (1786).

Cornelia Atwood Pratt. *Critic* 38 (April 1901), 368–70.

"The Sacred Fount" is sublimated gossip. The experienced reader does not need to be told that gossip plus Henry James changes its substance and becomes incorporeal, dazzling, and, to the vulgar, impossible. Doubtless Beyond, man will gossip thus.

The book is another of Mr. James's incredible feats. Its foundation—if it can be said to have anything so solid—is quite simple. The story relates the mental adventures of a nameless man who goes down for the week's-end to Newmarch, a country house whose occupants pride themselves—obviously not without reason—upon the intellectual acuteness of their guests. In the train, on the way down, the narrator meets two people to whom unprecedented things have happened. There is Gilbert Long, who used to be "a fine piece of human furniture," handsome, beefy, stupid; he has gained in ease of manner and in intellectual perception; he has acquired a mind and a tongue. There is also Mrs. Brissenden, a woman of forty-two or -three, who is married to a man barely thirty; she is now distinctly handsome, whereas she had been plain, and she is "prodigious" in the youthfulness of her aspect. While this lady is talking to some one else, the narrator makes out, with the assistance of Mr. Gilbert Long, that for Mrs. Brissenden the clock stopped on her marriage; her husband's youth became her own. And while Mr. Long is occupied

with a newsboy, he consults with Mrs. Brissenden and learns that the former has been altered from a "heavy Adonis" into an intelligent human being with lively mental reflexes through the particular interest taken in him by some clever woman. Arriving at Newmarch this psychical detective further discovers that Mrs. Brissenden's resplendent, almost insolent, assumption of youth is matched by the way in which her husband has piled up the years; "it was as if he had discovered some short-cut to the common doom." Pondering these appearances, he finds himself on the track of something ultimate—of a law whereby a supreme affection is permitted to work miracles in behalf of the beloved object. The next step, naturally, is to revert to the miracle of Mr. Gilbert Long. Who has offered at his shrine an affection so immense that it has literally re-created him? Not, surely, the hard and ostentatious Lady John to whom Mrs. Brissenden has ascribed the feat. No, judging from the analogy of the Brissendens, the woman who is responsible for Long's accession of wit must have parted with her own. The question of discovering her, then, becomes one of finding a woman once brilliant who gives the effect of having become an intellectual bankrupt.

Thus far, and, indeed, not a little farther, the reader goes willingly. "This is a new game," he says to himself, "but the rules seem simple enough, and yet, as Mr. James plays it, it is an absorbing mental diversion; there is more science in it than in any of the other clever games—their name is legion—which we have played with Mr. James. Let us see how it comes out."

What happens is that the narrator, pursuing his detective work, takes the foregoing appearances and inferences and uses them as a child uses soapsuds and a clay pipe. He blows an immense, brilliantly variegated brain-bubble and represents it

352

to himself as a world of truth which he has put together. The bubble grows bigger and bigger; the colors chase themselves over its surface more furiously. Just as those black swirls across the color which denote the limit of expansion appear—something happens! Either the bubble bursts, or it is whisked out of sight. You may choose your own interpretation. It is possible to be an abject admirer of Mr. James and yet to feel one has not been treated fairly here.

We have all had flashes of intuition and had them confirmed by our own interpretation of subsequent events; this gives us the basis for appreciating the constructive joy of the "conscientiously infernal" narrator who adds one subtle sign to another and "makes out" otherwise unattested marvels with unholy glee. He is conscious by flashes, this over-curious mind, that he is something of a cad, even if his prying is on the physical and not the material plane; he has his reluctances, his intervals of sanity, when he feels that his complicated perceptions are extravagant, that his whole idea is a ridiculous obsession, but most of the time his plunges of insight so exhilarate him as to leave no room for misgiving. He feels "the joy of the intellectual mastery of things unamenable, the joy of determining, almost of creating, results."

The reader, too, has an obsession. It is to keep up with the story-teller, to "make out," to take it all in, to believe in the brain-bubble. At first this is easy and delightful, but before the end it becomes almost a nightmare. He hypnotizes himself into holding the mood of acceptance while the book lasts, but when Mrs. Brissenden says to the psychological detective on the last page, "My poor dear, you *are* crazy!" the reader breathes a sigh of relief. He is not sure he agrees with her, but even the possibility is refreshing!

In other words, to keep up with Mr. James in this story strains even a willing intelligence to the breaking point. This is,

perhaps, because the book has none of those intimate relations with the world of ethics which usually enrich by implication this writer's art. Usually he holds up the torch and illuminates the dark places of life and thought in one way or another, but "The Sacred Fount" is a pure *tour de force*. It takes away our breath with astonishment and gives us nothing in return. It is wonderful, but is it worth while?

"Mr. Henry James' New Novel." Current Literature 30 (April 1901), 493.

"The way you get hold of things," says Mrs. Brissenden in The Sacred Fount, "is positively uncanny." Mrs. Brissenden is not speaking to us. We do not get hold of things. We do not pretend that we do. Mr. F. Marion Crawford says that he does. No one else outside the book has as yet made the claim.

The publication of Mr. Henry James' new novel has been probably the literary event of the month—an event in its result most exasperating. Mr. James has out-Jamesed himself in a book which must stagger some of his most unflinching admirers, and of which the effect upon the reader first making the acquaintance of his work could be only a conviction of its absolute lack of sense. It is all about a secret—of course a psychological one. It all happens in a single day—a solitary, eventless day in which nobody does anything. Everybody talks, however, in that brilliantly tedious tongue which the James characters always use, filling three hundred pages with abstractions, inuendoes, hair-splitting distinctions, and what are probably epigrams, all so arranged that it is quite possible to read three pages without getting a scintilla of an idea as to what they are driving at. These people are discussing each other, and the impersonal narrator is discussing them all—a preternaturally acute narrator, an X-ray-eyed narrator, who does not need to have anything told him, who understands the most complicated situations in half a word, and revels in a seventh heaven of subtilty.

Mary Dear.
"*The Sacred Fount*."
Indianapolis *News,* 13 April 1901, p. 5.

"The Sacred Fount" is by Henry James, a man who writes for those only who like to read his books; a new book of his acts like enchantment on his own readers.

"The Sacred Fount" opens with one of Henry James's good beginnings. The commencement is the taking of a train at London to join a party at a great English seat, of the sort that figures so delightfully in his novels. There at the station is the English railway carriage, not a thing to climb into at one end and fall out of at the other, but a carriage, to be stepped into on a level with the fine stone platform of the station; a comfortable carriage, at whose door you are not jostled by a crowd of barbarians, for only your own party enters with you; a carriage into which no lamplighter, no brakeman, no conductor, no peanut vendor and nobody that wants to drink water, ever enters, and a carriage that runs on its metals without swaying, without jarring. O comfortable memory to us American travelers!

Around the door of the English railway carriage in the story lingers a group who are going down to the country-house to meet, on the morrow at breakfast, various other persons, some bleak, some charming, some strangers, some old friends, some half remembered—all elegant. Among them is one of Henry James's heroes, a six-footer, with a blooming face and a low-growing, tight-curling hair, a fine piece of human furniture, who makes a small party seem more numerous. A porter is called to shift their luggage, they enter their train; they chat of whom they are to meet. Several of those wonderfully beautiful middle-aged women, who are the pride of England, figure in the narrative. At the termination of the short, dustless railway journey, which does not require a fresh toilette on the part of the travelers, follows the long afternoon of renewals of acquaintanceship, the sitting and strolling, for snatches of talk, in the shade of great trees and through the straight walks of old gardens, while fresh accessions of visitors enrich the pictures, among them many who promise to be interesting. All face [*sic*] for the house at twilight, to dress for dinner, and all go to their rooms, finding their cards on the doors of the chambers they are to use.

The splendor of the dinner and the beauty and elegance of the guests form a finish to the first day of the story. One lady is slim and fair, with pale eyes and auburn hair; they do not break out right and left with assertions and reflections; in fact, their talk is rather dull, to the sense of an American.

Next morning all within the house is clear dimness and rich gleams. All without is sunshine and August. Tall windows stand open upon shaded terraces, pink parasols are put up for sauntering in the great spaces of landscape gardening on a grand scale. The day as it develops is hot, and brilliant with a splendor of summer, and the company are spared organized amusements; life is a mere ramble and lounge for them, and the grandeur of the place where they are grows on the reader. Great, dim chambers indoors and great sweeps of view without, tea on the terraces, arbors far from the house, long vistas, at the end of which the mansion always rears its front; open, verdurous circles among trees with the sky above and with ancient stone seats about, and lengthening arching recesses of shade stretching away from these green circles, form parts of the picture. The company is gathered together to be handsome and happy, to be really what they look, and to look tremendously well; the ladies wear fresh dresses and jewels at dinner every day.

If anyone is ugly he is like some fine old Velasquez portrait, a presentation of ugliness and melancholy that is royal to behold.

After dinner long vistas of chains of rooms remain open and lighted in the great house for those who wish to talk into the small hours. The smoking-room where gentlemen gather late at night, is partly lined with books in warm bindings, admirable for old gilt and color, and there clusters of men smoke, contented, on easy seats among popped corks. In going from drawingroom to smoking-room you tread over marble and velvet, through twists and turns, among glooms and glimmers and echoes.

The conversations in "The Sacred Fount" are not up to the setting of the story. The house is immense, but the talk is not. The book is one of Henry James' minor works. Nobody can read it through save those who remember the author's better works, or those inveterate novel-readers who can never find enough novels to read, and go through pretty dull ones. The dialogues are not good enough to match the high tree tops and pinnacles, the long crests of motionless woods and chimneyed roofs that rise in the golden air

of the story. Charming manners are there and the refined, but exaggerated, glee that is frequent in high companies and light colloquies, but the high sport of intelligent talk between gentlemen, the play of lively expression and sociability, are not there. You are glad when the two days' visit is ended and the visitors begin to make arrangements for meeting in town; their talk has bored you. If Henry James' style becomes much more involved, he can not be read at all.

Saturday Review [England] 91 (4 May 1901), 574.

Confirmed readers of Mr. Henry James' novels must have, one would think, something of the same strenuous contempt for the adherents of all easier forms of fiction as some ostrich, blandly assimilating a breakfast of telegraph wire, must feel for such poor-spirited creatures as demand an effeminately eupeptic diet of green things or hay. "The Sacred Fount" requires of the reader a degree of concentration about the same as do the tougher passages of Aristotle's "Metaphysics." Its motive is a kind of grimly ingenious proposal on the part of a narrator who dimly writes himself an ass that social intercourse should be regulated on the vampirish suggestion that it is possible to exhaust the "sacred fount" of a husband's or other casual acquaintance's vitality for the mental and physical rejuvenation of oneself and one's friends. The pursuit of this theory is conducted with characteristic litheness of thought and subtle finish of style, in which every word is fraught with deliberate meaning. To such persons as may prefer even in novel-reading to "crush the wine of victory from the grapes of toil" this book is recommended with the utmost sincerity.

London *Times*, 4 May 1901, p. 5.

In an assembly of wise men a certain sage once propounded the question, "Whether a work of humour could ever be conceived and executed with such subtlety as should hinder the whole world from perceiving its aim?" After some disputation it was agreed that the possibility existed. Whereupon an Average Person who chanced to be of the company inquired what object such a work could have, and the sages answered that to the writer, on the one hand, this super-subtlety might afford entertainment, but, as regarded the readers, it was just as if they conned the writings of a dullard. Very respectfully we would venture to commend this apologue to the notice of Mr. Henry James. We have read THE SACRED FOUNT (Methuen) with care, as becomes those who value Mr. James's talent, and who have in the past—even in the quite recent past—derived pleasure and refreshment from his novels. The exact intention of the author having seemed to escape us upon a first reading, we read it again. Still finding ourselves hazy about the meaning, a third perusal was adventured. And now, after so much hard, mental effort, after solitary wrestling, and after consultation with other readers, we are bound to admit that we have the dimmest of notions as to what "The Sacred Fount" is all about. The only explanation that seems possible is that Mr. James, annoyed by the folly of shallow admirers, who praise his books for their least praiseworthy qualities, has gone about to parody himself, and that he is now laughing in his sleeve at the sham enthusiasts who pretend to think is a great work. If there were really any danger of finding oneself among such people as fill the pages of "The Sacred Fount" with cryptic elliptical snatches of conversation, the only thing to do would be to join the Trappist Order and live under a vow of perpetual silence. Since no such people exist, it scarcely seems worth while to go to the trouble of inventing them.

Checklist of Additional Reviews

"Mr. James' Unrevealed Secret." Chicago *Evening Post*, 9 February 1901, p. 5.

New York *World*, 9 February 1901, p. 8.

Brooklyn *Daily Eagle*, 16 February 1901, p. 7.

New York Times Saturday Review of Books and Art 6 (16 February 1901), 112.

Henry Austin Clapp. Boston *Daily Advertiser*, 23 February 1901, p. 8.

Detroit *Free Press*, 23 February 1901, p. 11.

Literature [England] 8 (23 February 1901), 144.

Boston *Sunday Post*, 24 February 1901, p. 30.

Detroit *Evening News*, 24 February 1901, section 2, p. 17.

Providence *Sunday Journal*, 24 February 1901, p. 15.

Springfield [Mass.] *Republican*, 24 February 1901, p. 15.

"House of Cards." *Pall Mall Gazette*, [England] 26 February 1901, p. 4. Reprinted in James W. Gargano, *Critical Essays on Henry James: The Late Novels* (Boston: G. K. Hall, 1987), pp. 42–44.

Carolyn Shipman. *Book Buyer* 22 (March 1901), 148.

Congregationalist 86 (2 March 1901), 353.

Outlook 67 (2 March 1901), 554.

Spectator [England] 86 (2 March 1901), 318–19. Reprinted in Roger Gard, ed., *Henry James: The Critical Heritage* (London: Routledge & Kegan Paul, 1968), p. 306.

Cleveland Plain Dealer Sunday Magazine, 3 March 1901, section 3, p. 8.

San Francisco *Chronicle*, 3 March 1901, p. 28.

Literary World [England] 63 (8 March 1901), 218–19.

World's Work 1 (April 1901), 667.

Illustrated London News 118 (13 April 1901), 536.

Churchman 83 (4 May 1901), 552.

Harry T. Peck. *Bookman* [New York] 13 (July 1901), 442. Reprinted in Gard, p. 308; Gargano, pp. 44–45.

THE WINGS OF THE DOVE

"Mr. Henry James's Novel."
London *Daily Chronicle*, 29 August 1902, p. 3.

The reader who comes victoriously to the end of this extraordinary book may plume himself on something more than an uncommon feat of application. He has some title to be considered joint author. Mr. James has contributed close upon six hundred pages. The reader, who has to read all the time between the lines, may think that his share of the composition reaches an equal quantity of matter. Mr. James, at any rate, does him the honour of leaving to his intelligence the solution of a vast number of minute problems. Seldom do any of the characters in the story decide upon matters even of the smallest consequence. The reader is placed inside their minds, and left to discover from the infinite complications of the mechanism what they would be at. If he were shut up in a factory to find out for himself the co-operative action of all the whirring wheels, the effect could be scarcely more bewildering. Bewilderment, however, must be brief if the reader is to be worthy of collaborating with Mr. James. He must have his wits about him, not his ordinary wits, not the wits that earn his respectable livelihood, but an almost uncanny acuteness. Mr. James has a sly allusion to the heroines of New England fiction, who can see "round several corners." His readers must have the same gift of vision, and must employ it in a singular way. His characters rarely allow a fact to do anything so rude as to stare them in the face. Perceiving its approach, they promptly encircle it with masses of vapour, with all manner of cloudy and attractive corners, and the devoted reader must see round these with a growing conviction that no fact ought ever to be disclosed in the crudity of naked outline.

It must not be inferred from all this that Mr. James has no story to tell. He happens to be, amongst other things, a story-teller of the first order, even when he seems to be most occupied with making his personages interpellate one another's nerves, as if through a telephone exchange not in perfect order. The story of "The Wings of the Dove" is sufficiently remarkable, especially when we consider the efforts of everybody concerned to keep it dark. Kate Croy, handsome, a little cold and hard, "lucid and ironic," brutal sometimes, but not "brutally brutal," is left motherless with a widowed and helpless sister, and a scamp of a father. "Papa has done something wicked." What it is we are not permitted to know, but it has removed him beyond the pale of society. Kate, who is capable of singular sacrifices, offers to live with this irredeemable parent. He rejects the proposal with contumely, seeing no personal advantage in it, and the young woman is taken under the roof of a wealthy aunt, who will have nothing to do with the rest of the family. Aunt Maud has ambitious schemes for her beautiful niece, and frowns upon the young journalist, Merton Densher, to whom Kate has plighted her affections. We have a strange liking for Aunt Maud. She startles us with one of the few direct and emphatic statements in the book. "I lie well, thank God!" says Aunt Maud. The sentiment is immoral, but it is not without a certain refreshment, quite harmless, seeing that she does not lie at all. A constant guest is Lord Mark (the family name of this nobleman is unrevealed), who is best described by the impression he makes on the journalist. Introduced to Densher, he simply said, "Oh!"

Densher said nothing, occupied as he mainly was on the spot with weighing the sound in question. He recognised it in a moment as less imponderable than it might have appeared, as having, indeed, positive claims. It wasn't, that is, he knew, the "Oh!" of the idiot, however great the superficial resemblance; it was that of the clever, the accomplished man; it was the very speciality of the speaker, and a deal of expensive training and experience had gone to producing it. Densher felt somehow that, as a thing of value, accidentally picked up, it would retain an interest of curiosity.

Lord Burleigh's nod was nothing in point of significance to Lord Mark's "Oh!" But even this accomplishment does not advance this young nobleman's suit, either with Kate or with Milly Theale, the American heiress, who appears on the scene when Mr. Densher is away on a mission from Fleet-street to the United States. She had met him in New York, and conceived a hopeless passion for him. She is a beautiful and gentle creature, literally dying of love, and keeping the secret almost to the end from herself, her friends, the breathlessly attentive reader; from everybody, in short, except the eminent medical man who divines the mystery, but contrives to say nothing about it.

It is impossible to give the faintest idea of the skill with which Mr. James handles this delicate theme. Milly dies through three parts of the story. She dies by inches, by pages, by whole chapters. It would be intolerably painful, but for the art which wraps it all in a softening mist of elusion. There is only one way of saving her life, and that is by marriage with Densher before it is too late. This young man finds himself in a notable dilemma. Kate, with her instinct for sacrifice, begs him to marry the girl. Should he become a wid-ower, well, he will have a fortune, and there will still be Kate. Needless to say, this proposition is not put with such explicitness. Again Mr. James's consummate evasion almost obliterates the suggestion of the "brutally brutal." Perhaps it is not brutal at all, for such a marriage would differ considerably from the marriage of convenience. But we are relieved to find that the journalist does not become Milly's husband, though he solves the problem in ethics by a compromise, which, if we understand Mr. James's intention, touches a still more striking pinnacle of audacity. Readers must take what view they please of Mr. James's intention, and of Miss Croy's incidental behaviour. There is, at all events, no sordid acceptance of dollars, and Kate and her lover are left at the end perched upon an altitude of self-denial. Such is the story, which we are almost ashamed to put in the form of a comparatively plain, unvarnished tale. It is an astonishing example of Mr. James's later method, not a method suited to all tastes, not a method which always achieves its own object. "My dear child, we move in a labyrinth," said a friend of Milly's. "Of course we do. That's just the fun of it!" said Milly with a strange gaiety. Then she added, "Don't tell me there are not abysses. I want abysses." Mr. James wants abysses overmuch. It is impossible for ordinary human beings to be so prodigiously deep as he would like to make them. Real people to begin with, his characters are apt to lose their reality in the minutiæ of an incredible observation. They become phantasmal intelligences. This seems to us the effect of Mr. James's method in its present excess. His book is too long, and far too meticulously elaborate. But it shows him as a writer of extraordinary amplitude of mind, with insatiable curiosity of research into the byways of human nature, and as a craftsman who has made fiction the subtlest of the arts.

Henry B. Fuller. "Latest Novel of Henry James Is a Typical Example of His Art." Chicago *Evening Post*, 30 August 1902, p. 4.

It is apparently the impression of both Henry James and his publishers (if one may judge from the preliminary announcements) that Mr. James in his latest novel, "The Wings of the Dove," has come down to the people—has made some such recognition of plot and incident as he was willing to concede in earlier years, and has produced a work which is susceptible of comprehension, not only by the more studious and determined members of his own profession, but even by the careless and unillumined laity. There seems to be a more or less open claim that Mr. James has "returned," and an intimation that those who have known him and left him may return on their part, too, as well as an assurance that those who have never known him may hope, at last, to know him now.

But, really, few men "return," despite Nietzsche's doctrine of the eternal recurrence; they move on—with such a difference, great or slight, as may be. The difference in Mr. James is very slight indeed. He may have thought to condescend—to dip down so far as to prejudice his own artistic integrity; he may have felt that he was risking such mortification as must ensue upon the grazing of the obvious; but, after all, the change is more in his intention than in the result, and those to whom Henry James has hitherto been an enigma will probably find him an enigma still.

The connoisseur who invites you to his rooms may pursue one of two courses. He may turn up the lights at the very beginning, thus aiding you to a general survey of his quarters and inviting you to a clear, easy, detailed inspection of his collections. Or he may cut off the light and muffle up the windows and allow you to jolt and grope and flounder among his possessions until, at the expense of bruised elbows and bewildered brain, you shall have acquired a dusky, theoretical knowledge of the shape and size of his apartment and of the disposal of his possessions through it.

The former method is that of the common North American novelist; the latter is the method favored by Mr. James. It is an intellectual exercise of a somewhat heroic type. It cultivates and strengthens both the power of synthesis and the power of analysis. And when, at the end, your host turns up the gas—if he does—you have a certain pleasure in finding your guesses substantiated and your conjectures confirmed. But this is not precisely the sort of pleasure that a work of art is expected to yield.

In the present instance Mr. James's cabinet is unusually crowded, so let us have the lights turned up to start with. We may even venture to disclose his plot, without doing an injustice—since no one would dream of reading Mr. James for plot primarily, or even secondarily; and the plot once disposed of, the ground is cleared for higher enjoyments.

His Dove, then, is Miss Mildred Theale of New York, who is dying, en princesse, in an old Venetian palace, under the paternal care of a great London physician. She is dovelike in name, and still more dovelike in nature—a gentle, exquisite, immaculate young creature upon whom her creator seems to have lavished all the stored-up sympathies of his sixty years.

Her Wings are financial, monetary, formed of bonds, one might say, and

363

feathered with coupons—not the pinions upon which one may fly away and be at rest, but those that constitute the spreading defense of brooding affection. A swift succession of calamities and fatalities has left her sole mistress of a prodigious fortune, and her foreign travels bring her into relations with the impecunious pair of young English lovers whose defenseless heads she is to cover at the expense of her own unsatisfied heart.

Merton Densher is a London journalist of limited means and unpromising future. Kate Croy is the daughter of a dispersed and ruined family, and is dependent upon the good will of a wealthy aunt. The aunt prefers that she marry Lord Mark—the equivocal designation of a nebulous and dubious nobleman—but Kate secretly engages herself to Densher. Milly Theale, unaware of this engagement, falls in love with Densher. Lord Mark, repulsed by Kate, proposes to Milly. Refused by her, he tells her the tale of the secret engagement. That is Milly's coup de grace. She dies, having made a will in favor of Densher. Thus does she stretch out her wings.

Kate and Milly are intimate friends. Kate proposes to Densher that he shall marry Milly, thus securing her fortune and making their own marriage possible later. Densher rises above the temptation. After Milly's death Kate accuses him of having been in love with her. He denies it.

"Your word of honor that you're not in love with her memory. . . . Her memory's your love. You want no other."

"I'll marry you, mind you, in an hour," he said.

"As we were?"

"As we were."

But she turned to the door, and her headshake was now the end. "We shall never be again as we were!"

And that is the finish.

To reach this finish requires ten "books," aggregating 770 pages—a labyrinth that might well require a clew. It is a veritable fog of words; the more matters are explained the more urgent does still further explanation seem to become. Mr. James repels with as much of disdainful decision as ever the advances of the obvious, the banal, the derivative. In point of conception, of execution, of diction, of all the rest, he is himself—the self-expresser par excellence; the master of initiative; and not only "of the center," as Matthew Arnold phrases it, but at the very center of the center. Yet to reach this goal and to hold it to his own satisfaction requires— words, and again—words, and yet again—words: a many-syllabled multiplicity of shadings, discriminations, qualifications and analytical niceties to cope with which the reader must combine the best points of the clairvoyant, the psychologist and the detective. Some of his effects are magnificent—nobody else in the world could fetch them off—yet as often as not they leave us dazed and more or less exhausted.

The chief of these effects in "The Wings of the Dove" is the psychology of Kate Croy. A brief resumé of the story may seem to make her out little less than a "villainess." Nothing, however, could be farther from the truth. Her earlier aspects are those of a veritable heroine, and the end, as we have already seen, leaves her a heroine still; but whether all her intermediate functionings are in accord with this lofty role, or indeed in consistency with one another, some more expert psychologist must decide. One might venture to say, however, that a girl who would propose an intermediate marriage (quite of the sort that moved our laughter in "The Mikado") would scarcely be very exigent regarding her lover's state of mind toward the memory of the bride that was to have been. But, as I have said, Mr. James studiously avoids the too apparent and the commonplace.

His technique remains as excessively Whistlerian as ever: myriads of infinitesimal touches fall like dim flakes upon his canvas; the longer he labors the more confusing do his labors become: the picture continually darkens and constantly sinks farther into its frame; and the poor limited amateur, though he have the best will in the world, is finally compelled to give the master up.

The world moves and of course the growing artist must move with it; but that twenty-two years should have led us on from "The Portrait of a Lady" to "The Wings of the Dove" is a matter more for amazement than for pleasure. As one of the old guard, I shall still profess a loyalty to the earlier books. Isabel Archer is just as attractive in her tender young dignity as Milly Theale, and rather easier to get at; and Lord Warburton is worth a dozen Lord Marks; and old Mrs. Touchett has much more definition and brio than Aunt Maud Lowder; and Henrietta Stackpole is just as stanch a friend as Susan Shepherd Stringham, and much better fun; and quaint, blessed Ralph Touchett is worth all the Merton Denshers that ever could be invented; and Gardencourt is vastly more of this world than is the vague Venetian palace wherein Milly Theale wore her ropes of pearls and held her pathetic little court.

Comparing these two books of two different periods, one feels that Mr. James has gone along refining on his own refinements until the delicate has become the impalpable, and the elusive the intangible, and the exquisite the all but imperceptible. To such lengths may we be led by our pursuit of the exact nuance in thought and the mot juste in expression, by the desire to compass the absolute where others make shift to rub along with the merely approximate, and by a determination to

be choicely, immitigably individual at whatever sacrifice of the social qualities and the instinct for solidarity. All these characteristics are growing on Mr. James, and they make it unlikely that, with the best will in the world, he will produce a book that the general reading public, even in its upper grades, can greatly care for. But his earlier books still remain, and some of these no fairly discriminating reader would wish to lose.

"Mr. Henry James's New Story."
London *Daily News*, 8 September 1902, p. 6.

We are sometimes tempted during the course of our reading of "The Wings of the Dove" (Archibald Constable and Co. 6s. 576 pages) to address the author, Mr. Henry James, somewhat in the words used by the immortal Mr. Yellowplush to Bulwer Lytton: "Now, what do you mean, Bart?" The story is very slight, concerning itself with some half-dozen people. The delicacy of its writing, the elusiveness of its treatment, are so tenuous that often we can no longer follow them. The intricacies of emotion, the play of light and shadow are so complex, so broken up into a thousand currents and cross currents, that we lay down the book completely at sea as to their meaning. We feel that our intellect and our capacity for emotion are altogether too clumsy to deal with them. Nothing so brutal and bald as an event is allowed, and yet there are pages of great beauty that are all alive with the finer vibrations of the spirit. The theme is shadowy, but to it is attached something of the passion of the universe.

The romance turns round an American girl, Milly Theale, a "slim, constantly pale, delicately haggard, anomalously haggard, agreeably angular young person, of not more than two and twenty in spite of her marks, whose hair was somehow exceptionally red even for the real thing which it innocently confessed to being, and whose clothes were remarkably black even for robes of mourning, which was the meaning they expressed." Milly goes to Europe with Mrs. Stringham, a writer of short stories, whose sympathy and admiration she has enlisted at first sight. The analysis of the character of Mrs. Stringham—indeed, we may say of every character in the book—is quite admirable. There are three or four pages devoted to the lady that cannot be surpassed as a study. But the impression we derive from them is frittered away by the excess of analysis before we have got through half the volume. Milly Theale has an immense love of life, a soul athirst for all its beauty and all its love, and she is dying of some mysterious disease. The touches with which the sense that she is mortally attacked is brought home to the girl, are all wonderfully to the point, and are all wonderful in their truth and pathos. But it is only on re-reading the ponderous volume that their values tell. It is difficult to understand at first what all these broken phrases, these half hints mean, and what they have to do with the thread of the story. Almost the first glimmer of a mystery is given to us when in Switzerland Mrs. Stringham goes to seek the girl and finds her on a mountain peak, sitting on the slope of a jutting rock, from which a single false movement, the turn of the head, might precipitate her into the depths below.

It gave her time to receive the impression which, when she some minutes later softly retraced her steps, was to be the sharpest she carried away. This was the impression that if the girl was deeply and recklessly meditating there, she was not meditating a jump; she was, on the contrary, as she sat, much more in the state of uplifted and unlimited possession that had nothing to gain from violence. She was looking down on the kingdoms of the earth, and though indeed that of itself might well go to the brain, it wouldn't be with a view of renouncing them. Was she choosing among them, or did she want them all.

In London, Milly consults the foremost physician of the day, accompanied by a friend, made quite recently, Kate Croy, and asks him if she is dying. He does not answer definitely, but tells her she wants joy, she must be as happy as she can be. Milly thankfully accepts the great man's verdict, and sets herself to be happy. She lives by the will—the will to live. She is in love with a young journalist, Merton Densher, whom she had met in New York before starting for Europe, and he is secretly engaged to be married to Kate Croy. Both these characters are very finely and clearly drawn. Before he had gone to New York

They had exchanged vows and tokens, sealed their rich compact, solemnised, so far as breathed words and murmured sounds and lighted eyes and clasped hands could do it, their agreement to belong only, and to belong tremendously, to each other.

Mrs. Lowder, Kate's aunt, with whom she lives, is colossally vulgar and colossally rich. She ignores the situation. By acting the part that her niece is not in love she thinks she will destroy the feeling. Kate has a mysteriously unclassed father, and a sister, the widow of a curate, who is very poor and mercenary, and it is imperative for Kate to remain with her aunt. She meets Milly and falls under her spell, the spell of the dove. The story with all its fantastical complications, its shadowy crisis, the terrible tide of passion that actuates its characters, needed the most lucid treatment to enlist our sympathy. It is not for us to tell the piteous end nor its enigmatical conclusion. If Mr. James had devoted half the space to his story, told it with no unnecessary mysteries of language and of thought, he would have written one worthy of his genius. As it is, his style has run to seed, he holds to the delight of trying to say the impalpable. He indulges in all sorts of allusiveness in curious obscurities, in a strange wit, in far-fetched humour, in a twisted and perplexing fancifulness.

"Mr. Henry James's New Book." Manchester *Guardian*, 10 September 1902, p. 7.

Mr. Henry James's latest work, THE WINGS OF THE DOVE (A. Constable and Co., pp. 576), exhibits in a heightened degree the qualities both for good and ill which have previously been noticed in these pages, and which are familiar enough to his own public. Never before has he been more demoniacally clever, more suggestive; never more allusive, more cryptic, more insatiate in his demands on the attention and intelligence of his readers. It is plain enough that he has long ago given up appealing to a wide audience. He is writing for a clique, for readers "fit if few," for those who have been trained to his mannerisms, who have learnt to read constantly between the lines. In his earlier days there was perhaps no writer whose English was more pellucid, more instantly intelligible, but he has developed a later style which is always a little difficult and is often quite obscure. He distracts the attention by frequent parentheses, often put in the form of rhetorical questions, or he taxes it by throwing his words into an unnatural order, so that the sentence has to be read twice over before its meaning is grasped. "What somehow in the most extraordinary way in the world had Kate wanted but to be of a sudden, more interesting than she had ever been" is a sentence whose sense is intelligible enough with a little care, but it wants care, and it is not worth the trouble it calls for. And this goes on for more than five hundred and fifty pages. Mr. James was always addicted to little tricks of phrase and idiosyncrasies of vocabulary with which it is necessary to become familiar. In this story he pushes the tendency to excess. Everyone is "immense" or "stupendous" or "glorious," an exuberance which may be natural enough in the mouth of Americans, but which is foreign to the habits of his English characters. Occasionally he descends to slang, and the effect is strangely incongruous. Kate tells her lover to "buck up," and spoils a scene and mars our impression of her character. He no doubt has become discontented with or tired of his old manner. He wishes to take hold of language with a new grasp and compel it to effects of which it is not safely capable.

The same tendency is discernible in Mr. James's psychology. He has of course always found his main interest in human character. But it may be questioned whether the characters which he now describes always appear as human. After making all allowance for the complexity of the female mind, can it be said that Kate moves within the bounds of human possibility? Other characters are dissected with such subtlety, which such reiteration, that their personality almost evades us. "The Dove" remains impalpable, if suggestively beautiful, to the end. For every page of dialogue, for every ten lines of action, Mr. James has twenty pages of suggestion and criticism, of explanation or apology. His art is too much with him, probing into unnecessary "abysms of personality" with a superfluity of conscientiousness which prevents him from "getting on." And yet, somehow and slowly, he gets on. Through dams and obstructions which with any other writer would have stifled the story, by this writer's unique art there trickles a thin coherent rivulet of narrative, which gathers strength as it proceeds and at times almost promises to flow free. If only this wonderful story-teller would think more of the matchless tales he has to tell. But that is not what interests him. In the same way, it is not the events in which they participate which interest his characters. It is only their own attitude to them with which they are concerned, their own pose—"where they are" just now or then, as Mr. James rather tediously puts it. Of the story itself, as we have already implied, it is impossible to speak too highly, where it emerges into view. There are times when we seem to be moving in worlds unrealised by the masculine consciousness, worlds wherein honour and truth and good faith appear in strange forms. But we are willing to believe Mr. James (for we cannot always be certain of his meaning) that all is well in the end, and that Kate should stand justified in our eyes, as well as in the eyes of her lover, by virtue of an insight, perhaps, which she possessed by right of sex, into the real bearings of the situation, which is denied to the perplexed reader.

F. Prevost Battersby. *"The Wings of the Dove."* London *Morning Post,* 11 September 1902, p. 2.

It would not be easy in enumerating the qualities of Mr. Henry James as a novelist to put the finger definitely on one in which pre-eminently his charm lay. He has a style completely, one might almost say inimitably, his own, a style the facility, the dexterity of which offers of itself an absorbing study, yet he can contrive on rare occasions, even in his easiest and most dexterous moments, to be dull.

So far from his interest being dependent on subject, he seems to revel in subjects which would paralyse any other writer of fiction. Who but himself would have seen in such a theme as is handled in "The Spoils of Poynton" the possibilities of passionate romance, and who, had he seen it, could have treated it with such delicate intensity, such surprise of feeling?

Nor is the instance exceptional, since from "Washington Square" to "The Sacred Fount" one could mention a dozen stories whose subjects seem, until he has touched them, either defiantly sterile or unlikely, should they prove productive, to yield any resemblance to the emotions which he makes them contribute. Even if one falls back for a reason on that exquisite correspondence with life which is the most intrinsic quality of Mr. James's work, that wonderful tenderness of tone and intricacy of motive which renders, as by no other it has been rendered, the latency, the hesitations, the illusiveness of life itself—even then one is sometimes at fault, for, though he never neglects that correspondence, he at times achieves it without producing the fine impression of

368

reality on which the attention always lays a hold.

"The Wings of the Dove" suggests more especially these reflections than, perhaps, anything else that Mr. James has done. It is long, almost wilfully long, but not longer than "The Portrait of a Lady," or than the wonderful "Tragic Muse." It loses all the way with which it starts in its first admirable chapter by a discursive analysis of as yet unrealised personalities, but "The Bostonians" makes a very similar, though unsuccessful, bid for torpidity. Its action is slow and very circumscribed, but a score of instances could prove the author entirely indifferent to the aid of action. Its most adequately drawn and finely-studied character, handsome Kate Croy, who carries for a long way on her capable shoulders the chief interest of the story, betrays the trust we have placed in her integrity, and breaks the spell which her rare intelligence, no less than her beauty, has woven for us by a scheme which, in spite of her reticent and suggestive shading, stands out as odious. Yet Rose Armiger in "The Other House," a woman not more handsome nor more rarely endowed, stooped to an act, in intention not less mean and in execution far more terrible, without ill effect to our interest in the story she so completely spoilt. The vacillations, too, of Merton Densher, accomplice to the scheme, who for a meeting with his mistress consents to play the lover to poor lonely Milly, yet declines, even though it hasten her end, to give in words that assurance of his freedom which his every action seemed to guarantee—what are they but part of that mental libration which it is Mr. James's accomplishment so notably to illustrate? No! if the book fail to interest—and by such a requirement one applies only the test of personal preference—one must look elsewhere for a reason. It is wrought with the perfect sense of being and of style which

Mr. James has acquired in his later years. Each character is drawn with a fulness of detail, an assurance of intimacy which is little short of astounding. Mrs. Lowder, Susan Stringham, Merton Densher, Kate Croy, and her unspeakable father—each one is finished with a knowledge, an acquaintance which seems never at fault. Many of the scenes are quite perfectly carried through; the dialogue not only working out its argument, but revealing, betraying, as only dialogue can, the reluctances, the indecisions of the mind behind it. The interview in the first chapter between Kate Croy and her father is an almost perfect example of how the thing should be done. Not only is everything said of essential significance, and everything not said of exquisite suggestion, but the very sequence and alternation of the sentences convey an intimation and complete the portraiture. Even the hints by which the scene is marshalled give with brilliant terseness just what is required.

"No relation with him (Lionel Croy) could be so short or so superficial as not to be somehow to your hurt." "Those who knew him a little said, 'How he does dress!' Those who knew him better said, 'How does he?'" "Nothing, however, was more wonderful than what he would sometimes take for offence, unless it might be what he sometimes wouldn't."

The book, had it fulfilled the promise of its first chapter, would have been a masterpiece. It would have been that, had it remained on the level of the scene at Milly Theale's reception between Kate Croy and Densher, when she discloses to him the extent of her schemes for poor Milly's delusion. So magnificent is her attitude, despite its horror, in handing over her lover as a temporary husband, in order to crown later on her own union to him with all the splendid emoluments of marriage, that our admiration is extorted by the courage, cool, ruthless, and passionate, of her ambition and her love. But nothing else in the book is equal to these two scenes, and the first of them might have been omitted almost without detriment to its evolution.

It is, indeed, with the mention of omission that one touches the book's weakness. There are no omissions. Everything is wrought with what one might call a passion for the particular. The detail is wonderful, but the detail is often not only wasted but wasteful. It spoils the quiet breadth of an effect quite as often as it contributes to its decoration. And detail is treated throughout as of a uniform value. The detail of Susie Stringham is worked to the same finish as the detail of everything else. It is all marvellously interesting, often even marvellously cunning, but it spoils the continuity, it destroys the proportion of a work of art. And often when we crave instruction we are left without it. There are steps in the deterioration of Kate Croy which are almost concealed from us; we only, as it were, find they are there by being precipitated down the whole flight. Perhaps they are visible, but, if so, they are lost to a reviewer's goaded scrutiny in the universal embellishment. Kate Croy's decline, from the splendid figure that confronts us on the first page to that other, sad and shamed, that slips from the last, is of an immense fascination. She is a book in herself, a book which Mr. James has almost written once or twice before. But he has never painted her with such a richness, with such an audacity, and one may almost, despite one's disappointment, add with such a subtlety as in this story. And it is by no mere description that we are captivated, by no trick of the novelist. She is built up for us as a figure is built from the clay, with all her fineness, her ingenuities, her responsiveness, her passion taking shape under her eyes.

Only the hand of a master could so have made her, and if we are left with unsatisfied understandings we are left with an abiding sense of her personality, which will prove a permanent addition to our memories of women. Beside her Milly Theale, the Dove, in her blackness, her whiteness, and her flaming hair, is thin as a wraith; but her faintness, her frailty, her almost evanescence are but a further tribute to Mr. James's mastery of his means, of his exquisite variety in the art of portraiture.

Illustrated London News 121 (27 September 1902), 464.

Mr. Henry James is a voluminous writer, but his work betrays no signs of rapid production. He becomes, if possible, more fastidious and abstruse. He is more than ever concerned with the infinitesimal shades of feeling, so that a perfectly ordinary conversation at a dinner-table is made to appear as if the persons engaged were exchanging the subtlest delicacies of thought. Every one of his characters is constantly examined by Mr. James through a microscope, and all the brain-cells, the minutest palpitations of the nervous system, are presented for the reader's inspection. It is beyond question an astonishing feat of literary art; but we fear that the substantial value of this method of vivisection is not in proportion to its elaborate penetration. When we know all the nervous systems down to the smallest particle, we are not conscious of an abounding wisdom. The characters do not live for us with a human interest commensurate with all this labour. Nothing could be more admirable than the opening. Kate Croy has a scamp of a father, whose special iniquity is never explained. An exhilarating air of mystery surrounds this pleasant-looking old gentleman, who bluntly declines the companionship of his daughter because she has committed the unpardonable fault of making over most of her money to her widowed sister. You expect to see a good deal more of a man who is like a striking figure in Balzac, but he vanishes out of the book, and the slowly developing story concerns itself with the struggle of a consumptive American heiress to find the love which alone can prolong her life. What Mr. James does with this theme is simply marvellous. It is original; it is marked by exquisite sensibility; but the reader finds himself wrapped in clouds of gossamer, and longs for a good solid incident to give him a foothold and a resting-place. All the same, "The Wings of the Dove" is a book that should be read as a mental exercise. It should be taken leisurely and steadily for an hour a day. At the end of this treatment the reader may feel that his intimacy with Mr. James's characters has not made them very diverting company; but he will certainly feel that his own perceptions are vastly more alert.

A. MacDonell.
"Mr. James's New Story."
Bookman [England] 23
(October 1902), 24–25.

A long and very ardent admiration for Mr. James's work has probably not prepared us for an adequate judgment of his latest novel. We say so without too great humility; for we came to it with eagerness, threaded its labyrinths with patience; and if we have not understood what it is all about, we are not ashamed. Mr. James has provoked in us an aggressive Philistinism;

and if it wrongs him, we are not repentant. Let him give us all the real subtleties he can conceive, and we shall follow him or not according to our capacities, and when we leave him it will be humbly regretful of our dulness. But here we presume to deny the subtlety, having a kind of assurance that by dint of hard labour we have understood his situation and the motives of his characters. If we are right, these are extremely simple, adequate enough, human enough, to interest and to touch us, if plainly expressed, as they might well be, in thirty pages. He hides them up in the close type of five hundred and seventy-six, through which we travel, now with an honest hope that the length is to be justified at last by a real mystery, or some genuine difficulty, now with a dull suspicious anger that we are being bamboozled. But the justification never appears; and yet the subject, which is pathetic, hardly allows us to think that Mr. James has perpetrated an elaborate joke. We do not deny the complications; and are positively certain Mr. James was puzzled by them as much as any of his readers. The multiplication table might seem very complicated if written in some unknown *patois* or slang. And a great deal of this book is written in what may be called slang, a very refined, very individual slang, but slang, none the less, certain vague words like "wonderful" or "beautiful" being made to do duty for and to summarise all sorts of varied things, ideas, and circumstances which have nothing to do with either marvels or with beauty. This slang is not meant to illustrate the inarticulateness of a fashionable coterie. It is all part of, and very nearly the whole of, an elaborate game. It is dictated by the laws of game, and the players use it for counters. Imagine a group of six or seven persons, of different nationalities, temperaments, professions, and motives, all sworn never to say the thing they mean when they are most in earnest, but always something else which may mean whatever you like. Everybody joins in and plays frenziedly, feeling that the most incoherent will be the winner. The American heiress, her *dame de compagnie,* the early Victorian, solid Mrs. Lowder, her handsome niece—but we own it is the native speech of that detestable young woman—the fashionable physician, the naturally straight-forward young journalist—one and all are as cryptic as if they were rival diplomats. Of course confusion reigns in the end—but so unnecessarily! There is one straightforward person who hasn't learnt the game—bless him!—Lord Mark. He blurts, being, as he is called, "adequately human"; and his blurting kills the heroine—and clears the atmosphere. We long to blurt, too, our discoveries—for so we think them—that the tactful, clever Kate, with the "talent for life," is no complicated, subtle, modern heroine, but only a vulgar schemer of a well-known type, and that Milly, stripped of her diaphanous draperies and her millions, and brought out to the light of common day, would not be much fallen in love with. Pathetic she is in that she has millions and no health; but the millions are made to play too great a part in her supposed charm and pathos. And Mr. James, by his roundabout reticence concerning her disease, rouses the uneasy suspicion that she must be a leper at least. Well, it is a *tour de force* to spin thirty pages out to five hundred and seventy-six, and to hang half a dozen commonplace people round with so many wrappings that they deceive themselves, and their creator, and almost the reader, into believing that they are subtle mysteries. The book may be something more, and better, but hard labour has not revealed it to us; and so, to quote Mr. James when a page or two's indirect and elliptical expression has landed him approximately at the truth, "let us leave it at that."

Montgomery Schuyler. "Subtle Mr. James." *New York Times Saturday Review of Books and Art* 7 (4 October 1902), 658.

There is still a certain number of readers to whom the appearance of a new novel by Henry James is the most interesting event in current fiction. We say "still" advisedly, for it is doubtful whether there are as many of them as there were ten years ago. In time of temptation they fall away. The novelist has never spared his readers any more than himself, and of late years he has become a harder taskmaster than ever. His exactions cannot be evaded except by strictly leaving the book alone, and nothing could more unfit a reader for the intent attitude of mind proper to studying his psychology than the languid perusal which is all that most contemporary fiction requires or repays. And this professor of psychology is increasingly indifferent to the comfort of his students. It is perhaps mainly in consequence of this indifference that the first living master of psychological fiction, at least in the English language, after a career of a generation, finds himself compelled to flit from publisher to publisher. The work explains why any human publisher, as Carlyle had it, should view it with apprehension and alarm, and why a conscientious publisher's reader, even though personally an enthusiast, should freely qualify and attenuate his recommendation.

And then there is always the chance that the new novel will be a failure from its own point of view. Does anybody, do the convinced students of Mr. James, "few and faint, but fearless still," regard "The

Sacred Fount" as a success? That was one of the mere fantasies, like "The Private Life," which do for an essay or a "skit," but simply refuse to be realized and become impossible exactly in the measure in which it is sought to make them possible, to "document" them and verify them and stand them on their legs. And yet "The Sacred Fount," according to the present reviewer's apprehension, is but an interlude of failure between two distinct and striking successes, between the "The Awkward Age" and "The Wings of the Dove."

There have been occasions on which it seemed that Mr. James was bent on demonstrating that fiction also is one of the arts in which the subject is nothing and the workmanship everything, and that a novelist who knew his business could do without a subject, just as some composers make "interesting modulations" do duty for tunes. But that is by no means the case with "The Wings of the Dove." Distinctly the author has this time a story to tell. The theme is the frequent, one may almost say the usual theme of Mr. James in his "third manner," the materialism and worldliness, essentially to the point of grossness, with all its superficial polish, of the world of London, and the manner in which these earthy qualities impose themselves. This lesson begins at the beginning, in the introduction of the impossible father of Kate Croy, who thereupon goes hence and is no more seen, after inculcating upon her the moral with which he is charged that poverty is the worst of evils, a moral also inculcated by her shabby and querulous widowed sister, who stands palpably convicted of the crime of unsuccess, and acts as social Helot for her as yet virginal sister, the heroine. How can the girl, how dare she, marry the man she loves, convicted before the fact and in his own mind of unsuccess, in the face of these object lessons, not less impressive than the solemn state of Aunt Maud, surrounded with all the trophies of British triumph? A lingering and conditional engagement, till Aunt Maud relents, which she will plainly never do till she dies, in which case also we foresee that she will have taken her precautions—till, in fact, something turns up—is all that is left to these London lovers. But something does turn up in the arrival of the delightful American heiress, Milly Theale, and her equally delightful duenna, who come, as they often do in Mr. James's novels, bringing their ideals to confront British institutions, to aerate and spiritualize the atmosphere of the materialized society they join. Visibly and markedly Mr. James's American women in London are pilgrims "from a brighter sphere." It is let be seen that Kate likes Milly, but not less that she finds Milly's money very charming. And when it appears that Milly has a mortal malady, and that Kate's conditionally accepted lover is Milly's most acceptable nurse, the notion arises, in an indurated London imagination which shrinks from nothing, that Merton Densher shall make love to Milly's money, which shall subsequently enrich Kate. The consent of the male lover would seem to be the hardest condition in this pleasing scheme to fulfill. But it is, in a manner, obtained. He will not quite make love, but will consent to "offer the check" upon certain amazing conditions, one being that his betrothed temptress shall make an irrevocable commitment and take a bond of fate against the jealousy which he foresees is likely to break out in spite of her if her cold-blooded scheme goes into operation.

Of course, stated crudely, this is what Shakespeare described as "a most filthy bargain," and all Mr. James's skill is taxed to make it clear of a man who is distinctly not a blackguard. There is the concurrent advice of Milly's best friend, the admirable Susan. There is the acquiescence of Aunt Maud in being hoodwinked. (Was Aunt Maud really hoodwinked?) There was even, in effect, the best medical advice that this was the best to do for Milly. In fact, the broad way that leadeth to destruction is made by the astonishing society of the novelist's art, the path almost of duty, certainly of humanity, though Densher cannot quite persuade himself that it is the path of honor. Milly does die, as per agreement, and does leave the money to the consoler of her declining hours, although her death is precipitated at last by the announcement of the pleasing Lord Mark, who has pursued her from London to Venice to make it, that Merton and Kate are still engaged, and that she, being duped, had better reconsider her refusal of himself. She does, we say, leave the other girl's lover the money, with which he restores the self-respect that has necessarily been more or less frayed at the edges from all this wear and tear promptly, at last, refusing to have anything to do with it. But he finds that, between the avarice which has been imposed by London on his betrothed, and the jealousy which, after all, she had not, when it came to the point, been able to repress, she will take him with the money, or she will take the money, the captive of her own bow and spear, without him, but, in spite of the commitment, which, almost more amazingly than that it should have been made, turns out to be after all, revocable, him without the money she will not have. And, as all these characters are all the time saying, "And there you are." The rehabilitated victim and legatee depart to make room, one imagines, for the final tableau, in which Lord Mark reaches out a shapely, aristocratic hand for Kate's, which clutches the envelope containing Milly's money, while Aunt Maud, in her character of Britannia, extends the aegis of her umbrella and her benediction over the happy and deserving pair.

This crude statement of "the argument," of course, does great injustice to the book. But so, also, one is bound to say, does the author's elaboration, for the purposes, at least, of "the general reader." It is not in laboring to be brief that Mr. James has become obscure. Often the obscurity seems willful, even perverse, certainly defiant. One is tempted to say, in his haste, that the sentences are in the minority that do not require to be read over twice. And there are very many whole pages that do require so to be studied. Mr. James seems to have become sensible to the accusation of "parenthesitis" that has been brought against his riper manner. There are not so many formal parentheses in these pages, but there are some thousands of sentences which are really parenthetical, though grammatically consecutive. And these are not by any means negligible. On the contrary, like the small claws of the lobster which the hasty eater refuses to occupy himself with, the leisurely student finds them the most toothsome morsels. But in a novel one feels that he is at least entitled to a "scenario." He feels that he has a right to repine when it is only after two pages that he finds that the function at which he is assisting is taking place at a "great historic house," and only after a page or two more that he makes out it is Lord Mark's own house, to which that astute and impecunious scion of the British aristocracy had invited the American heiress, that she might be stunned and dazzled with its evidences of antiquity and its implications of "race," while he himself was sedulously understating his advantages. Mr. James's "proposals" are not apt to be vociferous, but Lord Mark's to Milly is perhaps the acme of the unemphatic:

"Perhaps a part of what makes me remember it," she pursued, "is that I was quite aware of what might have been said about what I was doing. I wanted you to take it from me that I should

374

perhaps be able to look after you—well, rather better. Rather better, of course, than some other persons in particular."

Mr. James's own comment, characteristically made four pages afterward, is evidently warranted:

As a suggestion to her of a healing and uplifting passion it was in truth deficient; it wouldn't do as the communication of a force that should sweep them both away.

The subtleties of analysis which the novelist goes into might do if there were a "public" of mighty poets and subtle-souled psychologists. But when the plain man finds what looks to him like an attempt to decompose immediate intuitions and trace their steps, when by hypothesis they haven't any, it is no wonder the plain man revolts. Whether it is "worth going through so much to learn so little" is a question that each reader must and will answer for himself, the common devourer of novels no doubt by abstaining. And one notes with interest that the strain has told upon the intellect of the very proofreader, who has groaningly submitted to obvious misprints of which the correction only was not obvious. Sometimes, under the strain of trying to make it out, the poor man, like Johnson's "laborious commentator," "at some unlucky moments, frolics in conjecture," as when he introduces into the astonished English language such a vocable as "namble." And small blame to the proofreader!

But, after all, none of this subtlety or of this ingenuity is wasted for the right reader. None of it is fantastic as Mr. James's failures are fantastic. These are real people—Kate Croy and Milly, the dove, and Susan Shepherd Stringham, and Aunt Maud and Densher and Lord Mark, really observed, really presented, worthy

of all the elaboration that has been lavished upon them, and there is not a stroke that does not "tell." The lesson about London is as clear as in the "Awkward Age." Each is a "society drama," only the earlier is polite comedy and the later a rather sordid tragedy of low life above stalls. These latest accessions to Mr. James's portrait gallery are as credible, and as creditable, as any of their predecessors on the walls, and distinctly "The Wings of the Dove" is one of the author's high successes.

"Individualism."
Pall Mall Gazette [England], 7 October 1902, p. 4.

We are never quite certain how far any justification, considering the limitations of the art of fiction, and the work which the masters have, within those limits, accomplished, is to be found for Mr. James. His style is generally described as exquisitely careful; it is not really careful; he has an extraordinary passion in style for trouble; if it be possible to say a thing in three words, Mr. James will generally use thirty, and use them so well that you forget what the three words were, or, indeed, that there was any mode of expression save that adopted by him. If Mr. James was the only author we had, we have little doubt that we could the more easily appreciate him at the rate which his keen psychology and amazing cleverness demand from us; but with ordinary criteria of language and style before us, what are we to make of a passage like this?—

The difficulty with Densher was that he looked vague without looking weak—idle without looking empty. It was the accident, possibly, of his long legs, which were apt to stretch themselves; of his straight hair and his well-shaped head, never, the latter, neatly smooth, and apt, into the bargain, at the time of quite other calls upon it, to throw itself suddenly back and, supported behind by his uplifted arms and interlocked hands, place him for unconscionable periods in communion with the ceiling, the tree-tops, the sky.

In the last sentence there are fourteen commas to about seventy words. A long course of Mr. James (and "The Wings of the Dove" has 576 pages) makes one hunger for the period when there were no stops. And yet it is with a certain amount of shame that we indulge in all this carping criticism; for, truth to tell, this story has given us, in the reading, so keen a pleasure, and that with the memory of one or two masterpieces of this author before us, that it seems almost wicked to grumble at the punctuation of the book.

Now that Mr. Meredith has stopped from giving us fiction, there is no novelist whose brain one can watch working as one watches Mr. James'; he sits in the remoteness of his knowledge and analyzes the children of his brain—Kate Croy, Merton Densher, her lover, the unmentionable father, the colossal aunt, and the panting shadow of the American girl, Milly, so subtle a foil to her companion, Susan Shepherd Springham. The life that these characters lead is almost mystically awful; they are so ordinary, and yet so terribly and wonderfully beautiful; and they move about in this odd ordinary world of Mr. James, and underneath are depths—depths such as the author once portrayed in "The Turn of the Screw." The cry of Milly Theale, "Don't tell me that there are not abysses. I want abysses," is the defining legend of Mr. James's philosophy; he lives in the fear that after all there may be no abysses. It is impossible not to yield finally to the atmosphere of this book. It is an enormously fascinating book; and what matters if whether the fascinator pipes one tune or another?

J. P. Mowbray. "The Apotheosis of Henry James." *Critic* 41 (November 1902), 409–14.

Mr. Henry James's latest book may easily wear the distinction of being more so than any that preceded it. We adjudge it to be the logical ultimate of that specialization of talent to which he has so persistently devoted himself. In this sense if in no other it is consistent and is obedient to the laws of development. To have written any other kind of book would have disturbed our faith in the inevitableness of evolution. It may therefore be said that in "The Wings of the Dove" Mr. James, without allowing anybody else to arrive, has come to his own, and those of us who for years watched him with genuine admiration, must concede that in loyal obedience to an early determination of talents he has now successfully lost himself in the ultimate azure of himself.

We recall with a pensive memory that in every new flight he required of us larger instruments of observation, not that the field of vision grew larger, but that the terrestrial light grew less. We were not so ill-advised in sidereal remoteness as not to know that the blazing sun which, in its recessions, takes on to our vision the diminished importance of an asteroid, may still be a blazing sun to other systems. What chiefly concerned us was the growing unimportance of it to our system.

The orbit of Mr. James's endowment always promised an occultation. It was from the start predictable that if he held blazingly to his course the early light would get beyond even the reach of the Lick Observatory.

Out of sincere respect for receding if not for departed worth we have called this an apotheosis. We hold resolutely to the belief that there are systems somewhere to which Mr. James is an undiminished sun. But they are not ours.

If this similitude appears to be forced, in view of the fact that Mr. James had less to do with the starry realities of an upper world than any writer of the Victorian age, we may be permitted to drop the figure of a flight and come squarely down to a fashioning. If Mr. James has achieved indefiniteness it is not owing to the square of the distance but to the yards of fine-spun literary integument with which he has enswathed himself.

What criticism has to say of him, when it applies the comparative method, must be more or less deferential and acknowledges at once that there is not less imagination in his last book than in his first—indeed, it goes without saying that there could not be less—but there is more of Mr. Henry James, which, perhaps, is equivalent to saying that the feat of writing the last book—to use one of his own felicities—"throws a harmonizing blurr" over the inadequacy of that which is written about.

Time was when this gifted author was content to keep his rare personality in leash while his personages were talking. With a young discretion which he has now outgrown, he suffered himself at times to peep and mutter most charmingly, always intimating that there were other depths that he could let us into were he so inclined, and as he was not wholly inclined,

we forgave him. But now we must confess to some astonishment at a finite omnipresence that insists upon filling the stage, and not only pouring its asides into every ear but demands that every mortal soul of them shall use his patois and adopt his idiosyncrasies and carry his broken candy in its mouth not only to the utter discomfiture of differences but to the unique accomplishment of an edulcorated uniformity.

We enter upon what purports to be an ideal path, only to meet the accomplished fixity of Mr. James. We cannot well get on for the cunning barricades of him. When we would saunter through his meads of asphodel they are tunnelled with subways of Mr. James. He is continually present suggesting deeper and more perplexing chasms of Henry James. It does not seem to occur to him that in an urgent hour like this there is a much more expeditious and merciful way of accomplishing his purpose than in writing a two-volume novel—and it is to present his photographs to the ravening multitude and let them figure out the two volumes for themselves and go their ways.

If we look back to the earlier and deeper impressions which Mr. Henry James made upon us when he had not wholly lost the naïveté of objective existence, we shall, perhaps, find lurking there a slightly grave fear that Mr. Henry James stood in some danger of mistaking Mr. Henry James for Life itself and was in a fair way of falling into the belief that saying things out of himself must in time, by mere nimbleness of utterance, come to take the place of things themselves.

One, of course, dislikes to refer to this now, because it gives one a rather preposterous air of prophecy, seeing that "The Wings of the Dove" are spread before us, and yet, here is Mr. Henry James taking 768 pages to say things and provoking his admirers to ask—not indeed if it were worth while to take two volumes to say these things—but was it worth while to say them at all. As persistent admirers, clinging still to him through all the progressive convolutions of his introspective genius, we cannot help feeling that it is somewhat unkind to sweat our appreciation to the utmost and tax our endurance on his decorated treadmill because he insists that it is a chariot.

In "The Wings of the Dove" a story is assumed, but the assumption requires a strong effort of faith. The ordinary and necessitous ongoing of events and the unfolding of character in action which we naturally include in the invitation of the book, meet continually with the obstructing laboratory of the chemical Mr. James, joyously intent not on getting on, but on demonstrating to us the infinite divisibility of literary matter. We cling resolutely to the faith that there *is* a story stalled somewhere in the labyrinth of Mr. James's bottles and pumps, and that it would lumber on somehow if he would only consent to stop pumping and move a little out of the way. But that he never does. How indeed can he, when he is himself the story and has come to believe that the constructive or co-ordinating ability to deal with material is of less account than the exhibition of a superb dexterity in keeping the material in the air.

There are, it is true, intelligent minds that invariably estimate the excellence of a book, a picture, or a symphony, by its unintelligibility. It is not that they are humble enough to suspect that what may be unintelligible to them may be clear to others, but that the more incomprehensible a thing may be to common sense, the more uncommon is the sense that assumes to know it all, and this order of intelligence has a tendency to form the tail of every comet that excites our wonder by its eccentricity, and it is an order of intelligence, we regret to say, which is more interested in the adroitness of the juggler than in the craftsmanship of the worker. Moreover, it is this resonant kind of intelligence which will fall upon the futilities and foibles of Mr. James's latest exploit and declare that it must be esoteric art because nobody else can understand it. But we feel assured that there are other intelligences of no mean order, who cannot scrute the inscrutable in this instantaneous manner; minds that have imbibed with appreciative delight the debonair volumes of Brio on Elliptic Functions; revelled, let us say, in Neumann on the Infinitesimal Calculus; seized with sportive avidity the whole of Calvin's "Institutes," and drank in "The Ring and the Book" as the bird drinks the transparent dew,—but who will come to the diluted high-jinks of Mr. James's dialogue baffled and abashed at the narrowness of their mental grasp.

It is not within our jurisdiction to shut Mr. James out of the domain of Art, for there is an art of carving cherry-stones and making a pudding in a hat, no less than an art which "carries on the dream of God" and breathes the breath of life into the dust of romance so that the children of the parturient imagination live and move and have their being among the populations of the finite mind as the sons of men have inhabited the zones of the earth. But it does seem to be within our privilege to say that the perfection to which Mr. James has now brought his method is beyond all endurance wearisome to the ordinary sanity of serious minds which have by actual contact with life itself learned humbly to estimate its invincible scale of values, and such a result presents a question of the kind of art and the use that is made of it. It is not its deficiency, but its superabundance that weighs upon us. To go no deeper than this, the reader of "The Wings of the Dove" will, we think, suffer from a surfeit of Mr. James.

That he was free to detach himself from

the complex which we call life and make a domain of his own and live and breathe in it, no one can dispute, but when he asks us to follow him, the question of art must give way to one of oxygen. We are quite willing to admit that it is a remarkable feat of disembodiment to live and flourish in so thin an atmosphere, but when it comes to living in it ourselves, art will not take the place of lungs.

To have lived with him even for twenty-four hours as we have done, not from any irresistible impulse of our own, but in obedience to the request of the editor of this magazine, invests us with a duty if not with a distinction that is unique. There are few persons, we cannot help feeling, who will undertake the flight without the extra wings which the editor has furnished, and coming back to the objective world, we shall be pardoned if we feel like the resuscitated man who, after being rolled on a barrel, is expected to reveal something of the mysterious midway between this and another state of existence. Nor is the analogy extravagant, for we have lived during those twenty-four hours in a domain peopled only by shades and ruffled only by the see-saw of Mr. James's subtlety. What they were all up to we could by no means make out. They seemed to be mainly intent on analyzing each other. Existence, such as our environment had emphasized it, had ceased. All the larger springs of action: those grandiose rhythms of propulsion and attraction; the centrifugal and centripetal swing of primal forces; the majestic tropical movements of passion; the pressure of inheritance and of duty—all were stopped in a pallid inquisitorial equilibrium.

And all this is very unlike that equally mysterious and far more beautiful borderland which, thanks to the creative imagination of literature, we always have with us. In this field of life, vexed with storm as well as garlanded with beauty, genius has most triumphantly walked in imitation of the archaic Father Who took the cool of the day for it and Who, seeing that His work, once having the inspiration, moved and acted and aspired and struggled—pronounced it good.

To that old legend the finite creations of imitative man are arbitrarily and benignly held. He must inspire the dust of his material and the in-breathing of the procreant flame must people the pages. No device of art can make a continual out-pulling serve as a substitute.

In any examination of genius itself that is dealing potentially with the elements of humanity, it seems in its best estate to have moments when it is no longer compelling, but is compelled. The mute stuff of story, co-ordinated after the fashion of the divine original, but with much travail, must somewhere in the awakening take on the free will of finite creatures and begin to move with the impulses or the projection of its inheritance, its appetences, and its destiny. How else can it be life than by carrying in some measure in its system the energizing predisposition and the divine restrictions which turn life into stress and both punish and crown it?

This is the true test of Mr. James's progeny. Do they indeed live and move and have their being? Nothing can be more beautiful or more wondrous in the experience of literary genius than that first throb of independence in his assembled vessels of clay. They begin to palpitate and assert themselves in obedience to the fore-ordained canons of creation which he has summoned. After that, development takes the place of fiat. He can no longer ordain, only gently guide, and the great masters of literature have thus been surprised in their work by the fact so beautifully expressed long ago, that a little child shall lead them.

The free movement of duly commissioned human souls is no longer enjoyable in the personages who try to people Mr.

James's pages. We miss not only the complexity but the determinism of actual existence—two essentials which invariably furnish for us in all romantic literature the conflict and the web of interest. So completely are results submerged in processes that we are sensible of a continual protest that this is not life but a hypothesis of life formulated and worked independently of the thing itself to no end, so that what should be vitality is content to be vivisection and a continual flourish of tools.

That which assumes to be psychologic wears a phraseologic stress. Its constant dependence upon arbitrary forms robs it of that naïve honesty which is always its own best simplicity. Nor is the shade of thought when finally balanced adverbially between colons, determinative of character or indicative of purpose. It seems always to accomplish its end in behavior.

Our author has thus reached a perfection of diction which exacts something of his own athleticism from the reader, who is compelled to leap the five-barred gates of his parentheses at every turn if he would keep him in sight. And yet, notwithstanding all this show of dexterity in arbitrary appliances, so averse is the author to action in what after all should be the real movement of things, that the predicates of his sentence hang fire as if ashamed of themselves, and conclusions run up against dashes and breaks as if our perplexity could by any means take the place of his deliverance. His generous belief that his reader is gifted not only with his agility but with a supernatural acumen to discover what he means without his saying it, is not as preposterous as his confidence that the reader will understand it when he does say it, and both these amiable qualities of the author sink into insignificance by the side of the superhuman faith that the reader will think it worth saying when he has said it. He is so apprehensive when dealing with one shade of thought or emotion that there may be other subshades that he will miss and that he must clutch as he passes, that he frequently produces the effect of a painting niggled and teased out of all frankness by manipulation, and this, as we have already said, belongs as a method rather to chemistry than to art and takes us back as far as Hahnemann, who, if we mistake not, had a theory that there was potency in pounding. But it must be said at the same time that Mr. James's style is in great measure the result of his indiscreet admirers' praise, for they have held him and incited him to a purely decorative endeavor, applying constantly to his work the criteria by which they judged work in another field of art, thus convincing him that the meaning is of less account in literature as well as in painting than the treatment. Here we suspect is to be found the determining mistake of Mr. James. It is that he is trying to make articulate speech, which deals primarily with ideas, follow the aesthetic laws of beauty in the treatment of tone and color, which do not and cannot deal with definite concepts at all.

Definitive and conclusive expression is indeed the corollary of definite purpose and clear ideas, and to leave a sentence balancing on a "two-em" dash, as Mr. James frequently does, is more apt to betray the evasion of incertitude than the charm of subtlety.

Unerring precision of statement is certainly not as easy of accomplishment in dealing with the intricacies of a self-conscious girl's gossiping vagaries, as in dealing with determinable facts, but even in this pastime it is certainly necessary to be at least intelligible, and Mr. James is certainly not intelligible at all times. What, for example, does he mean by telling us in his opening chapter that Kate Croy has come to see her father in his lodgings, and is waiting along, examining her heart, her conscience, and her other appurtenances, and then telling us: "He [her father] had not come down from his room, which she [his daughter, waiting alone] knew to be above the one *they* were in"?

Here the subtlety surpasses our comprehension—but that is easy. It defies physics, and that is hard. The fact is, Mr. James's pronouns are the most American things about him. If they have any antecedents they are apt to show a democratic indifference for them as if they might be social instead of being syntactical. On page 207 the nominative and the objective waltz together indiscriminately, and if you do not keep your eye on them with the cool scrutiny of a dowager, there will be a mésalliance. Miss Milly in this book has more money than she knows what to do with. But this is offset by more self-consciousness than falls to the lot of most real girls. She is oppressed by a vague sense that true happiness can alone be achieved secretly by kicking introspectively against the bliss of having it. Her own words, wrung from her in answer to the anxious question, "What is it you think you haven't got?" are:

"The power to resist the bliss of what I have."

This is plainly an echo of the author's predicament. Milly goes about with an unbearable load of happiness, always wondering what she "was begun for," and never suspecting that it was to turn herself inside out.

The insufferable determination of all the persons in the book to forswear all peculiarities except those of the author, follows them with all his conceits and devices of expression. For example, he says, on page 416: "She suffered, but she could n't not question."

It is odd, to say the least, but it is an oddity that he cannot keep to himself. "Yet," says the travelled and refined hero, "yet, I could n't, could I, not have come?"

and the answer of the heroine is: "No, you could n't not have come." Then elsewhere we observe that Kate "waited as for how to say it," as if the author had left her any choice, and my lord "looked exactly as much as usual," and the literary lover in wooing Kate (he is a newspaper man and an Englishman) adopts this style of blandishment: "For young persons of a great distinction and a very high spirit, we 're a caution"—a form of dalliance that died with Sam Slick. Mr. Densher always insists *to* being a Briton; Lord Mark always "goes for" that which he would accept. The lover says, "I am 'gone for you'" when he would acknowledge his passion. They all of them insist that ideas like string-beans shall be "in the connection," and we learn in one place that Miss Milly will execute the incredible feat of paying a hundred per cent. "through her nose." When it comes to being spontaneous and frisky, Mr. James positively creaks and his merriment reminds us of an Amherst professor in a cake-walk.

But these specks taken separately are trivial beside the ensemble of them in interminable and indeterminate dialogue, where indeed Mr. James seems to have reached the fourth dimension of space— dialogue in which the speakers not only tell us what they think and what others think, but what they might have thought and did n't. Sometimes, as when Lord Mark has the floor, the choppy and spumy ambiguity and purposelessness of it all puts us to our wits' end for the word that fits it, and not having the moral courage to call it gibberish we fall back upon our fiery friend's—Mr. Crosland's—vocabulary, and admit that this must be "blithering"—a noble word that, with no rugged corners of definition—but *such* a comfort.

In trying to form anything like a comprehensive estimate of Mr. James's mature work, the effeminacy of it has to be counted with. One cannot call it virile, and—with the best examples still with us—hardly Saxon. In the selection of theme he appears to turn instinctively to the boudoir side of life, and to give himself, with a perspicacity and a zest that have been held to be characteristic of the other sex, to the intricacies of matchmaking and the silken embroideries of scheming dowagers and tender protégés. If there is any finesse or delicacy in the treatment, the merit we suspect is owing to the indisposition of a mind to contemplate more rugged aspects of humanity and content to loiter with a strange industry amid the foibles and fashions of mere intellectual coquetry.

One calls this "womanish" at some risk, at a time when woman, so far as literature is concerned, is taking events into her own hands, and, armed cap-a-pie, is flourishing a sword in her imagination and crying lustily, "Have at you, gentlemen." But it is none the less true that if we are to preserve the sweet tambour work of gentle dames there should be room somewhere for the delicacy of Mr. Henry James. The only question then worth considering will be, can he do the work as sweetly as Laura Matilda herself could do it if she were alive and could use the improved method?

"Mr. Henry James." *Independent* 54 (13 November 1902), 2711–12.

Mr. James becomes more tantalizing with every novel he writes. His latest, *The Wings of the Dove*, reminds us of a story we read once upon a time, about a little serving lad, who, like the critics, had a very bad habit of asking impertinent questions. One day certain who had suffered most from his inquisitiveness, having caught him, shaved his head, and after painting or seeming to paint a legend thereon, turned him loose to wander miserably about the court, distracted by his curiosity and begging every one he met to read his pate for him. But one and all persisted in replying, "There's nothing there," until at last, made ingenious by desperation, he succeeded with some difficulty in arranging a series of mirrors and reading for himself to the same effect. Very similar has been the result of our experience with the kind of writing Mr. James affects. After craning our necks almost to dislocation we have no more for our pains than had the hero of our little apologue, tho to be sure there is just enough ambiguity about the sentence to keep us unflaggingly on the search.

The truth seems to be that Mr. James has begun to show his age. There is a general impression that advancing age sees simple. Nothing of the kind; every year adds a facet to the human eye, and man in accumulating wisdom becomes ever more speculative, more disposed of talk about his experience rather than of it. So with Mr. James, the habit of contemplation, to which he was always addicted, has grown upon him with indulgence to such an extent that he not infrequently loses sight altogether of the object, which the reader is obliged in consequence to reconstruct for himself as best he can. It is this that we find so afflicting: that it, whatever it may be, is all in the air, in Mr. James's mind or elsewhere, we have no way of knowing. His situations appear to be interesting, as far as we can make out from the indications he allows to escape him; at all events we are prepared to be interested, if he would only refrain from wrapping them away in what we must consider the mummy clothes of irrelevant reflection. In the seven hundred and fifty odd pages of the book before us, for instance, there are, to trust our impression, barely four score of dialog; while as for action, which one would expect to divide a novel, there is none worth mentioning. There is, indeed, little else but long, dull paragraphs of emotional tergiversation, wherein one loses all sense of direction for lack of one little clue, one single clear straightforward word, which would, to be sure, if it were there, dispel the greater part of the story like a mirage.

To a plain man, such doings will inevitably appear but the exercises of a mistaken ingenuity. But in reality they are not altogether so, they are rather more serious than that. In his essay on Flaubert he regrets that to this artist the spiritual should have offered little or no "surface." "He should at least," says Mr. James, "have listened at the chamber of the soul." And the stricture, while it may not be quite just to Flaubert, does at least serve to suggest the meaning of Mr. James's own attitude. He is listening "at the chamber of the soul." And tho we might wish that his posture were a little less cramped and his message were a little more intelligible, still his intention is perfectly plain. Life is composed of two parallel currents, the stream of circumstance and the stream of consciousness. For obvious reasons, chiefly because such is the way of nature, it is the general practice of novelists to keep on the whole to the former, leaving the reader to take up for himself as much of the latter as he has inclination and capacity for. And if Mr. James reverses the natural order, suppressing incident and leaving the sequence of events to be pieced out by the reader's ingenuity, while he insists upon following the series of reactions which these hypothetical events are supposed to set up in the minds of his characters, he does so obviously in the hope of catching those subtle "psychic" states which he reproaches Flaubert with having neglected.

Now it would be fair to inquire of all this sort of thing whether "psychic" states were not fitter subjects for descriptive psychology than literature, whether, indeed, this conception of fiction does not show another of those strange confusions from which so many of our ideas appear to be suffering at present. At all events a writer who takes to such devices would seem guilty of throwing away his means of interest with a prodigality deserving, in case of bankruptcy, of no very great amount of sympathy; for it is just the advantage of the more usual and natural method that the reader has appetite only for a certain limited amount of subjective experience, precisely as much as he can get for himself, and no matter how much more is forced upon him is unable to digest it. But not to raise these moot questions, it is perhaps sufficient to point out that Mr. James's procedure, whether or no it is legitimate in theory, does at any rate in actual practice fail to accomplish its purpose and results simply in the bewilderment of the reader (or should we call him student?) and in the deformation of the novel to which it is applied. Art must always be in a very large measure representative; it must for the most part deal directly with the thing in itself, and if its substantial body be attentuated beyond a certain point it becomes a mere mist in the brain, a figment, a false illusion without reality or significance. The soul is all very well in its way, but to impoverish its body is certainly not to increase the efficiency of its manifestations. And further, in connection with the plot, to call it so, of this particular book, over which reigns a singular moral confusion wherein all natural feelings of pity and shame have been juggled away by some curious antic of the mind, it is worth while to notice the profound truth, that there is nothing so prone to depravity as unrelieved speculation, which, just because it has no issue and hence no corrective in conduct, tends of itself to become utterly dissolute and irresponsible. The fact is that Mr. James, together with some of his European neighbors, in forcing his "art," as he likes to call it, to such a point of refinement that its interest has come to be almost solely technical, has demonstrated incontestably the radical fallacy of *l'art pour l'art,* of art for art's sake, for art must exist for something besides itself or else be reduced finally to the composition of rhetorics.

Checklist of Additional Reviews

Times Literary Supplement [London] 34 (5 September 1902), 263. Reprinted in Roger Gard, ed., *Henry James: The Critical Heritage* (London: Routledge & Kegan Paul, 1968), pp. 319–321; J. Donald Crowley and Richard A. Hicks, eds., *The Wings of the Dove: Norton Critical Edition* (New York: W. W. Norton, 1978), pp. 481–83.

Academy and Literature [England], 1583 (6 September 1902), 235.

Springfield [Mass.] *Republican,* 7 September 1902, p. 19.

Athenaeum [England] no. 3907 (13 September 1902), 346.

Elia W. Peattie. "Henry James' Sordid and Ineffective English Romance." Chicago *Tribune,* 13 September 1902, p. 18.

"Henry James' New Book." Louisville

Courier-Journal, 13 September 1902, p. 5.

New York *Sun,* 13 September 1902, p. 8.

New York *Tribune,* 13 September 1902, p. 10.

" 'The Wings of the Dove.' " San Francisco *Chronicle,* 14 September 1902, Supp., p. 4.

Detroit *Free Press,* 20 September 1902, p. 11.

New York Tribune Weekly Review 1 (20 September 1902), 13.

Cleveland *Plain Dealer,* 21 September 1902, sec. 3, p. 6.

Chicago *Inter-ocean,* 22 September 1902, p. 7.

Churchman 86 (27 September 1902), 364.

Public Ledger and Philadelphia Times, 27 September 1902, p. 11.

Book News 21 (October 1902), 68–69.

Review of Reviews 26 (October 1902), 446.

Chicago *Record-Herald,* 4 October 1902, sec. 3, p. 3.

Speaker [England] (4 October 1902), 108–9. Reprinted in Arthur Sherbo, "Still More on James," *Henry James Review* 12 (1991), 108–9.

Spectator [England] 89 (4 October 1902), 498–99. Reprinted in James W. Gargano, *Critical Essays on Henry James: The Late Novels* (Boston: G. K. Hall, 1987), pp. 46–47.

Literary World [England] 66 (10 October 1902), 245.

Boston *Sunday Post,* 12 October 1902, p. 18.

[Annie R. M. Logan]. *Nation* 75 (23 October 1902), 330–31.

Indianapolis *News,* 25 October 1902, p. 6.

Frank Moore Colby. *Bookman* [New York] 16 (November 1902), 259–60. Reprinted in Gard, pp. 339–41; Gargano, pp. 47–48.

Contemporary Review [England] 82 (November 1902), 756–57.

Academy [England] (8 November 1902), 493–94.

Outlook 72 (6 December 1902), 789.

[Harriet W. Preston]. *Atlantic Monthly* 91 (January 1903), 77–82. Reprinted in Gard, pp. 332–34.

"The Novelist's Art and Mr. Henry James." *Saturday Review* [England] 95 (17 January 1903), 79–80. Reprinted in Gard, pp. 322–23.

THE AMBASSADORS

"*The Ambassadors*." London *Daily Telegraph*, 9 October 1903, p. 6.

Mr. Henry James can be an exasperating writer. Super-subtle he always is, but sometimes from those innumerable little subtle touches grows as if by magic a portrait with an unforgettable charm. And face to face with the masterpiece we forget the maledictions which we uttered in the weariness of the way. But in "The Ambassadors" the way is weary enough—for the first hundred pages it is tedious beyond belief—and after all we are entirely unrewarded, for though we become fairly well acquainted with some half a dozen men and women, without exception they are entirely destitute of the smallest atom of charm. What has Mr. James been about? It is unlike him to be so unrelenting. True, he sketches lightly two pretty girlish portraits, Jeanne de Vionnet, delicate and fragile as a snowflake, so perfect that a touch would spoil her, and Mamie Pocock, a perfectly healthy, self-reliant, but almost too finished specimen of the young American girl. Jeanne makes, however, only one appearance; Mamie scarcely occupies twenty pages out of four hundred and fifty. All the rest of the time we are following with entire bewilderment, but with neither excitement nor sympathy, the mental struggle of an elderly American to understand himself and the people who sent him, and the young compatriot in Paris to whom he was sent. Shall this young man, Chadwick Newsome, forsake the Paris which suits him and the lady who has "made" him, and return to Woollett, Mass., to take up the business of advertising as a fine art? Is his relation to the lady "virtuous" or not? Shall the elderly Mr. Strether work for the American mother, whose husband he is to become, or for Madame de Vionnet, who tries to enlist him on her side? It might all be interesting enough if Mr. James had made us feel the charm of Madame de Vionnet as he made us feel the charm of Daisy Miller, of Isabel in "The Portrait of a Lady," of the Princess Casamassima, or even only last year of Milly in "The Wings of a Dove." But we feel nothing of the kind, and as to some of the subsidiary actors, Waymarsh, Miss Barrace, Maria Gostrey, they strike us as preposterous. Was there ever anywhere a world where people behaved like that? Can it be that Mr. James is becoming so involved in the maze of his own creations that he is losing touch with real men and women and with the motives which actuate them? We can forgive him his peculiar phraseology, "she embroidered, she abounded," "she took it wonderfully," and all the rest of it; but we do really find it hard to forgive the almost vulgar outspokenness with which, on a short acquaintance, his characters question each other on the most delicate love affairs. Strether's position, relative to the lady who sent him to rescue her son from Paris, is of the most delicate. His attitude to his new friend Maria Gostrey is only a shade less difficult to characterise. Yet both relations are alluded to by various people on various occasions, and he positively permits the allusions, certainly a form of "taking it wonderfully," though not perhaps quite in Mr. James's sense. It may be that Mr. James's relation to life is like Whistler's to Nature, and that we are still too blind to see what the great artist is trying to show us. One might almost hope so, if it were not that the world will be an amazingly uncomfortable place to live in when it has finally rearranged itself upon the lines of Mr. James's art.

"The Genius of Mr. James."
Pall Mall Gazette [England], 13 October 1903, p. 4.

That saying of William Blake, that the Venus of Milo was not carved but released from the block, is profoundly true of every work of art, and not least of imaginative literature. All the stories that ever shall be written are somewhere latent, and the business of the story-teller is less to create than to evoke. Evocation is peculiarly the method of Mr. Henry James; he does not tell a story, he divulges it, and nowhere is his method brought to a more perfect finish than in this his last and finest novel. Perhaps not the worst way to estimate the quality of an artist is to define what he is not, and the precise position of Mr. Henry James in contemporary literature becomes clearer by reference to other great living writers. In reading "The Ambassadors" you do not, as in reading a story of Mr. Thomas Hardy's, feel the breath of a woman on your cheek, nor are the situations stamped upon your brain, as by the ironic lightning of Mr. George Meredith. In "The Ambassadors" you are kept always a little aloof from the picture; you do not feel that the writer is in the least responsible for the creation of Mme. de Vionnet, or Strether, or Chadwick Newsome; he reveals them to you by the gradual stripping off of the veils which hitherto obscured them from your vision, or, rather, by his kindly though ironical correction of your own eyesight. It is with a shock of surprise that you remember to have been told by a distinguished man of letters of his own nationality that Mr. James belongs to the school of the Realists. Realistic in effect "The Ambassadors" undoubtedly is, but not at all in method; it is by the liberation of essential ideas, and not by the patient enumeration of facts, that the story is put before you. Consequently it impresses you as overwhelmingly like life, and the difference between this and realism is just the difference between truth and accuracy. Truth presupposes vision, but the accurate delineation of facts does not imply even observation. Now "The Ambassadors" affects you as the result of intense observation—a long time ago. The facts observed have been dissolved in the writer's consciousness, and are only now recrystallised out in a series of images coloured by just that tincture of the *menstruum* which makes the revelation in the truest sense personal and Mr. James's. Nor are the images, as might be supposed, indefinite. A crystal is even more definite than a cut-glass lustre, only the history of its formation is entirely different, a crystal being the essential idea of the solution in which it secretly grows. As an example of the occult yet unwavering growth of Mr. James's characters into tangibility take Waymarsh. He looms through the earlier part of the book with his heavy speech and heavier silences, felt rather than seen, until he finally crystallises out from the lips of Miss Barrace as "Sitting Bull." After that it is impossible to think of him in any other form. The other characters and their surroundings emerge in the same magical way, and very often precisely because they are not stated. They become apparent, say, as green becomes apparent to the eye fatigued with red; they are complementary to the thing described. In considering the thing spoken of you are conscious, in Mr. James's own words, of "the obsession of the other thing," and it is often enough the other thing which is essential to the story. Thus, you are never taken to Woollett, the American town from which Mr. James's "Ambassador," Strether, is sent to Paris to reclaim Chadwick Newsome, nor are you introduced to Chadwick's mother; yet in the recital of Strether's impressions of Paris, more particularly of the personality and surroundings of Mme. de Vionnet, who represents the disastrous entanglement Woollett supposes, you are made vividly to see the vulgarity of Woollett refinement and the essential inferiority of Mrs. Newsome. So vividly, indeed, that you go farther, perhaps, than the writer intends, and in recognising the crass "culture" which Chadwick so happily escapes, you are taken with curiosity to know the private emotion of, say, Boston over this book of Mr. James's, though, truly, there is the afterthought that just as Woollett, through the eyes of Mrs. Pocock and therefore implicitly of Mrs. Newsome, failed to see what Chad was become under the gracious influence of Mme. de Vionnet, so Boston would remain after all unmoved.

In considering Mr. James's revelation of his characters, we may, perhaps, be permitted to express what is likely enough a private grievance due to dulness. It needs the writer's explicit statement that Strether was fifty-five years of age to conquer our belief that he belonged on the right side of forty. It is not that Strether talks younger than his years, or acts as such; on the contrary, his words and actions come always as a surprise from one so young, and it would seem as if Mr. James himself were on guard against perplexity in the mind of the reader, since at least twice in the course of the story he reminds him that Strether was fifty-five years old.

For the business of evocation, for the development, as it were, of the latest images of his characters, Mr. James uses a style which, as the verse of Shelley is the very stuff of poetry, may be described as the delicate essentials of prose. He adds word to word warily, as a chemist would use a reagent to bring down a visible precipitate. He does not construct with words in the ordinary sense, because for him, as for every great artist, words are symbols rather than building materials. In relation to the ideas they betray they are as the visible peaks of submerged, deep-rooted mountains. The peaks are apparent, the mountains implied. Some of Mr. James's phrases positively make you jump. This, for example, of Waymarsh: "He met you as if you had knocked and he had bidden you enter." Yet for all the alertness of his style, it is not as if he performed before you, but rather as if you overheard a very old man murmuring to himself.

"Mr. Henry James's New Novel." Manchester *Guardian*, 14 October 1903, p. 5.

It is a curious consideration that Mr. Henry James once condescended to the vulgarisations that are necessary for the purposes of the stage. The concession was declined by a public which prefers its own familiar conventions; and though there have been later exercises in dramatic form, it seems unlikely that such interesting experiments as "The American" and "Guy Domville" will be repeated. Rather Mr. James seems to have deliberately widened the breach that separates him from the play-goer or average man. THE AMBASSADORS (Methuen and Co, pp. 458, 6s.)—to use the word which he writes with a whimsical frequency—is "wonderful," but to many readers it must be, we fear, even impossible. Mr. James's simplicity was always rather deceptive, but here a story of simple outlines is so obscured that the relations are sometimes difficult to maintain. There is so much to apprehend that we read with the anxious sense of missing something. Probably Mr. James has never exercised such care in withholding definite information. His dialogue avoids, indeed, the effective finalities of wit in its widespreading allusiveness. We are baffled by easy colloquialisms when words are used as an aid to a kind of telepathy between persons of an extraordinary sensitiveness. Literature seems to approach the plastic arts when the relations of words to things are enriched by Mr. James's infinite modulations. It seems almost a grossness to attempt to state the bare facts that loom through the obscure medium. Told at many removes and from various points of view, the story is of the delightful Strether, an elderly American gentleman, sent out by Mrs. Newsome, of the typical American town Woollett, to reclaim her son Chadwick from the entanglements of Paris. The reward, it is indicated, would be no less than Mrs. Newsome's hand with all the accompanying privileges and emoluments. Strether's first accomplishment is to encounter and annex at Chester a compatriot lady, and this fantastic instance of love at first sight—raised to a plane far removed from the conventionally romantic—gives to Strether a constant resource and touchstone during his subsequent adventures. Their intercourse has the reticences that are necessary to give it piquancy, and the reticences of the story throughout are a miracle of artifice. The people taste every sensation to the full, but they take infinite precautions to avoid the mere facts of the matter. The game is not precisely life, but an extremely curious and fascinating analogy; it is life raised to Mr. James's mystical terms, and it is played with a delighted consciousness by actors who applaud one another with liberal frequency. There is al-

ways the sense of comedy, and it is comedy of a very high and noble kind. The degrees of Strether's education are carefully but not too precisely marked. He begins with little Bilham, Chad's friend, who "looked out, as it had first struck Strether, at a world in respect to which he hadn't a prejudice. The one our friend most instantly missed was the usual one in favour of an occupation accepted. . . . Strether had gathered from him that at the moment of his finding him in Chad's rooms he had not saved from his shipwreck a scrap of anything but his beautiful intelligence and his confirmed habit of Paris." Strether is a kindly soul, and he begins to see that, as Mr. James might say in one of his colloquial concessions, there is something in it. The "sharp rupture of an identity" on the part of his young friend Chad, who had not been the most hopeful of cases, convinces him that there is even a great deal in it. Of course a woman is concerned, and the moral issue is not a simple one. Strether finds, however, in place of the crying need for admonishment and recall, "a new appeal, a new revelation, a new predicament for him." The letters in which he explains and defines to Mrs. Newsome what is, in truth, the expansion of his own spirit give no satisfaction to that austere lady. She sends fresh emissaries, of which her daughter is the most formidable, and the battle for the possession of Chad takes on new conditions. What we may describe as Mr. James's flesh-and-blood Americans are excellent, and the huge complication of relations is worked out with a master's hand. The generous Strether realises his own lost opportunities, and he has a strange after-taste of the youth that he has missed—

All voices had grown thicker and meant more things; they crowded on him as he moved about—it was the way they sounded together that wouldn't let him be still. He felt, strangely, as sad as if he had come for some wrong, and yet as excited as if he had come for some freedom. But the freedom was what was most in the place and the hour; it was the freedom that most brought him round again to the youth of his own that he had long ago missed. He could have explained little enough to-day either why he had missed it or why, after years and years, he should care that he had: the main truth of the actual appeal of everything was none the less that everything represented the substance of his loss, put it within reach, within touch, made it, to a degree it had never been, an affair of the senses.

It may seem that Strether's liberal sympathy assured nothing very solid for Chad, but Mr. James is guiltless, of course, of any obvious moral stress or closely defined result. Strether has had his experience, and he retires on a note of renunciation. It is characteristic of him "not out of the whole affair to have got anything for myself."

We have suggested that Mr. James's book must remain caviare to the general. To a select band it will be, we may believe, a pure delight. Perhaps a larger number of his admirers may think that this fine piece of work might without loss have been reduced to simpler terms. The diction of "The Ambassadors" is of greater accomplishment than that of "Roderick Hudson" or "The American," but we are not sure that its significance maintains proportion with its elaboration. Passion is hardly recognisable through such an envelopment, and an admirable design seems a little clogged by a medium so opaque. As Mr. James says, we move "in a maze of mystic, closed allusions," and with a thousand perfect niceties and delicacies of effect there are some passages that seem a little teased. Mr. James's style has never been more intimate, and he is full of slight, subtle analogies that are surprisingly apt and enlightening. His patience is so extraordinary that it would seem churlish for the reader to fail in this necessary quality. Merely as a performance the book is brilliant and prolific in the extreme, but it is not a mere performance. It has the significance of fine art and a moral interest of an extraordinary kind. There is all Mr. James's quality of economical invention, which rarely, indeed, does violence to our conceptions of cause and effect. Especially, for those who appreciate it, there are Mr. James's peculiar graciousness and benignity, the combination of qualities that we admire in Strether, and must always admire when Mr. James writes, as it were, from the fulness of experience.

Times Literary Supplement [London] 92 (16 October 1903), 296.

The severest judgment that Mr. Henry James, when he turns critic, can find to pass on any work of imagination coming under discussion is that "it has no thesis." No one ever hoist Mr. James with his own canon. He is all thesis; and THE AMBASSADORS (Methuen, Co.) is as conspicuous for that almost perverted fidelity to the theme's essential morals as say of its ingenious predecessors. The tissue of the tale is largely composed of conversations carried on in brief antiphonal replies and rejoinders, as precise in their way as the stichomyth proper, though they depend for their point on verbal quip or adventitious wit, not even on the thing expressed, but solely on such allusive meaning and emphasis as only the spoken word is thought to be able to convey when you have a close knowledge of the speaker's character. But that the written word may rival the spoken, Mr. James demands unswerving and intense attention from his readers. Skip half a page and the next page or two are at once reduced to gibberish. Stop in the middle of a dialogue for a few hours and you risk losing half the salience of the whole. It were as fatal to interrupt an interview as to read, say, "Bishop Blougram's Apology" in instalments. The cleverness is baffling. Mr. James so respects his thesis that he dare not let you cross a full stop with a half truth in your mind, and he must drop in adverbs and parentheses and words between commas to qualify every part of the sentence to the quality of the whole. And the style is of the stuff of the tale. Acquaintance with the movement of the story is never imposed by the author as a contribution from his own knowledge as creator. We must become acquainted with the psychological progress according to the manner in which it dawned in the experience of the characters. The method, however true to art, may give sometimes an impression of undue dilatoriness in undoing a simple knot. But it is beautifully done; the strands are never mixed; the knot is never cut; nor, again, is there ever a period of arrested progress. Mr. Henry James never marks time, never stands easy, though you may hardly perceive till you reach the end how steady the progress was. "The Ambassadors" is even an audacious example of Mr. James's art. The narrative is—where? The *dénouement*—what? One takes a delight in boiling down the material to its elemental state. A lady, of New England, sends an ambassador to Paris to save her son from a supposed entanglement. Further ambassadors are sent to bring back both son and ambassador; and nothing is achieved. Perhaps in the sequel some men marry some women; one is not sure, though the balance of evidence, if it be carefully weighed, is on the whole in favour of the view. But it is quite certain that this issue does not much matter. The interest, if you are faithful to the rigour of the text, is immeasurably superior to incident. Every character betrays what Mr. James calls "a basis of intention," and the tangling and ravelling of the complications, which come principally from the abrupt contact of New England and Parisian standards of feeling and behaviour, acquire a vastly keener poignancy than if they were translated from psychology into terms of duels or elopements. Everything is seen to be significant, especially perhaps the insignificant; a dialogue doubles its meaning because it is held on the same settee as a previous dialogue; and it is imperative to know the intonations of the voice, to mark the gestures. No doubt Mr. James has the defects of his virtues in pronounced form; tricks of precious expression; an affected scorn of repetition; an excess of allusiveness that conceals its own foundation; a failure to give every one a concrete character. Miss Barrace, for example, is a sort of Cheshire cat; and the great sculptor and others of the minor characters are so exclusively used for their psychological value that they seem to have no persons; they evade the grip of our senses. But were Mr. James as "impossible" as some mere tasters of his work would have it, he would still have proved the novel to be a vehicle for a department of thought, almost neglected through all literature; and Mr. James thinks very hard indeed.

"The Deeps of Henry James."
London *Daily Chronicle*, 21 October 1903, p. 3.

Mr. Henry James is an almost unique example of the voluminous writer whose ideas grow more abundant with advancing years. A collected edition of his works would be massive in bulk, and bewildering in variety. This is the third volume of fiction he has given us in the present year; and yet he is so far from writing himself out that the new story is perfectly original; it contains at least two of his best characters, and there is no sense of repetition save in the peculiarities of the style. As usual, the reader wanders, as it were, in an enchanted wood, by devious paths which seem to be leading to nothing until he bursts suddenly into a friendly clearing, and understands at last that the wood is a mighty maze, but not without a plan. Mr. James himself supplies an "image" which may be cited, in no spirit of carping, as still more characteristic of his method. The chief ambassador in the story is Mr. Lambert Strether, from Massachusetts, who is engaged with his friend Waymarsh, a delightfully typical American from the same State, in elucidating the mystery of Mr. Chad Newsome's career in Paris. Mr. Newsome's mother is a widow, to whom Mr. Strether is provisionally engaged to be married. She has supplied the funds to carry on a periodical of which he is editor. His name is on the cover, and that appears to be the extent of his literary repute. The review, as he humorously remarks, is "sweetly ignored" by the reading public of America. His real probation with the widow is this mission to Paris. Her son, she believes, has been leading a deplorable life for years, and Mr. Strether is expected to rescue him, and bring him home. But when he tries to grip the nature of the entanglement which keeps Chad in Paris, away from a thriving manufacture bequeathed by his father, Strether finds it mysterious, impalpable.

Waymarsh himself, for the occasion, was drawn into the eddy; it absolutely, though but temporarily, swallowed him down, and there were days when Strether seemed to bump against him, as a sinking swimmer might brush a submarine object. The fathomless medium held them—Chad's manner was the fathomless medium; and our friend felt as if they passed each other, in their deep immersion, with the round, impersonal eye of silent fish

The reader also is conscious very often of swimming about in a fathomless medium; but there the comparison ceases. There is nothing impersonal and fishlike in Mr. James's characters. The people who surround Strether give one the idea of suppressed individuality, the idea that if they rose to the surface—came up to "blow," like whales—they would have a tremendous lot to say. Some of them do rise now and then, and the effect is striking. Face to face with Chad, the first impulse of the simple gentleman from Woollett (Mass.) is to telegraph to the anxious mother, "Awfully old—gray hair." Greatly changed is Chad. The ambassador remembers him in knickerbockers. "Yes, it was knickerbockers. I'm busybody enough to remember that, and that you had, for your age—I can speak of the first, far-away time—tremendously stout legs." But now the young man has an attractive maturity which makes Strether feel like an uncomfortable junior. It cannot be due to the influence of Mimi or Musette. No young person of that kind can have moulded these graces. They would never have grown at Woollett

(Mass.). Chad has "got an inscrutable new face somewhere and somehow." He is "the young man marked out by women," and the character has dignity, and even "comparative austerity." There is a hint of "some self-respect, some sense of power oddly perverted, something latent and beyond access, ominous and perhaps enviable." But perfectly staggering to the poor ambassador, who has come on a mission of rescue! Not much is to be extracted from the enigmatic Chad, who, to a direct question about women, replies, "One doesn't quite know what you mean by being in women's 'hands.' It's all so vague. One is when one isn't. One isn't when one is. And then one can't quite give people away."

Mr. Newsome has good reason for this reserve, as the reader discovers when he arrives at the next clearing. There is a certain Mme. de Vionnet, judicially separated from her husband. She has a charming daughter. They live in a most agreeable circle, where there are not "too many bores." Here the ambassador has a cordial welcome; he enjoys the life immensely; but his speculations about the mother and daughter and Chad are continually baffled. Everybody watches him with a friendly and slightly sardonic curiosity. His letters to Woollett are deemed so unsatisfactory that a fresh embassy is dispatched. One of the new envoys is Chad's married sister, and she promptly forms a very definite conclusion as to her brother's relations with Madame de Vionnet. That lady is indeed the key to the riddle of Chad. She has moulded those astonishing graces out of the raw material from Massachusetts. But for her Chad would have fallen captive to the bow and spear of Mimi or Musette. In the Parisian, but not the Woollett sense, she has saved him. The penalty she has to suffer is described by Mr. James with infinite delicacy and charm. It distresses the kindly Strether so profoundly that in the endeavour to avert it he cheerfully faces the pillory of Woollett (Mass.). "She was as much as ever the finest and subtlest creature, the happiest apparition, it had been given him, in all his years, to meet." Apparition is, perhaps, the most felicitous of all words for this winning and pathetic figure. We see her fading away in a sorrowful adieu, while Chad is busy with furtive preparations to take up that thriving manufacture in America, and give it the "boom" of scientific advertisement.

What is the manufacture? We are never told. Mr. James hovers over it with tantalising irony. "We constantly talk of it," says Strether to an inquisitive lady: "we are quite familiar and brazen about it. Only as a small, trivial, rather ridiculous object of the commonest domestic use, it's rather wanting in—what shall I say? Well, dignity or the least approach to distinction." The inquisitive lady tries clothespins and shoe-polish, but is cheerfully warned that she is not likely to guess it. It is right down at the very bottom of the fathomless medium, where it seems to grin at us with grotesque mockery of the patient devotion which transformed Chad into an ornament of society. Chad's perfections are now employed to stimulate the circulation of this commodity through the households of the United States. Of course, Mr. James leaves us to surmise that. It is no part of his system to tell us definitely what happens to anybody. If you like, you can believe that Strether does not venture to show his face in the scornful market-places of Massachusetts. Wherever he is, we shall always think with pleasure of his companionship through many pages, in which the psychology of his wistful good nature is unfolded with the most suggestive art.

Saturday Review [England] 96 (31 October 1903), p. 551.

Mr. Henry James grows cleverer and cleverer. Soon he will write a book of the nature of a recent work on Egypt which only four men were said to be able to understand and only one to appreciate. One regards this last product with the sort of astonished admiration reserved for those ingenious ivory toys, containing a ball within a ball, on which a Chinaman will spend a lifetime. The patience, neatness, precision, and ingenuity pass understanding; but with Western Philistinism one is disposed to wonder why in the world anyone did such a thing. It is impossible for anyone who has once concentrated attention on "The Ambassador" [sic] to withhold admiration from the artist. The intricacies and subtleties of motive and character are twined so deftly, the ravelled web so trimly knit. But like little Wilhelmine we should like to ask: what good came of it at last? The scheme is simple enough. A New England lady, one gathers a rather heavy patroness of men and things, sends over to Paris an ambassador to withdraw her son from some imagined liaison. While the ambassador, for whom his patroness has an unreciprocated affection, delays and another set of ambassadors are sent over to judge the situation and reclaim the first ambassador. That is the whole plot; for nothing particular happens in the sense that the romances are brought to a definite conclusion. But Mr. James succeeds in investing with amazing interest the slow change in the mental attitude of the ambassador, whose New England standards slowly fall before the larger, livelier standards of Europe. It were easy to scoff at the persistent ingenuity brought to bear on the thesis. We confess to a not infrequent ignorance of the full intention of pages of close dialogue; but Mr. James, as Nature, does nothing per saltum; and what is sometimes unintelligible in process gathers meaning in the result. Even if we do not know what Mr. James means, we are sure he means something; and the clear presence of significance is not common enough to be despised. Above all, the unravelling of the skein, under the guidance of Mr. James' two hands, is an intellectual amusement altogether enthralling. Only—let no one inquire why it enthrals; for we certainly could not tell.

"An International Novel." New York Times Saturday Review of Books and Art 8 (14 November 1903), 818.

It is rather cheering to find the inventor of the international novel, for such Mr. Henry James unquestionably is, returning to his first love after his recent and numerous excursions in London society. In "The Ambassadors," which has just been put between covers, after finishing a year's course in The North American, he makes this return.[1] It should be interesting to many readers whom the usual problems of Mr. James do not interest to see themselves as others see them. And to readers who make a point of reading everything that Mr. James writes it is particularly interesting to see how much more comprehensive is his vision, as well as how much riper in his art, than in the days of "Daisy Miller" and "The American" and "The Europeans" and "The Portrait of a Lady."

Like an artist, Mr. James is much more interested in putting questions than in answering them. The question put in "The Ambassadors" amounts to a confrontation of two civilizations. The prodigal son, from a Massachusetts town, is rumored to be feeding upon husks in Paris. To his family there is urgent need that he be reclaimed. And so Ralph Waldo Emerson, so to speak, is sent out to reclaim him and bring him home. At Liverpool he meets Daniel Webster, as it were, who is in Europe about his own occasions, and who does not count for much in the story, except to apply faithfully the standards of New England to the procedures of all other lands, and to find these wanting. But Ralph Waldo, being of an opener mind, cannot help observing and admitting that husks have agreed excellently with the prodigal. Of course he has been charged especially to "look for the woman," and he finds that it is the woman who has wrought the miracle of improvement he finds in his young friend, and this in spite of a relation, of which the irregularity, at first denied and dissembled, becomes at last incapable of disguise. He does not for that go back upon his conclusion that his ward is both reclaimed and irretrievably committed, and that for him to consent to be saved would be to consent to be damned. Meanwhile his own recreancy to his trust having been established, other missionaries come out, and chiefly the prodigal's sister. Her clear New England intelligence and her inflexible New England conscience refuse to be perverted by any sophistries. The improvement in her brother she finds mere degenerations and the relation which has wrought it simply "hideous." But she and Daniel Webster are the only two characters who retain their integrity in the presence of the allurements and the snares to which the young prodigal has gladly succumbed. And it is left in doubt whether their superior virtue is not merely superior density, density with a dash of hypocrisy.

It is really a diabolical dilemma that Mr. James has constructed, and of which he offers to his readers the choice of horns. Somewhere, in another book, he has recorded his regret at not having paid the homage he feels inclined to render to the French spirit. It seems that in "The Ambassadors" he has squared that account. For the confrontation of standards in the book is of New England and of France.

In almost the first chapter it is remarked that "Woollett,"—that is the name of the Massachusetts town—"Woollett is not sure it ought to enjoy." In one of the last, in speaking of the "text" given out by a scene of rural France, it is remarked:

> The text was simply, when condensed, that in those places such things were, and that if it was in them one elected to move about, one had to make one's account with what one lighted on.

In the earlier novels, although some dull persons accused him of Anglomania about them, the novelist commonly saw to it that "Europe" did not have the better of it, and flattered the patriotic pride of the American reader. In this the American reader must entertain an uneasy suspicion that the joke is on him, or at most that honors are easy. As with most of Mr. James's recent problems, the subject does not invite discussion at tea parties. But without any doubt he has woven a delightful story about it. He is not to blame if he found the subject altogether too irresistible to be resisted, and except by Sarah Pocock he will be acquitted of an intention to corrupt anybody's morals.

Note

1 *"The Ambassadors," North American Review* 176 (January–June 1903), 138–60,

297–320, 459–80, 634–56, 792–816, 945–68; 177 (July–December 1903), 138–60, 297–320, 457–80, 615–40, 779–800, 947–68.

Edward Garnett.
Speaker [England] new series 9 (14 November 1903), 146–47.

Mr. Henry James's handling of his public recalls to our memory nothing less than the high finesse of a sagacious old apple-woman who was used to dispose of her goodies to us schoolboys by a deeply simple plan. Her stock of piled-up sweets and sours lay there inviting to the hesitating hand and greedy eye, but the boys had to plump their pennies down, in faith, leaving her to choose and make up the "penn'orth" with a strange handful of fruit, some edible, some most inedible. Thus it is that grumbling we go away, at times, with sleepy pears, good in parts *(The Wings of the Dove)*; but at the next purchase *(The Ambassadors)* the fruit is mellow, most fine flavoured. What other stall sells goods so spicy to the taste? Taste is indeed the word that makes any dealing with Mr. Henry James a delightfully perilous business. The tendency of every artist of marked idiosyncrasies, after he has passed his meridian, to overstrain his own method is a danger against which we can scarcely expect him to be on his guard. He penetrates into life in such a way: he delights in penetrating in such a way: insensibly he practises his method more and more for its own sake, like a great specialist who is tempted to perform his favourite operation on all varying cases. Life so tied down indeed may be lost under the clever

shredding knife, but the famous method flourishes! So in *The Wings of the Dove* Mr. Henry James pushed so triumphantly along the tortuous path of his demonstrations that in the end he was left standing with one character, Milly, surviving still the strains and harassed ordeal of the exacting journey. In *The Ambassadors*, however, Mr. James has returned straight on his tracks, and, with the immense cunning of his artistic resources, has coaxed his readers, to set forth on a new, entrancing, and diverting journey. He has, in fact, like the aged apple-woman of our youth, arranged afresh his stall with such a sagacious eye for human appetite that the reader will find it impossible not to yield himself up for better or worse to his artistic dispensations. And in *The Ambassadors* we are fobbed off with no large handfuls of hollow walnuts or over-ripened pears.

The theme of this book is one rich in malicious human comedy. It is, to put it baldly, the collision between the crudity of the American mind and the finesse of Europe's old-world civilisation. Strether, the ambassador, an inexperienced but subtle American of fifty-five, is despatched by his *fiancée*, the imposing Mrs. Newsome, the presiding genius of Woollett, Mass., to rescue her son Chad from the feminine seductions of Paris, in which he has been "lowering himself" for five years. But on arriving in Paris Strether discovers that Chad has gained incomparably in refinement, in "tone," in breeding and bearing; that he has, in fact, scaled heights of culture quite uncomprehended at Woollett, Mass., and that the agent of Chad's social transformation is a certain French Countess, Mme. de Vionnet, for whom he has "a virtuous attachment." Strether is acute enough to pay full homage to the exquisite fascination of Mme. de Vionnet's charm, and to recognise that she is the consummate flower of European civilisation, and soon, turning traitor to Woollett and Mrs. Newsome, he throws his weight against Chad's departure for America. But Woollett despatches further "ambassadors"—Jim, Mamie and Chad's sister, Sarah Pocock—to bring back post haste the weak defaulter Strether to be disciplined finally by Massachusetts's and Mrs. Newsome's vigorous embraces. The terrific impact of the Americans on Strether's high altruism is cleverly set off against Chad's brilliant reception of this new "mission"; but suddenly the crash comes. Strether discovers, through a face-to-face encounter, what is known to everybody else, that Chad's "virtuous attachment" to Mme. de Vionnet, is, in fact, a *liaison;* and at this juncture Chad shows ominous signs of forsaking the woman who has made him, shaped him, polished him, and transformed him from Woollett's raw product into a man of taste and accomplished understanding. Strether takes the double revelation hard: his mission has broken into pieces, his self-sacrifice is futile. After abjuring Chad never to forsake Mme. de Vionnet, and being assured that he is not "tired" of her, he returns to Woollett to receive "the great difference" in his future at the hands of Mrs. Newsome.

From this meager menu of the plot the acute reader will guess the piquant flavour of the cosmopolitan dish Mr. Henry James has compounded for him. The reader, if he is wise, will surrender himself to the exciting bill of fare, and will not haggle as to the price he must pay in losing here and there the illusion of art. For it is obvious that the author's latter-day art is so finely experimental in its modern appeal, and is so shaded and blended with an exacting psychological inquisition into our vaguely lurking feelings, that the reader must make *his* handsome concession before he can take hands with Mr. James and be drawn into the thickening mesh of the sensitive web spun for his delectation. The reader, in short, must be ever ready to discard the visible, audible world of natural appearances for that mazy psychical world of our haunting apperceptions, the veil of which is constantly being drawn and shaken and shifted by Mr. Henry James's characters, of set purpose, in their clairvoyant talk. If the reader will make this single concession—and it is not an unreasonable one—he will be astonished to find how easily this subconscious world of our psychical intuitions can glide into and impinge on our vision of the world of natural manifestations. A good example of this called-for concession on the reader's part is afforded by Chapter XXXIII., where the disconcerted Strether receives the seal of Mme. de Vionnet's sacred confidence. Here the effect on the reader's nerves is the doubling of thought-reading with a scene of natural life. The conversation is carried on not so much by the natural words and gestures of the man and woman as by their secret comprehensions, it is a mute conversation, so to say, between their lively apperceptions analysing each other's situation, a spiritual interchange which Mr. Henry James has tried to render by conversation. Of course, if we judge the scene simply by its truth to nature and artistic inevitability, we simply do not believe in Mme. de Vionnet's actual self-abandonment. It is to the American's uncanny detection of the secret weakness within Mme. de Vionnet's soul that Mr. Henry James has devoted his fine analysis, and it is the American's typical thinness of feeling wherever passion is concerned that the author, half-unconsciously, has brought out in the following passages:

"'Selfish and vulgar—that's what I must seem to you. . . . It isn't that.'" (p. 429.)

This may be how some people think, but it is not how any people talk. Apart, however, from its naturalness, the effect on the reader is of Mme. de Vionnet's self-regarding soul detaching itself for Mr. James's purposes. It isn't life here painted for us; it's life decomposed. And as though to atone for the inevitable artistic dangers of his insistent analysis of the successive layers of his characters' inner consciousness, Mr. Henry James has accomplished extraordinary feats of skill in bathing each scene in the actual flaring atmosphere of life, in visualising, by exquisite little peeps and snatches, the country and streets and rooms in which his characters walk and talk, in flooding our senses with mysteriously-wafted suggestions of the gracious shades and forms, colours and moving harmony of the old-world civilisation of Paris:

"The house to his restless sense was in the high homely style of an elder day, and the ancient Paris that he was always looking for—sometimes intensely felt, sometimes more acutely missed— was in the immemorial polish of the wide waxed staircase and in the fine *boiseries,* the medallions, mouldings, mirrors, great clear spaces, of the grayish-white saloon into which he had been shown. . . . She was seated near the fire, on a small stuffed and fringed chair, one of the few modern articles in the room; and she leaned back in it with her hands clasped in her lap, and no movement in all her person but the fine prompt play of her deep young face. The fire, under the low white marble, undraped and academic, had burnt down to the silver ashes of light wood; one of the windows stood open at a distance to the mildness and stillness, out of which, in the short pauses, came the faint sound, pleasant and homely, almost rustic, of a plash and a clatter of *sabots* from some coach-house on the other side of the court." (p. 182.)

This exquisite gift of rendering a scene and its just atmosphere by a supreme sense for selection is, however, matched by the author's power of breaking up a mental atmosphere, by indicating the strange little gusts and eddies of forerunning changes. The two pages (pp. 449–450) in which Chad's hidden character works easily up to the surface before the astounded eyes of Strether, disclosing the insidious, bottomless gulf between Chad's and Mme. de Vionnet's natures, is an achievement which only two or three living authors could approach and none could surpass. All the fatality of life is disclosed behind the yawning vulgarity of Chad's revelation. The figure of Weymarsh [*sic*], again, brushed in with a few loosely fluid touches, is of continental significance. The disquieting secret of this transplanted American, for ever out of place in Europe, looms cloudily before our disconcerted eyes, suggesting migrant horrors swarming long before and long after us. Were the American intelligence permeable to such ironic testimony, the malicious creator of Weymarsh might suffer under the patriot's knife. Sally Pocock, the American woman, is again so much "one of the best, the real and the right," "the very thing itself," that Europe and America will put up a fervent prayer for her creator who has focussed her figure in this cruel immortal flash. Strether, the hero, is a type rather far-fetched for artistic purposes, but his over-lucid perceptions must be conceded to Mr. James as the necessary developing bath in which his negative of cosmopolitan values "comes out." And this brings us to one conclusion—that wherever the author's latter-day art weakens and comes near to disintegration, it is where he has put far too much of his own subtlety into his types and read into them meanings their figures cannot naturally carry. Densher, in *The Wings of a Dove* [*sic*], and the heroine of *In the Cage* soon become false and unnatural figures, untrue to type, by the sur-plusage of mental feats Mr. Henry James insists on coaxing out of their brains. When, as the story rolls on, we see the main chain of fine quivering sensibilities coupled hastily on to everybody's senso-rium alike, the illusion of life and the illu-sion of art break up and vanish. But where the author finds types plausibly true to life, as Strether and Miss Gostrey, in *The Ambassadors,* serving as complex mental mirrors in which the society round them can be refracted to us, then his art carries all before it. If some of his short stories present to us a more perfect illusion of life than does *The Ambassadors,* the latter is the most maliciously fine and withal the most broadly significant picture of mod-ern cosmopolitan life he has painted. Whether other generations will take trou-ble enough to find the right keys in the bunch that unlock the labyrinthine cham-bers of his art may be questioned, but *The Ambassadors,* we hold, will rank as the finest and subtlest piece in the long gallery of his many achievements.

Elia W. Peattie. "James' *The Ambassadors*: Four Hundred Large Pages in Which Little Happens." Chicago *Tribune,* 21 November 1903, p. 13.

I have been thinking a good deal the last few hours of the penalties and pleasures incurred in reading Henry James, our most distinguished if our most expatri-ated novelist.

To begin with, there is, in opening a new volume of his, such as "The Ambas-sadors," newly from the press of Harper & Bros., a satisfaction in the mere bulk of the book. From the outset the reader feels that he is undertaking a book written by a man of splendid leisure, who pays the reader the compliment of supposing that he has the same. Art is long and yet longer with James, and he is not tempted—however incoherent he may be—to prove scrappy. He enters upon a theme with dignity and repose. He deals with it after his own fash-ion, which involves an unrivaled delibera-tion. He has reached the place where he can refuse to try to interest a trivial or a hurried audience, and he has long since been oblivious to a provincial one.

He is, personally, far too much a man of the world to permit himself to have any ideas, and the reader has a suspicion that James regards ideals as something dis-tinctly American, not to say middle class. It is not with the middle class that James enjoys himself, except, perhaps, as he per-mits representatives of it to visit Europe, with mouth and eyes agape, for the pur-pose of being instructed by the Europeans. James cannot emerge from his wonder himself, apparently, and above all other ideas he holds this one, that Europe is the wonderful thing on this round world.

It is impossible for a person who has just finished "The Ambassadors" to avoid the use of the word "wonderful," for it oc-curs with amazing—I had almost said wonderful—frequency in the pages of this book. At frequent intervals the characters look at each other and cry: "But you are wonderful, wonderful!" Or one character, speaking of an absent one, says: "But, of course, she was wonderful. She is always that." Or one character says to another: "But whatever else she was, she must have been wonderful!"

These suppositions are always precisely right. In all circumstances this group of men and women who play at cross purposes, who are habitually indirect, who never arrive at anything vital, who have turmoils which are not of the spirit but of that curious substitute for it which accomplished Parisians and their friends devise, are wonderful and yet wonderful. It is, to begin and end with, wonderful how they can talk so much and say so little, how they can live so long and move so inappreciably.

The ambassadors are the representatives of a family in Woollett, Mass., who are sent abroad to discover why the son of the house does not come home, he being indefinitely stationed in Paris. This young American prince, Chad Newsome by name, is engaged in drinking in his Paris, and the draft has worked a transformation in him. No one living or dead is better qualified to describe the character of this transformation than is James. It seems brutal and unwarrantable, indeed, to say in crude English that the young man is among other things, converted into a liar, for by such circuitous paths is the reader brought to this conclusion, and so pleasantly does he wander from salon to boulevard, from country retreat to opera, with this engaging Mr. Newsome that he as well as Strethers [*sic*], the chief of the ambassadors, is reasonably well deceived. When Chad's garments of morality prove to be only glittering sequins which, however dazzling, are sewed upon miserable rags, a certain disgust for life is experienced by the reader. That is, no question, precisely what James intended. He is never so disingenuous as to permit the reader to weep. Neither does he at any time permit him to rejoice. He gives, with much circumlocution, his immaterial facts, and the reader is made to feel, in view of a catastrophe, the same emotions that one of James' characters would feel. Disgust of the world and distrust of all living creatures is the sense that overwhelms the reader at the end of this book. The moral of civilization appears to be, "Do not become civilised." Yet it would appear that none of those who have tasted of this tree of knowledge may ever return to ignorance and peace. The complicated, indirect, nonessential point of view appears to [be] all that remains to them. They are bound to a wheel of folly and deceit, and cleverly as they refer to their tortures they are not able to disguise the fact that they suffer tortures.

It is a view of life peculiarly irritating to the American, who, child that he is, really likes the fundamental and the honest things—at least in books. Perhaps it comes about because he is not mentally equipped for the reading of a book such as "The Ambassadors." Maybe the American is not up to the novel which is qualified to be judged by international standards. For it is an undeniable truth that Mr. James is one of the three or four Americans whose books can, frankly, be judged by international standards. The critics and the public approach almost all American books with commingled tolerance and expectation. Gay or somber, long or short, they present a universal naïveté, and have about them an appealing wistfulness.

"Behold me," each new one appears to say, "am I not really a book? Have I, perhaps, the constituents of a novel? Pray, am I not smart—have I not the accustomed air?"

James has the accustomed air. He is acquainted with the sophisticated world, and he is himself utterly sophisticated, so much so that he makes a whole book upon the most questionable of subjects— the entrapping of a provincial young man by a cosmopolitan woman, and the futile efforts of his kinsmen to break off the affair. Into this story, so unlovely, and in many ways so base, are interpolated estimates of character, striving and adroit phrases and glimpses of almost intensively intimate familiarity with the fickle souls of men and women. The touches of a master are apparent in his perplexing masterpiece—this masterpiece which lacks to a degree all of the elements which go to constitute a noble book, and which yet, by the variety of its knowledge and independence of expression, as well as richness of experience, makes it a great book. And this, too, when it irritates the reader at every page and tempts him to pronounce it anything but great.

It is no longer possible to be coherent about James because he is not, by any possibility, coherent about anything. Yet out of his incoherency, his provoking affectations, and his elaborate mistiness, emerge unforgettable figures of men and women—sinners all—as ships slip from the vacuity of the fog into a semi-visibility, and then slip back again. They are but half seen—or not so much as half—yet by that fact perhaps the impression of their power and speed is increased. They sweep on their way into the vaporous opacity from which they came, wending their blind way across the paths of the sea.

Lastly, as the preachers say, the reader of "The Ambassadors" is made envious. The thing he is envious of is the alert sensibilities, the answering eye, the subtle comprehension, the inimitable intuitions of James' men and woman. Where, in a dull and literal world, may the rest of us find such friends? Such companionship is dreamed of by all of us, but never attained. If, in one direction, we speak the language of the initiates, at another we fail. This aristocracy which James pictures, this privileged class, are provocative. The reader, attaining to their facile powers, does so only in imagination. His actual life must seem awkward in contrast, no matter how much more virtuous or straightforward it may be.

Inevitably, we provincials are disturbed

by this man who was once of us, and who is now so no more. He does not even look back with affection upon the time when he was as innocent, as dull, and as coherent as the rest of us. He is content to be of the cognoscenti, and to deal with life indirectly, by means of an evasive philosophy, a patronizing cynicism, and an iridescent eloquence, in which colors appear but to fade, and in which facts have no more substantiality than have the sides of a Venetian crystal, which may be crushed in the impatient hand.

"*The Ambassadors:* A Study of Two Codes of Morality." Chicago *Evening Post,* 28 November 1903, part 3, p. 5.

Mr. James loves France and the French genius, and in a contest between Woollett, Mass., and France, when described by him, you scarcely expect Woollett to come out with flying colors. Yet Mr. James is a loyal New Englander, and he knows that there is much to be said for Woollett.

Ah, with Strether and Mamie—and shall we add Chad?—to represent it, Woollett need not hang its head in shame even before enchanting Paris. And, after all, was not Woollett instinctively right, as to the facts, at least, if not as to the philosophy of them?

"The Ambassadors" is a study of two views of life—two codes of morality. A young American, made to please, we gather, goes to Paris and refuses to return to take charge of a successful business— the manufacture of an article too vulgar to be named (and, of course, left unnamed in the novel). His mother hears of a shocking connection with a "dreadful" woman, and sends an ambassador to save the youth and bring him back to Woollett—and to charming Mamie, the sister of his brother-in-law. The ambassador is in a sort of way engaged to this dame—a philanthropist, patroness of art and culture, stern moralist, and all that. She publishes a review, which the ambassador edits by her sufferance.

Well, Strether, the Woollett messenger, arrives in Paris and finds Chadwick Newsome, the prodigal son, transformed and—saved! The spell of Paris, and of Chad's society, plays havoc with Woollett's ideas. Strether is soon on Chadwick's side. He meets "the woman," sees nothing but beautiful friendship in the relationship and betrays Woollett—ignorant, narrow Woollett! Not so ignorant as you think.

Other ambassadors are sent—Mrs. Pocock, the daughter of the austere dame; "Him," her husband, Woollett's leading "business man," and Mamie. Things happen to them, too, in Paris, though not of the kind that happened to Strether. We do not care to tell more of the story, for that would deprive the reader of nine-tenths of the pleasure to be had from discovering Mr. James's meaning. But it may be said that poor Strether in the end stumbles upon the truth that vindicates Woollett. He remains on Chad's side in spite of it, and returns sans anything, and without hope or prospects. The mission fails, but the ambassadors, Mrs. Sarah included, bring something of Paris to Massachusetts, each what he or she can bring.

We do not advise the "mechanical" reader to tackle Mr. James's novel. The born reader will devour it without advice. But the volitional reader, if he has a very decided love for mental exercise, should find

it a rare treat. Mr. James, to use his own favorite word, is "wonderful," and every human creature is wonderful to him. How much he enables us to see in the most commonplace character, in the simplest action! He is amazingly ingenious and subtle, but if the proper study of mankind is man, his is the right method of analyzing and revealing the play of motive and impulse back of our daily and hourly transactions.

To read him understandingly is not easy. It requires as much application and attention as Kantian metaphysics, but the effort is richly rewarded. The art of fiction is not for the unskillful and idle alone; there is room for a James and a Meredith.

"The Ambassadors" is a finer novel than "The Wings of the Dove." It is a study of atmosphere as well as of character, of shades, nuances and "tones of time" and place. We should call it a masterpiece were not this an utterly un-Jamesian term. To the elite of fiction readers it is a thing of exquisite beauty and a joy forever.

H.C.
Literary World [Boston]
34 (December 1903), 348.

Many will be frightened away from Mr. James's latest novel on account of its size. And it certainly is an appalling book to contemplate—432 extra large, extra solid, printed pages! Few but the confirmed admirers of Mr. James, and the adventurous, will attempt to read this, what appears to be, ponderous novel. To the admirers, the size will be but an added pleasure: to the adventurous, the very idea of "tackling" such a feat will prove stimulating, as an extremely high mountain lures the adventurous climber. Frankly I am an admirer, likewise I am adventurous so far as novel reading goes, therefore it was with the greatest pleasure that I took up "The Ambassadors" and sat down to read and enjoy it. After hours (this novel is not one to be read at one sitting, or even at two) of delighted enjoyment, I put the book down, saying to myself, "This is the real thing once more. Once more has Mr. James proved himself the master hand. While we have him and Edith Wharton and Joseph Conrad (Mr. Meredith no longer writes), we need not fear for English fiction, despite the historical novelists."

The scheme of the story is delightful: even the barest outline will tell any one of discernment what a joy the book must be. A young man from a small Massachusetts town has been living in Paris five years, and his mother thinks it time for him to come home and go to work, make money, marry and settle down; in other words, to become a good American citizen. She sends an old friend, a middle-aged, quiet, unsophisticated man, over to get him, promising, as a bribe, her own hand in marriage, if he is successful. This man, Strether, is the first of the ambassadors. He finds the son, Chad Newsome, vastly improved; Paris and its fascination lay hold of him, and he lingers, lost in the pleasures of refinement and the companionship of Chad and his friends, and particularly of an expatriated American, Maria Gostrey. The mother, noting this failure, sends over, as other ambassadors, her daughter and her husband and the husband's sister, whom Chad is supposed to marry. These fail likewise, and the young woman for the same reason that Strether did. This is practically all the plot there is; nothing "happens," and the entire time of the story is but three months. But the joy of the character work! The subtle charm that Mr. James spreads over the

reader, as Paris absorbs the ambassadors,—all this is worth a hundred plots.

Never has Mr. James drawn two more real, more delightful, more finished, and perfect characters than Strether and Maria Gostrey. From the first moment of their meeting to their pathetic parting, they absorb the attention and delight the mind. She is the finished product of sophisticated life; he is the pliant material which you see formed before your eyes into the completed man. Circumstances had kept him narrow till he came to Paris, then he began to live. He says to Miss Gostrey: "It's a benefit that would make a poor show for many people; and I don't know who else, but you and I, frankly, could begin to see in it what I feel. I don't get drunk; I don't pursue the ladies; I don't spend money; I don't even write sonnets. But nevertheless, I'm making up late for what I didn't have early. I cultivate my little benefit in my own little way. It amuses me more than anything that has happened to me in all my life. They may say what they like, it's my surrender, it's my tribute to youth." If this short quotation (the epitome of the whole book, in a way) does not appeal to you, do not try to read "The Ambassadors." It will bore you.

This book could never be popular, even as Mr. James's other novels are popular, for its class of appreciative readers is so very limited. No really young people could understand it; no "simple people" would know what it was all about; no unsophisticated person could enjoy it; no "patriotic" American could stand it; few women would like it; no business men could find the time to read it; no one lacking a sense of humor could follow it. This leaves a very small class—the knowing—to appreciate the book. But for these it will be a marvel, a perpetual and high delight. For them there has been nothing like it in years.

In 432 pages of fine type, divided into
twelve parts, Henry James gives us the impressions of three or four Americans who
spend a few weeks in Europe, dividing
their time between London and Paris and
allowing their thoughts and impressions
to run the entire gamut of emotions and
probabilities. Flippant book reviewers
have long been at their best in flinging
sneers and cutting remarks at Mr. James'
literary productions, but the fact remains
that he is still recognized as the greatest
living English novelist. Remembering this
fact, the conscientious reviewer is forced,
almost, to take it as a reflection upon his
own powers of perception when he becomes hopelessly lost in the vagueness of
some of Mr. James' descriptive sentences.
By the same token, the reader who convinces himself that he understands just
what Mr. James is writing about and
grasps his meaning thoroughly congratu-
lates himself and scorns the weaker intel-
lects that refuse to rise to the grandness of
it all. This reviewer is forced to the humili-
ating confession that he has not been able
to indulge in any self-congratulation. For
the purpose of making this condition of
bewilderment clear, let us look at the
opening paragraph of the story:

> Strether's first question, when he
> reached the hotel, was about his friend;
> yet, in learning that Waymarsh was not
> to arrive until evening, he was not
> wholly disconcerted. A telegram from
> him, bespeaking a room "only if not
> noisy," with the answer paid, was pro-
> duced for the inquirer at the office, so
> that the understanding that they
> should meet at Chester rather than at

Liverpool remained to that extent
sound. The same secret principle, however, that had prompted Strether not
absolutely to desire Waymarsh's presence at the dock, that had led him thus
to postpone for a few hours his enjoyment of it, now operated to make him
feel that he could still wait without disappointment. They would dine together at the worst, and, with all respect to dear old Waymarsh—if not
even, for that matter, to himself, there
was little fear that in the sequel they
would see enough of each other. The
principle I have just mentioned as operating had been, with the most newly
disembarked of the two men, wholly
instinctive—the fruit of a sharp sense
that, delightful as it would be to find
himself looking, after so much separation, into his comrade's face, his business would be a trifle bungled should
he simply arrange that this countenance should present itself to the near-
ing steamer as the first "note," for him,
of Europe. Mixed with everything was
the apprehension, already, on Strether's
part, that it would, at best, throughout,
prove the note of Europe in quite a sufficient degree.

It takes a good while for that to soak
in and percolate through the clogged passages of an ordinary brain, and when you
have once mastered it, after several read-
ings, you wonder why he did not tell it all
in a sentence, and bring on dear old
Waymarsh. After you get further into the
story you find paragraphs two pages long,
and sentences that wander along and side-
track, and back up, and switch out a few
cars of words, and then pull out again on
the main track, and travel in a leisurely
way to the end of the division. But persistence in this study is rewarded, as persistence always is, and the meat of the story
is secured. It is a story of international re-

lations, the meeting of the New England conscience with old England facts and conditions. It is a picture of the transformation in character of a Massachusetts lad who succumbs to the allurements of life in Paris and other gay European capitals. An ambassador is sent from the Massachusetts home to rescue him. Other ambassadors are also necessary to accomplish the purpose, and the lad is finally rescued, with his New England conscience seared, his moral tone lowered, and his ideals shattered. Into this story the author injects estimates of character and throws sidelights on the frailties of men and women. In this Mr. James' master hand is recognized. He shows us glimpses of familiarity with fickle souls such as no other writer is able to do. He emphasizes the frailties of men and women, deftly etches the steps by which consciences are smothered and sensibilities deadened and character educated to living en masque. All of this comes, to the patient reader, out of Mr. James' incoherency, his vagueness, his elaborate mistiness, and his positively provoking affectation in style and word selection. Trimmed of these annoying, pestiferous objections, the book is a great one. The James admirers will revel in it. The rest of us, who find patience and perception sufficient to read it, will enjoy it, under protest.

"Henry James' Latest." Louisville *Courier-Journal*, 26 December 1903, p. 3.

A young fellow from Woollett, Mass., goes to Europe; he fails to return as soon as expected, so his widowed mother, fearing romantic entanglements, sends out an ambassador to reclaim him in the person of Lambert Strether, who, if his quest is successful, is to be rewarded with her beautiful hand and fortune. Paris is the whirligig whose centripetal force holds Chad spinning around charmed in its alluring mazes. Lucklessly the ambassador himself falls under the spell of the siren-city, and a few other missionary agents are sent to win back both truants. Considering they are all grown-up persons— Strether is fifty-five—this would seem a simple enough matter; the runaways might be supposed immediately to submit or to resist, and that would be all about it. But Mr. James has the telling of the story, and never in these latter days of his most finely spun method of dealing with motives obvious and recondite, never has he the mind to rise from his loom till he has woven over his warp every shred of thought, feeling, and even elusive imaginings that directly or indirectly concern his chief characters. So through four hundred and thirty-two closely printed pages, too closely printed in Messrs. Harper's edition, it is the mitigated pleasure of Mr. James' admirers and the mitigated pain of his enemies (for there is much to delight even these), to see the threads of the destinies of several more or less interesting people cross and recross each other, now getting pitifully tangled, now apparently smoothed out, till all of a sudden the author snaps the thread and leaves what? Everything still in a maze— lovers in qualms of uncertainty about hoped for reciprocities, a few left all alone in the world. Strether, the generous, sent up into midair, with the reader wondering when and where Strether will alight and fearing he will in any event fail of due reward for his sacrifices save the futile devotion of a few women to the tune of whose compliments, "wonderful, magnificent, of an absolute charm," he has pursued his uncomplaining, thankless way through the story.

The novel offers Mr. James opportunity for some of his best and some of his most characteristic work. With the touch of the artist that he was with his brush, and that he can be with his pen when his manner is free and not perversely knotty, had has rendered the poetry and glamour of a few phases of Paris and its environments; his charming wit has had golden chances to disport itself, notably in contrasting the unsophisticated folks from Woollett with the cosmopolites in Paris; to its utmost his subtlety in tracking motives to their remotest lairs has been exercised.

In "The Sacred Fount" and "The Wings of a Dove [sic]," James has seemed to be ranging himself somewhat on the side of the "Children of Darkness"—in men whom men condemn as ill he finds, if not so much of goodness still, certainly a great deal of attraction. A late writer in the Quarterly has been showing how in these latest days of roaring contemporary life a certain sympathy has been awakening for craft, worldliness and materialism that strive so heroically on their thorny, hungry way. This phase of modernity Mr. James seems getting particularly anxious to portray. There is no doubt of the tragic, at least, pathetic elements in the baffling of assiduous force, especially when, though the end be not the most ideal, the conditions out of which the pent force struggles to escape are ugly, squalid, cramped; there is no doubt of the dramatic possibilities it offers to the story-teller, witness Milton's use of Satan. But Strether tells a truth one does not have to be a preacher to appreciate when he says of Chad's brother-in-law, his wife and mother have as in honor bound no patience with such phenomena late or early. The pilgrim fathers of these people from Woollett, Mass. would turn in their graves at some of the talk, some of the situations in "The Ambassadors." The reader can fancy Henry James' antecedents marveling at his letting such a man as Strether get

under the spell of Madame Le Viannot, alluring, but something of a minx. It is certainly very skillful of Mr. James to capture in his pages these reflections of his time, but his sophisticated cosmopolites often make one sign for the deeper, more serious, more enduring touch that drew the "Altars of the Dead [sic]," the "Unfinished Madonna" or some of those earlier longer stories when Mr. James was more of a New Englander and less the accomplished omniscient citizen of the world.

The diction of "The Ambassadors" is in advance of that in "The Wings of the Dove" and "The Sacred Fount." Though subtle and exact enough, dear knows, it is more fluent, not so mathematically precise as before. It is riper, richer, more poetic on the whole. The little chapter on Strether's country excursion is a delight. But on the other hand, as usual, this master who has certainly been an influence in clarifying the English of American writers has exasperatingly performed in this new novel some of his old capers with the language. He tells somewhere of someone's "bepacing" the room. Maria Gostrey says that through her life she "jams down the pedal," supposedly the soft pedal, for the sake of others' nerves—even Maria might have used a more ladylike word than "jams." There is much "chucking" and "funking" what is disagreeable. This "smart" tale is continually exasperating—of course, people talk of the people James is writing of, but they oughtn't to, they have been better brought up—even Strether does it and he is represented as the editor of a ponderous, dignified magazine; James only aids and abets him and the others by carrying over their twaddle and jargon into what should be literature.

Checklist of Additional Reviews

Reader 2 (October 1903), 430.

Academy and Literature no. 1640 (10 October 1903), 387.

A. L. Lilley. "The Tribe of James." London *Daily News,* 19 October 1903, p. 5.

Literary World [England] 68 (23 October 1903), 304.

Illustrated London News 123 (31 October 1903), 652.

Reader 2 (November 1903), 619–21.

Boston *Daily Advertiser,* 14 November 1903, p. 8.

New York *World,* 14 November 1903, p. 8.

Graphic [England] 68 (21 November 1903), 704.

Atlanta *Constitution,* 22 November 1903, p. 10.

Public Ledger and Philadelphia Times, 22 November 1903, p. 13.

Public Opinion 35 (26 November 1903), 680.

Athenaeum [England] 3970 (28 November 1903), 714.

Philadelphia *North American,* 29 November 1903, sec. 7, p. 6.

Providence *Sunday Journal,* 29 November 1903, p. 21.

Book News 22 (December 1903), 395–96.

Lamp 27 (December 1903), 467–69.

Boston *Evening Transcript,* 2 December 1903, sec. 2, p. 18.

Detroit *Free Press,* 5 December 1903, sec. 2, p. 2.

New York *Commercial Advertiser,* 5 December 1903, sec. 3, p. 1.

New York Times Saturday Review of Books and Art 8 (5 December 1903), 892.

"*The Ambassadors.*" San Francisco *Chronicle,* 6 December 1903, p. 8. Reprinted in James W. Gargano, *Critical Essays on Henry James: The Late Novels* (Boston: G. K. Hall, 1987), p. 50.

Advance 46 (10 December 1903), 731.

J. B. Kerfoot. *Life* 42 (11 December 1903), 604.

Spectator [England] (12 December 1903), 1030–31.

Cleveland *Plain Dealer,* 13 December 1903, sec. 5, p. 10.

Chicago *Record-Herald,* 19 December 1903, p. 15.

St. Paul *Daily Pioneer Press,* 19 December 1903, p. 9.

Springfield [Mass.] *Republican,* 23 December 1903, p. 11.

F. T. Cooper. *Bookman* [New York] 18 (January 1904), 532–34. Reprinted in Roger Gard, ed., *Henry James: The Critical Heritage* (London: Routledge & Kegan Paul, 1968), pp. 359–60.

Dial 36 (1 January 1904), 22.

Indianapolis *Journal,* 17 January 1904, p. 7.

Churchman 89 (30 January 1904), 150.

[Annie R. M. Logan]. *Nation* 78 (4 February 1904), 95.

Standard 51 (6 February 1904), 14.

Congregationalist and Christian World 89 (27 February 1904), 302.

Atlantic Monthly 94 (September 1904), 426–27.

THE GOLDEN BOWL

H. W. Boynton. *"The Golden Bowl."* New York Times Saturday Review of Books 9 (26 November 1904), 797–98.

The publisher's official announcer characterizes "The Golden Bowl" as "an international story," of "thoroughly dramatic" character, which "will make a distinctively popular appeal, and is sure to attract the wider audience as well as the elect." Of course nobody pays much attention to remarks like this; they represent merely the ceremonial "sennet" immemorially used to proclaim the entrance of a fresh champion upon the publisher's list. It is just a chance that our official did not call it a "cosmopolitan story," of "delightfully romantic" character; but he could hardly have spared his "popular appeal" and "wider audience." Yet it is patent that the boundaries of Mr. James's audience were fixed long ago; certainly nothing could be less likely to extend them than a book like this. It quite lacks, indeed, a property which has undoubtedly done something toward attracting a grosser audience for some of his other books. "The Golden Bowl" makes no delicate overtures to pruriency; its most dubious passages suggest nothing more than the most ordinary improprieties.

In other ways it seems to me to present Mr. James at his worst, as its predecessor, "The Better Sort," presented him at his best.[1] There, in the smaller scale of such sketches as "The Beldonald Holbein," "The Tone of Time," and "Broken Wings," his art achieved its utmost: an effect both subtle and powerful. In "The Golden Bowl" we find, standing for subtlety, a kind of restless finicking inquisitiveness, a flutter of aimless conjecture, such as might fall to a village spinster in a "department store." Here is a bit of lace. How much is it? And does she want it? And there is some blue merino that would be just the thing if she could only recall what it would be just the thing for. She will ask the floorwalker; but he answers her absent-mindedly, in Greek, and there she is. Mr. James, the prolix, the inconsequent, the incoherent, the indecisive; it is of this Mr. James that we carry away an impression from "The Golden Bowl."

Of his manner we need say little. At best it is a kind of physical deformity, upon which he has been rallied quite enough. It has deprived him of some excellent company, and it has won him the adoration of not a few of the ingenious for whom verbal thickets have an irresistible attraction. The wider audience will never be more than willing to endure the imposition laid upon them by a Browning or a Mr. Meredith or a Mr. James. They do not like a diet all bones, though there is marrow in them; and paper frills are, under the circumstances, an added irony. Of mere mannerisms, certainly, they have a right to be impatient. Mr. James was informed of this long ago, but he has clung to them with an insistence that would be fine if the point at issue were not petty. How like ancient and tedious cronies the "wonderfullys" and "preciselys" and "adequatelys" and "competents" turn up on these pages—as a rule in places where no self-respecting adverb would choose to be discovered. And how well-prepared we are to hear that "it was quite positively for her as if she were altogether afraid of him," and that "she could almost have smiled at last, troubled as she yet knew herself, to show how richly she was harmless." Yet the writer who habitually deals in this kind of mincing awkwardness is capable enough of clean and vigorous expression, as we know. Here, for instance, is a human situation expressed in human terms:

> He was always lonely at great parties, the dear Colonel, ... but nobody could have seemed to mind it less, to brave it with more bronzed indifference; so markedly that he moved about less like one of the guests than like some quite presentable person in charge of the police arrangements or the electric light.

And here is one of those compact and nervous passages of description, which relieve, none too often, the burden of "psychological" speculation:

> The March afternoon, judged at the window, had blundered back into Autumn; it had been raining for hours, and the color of the rain, the color of the air, of the mud, of the opposite houses, of life altogether, in so grim a joke, so idiotic a masquerade, was an unutterable dirty brown. There was at first, even for the young man, no faint flush in the fact of the direction taken, while he happened to look out, by a slow-lagging four-wheeled cab, which, awkwardly deflecting from the middle course at the apparent instance of a person within began to make for the left-hand pavement and so at last, under further instructions, floundered to a full stop before the Prince's windows.

But we must delay no longer in getting at the substance of the book. It is, as would be expected, less a story than a study; its theme being the character and relations of six persons, namely:

> An Italian Prince, to be known as Amerigo; beautiful and indigent, betrothed and presently married to
> Maggie Verver, daughter of
> Adam Verver of American City, U.S., multimillionaire and connoisseur, secondarily married to
> Charlotte Stant of American blood, but of Italian birth and cosmopolitan accomplishment. Former sweetheart of Prince, who has not been able to marry her on account of said indigence. The fact of their old relation is for some time unknown to Princess, but has been long known to
> Mrs. Assingham, also acknowledged to be of American birth; a kind of poor-genteel dea ex machina, who has really made both matches above mentioned, and thereafter hovers over the scene with her hands up and her tongue going. To her is attached by law and apparently otherwise
> Colonel Assingham, a retired officer of the British Army, lean of person and frugal in all ways, understood to be good for more than appears on the surface; at worst, a patient listener.

All three male persons, it must be said, move somewhat dimly in the background of interest. The Prince has manners, as Mr. Verver has morals, which, admirably, never desert him. The beauty of the Prince seems of a vague, conventional sort, a little wooden, a matter of hearsay. He has no vices, he has no virtues, but the grand air. Nothing seems to concern him especially, not even the indiscretion of his attachment for Charlotte Verver. The most interesting thing his creator can say of him is that he had "the trick of a certain detached, the amusement of a certain inward critical life; the determined need, while apparently all participant, of returning upon himself, of backing noiselessly in, far in again, and rejoining there, as it were, that part of his mind that was not engaged at the front." Adam Verver is a mild ghost of disinterested benevolence, only intent upon effacing himself for the good of all concerned, and quite ready also to efface his fortune and connoisseurship, if that were possible. He does not altogether lack the power to qualify and to speculate, when fairly called upon; and so proves himself not quite unworthy our consideration.

The three women, whenever the verbal mists lift sufficiently, we are able to regard with somewhat stronger concern. Fanny Assingham is a sumptuous and rather bedizened matron whose compunctions and yearnings over her four victims are, though set forth with sufficient thoroughness, plainly secondary to her interest in her own progressive interpretation of the situation in which she has involved them. Col. Assingham's loneliness at those "great parties" seems to have been dubiously atoned for by audiences with his lady, prolonged almost beyond the small hours, in which it seemed his duty to be impressed with the brilliancy of her mental and verbal pyrotechnics. Charlotte Verver, née Stant, is by all accounts a remarkable and fascinating person. She has, to the most casual eye, the advantage of being absorbed less in the spectacle of her own sensations and more in their reality than her associates. She displays at times a faculty of prompt action which can but prove disconcerting to them. She intervenes with calculating untimeliness upon the eve of her lover's marriage to her friend. She does not scruple, from frankly interested motives, to marry the aging and multimillionaire father of that friend, or to "carry on" subsequently, up to the socially tolerable limit, with the husband of that friend. To the last page it remains matter for amused conjecture with Fanny Assingham, her Colonel, and the rest of us how far Charlotte and the Prince have at any time actually "gone."

The action of the story, if we choose to employ such a word as "action," consists in the arrival of these four people at the sensible conclusion that it is not profitable for them all to live together. The Ververs make off to America, leaving the Prince and the Princess, with their property Principino, in each other's arms. A pleasant conclusion which, it seems, might have been arrived at by a straighter path. The situation, in fact, could exist only in that land of dubiety which Mr. James himself has peopled. The dwellers in that land are clever enough, intricate enough, psychological enough; they merely lack common sense. They are dead in love with subtlety; they are mainly pleased with themselves and with each other as "cases." In the midst of their intrigue, at a moment sufficiently grave, one might think, the Prince and Charlotte are to be found dwelling fondly on the abstract merits of the situation.

> "Well, the Prince candidly allowed she did bring it home to him. Every way it worked out. 'Yes, I see, we hang, essentially, together.'
>
> "His friend had a shrug—a shrug that had a grace. 'Cosa volete?' The effect, beautifully, nobly, was more than Roman. 'Ah, beyond doubt, it's a case.'
>
> "He stood looking at her. 'It's a case. There can't,' he said, 'have been many.'
>
> "'Perhaps never, never any other. That,' she smiled, 'I confess I should like to think. Only ours.'"

So easily are people diverted from uncomfortable issues in this happy country of Mr. James. Only his. Mr. James has, we must agree, all the right in the world to occupy himself with the analysis of his subject or subjects; but in a work of art the elements are not given thought or voice to express what they stand for. The attempt to make them perform this function is suggestive of an imperfect impulse toward creation which now and then, as in "The Ring and the Book," produces work of great effectiveness, but not of absolute excellence.

The fact is pretty well enforced by the "case" of our Princess. Originally this Maggie Verver seems a nice girl, who stands in no need of any kind of galvanization into intellectual activity to make her worth knowing. It is hard not to feel a grudge against her author for having applied the superfluous wire. It seems to the robust intelligence that she might have been able to solve her appointed problems without recourse to intricate manipulations. That kind of method she might have left to the glory of Mrs. Assingham and the convenience of her more or less improper husband and his Charlotte. But no, she must not allow herself to be simple and straightforward. Even with her father she must not be frank and open; she must insinuate, she must equivocate, she must qualify. This, we are to understand, is the real test of her subtlety, of whether she actually deserves to be on intimate terms with Mr. James and with the other persons involved. She does not fairly make her standing good until the end of the first volume; it is the second which bears her name, and which we take to be a record of her existence as a fully naturalized subject in the land. She is now awake, and in full possession of faculties of qualification, of subterfuge, of circumvolution which enable her to beat the others at their own game, the clever Charlotte, the astute Prince, enable her even to out-Assingham the Assinghams. She has at last mastered the "case" notion of life. She accustoms herself to the manipulation of theories about questions which prompt and plain sense might have dealt with offhand. She learns to look upon her father, toward whom her attitude at the beginning had been so simple and fond, as an interesting specimen.

"His very quietness was part of it now, as always part of everything, of his suc-cess, his originality, his modesty, his exquisite public perversity, his inscrutable, incalculable energy; and this quality perhaps it might be—all the more too as the result, for the present occasion, of an admirable traceable effort—that placed him in her eyes as no precious work of art probably had ever been placed in his own. There was a long moment, absolutely, during which her impression rose and rose, even as that of the typical charmed gazer in the still museum before the named and dated object, the pride of the catalogue, that time has polished and consecrated. Extraordinary, in particular, was the number of the different ways in which he thus affected her as showing."

Well, the show is over eventually; and it must be confessed that we leave our named and dated objects, our pride of the catalogue and the rest, without keen regret. More than once in the course of the performance we may have had occasion to recall with malicious assent a certain vigorous exclamation with which Mrs. Assingham closes one of her most eloquent harangues. "Nothing—in spite of everything—will happen. Nothing has happened. Nothing is happening." We may, further, have discerned a more general application in the sentence which records a mood of the Princess's. "There was, honestly, an awful mixture of things, and it was not closed to her after-sense of such passages . . . that the deepest depth of all, in a perceived penalty, was that you couldn't be sure some of your compunctions and contortions wouldn't show for ridiculous." Let us say for our last word, however, that not a few pleasant human touches are admitted to the final scenes. Mrs. Verver goes not quite forlorn, not quite without hope of reward for her sacrifice, into her exile. And the Prince never shows so gracious as in that last moment when he registers at once his revolt against subtlety and his allegiance to Maggie.

"'That's our help, you see,' she added, to point further her moral.

"We left him before her, therefore, taking in—or trying to—what she so wonderfully gave. He tried, too clearly, to please her, to meet her in her own way; but with the result only that, close to her, her face kept before him, his hands holding her shoulders, his whole act inclosing her, he presently echoed, 'See? I see nothing but you.' And the truth of it had, with his force, after a moment, so lighted his eyes that as for pity and dread of them, she buried her own in his breast."

Note

1̇ *The Better Sort* (New York: Charles Scribner's Sons, 1903).

Elia W. Peattie. Chicago *Tribune,* 3 December 1904, p. 10.

Mr. Henry James has a new novel. It is in two volumes, is called "The Golden Bowl," and is about an Italian prince and a number of American women. Mr. James says of his prince and hero, almost at the outset: "He had done nothing he oughtn't—he had, in fact, done nothing at all." This may be taken as the shibboleth of the book. "He—she—they—had done nothing at all." And one agrees heartily when one of the three convoluting, evasive, loquacious, but uninforming heroines sighs: "Nothing—in spite of every thing—will happen. Nothing has happened. Nothing is happening." One wishes for one of those weird human repeaters devised by Maeterlinck in his most besotted moments of mysticism, who strike the hour of disaster with a parrotlike phrase. Were such an one interpolated in Mr. James' slow moving, unpleasant tale, to cry: "Nothing is happening. Nothing can happen!" it would take all responsibility from both critic and reader, and permit him to quit mid-misery.

I said the tale was unpleasant, but that is not quite just. It is about people who are no earthly good in the world—a prince who must needs marry an heiress, a woman who has no occupation but matchmaking, another woman who is subtle and the convenient recipient of the uttermost compliments from gentlemen who neglect to marry her, and an American heiress who is almost nice, but who contrives to be a good deal of a conformist to things not liked in the wholesome bourgeois world to which she was born, and some men who make money or spend it, and who are of no use, either. Nobody is of any use. It would have been better if none of them had been born. That in their useless lives they rend each other quite pleases the moralist. They are completely effete. But sometimes they are human, and at moments the coquettish prince is almost lovable. He is so at the end, when something of manhood blazes up in him, and he turns from feeble iniquities to an allegiance—transitory, one suspects—to true things. Here is a description of the prince, done, as is much of the book, in Mr. James' most exquisite form of portraiture—fine as if on old ivory, minute as if done through the most magnifying of lenses, sympathetic with a courtly, restrained sympathy, elegant with an elegance to which no other American writer has attained:

417

"The prince's dark blue eyes were of the finest, and, on occasion, precisely resembled nothing so much as the high windows of a Roman palace, of a historic front by one of the great old designers, thrown open on a feast day to the golden air. . . . It had been happily said of his face that the figure thus appearing in the great frame was the ghost of some proudest ancestor." [1904 Scribner's ed., pp. 43–44]

E.F.E.
"The Novels of Henry James."
Boston *Evening Transcript,* 21 December 1904, p. 18.

It is no easy task to assign Henry James his exact place in modern English literature. At one moment his genius seems unrivalled; at another moment he seems to have points in common with the veriest literary tyro. He writes at times as if he were inspired, only to become obsessed all too frequently by what appears to be a veritable demon of literary unrighteousness. Alternately clear and obscure in style, alternately verbose and succinct in form, alternately straightforward and eccentric in manner, he has obviously sought for himself an exceptional and unique position in the literary world. Unquestionably the most introspective of modern novelists— at least of those who write in English— he has never obtained the following which attaches itself to the train of those writers whose avowed purpose is to suit the popular taste. It is both because of and in spite of his faults that he has gained his present eminence, that he has been able to rank high as the spokesman of a small and select audience which is influential enough to exalt his reputation far above the fame of his more popular fellows.

In his two latest novels—"The Ambassadors," and "The Golden Bowl,"—Mr. James displays in their naked sincerity all those extraordinary mannerisms which have been growing upon him ever since the days when "Daisy Miller" first made his name familiar to the fiction-reading world. They offer still further evidence that heredity plays no small part in his intellectual and emotional make-up, and that the environment of an English birthplace combined with his American nativity has made him an undeniably picturesque and important literary figure. He is doing for fiction what his father did for philosophy, and there can be no question that he takes his art as seriously as the elder Henry James undertook his mission to reform the world by dabbling in the byproducts of science and religion. In quantity as well as in quality his labors have been enormous. Thirty-three years have elapsed since the publication of his first story, "Watch and Ward," and during that period his works, embracing long stories, short stories, plays, biographies, and essays, have grown in number until they now have almost reached the half-hundred mark. Among these "The American," "The Europeans," "The Bostonians," "An International Episode" and several others made clear the fact that Mr. James speaks through fiction more as a cosmopolitan than as an American. This quality, moreover, is especially prominent in "The Ambassadors" and "The Golden Bowl," in both of which Mr. James appears more than ever to detach himself from earth, and to write of human beings as if he were observing them from some faraway and inaccessible planet. For Mr. James is certainly even more than a cosmopolitan. He appears to dwell in extra-mundane regions of which he is the sole ruler.

To recount or even to suggest to our readers the contents of his two latest novels is a task wholly beyond our desires. Both deal with marriage and its complications, and both pursue their subject with an abundance of circumstance which admits no possibility of doubt or conjecture on the reader's part. That is, it would admit none, if Mr. James wrote the English language as other authors write it, or if he did not lose himself in a maze of thought out of which he is frequently unable to extricate himself through the medium of words. His characters, clear to his own mind, are by no means clear to the minds of others. He takes too much for granted; he pays too great a tribute to the insight of his readers. He imagines that they can see into his own mind and evolve out of their own consciousness the thoughts that are there. When he expresses thought clearly, he expresses it like the speaker who thinks that impressiveness lies wholly in the rotund manner. "When presently, therefore, from her standpoint, she saw the Prince come back," he writes in "The Golden Bowl," "she had an impression of all the place as higher and wider and more appointed for great moments: with its dome of lustres lifted, its ascents and descents more majestic, its marble tiers more vividly overhung, its numerosity of royalties, foreign and domestic, more unprecedented, its symbolism of 'State' hospitality both emphasized and refined." Page after page follows this majestic utterance with an elaborate description of a London social gathering, and at its conclusion we doubt if even the most clear-minded reader has any comprehensive idea of what the novelist has been dwelling upon at such great length.

Yet when Mr. James cares to leave the psychological and the verbose manner which persistently afflicts him, he is able to write a definite and compact description of this sort. "The March afternoon, judged at the window, had blundered back into Autumn; it had been raining for hours, and the color of the rain, the color of the air, of the mud, of the opposite houses, of life altogether, in so grim a joke, so idiotic a masquerade, was an unutterable dirty brown. There was at first, even for the young man, no faint flush in the fact of the direction taken, while he happened to look out, by a slow-lagging four-wheeled cab, which, awkwardly deflecting from the middle course, at the apparent instance of a person within, began to make for the left-hand pavement and so at last, under further instructions, floundered to a full stop before the Prince's windows."

Another brief specimen of Mr. James's style must suffice: "It now appeared, none the less, that some renewed conversation with Mr. Crichton had breathed on the faintness revivingly, and Maggie mentioned her purpose as a conception of her very own, to the success of which she designed to devote her morning. Visits of gracious ladies, under his protection, lighted up rosily, for this, perhaps, most flower-loving and honey-sipping member of the great Bloomsbury hive, its packed passages and cells; and though not sworn of the province toward which his friend had found herself, according to her appeal to him, yearning again, nothing was easier for him than to put her in relation with the presiding urbanities." Our readers need not imagine for an instant that we have misquoted Mr. James. This extract is the very concentrated essence of his singular literary style.

In these two novels, as in all of Henry James's work, there is much to study, much to linger over, much to reflect upon, nothing, indeed, that is not worth while from some point of view. We may not read it as we read Scott or even as we read Thackeray, and we may derive from our reading no mere pleasure, but we certainly may be able to have the satisfaction of seeing at least a short distance into the mind of a writer who knows what he wants to say, even if he be not always able to say it in the language employed by his fellow-countrymen.

Claude Bragdon.
"A Master of Shades."
Critic 46 (January 1905), 20–22.

A new book from the pen of Mr. Henry James is an event of importance, for since Meredith and Hardy have fallen silent, since Kipling has become the unofficial censor of the British Empire, the self-crowned laureate of torpedo boats and motor-cars, and since Barrie finds his greater profit in play-writing, Mr. James is the only Anglo-Saxon novelist of the first class remaining. In craftsmanship and sureness of intention his work bears about the same relation to the average current fiction that some fine and rare Oriental rug bears to a crazy-quilt. It cannot, however, be gainsaid that the figure in his carpet grows more obscure and intricate with the passing years; that it is woven with threads of a sometimes too gossamer fineness. His demands upon his readers are increasingly rigorous. Each successive performance has come to resemble less and less a diverting trick with cards, done with one eye on the audience, and more and more a game of solitaire which—for the reader—sometimes fails to "come out"; or it may perhaps be figured better as a labyrinth with a dozen wrong turnings in which it is possible to lose oneself, though to the attentive, leisurely, and sym-

pathetic reader (and Mr. James should have no other) the true path through the maze never ceases to be in doubt.

"The Golden Bowl" is conceived and written in this later, this esoteric manner of our author. It is addressed to the Cognoscenti, who are simply all those having, in any degree approaching Mr. James's own, an insight into those secret places of the human spirit which he essays to explore. Of this dim limbo he is assuredly the Sherlock Holmes.

The intense little drama upon which he this time focusses our attention has for its setting the London of Mayfair, with an occasional shifting of the scene to some stately country house set like a great jewel in the sweet English landscape. The action is restricted practically to four people: Amerigo, an Italian prince of an unnamed, decayed, but still illustrious house; Maggie Verver, a young American girl who loves him and whom he marries; Maggie's enormously rich and still youthful father; and Charlotte Stant, her brilliant friend, afterwards Mrs. Verver, who herself cherishes a fatal passion for the too fascinating Prince. In addition to this oddly related quartet, there are two others, Mr. and Mrs. Assingham, the parties of a happy international marriage, whose nocturnal colloquies, in the privacy of their own apartment, on the subject of the other four, perform something of the office of the chorus in a Greek tragedy.

After the marriage of Mr. Verver and Charlotte, which follows that of Maggie and the Prince, the real situation develops itself; the action, if such it can be called, begins to unfold. The four dwell together in luxurious idleness, with every outward amelioration and amenity; they are "nice" to one another without end, but beneath the surface, for each in a different manner, the crises crowd thick as in a Bowery melodrama. Charlotte and the Prince resume their old relations (whatever these may have been), now doubly illicit by reason of the marriage of each. Maggie's suspicions are aroused, and by a rare chance confirmed, and thereafter, throughout four hundred wonderful pages of so close and firm a texture that one may not miss a line, Mr. James carries the tale to its logical, to its surprising, end. Like some microscopist whose instrument, focussed on a pellucid drop of water, reveals within its depths horrible monsters feeding on one another, Mr. James shows forth the baffled passion, fear, jealousy, and wounded pride, the high courage and self-sacrifice which may lurk beneath the fair and shining surface of modern life in its finest and most finished manifestations. The transformation of the situation is effected secretly, without outward tumult of any kind; the change wrought is molecular, as it were,—invisibly, but none the less really, justice is done and wrongs are righted.

Like the Scarlet Letter of Hawthorne's romance, the Golden Bowl is an actual material object endowed by the author with a mystical, a metaphysical meaning with a skill worthy of the great romancer himself. An ancient carved and gilded goblet, cut from a single crystal, is discovered in a Bloomsbury shop by Charlotte and the Prince during a ramble which they take together on the eve of the latter's marriage. Charlotte is for having the Prince accept it from her as a souvenir of their more than friendship, then, as they both believe, irrevocably at an end, but he purports to have discovered that the crystal contains a hidden flaw which makes the cup not valueless merely, but (to his view) a thing of ill omen, unlucky to them both, and such in fact by a strange fatality it proves finally to be. The Golden Bowl is figured throughout as the crystal vessel of happiness for these four people,—"The bowl with all our happiness in it. The bowl without a crack," its hidden flaw being the secret intrigue which menaces that happiness,—"The horror of finding evil seated, all at ease, where one had only dreamed of good."

"Fanny Assingham had at this moment the sense of a large heaped dish presented to her intelligence and inviting it to a feast."

It is thus that I would express my own feeling about this remarkable novel: there are so many things in it—the obscure workings of hereditary traits, the seduction exercised by Europe on the American imagination, the regenerative power of married love, the differences in the "moral paste" of individuals—that like her I feel that to help myself too freely, to attempt to deal, in other words, with all these aspects in the space assigned me, would "tend to jostle the ministering hand, confound the array, and, more vulgarly speaking, make a mess," and so, like Mrs. Assingham again, I pick out for the reader's consideration "a solitary plum."

If it be true, as Schopenhauer affirms, that a novel will be of a high and noble order the more it represents of inner, and the less it represents of outer, life, this latest novel of Henry James must be given a high place. Throughout it is the inner life, the life of the passions, the emotions, the affections of four people which is presented—their souls' history, in other words, with only just enough of time and place and circumstance to give it verisimilitude, to make all vivid and real. The chronicle is accomplished with an art beyond all praise: by formulating the questions which the soul asks but which the lips fail to utter, by happy figures and comparisons which fall thick and golden like ripe fruit, by making all the characters impossibly articulate and lucid,—able "to discuss in novel phrases their complicated state of mind."

Those who lament the forsaking by Mr. James of his earlier themes, and the abandonment of his more direct and objective manner, perhaps betray the limit of their own interests and perceptions. Like all men of original genius arrived at maturity, the outward aspects of the world—manners, places, customs—no longer interest him exclusively. Little by little he has come to look for and to present the reality behind the seeming,—not circumstance, but the spiritual reaction of circumstance. Thus the Swedenborgianism of his father, like some pure, pale flower plucked from a cold Norwegian precipice, transplanted thence to a New England garden, blooms now in an English hothouse,—a thing to marvel at, a thing to be grateful for.

"The Golden Bowl." Independent 58 (19 January 1905), 153–54.

Henry James has written another novel: another two volumes of abstruseness, another long discussion of a situation that only scandal mongers are supposed to discuss; again the same old heavy respectability where nothing is bad because it is not named; again the heroic sweetness of two characters, that is always his saving grace, that makes us read him: for we do read him, we always will, we always must; the very greatness of his written work demands it.

The Golden Bowl is a similar contrast, a similar problem, to "The Wings of the Dove," published a year ago, in the fact that it is the subtle complicated European character brought up against the single-minded American crudity, to the advantage of the American in both cases. Let this be the unction of our souls. Henry James believes in the American, notwithstanding his acknowledged preference to live abroad. He heroizes the American uprightness and simplicity and makes it the touchstone of European sordid sophistication. It is Europe that is sordid for him always, and America that is romantic and heroic. In spite of our money and our bravado we to him represent the purity of youth. We have principles, we have honor, which, tho simple, is better in the end than old age wisdom, is better than the subtleties of art.

In *The Golden Bowl* the simple Americans presented are a father, a Western millionaire, who has retired and become a studied art collector, and his daughter, who has married into a title supplied by an Italian prince, tho one who is a resident of England, for the locus of the plot is English soil. This prince prior to his marriage has been in love with a friend of his wife and who later on marries the wife's father, whence the old relation is taken on again. This is the terrible situation of a family, where each is considerate of all the others, where each loves the others in subtle, fickle fashion and convinces himself he is acting for the best. There is no one like James to appreciate the good qualities of a villain, and in this case, tho he has not equaled Kate in "The Wings of the Dove," he has made a tolerable showing of Charlotte Stant, who plays her clever game with spirit. Charlotte, by the way, is not a European by blood, tho she is by birth and instinct and education. Mrs. Assingham, another English character, is also an American made over; but Maggie and her father are quite genuine, and they alone lift the book from degradation. They not only lift it, but they carry it with dignity and with silence uncomplaining. Indeed, we are forced to remark that if James can appreciate the good qualities of a villain he is familiar with hero stuff as well. And he does not work with shouts and declamation, but quietly and thoughtfully in full daylight. Nothing of limelight, of storm, or wilderness, but in the most ordinary of ordinary London houses, in the drawing room, in the dining room or in the garden the tragedy goes on with scarce a word that could not pass before the servants, with nothing named, with nothing said but commonplaces, and breaking hearts are talked of in terms of old art objects. Indeed, it is the conventional hobby, respectability, that saves the directful plot from wreck and ruin. It is because people refuse to speak, ignore the truth, that they are able to bridge the chasm and pass over. Their carriages are not so much as splashed with mud, tho they have taken their trembling occupants around the deep abysses; one foolish, thoughtless word not necessary, and the dignified procession would be precipitated; but every motion, every look, is with reserve, and the point is passed, the wide plain gained, with safety. Indeed, to a careless observer the complaint would be of a monotonous journey.

[Annie R. M. Logan]. *Nation* 80 (26 January 1905), 74.

The story contained in the two volumes entitled 'The Golden Bowl' is elaborately concealed. It is involved, swathed, smothered in many obscurities, obscurities inseparable from the author's method of presenting an inside and outside and all-round view; obscurities arising from excessive use of extended metaphor, from saying too much and saying too little, even from sentences too complex and too elliptical, too long and too short. To get the story you must pay the price, must attack and overcome the obscurities; and whether this be done in a spirit of happy satisfaction of delight in the obscurities

for their own sake, or of irritation, or of mere plodding determination to stick and pull through, in the end you have your reward—a story, a situation, which, as you think about it, pierces the obscurities and strikes you in the eyes, like the low red autumn sun pushing out of a mass of black clouds.

It is a short story and bitter. No one except Mr. James could tell it in English without grossness or vulgarity, without challenging our prejudices and prepossessions, without making us all out to be, in his estimation, no better than the French—a state of things we should hate to have forced upon our notice. And he doesn't literally tell the story; he only examines witnesses, comments on testimony, infers and speculates prodigiously, leaving us free to make what we can of the case, to grasp or miss its facts and its wide significance, according to our capacity for independent mental operations. To rehearse the facts is perhaps the most useful part that a reviewer can play between Mr. James and the public. Such preliminary knowledge doesn't impair interest which really lies in beating the bush with the author, sharing breathless moments when it seems that the game is about to break for the open, and long periods of doubt whether it hasn't, after all, tucked itself up and gone to sleep in perfect security. The facts at the bottom of 'The Golden Bowl' glare when you have found them.

Mr. Verver, a person so rich that his nationality may be taken for granted, buys for his daughter Maggie a husband, a Roman Prince, with whom she has fallen in love because he is beautiful and charming and because the history of his ancestors' follies and crimes is recorded in many volumes neatly ranged on a shelf in the British Museum. The Prince assumes responsibilities in good faith. He means to use the Verver money as his own, to be an agreeable husband, and perhaps, according to his subdued lights, a faithful one. Just before the marriage, appears in London Miss Charlotte Stant, a dear friend of Maggie's, an old love of the Prince's, a lady of great beauty, courage, and resource. She has left her own vast and uninteresting continent and crossed the Atlantic ostensibly to buy a wedding present for Maggie. Her real purpose is more sinister. The Prince, bound to secrecy, is obliged to assist in the hunt for a present, and when an apparently suitable one, a golden bowl, is found, it appears that the offering is intended for him, not for Maggie. The Prince refuses the bowl, making a pretext of a crack and a superstition about cracks. He is, indeed, as adamantine as a Prince may be to a fair woman with a past between them.

Charlotte, baffled, disappears, only to descend two years later upon an ideally happy home consisting of Mr. Verver, the Prince, the Princess and the Principino. The Prince, not yet sated with the sensation of rolling in money, finds the moment opportune for retiring with his Princess to one of his Italian hill places, leaving Charlotte to console Mr. Verver as "Fawns," another of his splendid acquisitions. When Mr. Verver buys Charlotte for a wife, the fat is conspicuously in the fire. At the end of the first volume the Princess wakes from bliss to perceive that her stepmother is also her husband's mistress. The Golden Bowl is sharply cracked, and the spectacle of the second volume is the struggle of all concerned to prevent the crack becoming a fissure so wide and deep that neither love nor cunning may avail to preserve an illusion of soundness.

Essentially a hideous struggle, it is difficult to accept all of Mr. James's embroidery of it in representation. The Prince's behavior is perfectly in character. As soon as he knows his wife's suspicions, he is on the defence. He initiates nothing; he waits for tips. He emphatically means in the last resort to abandon nothing for Charlotte, to "stay bought." He has, by nature, handed down through generations as surely as his title and his manners, a familiarity with unspeakable situations, a facility for handling them with what his wife called high decency. The phrase sounds his deepest moral note. Experience of life's shady ways has fitted Charlotte to play pretty well up to her noble partner; and when, in an agony of conscious loss, she shifts the burden of wrong from herself to the Princess, she really earns the epithet "splendid" so lavishly bestowed on her. In the prolonged game of bluff, it is the unsophisticated Ververs who strike us as inhumanly deep. Why, if Mr. Verver could suspect, should he have let things go so far? How, if he had not suspected long and shrewdly, could he have solved the situation by carrying Charlotte off to America, meaning that she should stay there eternally—a proceeding equivalent to declaring: "I know all about this rotten business. I've been waiting to see what my daughter really wants. She wants to have her Prince at any price. She shall have him. Trust me now to keep Charlotte muzzled."

There is a Mrs. Assingham who flits about the Verver establishments, always in the thick of things, useful in explaining to the Prince the strange race with which he has allied himself; useful also to the reader as a fairly correct indicator of the true state of affairs. She is very positive that Maggie knows no evil, is of a delicate stuff born not to know evil. Such is the impression of Maggie distinctly made up to the moment of the crisis. It is almost incredible that, suddenly confronted with evil which might have made a hardened sinner scream with a sense of insult and disgust, she could meet it with stoical reticence, set herself to compromise, to minimize, to hush up things with the patience and wariness of a practiced diplomatist. The assumed motive is her love for her father;

and underneath that, of course, is the personal power of the charming Prince. But recognition of the mutual affection of father and daughter and of their horror of "hurting" each other does not suffice to make us believe either that Verver kept on smiling at the Prince through thick and thin, or that Maggie let Charlotte go off scot free with her head high. It is certain that Maggie meant to keep the Prince, but one is constantly sceptical of her ability to conduct the campaign for possession of his person with such consummate repression of natural instincts. Of course, Verver, at least, was supported through the ordeal by confidence in what his money could do. It had bought the Prince, it had bought Charlotte; why should it not keep the one where Maggie wanted him, beside her in England, and the other where Maggie wanted *her,* beside him, Verver, wandering vaguely in America, yet held in leash?

The appalling power for moral disintegration, if not corruption, implied in the possession of immense wealth could hardly be more impressively illustrated than it is in 'The Golden Bowl.' Lest any reader should miss the persistent undercurrent, we quote a passage near the end. The Ververs have come to take formal farewell of the Prince and Princess. Father and daughter are looking about the drawing-room at the beautiful things which their money had bought:

> "Their eyes moved together from piece to piece, taking in the whole nobleness—quite as if for him to measure the wisdom of old ideas. . . . You've got some good things." [1904, Scribner's ed., pp. 368–69]

"What Maggie Knew." London *Morning Post,* 9 February 1905, p. 2.

To tell the story of a novel by Mr. Guy Boothby or Mr. William Le Queux is unkind to the author and his intending readers, but in the case of a novel by Mr. Henry James one need have no scruples on the point. The story is a thing of minor consequence with him, and those who read novels for excitement and shock are not among his admirers. "The Golden Bowl," then, is the tale of Maggie Verver, an American heiress, who, having married a poor Italian Prince, discovers, with the aid of the bowl—which is not golden but gilt—that Charlotte Stant, a girl of great character and beauty, with polyglot gifts, has been in love with the Prince, and, but for mutual poverty, would have been his wife. Before Maggie knows all about the matter she has persuaded her father and Charlotte to get married, and as it is evident later on that Maggie will be happier with her husband if Charlotte is away Mr. and Mrs. Verver arrange to live in America. When their carriage is out of sight Maggie buries her face in her husband's breast. It seems, and is, a simple little story, but of course it is anything but a simple little book. Even if you would only fix the story you must extract it by close and anxious reading, weigh the meanings of many obscure phrases, and trace back misty allusions to their parent clouds. Otherwise, when you get to the end you will have done nothing, for, as the bric-à-brac dealer says about the supposed flaw in the bowl, "If it's something you can't find out isn't it as good as if it were nothing?"

The fascination of the book works

most strongly when the two married couples, Maggie and her Prince, Maggie's father and her Prince's earlier love—we must use these crude words to save space, though the author would never write of "earlier loves"—begin, "a party of four, to lead a life gregarious, and from that reason almost hilarious, so far as the easy sound of it went, as never before." The Princess is a dear little thing—crudity again—but Charlotte is the finer, more intellectual woman of the two, a "lonely, gregarious girl," to whom, therefore, the gregarious life was half adapted. If Maggie had not been "gorged with treasures," with "a million a year" to give him, the Prince would not have married her for her *beaux yeux,* that is clear. His own "dark blue eyes were of the finest, and, on occasion, precisely, resembled nothing so much as the high windows of a Roman palace, of an historic front by one of the great old designers, thrown open on a feast-day to the golden air." Now, it needs a strong character to live up to a husband with such an imposing front as that, and Maggie, until her stepmother departed for the States, was hardly equal to the task. Whether she could have been quite happy with Charlotte and the Prince in the same flock together, even if she had not known the story of the golden bowl, we do not need to ask. Charlotte had to go, and one of the finest of her fine acts, done in the grand manner, was her going. Nature meant her to be splendid, with "her special beauty of movement and line when she turned her back, and the perfect working of all her main attachments." These are the three chief characters—the Prince, the Princess, and the stepmother. But the father, even when he lives "inscrutably monotonous behind an iridescent cloud," is a charming middle-aged millionaire of the collecting type. We do not like him, however, so much as we like Colonel Bob Assingham, the husband whose clever wife tries to act the part of good fairy to the mixed lovers, and declares that the colonel, when he cannot quite follow her voluble arguments, has "no play of mind." The colonel is a little eccentric. He dresses in clothes of "queer light shades and of strange straw-like textures, of the aspect of Chinese mats." He is, for all that, a very pleasant person. Looking back over the book we find that the passages that shine most brightly are the conversations of the colonel and his wife concerning Charlotte's relations with Amerigo (the Prince) and of Maggie with her father when she wants him to propose to Charlotte. There is no other living novelist save Mr. Meredith who could have imagined and expressed these duologues, and there are many other passages in the book which, both in idea and in artificiality of language, are distinctly Meredithian. Mr. Henry James may take a chapter to tell us what most other novelists would have told in a page; he may have little plot and few "situations." But he is an artist always, his every phrase is worked and cut, and for those who have the taste for his novels and do not read them because they ought we can commend "The Golden Bowl" as one of the finest results of his craftsmanship, and as something far above the general level of the successful fiction of the time.

"The Impalpable People." *Pall Mall Gazette* [England], 23 February 1905, p. 3.

This is not an age in which to complain of an author putting intellectual strain upon his readers. The novel that stimulates thought instead of merely ravishing the nerves is the novel that we all desire to see drawing homage from the perverse crowd. But Mr. Henry James is almost enough to excuse any amount of blasphemy and desertion to the Philistines. It has been long established that he can extract psychology from an afternoon call in the same profusion that a conjurer draws pink ribbon from his own mouth. But when the analysis of motive becomes so luxuriant as to strangle narrative power and destroy the sense of dramatic unity, the faculty is more wonderful than precious. Mr. James has come perilously near to this development. It requires a clear and steady head not to succumb to dizziness long before the end of "The Golden Bowl." The meticulous study of personality makes it extremely difficult to retain any sense of continuous interest. Individuality cannot survive the microscope, and in such minute inspection of the mood we are apt to lose all feeling for the man. It is hard to think of any of the small group of characters except as laboratory subjects. There is a sweet American girl at the opening of the book on whom one is prepared to expend sympathy. But before many chapters are over she has become a mere cancelling problem in emotions. The others are only refinements of boredom from the first. They exist to talk about themselves and each other, and for the paternal author to talk about them all. Their anæmic caricatures of the *genus homo* banish all sense of a real world, in which such types would have no function. It is irresistible to ask to what end all this ingenuity of dissection has been expended, for in the sense of real art the result appears to be sheer futility. None of these shadowy people is worth knowing, or signifies anything when known. They leave the imagination as hungry as before, and chill every emotion that would go forth to greet them. Verily, the crude and untimely births of the melodramatist and the mystery-monger are better than they.

Athenaeum [England] 4038 (18 March 1905), 332.

The theory of Impressionism has been summed up in the dictum of Monet, that light is the only subject of every picture. The theory of Mr. Henry James's art might also be put in a formula: "Human thoughts are the sole material of the novelist." Whoever fails to realize this elementary principle is sure to come to grief in the effort to follow a master never other than difficult. This principle alone accounts for the order in which events are narrated—or rather, they are not narrated at all. They are delineated only in so far and at such times as they are producing an effect on the inward life of one of his characters. Consequently they are never seen in a clear dry light, such as serves to display the events of Scott, or even Thackeray. We learn them always through the refracting medium of some person's mind— and that often is rather not his notion of the event in itself, but his suspicion of somebody else's notion of it. Now this is in reality the only way in which events, whether personal or historical, exist for any of us. "A fact when it is past becomes an idea," said Creighton. This truth, forgotten alike by most novelists and nearly all historians, is the justification of Mr. James's method. It gives us, of course, no ground for asserting his success. But one reason why some folks give him up is that they refuse to see that he is attempting what, to the best of our belief, has never been attempted before, even by the most "psychological" of novelists or poets, such as Browning. For even Browning's characters always display themselves to an audience. Not so with those of Mr. James. Here we are shown not the human heart under a microscope, as with the ordinary analytical novelist, but the soul developing itself from within, finding in other persons, circumstances, and happenings nothing but the matter of its thought. It is objected that Mr. James is supersubtle, and trails an idea through far too many windings, sets it in too many lights, refines and explains and exiguates, so to say, *ad nauseam*. This book will awaken this objection more than ever. But let any one reflect on his thought upon any matter that concerns him personally; let him take only half-an-hour of it, and try to retrace all its involutions, and he will find himself ten times as full of distractions, of strange backward twists, of hesitations, of reasons and imaginings, as any of Mr. James's characters. The fact is brought out in this new book, for none of the *dramatis personæ* is at all extraordinary. The impecunious but charming Italian prince who marries the daughter of a widowed American millionaire, his wife, his father-in-law, and his lover (the American girl of brilliant social qualities who marries the millionaire), are all commonplace persons enough. Indeed, the lack of greatness in his characters—their essential littleness—while it may enhance the realism of Mr. James's work, strikes us as one of its serious defects as great art. The father continues so wrapped up in his daughter that the two former lovers are naturally brought together, and the plot turns on a peculiarly treacherous adultery. The gradual discovery of this by the princess, her desire to shield her father from the knowledge of it; his discovery of it, and desire to shield her; her success in finally severing her husband

from his paramour and in securing his love, are the theme of the story. It is told—or, to be correct, it works itself out—with all the convincing realism of which Mr. James is a master. But it is very difficult, for everybody is occupied in concealing from every one else what he or she knows; and even when they desire to convey the truth, it is commonly done by the statement of something else. The triumph of this method is shown in the scene between Maggie and her father, when, as a result of what she omits to say, the millionaire resolves to pack his traps and take his wife back for good and all to America. But for the "chorus work" of Bob Assingham and his wife the whole thing would be scarcely intelligible. As it is, the book is clear to those who think Mr. James worth a little trouble. The method, in spite of its "inwardness," is detached, cold, and, if the word is possible, a little cruel. But its mental agility, its likeliness, its atmosphere, are perfect. Why Mr. James should require so very disagreeable a situation to develope his study we cannot understand, but that he has elaborated it as no one else could, we are sure; indeed, we should have liked two more books in the novel, one giving the story as it affects the mind of Charlotte, the brilliant, hard, repulsive woman, and the other showing it in the mind of the millionaire, strange compound of shrewdness and simplicity, inexorable decision and inexhaustible kindliness. Mr. James can hardly achieve a greater success than that of making even one of his readers desire that the book were double its length. At the same time we trust that in the next book which he writes he will purge himself of certain mannerisms that are little more than affectations. He overworks the word "lucidity" even more than writers of an earlier age did that of "sensibility." He plays upon the phrase "There you are" as though the words were the strings of a violin. He puts the commonest and most obvious expressions in inverted commas, and we dislike his too frequently interrupting adverbs. Doubtless all are defensible as necessary on the hypothesis of the method. We grant the method, but deny the necessity. All the same, we admit that Mr. Henry James is at his best throughout this book. The final month at Fawns, especially the two scenes between Charlotte and Maggie, is a veritable triumph. We quote one description—that in Maggie's mind of a card-party:—

> "Meanwhile, the facts of the situation were upright for her round the green cloth and the silver flambeaux; the fact of her father's wife's lover facing his mistress; the fact of her father sitting all unsounded and unblinking between them; the fact of Charlotte keeping it up—keeping up everything, across the table, with her husband beside her; the fact of Fanny Assingham, wonderful creature, placed opposite to the three and knowing more about each, probably, when one came to think, than either of them knew of either. Erect above all for her was the sharp-edged fact of the relation of the whole group, individually and collectively, to herself—herself so speciously eliminated for the hour, but presumably more present to the attention of each than the next card to be played."

"Letters in Gold Filigree."
Saturday Review
[England] 99 (25 March 1905), 383–84.

The years are past when one's interest, one's concern, in opening a new book by Mr. Henry James was to discover how far he had retained or by how much he had modified his wonderful manner, which, first revealed to us in "The Tragic Muse", seemed to attain completeness in "The Spoils of Poynton". That manner, which has, as it were, shut a water-tight door on Mr. James' admirers, and made them feel themselves, unfortunately, but inevitably, a little community of the elect, is now as surely a part of his speech as a tone of voice or an alien accent, and one's preoccupation, with each fresh presentment, has been transferred to the material on which it is to be used. And for this reason. Wonderful as the manner is, intrinsically subtle, hyperæsthetically discreet, it is exposed alike by its subtlety and its discretion to a too easy satisfaction in its sources of interest. With existence so absorbingly perplexed, so prismatically transfigured, the subject matter of romance becomes of a quite serious unimportance to the adroit manipulator; indeed, as his sense of the magic colour in every part of its web grows insistently acute, he is even led to avoid those parts of it which are impressed with the big dramatic patterns, lest these should divert attention from the exquisite intricacy of texture on which his thoughts are set. Such a danger confronts every writer who is primarily interested in what is to his public of only secondary account, and it is the greater danger to Mr. James, since his genius is essentially dramatic and, lacking the saliencies of drama, as high mountain peaks, to lead him from one wide outlook to another, is apt to keep up too long wandering in valleys beneath mountain mists of hypothesis and speculation.

The dramatic quality of Mr. James' work may not be obvious to readers who measure dramatic force rather by its disturbance than its significance. The stage, always eager for the obvious, has publicly affianced drama to a fury of gesture and a high voice, preferring its spent forces to its springs; but to productive intensity, the pregnancy of action is of more importance than its barren effect, however astounding; and thus putting a knife into one's pocket may have in it more of drama than putting it into a man. It is by the exhibition of what one may call deferred action that Mr. James achieves his dramatic effects, and by it he practically tells the whole story.

This is why the success of his method depends on the significance and variety and, one might add, the humanity of the dramatic moments arising naturally from his theme, and why, too, being such a perilous and impossible author to "skip", he is represented so often by professional skippers as an extremely involved and difficult writer. Yet, with the exception of an occasional sentence which has been asked to carry more than it conveniently can, Mr. James is, considering all he has to say, very easily followed by those who read him.

But he is so exact, so continuous in his presentation of ideas, that often the omission of a single sentence may confuse the purpose of a page, and the omission of a page render unintelligible the dramatic moment—even if that be not missed too—on which an interpretive interest in the tale depends. For though these moments are few, they are tremendously led up to. Between the curtain's rising on each fresh tableau there is an intricate and indefatigable training of our perception to obtain the full effect of it. Without such training, indeed, the tableaux would not count for much; for pregnant as they are with action, they are themselves often so still, so slight, so dependent on, perhaps, the lifting of an eyebrow, or the length of a glance, that unless announced in Mr. James' deliberative way, one might scarcely notice them. Take the first meeting of Charlotte Stant and the Prince—the first, that is, of which we are spectators.

As she enters the room, "she could have looked at her hostess with such straightness and brightness only from knowing that the Prince was also there". Such a regard may not seem much of a clue; yet to the Prince "that immediate exclusive address to their friend was like a lamp she was holding aloft for his benefit and for his pleasure. It showed him everything". It is to show us everything too, though we have never seen before and scarcely heard of Charlotte, and have spent a short half-hour with the Prince; everything, even to her having once so loved him that "she might have been anything she liked—except his wife". The peculiar significance of Charlotte's address is not a fair example of the author's wonderful manner, since it occurs at the opening of the story, and our intelligence, instead of being prepared, has to be coaxed back to appreciate it; but it quite fairly represents the claim he makes on our attention, and the delicacy and energy of suggestion he obtains from his effects.

The most revealing and dramatic moment of the book is a woman's mere leaning out of a window. "Something in her long look at him now out of the old grey window"—it is again Charlotte and the Prince—"something in the very poise of her hat, the colour of her necktie, the prolonged stillness of her smile, touched into sudden light for him all the wealth of the fact that he could count on her". And it does, yes, just as wonderfully, touch into sudden light the fact for us as well, so that the rosebud she throws down to him has, by comparison with her appearance, no meaning at all. Hence it is that one has come to measure Mr. James' success by the amount and intensity of dramatic action which a theme will yield him. It is rather curious, perhaps no more than a coincidence, but the change in his manner, his substitution of implicit for explicit action, dates from days when he was a good deal occupied with that school of action, the stage. One would like to think that hours one so intensely grudged to that occupation have yielded so unlooked for a reward. Be that as it may, the somewhat surprising fact remains that the basis of Mr. James' later manner is dramatic, not didactic; and its drama is always, at its best, of a high and simple human interest.

It is true that the drama is often hid, like some secret queen, at the centre of a maze, a maze of fine shades and ultra-sensitive perceptions, which one might almost fancy to be here put half-humorously before us in the involutions of Mrs. Assingham. "She was a person for whom life was multitudinous detail, detail that left her, as it at any moment found her, unappalled and unwearied." "My first impulse," she declared, "is always to behave, about everything, as if I fear complications. But I don't fear them. I really like them. They're quite my element". They are also, unquestionably, quite the element of Mr. James. It is almost impossible to conceive him placing a fact before us without its attachments. His vision of the social mechanism is so discriminating and so tenacious that one occasionally follows its amazing flights, as Bob Assingham did those of his wife's intelligence, "very much as he had sometimes watched, at the Aquarium, the celebrated lady who, in a slight, though tight, bathing suit, turned somersaults and did tricks in a tank of water which looked so cold and uncomfortable to the nonamphibious", and feel, as Mr. Verver felt when dealing with that same intelligence, "never quite sure of the ground anything covered". But that insecurity is for some of us, one of the author's most seductive charms, even though he not infrequently seems to resemble the Prince "in liking explanations; liking them almost as if he collected them" and with the Prince also to share an "inability, in any matter in which he was concerned; to

conclude". The book itself is evidence of that inability, for one sees, without wishing a word of it away, what its story might occasionally gain by a somewhat closer handling. Even to hint at that story would spoil the pleasure of the fortunate ones who have yet to follow its unfolding, for though Mr. James' dramatic effectiveness depends so largely on an historic vividness of emotion, it is in the exquisite flower-like opening of the fine petals of human feeling to the light, and in the atmosphere often so oppressively intense which he distils from character that his art displays its most essential quality.

What of atmosphere could be more wonderfully wrought than the breathing of Adam Verver's gentle influence, his spirit of the connoisseur, which seems to touch to a rarity of beauty the shapes and colours of all things about him? Charlotte, with that shade of tawny autumn leaf in her hair which suggested at moments, "the sylvan head of a huntress"; her free arms, with "the polished slimness that Florentine sculptors, in the great time, had loved"; the Prince, with his dark-blue eyes like "the high windows of a Roman palace, of an historic front by one of the great old designers, thrown open on a feast day to the golden air"; or Maggie, with "the blurred absent eyes, the smoothed, elegant, nameless head, the impersonal flit of a creature lost in an alien age and passing as an image in worn relief round and round a precious vase";—what are these, with their air of the antique, but a subtle diffusion of Adam Verver's fine perception to steep the more threatening edges of the story in the glamour of his tender soul! What Mr. James can thus achieve may be set forth, in conclusion, by one astonishing example. He is showing us the effect on a wife's mind of the "awfulness" of the relation between her stepmother and her husband. "The situation had been occupying, for months and months, the

431

very centre of the garden of her life, but it had reared itself there like some strange, tall tower of ivory, or perhaps rather some wonderful, beautiful, but outlandish pagoda, a structure plated with hard, bright porcelain, coloured and figured and adorned, at the overhanging eaves, with silver bells that tinkled, ever so charmingly, when stirred by chance air."

Checklist of Additional Reviews

Burton T. Beach. "Henry James's Novel Published at Last." Chicago *Evening Post,* 19 November 1904, p. 6.

Book News 23 (December 1904), 275–76.

New York *Sun,* 3 December 1904, p. 7.

New York *Tribune,* 3 December 1904, p. 10.

Outlook 78 (3 December 1904), 865.

Cleveland *Plain Dealer,* 18 December 1904, sec. 6, p. 2.

"International Society as Mr. James Sees It." Chicago *Evening Post,* 24 December 1904, p. 4.

Ethel M. Colson. Chicago *Record-Herald,* 29 December 1904, p. 8.

New York *Herald,* 31 December 1904, p. 12.

American Monthly Review of Reviews 31 (January 1905), 116.

Bookman [New York] 20 (January 1905), 418–19. Reprinted in Roger Gard, ed., *Henry James: The Critical Heritage* (London: Routledge & Kegan Paul, 1968), p. 391.

Alice Duer Miller. *Lamp* 29 (January 1905), 583.

World's Work 9 (January 1905), 5766.

New Orleans *Daily Picayune,* 1 January 1905, sec. 3, p. 9.

"Henry James' Latest Novel." San Francisco *Chronicle,* 8 January 1905, p. 8.

Springfield, [Mass.] *Republican,* 8 January 1905, p. 19.

Reader 5 (February 1905), 380–82.

Times Literary Supplement [London] 161 (10 February 1905), 47. Reprinted in Gard, pp. 374–75.

Francis Thompson. *Academy* [England] (11 February 1905), 128–29. Reprinted in Gard, pp. 376–77; *Literary Criticisms by Francis Thompson,* ed. Terence L. Connolly (New York: E. P. Dutton, 1948), pp. 298–301.

London *Daily Telegraph,* 15 February 1905, p. 12.

Manchester *Guardian,* 15 February 1905, p. 5.

Illustrated London News 126 (25 February 1905), 268. Reprinted in Gard, p. 378.

Churchman 91 (4 March 1905), 334.

"The Golden Bowl." London *Daily News,* 4 March 1905, p. 4.

Graphic [England] 71 (4 March 1905), 264. Reprinted in Gard, pp. 379–80.

Literary World [England] 71 (15 March 1905), 60.

[Mary Moss]. *Atlantic Monthly* 95 (May 1905), 696. Reprinted in James W. Gargano, *Critical Essays on Henry James: The Late Novels* (Boston: G. K. Hall, 1987), p. 57.

Advance 49 (4 May 1905), 563.

THE AMERICAN SCENE

"*The American Scene*." London *Daily Telegraph*, 1 February 1907, p. 12.

Not long ago appeared the impressions suggested by Mr. H. G. Wells's flying visit to America; we have in the present volume the result of "the return of the native," Mr. Henry James, after an absence of twenty-five years.[1] The two books are, perhaps, even more illuminative of the writers than of their common subject. That it is so is certainly no matter for regret in this instance, for Mr. Henry James is quite as interesting as America, and not more difficult to understand. Being an American born and bred, and having lived in Europe most of his working life, there is no one who understands the New and the Old World as well as he, and few have such an appreciation of the attributes of modernity or such a love of old cities and countries. These qualities, apart from others, give the creator of Roderick Hudson, Christopher Newman, the Bellegardes, and the rest of the marvellous host, a unique point of vantage. His outlook differs diametrically from that of Mr. Wells. To the latter the sight of a boy suggests a by-law; a woman, a factory Act, a house, a municipal council. To Mr. Henry James a house suggests the people who built it and inhabit it; a pillar-box connotes the postman and the million people whose correspondence he carries. Everything, still life as well, as humanity, is intensely individual to him; he sees in all the work of man and deduces from all amazing theories and endless speculations as to man's peculiarities. We may trust Mr. Henry James to choose the exact phrase, and he rightly dubs himself throughout the volume "the restless analyst." Restless analy-sis is the keynote of the book, and though in the reading of it we are sometimes bewildered by the intricacy of the thought and minuteness and refinement of the classifications, the relentless "hedgeing" and pruning; yet when we have finished the reading we find we have a perfect picture drawn with a skill and completeness possible only to the amazing cleverness of this author. He himself says, that when he determined to collect and record his impressions of his native country, revisited after so long an absence, "I became aware, on the spot, that these elements of the human subject, the results of these attempted appreciations of life itself, would prove much too numerous, even for a capacity all given to them for some ten months; but at least, therefore, artistically concerned as I had been all my days with the human subject, and with the consequent question of literary representation, I should not find such matters scant or simple." The whole book is proof of Mr. James's determination to be baffled by no difficulties, but to probe every problem, present every facet, and find the solution of the puzzling kaleidoscope of American life. The result is America as no writer has ever before been able to show it, a book into which all who propose to treat it in future should dip deeply, for by studying it we can evolve not only what America is, but what Europe is also.

To particularise about a book which must be read as a whole, and cannot be judged or get its proper effect till the whole has been mastered as completely as possible, is a difficult task, and not perhaps a very valuable one. It will be sufficient to point out some of the excellences of a piece of work which is eminently undetachable. Naturally happy phrases, strangely chosen similes, abound. Here is a characteristic description of the inscrutability of the houses in the village street of Farmington: "What they seemed to say is what I have mentioned; but what secrets, meanwhile, did the rest of the scene keep! Were there any secrets at all, or had the outward blankness, the quantity of absence, as it were, in the air, its inward equivalent as well!" All buildings seem to Mr. Henry James as human beings. Again and again he compares them to women; they speak to him about themselves, they present themselves to him in human attitudes. "Any building that, being beautiful, presents itself as seated rather than as standing, can do with your imagination what it will." Is that fantastic? Is it not rather suggestive?

New York occupies many pages, and the picture is not a pleasant one. How should it be when drawn by a man who says, "it takes an endless amount of history to make even a little tradition, and an endless amount of tradition to make even a little taste, and an endless amount of taste, by the same token, to make even a little tranquillity." There is no tranquillity in New York, though Mr. James admits "the grace of a city where the very restaurants may on occasion, under restless analysis, flash back the likeness of Venetian palaces flaring with the old carnival." He sums up the city by confessing that "ambiguity is the element in which the whole thing swims for me." Of the American cities of the large type, Philadelphia was the only one which did not bristle, just as Chicago was the worst offender. Philadelphia had a society, settled, content, serene; Philadelphia "was not a place, but a state of consanguinity, which is an absolutely final condition." It has also a character of its own in contradistinction to New York, which borrows from every source "like some simple childless mother, who consoles herself for her sterility by an unbridled course of adoption." Mr. James is continually beset by the disadvantages of the new country,

remembering the charms of older civilisation; the absence of manners, the enforced speculation as to what the alien will become when he is absorbed into the land of his adoption, so that you have to take consolation in "the blest general drop of the immediate need of conclusions."

What, then, is the verdict on the mass of "restless analysis"? It is the most perfect picture of the social aspect of a State which it is humanly possible to give. Of necessity bewildering by its very nature and the conscience of the artist who has made it, the illuminating eye and acute diagnosis make it one of the most remarkable as well as one of the most instructive pieces of work to be met with. The true humour of the author, combined with his shrinking from crudeness and an absence of "manners," and his burning love of beauty, make it complete. All he treats with unerring appreciation, from the old cemetery of Charleston—"the golden afternoon, the low, silvery, seaward horizon, as of wide, game-haunted islets and reed-smothered banks, possible site of some Venice that had never mustered"—to the Bowery play illustrative of "our Anglo-Saxon policy, or our seemingly deep-seated necessity, where 'representation' is concerned, so far away from the truth and the facts of life as really to betray a fear in us of possibly doing something like them should we be caught nearer." It will satisfy and astound all but the author himself. We may be sure that he will never be able to say as much as he wants to say, or perhaps, as we ought to add, speak intelligibly for the ordinary listener.

Note

1   H. G. Wells, *The Future in America* (1906).

436

[Edmund Gosse]. "America: Mr. Henry James's Impressions." London *Daily Mail,* 2 February 1907, p. 3.

When it was known that the most original and the most ingenious of contemporary American writers had broken the continuous exile of nearly a quarter of a century, and had deliberately returned across the Atlantic for the purpose of making investigations and of recording perceptions, hope ran high. We now receive, in a stately volume, the earlier or purely Eastern results of this excursion, and the first thing to say about them is that hope did not run too high. This diorama of "The American Scene" is astonishingly vivid, generously candid, picturesque beyond all precedent. We have no hesitation in saying that no one before Mr. Henry James has produced a picture, or a series of pictures, of what the Atlantic States of America have to present to-day, which is comparable with his for fulness and variety. No one has clothed his impressions with anything like such a tissue of exquisite and ingenious style. If there is sometimes a difficulty in reading the book continuously, if the texture of it is sometimes rather dense, this density comes from the very richness of the material, from its conscientious and sedulous avoidance of all *clichés* and the commonplace.

To "review" this book, in itself the most superb of "reviews," would be impossible. All we can do is to give, in our brief space, some light notion of its character and contents. To do this we must explain at once that statistical enumerations, tabulated data, obvious explanations, do not come within Mr. James's scope at all. He keeps, quite resolutely, to his determination of penetrating as far as possible below the surface, of detaching the perfume and colour and sound from the mere material facts, and keeping continuously to the study of these. And we notice, first of all, skimming the book hastily, as here we must, the most rare, the most persistent sense of the physical beauty of the Transatlantic landscape. There has been a vast American solitude, a delicate, early American civilisation, and these have not yet wholly vanished. Wherever he finds them, even in desuetude, Mr. Henry James feels every fibre in his spirit leap out in appreciation of their exquisite quality. But the solitude is being ravaged, the early charm crushed beneath forms of "advance," at the mandate of a "pretended message of civilisation," and to the appalling consequences of this crude revolution, he finds Americans of all classes deplorably blind and deaf. Encased in their singular national self-sufficiency, they heed no appeal that comes to them with a cry, "Stop your hands! You are not advancing and improving; you are wounding, disfiguring, destroying!"

It would be wholly unjust to take this brief summary as covering the scope of Mr. James's wonderful book, which is full of other things than these; but we believe we do no wrong to his subtle consciousness of what America to-day means when we sum it up in this alternate discovery of how much beauty there is, and horror of how wantonly it is being destroyed. To speak of "The American Scene," however, is to wish to quote incessantly; not otherwise could we reproduce the charm. Here is, at all events, a characteristic fragment which we detach from the series of lovely vignettes sketched rapidly in as the writer traverses the heart of New England:

... The full, vertiginous effect of the long and steep descent, the clinging road, the precipitous fall, the spreading, shimmering land bounded by blue horizons. ... Again and again the land would do beautifully, if that were all that was wanted, and it deserved, the dear thing, thoroughly, any verbal caress, any tenderness of term, any share in a claim to the grand manner, to which we could responsively treat it. The grand manner was in the winding ascent, the sudden rest for wonder, and all the splendid reverse of the medal, the world belted afresh as with purple sewn with pearls—melting, in other words, into violet hills, with vague white towns on their breasts.

On the other hand, the crudity and waste of American cities, the insincerity of effects, the absence of finality, these are dwelt upon in eloquent and striking pages, from which we regret that it is impossible for us to quote at length.

"The new Paris and the new Rome do at least propose, I think, to be old—one of these days; the new London even, erect as she is on leaseholds destitute of dignity, yet does, for the period, appear to believe in herself." The flagrant vice of Boston and New York, architecturally, is that even when these cities smell most of their millions, they affect you with the sense that they are "coming down." They have learned the unhappy lesson of how not to suffer the consecrating association so much as to begin.

It is in portraying some of the less dominating cities that Mr. Henry James achieves his greatest miracles of art. Philadelphia, with its persistent Quaker drab, still visible in its primitive monotone, in spite of all the "bestitching of the drab with pink and green and silver"; the almost ecclesiastical sweetness and harmony of Baltimore, dreaming in its "cit-ronic belt"; Richmond, blank and void, drained of its life-blood, like "a page of some dishonoured writer"; the affronting witlessness of Newport, full of "white elephants," "all cry and no wool, all house and no garden," spread along three or four lamentable miles of "distressful, inevitable waste"; St. Augustine, charming, shy, and vague, with its Spanish "ghost of a ghost," desiring to communicate, and yet really too weak to express anything. We could pursue these sips indefinitely whirring from corolla to corolla like one of the authentic Floridan hummingbirds, but the reader needs but our hasty indication, and will drink deeper for himself.

Mr. Henry James constantly poses the question why, with so many elements of distinction and beauty scattered about it, with so curious and even pathetic a desire for taste implanted in the inhabitants of it, the American scene does, none the less, remain so heart-breaking a combination of the confused, the unbalanced, and the frustrated. He asks what answer the great palaces of the South, "inflated with the hotel-spirit and exhaling modernity at every pore," have to give to the inquirer. The enterprising American touches "the great lonely land—as one feels it still to be—only to plant upon it some ugliness, about which, never dreaming of the grave of apology or contrition," he then proceeds to brag with a cynicism all his own. This is the central discord which spoils the music of so much American enterprise, "development," and push.

This strange and eloquent book, divided by such a chasm from all ordinary impressions of travel made by the competent and intelligent stranger, is highly typical of Mr. James's later manner of writing. It is produced in that curious mode of his, by which an infinity of minute touches, each in itself apparently unemphatic, are so massed and arranged that out of them arises, when the reader least expects it, perhaps—a picture which absolutely controls the imagination. We are much deceived if this is not a durable contribution to literature, and in its evidence of intense solicitude for truth, of scrupulous fairness, the severity of the judgment it passes on the rush and roughness of the new American ideals is not to be avoided. "The American Scene" may be read by some Americans with bewilderment and impatience, but it constitutes the most durable surface-portraiture of an unparalleled condition of society which our generation is likely to see.

"The American Scene." Times Literary Supplement [London] 265 (8 February 1907), 44.

For some months past Mr. Henry James's admirers have been in the habit of searching the monthly magazines, English and American, for foretastes of the book which he now presents to us.[1] Those scattered, isolated chapters had all the expected flavour—the extraordinary sensitiveness to impressions, the easy mastery over them, the packed richness of expression. But now that we have them in a bunch, something more emerges, the unique attraction, that is, of the general point of view. The attraction is that of watching Mr. James the novelist in the act of collecting and sifting the novelist's material. He describes the American scene, and describes it as only he could, but he never stops short at the mere felicitous rendering of the impression. That is the first step, but, the scene once rendered he has innumerable questions to put to it—what does it stand for, what does it imply, what is its relation to other scenes, where does it come in the scale of things? It is plain enough that these cross-examinations are not conducted in the spirit of the statistician or the reformer. The fact is, as we presently realize, that the novelist is at work. Mr. James has watched and long ago mastered and given shape to America as projected upon the background of Europe. Now he revisits the American scene itself and takes the same method with him. Other masters of fiction, when they write their *sensations de voyage,* generally treat the occasion as a kind of æsthetic holiday, an irresponsible excursion outside their proper field. Wistfully or languidly or ecstatically they describe the interlude, but they know, and we know, that their real work awaits them elsewhere. What fundamentally divides Mr. James's book from theirs is that he pursues his art as he goes, that he observes in order to analyse, and analyses in order to construct. The dispersed elements of the scene hurry forward to offer their help and to answer his questions. Sometimes he has to tell them, not angrily but condoningly, that they can be of no use; they are not stones with which an artist can build. But now and then we positively see him on the brink of building with them before our very eyes. For instance:—

> Nothing, meanwhile, is more concomitantly striking than the fact that the women over the land—allowing for every element of exception—appear to be of a markedly finer texture than the men.... The superiority thus noted, and which is quite another matter from the universal fact of the mere usual female femininity, is far from constituting absolute distinction, but it constitutes relative, and it is a circumstance at which interested observation snatches, from the first, with an immense sense of its *portée*.... It is, at

all events, no exaggeration to say that the imagination at once embraces it as *the* feature of the social scene, recognizing it as a subject fruitful beyond the common, and wondering even if for pure drama, the drama of manners, anything anywhere else touches it.

To read these sentences is like watching a pianist seated before a keyboard which he is hindered for the moment from touching; all his fingers itch to strike the notes. We can only hope that the right moment may duly come.

Meanwhile it is this attitude towards the material collected by the way that gives the book perhaps its rarest distinction. It is a book of personal impressions, of course, but they are impressions gathered in a constructive and not in a merely eclectic frame of mind. And as for the innumerable pictures themselves which are thus brought side by side, it is difficult to say which is the greater, the responsive swiftness with which they are caught and fixed, or the dexterity with which they are kept in their places and prevented from taking more than their proper share of the field. There is no one to touch Mr. James as an impressionist. He alone can not only detect every aspect of a scene, every significant hint which it lets drop, but can render them all, and not only render them, but set each one in its right relation to the whole picture. If someone ignorant of Mr. James's way were to open the book and burrow into a page at random (it takes some burrowing—Mr. James's texture is very close), he would probably find himself, long before the end of the paragraph, entirely bewildered by the network of fine discrimination, suggestions, images, with which the effect is produced. Those who know their author best know that it is only possible to begin at the beginning; the atmosphere later on becomes far too highly charged with references to what has

gone before, to make it possible to cut in by the way. They begin at the beginning, and are led on step by step, each sentence adding some minute touch and preparing the way for the next, no superfluous word allowed and no necessary link omitted— sometimes diverted along some side issue, till it seems as though the main journey must have been forgotten, but always led back again and set safely in the right path—till at the end they find that all the details which had crowded round them so thickly, all the qualifications and all the metaphors, have between them produced a big luminous picture, as broad in its effect, for all its richness, as if it had been painted with two strokes of the brush.

Mr. James readily admits that a good deal has to be put into the American scene before anything can be taken out of it. He was reminded, he says, "of the wonderful soil of California, which is nothing when left to itself and to the fine weather, but becomes everything conceivable under the rainfall. What would many an American prospect be for him, the visitor bent on appreciation frequently wonders, without his preliminary discharge upon it of some brisk shower of general ideas?" There is no difficulty, as may well be imagined, about the preliminary shower in the case of this traveller. In New York, in Newport, in Boston, early memories swarm about the "restored absentee," and under their vivifying influence the very stones begin to cry out. Mr. James is a past-master in the art of interpreting their voices when they have anything to say; at other times he is equally skilful at exposing their helpless and hopeless case. "It's all very well," he says to the great Fifth Avenue palaces, "for you to look as if, since you've had no past, you're going in, as the next best thing, for a magnificent compensatory future. What are you going to make your future *of,* for all your airs, we want to know?" The question entirely silences Fifth Avenue,

440

who can only tacitly admit that "for all her airs" she has nothing assured, nothing stable, to build a future with. The provisional, the expensively provisional, is indeed òne of the principal "notes" which Mr. James encounters; the sky-scrapers, the pervading "hotel-spirit," the huge deserted villas of Newport, all tell the same story; scarcely anything seems to flatter itself for a moment that it has any chance of permanence. Indeed after a visit to Ellis Island, the gate through which the incredible stream of alien immigration pours daily into the States—after watching the process by which a whole population (as it seems) of Hungarians and Armenians and Italians is being steadily tilted into the lap of America—what meaning, asks Mr. James, can before long attach to the very idea of the national character itself? That is a question which even the novelist—though it lies beyond his domain—cannot help putting, and which even Mr. James cannot answer. Among so many uncertainties and makeshifts, he falls back all the more eagerly upon the indications of a past, numerous though unobtrusive, which New England has to offer. The old Newport, which had its sedately cultivated, mildly cosmopolite little society before ever the millionaires swooped down upon it, evokes a chapter in which the charm of the vanished life is all enticed back again under the writer's light and loving touch. The embowered home of Washington Irving, in the heart of the country, is a place where the "restless analyst" (as he loves to speak of himself) can for once rest in uncritical felicity. Salem and Concord are a little disappointing; the spirit of Hawthorne is not so fortunate as that of Irving. The interest there is different; who but Mr. James could have felt it, much less described it, like this?:—

It is always interesting, in America, to see any object, some builded thing in particular, look as old as it possibly can; for the sight of which effort we sometimes hold our breath as if to watch, over the course of the backward years, the straight "track" of the past, the course of some hero of the foot-race on whom we have staked our hopes. How long will he hold out, how far back will he run, and where, heroically blown, will he have to drop? Our suspense is great in proportion to our hope, and if we are nervously constituted, we may very well, at the last, turn away for anxiety. It was really in some such manner I was affected, I think, before the Salem Witch House, in presence of the mystery of antiquity.

Thus, with a sympathetic hand ready for every admonition from landscape or people or thoroughfare, seldom refusing a tempting digression, but never losing his thread, Mr. James pursues his way southward. His characterizations of Philadelphia, of Baltimore (where the houses, in certain secluded squares, "suggested rows of quiet old ladies seated, with their toes tucked up on uniform footstools, under the shaded candle-sticks of old-fashioned tea parties"), and of Washington are as inimitable as the rest. At last, in Richmond, he reaches the South. Here, after indicating all that this word means to an American of the Northern States, the old unhappy far-off things, memories of valour, an impossible cause, a paralysing defeat—the restless analyst searches the face of the town for tokens of all it has seen and suffered. He had counted, he says, on finding "a sort of registered consciousness of the past, and the truth was that there appeared for the moment, on the face of the scene, no discernible consciousness, registered or unregistered, of anything." Richmond for the first moment seemed blank and void, but very soon the illumination came. It was exactly this blankness that constituted the real tragedy and the real appeal of the Southern States; no positive features could have testified so eloquently to the full meaning of the perversity and disaster through which their history has led them. Before this aspect of the scene, and under the ominous shadow of the negro problem, the tone of the book changes for a moment from its usual self-possessed serenity. In a few grave pages the essence of the tragedy is indicated with profound sympathy and with full consciousness of the fact that the outsider, the Northerner, cannot presume either to chide or to advise. The book ends in a lighter vein with studies of Charleston and Florida, two perfect examples of Mr. James's penetration and humour—Charleston, so hushed and refined, but so unutterably empty, and Florida, adorably mild and sweet, but also, "ever so amiably, weak." Not the least agreeable page is that on which we have a hint of further scenes to follow—from that Californian coast, to which, we are told, the coast of Florida is related "much as a tinkle is related to a boom."

Here, however, for the present ends this crowded, sensitive, intricate book, probably the most remarkable book of impressions of travel which we possess. It cannot be pretended that it can be read without considerable concentration of attention; once drop the fine-spun thread, and you are lost. But to follow it out to the end is to have a positive revelation of the amount of insight and exactness of expression which can be packed between the covers of a single book.

Note

1 Parts of *The American Scene* had previously appeared in *North American Review, Harper's Magazine,* and *Fortnightly Review.* See Leon Edel and Dan H. Laurence, *A Bibliography of Henry James. Third Edition* (Oxford: Clarendon Press, 1982), no. A63.

"The Return of the Native."
Pall Mall Gazette [England], 11 February 1907, p. 4.

The chief impression one brings away from the study of these impressions in "The American Scene" is the perfect balance, the due correspondence between thought and expression which are distinguishing features and excellences of Mr. Henry James's masterly style. The intricacy of the phrasing is well fitted to the complex thought of a yet most lucid thinker. The delicacy of its turning and its subtle involutions are admirably adapted to the fineness and the light and elusive quality of his humour. That frequent adverb or adverbial expression, so placed that it must arrest our attention, is of the largest and most illuminative significance, for without it we had lost half his meaning. Those rare locutions and rare or new-coined words, such as "ancientries," are employed, we feel, not so much out of wanton eccentricity, but once again to compel attention and *emphasis gratiâ.* This adaptability of style to meaning will more than ever be gratefully appreciated here by those who, like the present reviewer, are unfamiliar with the scenes on which "the brooding analyst," as Mr. James call himself, meditates.

We have become so accustomed to regard him as wholly English that it is with something of a shock that we are here reminded of his nationality, and not in the least surprising to find that in Florida, as a negro was depositing his baggage in the mud, he was hailed as a Britisher by a Southerner boasting of America's travelling facilities. At any rate, he displays filial affection for the land of his birth. The unspeakable bagmen of the south ("they insisted, I say, with the strange crudity of their air of commercial truculence, on being exactly as low as they liked") may stir him to animated protest, but the people most concerned will not understand him. He regrets and condemns America's grievous lack of "the decency or dignity of a road"; he may condemn, too, the "criminal continuity" of the railway track, that "makes but a mouthful of the Mississippi," yet he betrays his pride in the bigness of the feat. He denounces rightly enough in one place New York's skyscrapers as grossly tall and grossly ugly, but shortly before he finds some sort of excuse for them. He is, perhaps, most astonished, after twenty-five years' absence from the States, at the ubiquity of the alien, from whom there seems no escape, for even when he lost his way in the New Hampshire hills, he asked it from the first person upon whom he came, and he was an Armenian. It is, perhaps, in his account of the autumnal beauties of this district that he charms us most. The description of the single scarlet maple as the "daughter of a noble house dressed for a fancy ball, with the whole family gathered round to admire her before she goes," and of nature there as "feminine from head to foot, in expression, tone, and touch, mistress throughout of the feminine attitude, and effect," will not away from the memory. But always and above all, it is the style, the touch of this master hand, which ministers to our delight.

J.A.H.
"The American Scene." Manchester *Guardian*, 12 February 1907, p. 5.

A quarter of a century's continuous absence from his native land has served as preparation for this book. A mind of unique sensibility has thus been launched into the wide medley of American life. The result is, of course, impressions differing in kind from those with which we are familiar either through the pen of skilled foreign impressionists like Mr. Wells or keen semi-detached residents like Professor Münsterberg.[1] Mr. James steps into an America which is to him in many pressing external features entirely new—a New York rebuilt with body of steel and electric soul, hoisted mid-air; a vast polyglot Boston, with its historic streets disappearing under the tireless arts of the improver; a Washington of new palaces and magnificent distances; a land visibly dominated by railroads, full of new monstrous "problems," the ethnic stew, the octopean Trust, the resurrected negro question; and everywhere rumbling in the background the indignation of the thwarted people at the flaunting luxury of a material ostentation never rivalled in its scale and provocative display. With these problems, set as such, Mr. James does not much concern himself; it is where pieces of them press upon his vision or get entangled in his analysis of some concrete "document" that he is forced to handle them. Indeed, of the great social problems the alien immigration is almost the only one he treats directly and explicitly, because of its manifold dramatic appeal.

The work throughout is that of the restless, brooding analyst, concerned not primarily with objective facts, even when he handles scenery, but with their reaction upon his mind. He tells with unique but not always intelligible refinement how everything in a series of carefully chosen representative scenes affects him. This of course, in a sense, is what every narrator does; but a plain man of any "standard" sort gives what may be considered representative impressions, whereas every item in these scenes is coloured by the extraordinary personality and literary setting of one of the rarest of our modern writing men. To most English readers the book will be interesting more as a study of Mr. James (and an example of his later literary manner) than of America. But, nevertheless, a great many true and interesting things are said about America, and keen, penetrative glances at common objects are made to yield important disclosures of human nature in America. "Manners," in the broad acceptation of the word, are his chief subject; the play of "summer girls" with "a summer boy" in a country drive, the amazing little world of the Waldorf-Astoria, the wide-open doors and lack of privacy in the structure of the American club, the physical and mental gregariousness of city life in a hundred illustrative details—such are the themes in which he lets his quick reflective mind play, as it works through in a rich tangle of brilliant phrases. Ever and anon he wanders into the two topics which most engage the interest even of the casual visitor to the United States, the social omnipotence of woman and the pecuniary theory of life, churning them up into a rich mess of psychological reflection. There is no real endeavour to suggest causes or solutions, and one has a feeling that such treatment is shunned as alien from artistic method and belonging to the obviousness or directness of science. Indeed Mr. James carries much further his purposed or instinctive avoidance of the obvious, preferring

to insinuate himself by some side-entrance not merely into his subjects but into the very structure of his sentences. This elusive, mysterious, and oft-times finnicking style of composition is of course familiar to all readers of his later stories, forming the appeal of a certain exclusive cult it has won for him. It is sometimes exasperating in its waste, as in the opening pages, where several thousand words are spent in telling that "expensiveness" and "publicity" are the characteristics of upper New York life, though it yields occasional compensation when a straight thought, bluntly or even rudely put, suddenly obtrudes from the soft literary maze and makes its shock.

Regarded as a criticism, the treatment fails to do justice to the great interests of the struggle for order, political, economic, intellectual, and moral, that is going on in America, and the rich human qualities manifested in this struggle. Mr. James does not, indeed, ignore these strong aspects of "the will to live," but he does not give them a fair show in the American Scene.

Note

1   Hugo Münsterberg, *The Americans* (1905).

Boston *Evening Transcript*, 20 February 1907, p. 19.

Nothing in the modern literature of travel could be more distinctive than "The American Scene," wherein Henry James gives voice to the feelings that beset him upon his return to his native land after an absence of twenty-five years. But "The American Scene" is of course only superficially a book of travel. It brings to light certain aspects of America, to be sure, but it also reveals to us with still further emphasis the strong characteristics of thought and style that have made Mr. James a unique figure in English literature. From time to time during Mr. James's sojourn among us last year we reprinted at length, as they appeared serially in the North American Review, some of the impressions that go to the making of this volume, and it therefore only remains to us now to call attention to their appearance in permanent form. The volume is a small octavo of over four hundred pages, and it takes the reader from New England to Florida in the course of a series of sixteen chapters. Through them Mr. James gives us an autumn impression of New England, a spring impression of New York and the Hudson, social notes of New York, a view of the Bowery and thereabout, a survey of New York revisited, a study of the scenes of Newport, leading us thence through the streets of Boston, Concord, Salem, Philadelphia, Baltimore, Washington, Richmond and Charleston.

What more American, and at the same time what more European, indeed what more cosmopolitan, scene could Mr. James possibly visit than the Bowery? Strangely enough, the first landmark of the Bowery to which he leads us is the Bowery Theatre, a "vast, dingy edifice" that calls up memories of an illustrious past, but which is now sadly fallen from its high estate. Thither he "electrically travelled"—could apt phrase be more Jamesian?—and as he rolled down the Bowery towards the doors of the ancient playhouse he realized that the Bowery, like all else, had changed since his boyhood into something new and strange. It is the elevated railroad that thus impressed him, but who else would phrase his feelings of "a strange, sinister overroofed clangorous darkness, a wide thoroughfare beset, for all its width, with sound and fury, and bristling amid the traffic with posts and piles that were as the supporting columns of a vast, cold, yet also uncannily animated, sepulchre." But with his inspection of the Bowery drama Mr. James was by no means done with the Bowery itself. The many nations clustered there held him in their grasp, and physiognomy, language and character alike gave him opportunity to linger and study. There he observed "quiet couples, elderly bourgeois husbands and wives," over their "belated sausage and cheese, potato salad and Hungarian wine," and there also, as might be expected, he found the "exotic boss" speaking "fluent East-Side New Yorkese," and presenting himself "as a possibly far-reaching master-spirit."

Elsewhere in New York Mr. James found equally picturesque scenes amid the "elegant domiciliary" of the metropolis. What struck him most obviously, and sometimes full in the face was the braggart, blatant appalling newness of the great city. "There are new cities enough about the world, goodness knows," he remarks, "and there are new parts enough of old cities—for examples of which we need go no further than London, Paris and Rome, all of late so mercilessly renovated. But the newness of New York—unlike even that of Boston, I seemed to discern—had this mark of its very own, that it affects one in every case, as having treated itself as still more provisional, if possible, than any poor dear little interest of antiquity it may have annihilated. The very sign of its energy is that it doesn't believe in itself; it fails to succeed even at the cost of millions, in persuading you that it does." And although when Mr. James reached Charleston, he found "no very finished picture," yet it was "even so different in aspect and 'feeling,' and above all in intimation and suggestion, from any passage of the American scene as yet deciphered."

445

Richmond, however, was saddened by its memories as the capital of the Confederacy, by "the humiliation of defeat" and its involving bereavement and bankruptcy. "These afflictions are still admirably ventilated, and what is wonderful in the air today is the comfort and cheer of this theory of an undying rancor. Practically, and most conveniently, one feels, the South is reconciled, but theoretically, ideally, and above all for the new generation and the amiable ladies, the ladies amiable like the charming curatrix of the Richmond Museum, it burns with a smothered flame."

As Mr. James penetrates the heart of present-day Southern feeling, so does he penetrate the heart of the entire American scene. He shows us ourselves and our country, through the medium of his own eyes and his vigorously individual powers of expression, ourselves as we are, ourselves as we want to be, and ourselves as we frequently do not want to be revealed. As thoroughly imaginative as any of his novels, "The American Scene" is at the same time a record of stern and undeniable fact. It comes from the press with the imprint of Harper & Brothers.

"Impressions of an Artist: Henry James' Beautiful Convolutions around American Scenery, Cities and People."
Louisville *Courier-Journal*, 23 February 1907, p. 5.

It would be well to go abroad if absence could so quicken thought and sensi-

tiveness as it has in Mr. James. After twenty-five years' life with over-the-ocean scenes and types, he lands in New York much as a stranger might, yet with a memory of past impressions that he is prepared to find subverted. In a sense it is the same New York, yet he quickly discerns the difference which is owing principally to invention and scientific progress.

Journeying past the homes of the multimillionaires, his chief impression seems to be that a cat can look at a king—there is no protection to the houses—"The most yet accomplished at such a cost was the air of unmitigated publicity, publicity as a condition, as a doom, from which there could be no appeal . . . no achieved protection, no constituted mystery of retreat, no saving complexity, not so much as might be represented by a foot of garden wall or a preliminary sketch of interposing shade."

How good the above is and what other writer could so have expressed it! "Not so much as a lodge at any gate." The no-fence idea is so American, and seems painfully unhomelike and public to eyes accustomed to the seclusion offered by high garden walls guarding the privacy of the family. He thinks that in such a condition there cannot be any manners to speak of. The owners affirm their wealth in their homes but nothing else, the crudity of this wealth striking him with direct force— their houses have the air of costing as much as "they knew how," is the fine reflection.

"The highest luxury of all, the supremely expensive thing, is constituted privacy—and yet it was the supremely expensive thing that the good people had supposed themselves to be getting." Unfortunately these people can neither read nor understand Mr. James, so the lesson is lost to the class that would be most benefitted.

Then he goes to New Hampshire, and his description of the New England scenery is one of the best things he has ever done. Again in New York, after New England impressions, he questions whether the American spirit be not the hotel spirit as evidenced in the Waldorf-Astoria, which seems to have pleased him. Here in America every one is practically in everything, while in Europe it is only certain people who are in anything. "This one caravansary makes the American case vivid, gives it, you feel, that quantity of illustration which renders the place a new thing under the sun." The Waldorf-Astoria, he thinks, is an expression of the gregarious state, breaking all but two barriers—one being pecuniary, the other being the condition that all dwellers must be "respectable."

The high buildings are not subjects for veneration. One can venerate an old staircase "consecrated by the tread of generations," and they are often lovely in themselves. "You'd be ashamed to venerate the arrangement of fifty floors," or an old elevator or an old omnibus. This building up and down, he hints, "blights the superstition of rest." "Houses of the best taste are like clothes of the best tailors—it takes their age to show us how good they are." Cases of real refinement he mentions that have escaped the spirit of the age—the City Hall that has been saved and the house on the corner of Washington Square and Fifth Avenue.

Going south he found Baltimore "sympathetic" and "amiable." Washington was charming, Mount Vernon exquisite, not expressed in terms so plainly to be read, but to be delved for among multitudinous sensations.

In Richmond one finds the author in his best mood, he seems to present the city, in the point of view of the unprejudiced stranger, better than has ever been done before. His impression of the statue of Lee stands forth, also his disappointment over the poor little relics of the war. The negro "had always been and could absolutely not fail to be, intensely 'on the nerves' of the South." And so on.

He saw the social tone in the person of a little old lady who was the custodian of the Confederate Museum, "a person soft voiced, gracious, mellifluous, perfect for her function, who, seated by her fire in a sort of official entrance, received him as at the gate of some grandly bankrupt plantation—he had not surrendered to this exquisite contact before he felt himself up to his neck in a delightful, soothing, tepid medium, the social tone of the South that had been." This lady was the only beautiful thing in the museum. "No little old lady of the North could, for the high tone and the right manner, have touched her, and poor, benumbed Richmond might now be as dreary as it liked ... my pilgrimage couldn't be a failure."

Richmond's poverty (of impressions especially) is historic poverty. It is in the condition of having worshiped false gods. "As I looked back, before leaving it, at Lee's stranded, bereft image, which time and fortune have so cheated of half the significance, and so, I think, of half the dignity of great memorials, I recognized something more than the melancholy of a lost cause. The whole infelicity speaks of a cause that could never have been gained."

Mr. James' prose has a strange effect. Beguiled and baffled one rambles along, often wondering what it all means, but after persevering one finds suddenly the sense of a delightful picture, of special atmosphere, a combination of color, that can never afterwards be separated from the thing he has described. This pastmaster of phrase may seem obscure and involved as to thought; in the final, lasting effect he is clarity itself.

Y.Y.
"The American Scene."
Bookman [England] 31 (March 1907), 265–66.

Mr. Henry James has spent a holiday in America, and like other scribblers, better and worse, would fain recover his traveling expenses, by printing his impressions. Only that—and nothing more! How much that means, those who are familiar with Mr. James's little ways know but too well. Yet peradventure some there be, nay, my impressionist brain hovers between a strong improbabalistic certainty, and a vague, nebulous, sharply defined suspicion, pale as the Dawn over a sky-scraper and elusively pink as an inadequately boiled lobster, that they are many—(oh! this terrible Jacobean jargon! it is an influenza, and you see that I have caught it already)—who have not yet gone through the fire to his pinchbeck Molochs or bowed the knee in the obfuscatorily tenebrose coal-cellar of his fuliginous Rimmon. (By an effort I shake off the sesquipedalian paroxysm and resume my pedestrian jog-trot.) Well, if these unspotted souls demand some description, some criticism of "the American Scene," it could be adequately, exhaustively, finally summed up in a single impressionist word, monosyllable or dissyllable—for there is choice of synonyms—which they at least would understand—"and with an ill-bred whisper close the Scene." One word—one little word!—and the Editor suggests "about 1,600"! What is to be done? Suppose that, rejecting modernisms—for I detest the XXth century, even to its slang—we choose for our little word a synonym respectable for its antiquity and sanctioned by the highest literary authority—

the oracular "Fudge!" of good Mr. Burchell—very willingly could I expand it into 1,600, or 16,000 words, by condensing just a very few of my impressionist impressions of Mr. James and other One-eyed Kings among the Stone-blind; but that I must not. Or I might impressionize his impressions after his own manner—which is easy enough to parody—in a rigmarole as prolix as his own; but that I will not. It would only please the Jacobeans, whom I want to snub.

Though Mr. James's "American Scene"—and probably much of his later work—is sad rubbish, I shall ever retain my deep and unfeigned admiration for his consummate talent. Several of his early works I reviewed, and no doubt dwelt upon their many excellences, but certainly I pointed out the rocks on which his genius was fated to make shipwreck. The dread propensities were already growing fast when I took my last view of him with an impression—for even we poor simple souls have our impressions—as of a gallant craft which, dimly descried through the yeasty surges of his own jargon, had got out of his course, wallowing helplessly in a sea of spurious "Analysis." And after many years I find to-day his shivered timbers and cargo of soft goods and mixed notions cast up in dire ruin on the American coast. (Jacobean metaphors again! Pardon and pity!) In plain words, I dropped Mr. James because he no longer promised more than variations on his old triumphs, while his growing tendency to falsetto alarmed and disgusted. From time to time stray notices in the press seemed to record the stages in his deterioration. So Henry James survived only as a memory—the memory of a distinguished novelist who flourished somewhere between 1870 and 1890; whether since then deceased or still amusing his well-earned leisure by throwing dust and pepper in the eyes of his public mattered not. No one, I presume, has ever denied his remarkable native gifts, or his fine, literary accomplishments, and it is an impertinence to say—yet it has been said—that he is a genius who might have done great things. He has done great things. True, not even his best books are great, or even good, because they all are marred by grave defects, but they do contain work so superlatively good in its way as to claim the palm of greatness. Even in this last volume you may with effort disentangle from the verbiage strands of perception as vivid and of thought as tense as of old; and now and then you will find him, in his chosen domains—scenic impressions and human motive—forgetting his pose and falling back perhaps for a whole sentence, into exquisitely sympathetic or arresting expression.

What from the very first—from "The Lady of the Aroostook"[1]—vaguely repelled me in Mr. James was not his monomania for what he calls, and evidently believes to be, Analysis, but a certain conscious though concealed want of moral ballast, lack of ethical faith—what shall I call it? It seemed as though he were rearing his airy palaces so light yet strong—slight nervous steel girders, intricate wire trellis, glittering glass—because he suspected that he was building on treacherous foundations—quicksands, morass, or volcano crust. He analysed and discussed the motives and actions of his personages—or made them do the business for themselves—always in terms of conventional morality, but it was rarely clear when we were expected to approve or disapprove, and Mr. James seemed as much befogged as ourselves. I suppose modern Art forbade him to use the old didactic moral labels, but if he did not know which to call right or wrong, he should either have said so frankly, or else concealed his hesitancy more artistically—and successfully. One felt somehow that at the bottom of it all there was something dubious, unsettled and unsettling—something perhaps bordering on evil. But after all, this vague air of insincerity he shares with some other typical writers of his transition period, who may have felt their minds not yet clear enough on fundamental ethics, or may have judged the time was unpropitious for speaking out. And that is why they appear—unjustly appear—as irresponsible amateurs compared to the Old Masters, who, though they sometimes built on sand, firmly believed it to be solid rock, and so their magnificent assurance dominates and convinces to this day.

Impressions twenty-five years old! Yet they have lingered in the memory, so must have been strong and definite. One is of surprise—bewilderment—then admiration. Here was something new and strange. Was it mere eccentricity? Was it impudent mystification? Many features recalled older masters—I do not say, were derived from, for I hate all that "deriving," "tracing," evolution-business—Dickens, for instance, in the accentuation of odd characters, Balzac the dissecting surgeon of the heart, and the rest. But the general effect, good or bad, seemed distinctly original and individual. Mr. James has had some rivals and many imitators in his enterprise, but can you point to a single previous work which could possibly be for one moment mistaken for his? I think not. Again, though from the very first unto this last we trace the progress of his maladies—his fidgety, niggling handling of cases of conscience, his pryings and pokings and probings and fumblings—he had received the rare natural gift of the Seeing Eye. It is all in a nutshell. He gazed on his fellow-men. He saw in clearest light their clothes—their social environment; through these he saw less distinctly the naked form—the physical constituents, proclivities, and so forth—and piercing the envelope of flesh his eye discerned something—not much, but far more than yours or mine could see—something of the Something in the central-shrine—the Secret of the Soul. But he wanted to see more—farther, deeper, clearer. Alas, he *could not.* So he *pretended to.* And by means of the faculty called Faith, he easily half-persuaded himself into believing that he really *did.* A few doubted, contemptuous of this amalgam of pretense and self-delusion. But many believed and cherished him, for *"parmi les aveugles le borgne est roi"*—be he novelist, scientist, or theologian. All in a nutshell!

Yes, Mr. James sees and knows a lot about human beings. And the proof is that he can invent them. Some characters live in his pages, who certainly never could have lived out of them. His humour, too, more English than American, is genuine, though here he neglects his powers. But to me his charm lay in his somewhat rare but brilliant flashes of the modern French *esprit*—it goes back no farther than Voltaire—which few English can understand, and far fewer imitate—that impish protervity of thought and phrase, grave yet sportive, delicate yet impudent, lightsome but profound, fantastic yet severely true. For Mr. James at his best could be enchantingly odd, and that best I found and praised in a short story called "Lady Barberina," a little masterpiece in spite of its exaggerations and burlesque.[2] Shelves, libraries of European fiction studied in those days have faded from my mind, but that tale survives still fresh and clear. Enough remains to fill several pages—the entire plot, all the characters and scenes, some conversations, and many of the quips and cranks which tickled me most. Yes, I admit that Mr. James has chosen to do poor work, and that if he had hearkened to his own genius instead of to the busy flatterers, he might have done better, and the best. But with this old spell still strong upon me, it would be ungenerous to deny that, for me at least, he has done great work—work of forcible, of abiding, of indelible impress.

Must we again lift the curtain on the dreary "American Scene"? Sad rubbish!—what more would you know? I cannot read it through; nor could you—perhaps no one ever will. There are 465 pages; 14 chapters, each, nominally, dealing with some city or district. Study a few pages carefully, pick out what sense there is, and you will find that Mr. James is quite sound on American bigness, nastiness, and social barrenness. But so are other people; so should be all who see to-day the Spread Eagle gloating over the corruption of a gang of low millionaires not fit to associate with decent niggers. If you want to know about the States, read Basil Hall or any other intelligible old writer. Their facts may be obsolete—no matter—they are less unsavoury. Mr. James tells me very little about America, but 465 pages more about himself than I want to know. His Impressionism and Analytics are, to speak bluntly, pure Humbug. The Perfect Impressionist pretends to seek the Mystical Affinities and Inner Meaning of everything. Gazes on a cloud and wonders is it humped like a camel—or meant for a whale—a five-pound note—or a greenback—or possibly a piano, or a mother-in-law? Or he stares at a blank wall—what mystery does its blankness import? The House of Commons? shrimps for tea? a fall in Kaffirs? Miss Terry with her back hair down? No! something greyer, more brickdusty, more Rhadamanthine than any of these. Really most puzzling! Then sometimes comes the supreme joke. After driveling on with nonsense like this for a page or two, muddled and muddling, Mr. James is sorry to say he cannot "at present" interpret that particular brick wall—his "mood" is not propitious maybe—and he has the impudence to promise to look at it another day "in a different light," and favour us with the result later on. If only they *were* meant for burlesque, I should hugely relish these candid confessions of failure. And this twaddle he calls Analysis. It is nothing of the kind. Analysis is getting sense out of something, not putting nonsense in. And he pumps out his nonsense in a flood of jargon which really beggars description, in a style clumsy, slipshod, pretentious and "deliberately unintelligible"—as he would say, for long words are as dear to him as his crabbed Impressionist shibboleths. I tried the Sortes Jacobeanæ, and opening the leaves at random, noted down a few sentences, each more astounding than the last, and meant to make fun of them. But I forbear. You cannot trust me? Very well, take the first (page 2) and see how you like it! Mark the style, the sense, the chaste imagery. It is a first impression of New York, below which two rivers meets—"the serried bristling city, held in the easy embrace of its great good-natured rivers very much as a battered and accommodating beauty may sometimes be 'distinguished' by a gallant less fastidious, with his open arms, than his type would seem to imply." How far he goes to fetch—well, coarseness! And note, there are two rivers, so there ought to have been two gallants, "distinguishing" one on each side—which is absurd—and revolting. Lower down I find the sun "resting on that dull glaze of crimson paint, as thick as on the cheek of cruder coquetry, which is, in general, beneath its range, the sign of the old-fashioned," whatever that may mean. Again on page 16—"the hidden ponds over which the season itself seemed to bend as a young bedizened, a slightly melodramatic mother, before taking some guilty flight, hangs over the crib of her sleeping child." Thus much of his delicate virginal similes—seek for yourself specimens of his crack-jaw jargon. And worse—the very worst—the pump is not yet dry. In a later volume the mystery of the, at present, insoluble paving-stones, straw hats and gaspipes will be revealed. Enough! A long farewell to the Impressionist and his impressions! The only impression I retain of them is that of a Remorseless Bore.

Notes

1 Y.Y. Is mistaken. *The Lady of the Aroostook* (1879) was written by William Dean Howells, not James.
2 "Lady Barberina," *Century Magazine* 28 (May–July 1884), 18–31, 222–34, 336–50. Reprinted in *Tales of Three Cities* (1889).

"Mr. Henry James on America."
Spectator [England] 4105 (2 March 1907), 334–35.

Mr. Henry James has issued to a highly curious world the first instalment of his impressions of America. The visit of such an inquirer to his native land after an absence of a quarter of a century is a notable event in the history of letters. Of late we have had many impressions of America, in which the manifold life of a vast continent was apt to condense itself into a few epigrams. Mr. James knows too much to begin with to attempt any facile generalisations. He has his former memories as a standard of comparison, and such an equipment would have given the ordinary traveller material for a neat antithetical summary. But Mr. James is far too acute and far too sincere to be content with such a surface view. In this book he is still groping among strange things, catching sight of a shape here and there, but for the most part only conscious of an immense and

451

amorphous environment. It is the most original book of travels we have ever read, and to the careful reader one of the most illuminating. The faults we have to find with it are only the faults which cling to all Mr. James's recent work. He is exceedingly difficult to read. In one page he will have sentences shapely and musical, and sentences which come to an end only by the grace of God. He is apt to hang too often on the same metaphor, and he has an inordinate love of the adverb "quite," and of words like "virtues," "values," and "precious." The first pages of all give one an example of the author at his tortuous worst, and then we are transported to the New England highlands, where the descriptions of landscape are a model of luminous and exquisite prose. The style varies much, but one thing never varies—the sustained intellectual power of the analysis.

No casual reader can get even a glimmering of Mr. James's meaning. His reasoning is close, his perceptions subtle and evasive, and his conclusions often surprising, so that he must be read sentence by sentence and page by page. He does not make the path easy for his followers, for while he has many brilliant generalisations, they remain unconnected, still in the baggage of the traveller rather than set out in the museum on his return. He is, as he calls himself on many occasions, the "restless analyst," "the ancient contemplative person," and his quest is always for the truth. He never says a thing for the mere sake of saying it brilliantly, though brilliance is often enough in attendance. Though he is far removed from the ordinary impressionist, phrases could be selected from his pages which would make a brilliant impressionist picture. But he is too philosophic to rest content with word-painting when the heart of the matter still awaits discovery. In landscape, in character, in customs, he seeks for guiding prin-ciples, for the type, the characteristic. Sometimes it evades him, and he leaves in bewilderment; sometimes, as at New York, it is almost too simple to be interesting. At the Waldorf-Astoria, for instance, "the air swarms, to intensity, with the *characteristic*, the characteristic condensed and accumulated as one rarely elsewhere has had the luck to find it." Mr. James, it will be perceived, is a moralist above all things. He is not content when he is told that America is this or that in material statistics. He still asks: "What does it all *mean*, what is its *virtue*, its *value?*"

First for Mr. James's conclusions. Mr. Wells was very clear in his verdict. The power and the will to create went down to the profit account of America with civilisation, and "State-blindness" to the loss. Mr. James reaches the same general conclusion by far subtler means, and he works out his doctrines to a fractional result impossible with Mr. Wells's more hasty methods. We may best describe his plan by calling it the detection of tendencies rather than the chronicle of facts. He sees forces in movement, and devotes himself to their analysis, leaving their immediate material effect for more superficial students. In America one may observe how the "short-cut" works, and "if there be really any substitute for roundabout experience, for troublesome history, for the long, the immitigable process of time." A little later he sees the *will to grow* everywhere, "at no matter what or whose expense." This, it will be observed, is not quite Mr. Wells's "will to create," for it involves destruction of the past, and growth, unlike creation, implies no conscious object. At the Universities he is struck suddenly by the fact that the women in America are monopolising all the "distinctions," in the physiological sense, and he is impressed by the wonderful possibilities the thing has for the art of the novelist. The alien leaves him bewildered. He meets him everywhere, and penetrates to his own East Side haunts in his quest for enlightenment; but he can come to no conclusion save that these newcomers have all the air of having acquired something new, and of having lost much of their former identity. They are both a kind of American and a kind of Italian, and their future is dark. Anyhow, the fact of their numbers makes Mr. James sigh for "the luxury of some such close and sweet and *whole* national consciousness as that of the Switzer and the Scot." On the question of poverty he admits the general betterment, but doubts its continuance in the face of the new anti-social forces. Freedom in the United States may end by being only "freedom to grow up blighted." On the worship of money and the position of woman Mr. James tells the old tale: travellers do not differ in their reports on these matters:—

"To make so much money that you won't, that you don't 'mind' anything—that is absolutely, I think, the main American formula. Thus your making no money—or so little that it passes there for none—and being thereby distinctly reduced to minding, amounts to your being reduced to the knowledge that America is no place for you."

And the fact that America produces no kind of man in large quantities except the business man, while the woman, created by a woman-made society, is wholesomely differentiated, leads to some curious speculations about the end of it all. Mr. James surveys the scene where Democracy, unfettered and colossal, is having her own way, and is left questioning. America, having no past, hopes for a future; but of what stuff is the future to be? It is a great lonely land of which civilisation has only scratched the surface. The sense of "margin" presses in on him and gives him hope;

but when he considers the ugliness of the scratching he again despairs. There are two lessons, quite obvious and simple, but singularly neglected, which America has got to learn. One is that "production takes time, and that the production of interest, in particular, takes *most* time." The other is the very old truth that the whole material world is unprofitable if the soul be lost. "In the early American time, doubtless, individuals of value had to wait too much for things; but that is now made up by the way things are waiting for individuals of value." We apologise for the banality of the act in putting Mr. James's subtleties into a crude moral; but that, after all, is the gist of them.

We have little space to notice the other aspect of the book, the wholly delightful travel sketches. Out of the bland and lingering sentences pictures of the landscape build themselves up with clear outline and all the atmosphere of reality. We have already noticed the beautiful New England pictures, where the dominant note, says Mr. James, is the country's "amiability." Memories of Lowell and Mr. Howells and Washington Irving give Mr. James occasion for certain charming pages. Thence he goes to New York, whose character is extravagance, pulling down to make larger, and building nothing intended to endure. The poor pilgrim wanders in the elder New York, and sees in Washington Place and certain old buildings the ghosts of a once civilised past. He finds that the great hotels provide just the "prodigious public setting" which the modern city life demands: "an expression of the gregarious state of breaking down every barrier but two,"—*i.e.*, wealth and reasonable respectability. Then we pass to memories of old Newport and an acid picture of the new; to Boston, where his complaint is the opposite of that of Mr. Wells; to Philadelphia, where he is charmed by the Quakerish gentility of the city and awed by the scandals of its public life; to Washington, where the men are allowed to rank almost with the women; and lastly, to the South. The chapters on Richmond and Charleston are perhaps the most wonderful in the book, for in the South Mr. James has a more congenial task, since it is the decline of civilisation which he analyses, not its advance. Take such a passage as this:—

> "The place was *weak*—'adorably' weak; that was the word into which the whole impression flowered, that was the idea, evidently, that all the rest of the way as well would be most brought home. . . . . . I can doubtless not sufficiently tell why, but there was something in my whole sense of the South that projected at moments a vivid and painful image—that of a figure somehow blighted and stricken, discomfortably, impossibly seated in an invalid-chair, and yet fixing one with strange eyes that were half a defiance and half a depreciation of one's noticing, and much more of one's referring to, any abnormal sign. The depreciation, in the Southern eyes, is much greater to-day, I think, than the old lurid challenge; but my haunting similitude was an image of the keeping-up of appearances, and above all of the maintenance of a tone, the historic 'high' tone, in an excruciating posture."

And so this very candid and analytical traveller finally comes to an anchor among the palm-trees of Florida, and leaves us with the news that he has not done with the States, and that it is now the turn of California and the West. Mr. James writes with such urbanity and so genuine a love for the land that the most nervous patriot could not take offence at his pages, while to a certain limited class of readers they will be a source of acute intellectual pleasure.

Francis Thompson.
Athenaeum [England] 4141 (9 March 1907), 282–83.

To read this latest book of Mr. Henry James is like tackling one of those exasperating puzzles called "mazes," with a little arbour in the middle, and a tangle of ways which all run up against something—unless you hit on "the only way." The things you run up against are of course connected with Mr. James's style and (what is largely the same thing) his way of thinking. Readers may conceive that, having mastered his novels, they can be daunted by nothing more. But in the novels the necessity of narration does sometimes oblige Mr. James to write almost like the kindly race of men. Here, "story, God bless you! he has none to tell, sir"; and throughout four hundred and sixty-five broad pages there is no oasis in the level, unbroken expanse of Jacobean style. He has seized so rare an opportunity relentlessly, and holds his audience in the toils like the Wedding-Guest; "the Mariner hath his will." Nor has his style improved with years. In this latest example it has an irritation once absent; for to the defects of his own qualities he has added carelessness. "There's no step," he writes, "at which you shall rest, no form, as I'm constantly showing you, to which, consistently with my interests, you *can*." Which seemingly means that there is no form *to* which we can rest—a construction scarcely to be dismissed as a grammatical licence. Later we read, "The great thing is not to suffer it to so much as begin," and meet sentences like this: "The present Public Library, however remarkable in its pomp and circumstance, *and of which* I

454

had at that hour received my severe impression." Extremes meet. By the road of fastidious and defiant individuality Mr. James has, in fact, arrived at some of the results which the callow novelist achieves as a child of nature. With this he has the curiously contrasting vice of the Gallic use of the word "so": "From his so interesting point of view"; or again, "New York, with the so ambiguous element in the launched foreign personality," &c. This manner of idiom is sometimes harassingly frequent. Against the appearance of such symptoms in Mr. James's writing his admirers (among whom we are not the least sincere) have a right to protest; for these are not vices of style, but result from the want of it.

Though, however, they fret and exaggerate (by their needless slovenliness) one's sense of the difficulty, they are not the difficulty. That is in Mr. James's manner of thought. If you expect from him a guidebook to America, or a record of sightseeing as people in general understand sightseeing, you may close the book. It is an elaborated impression of America as it vibrates on the very conscious consciousness of Mr. Henry James—an impression on a minutely large scale. Yet it is not even impressionism as usually understood— the immediate sensitive impression of eye and emotion, stripped of afterthought and analysis. That would not be Mr. James, who is nothing if not analytic. Rather, it is the application to sightseeing of the methods of Mr. James the novelist—an endeavor first to capture, then to tease out and analyze the elusive subtleties of human atmosphere and suggestion in scenes and localities. We say "human atmosphere and suggestion," since for nature, apart from its connexion and reciprocal interaction with man, the novelist can spare little interest. And the novelist in Mr. James is always hankering after elusive subtleties, always aiming at them, even when he fails

to get them. The result, whether one thinks it successful or not, is something curious—and very tough reading. For, despite this inveterate quest of the elusive, gendered in him by the calling of a lifetime, the ideas suggested to Mr. James by a revisited "American scene" are inevitably, at bottom, often much what might occur to any other reflective observer. But the expression does not accommodate itself to the relative obviousness of idea. That must still preserve all the paraphernalia of elusiveness, though there is nothing which eludes. He must still write about and around it, and every way but *of* it—must approach it by stealth and tortuous indirectness, and deck it with the most elaborated precisions of impreciseness, as. if it required hinting afar off. He must (habitual microscopist!) still use his delicate microtome, though only to make sections of butter. The language invented, and the manner of thought developed, for his psychological subtleties he uses for matters the most familiar, and so reduces them to a strange, phantasmal abstraction of their workaday selves, bafflingly implying subtlety which is not in them. It is more difficult to follow than really inherent subtlety. For through the swathings you laboriously arrive at relative commonplace, and strenuous attention exerted to such a result exhausts one more than if the evasive expression had been compelled by a true evasiveness of idea.

Mr. James for example, staggered by the huge alien masses of the United States, and especially of New York, wonders, like other thinkers, what will issue from the Americanization of them which is furiously going forward, and recoils from answer. He tells you that, among the vast numbers newly cast into the machine (so to speak), the most striking feature is their featurelessness, the dead blank of monotonous uniformity which has resulted. He regrets, in particular (and with a special eye on the Italians), the loss of those racial amenities which make various nations engaging to the traveller's observation in their own land. The Italian has no longer the soft and amiable address universal in Italy. And these traits of national charm go with instant swiftness and absolute completeness: they are cast off on contact with the soil, as if they were contraband, and confiscated at the custom-house. This, in effect, Mr. James has to say. It is interesting, but not very difficult to say, one would think. Mr. James contrives to say it at great length, with an accumulation of every Jacobean resource for uttering the unutterable; so that when you exhaustedly look back and note what he *has* said, you can scarce credit your memory that this, essentially, is all.

To render any account, any description, of a book so written is manifestly impossible. It is not to be read through like other books, but should be taken up and read slowly by portions, when one is in a mood for the effort. So doing, you will find suggestion enough and to spare. For it is, after all, Mr. James; and what counts in it is less the subject than the author. The point is that such is the way things affected Mr. James. It happens to be America—it might have been Astrachan or the Samoyedes; the main interest would have been the same, so long as there were men, and Mr. James, insatiably curious, watching them. He does not describe, he gives no information; he exposes himself to impressions, and discusses and analyzes the result. Very characteristically, he mostly ends by leaving the result an open question; he is indisposed to commit himself even as to what his impression is after all. His attitude is curiously dispassionate, critical, and a-patriotic rather than unpatriotic. The colossal utilitarianism and restless mutability of the American atmosphere stir him to perpetual hostility. Everywhere he finds the America of his own

day "coming down," and declares "coming down" to be the law of American life, fatal to all association. America is a top, which stands only on condition that it perpetually "hums"—in the most American sense of that word. Yet it interests him, even the modern city with its "skyscrapers" that provoke him to blasphemy against the American idea; for it is human, and the novelist in him perpetually speculates on the possibilities of its evolving charm. It is a gigantic note of interrogation; he can neither answer it, nor cease from subtilizing on what answer the future may give. A good example of his manner is the chapter on the Bowery, with the contrast between the alien audience of its theatre, munching sausages as in their German homes, and the conventionally American play at which they stare; or the account of the immense impression made on him by the Ghetto of New York, prosperous, a New Jerusalem, the strong Judaic features dominating its streets with aggressive vitality. These things are impressions, singularly communicated, of a singular commixture, yet only possible from a unique personality.

Never can one forget the novelist. The book has an effect as of a man who in a dream makes struggling motions of running. We have the feeling that we should know better Mr. James's revised perceptions of New York or Boston if he made those cities the scene even of a short story, than we do from this minutely complex *compte rendu* of them. Further, he seems (to us) always wanting to write that story. He says of himself that he was always wanting to *get inside* the picture. When he quits the city for the country, where poet or painter would be content with the solitary charm of nature, he is restless to penetrate its human meaning, to discover in it the soul of its inhabitants: lonely loveliness which will surrender no such message leaves him but half-pleased. Were he not busy with other matters, no man could give you the impression of it in fewer touches. Read, for instance, this of Cape Cod:—

"A broad band of deep and clear blue sea . . . limited in one quarter by its far and sharp horizon of sky, on the other by its near and sharp horizon of yellow sand overfringed with a low woody shore; the whole seen through the contorted crosspieces of stunted, wind-twisted, far-spreading, quite fantastic old pines and cedars, whose bunched bristles at the end of long limbs, produced against the light the most vivid of all reminders. Cape Cod, on this showing, was exactly a pictured Japanese screen or banner."

He throws off Cotuit with a pen-scratch or two:—

"The little white houses, the feathery elms, the band of ocean blue, the stripe of sandy yellow, the tufted pines in angular silhouette, the cranberry-swamps stringed across, for the picking, like the ruled pages of ledgers."

You retain a distinct impression of the New Hampshire villages: the long straight road, the double file of verdurous branching elms, the white-painted wooden walls splashing the shadow with bright coolness, the far horizons that "recall the Umbrian note." But from all this, and through all this, he zigzags and feels his verbose way to the hesitant conclusion that these are the paradise and sphere of the "common man" and woman, the passive and negative people who "simply invest themselves for you in the grey truth that they don't go to the publichouse." That description of them is in turn debated into dubiety, with as meticulous an earnestness. The rest is a felicitous incident: this it is that interests him. He is throughout instinctively seeking psycho-logical problems as a dislodged limpet seeks a rock or stone to fasten on. You will be gratified with all manner of incidental felicities by the way, such as the half-revealed glimpses of the delicate shyness of Newport; but you must go problem-seeking to get them. Nor must you care overmuch about the results reached. We doubt whether the tabulated conclusions of the whole book (but who shall formulate them?) would yield much new light on the States or even their possibilities. The pleasure of the chase must content. Distinctly it is the process rather than the result that fascinates Mr. James, and you must let it fascinate you. That is how we are reduced to take this tantalizing, endlessly clever, engaging, perverse, compelling and repelling byproduct of the most fastidiously probing mind in present literature. As the peculiar and specialized methods of a novelist applied to a purpose outside fiction, it may or may not be successful. Interesting it must be—with the interest Browning felt in Dante's drawing of the angel, and we all feel in the essay of a great specialist in an art outside his own. Not even slipshod blemishes can make Mr. James's style other than distinguished, as Mayfair may drop its *g*'s, which Bayswater neglects at its peril.

"*The American Scene.*" San Francisco *Chronicle*, 17 March 1907, p. 9.

Those who have patience to go through Henry James' long and involved sentences will find much to reward them in "The American Scene," which includes the chapters he has written for various publications, summing up his observations on American life after over twenty-five years spent abroad. When Henry James first went abroad and wrote "The American" and "The Portrait of a Lady," he was the master of a beautiful style—clear, limpid and perfectly intelligible to the man in the street. But year by year he has sought to perfect the style and to attempt to define more exactly his opinions and impressions. The result has been to spoil his style. He is not content with a simple, direct statement; he must refine it, dwell upon certain features, involve the whole in a maze of words, with parenthetical clause within clause. It is no exaggeration to say that one must read some of these sentences two or three times to grasp their meaning, and even then it is not clear.

Besides this defect of language, Henry James comes back to his native land with certain preconceived ideas that are foolish because they are founded on English or French slanders. Thus he was much exercised because American men wear so much better shoes than hats. He evidently detests the derby or the soft hat and would have all well-dressed men adopt the silk hat, which is probably the most disagreeable head covering ever invented. What he has to say, however, about the undue devotion to business among American men and about our national propensity to plume ourselves on great material conquests while leaving intellectual things in neglect—all this is very true and very well put. Mr. James' description of the great American cities are fine specimens of descriptive, but they would be far better if they did not exact such close attention from the reader. The book is interesting, despite its style, because it contains the conclusions of one of the keenest of modern observers who is absolutely unprejudiced.

"Henry James on America."
Nation 84 (21 March 1907), 266–67.

Mr. James is a native American, and there are passages in this book which certainly could not have been written by one born under other skies. And yet, in general, he appears as a curiously alien observer, one who has been unable to realize in his own breast the feeling indicated in Goethe's words. "Hier oder nirgends ist Amerika." Mr. James's chief interest lies in the hallowed associations of what he terms the "whole precious past"; he has little but misgiving and suspicion for the new and untried. The interest offered by the "promiscuous packs and hustled herds" of America is to him simply, or at any rate predominantly, "queer." He assumes that the greater depth and urgency of his own sentiment about the past are in themselves proof that such past is more interesting than the present; the early associations of the Boston Athenæum, for example, far outweigh the connotation of the Boston Public Library. Human beings without an imaginative recognition of the past are to him almost a negligible quantity, and he fails to see that the indulgence of this view is practically to ignore the great bulk of Americans. He comes to his task saturated with the conventions, the ideas, and the ideals of an older and more sophisticated civilization, of a sheltered and intellectually fastidious *milieu;* and by this standard he insensibly measures all American institutions and tendencies. Thus it is that there have been foreign observers, such as James Bryce, who have been, so far as sympathetic insight goes, more American than Mr. James.

Mr. James repeatedly refers to himself as the "Restless Analyst"; and this phrase gives the reviewer an excellent clue for his summary of the book. "The American Scene" is a work of marvellously keen and subtle analysis; it transfixes the defects and shortcomings of American civilization with unerring thrusts; but it is less successful on the positive and synthetic side. Its vision is, if anything, too personal, too microscopic. We are driven to accept Mr. James's own statement that he has a bad habit of receiving through almost any accident of vision more impressions than he knows what to do with. As a result, we gain a hugely interesting reflection of what America seems to Mr. James, but we cannot help feeling at times that the camera obscura is an observer merely, not an interpreter.

Taking the book simply for what it is, however, we can surely describe it, if not as one of the greatest works on America, at least as one of the most fascinating to which the subject has given rise. The passages reminiscent of the scenes of Mr. James's boyhood are charming; and we are grateful for certain little fragments of autobiography. Nothing can be more vivid and discriminating than his descriptions of American scenery, such as of New Hampshire or Florida; nothing more happy than his reproduction of the atmosphere of such a place as Concord. His characterization of the different American cities is extraordinarily acute. No other writer on America has made shrewder observations or gathered up certain classes of facts under more illuminating labels. He is deeply sensible of the obtrusiveness of wealth in the United States, where he finds the main formula to be to "make so much money that you won't, that you don't 'mind' anything." He resembles other commentators on America in his preoccupation with the question of Woman; but none has equalled the aptness

of phrase in which he crystallizes his impressions. He sees that the sexes "fail to keep step socially." He notes that the rustle of American petticoats is "too distinguishable from any garment-hem of the sacred nine." It is, perhaps, characteristic of his point of view that he seems to regret the absence of any male presence of native growth to whom the wearers of American tiaras might suitably curtsey. "Woman is two-thirds of the apparent life—which means that she is absolutely all of the social." In Washington alone does man enjoy enough of social existence (*i.e.*, one independent of the market) to make it conceivable that he will ever catch up with woman. Apropos of the American failure to appreciate the blessings of privacy, Mr. James is tempted to ask whether the hotel spirit is not the "American spirit most seeking and most finding itself." In Europe there are endless things behind and beyond the hotel, in the States (he uses this, to the American, objectionable name) the hotel itself constitutes for vast numbers of people the richest form of existence. Mr. James's treatment of the South, in his chapters on Richmond and Charleston, is especially subtle and sympathetic. It is interesting to find that he regards "The Souls of Black Folk," by W. E. B. Du Bois, as "the only 'Southern' book of any distinction published for many a year."

Of the verbal felicities, marked for possible quotation only a very small selection can be given: The first scarlet maple of the fall is like "the daughter of a noble house dressed for a fancy ball, with the whole family gathered round to admire her." The streets of Boston and Cambridge present a picture of "extraordinary virtuous vacancy." The university is the "place inaccessible to the shout of the newspaper." New York, seen from the river, is a "pincushion in profile." The Ocean Drive at Newport is "a proof of the possible appeal of scenery, even to the dissipated."

Whether or not the general style of the book is found acceptable, must depend largely on the temperament of the reader. Its verbal subtleties sometimes remind one of a swordsman, who, having exhausted all the legitimate arts of his profession, now shows his skill by using his weapon as a vehicle of legerdemain. We find ourselves at one time half resenting the apparently needless amplification of theme, at another wondering whether, after all, the desired cumulative effect could be attained in any other way. If one owns to a more frequent experience of the former state, it is at least easy to sympathize with those who take the opposite view. When Philadelphia is admirably pigeonholed as the only large American city that doesn't *bristle*, we feel some sense of exasperation on finding that nothing is left to our imagination and that the idea is beaten out thin over several pages of explanation.

In conclusion, we come back to our initial impression that Mr. James is fundamentally incapable of getting inside the skin of the average American or of realizing that the outlook to such a citizen is by no means so dreary and "common" as to himself. He writes of America as an able but unsympathetic adult might write of the games of a child; the effect is as of a study of human nature by one to whom a refined and sophisticated elderly gentleman is the only type of interest. Given this point of view, the book is as fascinating as it well could be.

"The American Comedy." *Saturday Review* [England] 103 (30 March 1907), 395–96.

That Mr. Henry James is considerably intrigued by the American problem is evident throughout his book, but its title declares the intensely personal and contemplative fashion in which he essays to state it. His susceptive and intricate rendering of the "scene" announces to the inquirer not only the novelists "bad habit of receiving through almost any accident of vision more impressions than he knows what to do with," but his conviction that a mastery of all the elements in that scene, of how and what America has come to be, is the only base on which can be built any profitable conjecture as to her future. In pursuit of that idea he has, however, taken a way entirely of his own: he has written not a guide-book, but a drama, the drama of a continent; and he has contrived with illuminating subtlety that the "persons" of it shall be not the varieties of humanity upon its surface, but the evidences, the more or less enduring records of their aspiration and their content. True, he shows us occasionally the men and women, and he draws them with that fine conjectural penetration which so distinguishes his fiction: but we only see them as small moving things among the monuments of their collected activities to which he puts his questions, and from which he helps us to the nearest thing to a conclusion of which his deliberate consciousness will allow. These things, invested with personality by his art, take on before us a strange immense significant identity. They are like the monstrous creatures in a pantomime come true.

"The ample villas, in their full dress, planted each on its little square of brightly green carpet, and as with their stiff skirts pulled well down, eyed each other, at short range, from head to foot." "The huge new houses, up and down, looked over their smart short lawns as with a certain familiar prominence in their profiles, which was borne out by the accent, loud, assertive, yet benevolent withal, with which they confessed to their extreme expensiveness."

The intention clearly is that we shall see these buildings not only as a plain brick and stone, but as ideographs, as it were, of the men who built them. These houses with their "candid look of having cost as much as they knew how" are part of "the great adventure of a society reaching out into the apparent void for the amenities," an adventure which we follow with Mr. James across the entire continent. We question the houses again at Newport, the "monuments of pecuniary power" which have been planted thick and close that their occupants may remark from the windows to each other on the solitary and sympathetic charm of their sites. We ask the New York that "lies looking at the sky in the manner of a colossal hair-comb turned upwards and deprived of half its teeth" of what, for all its airs, it is going to make its future; and we find in its handsomer regions "the suggestion of a crowded 'party' of young persons," "the collective alertness of bright-eyed, light-limbed, clear-voiced youth, without a doubt in the world and without a conviction." From "wonderful little Baltimore," seated "as some quite robust but almost unnaturally good child might sit on the green apron of its nurse," we carry chiefly the impression of the little ladylike squares and the little brick-faced, protrusively door-stepped houses overhung by trees, like "rows of quiet old ladies seated, with their toes tucked up on uniform foot-

stools, under the shaded candlesticks of old-fashioned tea parties;" while Richmond, tragic ghost-haunted Richmond, affects us by its utter failure to fill out our conception of tragedy, by its void blankness, its lack of any discernible consciousness, its "very dim smile of modesty, the invalid gentleness of a patient who has been freely bled."

Torn from the fabric of the book, from the intricacy of its dexterous and elaborate design, these descriptions may seem but impressionist studies of architecture and fail even to suggest that peopling of a continent with the vague shapes of its incarnated activities which Mr. James has so marvelously achieved. No elucidation of that achievement is possible in a review, since its success is dependent to a quite incommunicable degree upon an atmosphere, diffused from every page, by which the effects have been created. That atmosphere can be breathed only by those who read the book, and who read it moreover from the beginning. It is a book into which it is almost impossible to "dip;" its pages are as resistant to any effort to penetrate them casually as is a coat of mail. We would risk the assertion that not one page in the entire volume is intelligible by itself; in none certainly can the argument be followed or the impression received if a single paragraph be omitted. Insistence on this curious fineness and closeness of texture is a reviewer's duty, as much to himself as to his readers. It is his excuse for failing to communicate any measure of its charm; it limits his recommendation to the seriously-minded. Its chapters doubtless may be separately studied for delineations of the dozen States and cities with which they deal; but only those who read them all, and read them in order, will receive the author's vision of the American scene. Even then they will feel their knowledge incomplete and be conscious of something withheld in his impression, something which one trusts he still intends to communicate.

What one chiefly gathers from that impression, so far as it is revealed, is a sense of impermanence, a sense pervading not the onlooker's consciousness but that of the nation itself. Its very magnificence is provisional, it does nothing with an illusion of finality, its constructiveness quite as much as its destructiveness seems intended to "blight the superstition of rest." "The very sign of its energy is that it doesn't believe in itself; it fails to succeed, even at a cost of millions, in persuading you that it does." The lack of any illusion of finality is reflected from every arrangement of its social affairs. The author draws a humorous but sympathetic picture of the social effort to imitate the habits of older civilisations while lacking their resources. He depicts in his intimate fashion the collapse of the social impulse at the most regal hour of the night from sheer lack of something to "go on" to, or with the opera alone offering on such occasions—occasions that have contributed all conceivable splendours of attire—"the only approach to the implication of the tiara known, so to speak, to the American law." "In worlds otherwise arranged," he remarks delightfully, "the occasion itself, with its character fully turned on, produces the tiara. In New York this symbol has, by an arduous extension of its virtue, to produce the occasion."

But he doubtless sees that the occasion will have to wait for something else, since one sex only in the American world may be said to have risen to the "implication of the tiara," and the "failure of the sexes to keep step socially" is as fatal to the attainment of "functions" as it is illustrative of the foredoomed *grope* of wealth.

But with his eye chiefly occupied with the costlier exponents of that drama, Mr. James has not been unconscious of the significant and incalculable changes taking place in the strata on which its foundations at present indifferently repose. The menace of immigration does not move him quite to the extent of Mr. Wells' misgivings, but he finds it not a whit less suggestive; and of his luminous comparisons not the least is that which likens the Americanising of the immigrant, and the loss, "after a deep inhalation or two of the clear native air," of all his charming and apparently indelible qualities, to the immersion of a piece of bright-hued stuff in a tub of hot water, which fails however to exhibit any traces of the dye which it extracts. America "rubs off" the Italian's manners without in any way affecting the complexion of its own.

These elements of the drama only prove the author's acquaintance with every contributory factor to the scene, and but add, as his exquisite appreciations of its scenery, to the variety of its colour. Our completed sense of the scene is of a comedy of manners portrayed with an incomparable delicacy of definition, but of a comedy to which he has still to add the most exacting touches.

E[lizabeth] L[uther] C[ary].
"Henry James."
New York Times Saturday Review of Books 12 (6 April 1907), 221.

In approaching the pages on which Mr. James has recorded his impressions of America it is natural to experience a kind of wonder at the extraordinary concatenation of circumstances by which a vision at once so ripe and so fresh, so initiated and so sensitive, so broad and so intimate, was brought to bear upon us. The American individual has too often been the hero or heroine of his novels for us to consider seriously that Mr. James has lost interest in his countrymen through being removed from the land of his birth. He has, in fact, treated his Americans with such a tender and beneficent justice as to make us feel that we seemed to him a peculiarly rewarding type. But for many years he has seen us against the English or the Continental background and who can say what that complicated pattern may not have done for our simple lines, what the dimness of that old tapestry may not have done for our fresh and youthful coloring. He has seen us now, at all events, against our own background. He has seen not only the modern American, but modern America, and it is amazingly interesting to note how he has been affected by the experience.

For one and the first thing, he seems to have been arrested by the fact that he found us not ourselves at all, but so mixed up and mixed in with other races as to present a curiously ambiguous countenance to the traveler returning to the home of his childhood. In his home, on its threshold and in all the inner-rooms through which he passed, he was met by the alien installed and as much at home as he. Nor did the alien wear for him the more or less familiar alien aspect. All foreigners on reaching our shores put aside certain characteristics by which at home they were especially signalized, and this sudden dropping of color moves the observer who has seen them in the rich bloom of their native beauty to reflect upon ultimate possibilities for them:

What does become of the various positive properties on the part of certain of the installed tribes, the good manners, say, among them, as to which the pro-

cess of shedding and the fact of eclipse come so promptly into play? . . . It would be for them, of course, in this event, to attest that they had been worth waiting so long for; but the speculation, at any rate irresistibly forced upon us is a sign of the interest, in the American world, of what I have called the "ethnic" outlook. [1907 Harper ed., pp. 129–30]

It is these "positive properties" of the Americanized alien, those to which Mr. James refers as having promptly been dropped, and others to which he elsewhere refers which are retained quite stubbornly, and which appear to resist the process of amalgamation that make our ethnic problem one that the most passionate analyst may give up without reproach. That Mr. James does give it up after turning it to the light on many sides and examining it with scrupulous solicitude, is proof not only of its complication but of his high intelligence as well.

With the social question in the more circumscribed classes the inquirer may move in a freer air and indulge himself in livelier generalizations. It is with the social question, of course, that Mr. James has dealt most largely on the pages of his remarkably truthful fiction, and the ramifications of international and intersocial relations have been explored by him with such thoroughness that we can very well imagine him astonished by nothing so much as by a social relation of translucent simplicity. Such a one presented itself in the whirling gayeties of New York life despite the innumerable items that went toward its making. To detach from all the wise comments on that mad life the one that most has struck us with its wisdom is, no doubt, to bring it into a more or less misleading conspicuity; but when the word that fits a situation perfectly has once been found it is impossible not to announce it and return to it at the risk of spoiling the fit by stretching it unduly. When Mr. James characterizes the New York social movement of the day as analogous in its elements to a child's "party," it is difficult not to subscribe with a too riotous enjoyment to the phrase.

What, for example, could more brilliantly illuminate the scene of our kaleidoscopic Winter occupations than such a passage as this:

> It comes home to the restless analyst everywhere that this "childish" explanation is the one that meets the greatest number of the social appearances. . . . The immensity of the native accommodation, socially speaking, for the childish life, is not that exactly much of the key of the spectacle?—the safety of the vast flat expanse where every margin abounds and nothing too untoward need happen. [1907 Harper ed., p. 171]

If there must needs be a kind of grimace of chagrin with the smile this characterization inspires, if we have to say to ourselves rather sturdily that to be a child is presumably to have a long life before you, and at any rate is to be innocent and vigorous and smooth of skin, which is not so bad in comparison with being sophisticated and feeble and more or less sere, as some of our European friends among the countries are, we are released from any necessity of braving it out when we arrive with Mr. James at Concord and again at Washington, and still again at Baltimore, at Cambridge, and at Philadelphia. Never have we been more conscious of our precious links with history than when standing with an American to whom our present is a maze of perplexities in the presence of our past, to which he pays tribute with a tenderness so deep as to cast our own familiar acceptance of our history into a shade which to our awakened consciousness seems one of

shame. At Concord, not only Emerson and Thoreau and the Concord "school" solicited him with a depth and warmth that find a peculiarly moving expression in his fastidious prose stirred to eloquence by the strong emotion.

It would be impossible within reasonable limits to give much idea of the rich and fantastic humor that plays about the revisited towns of America, leaving behind it suggestions to awaken our serious thought. It is possible only to record how steadily for the attentive reader the Muse of History presides over the impressions received by the "restless analyst" returning to a country which in his youth was busy with wars. In Concord, at Mount Vernon, at Baltimore, at Richmond, wherever the past had vibrated to historic interests and passions, he yielded himself to the ghostly associations. Our tearing down and building up, our extravagance and haste and irresponsibility could hardly claim, even from the embodiment of courtesy extraordinary tolerance. But our intimate past, where it has been permitted peacefully to take on its mellow tone, entreats him persuadingly, and we should have difficulty in finding anywhere in literature portraits more delicately synthetic and vital than those of our National heroes that are sprinkled through the pages like illustrations to the text by a master of the rare art of illustration. What for example, could be more in the golden style of portraiture than this of Franklin:

> He seemed to preside over it all while one lingered there, as if he had been seated at the mahogany, relentlessly enough, near his glass of madeira, seemed to be "in" it even more freely than by the so interesting fact of his still having in Philadelphia, in New York, in Boston, through his daughter, so numerous a posterity. The sense of

life, life the most positive, most human and most miscellaneous, expressed in his aged, crumpled, canny face, where the smile wittily profits, for fineness, by the comparative collapse of the mouth represents a suggestion which succeeding generations may well have found it all they could do to work out.

Frederic Taber Cooper. *"The American Scene."* North American Review 185 (17 May 1907), 214–18.

There are certain volumes in which the personal equation so frankly and agreeably obtrudes itself that they ought in fairness to be reviewed, not as separate and complete productions, but as links in the chain of an author's self-revelations, significant factors in the rounded sum of a lifetime's accomplishment. "The American Scene," by Henry James, is essentially and peculiarly a book of this class, the more intimate charm of which must elude those readers who choose to regard it as an isolated volume of travel, and who fail to recognize the continuity of thought and mood which binds it with his novel, "The Ambassadors," and his "Life of William Wetmore Story," into a kind of strangely assorted trilogy.[1] Indeed, one may venture to hazard the opinion that, when the time comes to draw up a final balance-sheet of the life achievement of Mr. James, these three works will prove to be that portion of his writings which his future biographer can least afford to neglect; because they reveal, from three several standpoints, the chief preoccupation of the author's mind, the dominant motive of his migrations and his habits, the recurrent burden of his literary product.

Mr. James has long been accredited with the invention of the International Episode. Yet "invention" is scarcely the correct word; since, before he had reduced it to a formula for fiction, he himself was, from deliberate choice, living and breathing the International Episode, studying, analyzing, vivisecting it in the experiences of himself and of others, allowing it gradually to dominate him like a strangely stimulating obsession, full of infinite and tantalizing suggestion. It was "Europe," to borrow his own words,

"that had, in very ancient days, held out to the yearning young American some likelihood of impressions more numerous and varied and of a higher intensity than those he might gather on the native scene; and it was doubtless in conformity with some such desire more finely and more frequently to vibrate that he had originally begun to consult the European oracle."

Such is Mr. James's characteristic way of explaining the impulse which led him to make his domicile "in the very precincts, as it were, of the temple"; and, through all the years which followed, the study of the racial, social and æsthetic relation of the American world to the European, seems never, for him, to have lost its original zest. The subtle note of the cosmopolitan spirit, in its finer sense, is what binds together his most divergent works, with the unmistakable tie of kinship. Viewed from his standpoint, his biography of the artist Story ceases to be merely the life of an individual. It becomes the solution of a problem which many a man with the inborn artistic temperament has had to confront; it is a luminous and fascinating interpretation of what Europe may mean to the expatriated American, the American who has strongly taken his life into his own hands, and chosen to live it out in the environment for which his nature has best fitted him. In one novel after another, from "Daisy Miller" onward, sometimes as the *Leitmotiv,* sometimes as mere side-issues, we find, in all its possible variations of form and degree, the insistent, recurrent, dominating question of what Europe "connotes" for the compatriots of Mr. James. And notably in "The Ambassadors," which one is tempted to single out as the author's supreme achievement in fiction, we have a picture drawn with infinite understanding and sympathy, of the type that forms the antithesis to the artist Story, the man of weaker nature, the "frustrated American" who has not had the courage to choose his own environment, and who realizes, when he has crossed the threshold of middle age, the golden opportunity that he sacrificed to heredity and convention. One conjectures that, in the character of Strether, Mr. James sees himself as he might now have been had he too crushed down the adventurous spirit and consented to a lifetime in "Woolett" along the line of least resistance. And, lastly, comes "The American Scene," as a logical, inevitable sequel, a final summing up, for himself and for the world, of what America "connotes" for the "restored absentee." It is this connection of thought and mood which leads one to group these three widely divergent volumes into a strangely assorted, and yet intimately related, trilogy of Expatriation.

The first point, then, to insist upon is that "The American Scene" is from first to last intensely subjective. Yet this is no more than to say that, in writing impressions of travel, Mr. James follows the same method that he does in fiction, seeing the outside world strictly through the medium of some one temperament. For instance, in "What Maisie Knew," the field of vision is limited, in a manner which compels wonder, to the narrow segment of life that comes within Maisie's personal knowledge. Whenever the other characters pass beyond her ken, they disappear as completely from the reader's sight as the germs that wriggle from beneath the lens of a microscope. In "The Ambassadors," through all that amazing intricacy of human hopes and desires, all that we are allowed to know is what Strether himself knows— what he sees, what he thinks, what he is told that other people think. There are countless questions we long to solve, doors we would like to open, corners we would like to turn; but Mr. James will not permit it; he forces us to see life through the eyes of the none too alert Strether.

In "The American Scene" the method is the same, excepting that the temperament through which we behold places and people is that of the author himself. Moreover, it is a keenly self-conscious temperament, tremendously interested with its own sensations, and with finger constantly on pulse, to detect and record every momentary quickening. On every page one reads between the lines a tingling curiosity on the author's part to discover whether, among the emotions awakened by his "repatriation," there is a lurking regret, a single fleeting wave of nostalgia for the home of his early years. Without a full recognition of what the volume stands for in a personal way, its prime significance as an interpretation of a people will be largely missed. It is not enough to accept it as a minute and unflinching analysis by a trained psychologist, an acute observer of life and of places. More than that, it is written by one who long ago weighed America in the balance and found it, for his own personal needs and desires, quite definitely wanting as an abiding-place, and who now, returning after long years, finds that his choice was wisely made. There have never been written subtler, keener, more luminous studies of the cities of America—but we see them through the medium of a temperament which, if not antagonistic, is at least aloof. To appreciate their marvellous delicacy of intuition, their sanity, their inherent justice, one must share in no small measure the broad, contentedly cosmopolitan spirit of the author himself. His Boston and his New York are never quite those of the complacent Bostonian and New-Yorker, any more than they are those of the critical foreigner. His observations, whether of censure or approval, are always those of the "restored absentee," and equally removed from the exaggerations of patriotic pride and the depreciation of foreign jealousy.

A great deal of complacent folly has been written about the obscurity of Henry James's style. Granted that his tricks of speech, his curious little verbal twists, have grown to be mannerisms so pronounced as to seem at times to be little less than deliberate affectation; yet these alone would never make a single page of Mr. James obscure. It is the thought behind the words which is often difficult to grasp. Indeed, thought is too definite a word to apply to those elusive mental states that he so often tries to interpret. Mr. James is seldom content to analyze thoughts, and never less so than in "The American Scene." He is continually reaching back to those obscurer, more complex phases of transition, vague, instinctive impressions, the forerunners of conscious thought. Many readers are apt to find the later chapters of this volume especially admirable, the chapters on the Southern cities of Baltimore, Richmond, Charleston, where, because they are practically an unexplored territory, his impressions are fresh, clear, definite. Far more difficult and more profound are his inimitable chapters on New York, where every new impression blends with old memories, until every page suggests a palimpsest, with the vague, time-obliterated records revealing themselves beneath the freshly written

script. It is New York which makes the most potent appeal to old associations; it is New York which, at the same time, most violently antagonizes him with its typically American note of the power of money and the pervading sense of instability and transition; it is New York which convinces him that "to make so much money that you won't, that you don't, 'mind,' don't mind anything, is absolutely the American formula," and that "your making no money—or so little that it passes for none—and being thereby distinctly reduced to minding, amounts to your being reduced to the knowledge that America is no place for you." In other words, it is New York, more than any other American city, that confirms Mr. James in the inherent wisdom of his own life, and enables him to return to the precincts of the temple, more than ever "contentedly cosmopolite." There is but one way in which to read "The American Scene": refuse to let it antagonize you, remember constantly that it is the utterance of a "restored absentee"; and, with every page, you will come more and more under the charm of his descriptions and the subtlety of his judgments.

Note

1 *William Wetmore Story and His Friends* (Boston: Houghton, Mifflin, 1903).

E.M.
South Atlantic Quarterly 6 (July 1907), 313–14.

Mr. Henry James, who, after an absence of nearly twenty-five years, returned to this country for a visit of several months, has in this volume given his impressions of his native land. As a young man he went to live in Europe to enjoy the impressions, more numerous and various and of a higher intensity than those to be gathered here. Having lived for long years "in the very precincts of the temple" of art and beauty, he sought romance and mystery in the native, the forsaken scene, "now passing, as continual rumor had it, through a thousand stages and changes." America would now be romantic, because she was different from Europe. He writes not so much of the human life he met with—suggesting that he may do so in another volume—as of the external characteristics of New York, Boston, Philadelphia, Newport, Concord and Salem, Washington, Baltimore, Richmond, Charleston and Florida. The point of view is that of the "restless analyst," the "expatriated observer," charmed with the signs of the antique and the picturesque, rather than with the more obvious aspects of our commercial and democratic life. Mr. James is frankly out of sympathy with "the eternal American note."

In Boston he is struck with the overwhelming number of aliens that have destroyed the homogeneity of the old population with which he was familiar as a boy, and he has but little sympathy with the new Boston of Commonwealth and Marlborough avenues as contrasted with the crooked streets and picturesque sidewalks of the old Boston. The Public Library in no sense takes the place of the old Athenæum. The ampler resources and buildings of Harvard and the elaborate system of parks along the Charles look but mean and vulgar by the Harvard and Cambridge of Lowell, Longfellow and Howells. Concord alone keeps the look, the feeling, the air of the olden time. With infinite relief the author passes from New York or Newport to the Hudson of Washington Irving, or to Philadelphia and Baltimore.

To a Southerner the chapters on Richmond and Charleston are especially suggestive and interesting if, indeed, they are not the best chapters in the book. Mr. James came South with every desire to be "romantically affected"—here he would find in abundance the survivals of "old unhappy far off things." Unable to understand or to see with the eye of imagination the forces that are making the new order, he hoped to feel in the most poignant manner the beauty and tragedy of the old order. In Richmond he found only a void, a blank—not only no survivals, but no worthy record in any form of art. In Charleston, with the author of "Lady Baltimore" as his guide, he was satisfied as perhaps nowhere else in the country save Concord. St. Michael's church and the old cemetery raised him to "the highest Carolinian pitch."

Mr. James' style, like his thought, is baffling. The mingling of cold analysis with a dreamy sentimentalism is an unusual phenomenon in writing. His criticism is extremely disinterested rather than wisely sympathetic, but for that reason the book should be read by intelligent Americans. There is no use getting mad at what he says—better be sure that he is not right.

Checklist of Additional Reviews

C.R. "The Return of the Native." London *Daily Chronicle*, 30 January 1907, p. 3.

C. F. G. Masterman. "America." London *Daily News*, 30 January 1907, p. 4.

Jeannette L. Gilder. Chicago *Tribune*, 2 February 1907, p. 9.

New York *Sun*, 16 February 1907, p. 7.

New York *World*, 16 February 1907, p. 8.

Albany *Evening Journal*, 20 February 1907, p. 3.

British Weekly: A Journal of Social and Christian Progress 41 (21 February 1907), 545.

Chicago *Inter-Ocean*, 23 February 1907, p. 7.

Francis Hackett. "America Revisited." Chicago *Evening Post*, 23 February 1907, p. 7.

Portland *Sunday Oregonian*, 24 February 1907, p. 51.

Edward Marsh, *Bookman* [New York] 25 (March 1907), 188–90.

Academy [England] 72 (2 March 1907), 214–15.

Carl T. Robertson. Cleveland *Plain Dealer*, 3 March 1907, p. 7.

Boston *Daily Advertiser*, 6 March 1907, p. 7.

Hartford *Courant*, 6 March 1907, p. 19.

San Francisco *Argonaut* 60 (9 March 1907), 504.

J. B. Kerfoot. *Life* 49 (14 March 1907), 388.

Literary World [England] 73 (15 March 1907), 103.

Percy F. Bicknell. "Home Impressions of an Expatriated American." *Dial* 42 (16 March 1907), 176–77.

Outlook 85 (16 March 1907), 622–23.

New Orleans *Daily Picayune*, 18 March 1907, p. 14.

St. Paul *Daily Pioneer Press*, 18 March 1907, p. 5.

Churchman 95 (22 March 1907), 428.

Springfield [Mass.] *Republican*, 24 March 1907, p. 23.

New York *Evening Post*, 30 March 1907, supp., p. 6.

Desmond MacCarthy. *Albany Review* 1 (April 1907), 479.

Congregationalist and Christian World 92 (13 April 1907), 503.

Bellman [Minneapolis] 2 (20 April 1907), 476.

Asi. G. *Putnam's Monthly* 2 (May 1907), 164–70; (July 1907), 433–42. Reprinted in Gard, pp. 432–49.

Current Literature 42 (June 1907), 634–36.

Reader [New York] 10 (July 1907), 215–16.

"Euphues and His America." *Independent* 63 (11 July 1907), 95–96.

Literary Digest 35 (20 July 1907), p. 96.

Atlantic Monthly 100 (October 1907), 566–68.

Papyrus: A Magazine of Individuality 9 (October 1907), 27–30.

Index

Bridges, Robert, xiv, 203, 213, 298
British Quarterly Review, 18, 45, 78, 91, 137, 160
British Weekly: A Journal of Social and Christian Progress, 469
"Broken Wings," 413
Brontë, Charlotte, *Jane Eyre*, 108
Brooklyn *Daily Eagle*, 278, 298, 334, 356
Brooks, John, xxii n. 18
Brown, Alice, 332
Brown, Edith Baker, 255
Brownell, W. C., 90, 145
Browning, Robert, 351, 413, 428, 457; *Bishop Blougram's Apology*, 394; *The Ring and the Book*, 320, 378, 415
Bryce, James, 458
Buchanan, Robert, 216, 217 n. 1
Buckstone, John Baldwin, 301
"Bundle of Letters, A," 107, 115, 227
Burke, Edmund, 143, 146
Burlingame, Edward L., 45

C., H., 405
Caine, Hall, 284
Californian, 97, 138
Calvin, Jean, *Institutes*, 378
Cambridge Review, 217
Carlyle, Thomas, 146, 372
Carpenter, Millie W., 334
Cary, Elizabeth Luther, 462
Catholic World, 142, 172, 195, 208
Century Magazine, 157, 166, 451 n. 2
Cervantes Saavedra, Miguel de, *Don Quixote*, 90
Chamberlain, Joseph Edgar, 339
Chap Book, 286, 287 n. 1, 295 n. 1
Charleston *News and Courier*, 149, 194
Chautauquan, 240, 259, 312
Cherbuliez, Victor, 54, 55 n. 2
Chicago *Evening-Post*, 259, 264, 326, 356, 363, 404, 432, 469
Chicago *Inter-Ocean*, 17, 64, 118, 149, 172, 217, 240, 258, 278, 384, 469
Chicago *Record-Herald*, 384, 410, 432
Chicago *Times*, 45, 97, 172, 195, 208, 240
Chicago *Times-Herald*, 298, 333
Chicago *Tribune*, xiii, xvii, xix, 8, 45, 52, 101, 149, 160, 240, 251, 266, 290, 320, 346, 384, 402, 417, 468
Christian Union, xvi, 64, 94, 204, 217, 221
Churchman, 149, 208, 217, 240, 279, 334, 357, 384, 410, 432, 469
Cincinnati *Commercial*, 149
Cincinnati *Commercial Gazette*, 172, 195, 208, 240
Cincinnati *Commercial Tribune*, 298

Clap, Henry Austin, 356
Clare, Ida, 148
Clark, Kate Upson, 241
Cleveland *Plain Dealer*, 117, 172, 194, 240, 278, 357, 384, 410, 432, 469
Clough, Arthur Hugh, "Amours de Voyage," 85, 86 n. 1
Colby, Frank Moore, 384
Coleridge, Samuel Taylor, "Rime of the Ancient Mariner," 454
Collins, Wilkie, 15
Colorado Springs *Weekly Gazette*, 149
Colson, Ethel M., 432
Confidence, xiii, xiv, xv, 79–97
Congregationalist, 259, 298, 357
Congregationalist and Christian World, 410, 469
Connolly, Terence L., 432
Conrad, Joseph, 406
Contemporary Review [England], 171, 385
Coolidge, Susan, 92
Cooper, Frederic Taber, 410, 465
Cooper, James Fenimore, *The Pioneers*, 156
Corelli, Marie, 284
Cornhill Magazine, 70
Correspondance of Henry James and the House of Macmillan, 1877–1914, The, xxii nn. 6, 14–16, and 21, xxiii n. 23
Correspondence of William James The, xxi n. 1, xxii nn. 2, 4, 7, 18, and 22, xxiii n. 24
Cosmopolis, 259, 318
Cottage Hearth, 241
"Covering End, The," xvii, 301, 303, 305, 307–10, 312
"Coxon Fund, The," 270
Crawford, F. Marion, 265, 353
Crébillon, Claude, 107, 129; *Tanzai et Néadarné*, 129, 130 n. 2
Critic, xiii, 126, 149, 164, 190, 208, 215, 229, 240, 254, 276, 295, 313, 330, 352, 376
Crowley, J. Donald, xxiii n. 31, 384
Current Literature, xix, xxiii n. 25, 257, 353, 469

Daisy Miller, xii–xiii, xvi, xxi, 16, 49, 59, 65–78, 87, 94, 95, 101, 106, 110, 117, 125, 143, 147, 205, 227, 236, 258, 323, 328, 331, 348, 389, 397, 418, 466
Dankleff, Richard, "The Composition, Revisions, Receptions, and Critical Reputation of Henry James' *The Spoils of Poynton*," xx
Dante Alighieri, 457
Daudet, Alphonse, 153; *Le Petit chose*, 54, 55 n. 1, 229
Davies, James, 97

Dear, Mary, 354
Defoe, Daniel, 133
Detroit *Evening News*, 172, 194, 356
Detroit *Free Press*, xxii n. 12, 45, 97, 149, 161, 176, 217, 312, 329, 356, 384, 410
Dial, 102, 149, 172, 195, 240, 279, 334, 410, 469
"Diary of a Man of Fifty, The," 143
Dickens, Charles, 5, 182, 184, 212, 286, 348, 449; *Great Expectations*, 132; *Martin Chuzzlewit*, 60, 201; *Pickwick Papers*, 128
Disraeli, Benjamin, 101, 319
Dixie, 313
Dostoyevsky, Fyodor, 153, 175
Doyle, Sir Arthur Conan, *The Adventures of Sherlock Holmes*, 350, 351, 420
"Droch," *see* Bridges, Robert
Dublin Review, 195, 206, 238
Du Bois, W. E. B., *Souls of Black Folk*, 459
Dumas, Alexandre, 3, 184, 348
Du Maurier, George, 101, 102, 293, 294 n. 1, 326

E., E. F., 418
Eclectic Magazine, 44, 56, 94
Edel, Leon, xxii n. 1; *A Bibliography of Henry James*, 295 n. 1, 442 n. 1
Egan, Maurice F., 195
Eliot, George, 117, 122, 132, 139, 140, 146; *Daniel Deronda*, 38 n. 1; *Middlemarch*, 111, 147, 257, 258 n. 1; *Mill on the Floss*, 140; *The Spanish Gypsy*, 43, 44 n. 1
Eliot, T. S., xxiii n. 33
Embarrassments, 246–247, 251 n. 1, 255, 318
Emerson, Ralph Waldo, 146, 398
Epoch, 195, 208, 217, 241
Europeans, The, xi–xii, 16, 47–64, 71, 91, 104, 106, 111, 143, 397, 418

F., E., 278
Feuillet, Octave, *Julia de Trécoeur*, 50
Fielding, Henry, 122; *Tom Jones*, 146
"Figure in the Carpet, The," 317, 318 n. 1
Flaubert, Gustave, 383; *L'éducation sentimentale*, 175, 176 n. 1
Fogel, Daniel Mark, xxi
Foley, Richard Nicholas, *Criticism in American Periodicals of the Works of Henry James from 1866 to 1916*, xx
Fortnightly Review, 442 n. 1
"Four Meetings," 16, 70–72, 74–75, 77
Fragonard, Jean Honoré, 216
Franklin, Benjamin, 464
Frederic, Harold, 348
Freeman, Mary Eleanor Wilkins, 332
French Poets and Novelists, 50, 52 n. 1, 56

Fuller, Henry B., 363
Fullerton, William Morton, 217

G., Asi. 469
"Gabrielle de Bergerac," 27, 28 n. 1
Galaxy, 3, 7 n. 1, 32, 40 n. 1
Gard, Roger, *Henry James: The Critical Heritage*, xxi, xxiii nn. 28 and 31, 18, 64, 97, 118, 149, 172, 194–195, 208, 240, 241, 297, 313, 333, 334, 357, 384, 385, 410, 432
Garfield, James A., 128
Gargano, James W.: *Critical Essays on Henry James: The Early Novels*, xxi, xxii n. 18, 17, 18, 45, 64, 97, 118, 149, 172, 194, 195, 241; *Critical Essays on Henry James: The Late Novels*, 334, 356, 384, 410, 432
Garnett, Edward, xix, xxiii n. 32, 399
Gasparin, Agenor, Comte de, 63, 64 n. 1
Gautier, Theophile, *Captain Fracasse*, 94
Gilbert, Sir W. S., *The Mikado*, 364
Gilder, Jeannette L., 468
Gissing, George, *Demos*, 185, 186 n. 1
Godey's Lady's Book, 228
Goethe, Johann Wolfgang von, 128, 458
Golden Bowl, The, xix, 411–432
Goldsmith, Oliver: *She Stoops to Conquer*, 38 n. 1; *The Vicar of Wakefield*, 234
Gosse, Edmund, xv, xix–xx, xxii n. 19, xxiii n. 34, 437
Graphic [England], 17, 45, 53, 75, 172, 184, 199, 217, 241, 259, 313, 410, 432
"Guy Domville," 391

H., J. A., 443
Hackett, Francis, 469
Hall, Basil, 450
Hardy, Thomas, 109, 146, 348, 390, 420; *Jude the Obscure*, 285; *A Laodicean*, 130–131
Harper's New Monthly Magazine, xxii n. 18, 64, 78, 97, 101, 102 n. 1, 109, 149, 193, 208, 294, 442 n. 1
Harte, Bret, 122
Hartford *Daily Courant*, 45, 64, 78, 97, 117, 148, 208, 217, 298, 469
Hawthorne, 85, 86 n. 2
Hawthorne, Julian, *Love—or a Name*, xxii n. 13
Hawthorne, Nathaniel, 52, 85, 109, 127, 230, 303, 441; *The Blithedale Romance*, 169; *The Scarlet Letter*, 421
Hay, John, xv, xxii n. 16, 68, 134, 234
Hazeltine, Mayo Williamson, 97, 122, 162
Henley, W. E., xii, 16, 49

Henry James Letters, xxii nn. 1, 5, 17, and 20, xxiii n. 29
Henry James: Novels 1871–1880, xxi, 83, 93
Henry James: Novels 1881–1886, xxi, 126, 135, 136, 161
Henry James: Novels 1886–1890, xxi, 187
Henry James Review, xxiii n. 32, 217, 297, 333, 384
Herzen, Alexander Ivanovich, 175, 176 n. 1
Hewitt, Rosalie, xx
Hicks, Richard A., xxiii n. 31, 384
Hill, Mrs. F. H., 78
Holmes, Oliver Wendell, 75, 76
Homer, 245
Horace, 156, 245–246
Howells, William Dean, xi, xii, xiii, xv, xxii nn. 1 and 17–18, 52, 117, 146, 159, 193, 221, 234, 328, 347, 348, 453, 468; *A Hazard of New Fortunes*, 221, 222, n. 1; *The Lady of the Aroostook*, 59, 449, 451 n. 1; *A Modern Instance*, 204 n. 1; *The Rise of Silas Lapham*, 170, 204 n. 1; *The Shadow of a Dream*, 233; *The Undiscovered Country*, 159.
Hugo, Victor, 101
Huntington, H. A., 149
Hutton, R. H., 18, 118, 149, 186, 208

Illustrated London News, xviii, 294, 357, 370, 410, 432
In the Cage, 302–303, 304 n. 1, 308, 327, 401
Independent, 17, 45, 54, 97, 140, 166, 185, 208, 259, 279, 298, 313, 350, 382, 469
Indianapolis *Journal*, 45, 149, 172, 195, 217, 240, 278, 410
Indianapolis *News*, 323, 354, 384
"International Episode, An" 70, 73–75, 77, 143, 418
International Review, 64, 78
Irving, Washington, 441, 453, 468; "Rip Van Winkle," 319

James, Henry, *see titles of individual works*
James, Henry, Sr., xi, xxii n. 1, 3, 21, 418, 422
James, Mary Robertson Walsh (Henry James's mother), xi, xii, xxii nn. 1 and 5
James, William, xi, xii, xvi, xxi n. 1, xxii nn. 2, 4, 7, 18, and 22, xxiii n. 24
Jeune, Sir Francis, 319
Jewett, Sarah Orne, 332
Johnson, Samuel, 109, 375

Kant, Immanuel, 405
Kerfoot, J. B., 410, 469
Kimbrough, Robert, 312, 313

Kipling, Rudyard, 348, 420
Knight, Lucian L., 334

"Lady Barberina," 450, 451 n. 2
Lamp, 410, 432
Lang, Andrew, 179, 259
Lang, Leonora B., 113
Lanier, H. W., 307
"Last of the Valerii, The" 38, 40 n. 1
Laurence, Dan H., *A Bibliography of Henry James*, 295 n. 1, 442 n. 1
Lemay, J. A. Leo, xxi, xxii n. 11
Le Queux, William, 425
Library Table, 45
Life, 213, 298, 305, 469
Lilley, A. L., 410
Lippincott's Magazine, xxii n. 10, 118, 143, 172, 195, 241
Literary Digest, 469
Literary Review, 278
Literary World [Boston], 37, 64, 92, 118, 149, 172, 189, 205, 214, 240, 258, 279, 293, 334, 405
Literary World [England], 149, 172, 217, 240, 279, 298, 313, 334, 357, 384, 410, 432, 469
Literature [England], 297, 356
Littledale, Richard F., 200
Logan, Annie R. M., 191, 206, 217, 239, 278, 297, 313, 384, 410, 423
London *Daily Chronicle*, xix, 349, 361, 395, 468
London *Daily Mail*, xx, 437
London *Daily News*, xviii, 78, 153, 341, 365, 410, 432, 468
London *Daily Telegraph*, 149, 176, 199, 214, 389, 432, 435
London *Echo*, 298
London *Examiner*, 64
"London Life, A," 221, 222 n. 3
London *Morning Post*, 368, 425
London *Review*, 309
London *Times*, xix, 97, 118, 131, 167, 181, 202, 259, 298, 311, 321, 334, 356; see also *Times Literary Supplement*
Longfellow, Henry Wadsworth, 468
"Louisa Pallant," 211, 212, 213, 216, 217
Louisville *Courier-Journal*, 45, 117, 172, 240, 298, 347, 384, 408, 446
Lowell, James Russell, 453, 468
Lytton, Baron (Edward Bulwer-Lytton), 101, 351, 365; *The Haunters and the Haunted*, 311

M., E., 467
Mabie, Hamilton W., 313
MacCarthy, Desmond, 469

MacDonell, A., 371
Macmillan, Frederick, xv–xvii, xx, xxii nn. 6 and 14–16, xxiii n. 23
"Mme. de Mauves," 13, 38, 40 n. 1
"Madonna of the Future, The," 38, 40 n. 1, 409
Madonna of the Future and Other Tales, 81, 84 n. 1
Maeterlinck, Maurice, 257, 417
Mallock, W. H., 61; *The Old Order Changes*, 194
Manchester *Guardian*, xvi, xviii, xxiii n. 26, 225, 269, 283, 312, 317, 347, 367, 391, 432, 443
Marivaux, Pierre Carlet de Chamblain, 129, 130 n. 1
Marryat, Frederick, 182
Marsh, Edward, 469
Masterman, C. F. G., 468
Meredith, George, 227, 253, 275, 284, 305, 348, 376, 390, 405, 413, 420, 426; *Diana of the Crossways*, 190
Mérimée, Prosper, 82, 84 n. 2
Merrick, Leonard, *One Man's View*, 290
Miller, Alice Duer, 432
Miller, Joe, 324
Milton, John, xvii, 409
Minneapolis *Tribune*, 149, 334
"Modern Warning, The," 211, 212, 213, 216, 217
Monet, Claude, 427
Monteiro, George, *Henry James and John Hay*, xxii n. 16
Moore, Rayburn S., xxii n. 6, 19
Morrison, Arthur, *Child of the Jago*, 290, 291 n. 1
Moss, Mary, 432
Mowbray, J. P., 376
Munsey's Magazine, 312
Münsterberg, Hugo, 443; *The Americans*, 444 n. 1
Murray, Donald McLeish, "The Critical Reception of Henry James in English Periodicals, 1875–1916," xx
Murray's Magazine, 208, 236
Musset, Alfred de, 84, 85 n. 3

Nation, 13, 28, 45, 78, 84 n. 2, 85 n. 2, 90, 145, 172, 191, 206, 217, 239, 259, 297, 313, 334, 384, 410, 423, 458
National Observer [London], 258
National Quarterly Review, 97
New Orleans *Daily Picayune*, 78, 172, 194, 298, 313, 432, 469
New Review, 294, 295 n.1
New York *Commercial Advertiser*, 410

New York *Daily Graphic*, 17, 45, 64, 117, 149, 172
New York *Evening Post*, 97, 469
New York *Herald*, xiii, 9, 101, 245, 432
New York Observer, 259
New York *Sun*, 97, 122, 162, 208, 217, 240, 258, 298, 334, 384, 432, 468
New York *Times*, xii, xiii, xvi, xvii, xxii n. 8, 3, 26, 64, 67, 117, 125, 172, 178, 201, 217, 222; see also *New York Times Saturday Review of Books*
New York Times Saturday Review of Books, xxiii n. 30, 246, 265, 327, 356, 372, 397, 410, 413, 462
New York *Tribune*, xii, xv, xviii, 21, 64, 87, 103, 134, 149, 172, 194, 240, 245, 263, 291, 298, 312, 333, 337, 384, 432
New York *World*, 17, 22, 64, 172, 334, 356, 410, 469
"Next Time, The," 249, 251 n. 1
Nietzsche, Friedrich Wilhelm, 363
Noble, John Ashcoft, 149
North American Review, 17, 45, 57, 68, 84 n. 2, 208, 397, 398 n. 1, 442 n. 1, 445
Norton, Grace, 13
"Nym Crinkle," 172

O., L. R. F., 343
"Old Things, The," 263, 264 n. 1; see also *Spoils of Poynton, The*
Oliphant, Margaret, 149, 194; *Old Lady Mary*, 311
Other House, The, xvi, xvii, 243–259, 263, 264, 266, 268, 273, 325, 369
Outlook, 278, 298, 312, 333, 357, 385, 432, 469
Overland Monthly, 238, 258
Owen, F. M., 12

P., E. S., 149
Palestrina, Giovanni Pierluigi da, 317
Pall Mall Gazette [England], xiii, xv, xix, xxii n. 13, 18, 50, 72, 85, 111, 128, 155, 268, 283, 318, 356, 375, 390, 426, 442
Papyrus: A Magazine of Individuality, 469
Parker, Hershel, xxi
Parkman, Mary Eliot, 78
"Passionate Pilgrim, A," 13, 38, 40 n. 1
Passionate Pilgrim, and Other Tales, A, 10, 12 n. 1, 40 n. 1
Payne, William Morton, 172, 195, 240, 279, 334
Peattie, Elia W., 384, 402, 417
Peck, Harry T., 357
Penn Monthly, 149
"Pension Beaurepas, The," 107